JOHNSON

THE CRITICAL HERITAGE

Edited by
JAMES T. BOULTON
Professor of English Literature
University of Nottingham

BARNES & NOBLE, Inc.
NEW YORK
PUBLISHERS & BOOKSELLERS SINCE 1873

ISBN 0 389 041807

Printed in Great Britain

General Editor's Preface

The reception given to a writer by his contemporaries and near-contemporaries is evidence of considerable value to the student of literature. On one side we learn a great deal about the state of criticism at large and in particular about the development of critical attitudes towards a single writer; at the same time, through private comments in letters, journals or marginalia, we gain an insight upon the tastes and literary thought of individual readers of the period. Evidence of this kind helps us to understand the writer's historical situation, the nature of his immediate reading-public, and his response to these pressures.

The separate volumes in the *Critical Heritage Series* present a record of this early criticism. Clearly, for many of the highly productive and lengthily reviewed nineteenth- and twentieth-century writers, there exists an enormous body of material; and in these cases the volume editors have made a selection of the most important views, significant for their intrinsic critical worth or for their representative quality—perhaps even registering incomprehension!

For earlier writers, notably pre-eighteenth century, the materials are much scarcer and the historical period has been extended, sometimes far beyond the writer's lifetime, in order to show the inception and growth of critical views which were initially slow to appear.

In each volume the documents are headed by an Introduction, discussing the material assembled and relating the early stages of the author's reception to what we have come to identify as the critical tradition. The volumes will make available much material which would otherwise be difficult of access and it is hoped that the modern reader will be thereby helped towards an informed understanding of the ways in which literature has been read and judged.

B.C.S.

Contents

PREFACE   *page* xi
ACKNOWLEDGMENTS   xii
NOTE ON THE TEXT   xiii
INTRODUCTION   I

Johnson's Poems

1 JOHNSON seeking a publisher for *London*, 1738   42
2 WILLIAM MUDFORD on *London* and *The Vanity of Human Wishes*, 1802   44
3 JOHN AIKIN on Johnson's poems, 1804   49

Irene (1749)

4 *A Criticism on Mahomet and Irene*, 1749   52
5 JOHN HIPPISLEY (?), *An Essay on Tragedy*, 1749   57

The Rambler (1750–2)

6 Two early tributes, 1750   63
7 JOHNSON surveys his purpose and achievement, *Rambler*, 1752   64
8 ARTHUR MURPHY, *Essay on the Life and Genius of Johnson*, 1792   68
9 GEORGE GLEIG in the *Encyclopaedia Britannica*, 1797   72
10 MUDFORD on the 'moral utility' of the *Rambler*, 1802   74
11 ALEXANDER CHALMERS in *British Essayists*, 1802   81
12 HAZLITT on the *Rambler*, 1819   86

The Dictionary (1755)

13 JOHNSON's *Plan of a Dictionary*, 1747   90
14 Foreign notice of the *Plan*, 1747   94
15 CHESTERFIELD in the *World*, 1754   95
16 JOHNSON writes to Thomas Warton, 1755   102
17 JOHNSON's letter to Chesterfield, 1755   103
18 JOHNSON's Preface, 1755   105
19 ADAM SMITH, unsigned review, *Edinburgh Review*, 1755 115
20 HORNE TOOKE's *Diversions of Purley*, 1786   117
21 A German view of the *Dictionary*, 1798   118
22 An American view of the *Dictionary*, 1807   125

Rasselas (1759)

23 OWEN RUFFHEAD, unsigned review, *Monthly Review*, 1759   141
24 Unsigned notice, *Annual Register*, 1759   147
25 MUDFORD on *Rasselas*, 1802   148
26 MRS BARBAULD, *The British Novelists*, 1810   149

Edition of *The Plays of William Shakespeare* (1765)

27 JOHNSON's *Proposals* for his edition of Shakespeare, 1756   155
28 From Johnson's Preface to the first edition, 1765   157
29 GEORGE COLMAN, unsigned notice, *St. James's Chronicle*, 1765   162
30 WILLIAM KENRICK, unsigned review, *Monthly Review*, 1765   164
31 WILLIAM KENRICK, *Review of Johnson's Shakespeare*, 1765   181
32 JAMES BARCLAY, *Examination of Mr. Kenrick's Review*, 1766   189
33 VOLTAIRE, 'Art Dramatique', in *Questions sur l'Encylopédie*, 1770   194
34 SCHLEGEL, *Lectures on Dramatic Art and Literature*, 1808   195
35 COLERIDGE on Johnson's *Shakespeare*, 1811–16   197
36 HAZLITT, *Characters of Shakespear's Plays*, 1817   199

Political Pamphlets (1770–5)

37 Unsigned review of *The False Alarm*, *Critical Review*, 1770   204
38 Unsigned review of *The False Alarm*, *Monthly Review*, 1770   207
39 PERCIVAL STOCKDALE, *The Remonstrance*, 1770   209
40 JOHN WILKES, *A Letter to Samuel Johnson LL.D.*, 1770   211
41 JOSEPH TOWERS, *A Letter to Dr. Samuel Johnson*, 1775   216
42 Anonymous, *Tyranny Unmasked*, 1775   225

Journey to the Western Islands of Scotland (1775)

43 ROBERT FERGUSSON, 'To Dr. Samuel Johnson', 1773   231
44 RALPH GRIFFITHS, unsigned review, *Monthly Review*, 1775   234
45 Anonymous, *Remarks on a Voyage to the Hebrides*, 1775   237
46 JAMES MCINTYRE, 'On Samuel Johnson, who wrote against Scotland', 1775   240
47 DONALD MCNICOL, *Remarks on Dr. Samuel Johnson's Journey to the Hebrides*, 1779   242

Lives of the English Poets (1779–81)

48 EDWARD DILLY to James Boswell, 1777   250
49 Advertisement to the *Lives*, 1779   252

CONTENTS

50 EDMUND CARTWRIGHT, unsigned review, *Monthly Review*,
    1779–82   253
51 Unsigned review, *Critical Review*, 1779–81   270
52 WILLIAM COWPER's opinions of the *Lives*, 1779–91   273
53 FRANCIS BLACKBURNE, *Remarks on Johnson's Life of Milton*,
    1780   278
54 WALPOLE on the *Life of Pope*, 1781   284
55 WILLIAM FITZTHOMAS, *Dr. Johnson's Strictures on the Lyric
    Performances of Gray*, 1781   285
56 Unsigned review, *Annual Register*, 1782   293
57 ROBERT POTTER, *Inquiry*, 1783   295
58 SIR JOHN HAWKINS, *Life of Samuel Johnson LL.D.*, 1787   303
59 ROBERT POTTER, *The Art of Criticism*, 1789   306
60 ANNA SEWARD's opinions of the *Lives*, 1789–97   311
61 DE QUINCEY, 'Postscript respecting Johnson's Life of Milton',
    1859   313

Johnson's Prose Style
62 ARCHIBALD CAMPBELL, *Lexiphanes*, 1767   317
63 JOHNSON defends his style, 1777   323
64 WALPOLE, 'General Criticism of Dr. Johnson's Writings',
    c. 1779   324
65 ROBERT BURROWES, on 'the Stile of Doctor Samuel Johnson',
    1786   326
66 ANNA SEWARD on Johnson's prose style, 1795   343
67 NATHAN DRAKE on the influence of Johnson's style, 1809   344
68 SIR JAMES MACKINTOSH, private journal, 1811   349
69 COLERIDGE's opinions on Johnson's style, 1818–33   355

Biographical and General
70 CHARLES CHURCHILL, 'Pomposo' in *The Ghost*, 1762   357
71 JOHN WILKES, *North Briton*, 1762   360
72 BLAKE, 'An Island in the Moon', c. 1784   363
73 JOHN COURTENAY, *A Poetical Review*, 1786   364
74 JOSEPH TOWERS, *An Essay*, 1786   371
75 BOSWELL, *The Life of Samuel Johnson LL.D.*, 1791   383
76 ANNA SEWARD's general estimate of Johnson, 1796   412
77 GEORGE MASON, Epitaph on Johnson, 1796   415
78 RICHARD CUMBERLAND, *Memoirs*, 1807   416
79 SCOTT, *Lives of the Novelists*, 1821–4   420

CONTENTS

80 MACAULAY, review of Croker's edition of Boswell's *Life*,
     Edinburgh Review, 1831   423
81 CARLYLE, review of Croker's edition of Boswell's *Life*,
     Fraser's Magazine, 1832   432

    BIBLIOGRAPHY   449
    SELECT INDEX   451

Preface

The purpose of this volume is to document the development of Johnson's reputation by extracts from criticism written (with one exception, No. 61) during his lifetime and up to 1832. The terminal date is significant: by that time both Macaulay and Carlyle had published their reviews of Croker's edition of Boswell's *Life of Johnson*; in their essays was found authoritative expression of views about Johnson which remained virtually unchallenged almost until the present century.

Extracts are grouped chronologically under each of Johnson's major publications. Since his critics gave considerable attention to his style a separate section is devoted to that. Further, some extracts are most conveniently collected under the heading 'Biographical and General', either because they have historical significance without having exclusive reference to any single work by Johnson, or because of the scope of their authors' inquiry.

The main principles of selection were interest, historical importance, and representativeness. Literary or critical excellence was not the first criterion. Much critical writing in Johnson's lifetime and immediately after it was not distinguished; but his work had to endure criticism which ranges from the crude to the sensitive, and his character to tolerate both savage denigration and panegyric. The collection of extracts must therefore be qualitatively wide-ranging. In some cases, as with James Callender's notorious *Deformities of Dr. Samuel Johnson*, where the original publication was itself fragmented as well as coarse, and selection was almost impossible if the reader's pleasure was to count for anything, quotation has been confined to the introductory essay. No apology is necessary for quoting from Johnson himself: both as stylist and as commentator on his own works he outshines most of his critics.

Acknowledgments

The publication of this volume affords a welcome opportunity to acknowledge a number of personal debts: to the President, Librarian, and English Department at Hofstra University, New York, for hospitality and research facilities during my tenure of the John Cranford Adams Chair; to the library staff and the 'Johnsonians'—especially their doyen, Professor James Clifford—of Columbia University for their many courtesies to a frequent visitor; to Professor Donald J. Greene, of the University of Southern California at Los Angeles, for extensive bibliographical information; to Dr David Fleeman, of Pembroke College, Oxford, for his scholarly care in reading and making valuable improvements to the introductory essay; and to Mr W. R. Chalmers, of the University of Nottingham, for his patient help in solving problems in classical literature. For errors that still remain I take sole responsibility.

I am grateful to the Harvard College Library for permitting me to publish the text of their rare copy of *A Criticism on Mahomet and Irene*; and to the Trustees of the British Museum for permission to print Horace Walpole's 'General Criticism of Dr. Johnson's Writings' from the manuscript in their possession.

Note on the Text

Materials printed in this volume follow the original texts in all important respects; no attempt has been made to modernize spelling, punctuation, or capitalization, but typographical errors have been silently corrected. Lengthy extracts from Johnson's works have been omitted as clearly indicated in the text.

The following abbreviations have been used throughout:

Boswell, *Life:* James Boswell, *The Life of Samuel Johnson LL.D.*, third edition, 1799; for the reader's convenience page references are given to the edition by G. Birkbeck Hill and L. F. Powell, Clarendon Press, 1934–50.

Johnsonian Miscellanies: Johnsonian Miscellanies, ed. G. Birkbeck Hill, Clarendon Press, 1897.

Journey: Samuel Johnson, *A Journey to the Western Islands of Scotland* (with Boswell's *Tour to the Hebrides*), ed. R. W. Chapman, Oxford University Press, 1924.

Lives: Lives of the English Poets by Samuel Johnson, LL.D., ed. G. Birkbeck Hill, Clarendon Press, 1905.

Letters: The Letters of Samuel Johnson, ed. R. W. Chapman, Clarendon Press, 1952.

Poems: Samuel Johnson, Poems, ed. E. L. McAdam with George Milne, Yale University Press, 1964.

Shakespeare: Johnson on Shakespeare, ed. Arthur Sherbo, Yale University Press, 1968.

Introduction

Four years after Johnson's death in 1784, the essayist Vicesimus Knox remarked on the severity with which he had been treated by critics and biographers:

Few men could stand so fiery a trial as he has done. His gold has been put into the furnace, and really, considering the violence of the fire, and the frequent repetition of the process, the quantity of dross and alloy is inconsiderable. . . .

I think it was in Egypt in which a tribunal was established to sit in judgment on the departed. Johnson has been tried with as accurate an investigation of circumstances as if he had been judicially arraigned on the banks of the Nile.

It does not appear that the witnesses were partial. The sentence of the public, according to their testimony, has rather reduced him; but time will replace him where he was, and where he ought to be, notwithstanding all his errors, and infirmities, high in the ranks of Fame. . . . The number of writers who have discussed the life, character, and writings of Johnson, is alone sufficient to evince that the public feels him to be a *great man*.[1]

Here in summary form is the outline of Johnson's critical reception both during his lifetime and afterwards. Few writers have been subjected to an equally sustained, rigorous, and wide-ranging scrutiny for upwards of a century. Few have emerged from 'so fiery a trial' with such a secure reputation for greatness. The general nineteenth-century view of that greatness does not coincide with our own; but eminence of some kind was rarely denied him. He was constantly before the public: whether to acclaim or admonish, a succession of reviews, pamphlets, and books kept him there. It may have been merely an anonymous letter to the *Gentleman's Magazine* in 1774 in which he was cited as evidence that the ancients did not excel the moderns 'in elegance of stile, or superiority of knowledge'.[2] Or the swingeing attacks made on him by men like Charles Churchill, John Wilkes, Archibald Campbell and James Callender. Or such a book as Robert Alves's *Sketches of a History of Literature* (1794) which, because of its censorious attitude towards Johnson, forced the *Monthly Review* into a reappraisal of its critical view of him.[3] Or, on the other hand, it may have been no more than the casual sneer that occurs in Cobbett's *Tour of Scotland* (1832):

Dr. Dread-Devil (who wrote in the same room that I write in when I am at *Bolt-court*) said, that there were *no trees* in Scotland, or at least something pretty nearly amounting to that. I wonder how they managed to take him about without letting him see trees. I suppose that lick-spittle Boswell, or Mrs Piozzi, tied a bandage over his eyes, when he went over the country which I have been over. I shall sweep away all this bundle of lies.[4]

Whatever the nature of the reference or the authority of the commentator, the reading public were continually reminded that the character, writings, and reputation of Johnson were subjects for debate. Indifference to them was impossible.

Johnson was not indifferent to his reception: praise or censure, so long as it was published, was welcome to the professional author:

It is advantageous to an authour, that his book should be attacked as well as praised. Fame is a shuttlecock. If it be struck only at one end of the room, it will soon fall to the ground. To keep it up, it must be struck at both ends.[5]

Johnson never lacked admirers, but a review of his critical reception leaves the impression that the most persistent and clamorous were his traducers. Indeed one wants to believe, with Boswell, that Johnson's paragraph in the *Life of Blackmore* reflected his own character:

The incessant attacks of his enemies, whether serious or merry, are never discovered to have disturbed his quiet, or to have lessened his confidence in himself; they neither awed him to silence nor to caution; they neither provoked him to petulance nor depressed him to complaint. While the distributors of literary fame were endeavouring to depreciate and degrade him he either despised or defied them, wrote on as he had written before, and never turned aside to quiet them by civility or repress them by confutation.[6]

By 1779 (when this was written) Johnson knew from harsh experience how essential was this equanimity.

CONTEMPORARY RESPONSE: A GENERAL REVIEW

Substantial critical attention to Johnson's works was delayed until the publication of the *Rambler*, 1750–2. His two major poems attracted little notice. The *Gentleman's Magazine* printed brief extracts from *London* in May 1738 with the comment that the poem had 'become remarkable for having got to the Second Edition in the Space of a Week' (the third edition appeared on 15 July). Perhaps more significant was Pope's remark on the anonymous author that 'he will soon be *déterré*'.⁷ *The Vanity of Human Wishes* in 1749—the first work to bear Johnson's name —attracted even less attention. The *Gentleman's Magazine* printed extracts with no critical comment. On the other hand *Irene* (1749), his sole and unsuccessful attempt to write for the stage, was greeted by two pamphlets (Nos. 4, 5). Barely more than a fortnight after the first performance an anonymous sixpenny pamphlet was on sale, followed two weeks later by another, possibly written by the actor John Hippisley.

With the *Rambler* (1750–2) Johnson first caught the critics' attention on any important scale. The sales were not large—though recent research shows that the potential readership was greater than had been thought before—but critical interest in the essays began at once. Two early tributes were reprinted by the *Gentleman's Magazine* from the *Remembrancer* and the *Student* (No. 6); a third was reprinted from the *Daily Advertiser*. Charlotte Lennox, in the penultimate chapter of her novel *The Female Quixote* (1752), declared 'the Author of the Rambler' to be 'the greatest Genius in the present Age'. Joseph Warton included *Rambler* No. 37 in his *Works of Virgil in Latin and English* (1753); in the same year essay 53 on 'Essay Writers after Addison', in the *Gray's-Inn Journal*, referred to 'the admirable Performances of the Author of the *Rambler*' in his 'nervous, clear, and harmonious Stile'; and Goldsmith paid Johnson a handsome compliment in the *Bee*, 3 November 1759. A discordant note had been sounded, however, in the *Connoisseur*, essay 27, on 1 August 1754. Although the author does not refer directly to Johnson, in view of subsequent criticism of his style one suspects that the *Rambler* was the target of remarks on the 'new-fangled manner of delivering our sentiments':

As to Essays, and all other pieces that come under the denomination of familiar writings, one would imagine, that they must necessarily be written in the easy language of nature and common-sense. No writer can flatter himself, that his productions will be an agreeable part of the equipage of the tea-table, who writes almost too abstrusively for the study, and involves his thoughts in hard words and affected latinisms. Yet this has been reckoned by many the standard stile for these loose detached pieces.

A few days earlier a similar comment in the privacy of a letter from Lady Mary Wortley Montagu to Lady Bute certainly shows that the *Rambler* had roused the interest of the *cognoscenti*; it is also an early example of the distaste for the 'Laborious Author' (whose identity Lady Mary did not know) who plods after the *Spectator* 'with the same Pace a Pack horse would do a Hunter in the style that is proper to lengthen a paper'.[8]

The *Rambler* had crept anonymously into the world; the *Dictionary*'s arrival was carefully stage-managed and professionally 'puffed'. The *Plan of a Dictionary* had appeared in 1747; Dodsley, the publisher, had persuaded Lord Chesterfield (to whom the *Plan* was dedicated) to write two essays for the *World* (November–December 1754) to herald the forthcoming work; these essays were reprinted in three other journals,[9] and an extensive advertising campaign coincided with the publication of the *Dictionary* itself on 15 April 1755. The book was widely reviewed. The *Monthly Review* allotted so much space to its favourable notice (by Sir Tanfield Leman) that it omitted its usual monthly 'Catalogue of Books', 'notwithstanding the additional expence of *four pages extraordinary*'.[10] The *Gentleman's Magazine* reviewed it enthusiastically, and —like the *Public Advertiser* and *London Magazine*—printed Garrick's poem '*Upon* Johnson's *Dictionary*' celebrating his friend's superiority over the forty academicians of France:

> And *Johnson*, well arm'd, like a hero of yore,
> Has beat forty French, and will beat forty more.[11]

The practice of reprinting important notices—obvious in the case of Garrick's verses—was also employed in the case of Adam Smith's largely favourable article in the *Edinburgh Review* (No. 19). Abroad Johnson's *Dictionary* was presented in 1755 to both the French Academy and the Accademia della Crusca; at home suitable publicity was given to these events.[12]

The chorus of approbation was not sustained. As the more professional lexicographers entered the debate censure of Johnson mounted. John Maxwell led the way. In *The Character of Mr. Johnson's English Dictionary* (1755) he attacked the omission of certain classes of words, inadequate etymologies, and the unsatisfactory arrangement of Johnson's definitions. Later the notorious John Horne Tooke contemptuously dismissed Johnson's work as unworthy of serious consideration (No. 20); Herbert Croft in his *Unfinished Letter to Pitt* (1788) found the *Dictionary* 'defective beyond all belief';[13] George Mason in his *Supplement to Dr. Johnson's Dictionary* (1803) described his predecessor's book as abounding in 'inaccuracies as much as any English book whatsoever —written by a scholar';[14] and the American lexicographer, Noah Webster, following up his *Letter to Dr. David Ramsay* (No. 22), remarked in the introduction to his *American Dictionary of the English*

Language (1828) on Johnson's 'great defect of research by means of which he often fell into mistakes; and no errors are so dangerous as those of great men.' Only the German scholar, Johann Christoph Adelung, in one of his *Three Philological Essays* (translated by Willich in 1798), was able to retain enough critical objectivity to give a balanced appraisal of Johnson's achievement (No. 21).

Rasselas was published anonymously in April 1759 but no reviewer seems to have been in doubt about its authorship. Its initial reception was varied: the *Gentleman's Magazine* and the *London Magazine* were favourable; the *Critical Review* and Owen Ruffhead in the *Monthly* (No. 23) were censorious; and the *Annual Register* (No. 24) was mixed.

Until and including the publication of *Rasselas* Johnson's reception by reviewers had been largely favourable, certainly tolerant, even on occasions good humoured. But in the 1760s a degree of virulence and personal malice hitherto completely absent made its appearance. Charles Churchill opened fire with the portrait of 'Pomposo' in *The Ghost*, Book II, March 1762; before Book III appeared in October he had formed his friendship with the radical John Wilkes and Johnson had accepted a royal pension; consequently the second passage on 'Pomposo' in the later book is edged with a bitterness so far unknown in Johnsonian criticism (No. 70). Simultaneously—in August 1762—Wilkes joined in the attack on Johnson's alleged political apostasy and hypocrisy, in the *North Briton*, Nos. 11 and 12 (No. 71). In 1765 William Kenrick added his severity, first in a thirty-page review of Johnson's edition of Shakespeare in the *Monthly Review*, and then in a book-length excoriation of the same work (Nos. 30, 31). Though the *Gentleman's Magazine* expressed itself unable to explain the 'malignity' of Kenrick's second attack,[15] it must be owned that, for the most part, the *Shakespeare* was greeted with disappointment. (The reputation of the edition improved only towards the end of the following century.) But more virulence was still to come in the 1760s. In 1767 Archibald Campbell's *Lexiphanes* purported to 'restore the English tongue to its ancient purity' by exposing Johnson's 'affected style' to harsh ridicule and by applying 'that rod which draws blood at every stroke'.[16] This he followed with the *Sale of Authors* (1767) which intensified the assault on Johnson among others. Concentrated in this decade, therefore, was a series of vicious attacks which coincided with a notable rise in Johnson's popularity and authority; from now on personal, political, scholarly, and stylistic matters seemed equally legitimate for critical use.

Johnson played into the hands of abusive critics in the following decade by publishing four political tracts between 1770 and 1775. The first, *The False Alarm* (1770), was roundly condemned in the *Middlesex Journal* and *Political Register* as well as in the *North Briton* and three pamphlets, one by Wilkes, the man at the centre of the furore (No. 40).[17] *Thoughts on . . . Falkland's Islands* (1771) and *The Patriot* (1774) were received with similar hostility; but most bitterness was reserved for Johnson's contribution to the debate on the American colonies, in *Taxation no Tyranny* (1775). The *Public Advertiser*, *St. James's Chronicle* and *Whitehall* carried rebuffs from pseudonymous contributors;[18] at least ten pamphleteers denounced him; and though he was not without defenders, they were swamped by the voices of the opposition. So successful were his detractors that—backed by more than a century of misunderstanding of eighteenth-century politics—Johnson's political views have continued to be grossly misrepresented. To the detriment of his fundamental rationalism, scepticism, and humanitarianism, he was declared a high Tory out of sympathy with democratic principles. Equally false was the description of Johnson as a Jacobite. He was also vilified for his alleged support of arbitrary rule based on the divine right of kingship; he was in fact a monarchist but on pragmatic grounds and with a profound distrust of all political metaphysics. And on the American question, though he was denounced (by Joseph Towers among others) for defending tyranny, Johnson's intention in *Taxation no Tyranny* was quite otherwise. In that pamphlet he expounded rationally and logically the constitutional principle of the inalienable sovereignty of the British Parliament over the American colonies. He can be accused of being insensitive to the demands of practical politics in 1775, but his wholehearted approval of a policy of armed repression is certainly open to doubt. First, since he introduced textual changes into his pamphlet as a result of ministerial pressure, his original views cannot be exactly known; second, the use of armed force was inconsistent with his declared horror of war; and third, Johnson never believed that governmental tyranny was a practical possibility. 'Mankind will not bear it. If a sovereign oppresses his people to a great degree, they will rise and cut off his head.'[19]

In the mid-1770s attacks were directed from a new quarter—Scotland—on the *Journey to the Western Islands* (January 1775). Most London-based reviewers were favourably disposed towards 'the learned author' in whom 'every talent was united which could gratify the most inquisitive curiosity',[20] but not so the Scots. A poem by Robert Fergusson (No. 43) which appeared in the Edinburgh *Weekly Magazine* a month before the Doctor's tour was completed gave a foretaste of what was to greet the published work. The *Weekly Magazine* carried six hostile reactions by March 1775[21] and an anonymous pamphlet appeared before the end of the year. Other angry rejoinders followed, the most abusive being one of 370 pages by Donald McNicol (possibly with assistance from the indignant James 'Ossian' Macpherson).

Johnson's last major work (1779–81), the *Lives of the English Poets* (as they came to be known), inevitably attracted multitudinous commentators ranging from one anonymous contributor to the *London Packet* offering his views on the *Life of Milton* to another in the *Westminster Magazine* on the *Life of Smith*,[22] as well as more substantial critics. With such a variety of issues raised—chief among them being Johnson's alleged hostility to Milton and the lyric poetry of Gray—there was abundance of matter for critical scrutiny. The plethora of censorious pamphlets and articles continuing well into the nineteenth century must not, however, be allowed to obscure a generally favourable reception: 'It is a work which has contributed to immortalize his name.'[23] While, for example, abusive criticism of Johnson on *Paradise Lost* could readily be cited, account must also be taken of the *Monthly* reviewer: 'it is executed with all the skill and penetration of Aristotle, and animated and embellished with all the fire of Longinus' (No. 50). Similarly, though William Fitzthomas devoted an entire pamphlet to refuting Johnson's 'Strictures on the Lyric Performances of Gray' (No. 55), the *Critical Review* supported Johnson: 'Gray's Odes, as well as his other little performances, have been much over-rated' (No. 51).

The critical response of Johnson's contemporaries was, then, voluminous, searching, and frequently personal in view of the increasing dominance of the man who provoked it. Inevitably, too, because he was essentially a miscellaneous writer Johnson had to endure criticism of very diverse quality. His critics were innumerable. They were encouraged by newspapers whose volume and frankness impressed foreign visitors to London;[24] by the well-established system of journalistic reviewing; and by the avid interest in pamphleteering which Arthur Young said existed even among 'grocers, chandlers, drapers, and shoemakers of all the towns in England'.[25] Johnson's contemporaries could not remain unaware of his character, views, prejudices, and publications; cartoonists like Gillray reminded them of his appearance and of widely shared (even if not fully justified) attitudes towards him;[26] indeed their number cannot be estimated who, on his death, would ask

Richard Cumberland's rhetorical question: 'When will this nation see his like again?'[27]

POSTHUMOUS RESPONSE

Cumberland's was undoubtedly the implicit question asked by the majority of the interminable necrologists, biographers, recorders of Johnsonian anecdotes, and the like, after Johnson's death in 1784. Of many it could be said, as Thomas Tyers remarked of his own *Biographical Sketch*: 'His little bit of gold he has worked into as much gold-leaf as he could.'[28] Yet in virtually all the substantial biographies—as well as the avowedly literary-critical studies—some attempt was made to evaluate Johnson's writings. But Johnson the man could not be dislodged; his conversational prowess, religious devotion, benevolence, learning, and his exemplary struggle from obscurity to incomparable fame all kept him in the centre. Inevitably then, his biographers exerted a major influence on his literary reputation. Ironically the consequences were unhappy. Boswell fulfilled his role as biographer with such brilliance in 1791 that only forty years later Macaulay and Carlyle could express their own and their generation's fascination with Johnson the man, yet for his works, contempt.

Boswell did not bring about this revolution unaided. The changing critical climate hastened the process. There continued to be critics like Robert Burrowes and William Mudford who were, though severe, fundamentally sympathetic; creative writers there were, such as George Crabbe and Jane Austen, who responded to the influence of 'dear Dr. Johnson';[29] but there is no denying a growing distaste for him and all he represented. It could manifest itself in Jeremy Bentham's dismissive remark—'that pompous preacher of melancholy moralities'[30]—or, on the large scale, in the Romantics' realization that Johnson epitomized supremely the assumptions about 'man, nature, and human life' which had to be rejected if their own convictions were to prevail. Their determination to confront and dispose of the eighteenth century by attacking Johnson is particularly evident in Coleridge, Hazlitt, and later De Quincey in England, and Schlegel in Germany. It is vividly demonstrated in Hazlitt's decision to meet Johnson's challenge in the prefatory remarks to his *Characters of Shakespear's Plays* (1817) before advancing his own views; it is summed up in his comment that 'if Dr. Johnson's opinion was right, the following observations on Shakespear's Plays must be greatly exaggerated, if not ridiculous' (No. 36). Johnson provided a sacrificial victim essential to the success of the literary and moral revolution.

JOHNSON'S RESPONSE TO HIS CRITICS

Against contemporary attacks, with one exception, Johnson offered no defence. 'The only instance, I believe,' says Boswell, 'in the whole course of his life, when he condescended to oppose any thing that was written against him,'[31] was a reply in 1756 to Jonas Hanway's angry retort to Johnson's review of his *Essay on Tea*. Even there Johnson was unconvinced of the propriety of making any response:

It is observed in the sage *Gil Blas*, that an exasperated author is not easily pacified. I have, therefore, very little hope of making my peace with the writer ... indeed so little, that I have long deliberated whether I should not rather sit silently down under his displeasure, than aggravate my misfortune by a defence of which my heart forbodes the ill success.[32]

Johnson never repeated his folly. Rather he adopted Vida's advice to his pupil, quoted in *Rambler* No. 176, 'wholly to abandon his defence, and even when he can irrefragably refute all objections, to suffer tamely the exultations of his antagonist.' Moreover, Boswell believed that Johnson 'enjoyed the perpetual shower of little hostile arrows',[33] presumably on the grounds that he outlined in conversation on 1 October 1773.

He remarked, that attacks on authors did them much service. 'A man who tells me my play is very bad, is less my enemy than he who lets it die in silence. A man, whose business it is to be talked of, is much helped by being attacked. ... Every attack produces a defence; and so attention is engaged. There is no sport in mere praise, when people are all of a mind.[34]

Two years later he commented on the reception of *Taxation no Tyranny*: 'I think I have not been attacked enough for it. Attack is the re-action; I never think I have hit hard unless it rebounds.'[35] Both sets of remarks involve several considerations. As a professional Johnson was well aware that all publicity is good publicity; thus a writer becomes 'known' (as he triumphantly informed Chesterfield (No. 17)); and he becomes economically more attractive to the publishers. Again, as a writer who was perpetually a teacher—'a majestick teacher of moral and religious wisdom', Boswell called him[36]—Johnson sought the assurance that his writings drew some positive response even if it were hostile. And, thirdly, he had a high regard for the public's right to pass judgment on an author's performance: 'the public to whom he appeals must, after all, be the judges of his pretensions.'[37] If he sought their approval he must also be prepared to suffer their condemnation.

Although there is no firm evidence that Johnson—like his friend Burke in the *Enquiry into . . . the Sublime and Beautiful* (1757)—revised any of his writings to take specific account of criticism of them, this does not denote lack of interest. He could show mere amusement at the ineptitude of his opponents, as with McNicol's angry *Remarks on . . . Journey to the Hebrides* (1779): 'This fellow must be a blockhead. They don't know how to go about their abuse. Who will read a five shilling book against me? No, Sir, if they had wit, they should have kept pelting me with pamphlets.'[38] On the other hand, at least on two occasions, Johnson showed himself sensitive to criticism which sprang from the worthy motives of responsible men. According to Boswell[39] he was disturbed by the censure contained in a private letter from the Revd. William Temple and, probably more so since it was public, by Joseph Towers's *Letter to Dr. Samuel Johnson Occasioned by his late Political Publications* (No. 41). Towers's pamphlet was not virulent despite his profound disagreement with Johnson; perhaps its firm moderation, its respect for Johnson, and its basically moral disgust with his political views caused disquiet.

EDITIONS AND SALES OF JOHNSON'S WORKS

Evidence on these matters is necessarily incomplete. What is available seems to show a steady growth in Johnson's popularity in the early years, with a noticeable quickening of it in the late 1750s and 1760s. Indeed, while not disregarding the intrinsic achievement of the *Dictionary* and *Shakespeare*, it is likely that his delight in public criticism was soundly based economically; that the notoriety he acquired during the 1760s itself provoked an increased demand for his books.

Johnson's poem *London* could be described as a publishing success: a second edition within a week, a third within two months, and a fourth in the following year. Dodsley, the publisher, paid ten guineas for the copyright; Boswell thought the amount inadequate; but compared with the £7 Pope received from Lintot for the first version of *The Rape of the Lock* or the £15 for the second,[40] Johnson was fairly rewarded. By same token fifteen guineas for the *Life of Savage* (1744) and the same sum for *The Vanity of Human Wishes* (which was not separately republished in Johnson's lifetime)[41] was not inappropriate.

Irene was not a theatrical success; yet Johnson sold the 'copy' to Dodsley for £100 and received nearly £200 as his share of the profits. Nevertheless it was with the *Rambler* that his popularity increased significantly. The London sales of the twopenny issue each Tuesday and Thursday over the two years from March 1750 probably never exceeded 500. But, as R. M. Wiles has proved, through the practice of reprinting whole essays or extracts in provincial newspapers, 'more people in all parts of England had the opportunity of reading *Rambler* essays than saw the successive issues as they came from the press in London.'[42] From Bath and Bristol to Nottingham and Newcastle readers were able to enjoy at least 142 of the 208 issues of what the *Newcastle General Magazine* described as 'the best Paper of the present time'. Therefore, by 1752, when the collected edition of the essays was published, Johnson—with the aid of perceptive newspaper editors—had a potentially large and responsive audience. The fourth edition (of 1,500 copies) came out in 1756; three further London editions were produced in the 1760s; and the tenth was on sale in the year of Johnson's death. In addition Dublin had its unauthorized edition in 1752; Elphinstone published his (with permission) in Edinburgh, in 1750–2; and there were two further editions, probably from Edinburgh, in 1772 and 1776. For the essays Johnson received two guineas each, which compares favourably with the fee of two guineas for sixteen pages paid to contributors to the *Critical Review*.[43]

By placing his bust of Johnson on a solid volume marked 'RAMBLER', Joseph Nollekens, in 1777, accurately indicated the basis of his fame.[44] The consequent reputation—along with the publicity campaign conducted by the publishers—doubtless contributed to the success of the *Dictionary* in 1755. 'The Dictionary sells well,' wrote Johnson on 10 June 1755. It did. The reception of the first folio edition of 2,000 copies (price 90s. per copy) prompted a second in 1756, and concurrently the issue of the work in weekly parts at sixpence each for three and four sheets alternately, or at a shilling for seven sheets. Also in 1756 an octavo abridgement appeared; it went through ten editions (eight from London and two from Dublin) and approximately 40,000 copies in thirty years. Inevitably with this multiple choice of editions the expensive folio was not a best seller; yet by 1784 when Johnson died five editions had been required, totalling about 7,000 copies. The folio version was also reprinted in three quarto editions between 1775 and 1785, in London and Dublin.[45] When it is recognized that the public was, in 1755, offered as an alternative J. N. Scott's revision of the well-established *Universal*

Dictionary by Nathan Bailey, Johnson's success becomes even greater. In Boswell's estimation 'his clear profit was very inconsiderable';[46] he had been paid £1,575 (or perhaps £100 more[47]) but from this sum had to hire amanuenses, buy paper, and discharge other expenses; and he was paid £300 for 'improvements' to the fourth folio edition (1773). For his part Johnson insisted that publishers were 'generous liberal-minded men'.[48]

The cumulative importance of the *Rambler* to Johnson's esteem is further indicated by the announcement on the title-page of the third collected edition of the *Idler* (1767): 'By the Author of the Rambler'. His income from this edition is not known. From the first, in 1761, he had earned £84 2s. 4d., which represented two-thirds of the profit on the 1,500 two-volume sets printed. Equally important in the long term was the wide distribution of the essays through reprinting in London and provincial journals. The *Newcastle General Magazine*, for example, which had shown a marked enthusiasm for the *Rambler*, reprinted 28 numbers.[49]

The historian William Robertson remarked that 'an author should sell his first work for what the booksellers will give, till it shall appear whether he is an author of merit; or, which is the same thing as to purchase-money, an author who pleases the publick.'[50] This Johnson had done. By the late 1750s he was clearly an author who 'pleased'. Thus when he urgently needed money in 1759 Dodsley paid him £100 for *Rasselas* (which sold for 5s.); he added £25 more when a second edition was printed in the same year. For his part, Dodsley made a profitable purchase: the sixth edition was on sale in 1783. The work was also translated into Dutch (1760), French (1760), German (1762), Italian (1764), Russian (1795), and Spanish (1798).

The eight-volume *Shakespeare* of 1765 comprised 1,000 copies. In October, the month of publication, the *Gentleman's Magazine* announced that 'the rapid sale of the impression has already made a second necessary'; it appeared in November (750 copies). A pirated Dublin edition is dated 1766; authorized London editions followed in 1768, 1773, and 1778. It was only for the first three editions that Johnson had sole responsibility; other editors were also involved from 1773 onwards, though he continued to contribute notes and slight changes until Malone's *Supplement* in 1780. His total income from the venture has been estimated at £1,312 10s.[51]

All Johnson's political pamphlets met harsh criticism; all were anonymous; but the demand for them was obviously brisk. The publisher,

Thomas Cadell, brought out four editions of *The False Alarm* in 1770; two of the *Falkland's Islands* in 1771; two of *The Patriot* in 1774 and one in the following year; and four of *Taxation no Tyranny* in 1775.[52] Then, with the King's printer, William Strahan, Cadell reprinted the four pamphlets in a volume of *Political Tracts* (at 4s.) in 1776. The more clamorous the abuse, the greater the sales.

The same two publishers were responsible for the *Journey to the Western Islands* in 1775. They were doubtless encouraged by a reputed sale of 4,000 copies (at 5s.) in the first week; even if this exaggerates the speed of sale, Boswell corroborates the number sold.[53] Two editions in 1775 and three unauthorized Dublin editions (one issued in London with a bogus imprint) were produced. Then the demand ceased. Boswell was surprised; so was Johnson: 'in that book I have told the world a great deal that they did not know before.'[54] The register of borrowings from the Bristol City Library over the last eleven years of Johnson's life—the only one of its kind extant—confirms this impression of some initial enthusiasm followed by a steady decline.[55] A new edition of the *Journey* was not necessary until 1785 when Boswell published his own account of the tour and, one assumes, stimulated a demand for Johnson's. Six editions appeared in the next fifteen years.

Johnson's Advertisement to the *Lives of the Poets* (No. 49) clearly suggests that he underestimated either the magnitude of the task to which he committed himself in 1777 or his own enthusiasm as he proceeded with his commentary on a collection of poets who (except for four) were not of his own choosing. Some such explanation is needed to account for his naming 200 guineas when asked by the publishers to propose his fee. The publishers spontaneously added another 100 guineas; a further 100 were later paid to the author for corrections.[56] The sum was trivial in comparison with what Johnson at the height of his fame could have demanded—Malone thought 1,000 or even 1,500 guineas.[57] (It might be noted, for example, that Hugh Blair was paid £1,100 for his first three volumes of *Sermons*, 1777–90.[58]) Malone adds that the publishers probably made a profit of 5,000 guineas in twenty-five years. The succession of editions—seven before 1800 (and two from Dublin)—would seem to justify the assertion. And the Bristol Library registers corroborate the enthusiasm implied in the figures: in 1781–4 more borrowings were made of the *Lives* than of any other work in the 'Belles Lettres' section of the library. (It might be added that these borrowings exceeded those of Blair's *Sermons*, in the same period, by a ratio of eighteen to one.[59])

A compilation which, possibly as much as any, consolidated Johnson's reputation as a sage and moral teacher, as well as satisfying an audience unaccustomed to sustained and serious literary pursuits, was *The Beauties of Johnson*. It was published by Thomas Kearsley; the probable compiler was William Cooke, a member of the Johnson circle and author of the anonymous *Life of Johnson* published by Kearsley in 1785. The title-page sufficiently describes the contents of the work:

The Beauties of Johnson: Consisting of Maxims and Observations, moral, critical and miscellaneous, by Dr. Samuel Johnson. (Accurately extracted from his works, and arranged in Alphabetical Order, after the manner of the Duke de la Roche-Foucault's Maxims.)

The first volume appeared in 1781, at 3s.; a second volume was added and reprinted twice in 1782; and in 1787, at the 'seventh' edition, the two volumes were combined into one.[60] The reason for this, given in the Advertisement, is interesting:

The former Editions of this selection have been introduced into several of the most reputable schools, for both sexes, in the Kingdom; however, the Price of the two volumes (viz. *Five Shillings*) has been, by some, thought too much, the whole is therefore now brought into one Volume, under one Alphabet, and the Price reduced to Three Shillings and Sixpence.

Thus was Johnson made accessible to generations of young readers in a way that would certainly fix his image as a moralist from whose 'lips impressive wisdom fell'.[61] The book would have been highly appropriate at academies such as that conducted by Miss Pinkerton on Chiswick Mall.

The posthumous interest in Johnson was unprecedented. Dr Burney, reviewing Anderson's *Life of Johnson* in 1796, commented on the volume of it:

In the course of our reading or recollection, we do not remember a similar instance, either in antient or in modern times, of any man, however he may have distinguished himself by 'compass, pencil, sword, or pen,' having, within ten or eleven years from the time of his decease, been the object of so much literary notice.

The reviewer went on to prophesy that, however Johnson might have irritated some among his contemporaries, 'posterity will admire the depth, force, eloquence, moral purity, and originality of his writings, as long as the language of which he has made use shall remain intelligible.'[62] Publishers at first seemed to regard the potential readership for Johnson's writings as unlimited. An eleven-volume collected *Works*, with a 'Life' by Sir John Hawkins, was published in 1787; five years later another edition appeared in twelve volumes, prefaced by Arthur Murphy's 'Essay on the Life and Genius' of Johnson, and this was reprinted fifteen times by 1824.[63] A ten-volume edition was produced in Alnwick in 1816, and reissued in London in 1818. In 1825 there were five different editions: three from London, one from Glasgow, and another from Philadelphia. Then at last—and in view of the opinion expressed by Macaulay of Johnson's writings six years later it is not surprising—the demand in England apparently declined. The next edition—by Henry Bohn—was in two volumes in 1850 (republished in 1854). In America, however, the high rate of publication suggests at least that an interest was assumed to be continuing in Johnson's writings. A New York two-volume edition of 1832 was republished annually from 1834 to 1838, twice in the 1840s, four times in the 1850s, and again in 1873.

CRITICAL RESPONSE: AN ANALYSIS

In view of the indifferent quality of many eighteenth-century reviews —they ranged from something little better than publishers' lists to journals attracting contributors like Goldsmith, Dr Burney, and Johnson himself—Johnson's respect for them is perhaps surprising. But his view was probably a characteristic blend of generosity and realism: that theirs was a difficult function combining advertisement and critical evaluation, both of which were essential to the new class of professional writers. Without reviews books would not be known or bought, bad writers would not be chastised nor good ones acknowledged. He believed that reviewers wrote well 'in order to be paid well'[64]—which is sensible; but his claim that they were also impartial seems in flat contradiction of his own comments on the *Monthly* and *Critical*:

The Monthly Reviewers (said he) are not Deists; but they are Christians with as little christianity as may be; and are for pulling down all establishments. The Critical Reviewers are for supporting the constitution both in church and state.[65]

(One of his own definitions of 'impartial' is 'free from regard or party'.) He preferred the *Critical* reviewers on grounds other than their Toryism: even if they 'often review without reading the books through', they 'lay hold of a topick and write chiefly from their own minds. The Monthly Reviewers are duller men, and are glad to read the books through.' However, despite the alleged originality of the *Critical*, though review-criticism varied widely in quality it rarely approached the normal level of the *Edinburgh* and the *Quarterly* in the next century. The revolution of 1802—the founding of the *Edinburgh*—was still to come.

But in analysing the response to Johnson we must have regard for limitations other than those imposed by the lack of distinction in the majority of his critics. Attitudes existed or gradually developed, based primarily on prejudices of various kinds—social or religious, personal or political, as well as literary—which made it especially difficult for those critics to achieve the Arnoldian ideal of seeing the object as in itself it really was.

Johnson was from the beginning an outsider. He was poor and ambitious—and 'Slow rises worth, by poverty depress'd'; he was from the lower middle class in an age dominated by the aristocracy; he was coarse in a period jealous of its social refinement; and he had the proud aggressiveness (as well as the sympathy for the underprivileged) which is often associated with success founded solely on personal achievement. Like Burke he could have described himself as the 'novus homo'.[66] Both suffered for it. Burke scornfully repudiated the pretensions which accompanied aristocratic privilege, in his *Letter to a Noble Lord* (1796); Johnson wrote his famous letter to Chesterfield. Both men provoked sharp antagonisms. Indeed Johnson could have echoed Burke's Ciceronian retort made in the Commons in 1770: 'Novorum Hominum Industriam odisti' (which may be translated 'you hate the industry of self-made men').[67] The new man was hated not only for his industry but—as Pope had discovered—for his unaided success.

Social or class prejudices were, then, certainly active in some criticism of Johnson. His lowly origin and his professionalism frequently offered opportunities for a sneer or for a condescending explanation of his eccentricities. The jibe took various forms. It provided James Callender with an explanation for Johnson's emergence to fame: Johnson, 'not worth a shilling', was patronized by 'a phalanx of booksellers', 'protected' by Garrick, and indebted to Chesterfield; he thus gradually achieved 'the dignity of Independence'.[68] Archibald Campbell turned it the other way. He asserts that Johnson and his like—'authors by profession'—'reckon a gentleman who writes, or in the language of the shop, makes a book, an interloper who takes so much of their trade out of their hands.' Therefore 'they entertain a particular spite against noble authors.'[69] Thus Johnson becomes by turns a dependant or an inverted snob, a social climber or a literary tradesman. Sometimes the sneer that he wrote 'for gain or profit' was used to explain why he was better qualified for certain literary tasks than for others. William J. Temple, in his *Character of Dr. Johnson* (1792), describes his subject as 'the son of a petty bookseller of Lichfield, or some other provincial town' (which recalls Swift's contemptuous remark on Defoe—'the fellow that was pilloried, I have forgot his name'); he later explains why Johnson was best equipped for lexicography: 'Poverty and Solitude bar the door against liberal and enlarged observation and refinement of sentiment, but are peculiarly favourable to the compiler's labour.'[70] Sir Samuel Egerton Brydges accounts on similar grounds for Johnson's inability in the *Rambler* to match Addison's 'exquisitely nice touches of character'; his own creations, though 'full of good sense are coarse'. The explanation follows: 'Johnson had not in early life, like Addison, been familiar with the circles of polished society,'[71] and no amount of experience could compensate for that deficiency. Likewise Mrs Thrale, smarting under Johnson's rebuke for laughing at people who like to smell their food before eating it, generalized on the same theme:

These Notions . . . seem to me the faeculancies of his low Birth, which I believe has never failed to leave its *Stigma* indelible in every human Creature; however exalted by Rank or polished by Learning:—no Varnish though strong can totally cover primaeval meanness, nor can any Situation of Life remove it out of the Sight even of a cursory & casual Observer . . . no Flattery was so welcome to him, as that which told him he had the Mind or Manners of a *Gentleman*.[72]

Sir Walter Scott shrewdly detected a similar bias in Anne Seward:

Neither Dr. [Erasmus] Darwin nor Miss Seward were partial to the great moralist. There was, perhaps, some aristocratic prejudice in their dislike, for the despotic manners of Dr. Johnson were least likely to be tolerated where the lowness of his origin was in fresh recollection.[73]

Thomas Tyers, writing his *Biographical Sketch* in 1784, clearly recognized the class-prejudice operating against Johnson; he nobly repudiated it: 'His father . . . was an old bookseller at Lichfield, and a whig in principle. The father of Socrates was not of higher extraction, nor of a more honourable profession.'[74]

Scott's use of the word 'despotic' directs attention to another set of attitudes which militated against critical objectivity. Various elements were combined here. Envy of Johnson's successful emergence from

Johnson exhibits a striking likeness of a confident, over-weening, dictatorial pedant, though of parts and learning.'[81] And Sir James Mackintosh, in his journal for 1811, opens his account of Johnson with these words (No. 68):

Dr. Johnson had a great influence on the taste and opinions of his age, not only by the popularity of his writings, but by that colloquial dictatorship which he exercised for thirty years in the literary circles of the capital.

In varying degrees, therefore, commentators on Johnson were guilty of prejudiced and—if not vindictive—certainly personalized criticism. He appeared to his contemporaries a man of extraordinary stature whose influence became immeasurable and whose dominance of 'the literary circles of the capital' was absolute. They found it virtually impossible to dissociate his writings from his reputation and personality. To the extent that they considered his influence beneficial, they welcomed his rule; to the extent that they disapproved of authoritarianism in general and 'King Critic' (to quote Cowper (No. 52)) in particular, they repudiated it. Few were objective.

Turning to the criticism of specific works, one can say outright that throughout the period to 1832 the assessment of Johnson's poems was generally inadequate. In his lifetime little was said of them worth remark. Occasionally certain poems were commended. For example, in the early months of 1748 (before the publication of *The Vanity of Human Wishes*) Thomas Gray wrote to Walpole:

... (I am sorry to differ from you, but) *London* is to me one of those few imitations, that have all the ease and all the spirit of an original. The same man's verses at the opening of Garrick's theatre are far from bad.[82]

Or again, Goldsmith wrote a headnote for *London* in his collection called *The Beauties of English Poesy* (1767):

This poem of Mr. Johnson's is the best imitation of the original that has appeared in our language, being possessed of all the force and satyrical resentment of Juvenal. Imitation gives us a much truer idea of the ancients than even translation could do.[83]

Among his biographers most, like Boswell, rate Johnson highly as an 'ethick' poet; few analyse the poems in detail. William Shaw is an exception but his analysis is finicking; he looks for a Popeian kind of verbal economy and, failing to find it, censures what he takes to be tautologies. His conclusion is broadly representative of eighteenth-century opinion:

Johnson fortunately for his reputation was soon satisfied his *forte* did not lie in making verses. His poetry, though not anywhere loaded with epithets, is destitute of animation. The strong sense, the biting sarcasm, the deep solemnity, which mark his genius, no where assume that union, symmetry, or collected energy, which is necessary to produce a general effect. We are now and then struck with a fine thought, a fine line, or a fine passage, but little interested by the whole.[84]

Mudford in his *Critical Enquiry* is at least prepared to devote earnest attention to the poems; he succeeds in underlining some of Johnson's distinctive qualities but he too uses Pope as his reference point, to Johnson's disadvantage. Also, like Joseph Warton writing on Pope himself, Mudford finds Johnson unable 'to attain those heights of sublimity which astonish and delight' (No. 2). The assumptions (originally Burkean) behind this remark had secured wide acceptance by 1802. 'The mind that is not turned either to the sublime or the pathetic, cannot certainly rank in the first class of writers of imagination.'[85] Satire no longer commanded immediate respect; when written in couplets it was likely to attract the disapproval marked by Mudford's word, 'mechanical'. (Only a few years later Keats would speak of 'musty laws lined out with wretched rule'.[86]) If Johnson's poems were to find approval it was more probably on the basis of their morality. On these grounds John Aikin could place *The Vanity of Human Wishes* higher than Juvenal on account of its superior theology (No. 3). The only critic who showed notable sensitivity to Johnson's achievement in poetry was Anna Seward, not invariably one of his admirers. In her view it was only 'the gay and commiserating sensations' that he failed to touch in his verse; that he was unable to excite the 'passions' of any kind she totally rejects. Indeed she claims for Johnson 'nervous and harmonious versification . . . a quick and vigorous imagination, elevated sentiments, striking imagery and splendid language'. She continues:

Of the author who possessed those great essentials, it is surely not too much to say that he might, had he chosen it, have been perpetually a poet—a stern and gloomy one certainly; but yet a poet, a sublime poet, however the want of tender sensibilities might have closed all the pathetic avenues against his muse.[87]

Anna Seward, with other critics of *Irene*, dismissed the possibility that Johnson could ever have become 'a great dramatic writer'. There was unanimity among the critics whether they wrote—like the two quoted below (Nos. 4, 5)—in 1749, or in biographies published after his death, that whereas the play was morally unexceptionable, the verse was non-dramatic; the author reached the intellect but not the emotions of his audience. 'The very soul of Tragedy, *Pathos*, is wanting; and without that, though we may admire, our hearts will sleep in our bosoms.'[88] Had Garrick not been involved in the production or, for later writers, had Johnson not been the author, *Irene* would almost certainly have attracted less critical attention.

The *Rambler* 'was the basis of that high reputation which went on increasing to the end of his days' (No. 8). So wrote Arthur Murphy in 1792; the critical history of the work supports his claim. The second public tribute to the essays, in 1750—probably by Christopher Smart—contains in embryo most subsequent criticism: a comparison with Addison, a reference to 'high-wrought' diction, the appropriateness of style to sentiment, and the general vigour of the writing. Later critics were principally concerned to amplify or contest these points. One critical tradition contesting them begins in the *Connoisseur* (quoted on p. 3)—objecting to Johnson's abstruseness, 'hard words and affected latinisms'—and makes its way through Campbell's burlesque of his style in *Lexiphanes* to Hazlitt's complaint about his wordiness and stylistic monotony (No. 12). But for the most part, from the critic in the *Gray's-Inn Journal*, 1756, via Goldsmith and Anna Seward (in her letters of 1763-4) to Boswell, Murphy, George Gleig in the *Encyclopaedia Britannica* (1797), and Alexander Chalmers in *British Essayists* in 1802, there was a consensus of critical opinion. It was largely agreed that, though Addison was the safer model for imitation, Johnson had revolutionized and enriched the essay style. He achieved 'more vigour, more spirit, more elegance. He not only began a revolution in our language, but lived till it was almost completed.' As is true of so much criticism of Johnson, Chalmers is here praising him on grounds which he had himself already specified. In the final *Rambler* paper Johnson claims as his chief contributions to the essay tradition an increased refinement of language, greater stylistic elegance, and the inculcation of wisdom and piety. Again it is Anna Seward who proves herself particularly sensitive to his style. Few writers before the present century have commended Johnson's lavish 'use of imagery and metaphor' with equal force; few recognized the advantage he derived from his classically-based diction: 'Greek and Latin being so much higher voweled than English, a liberal intermixture of words springing from their roots, must surely render the style more graceful and sonorous'; and few better conducted the critical exercise of comparing Johnson with Addison:

The language of Addison appears to me as only possessing distinguished excellence from comparing it with that of his contemporary writers; and even then we should except some of them, Bolingbroke and Swift for instance, who wrote prose at least as well; that, compared with the style of our present essayists, it is neither remarkably perspicuous nor remarkably musical . . . Then he frequently finishes his sentence with insignificant words . . . [which] utterly precludes that roundness, that majestic sweep of sound, in which the Johnsonian periods so generally close: periods that my ear finds of such full and satisfying harmony, as not to need either rhyme or measure to add more sweetness. In truth, rhyme and measure are but the body of poetry, not its spirit, and its spirit breathes through all the pages of the *Rambler*.[89]

Great stress was also laid on one feature not mentioned by Smart: Johnson's distinction as a moral teacher in the *Rambler*. Again critics were paying tribute to his having achieved his stated purpose: 'to consider the moral discipline of the mind, and to promote the increase of virtue rather than of learning'.[90] It was recognized that he taught known truths but that, as Addison had remarked of Pope's *Essay on Criticism*, in 1711:

they are placed in so beautiful a light, and illustrated with such apt allusions, that they have in them all the graces of novelty, and make the reader, who was before acquainted with them, still more convinced of their truth and solidity.[91]

Hazlitt and his age no longer accepted the criteria assumed here; critics nearer to Johnson's time did. There was only one discordant voice: that of William Mudford. While he generally approved of the *Rambler*—judiciously edited, it would be 'the most estimable book which the English language can boast'—he took very strong exception to the misanthropic cast of the author's mind. The impression of mankind given in the essays is, he claims, of 'fraud, perfidy, and deceit'; Johnson overstresses the evils of mortal existence and underestimates its joys. 'This . . . greatly disqualifies the work for the hands of youth.' But Mudford is second to none in his estimation of the importance and popularity of the *Rambler*: 'where is the person who lays any claim to learning that has not read the *Rambler* of Johnson?' (No. 10). Indeed when Boswell (who writes some of his most spirited pages on the essays) perpetually thought of Johnson as 'the Rambler', he was acknowledging what he and his contemporaries recognized as among the most distinctive of the Doctor's achievements.

With the exception of the *Lives of the Poets*, no work raised a greater furore among the critics than the *Dictionary*. To indicate their range we can cite Callender on the one hand and George Colman and Joseph

Towers on the other. In the *Deformities* Callender delivers a bitter and sustained attack on Johnson's 'amazing ignorance', 'circumscribed reading', and 'negligence':

> We look around us in vain for the well known hand of the Rambler, for the sensible and feeling historian of Savage, the caustic and elegant imitator of Juvenal, the man of learning, and taste and genius. The reader's eye is repelled from the Doctor's pages, by their hopeless sterility, and their horrid nakedness.[92]

One is surprised only by the modicum of praise which precedes the damnation. Colman, writing in the *Gentleman* of July 1775, expressed his conviction that the *Dictionary* would ever remain 'a monument of the learning and genius of its author'.[93] And Towers for his part selected this (with the *Rambler*) as Johnson's most permanently valuable work. He acknowledges its faults—no man could 'suppose it possible that it should be without'; but adds:

> His Dictionary was a work of great labour, and great merit, and has not been praised more than it deserves . . . by the completion of it, with all its defects, he might justly be considered as having rendered a signal service to the republic of letters.[94]

Both professional and amateur criticism, with varying authority, fluctuated between these extremes. Once more Johnson had anticipated it: his Preface, a moving and honest appraisal of intentions and achievement, foreshadows much which both friends and detractors had to say.

The initial reception of the *Dictionary* was generally favourable; it did not involve professional lexicographers whose reactions took longer to formulate, but rather cultured amateurs who were moved (as is clear in Garrick's verses) by patriotism or were prepared (as Johnson suggests in his Preface) to estimate the work by its practical usefulness. Adam Smith, for example, considered the word-list ample and accurate; he urged its use since there was 'no standard of correct English in conversation' (No. 19). On these grounds, like Towers later, he was ready to pardon its defects. Not so the professionals. In their hands criticism became more detailed and cumulatively severe. Horne Tooke sneered, reinforcing his ridicule with political prejudice; Herbert Croft, despite his great regard for Johnson—'this great Philological Cook'[95]—lamented his extraordinary carelessness; and it fell to the German lexicographer Adelung to give a discriminating assessment. His account is the more convincing, not only because he fairly identifies Johnson's failures and his successes—his etymologies on the one hand, and distinctions between vulgar and polite usage on the other; but also because he is quite detached from all controversies relating to Johnson the man or 'literary despot'. Noah Webster was differently motivated. His onslaught on the *Dictionary* in the *Letter to Ramsay* was prompted by politico-sociological as much as by lexicographical reasons. In 1789—eighteen years before the *Letter*—he published his *Dissertations on the English Language* in which he spoke of Johnson 'whose pedantry has corrupted the purity of our language'; he went on to insist on the intimate relationship that should exist between the 'political harmony' of an independent America and the 'uniformity of its language':

As an independent nation, our honor requires us to have a system of our own, in language as well as in government. Great Britain, whose children we are, and whose language we speak, should no longer be *our* standard; for the taste of her writers is already corrupted, and her language on the decline.[96]

It is an easy step from rejecting a political system to rejecting 'the right often assumed by individuals who dictate to a nation the rules of speaking, with the same imperiousness as a tyrant gives laws to his vassals'. Here, manifestly, is a further example of the irritation with the despotic Johnson—Webster refers to 'literary governors' and lists Johnson among them—which was discussed earlier. Webster's fury at his countrymen in Charleston, South Carolina, who objected to his presumption in trying to improve on Johnson's *Dictionary* can be readily understood. It accounts in great measure, though not entirely, for the animus and rigour of his comments in the *Letter to Ramsay*.

Undoubtedly Johnson's growing reputation in other fields strengthened the authority of his *Dictionary*; his posthumous fame and the immensity of his lexicographical achievement, despite its flaws, gave it the status of an oracle. Consequently later lexicographers were constantly placed in the position of improving on Johnson, rarely—'until the notion of the standard and standardizing dictionary was called in question'[97]— of being able to produce original and independent work. Their frustration in having to repair the scholarship of the man who had pre-empted them, one they regarded as a careless if gifted amateur, at least partly explains their vindictive criticism.

Though Johnson 'had written nothing else', Boswell believed *Rasselas* 'would have rendered his name immortal in the world of literature' (No. 75). Yet the book attracted little independent criticism after its appearance in 1759.[98] Owen Ruffhead in the *Monthly Review* condemned it severely for the author's limited narrative ability, his pompous style (for which Johnson later fell foul of Campbell), the lack of discrimination between characters and of originality of design. To the extent that this criticism depends on naturalistic principles, Ruffhead was answered by the *Annual Register*'s reviewer who observed that the story is merely a vehicle for the moral content; thus vivid action and nicely discriminated characters should not be expected. Ruffhead's objections to Johnson's moral vision found support in Mudford. Ruffhead complained that by insisting on disappointment as endemic in human life, Johnson would exacerbate it by discouraging determined effort. Mudford thought Johnson's morbid melancholy not validated by general experience; therefore, despite admirable features of language and sentiment, he regarded *Rasselas* (as Johnson did *Paradise Lost*) as a work which the reader admires, puts down, and fails to pick up again. Mrs Barbauld, in 1810, added a further complaint. Proper to an age which was becoming acutely conscious of the social interdependence of all men, she asserts that to focus attention on a single individual, unencumbered by family or duty and seeking abstract good, falsifies the terms of a philosophical inquiry intended to have general relevance. Nevertheless she recognizes that Johnson's stylistic richness is appropriate to an oriental tale; she rightly protests that he had been underestimated as an imaginative writer; and she claims that his morality is 'perfectly pure'. Johnson had painted no 'luxurious bower of bliss': it is worth recalling that Mrs Grundy had made her appearance in 1798 and that Dr Bowdler's *Family Shakespeare* followed in 1818.

The edition of Shakespeare suffered initially from the expectations which had been aroused during the nine-year period since the *Proposals* were issued. Remarks by George Colman (himself a dramatist) and the *Critical* reviewer testify to the keenness of these expectations. Colman was tolerant: 'the appearance of any production of Mr. Johnson cannot fail of being grateful to the literary world' (No. 29). Not so the reviewer who considered the edition permanently damaged by the long gestation.[99] Other prejudices which Johnson encountered are clarified by reference to William Kenrick's *Review* (which followed his article in the *Monthly Review*). In line with Churchill and Wilkes, who had prepared the way, Kenrick lashes Johnson for accepting a pension; dominating the 'republic of letters'; enjoying the 'homage' of the King, universities, writers, and booksellers; and presuming to intrude into a field of scholarship in which he had no competence. Such personal abuse is now easy to shrug off, as it is with Pope who suffered greatly at the hands of Grub Street for his creative and social successes (but who expected 'the life of a Wit' to be 'a warfare upon earth'); but we must recognize its intensity.

Shakespeare editing was a literary minefield: four editions had appeared since Rowe's in 1709, and Johnson had not only to justify the need for another but also to withstand scrutiny from a highly critical and, in many cases, well-informed public. They expected an 'attempt to do justice to the [Englishman's] favourite poet' (No. 31): many were angry at Johnson's seeming rigour in exposing Shakespeare's weaknesses; they expected lavish textual emendations with notes to defend them: they found that, as Johnson 'practised conjecture more, [he] learned to trust it less';[100] they expected large-scale textual collation: they found that Johnson failed them on this score too. Even his young Oxford champion, James Barclay, before beginning his rebuttal of Kenrick's indictment, feels bound to admit that the editor had disappointed 'the expectations of the generality'; because of his reputation for learning, Johnson had been relied upon to provide 'a compleat commentary upon the works of their immortal bard'; his failure to satisfy this demand had provoked 'public censure' (No. 32). Joseph Ritson, irascible critic as he was, had some justification for remarking on Johnson's claim that originally he collated all the folios but 'afterwards used only the first': 'men who proudly expose and severely reprobate the crimes of their neighbours should effectually guard themselves against similar accusations.'[101]

The Preface to the edition was from the first treated with respect, often admiration: Edmond Malone considered it 'one of the finest compositions in our language'.[102] This did not, of course, protect it against critical scrutiny. When Schlegel, Coleridge, and Hazlitt sought to establish the Romantic view of Shakespeare, it was with the Preface that they took issue. We are then made aware of the antagonism between two centuries, traditions, and modes of criticism. Coleridge's scathing description of Johnson as the 'dogmatic Critic and soporific Irenist' (No. 35) underlines the lumbering conventionality and juridical heaviness, the lack of imaginative perception and the insensitivity to poetry for which the Romantics condemned him. His style, as well as his critical criteria, was Procrustean.

Comparable hostility was lavished on his political pamphlets when they first appeared. Doubtless there were some who shared Adam Smith's and the Tory *Critical Review*'s admiration for the moral sophistication shown in *Falkland's Islands*;[103] others no doubt had the high opinion expressed by a modern historian of Johnson's defence of the government's case in *Taxation no Tyranny*;[104] but it was in a review of this pamphlet in the *Monthly* that Edward Bancroft stated the attitude generally held:

Human powers and human knowledge are circumscribed within such narrow limits, that no individual can excell in all undertakings.—The writer to whom we ascribe the work before us, has on other occasions by the right application of his talents merited a large share of public approbation; and if his present effort has less claim to applause, it is not because his abilities have been impaired, but because they have been misapplied. We have before had occasion to regret that any motive should have influenced him to engage in political controversy, and we believe his present performance will yield no considerable addition to his credit.[105]

Great abilities but misapplied: sharpened by abuse in the case of Wilkes or by bitter disappointment at Johnson's treachery to the cause of 'candour, of justice, and of truth' in the case of Towers—that was the general response to the political pamphlets as a whole. Johnson's critics exhibited an interesting contrast in rhetorical methods. On the one hand there is the attempt—bolstered by abuse of Johnson's hireling pen—to translate into common speech what a newspaper correspondent called his 'intolerable fustian'[106] and thus to reduce his seeming authority. This is the method described by Wilkes as his 'humble but laborious province, to endeavour to reduce [Johnson's] lofty speculations to the level of vulgar apprehension' (No. 40). Towers, on the other hand, dispenses with all scurrility; his manner evidences greater liberality and refinement than Wilkes's; and his effect is achieved through a sternly abrasive statement of regret at Johnson's betrayal of the morality so finely communicated in his non-political writings. The rhetorical range also includes the middle way of *Tyranny Unmasked* whose author does not hesitate to make scathing accusations but tempers them with a serious attempt to grapple with Johnson's argument (No. 42).

The response to Johnson's *Journey to the Western Islands* divided by and large on national grounds. English reviewers approved highly of it; Scottish patriots challenged its accuracy and fairness. Ralph Griffiths in the *Monthly Review* found the author 'able and entertaining' (No. 44); the *Critical* reviewer, equally enthusiastic, observed that a travel-book must provide an investigation of 'the remote resources of the genius and character' of the people as well as topographical descriptions.

Such an enquiry can only be conducted by a person who is conversant in moral speculations, and is endowed with intellectual penetration capable of tracing the peculiarities of manners and action, through their various modifications, to the universal principles of human nature. In the learned author of this *Journey* every talent was united which could gratify the most inquisitive curiosity, or give elegance and dignity to narration.[107]

The Scots for their part felt both insulted and patronized. They were bitterly aware of the distrust of them entertained in England since medieval times and recently intensified by the three armed rebellions in the Highlands together with George III's unpopular choice of Lord Bute as Prime Minister. One recalls Boswell's timorous remark on first meeting Johnson: 'I do indeed come from Scotland, but I cannot help it.'[108] It is relevant to remember the mixture of pride with a sense of injury and inferiority in that remark when considering Scottish replies to the *Journey*. Moreover Johnson's supposed anti-Scottish prejudice was well known, as Fergusson's poem testifies. Unbiased responses could scarcely be expected north of the Border.

They were conveyed in undistinguished prose. The anonymous author of the *Remarks on a Voyage to the Hebrides* (1775) and McNicol are both on the defensive, both merely advancing objections and facts in opposition to Johnson's magisterial assertions; in fact both sound petty and irritable. However justified their claims, they appear humourless and as intolerant as Johnson was reputed to be. It is a case of pugnacious authority challenged by petulant chauvinism. Fergusson's poem is saved only by its wit, though this is somewhat smothered by his rhetorical device of inflating, for the purpose of burlesque, every simple term into a grandiose latinate monstrosity.

Beneath the fears and thus the severity of the detractors of Johnson's *Dictionary*, his political pamphlets, the *Journey* and, finally, the *Lives* lay a frequently stated apprehension which was expressed by the author of *Tyranny Unmasked* in these words:

the most straggling thoughts, when they are supposed to come from able writers, are apt to have an influence on many, beyond their specific moment in the question.[109]

Partly because the *Lives* were received with wide acclaim and would therefore exert 'an influence on many', critics who wished to object to them in whole or part could not be content with cursory or mildly-phrased rejoinders. They had to contend with a journalistic reception typified by the two leading reviews: 'In the walk of biography and criticism Dr. Johnson has long been without a rival. It is barely justice to acknowledge that he still maintains his superiority' (No. 50). 'It was a labour which . . . no man but Dr. Johnson would have performed so well' (No. 51). One can appreciate the frustration and impotence felt by those who thought otherwise:

The splendour of Johnson's literary fame, and of his *ignis fatuus* reasoning, co-operating with the natural envy of the ignorant, or rather half learned, will enlist a numerous army under his banners, overpowering by their numbers and by their clamour the generous few who have perceptions of excellence, and who dare think for themselves.[110]

Criticism was aimed at the *Lives* from two main directions: moral and political, and literary. Francis Blackburne in his *Remarks on the Life of Milton* (1780) exemplifies the first. He accuses Johnson of sympathy with authoritarian political views and therefore of working out a 'virulent malignity' against Milton's republican convictions under cover of a biography.[111] In the event he is more abusive than Johnson whose alleged abuse of Milton he roundly condemns; but he was not alone in his opinion. Cowper explains Johnson's antipathy to Milton on the same grounds; so does Towers in his *Essay*; and the same reasoning underlies the angry comment by the distinguished orientalist, Sir William Jones: 'I can't praise [the *Lives*], nor do I want to have the good word of a man who abuses all the friends of Liberty because they are so.'[112] But in the long term more important were the literary objections. Here too, as with the Shakespeare edition, we encounter a significant shift of critical perspective. Leaving aside the major Romantic writers, authors like Cowper, Fitzthomas, Potter, Anna Seward and, later, Mackintosh, accused Johnson of inadequacy when confronted with recent, especially lyric, poetry. Few disputed his good sense, varied insights, or boldness and independence of judgment; but many found him a 'husky dry commentator' with a mind 'in some respects as narrow as a crane's neck' (No. 59). In particular they found him wanting when faced with, for example, the 'romantic turn' of Prior's verse, the poetry glowing with 'enthusiasm' of Gray, or the 'romantic' ideas and the 'wild grandeur' of imagination in Collins (Nos. 52, 55, 57). The tone of rapturous pleasure in Potter's remarks on Shenstone and Gray's *Bard* (Nos. 57, 59) is indicative of a new critical temper; against the spread of this and the criteria which sustained it Johnson seemed to crouch like a dragon at the gate. Richard Graves commented: 'A new era or school of poetry seems to have commenced with Mr. Gray, as different from the simplicity of Addison, Pope, and Parnel, as Pindar's or Horace's Odes from Homer or Virgil.'[113] To many of his contemporaries Johnson appeared insensitive or hostile to this revolutionary change. Thus, though—as Potter remarked—probably the majority of readers in 1779–81 accepted Johnson as 'infallible', it was not difficult to discern the coming rejection of his authority represented by Keats's dismissive statement in 1818: 'that

"Monument of his Mortality the lives of the Poets" and his deadness to the exalted and excellent in Poetry'.[114] More than a century was to pass before T. S. Eliot viewed the *Lives* as 'a masterpiece of the judicial bench'.[115]

As there are no modern writings higher in public estimation than Doctor Johnson's, and as there are none which abound more in appropriate marks of stile, there are none which can with more advantage be made the subject of critical enquiry.

Burrowes's declaration (No. 65) is symptomatic of the interest taken by sympathizers as well as detractors in Johnson's prose style virtually as distinct from content. All commentators testify to its extraordinary influence—on miscellaneous writers, critics, orators, and historians; Courtenay, Nathan Drake, and Mackintosh speak of a Johnson 'school' of writers (the first two providing names of its members); and except those like Campbell, Walpole, and Webster who lament the passing of the style associated with the age of Anne, most welcome Johnson's influence. The views of derogatory critics may be summarized in Webster's remark: 'simplicity of stile is neglected for ornament, and sense is sacrificed to sound.'[116] Burrowes, on the other hand, attributes to Johnson the awareness that his mode of thought, careful moral discriminations, and desire to provide imaginative stimulus required of him a prose medium different from that of his predecessors. His prose is variously described by others, but none analyses it with greater thoroughness or precision than Burrowes. Mackintosh identified the 'Rhetorical' period of Johnson and his school as the successor to the 'Latin or pedantic age' of More and Clarendon, and the age of Dryden and Addison with its middle style 'between vulgarity and pedantry' (No. 68). Anna Seward, generous in her commendation of Johnson's prose style, pronounced it 'the most perfect example of eloquent writing'; she also made one of the earliest laudatory comments on his use of abstract terms 'which at once elevate his language and compress his sense'.[117] Only in our present century have the implications of this remark begun to be investigated.

In an age when imitation of great models was standard literary practice it was inevitable that Johnson's prose style would be numbered among the select. Its 'universally acknowledged beauties' (No. 65) ensured that. Boswell prints quotations from some of the 'serious imitators', including William Robertson, Gibbon, and Fanny Burney;[118] Walpole, Burrowes, and Drake warn their readers against the dangers of imitating such a personal, highly-wrought manner; and Drake (like Boswell) censures the essayist Vicesimus Knox, for example, for adopting John-son's style for 'subjects too delicate to support its weight' (No. 67). But the practice continued; according to Coleridge the 'common miscel-laneous public' required trivial thoughts presented in an uncommon way (No. 69). It took a stylistic revolution at the direction of Carlyle to effect the break-up of Johnsonian English.

POSTHUMOUS REPUTATION

Other factors operated to complete Johnson's eclipse as 'the first great literary character' of his own age and that which followed. Doubtless his detractors of whom, through his long writing career, there were scores, cumulatively brought about some erosion of his reputation as the 'literary Colossus'[119] of his day. Then, as Arthur Murphy declared in the *Monthly Review*, 'many who would have trembled to have assaulted him when living, have mustered up resolution enough to treat him with a hearty kick *after he was dead*.'[120] Thus we have W. J. Temple who pro-nounced Johnson narrow-minded, arrogant, insensitive, and pompous; Mason whose vindictive epitaph is printed below (No. 77); Hurd who despised the pedant with the 'swaggering' style;[121] or Blake who associ-ates him with slightly crude jokes and spurns any reverential attitude (No. 72). Chalmers also ruefully observes that the courage of Johnson's adversaries rose 'very considerably after his death' (No. 11); they dis-covered new faults in his writings; and, as is the case of Potter's second critical work, they became more aggressive when safe from rebuff. Yet his adversaries could not alone secure his eclipse. Paradoxically it was his biographers, pre-eminently Boswell, who helped to bring it about. 'Friends and foes' alike, Arthur Murphy commented:

have conspired in mangling his memory, in *drawing his frailties from their dread abode*, and in bringing him to an inquisition so rigid, that were the like practised in the courts of Minos and Rhadamanthus, no mortal could pass into the Elysian fields.[122]

A highly sympathetic memoir of the dead man at once produced its counter-balance; however well intentioned, the result was to expose Johnson's defects with added rigour. Thomas Tyers and Joseph Towers provide an illustration. The opening sentence of Tyers's *Biographical Sketch* sets the tone for the whole; it applies to Johnson Charles II's remark on the death of Cowley: 'that he had not left a better man behind him in England'. Two years later, in 1786, Towers in his *Essay* explicitly rejects this view: Johnson had many virtues but also too many 'apparent faults to be considered as a proper object of indiscriminate imitation' (No. 74). Towers must then justify his assertion. He therefore proceeds to present Johnson as a throwback to an earlier age of intolerance and bigotry, out of tune with the growing enlightenment of the later eighteenth century. Johnson remains 'among the best and ablest writers that England has produced' but, to Towers the moderate radical, an unsatisfactory model for imitation.

Hard on the heels of Towers's *Essay* came the *Life* by Sir John Hawkins (first edition March, second June, 1787). Although Hawkins considered himself sympathetic towards Johnson, his detractors (including Boswell) attacked the biography as malevolent, and it can indeed be read in that light. However, as Bertram H. Davis has argued, 'in the tradition of the magistrate, Hawkins considered it necessary to cast up the account of good and bad, of pro and con, and to base his judgement, not on some preconceived notion, but on the evidence as it was presented to him.'[123] Whatever his motives, Hawkins appeared ruthlessly to expose Johnson's weaknesses; his commentary on the writings provided little compensation.

Boswell was undoubtedly on the offensive against Hawkins, but he did not write a panegyric. 'I profess to write . . . his Life; which, great and good as he was, must not be supposed to be entirely perfect.'[124] He did not reveal 'warts and all' but he was guided by Johnson's own demands of a biography in *Rambler* No. 60: 'If we owe regard to the memory of the dead, there is yet more respect to be paid to knowledge, to virtue, and to truth.' Honesty can be claimed for both Boswell and Hawkins; but Boswell loved Johnson where Hawkins respected him. Like Johnson himself when writing the life of his friend Savage, Boswell, though he was truthful, was not coldly objective. 'My affection and reverence for you are exalted and steady'; 'how elevating it is to my mind, that I am found worthy to be a companion to Dr. Samuel Johnson':[125] such statements confirm Boswell's personal involvement.

Yet with the foregoing evidence of critical controversy in mind, it is clear that he had to declare his position on every one of Johnson's major writings. His opening sentence, that Johnson 'excelled all mankind in writing the lives of others', implies an attitude to censorious critics of the *Lives*; his sympathetic critique of the *Rambler* and defence of its perspicuity ranges him firmly against critics like Campbell; or his care to assemble testimonies from distinguished witnesses proves his anxiety to dissociate himself from fellow Scots who had denounced the *Journey*.

But his position on the political tracts is not far removed from Towers's; he frankly disowns Johnson's views on America and criticizes *Taxation no Tyranny*. Equally was he committed to participation in the 'inquisition' on his friend's personality. Public inquiry was too intensive to be ignored. His *Life*—though *sui generis* and in its own right a notable advance in the art of biography—was a contribution to a controversy. Consequently Boswell had to declare himself on, say, whether Johnson was prejudiced in politics and religion, whether he was vain, whether he lacked humour or was aggressive. His answers were given with affection as well as frankness; but help they did to draw Johnson's 'frailties from their dread abode'.

His skill in confronting (or seeming to confront) all the contentious issues raised over half a century became less significant as time blunted the sharp edges of the debate. Indifference also helped to blunt some of them. It is noticeable how relatively small is the attention paid to Johnson by the Romantics and—except for Byron, who thought he possessed the 'noblest critical mind'[126]—how completely adverse their judgement. What unmistakably remained from Boswell's achievement was his vivid presentation of a character. The results are evident in Scott, Macaulay, and Carlyle. Scott could not read a word of Johnson without the man being recalled to his imagination by Boswell: 'a personification as lively as that of Siddons in *Lady Macbeth* or Kemble in *Cardinal Wolsey*' (No. 79). Macaulay confidently pronounced on the 'indiscriminate contempt' with which Johnson was regarded as a critic, the 'fading' reputation of his writings, and the irrelevance of analysing his stylistic faults—'the public has become sick of the subject' (No. 80). With equal assurance he declared the permanent interest in the character created by Boswell. For Carlyle too Johnson's works were 'becoming obsolete'; he prophesied that their continuing importance would be as 'Prolegomena' to Boswell's *Life*, a book he rated 'beyond any other product of the eighteenth century' (No. 81). Johnson for him was a man, not a writer; a Carlylean hero distinguished by his courage, honesty, compassion and sense of purpose to become one of 'the guides of the dull host'; indeed, in Matthew Arnold's words, from *Rugby Chapel*, one of those

> souls temper'd with fire,
> Fervent, heroic, and good,
> Helpers and friends of mankind.

Though Carlyle could claim with some justice in 1832 that outside England Johnson's name was 'hardly anywhere to be met with', in this country it continued to be frequently invoked. But that Johnson was largely Boswell's creation; as a writer he suffered almost total eclipse. There were, of course, exceptions to the rule. Arnold had obviously read him, but in blinkers; Leslie Stephen had read him, yet it was the talk recorded by Boswell to which he listened most avidly.[127] In fact the predominant nineteenth-century attitude may be summed up in some words from the *Temple Bar* of June 1892:

Our knowledge of Johnson comes to us solely and exclusively through Boswell's spectacles. .... Not one man in a thousand ... has ever dipped into any single thing that Johnson wrote.[128]

Like Becky Sharp and her contemptuous treatment of the *Dictionary*, her contemporaries had flung Johnson's works out of the window as the carriage rolled away from the eighteenth century.

What remained and has persisted in the popular imagination is either a picture (Miss Pinkerton's) of '*The Great Lexicographer*', 'the late revered Doctor Samuel Johnson'; or one of a rather coarse conventional Tory with the astonishing conversational loquacity recorded by Boswell; or a mixture of the two. As recently as 1946 C. E. Vulliamy rejuvenated the grotesque Johnson in his *Ursa Major*; in the same year Robert Lynd reaffirmed the dependence of Johnson on Boswell. Lynd presented the principal subject of his *Dr. Johnson and Company* as 'the hero of the most permanently entertaining book in English literature', and Johnson and Boswell were 'as inseparable in our imaginations as Castor and Pollux. Each, lacking the other, would lack half himself.'[129] But what Bernard H. Bronson called 'the learned tradition'[130] has increasingly asserted its authority. No longer is it possible for a student of Johnson to give credence, for example, to Lytton Strachey's remark on the *Lives of the Poets* in 1906:

as serious criticism, they can hardly appear to the modern reader to be very far removed from the futile. Johnson's aesthetic judgments are almost invariably subtle, or solid, or bold; they have always some good quality to recommend them—except one: they are never right.[131]

The scholarly reappraisal of Johnson has meant that Strachey himself now appears demonstrably wrong; his wit has ossified his folly.

The development of the 'learned tradition' of Johnsonian studies effectively began with the notable advance in textual scholarship associated with the name of George Birkbeck Hill. Significantly enough, he first edited Boswell's *Life* and *Tour to the Hebrides* (1887); then followed editions of Johnson's *Letters* (1892), the *Johnsonian Miscellanies* (1897), and the *Lives of the Poets* (1905). L. F. Powell completed the edition of Boswell's *Life* with monumental thoroughness in 1934; D. Nichol Smith with E. L. McAdam Jr. published their edition of Johnson's *Poems* in 1941; and R. W. Chapman his editions of the *Journey to the Western Islands* and the *Letters* in 1924 and 1952 respectively. And in 1958 the first edition of Johnson's complete works since 1825 began to appear from Yale. Side by side with editing has gone bibliographical study. First in the field was W. P. Courtney whose work was revised and published by D. Nichol Smith in 1915; the numerous attributions of writings to Johnson since that time have been surveyed by Donald J. Greene in his essay 'The Development of the Johnson Canon'.[132]

Following Sir Walter Raleigh's pioneer work *Six Essays on Johnson* (1910) and Nichol Smith's chapter in volume X of the *Cambridge History of English Literature* (1913), innumerable critical studies have directed attention to Johnson's historical and permanent significance as a writer. Major biographical studies, delayed for so long by the supremacy of Boswell, have been undertaken by Joseph Wood Krutch (1944) and James Clifford (1955), but the most sustained effort has undoubtedly been devoted to literary-critical investigations. Johnson's influence on the very practice of literary criticism has been striking. When F. R. Leavis can regard him as discriminating 'with something approaching infallibility between what is strong and what is weak in the eighteenth century',[133] this is not surprising. T. S. Eliot, Leavis himself, and others named below, with their insistence on the necessity for close attention to the detail of a literary text, their studious avoidance of generalizations except on the basis of such detailed scrutiny, and their sensitivity to the relationship between literature and morality, all pay tribute to Johnson's critical procedures. The application of this critical mode to his own writings has produced results of great moment. Eliot, for example, in his introductory essay to *London* and *The Vanity of Human Wishes* (1930), declared the two poems as 'amongst the greatest verse satires of the English or any other language'. This revolution in the estimation of Johnson as a poet has been continued in the work of other writers including Leavis (*The Common Pursuit*, 1952); Donald Davie (*Purity of Diction in English Verse*, 1952); Ian Jack (*Augustan Satire*, 1952); and Chester Chapin (*Personification in Eighteenth-Century English Poetry*, 1955). By similarly detailed and sensitive examination of Johnson's prose, W. K. Wimsatt (*The Prose Style of Johnson*, 1941) and Donald J. Greene (*Johnson, Boswell and their Circle*, ed. M. Lascelles *et al.*, 1965) have sharpened our understanding of his

36

complex, subtle, and often imaginatively stimulating style. Close scrutiny of Johnson's other writings has been employed with great advantage. From approximately 2,500 items in the bibliographical surveys conducted by James Clifford and Donald J. Greene[134] selection presents acute difficulties, but even a brief list of significant criticism must include: James H. Sledd and Gwin J. Kolb, *Dr. Johnson's Dictionary* (1955); W. J. Bate, *The Achievement of Johnson* (1955); Arthur Sherbo, *Johnson, Editor of Shakespeare* (1956); Donald J. Greene, *The Politics of Johnson* (1960); Robert Voitle, *Johnson the Moralist* (1961); and, on Johnson as literary critic, Allen Tate in *Collected Essays* (1949), Jean H. Hagstrum's *Johnson's Literary Criticism* (1952), and Warren Fleischauer's 'Johnson, *Lycidas*, and the Norms of Criticism' (in *Johnsonian Studies*, ed. Magdi Wahba, 1962). These and countless other writers have contributed to the rediscovery and, in some respects, the discovery for the first time of what—in Boswell's memorable phrase—Johnson essentially provides: '*bark and steel for the mind*'.[135]

NOTES

1 *Winter Evenings: or, Lucubrations on Life and Letters*, 1788, i. 187, 190–1.
2 *Gentleman's Magazine*, xliv (1774), 298.
3 *Monthly Review*, xviii (1795), 377–80 (by Dr Burney).
4 *Rural Rides*, ed. G. D. H. and M. Cole, 1930, iii. 820.
5 *Journey*, 431; see Boswell, *Life*, v. 400.
6 *Lives*, ii. 253.
7 Boswell, *Life*, i. 128–9.
8 *Complete Letters*, ed. R. Halsband, 1967, iii. 66–7.
9 See head note to No. 15.
10 Op. cit., xii (1755), 324.
11 Op. cit., xxv (1755), 190.
12 For these and other details of the reception of the *Dictionary* see works by J. H. Sledd and G. J. Kolb, and by Gertrude Noyes listed in the Bibliography.
13 Op. cit., 9.
14 Op. cit., i.
15 Op. cit., xxxv (1765), 529.
16 Op. cit., xiii.
17 *Middlesex Journal*, 3 Feb. 1770; *Political Register*, vi (June 1770), 315–18; *North Briton*, 13 Nov. 1770.

18 *Public Advertiser*, 13 March 1775; *St. James's Chronicle*, 1 April 1775; *Whitehall*, 6 April 1775.
19 Boswell, *Life*, ii. 170. For a full analysis see Donald J. Greene, *The Politics of Samuel Johnson*, Yale, 1960.
20 *Critical Review*, xxxix (1775), 44.
21 On 9, 16, and 23 February, and 2, 9, and 22 March.
22 *London Packet*, 28 June 1779; *Westminster Magazine*, vii (November 1779), 591–2.
23 *Critical Review*, iv (2nd ser. 1792), 259.
24 Cf. Friedrich Wendeborn, *A View of England towards the Close of the Eighteenth Century*, 1791, i. 211–18.
25 *Travels in France*, ed. M. Betham-Edwards, 2nd edn, 1889, 237.
26 See M. D. George, *Hogarth to Cruikshank: Social Change in Graphic Satire*, 1967, plates 119–21.
27 *Memoirs*, 1807, i. 364.
28 See *Johnsonian Miscellanies*, ii. 380.
29 *Jane Austen's Letters*, ed. R. W. Chapman, 2nd edn, 1952, 181. See also B. C. Southam, *Jane Austen's Literary Manuscripts*, 1964.
30 *Works*, ed. John Bowring, New York, 1962, ii. 386.
31 Boswell, *Life*, i. 314.
32 *Literary Magazine*, ii (1757), xiv. 253–6.
33 Boswell, *Life*, iv. 55.
34 *Journey*, 344; see Boswell, *Life*, v. 273.
35 Boswell, *Life*, ii. 335.
36 Ibid., i. 201.
37 Ibid., i. 200.
38 Ibid., ii. 308.
39 Ibid., ii. 316.
40 *The Rape of the Lock*, ed. G. Tillotson, 2nd edn, 1954, 104 and n.1.
41 It was, however, included in several poetical collections; see *Poems*, 91, for details.
42 'The Contemporary Distribution of Johnson's *Rambler*', *Eighteenth-Century Studies*, ii (December 1968), 159.
43 Boswell, *Life*, i. 208 n.3; iv. 214 n.2.
44 See R. M. Wiles, art. cit., 156.
45 For full details see R. C. Alston, *Bibliography of the English Language*, 1966, v. 30–7.
46 Boswell, *Life*, i. 304.
47 Ibid., i. 183 n.2.
48 Ibid., i. 304.
49 *Idler and Adventurer*, ed. W. J. Bate *et al.*, Yale, 1963, xxii n.
50 Boswell, *Life*, iii. 334.
51 *Athenaeum*, ii (1909), 298.

52 Dublin editions of *The False Alarm, Falkland's Islands* and *The Patriot* also appeared in 1770, 1771, and 1775 respectively; New York had its edition of *Falkland's Islands* in 1771.

53 Boswell, *Life*, ii. 310 n.2.

54 Ibid., iii. 326.

55 Paul Kaufman, *Borrowings from the Bristol Library 1773-1784*, Charlottesville, 1960, 41.

56 Boswell, *Life*, iv. 35 n.3.

57 Ibid., iii. 111 n.1.

58 Ibid., iii. 486.

59 Kaufman, op. cit., 15, 99.

60 For a full bibliographical account see Allen T. Hazen in *Modern Philology*, xxxv (1938), 289-95.

61 See below, No. 73. (The *Beauties* was republished in 1792 and 1797; a 'new edition' appeared in 1828.)

62 *Monthly Review*, xx (1796), 18-19.

63 Two of these editions were published in Dublin, one in Edinburgh, and another in Boston, Mass. Murphy's 'Essay' was also published separately from the *Works* in 1792 and again in 1793.

64 Boswell, *Life*, iii. 44.

65 Ibid., iii. 32.

66 Burke, *Correspondence*, ed. Lucy S. Sutherland, 1960, ii. 128.

67 Ibid.

68 *Deformities of Dr. Samuel Johnson*, 2nd edn, 1782, v.

69 *Lexiphanes*, 2nd edn, 1767, xviii.

70 Op. cit., 1792, 7, 9.

71 *The Ruminator*, 1813, ii. 67-8.

72 *Thraliana*, ed. K. C. Balderston, 1942, i. 186.

73 *Poetical Works of Anna Seward*, ed. Scott, 1810, i. x. But see below, p. 421.

74 *Johnsonian Miscellanies*, ii. 339.

75 See James T. Boulton, 'Arbitrary Power, an Eighteenth-Century Obsession: a Lecture', University of Nottingham, 1967.

76 *Lives*, i. 233.

77 *Mac Flecknoe*, ll. 5-6.

78 *The Ghost*, IV, ll. 872, 997-8, 1679-84.

79 *Memoirs of the Life and Writings of . . . Johnson*, 1785, 189.

80 *Deformities*, 31, 46 n., 82.

81 *Memoirs of the Life and Writings of Richard Hurd*, ed. F. Kilvert, 1860, 254.

82 *Correspondence of Gray*, ed. P. Toynbee and L. Whibley, 1935, i. 295.

83 *Collected Works of Goldsmith*, ed. A. Friedman, 1966, v. 320.

84 *Memoirs*, 71.

85 *European Magazine*, xviii (November 1790), 331.

86 'Sleep and Poetry', l. 195.

87 *Letters*, 1811, i. 305.

88 George Colman, *Prose on Several Occasions*, 1787, ii. 99.

89 *Poetical Works*, i. xc.

90 *Rambler*, No. 8.

91 *Spectator* No. 253. (Cf. No. 9 below.)

92 *Deformities*, 58, 66, 72.

93 *Prose on Several Occasions*, i. 185.

94 *Essay on . . . Johnson*, 1786, 38.

95 *Unfinished Letter to Pitt*, 1788, 38.

96 Op. cit., ed. Harry R. Warfel, in 'Scholars' Facsimiles and Reprints', Gainesville, Florida, 1951, xi, 19, 168.

97 James H. Sledd and Gwin J. Kolb, *Dr. Johnson's Dictionary*, 204.

98 Nevertheless, on average, three editions of *Rasselas* (including translations into major European languages) have appeared every two years since 1759. Of this approximate figure of 600 editions, 400 are in the English language.

99 See head note to No. 30.

100 Preface, in *Shakespeare*, 108.

101 *Remarks, Critical and Illustrative, on . . . Last Edition of Shakespeare*, 1783, iii.

102 *Percy Letters: Correspondence of Thomas Percy and Edmond Malone*, ed. A. Tillotson, Louisiana State University Press, 1944, 249.

103 *Johnsonian Miscellanies*, ii. 424; *Critical Review*, xxxi (1771), 196.

104 Peter Brown, *The Chathamites*, 1967, 150.

105 *Monthly Review*, lii (1775), 253. (Edward Bancroft (1774–1821) was responsible for most reviews on American affairs in the *Monthly*, 1774–7. See *D.N.B.* and *Dictionary of American Biography* for Bancroft's remarkable career.)

106 *London Packet*, 22 January 1770.

107 *Critical Review*, xxxix (1775), 44.

108 Boswell, *Life*, i. 392.

109 Op. cit., 11.

110 *Journals and Correspondence of Thomas S. Whalley*, ed. Hill Wickham, 1863, i. 348 (Letter from Anna Seward).

111 Op. cit., 131.

112 Cited by Peter Brown, *The Chathamites*, 387.

113 *Lucubrations*, 1786, 218 n.

114 *Letters*, ed. H. E. Rollins, 1958, i. 385.

115 *The Use of Poetry and the Use of Criticism*, 1933, 64.

116 *Dissertations on the English Language*, 34.

117 *Letters*, 1811, i. 212; ii. 267.

118 Boswell, *Life*, iv. 388–92.

119 Ibid., i. 2.

120 Op. cit., lxxvii (1787), 457.

121 Temple, *Character of Johnson*, 10–13; *Memoirs of Hurd*, 296.

122 *Monthly Review*, lxxvii (1787), 457.

123 Hawkins, *Life of Johnson*, ed. B. H. Davis, 1962, xxiv.

124 Boswell, *Life*, i. 30.

125 Ibid., iii. 105, 439.

126 *Letters and Journals*, ed. R. E. Prothero, 1922–4, v. 564; see also ii. 356; iv. 488, 490.

127 *English Literature and Society in the Eighteenth Century*, 1963 edn, 114.

128 Quoted by James Clifford, *A Survey of Johnsonian Studies, 1887–1950*, reprinted in *Samuel Johnson, A Collection of Critical Essays*, ed. D. J. Greene, Spectrum Books, 1965, 47.

129 Op. cit., 23, 27.

130 In 'The Double Tradition of Dr. Johnson', reprinted in *Eighteenth-Century Literature: Modern Essays in Criticism*, ed. James Clifford, New York, 1959, 286.

131 *Books and Characters*, 1922, 68.

132 In *Restoration and Eighteenth-Century Literature*, ed. Carroll Camden, Chicago, 1963.

133 *The Common Pursuit*, 1962 edn, 113.

134 See Bibliography, page 449.

135 Boswell, *Life*, i. 215.

1. Johnson seeking a publisher for *London*

(published 12 May 1738)

Text from the *Gentleman's Magazine*, lv (January 1785), 4–5.

Two letters from Johnson in the early months of 1738 to Edward Cave, the proprietor of the *Gentleman's Magazine*. Johnson does not identify himself as the author of his poem; it was published anonymously.

Sir

When I took the liberty of writing to you a few days ago, I did not expect a repetition of the same pleasure so soon; for a pleasure I shall always think it to converse in any manner with an ingenious and candid man; but having the inclosed poem in my hands to dispose of for the benefit of the author (of whose abilities I shall say nothing, since I send you this performance), I believed I could not procure more advantageous terms from any person than from you, who have so much distinguished yourself by your generous encouragement of poetry; and whose judgement of that art nothing but your commendation of my trifle[1] can give me any occasion to call in question. I do not doubt but you will look over this poem with another eye, and reward it in a different manner, from a mercenary bookseller, who counts the lines he is to purchase, and considers nothing but the bulk. I cannot help taking notice, that, besides what the author may hope for on account of his abilities, he has likewise another claim to your regard, as he lies at present under very disadvantageous circumstances of fortune. I beg therefore that you will favour me with a letter to-morrow, that I may know what you can afford to allow him, that he may either part with it to you, or find out (which I do not expect) some other way more to his satisfaction.

[1] Probably Johnson's ode 'Ad Urbanum'.

I have only to add, that as I am sensible I have transcribed it very coarsely, which, after having altered it, I was obliged to do, I will, if you please to transmit the sheets from the press, correct it for you; and will take the trouble of altering any stroke of satire which you may dislike.

By exerting on this occasion your usual generosity, you will not only encourage learning, and relieve distress, but (though it be in comparison of the other motives of very small account) oblige in a very sensible manner, Sir,

your very humble servant, Sam. Johnson.

Sir

I waited on You to take the copy to Dodsley's;[2] as I remember the number of lines which it contains, it will be longer than *Eugenio*,[3] with the quotations, which must be subjoined at the bottom of the page, part of the beauty of the performance (if any beauty be allowed it) consisting in adapting Juvenals sentiments to modern facts and persons. It will, with those additions, very conveniently make five sheets.

[2] Although Cave liked the poem he suggested that Robert Dodsley should publish it.
[3] A poem (1737) by Thomas Beach.

2. William Mudford on *London* and *The Vanity of Human Wishes*

1802

Text from the *Critical Enquiry*, 68–80.

Mudford (1782–1848)—a journalist and later editor of *John Bull*—published his *Critical Enquiry into the Moral Writings of Dr. Samuel Johnson* under the pseudonym 'Attalus'. His 'essays' had previously appeared in the London newspaper, the *Porcupine* in 1801. See Introduction, p. 21.

. . . some lines may justly contest even the superiority with Pope. But *London* presents less of these than the *Vanity of Human Wishes*. Yet the former is said to have obtained the approbation of a man (Pope) well qualified to judge; who declared that the author of such an excellent work could not be long concealed.[1] This story is related, but is, I think, little deserving of credit. Pope, whose ear was accustomed to the nicest harmony, and who could easily discern the minutest deviation from propriety, can hardly be supposed to have overlooked the many weak lines and puerile tautologies which this presents; and if he saw them, it can as little be supposed that he would have conferred upon it such a disqualified commendation.*

It is an invidious mode of criticism to detect and expose trifling errors in a work, which otherwise abounds in beauties; it displays a mean appetence to detraction; and a mind void of sensibility. Yet as much indiscriminate praise has been lavished on this poem of Johnson's, and [it] has even been preferred by some to his *Vanity of Human Wishes*, and as its faults have been hitherto unnoticed, a few remarks may be offered without any disingenuous imputation. I am far from wishing to detract

* 'His poetry, though not any where loaded with epithets, is destitute of animation. We are now and then struck with a fine thought, a fine line, or a fine passage, but little interested by the whole. After reading his best pieces once, few are desirous of reading them again.' [William Shaw,] *Life of Johnson*, 1785, [71–2].

[1] Boswell, *Life*, i. 128–9.

in the smallest degree from the great fame of Johnson, and I am besides aware, that no examination of his poetry can do it, however severe it may be. He has been read, and praised, and imitated, as a philosopher, a moralist, and an elegant prose writer; but none yet ever did, or ever can, confer upon him the appellation of poet. I therefore only propose to myself, in exposing a few trifling errors, to give confidence to un-ambitious modesty, and to instruct the blind admirers of this stupendous genius that even *he* is not infallible.

It is always deemed unlucky to stumble upon the threshold. In the third couplet, however, Johnson has fallen into a manifest tautology.

> Resolved at length from vice and London *far*
> To breathe in *distant* fields a purer air.

This indeed was hardly to have been expected from the usual correctness of his language, which was in general scrupulous of the words adopted, even to a fault. Yet we have the same impropriety again, a few lines afterwards.

> With slavish tenets *taint* our *poisoned* youth.[2]

It is impossible to taint a body already poisoned. If there be a weaker line in the namby pamby verses of Philips, or the dull page of Tate,[3] I will confess my inability to discover it. It is indeed surprizing, that the perspicuity of Johnson's mind, which could so readily detect the deviations of other poets, should have been incapable of correcting his own.* But the fondness of a parent, rarely beholds the imperfections of his offspring.

The concluding line of this poem is remarkably weak, and the last part is indeed a mere languid iteration of the former.

These are a few of the faults of this imitation, and these are sufficient

---

* He did not often conform himself to his own precepts. In his Essay on Pope's Epitaphs, (which is indeed an invidious piece of criticism), he says, 'I think it may be observed that the particle *O!* used at the beginning of a sentence, always offends.'[4] Yet, in his translation of the dialogue between Hector and Andromache, he himself uses it.

> How would the Trojans brand great Hector's name,
> And one base action sully all my fame,
> Acquired by wounds and battles bravely fought!
> *Oh!* how my soul abhors so mean a thought.[5]

And in many other of his pieces, as his 'Lines to a Friend', 'To a Young Lady on her birth-day', &c. &c.

---

[2] Both this and the previous example of tautology were cited by William Shaw (*Memoirs of the Life of Johnson*, 51) to whom, it would appear, Mudford was often indebted.

[3] Ambrose Philips (1675?–1749) and Nahum Tate (1652–1715).

[4] *Lives*, iii. 266.

[5] *Poems*, 19.

to answer my purpose. I now hasten to the more agreeable task of pointing out some of its most striking beauties, which I trust will be more agreeable to my reader. The description of London is spirited and just; for who can deny but that

> Here malice, rapine, accident, conspire,
> And now a rabble rages, now a fire;
> [quotes to l. 18]

There is something colloquial and vulgar in the expression *talks you dead* (l. 18), which is not suited to the dignity of poetry. In these lines also, he uses the initial resemblances, or alliterations, though he censures them in his life of Gray.[6]

Johnson had the power of reasoning in verse, though he did not always reason with cogency, nor did he possess the vigour of Pope in condensing much meaning in a few words. That is a power granted but to few, and is not much the effect of study. But he is seldom more pleasing than in the following lines:

> But thou, should tempting villainy present
> All Marlborough hoarded or all Villiers spent,
> [quotes to l. 90]

After enumerating with indignation, the vices and snares of the metropolis, the poet takes occasion to break out into the following exclamation.

> Has heaven reserved in pity to the poor
> No pathless waste or undiscovered shore?
> [quotes to l. 177]

These are perhaps the beauties of *Johnson's poem*, but they surely are not the *beauties of poetry*.

The Vanity of Human Wishes is by far more energetic, and more pleasing than *London*.—Whether it be that the author had improved his taste or his judgment; whether he was seized with some sudden inspiration, or whether he was intent upon exposing what he had long beheld with pain and anxiety, I know not; but it certainly contains more masterly touches, more spirited delineations, more vigour of sentiment, and compression of language than his *London*. This was indeed his favourite topic.

His *Vanity of Human Wishes* was published the year preceding the

[6] *Lives*, iii. 439.

commencement of his *Rambler*.[7] It may therefore be expected to contain some of those sombre pictures, and doleful declamations which that work presents. And this expectation will not be disappointed, for it does in fact abound in them, and they are, in consequence, the most pleasing parts of the poem. Some of these I shall transcribe, as exhibiting more happy efforts of Johnson's poetic powers.

I will not vouch for the truth of the following lines, but must affirm, that they afford a rich repast to the melancholy mind, and to those whom disappointments have taught the necessity of patience.

> On ev'ry stage the foes of peace attend,
> Hate dogs their flight, and insult mocks their end.
> [quotes to l. 90]

There is much of keen satire and animated diction in this passage, and it would have been no disgrace to the pen of Pope or Dryden. It has indeed been the opinion of some, that had Johnson cultivated poetry, he would have equalled the former author in his versification, and in his language. Of this no one can be certain; and all conjectures are vain; but there exist no solid grounds for the inference. Those who regard poetry as mechanical, may perhaps believe it; but those who consider it as intuitive and not to be acquired, will reject it as idle. What Johnson could not attain at forty years of age, it is not likely he ever would attain afterwards. It is my opinion, that no labour or study, however assiduous, could possibly have ever rendered him equal to Pope, whose melody and genius yet remain unequalled.

[summarizes and comments on various passages from the *Vanity*.]

From these quotations it is, I think, manifest how far superior the present poem is to the *London* of Johnson. While the former contains nothing that is remarkable, this frequently presents striking lines and paragraphs, and is often laboured into dignity; the language is more pure, the ideas more vivid, and the versification more harmonious: yet Johnson's claim to poetry is very doubtful. He was too much given to reasoning and declamation ever to attain those heights of sublimity which astonish and delight. If he seldom offends by his harshness he as seldom exhilarates by his vivacity; and though he did not detract from our poetic dignity, he cannot be said to have added any thing to it. As his reflections were always melancholy, so his writings have the same cast: and as this is a disease which does not allow very vigorous or very frequent

---

[7] The poem appeared in January 1749.

excursions to the intellect, his images are not much varied; and analogous ideas are generally excited by events the most dissimilar. It was not in his power to assume much variety, nor did he seek to improve this inability by labour; for he was, I believe, little ambitious of the title of poet; an indifference proceeding, perhaps, from a consciousness of natural disqualifications for the exercise of that exalted function. The soft graces he never could attain, though he sometimes exhibits strength and elegance. He was, indeed, soon aware that his abilities did not consist in poetry; for he began it late, and abandoned it early:[8] and it is very probable that had he been exempt from want, he never would have produced the imitations of Juvenal. In short, his poetic character may be given in his own words: 'He is elegant but not great; he never labours after exquisite beauties; and he seldom falls into gross faults. His versification is smooth, but rarely vigorous; and his rhymes are remarkably exact.'[9]

[8] In fact poetry 'formed a major part of his writing from his school-days till his death'. *Poems*, xvi.
[9] *Lives*, i. 239.

3. John Aikin on Johnson's poems

1804

Text from *Letters to a Young Lady*, 273–8.

Aikin (1747–1822), brother to Mrs Barbauld (see No. 26), was a prolific writer though a physician by profession. The purpose of his *Letters to a Young Lady on a Course of English Poetry*, 1804, was to introduce his pupil to 'a course of poetical reading as may best conduce to the forming of [her] taste and cultivating [her] understanding'. Aikin's knowledge of Johnson's poems is more comprehensive than was evident among most contemporary critics. See Introduction, p. 21f.

An example of what may be done by strong sense, learning and cultivated taste towards producing valuable poetry, without a truly poetical genius, is afforded by several pieces in verse of the celebrated Dr. SAMUEL JOHNSON, whose great name in literature has been acquired by his prose compositions. The walk in which a writer so qualified is most likely to succeed, is that of the morally didactic. Energy of language, vigour and compass of thought, and correctness of versification, are the principal requisites for the moral poet; and few have possessed them in a higher degree than the author in question.

His imitations of two satires of Juvenal, under the title of *London*, and *The Vanity of Human Wishes*, are, perhaps, the most manly compositions of the kind in our language. The Roman poet is distinguished by the earnest and pointed severity of his invective, as well as by the force of his painting, and the loftiness of his philosophy; and the imitation does not fall short of the original in these respects, whilst it is free from its grossness and impurity. The *London* indeed, written in the earlier part of Johnson's literary career, while he was a warm oppositionist in politics, and had scarcely acquired that confirmed relish for the metropolis which afterwards characterised him, has a considerable mixture of coarse exaggeration. The other piece possesses more calm dignity; and the examples drawn from modern history to parallel those from antient history in the original, are, for the most part, well chosen. That of Charles of Sweden is written with peculiar animation. The conclusion, which is sublime in the Latin, is as much more so in the English, as the theology of the modern writer was superior to that of the antient. Nobler lines than the following were never composed:

[quotes *Vanity of Human Wishes*, ll. 357–64.]

Both these imitations have an excellence to an English reader not always found in compositions of this class—that of being complete in themselves, and not depending for their effect upon allusion to the originals.

The same vigour of thought and style has made Johnson the author of the finest prologue our language can boast, with the exception, perhaps, of Pope's to [Addison's] *Cato*. It was written on the occasion of opening the Drury-lane theatre in 1747, and was meant to usher in that better choice of plays which took place under the management of his friend Garrick. The sketch of the vicissitudes of the English drama is drawn with justness and spirit, and the concluding appeal to the good-sense and taste of the audience is truly dignified. Another prologue, to the benefit-play [*Comus*] given to Milton's grand-daughter, is likewise much superior to the ordinary strain of these compositions.

The Odes of Johnson have, I think, the same air of study, the same frigid elegance, which he has derided in those of Akenside. The sublimer flights of the lyric muse he has judiciously not attempted, conscious of his want of enthusiasm; his want of gaiety equally unfitted him for her sprightly strains. The pieces denominated from the four seasons of the year have little characteristic painting: he was, indeed, precluded by corporeal defects from any lively perception of the imagery of rural nature. The translation of Anacreon's 'Dove' is, however, very happily executed. Cowley would have done it with scarcely more ease, and with less elegance.

There is one piece, written, too, at an advanced age, which may be produced as an example of perfection in its kind—I allude to the stanzas on the death of Levett. I know not the poem of equal length in which it would be so difficult to change a single line, or even word, for the better. The subject supplied matter neither for sublimity nor pathos: the mature decease of a man in obscure life, and with no other quality than humble utility, was to be recorded; and who but Johnson could have filled such a meagre outline with such admirable finishing? Every line is a trait of character or sentiment. What a picture of life is given in the following stanza!

In misery's darkest caverns known,
His useful care was ever nigh,
Where hopeless anguish pour'd his groan,
And lonely want retir'd to die.

I confess, that much as I admire the flights of a poetical imagination, it is these sober serious strains to which at present I recur with most delight. Your taste may reasonably be different; yet I trust in the solidity of your understanding to lead you to set a just value upon that verse, which, while it gratifies the ear, also touches and meliorates the heart.

Farewell!

IRENE

16 February 1749

4. A Criticism on Mahomet and Irene. In a Letter to the Author

1749

Text from the Harvard College Library copy.

Irene was produced by Garrick at Drury Lane on 6 February 1749; it ran for nine nights and was published on 16 February. Five days later the anonymous '*Criticism on* Mahomet and Irene' was announced in the *General Advertiser*. Only two copies of it are known: one in the Hyde Collection, the other in the Houghton Library, Harvard (see Robert F. Metzdorf, 'A newly recovered criticism of Johnson's *Irene*', *Harvard Library Bulletin*, iv (1950), 265). The author, who is unsympathetic to heroic drama, makes some valid observations; others are easily refuted. See Introduction, pp. 21–2.

Sir,
You must not wonder that your Tragedy of *Irene* engross'd, for some Months before its Appearance, the Conversation of the Town, and every one was big with Expectation of seeing a Piece plann'd, and wrote up to the highest Pitch of a Dramatic Performance; but as they are, in some Measure, disappointed in both Particulars, you can't be surpriz'd they now grow clamorous in their Censures: And tho' some may take you to Pieces without Mercy, behind your Back, I think it more generous to do it to your Face, and will handle you as tenderly as the Nature of your Offence will admit of.—And that I may not destroy your Virtues among the Crowd of your Vices, I will singly call 'em before me, and convict 'em one by one.
The first Thing I have to enquire into, is your Scene; which, I think,

you have plac'd in the Garden of the Seraglio:[1] Nay, in the most private
and sequester'd Walks of it; which the Sultan, being deep in Love and
fond of Melancholly, had chosen for his own Retirement.—This, I think,
is the Place where your two *Grecian* Heroes, in *Turkish* Habits, open the
Play; which, I doubt not, amaz'd every Body, to think how they got
there: For the Seraglio being a Place so guarded by Slaves, and kept
sacred to the Sultan's Pleasures, how should it be possible two strange
Turks (suppose they were really so) durst appear, dress'd in all the Magnificence of eastern State, in the most retir'd Walks of the Palace Garden,
and never be enquir'd after? It is certain, there is not a Janizary upon Duty,
or Servant at his Labour, but knows every Person who has Authority to
frequent those Shades, as well as the Gate-Keepers do who has a Right to
ride through St. *James's-Park*.—I can hardly think their Friend *Cali* wou'd
place 'em there to be out of Sight. No; 'tis plain he knew better—for
when he was dispos'd to break his Mind to *Demetrius* ONLY, he very
cautiously advis'd his Friend *Abdalla* to a properer Place, as you have very
judiciously describ'd:

> —— *He seiz'd my doubtful Hand,*
> *And led me to the Shore where* Cali *stood*
> *Pensive, and list'ning to the beating Surge,* &c.
> [I. i. 126ff.]

This Shore mention'd, cou'd not be within the Bounds of the Seraglio;
for, it is well known, that Palace is guarded next the Sea by very strong
and high Fortifications, and no other Building near the Place. Here *Cali*
told *Demetrius* his Purpose; and, I suppose, desir'd to see his Friend *Leontius* for the same End, and, I shou'd think, at the same Place: But whether
Leontius was afraid of catching Cold, or daubing his Feet by the Water-
side, I can't tell; yet it is certain, the Place is chang'd from the silent Shore
to the Sultan's Gardens, where *Cali* meets him and his Friend, and they
talk Treason as loud as *Syphax* and *Sempronius* do in the Hall of *Utica*—
An Error very wisely remark'd by a deceas'd Critic.

In the Course of these Traitors Conversation, *Cali*, talking of tyrannic
Government, breaks out in an Ecstasy:

> *If there be any Clime, as* Fame *reports,*
> *Where common Laws restrain the Prince and People,* &c.
> [I. ii. 55f.]

If, quotha! There's a Statesman indeed! that cou'd not be certain

[1] In fact the scene is laid in a palace garden near the shore of the Bosphorus. See *Irene*
I. v. 1; II. ii. 36–9; III. ii. 50–2.

whether there was any Country, whose Constitution differ'd from his own—After that Confession of his Ignorance, I did not at all doubt, but he introduc'd the *Greeks* into the Palace to be private.

Cali here gives a very odd Account of the Sultan's Temper—Really, such a sudden, undeterminated Character he gives him, that we may, without great Absurdity, take him for a Madman.—He says—*Aspasia* being brought before the Sultan, he was so struck with her uncommon Beauty and Behaviour, that he immediately offer'd to make her his Queen; which she, from some nice Scruples of Conscience and Religion, join'd to her strong Attachment to *Demetrius*, refus'd. This so inflam'd him, that he was almost incens'd to offer Violence—But very lucky for her, *another Plunderer* (so he is stil'd) just in that Moment brought in *Irene*; upon which, the Sultan turn'd round, and offer'd, in the same Moment he was courting *Aspasia*, the Crown to her; and finding not so much Aversion there, as in the other Lady, pursu'd his Point with *Irene*, and never once thought of *Aspasia* more.—What wou'd this unhappy Monarch have done, if she had behav'd like *Aspasia*? Why, he must certainly, just in that Moment, as he was so violent in his Love, have married the first Wench he had met, or have perish'd in his own Flames.

The Scheme of over-turning the Government, and destroying the Sultan, being very well plann'd, and agreed to, I am a little puzzled how the Mutineers shou'd escape; for I can hear of but one Galley that was provided, and that wou'd not more than accommodate the Lovers and their Ladies, with proper Mariners to conduct 'em: For if *Purchas* may be believ'd, at the Time of *Amurath*, a *Turkish* Galley was look'd upon as very large, and of great Use, that wou'd carry eight Sailors (or Oar-Men) twenty fighting Men, their Officers, and Provision for two Months.—If this Account be true, what was to become of all the rest of the Associates? For, by *Leontius's* Account,

> *Above a hundred Voices thunder'd round him,*
> *And every Voice was Liberty and* Greece.
> [II. iv. 29–30.]

Which, by the Bye, was not quite so wise, to make such an Uproar so near the Palace. For Shouting and Hollowing will naturally bring People to enquire the Cause; and, had this happen'd now, the whole Plot had been unravell'd, and the *Grecians* lost their Liberty for a Huzza.

The Conspirators, in the Midst of their Consultations, are suddenly dispers'd by the Approach of *Mustapha*; who comes to tell *Cali*, that the Emperor is walking that Way, and wou'd be private.—The Emperor appears, and is met with a fine Panegyric from *Cali*, who receives it very kindly, orders a Counsellor to Death, and puts *Irene* into the Protection of the Bassa; not from any great Opinion of his Virtue, but because

> *His Blood, frozen with sixty Winters Camps,*
> *At Sight of Female Charms will glow no more.*
>
> [I. v. 5–6.]

The pious Bassa refuses this great Charge, and begs Leave to perform a Pilgrimage to *Mecca*; which the hasty Monarch denies, and perswades him rather to stay, spill some more Blood, and do a few more Mischiefs first; then, quoth he,

> *'Tis Time to think of Pray'rs, of Pilgrimage, and Peace.*
>
> [I. v. 45.]

Mahomet, tho' the greatest Man in the Play, I don't think the wisest; for when he hears of *Cali*'s Treachery, instead of instantly putting him to Death and secure his own Person, resolves to have a little Sport with him, by Way of hunting him round the World; as we turn Foxes loose, only to have the Pleasure of finding 'em again: And indeed, he proposes a pretty long Chase; I think, it is from Pole to Pole; and is determin'd to have him, tho' the North Wind shou'd stand his Friend—But *Mustapha*, who, it seems, was not so keen a Sportsman as his Master, is for making sure of him now they have him, and not trust to a future Chace.—Yet *Mahomet* was so much in Love, that *Cali*'s Crime slipt over, without any particular Notice taken of it—and tho' the Aga gives a long Description of the two Strangers he had seen with *Cali* in the Garden, *Mahomet* never gave himself the Trouble to have 'em enquir'd after, or even to ask who they were suspected to be.

The next Thing that struck me, was *Mahomet*'s uncommon Courtship of *Irene*; for instead of Flattery, and other gay Delusions to engage Affection, generally made use of by an eager Lover, he courts her out of the *Alcoran*; or, as my Lord *Foppington* says, seems to think a Woman shou'd fall in Love with him, for his endeavouring to perswade her she has not one single Virtue in the whole Composition of her Soul and Body[2]—In short, his Arguments are so strong, or her Understanding so weak, that at last she seems to be quite of his Opinion, and throws herself, without farther Trouble, into the Sultan's Embraces.—What Pity 'tis a virtuous Christian cou'd not make a better Defence against an amorous Heathen!

I was greatly surpriz'd at the sudden Passion of *Abdalla*, which broke

---

[2] Colley Cibber, *The Careless Husband*, 1705, III. 489–92.

out in such extravagant Gusts of Rage and Tumult, that one wou'd have thought the *Turk* had been seiz'd with a sudden Frenzy; and whatever *Mahomet* may think of his Passion, *Abdalla*'s is as much above him for Fire, high Flights, and precepitate Designs, as Champaign, in its Effect, is above the Operations of Small Beer.—'Tis well *Abdalla* had not *Mahomet*'s Power; for, if he had, we shou'd doubtless have seen the Palace, Gardens, *Cali*, and all his Friends in a Flame, in one Moment's Time.

His Passion (as I imagin'd it wou'd) prov'd fatal to the Scheme of Liberty; for we find his Rage set him upon Baseness, to the Ruin of old *Cali*, and the rest of the Conspirators, except *Demetrius*; and how he came to escape is a most surprizing Piece of good Fortune. What! the *only* Man at whom his Rage was levell'd, that he should be the *only* one that escap'd; nay more, had still Power enough to fetch his Mistress away, even when *Abdalla* was present?—who, instead of seizing the Lady, or destroying *Demetrius*, very kindly slipt aside, while the two Lovers whip'd into the Galley so often mention'd, and sail'd away.—This Incident, tho' very diverting, I must confess, savours greatly of the Marvellous.

The Death of *Irene*, tho' not approv'd of by some of the Spectators,[3] I think very natural and decent. The Reason for her Death, and the Manner of executing it, may be highly justified—*Cali*'s dying Confession, that *Mahomet* was to have been murder'd in *Irene*'s Chamber, must, doubtless, alarm a less passionate Monarch than *Mahomet*: Nor am I at all surpriz'd, at the speedy Vengeance he took of her—I doubt not, but some of our *Conoisseurs* expected, according to the old Story, to have seen her Head taken off by *Mahomet*, at one Stroke of his Scymitar; which when perform'd to the Height of Expectation, cou'd have been but a Pantomime Trick, and beneath the Dignity of a Tragedy; unless you cou'd suppose, the Hero was bred a Butcher.—As to the Trick, perhaps, some of our tender hearted Countrymen, wou'd have eas'd that Objection, by having her Head cut off in good Earnest, and so have had the Pleasure of a new *Irene* every Night.

But, I think it is better as it is, and the Tale finely adapted to the Stage. —*Irene*'s Innocence being prov'd to the Sultan, gives him Occasion to reflect upon his hasty Sentence, and may be the Means of preventing many an innocent Subject from falling unheard, under his Displeasure.

As to the Epilogue,[4] it is of too delicate, too refin'd, too noble, too

---

[3] At the first performance Garrick's intention to have Irene strangled on stage was thwarted by the audience; they stopped the play with cries of 'Murder'; and Irene had to be killed off stage.

[4] By Sir William Yonge.

eloquent, too witty, and too new a Kind to deserve Applause, or incur Censure. It is its own Satire, and he that has a mind to Burlesque it, has nothing to do but to Copy it.

> *I am,*
>
> > S I R,
> >
> > > *Your humble Servant,* &c.

5. John Hippisley (?), *An Essay on Tragedy, with a Critical Examen of* Mahomet and Irene

1749

Extracts from the Essay, 12–34.

This anonymous pamphlet—possibly by the actor John Hippisley (d. 1767)—was published on 8 March 1749. The author sets his criticism in the context of observations on tragedy as a genre; his principles are Aristotelian; and his view of tragedy has a traditional loftiness. 'Of the many species of dramatic Writings, there is none so noble in its nature, so useful in its end, as tragedy; 'tis this that gives the sublimest lessons of virtue and morality' (p. 3). See Introduction, pp. 3, 21–2.

In the first place then, my good reader, I spy a fault in the very title-page, *Mahomet and Irene is an errant misnomer, for 'tis evident (notwithstanding the author's intention) the episodical is in fact the principal action. Demetrius is the hero, Mahomet in point of character, but the second of the drama.

---

* Had the author taken notice of the title page, and head title, of the printed copy of the Play, he would have perceived that, tho' 'twas called *Mahomet and Irene* in the bills, 'tis only *Irene* in the book.

Another error, which is by no means inconsiderable, (and what I shall particularly consider, as it is the source from whence the principal faults in this poem arise) is the wilful deviation from History: for, although no author is under a necessity of adhering to it, when either for the embellishment of his work, or for the utility of the moral, he can depart from it with advantage; yet when the Plan is of itself compleat, interesting, and adapted to the stage, the least alteration, as it must be for the worse, argues an affected petulance, or a great weakness of judgment in him who suffers himself, by any inducements whatever, to attempt it.

And what story was ever more uniform, or truly dramatic, than that of the Fair Greek? How many affecting scenes? what an important moral it would have conveyed? Here follow the facts: my friends judge for yourselves.

Mahomet, Sultan of Turkey, inclined by nature, as well as stimulated by the ambitious precepts of the Koran, to aim at universal monarchy, pushes his conquests, with the utmost vigour and rapidity through the Grecian empire, in the midst of which he becomes so deeply enamoured of a captive Greek, that, dissolved in the soft dalliance of a Seraglio, and deaf to the repeated remonstrances of his soldiers, he neglects all imperial cares, as well civil, as military, till at last, their hopes of plunder being defeated, they break out into a mutiny, and, in high terms, loudly complain of the Emperor's inactivity. In this desperate emergency, he convenes the divan, and leading in the Sultaness, dressed with the utmost magnificence, to the council-chamber, where they were sitting, demands of them whether all publick concerns were not justly sacrificed to the enjoyment of so illustrious an object? and whether the whole world was not a trifling acquisition when put in competition with IRENE? They, struck with the commanding dignity of her Demeanour, the blaze of charms which darted from her whole form, and the brilliance of her appearance, acquiesced in the sentiments of their monarch, unanimously declaring that nothing inferiour to divinity could withstand so irresistable, so consummate a beauty. Upon this, the Sultan drew his sabre, and with a greatness and ferocity of mind truly Turkish, at one blow sever'd her head from her body; saying at the same time (in these, or words to this effect) 'Thus perish all private gratifications, when incompatible with the publick emolument: and learn how to esteem a King who sacrifices more than his life, his happiness, to his people's welfare.'

[expounds the Aristotelian view of tragedy and the tragic hero.]

And now 'tis time to see how far *Mahomet and Irene* tallies with these

[Aristotelian] rules, and where it is defective. And I must confess whatever beauties it may have, that of touching the passions is by no means to be allow'd it. IRENE's character is not badly drawn. Her apostacy is owing to predominating fears; and a feminine fondness for glare and splendor, a weakness so inseparable from the sex, that VIRGIL (who was an exact copier of nature) has given it to his favourite CAMILA; tho' in every thing else he has drawn her more than man, yet

> Femineo spoliorum ardebat amore. Aen. XI.[1]

Her disloyalty to ASPASIA, and the long train of deceit subsequent to that, are the necessary consequences of her apostacy, as one lapse from virtue, is generally the parent of another, according to that beautiful remark,

> The soul once tainted with so foul a crime,
> No more shall glow with friendships hallow'd ardour
> [quotes to III. viii. 20.]

But to return,

It is then universally allowed, that terror and pity are the two passions which every good tragic poet will in some measure affect,

> —They aim to draw the melting sigh,
> Or steal the trickling tear from beauty's Eye,
> To touch the strings that humanize our kind,
> Man's sweetest strain the Musick of the mind.[2]

But so languid and unaffecting is this poem, that I very much question, if one maudling girl squeez'd out a single tear, either at the theatre, or in the closet. The precipitate fate of Irene (who although innocent as to the crimes she suffers for, yet as guilty of others of a more malignant nature) makes no Impression on the audience: Unless that of a gloomy pleasure, in observing the just and swift-wing'd vengeance of heav'n overtake a wretch, who can be so impious to prefer the momentary charms of a transient splendour, with the wild chimeras, and extravagant fopperies of Mahometanism to the more durable, though less pompous satisfactions of virtue, and Christianity.

And here reader give me leave to remark that our author endeavouring to observe the τὸ πρέπον[3] of the stage, by strangling his heroine behind the scenes, has been guilty of a flagrant absurdity.

The Sultan, enraged at the supposed guilt of Irene, gives orders for

---

[1] *Aeneid*, XI, l. 782. ('[She] was afire with a womanly love of booty.')
[2] Henry Brooke, Prologue to Edward Moore's *The Foundling*, 1747.
[3] 'Propriety' or 'decorum'.

her immediate death, which sentence Abdallah (for any thing that at that juncture appears to the contrary) is sent from Mahomet to confirm, and hasten the execution of. To carry her out therefore, from the place where she is found, to another part of the gardens, merely to preserve a fancied decorum, is extreamly trifling and ridiculous.

Another fault that he has run into by the alteration of the story, is, that the love which is there truly great and noble, is here too mean and insignificant to deserve a place in tragedy, according to the opinion of a celebrated author among our neighbours. In order, says he, to make love worthy of the tragic muse, it must be an essential part of the plot, and not brought in at random, to fill up the void: It must be a passion truly tragical, considered as a weakness, and combated by remorse. Love must lead either to unhappiness or guilt, in order to point out the danger of that passion, or else virtue must triumph over it, to shew that it is not invincible: without these qualities, 'tis merely a pastoral, or comic love. See Voltaire's discourse on tragedy, in a letter to Lord Bolinbroke.[4]

The unities of time and place are preserved, even to scrupulous nicety: As indeed the unity of action: But that of character, which is certainly prior in dignity, is mangled in a miserable manner: Shakespear for the most part, religiously adhered to this, though he broke all the rest at will.

[comments on the leading characters.]

Now Mahomet, who is (or at least ought to be) the chief person of the drama, is represented so vague and undetermined, that it is impossible to fix any precise criterion, whereby to regulate our judgment concerning him: He is a madman, instead of an hero, a monstrous caricatura, rather than a just and proportion'd picture. Every thing he says, and does, is so *outré*, so odd, and unaccountable, that it is evident no such person ever had existence, but in the confused imagination of a romantic Quixot in poetry. In short, instead of *Mahomet and Irene*, I would have him give us a second edition of his tragedy, under the title of human nature burlesqued. . . .

Having thus far consider'd the conduct of the fable and characters, it is now time to speak to the diction and sentiments, which may not improperly be called the colouring and drapery of the piece. And here our author triumphs over almost every opponent. Never do any strain'd metaphors, unmeaning epithets, turgid elocution, high sounding rants, disgrace his scenes. He is sensible, that the true sublime does not consist in

4 'Discours sur la Tragédie' in *Œuvres Complètes*, Paris, 1859, i. 151. (The 'Discours', which forms the preface to Voltaire's *Brutus*, is addressed to Bolingbroke.)

smooth rounding periods, and the pomp of verse, but in just and noble sentiments, strong and lively images of nature: And to this for the most part he closely adheres: He seems fully convinced of the truth of that admirable precept of the great Boileau.

> Et que tout ce qu'il dit facile à retenir,
> De son ouvrage en vous laisse un long souvenir.[5]

And indeed rarely loses sight of it.

But as I have been pretty copious on the defective, so it is but scanty justice, that I should dwell a little on the unexceptionable parts of this poem, and enumerate their particular excellencies: And in order to [do] this, I know no better way, than to select some remarkable instances of the justness and propriety of his sentiments, the masculine and harmonious turn of his numbers.

And under the first head, I beg leave, in an especial manner, to recommend to the attention of every British reader, that beautiful apostrophe of Cali, to the civil constitution of these Kingdoms; and hope every dissatisfied malcontent, will particularly consider the severe sarcasm couch'd in the conclusion.

[quotes I. ii. 55–64.]

Nor is that charming dissuasive from that surprizing, yet too prevailing error of putting off to some future, the business of the present period, less worthy our notice. The visier Cali, and the captive Greeks, having resolved on the assassination of Mahomet, Cali is for delaying it till the morrow: upon which Demetrius breaks out in the following exclamation.

[quotes III. ii. 19–33.]

But the scene between Irene and Aspasia in the third act, is so truly great, so admirably calculated for the service of religion, abounds with such just observations on life, such strength of reasoning, such noble sentiments of virtue, that it would be an injury to the world, as well as ingratitude to Mr. Johnson, to pass it over in silence. But as there is no other way of doing it justice, I shall beg leave to transcribe it.

[quotes III. viii.]

It is now time to speak to the second thing proposed, namely, the

---

[5] *L'Art Poétique*, 1674, iii. 157–8. ('Everything he says should be easy to remember, leaving you with a permanent memory of his work.')

harmony of his versification; but having so largely expatiated on the excellence of his sentiments, I shall only select one passage (from many) and that is, the charming description that concludes the second act.

[quotes II. vii. 84–91.]

In a word, was I to give my sentiments in general of this tragedy, I should pronounce it a heap of splendid materials, rather than a regular structure: But whatever may be its faults, as its sole tendency is warmly to promote, and earnestly to encourage the practice of virtue and religion, it deserves the highest applause.

THE RAMBLER

6. Two early tributes

1750

Text from the *Gentleman's Magazine*, xx (1750), 4 65.

The first, from the *Remembrancer*, is the opening of 'an ingenious Rambling Letter' signed 'Dennis Ductile'. The second, believed to be by Christopher Smart, occurred in the final paragraph of an essay on 'Gratitude' in the *Student, or the Oxford and Cambridge Monthly Miscellany*, II. i. 1–3. Both were reprinted in the *Gentleman's Magazine* in 1750. Also reprinted (but not reproduced here) were laudatory verses 'To the Author of the *Rambler*, on reading his Allegories'. They were taken from the *Daily Advertiser*, 24 August 1750. See Introduction, pp. 3, 22.

(a) 21 April 1750, the *Remembrancer*: 'If a new writer, blessed with a vigorous imagination, under the restraint of a classical judgment, a master of all the charms and graces of expression, had not lately made his appearance to the public under the stile and title of *The Rambler*, I would myself have assumed that character, as the most suitable to my own.'

(b) 2 October 1750, the *Student*: 'There is one gentleman from whom we should be proud to borrow, if our plan forbad it not; and, since our text is GRATITUDE we beg leave to return acknowledgements to him for the noble and rational entertainments he has given us, we mean the admirable author of the RAMBLER, a work that exceeds any thing of the kind ever published in this kingdom, some of the SPECTATORS excepted—if indeed they may be excepted. We own ourselves unequal to the task of commending such a work up to its merits—where the diction is the most high-wrought imaginable, and yet, like the brilliancy of the diamond, exceeding perspicuous in its riches—where the sentiments enoble the style, and the style familiarizes the sentiments—where every thing is easy and natural, yet every thing is masterly and strong. May the publick favours crown his merits, and may not the English, under the auspicious reign of GEORGE the Second, neglect a man, who, had he lived in the first century, would have been one of the greatest favourites of AUGUSTUS.'

7. Johnson surveys his purpose and achievement, *Rambler* No. 208

14 March 1752

Text from fourth edition, 1756.

Ἡρακλειτος εγω τι με ων κατω ελκετ' αμουσοι;
Ουχ' υμιν επονουν, τοις δε μ' επισαμενοις·
Εις εμοι ανθρωπος, τρισμυριοι' οι δ' αναριθμοι
Ουδες· ταυτ' αυδω και παρα Περσεφονη.
                                    DIOG. LAERT.[1]

Begone, ye blockheads, Heraclitus cries,
And leave my labours to the learn'd and wise;
By wit, by knowledge, studious to be read,
I scorn the multitude, alive and dead.

Time, which puts an end to all human pleasures and sorrows, has likewise concluded the labours of the Rambler. Having supported, for two years, the anxious employment of a periodical writer, and multiplied my essays to four volumes, I have now determined to desist.

The reasons of this resolution it is of little importance to declare, since justification is unnecessary when no objection is made. I am far from supposing, that the cessation of my performances will raise any inquiry,

[1] Diogenes Laertius, IX. i. 16. The translation is by Johnson himself (see *Poems*, 255).

for I have never been much a favourite of the public, nor can boast that, in the progress of my undertaking, I have been animated by the rewards of the liberal, the caresses of the great, or the praises of the eminent.

But I have no design to gratify pride by submission, or malice by lamentation; nor think it reasonable to complain of neglect from those whose regard I never solicited. If I have not been distinguished by the distributers of literary honours, I have seldom descended to the arts by which favour is obtained. I have seen the meteors of fashion rise and fall, without any attempt to add a moment to their duration. I have never complied with temporary curiosity, nor enabled my readers to discuss the topic of the day; I have rarely exemplified my assertions by living characters; in my papers no man could look for censures of his enemies, or praises of himself; and they only were expected to peruse them, whose passions left them leisure for abstracted truth, and whom virtue could please by its naked dignity.

To some, however, I am indebted for encouragement, and to others for assistance. The number of my friends was never great, but they have been such as would not suffer me to think that I was writing in vain, and I did not feel much dejection from the want of popularity.

My obligations having not been frequent, my acknowledgments may be soon dispatched. I can restore to all my correspondents their productions, with little diminution of the bulk of my volumes, though not without the loss of some pieces to which particular honours have been paid.

The parts from which I claim no other praise than that of having given them an opportunity of appearing, are the four billets in the tenth paper, the second letter in the fifteenth, the thirtieth, the forty-fourth, the ninety-seventh, and the hundredth papers, and the second letter in the hundred and seventh.[2]

Having thus deprived myself of many excuses which candor might have admitted for the inequality of my compositions, being no longer able to allege the necessity of gratifying correspondents, the importunity with which publication was solicited, or obstinacy with which correction was rejected, I must remain accountable for all my faults, and submit, without subterfuge, to the censures of criticism, which, however, I shall not endeavour to soften by a formal deprecation, or to overbear by the influence of a patron. The supplications of an author never yet reprieved him a moment from oblivion; and though greatness has sometimes sheltered guilt, it can afford no protection to ignorance or dulness.

[2] For the authors of these contributions see Boswell, *Life*, i. 203.

Having hitherto attempted only the propagation of truth, I will not at last violate it by the confession of terrors which I do not feel: Having laboured to maintain the dignity of virtue, I will not now degrade it by the meanness of dedication.

The seeming vanity with which I have sometimes spoken of myself, would perhaps require an apology, were it not extenuated by the example of those who have published essays before me, and by the privilege which every nameless writer has been hitherto allowed. 'A mask,' says Castiglione, 'confers a right of acting and speaking with less restraint, even when the wearer happens to be known.'[3] He that is discovered without his own consent may claim some indulgence, and cannot be rigorously called to justify those sallies or frolics which his disguise must prove him desirous to conceal.

But I have been cautious lest this offence should be frequently or grossly committed; for, as one of the philosophers[4] directs us to live with a friend, as with one that is some time to become an enemy, I have always thought it the duty of an anonymous author to write, as if he expected to be hereafter known.

I am willing to flatter myself with hopes, that by collecting these papers, I am not preparing for my future life, either shame or repentance. That all are happily imagined or accurately polished, that the same sentiments have not sometimes recurred, or the same expressions been too frequently repeated, I have not confidence in my abilities sufficient to warrant. He that condemns himself to compose on a stated day, will often bring to his task an attention dissipated, a memory embarrassed, an imagination overwhelmed, a mind distracted with anxieties, a body languishing with disease: He will labour on a barren topic, till it is too late to change it; or in the ardour of invention, diffuse his thoughts into wild exuberance, which the pressing hour of publication cannot suffer judgment to examine or reduce.

Whatever shall be the final sentence of mankind, I have at least endeavoured to deserve their kindness. I have laboured to refine our language to grammatical purity, and to clear it from colloquial barbarisms, licentious idioms, and irregular combinations. Something, perhaps, I have added to the elegance of its construction, and something to the harmony of its cadence. When common words were less pleasing to the ear, or less distinct in their signification, I have familiarized the terms of philosophy by applying them to popular ideas, but have rarely admitted

3 *The Book of the Courtier*, 1528, II. ii.
4 Publilius Syrus, in *Minor Latin Poets*, ed. J. W. and A. M. Duff, 1954, 50.

any word not authorized by former writers; for I believe that whoever knows the English tongue in its present extent, will be able to express his thoughts without further help from other nations.

As it has been my principal design to inculcate wisdom or piety, I have allotted few papers to the idle sports of imagination. Some, perhaps, may be found, of which the highest excellence is harmless merriment, but scarcely any man is so steadily serious, as not to complain, that the severity of dictatorial instruction has been too seldom relieved, and that he is driven by the sternness of the Rambler's philosophy to more chearful and airy companions.

Next to the excursions of fancy are the disquisitions of criticism, which, in my opinion, is only to be ranked among the subordinate and instrumental arts. Arbitrary decision and general exclamation I have carefully avoided, by asserting nothing without a reason, and establishing all my principles of judgment on unalterable and evident truth.

In the pictures of life I have never been so studious of novelty or surprise, as to depart wholly from all resemblance; a fault which writers deservedly celebrated frequently commit, that they may raise, as the occasion requires, either mirth or abhorrence. Some enlargement may be allowed to declamation, and some exaggeration to burlesque; but as they deviate farther from reality, they become less useful, because their lessons will fail of application. The mind of the reader is carried away from the contemplation of his own manners; he finds in himself no likeness to the phantom before him; and though he laughs or rages, is not reformed.

The essays professedly serious, if I have been able to execute my own intentions, will be found exactly conformable to the precepts of Christianity, without any accommodation to the licentiousness and levity of the present age. I therefore look back on this part of my work with pleasure, which no blame or praise of man shall diminish or augment. I shall never envy the honours which wit and learning obtain in any other cause, if I can be numbered among the writers who have given ardour to virtue, and confidence to truth.

Αὐτῶν ἐκ μακάρων ἀντάξιος εἴη αμοιβή.[5]

Celestial pow'rs! that piety regard,
From you my labours wait their last reward.

[5] Dionysius, *Periegesis*, l. 1186. The translation is Johnson's (see *Poems*, 255).

8. Arthur Murphy, *Essay on the Life and Genius of Johnson*

1792

Text from Johnson's *Works*, 1792, i. 56–9, 155–62.

One of the most influential memoirists of Johnson was the dramatist and miscellaneous writer, Arthur Murphy (1727–1805), a man 'whom [Johnson] very much loved' (Boswell, *Life*, ii. 127). His *Essay* formed the prefatory matter to the 1792 edition of Johnson's *Works*. See Introduction, pp. 15, 22.

At the time of instituting the club in Ivy-lane, Johnson had projected the *Rambler*. The title was most probably suggested by the *Wanderer*; a poem which he mentions, with warmest praise, in the Life of Savage.[1] With the same spirit of independence with which he wished to live, it was now his pride to write. He communicated his plan to none of his friends: he desired no assistance, relying entirely on his own fund, and the protection of the Divine Being, which he implored in a solemn form of prayer, composed by himself for the occasion.

[quotes prayer. See Boswell, *Life*, i. 203.]

Having invoked the special protection of Heaven, and by that act of piety fortified his mind, he began the great work of the *Rambler*. The first number was published on Tuesday, March the 20th, 1750; and from that time was continued regularly every Tuesday and Saturday for the space of two years, when it finally closed on Saturday, March 14, 1752. As it began with motives of piety, so it appears, that the same religious spirit glowed with unabating ardour to the last. His conclusion is:

[quotes final paragraph of *Rambler* No. 208. See above, No. 7.]

The whole number of Essays, amounted to two hundred and eight. Addison's, in the *Spectator*, are more in number, but not half in point of quantity: Addison was not bound to publish on stated days; he could

[1] *Lives*, ii. 364–7.

watch the ebb and flow of his genius, and send his paper to the press when his own taste was satisfied. Johnson's case was very different. He wrote singly and alone. In the whole progress of the work he did not receive more than ten essays. This was a scanty contribution. For the rest, the author has described his situation:

[quotes 'He that condemns himself' to 'examine or reduce', from *Rambler* No. 208. See above, No. 7.]

Of this excellent production the number sold on each day did not amount to five hundred: of course the bookseller, who paid the author four guineas a week, did not carry on a successful trade. His generosity and perseverance deserve to be commended; and happily, when the collection appeared in volumes, were amply rewarded. Johnson lived to see his labours flourish in a tenth edition.[2] His posterity, as an ingenious French writer has said on a similar occasion, began in his lifetime. . . .

The *Rambler* may be considered as Johnson's great work. It was the basis of that high reputation which went on increasing to the end of his days. The circulation of those periodical essays was not, at first, equal to their merit. They had not, like the *Spectators*, the art of charming by variety; and indeed how could it be expected? The wits of queen Anne's reign sent their contributions to the *Spectator*; and Johnson stood alone. A stage-coach, says Sir Richard Steele, must go forward on stated days, whether there are passengers or not.[3] So it was with the *Rambler*, every Tuesday and Saturday, for two years. In this collection Johnson is the great moral teacher of his countrymen; his essays form a body of ethics; the observations on life and manners are acute and instructive; and the essays, professedly critical, serve to promote the cause of literature. It must, however, be acknowledged, that a settled gloom hangs over the author's mind; and all the essays, except eight or ten, coming from the same fountain-head, no wonder that they have the raciness of the soil from which they sprung. Of this uniformity Johnson was sensible. He used to say, that if he had joined a friend or two, who would have been able to intermix papers of a sprightly turn, the collection would have been more miscellaneous, and, by consequence, more agreeable to the generality of readers. This he used to illustrate by repeating two beautiful stanzas from his own Ode to Cave, or *Sylvanus Urban*:[4]

[2] Published in 1784.
[3] *Tatler* No. 12.
[4] This poem, 'Ad Urbanum', Johnson's first certainly known contribution to the *Gentleman's Magazine*, was printed in March 1738. For the poem and a contemporary translation, see *Poems*, 40–2.

[quotes last two stanzas, in Latin.]

It is remarkable, that the pomp of diction, which has been objected to Johnson, was first assumed in the *Rambler*. His *Dictionary* was going on at the same time, and, in the course of that work, as he grew familiar with technical and scholastic words he thought that the bulk of his readers were equally learned; or at least would admire the splendour and dignity of the style. And yet it is well known, that he praised in Cowley the ease and unaffected structure of the sentences.[5] Cowley may be placed at the head of those who cultivated a clear and natural style. Dryden, Tillotson, and Sir William Temple, followed. Addison, Swift, and Pope, with more correctness, carried our language well nigh to perfection. Of Addison, Johnson used to say, *He is the Raphael of Essay Writers*. How he differed so widely from such elegant models is a problem not to be solved, unless it be true that he took an early tincture from the writers of the last century, particularly Sir Thomas Browne. Hence the peculiarities of his style, new combinations, sentences of an unusual structure, and words derived from the learned languages. His own account of the matter is, 'When common words were less pleasing to the ear, or less distinct in their signification, I familiarized the terms of philosophy, by applying them to popular ideas.'[6] But he forgot the observation of Dryden: '*If too many foreign words are poured in upon us, it looks as if they were designed, not to assist the natives, but to conquer them.*'[7] There is, it must be admitted, a swell of language, often out of all proportion to the sentiment; but there is, in general, a fullness of mind, and the thought seems to expand with the sound of the words. Determined to discard colloquial barbarisms and licentious idioms, he forgot the elegant simplicity that distinguishes the writings of Addison. He had what Locke calls a roundabout view of his subject;[8] and, though he was never tainted, like many wits with the ambition of shining in paradox, he may be fairly called an ORIGINAL THINKER. His reading was extensive. He treasured in his mind whatever was worthy of notice, but he added to it from his own meditation. He collected, *quae reconderet, auctaque promeret*.[9] . . . Johnson had a fund of humour, but he did not know it, nor was he willing to descend to the familiar idiom and the variety of diction which that mode of composition

---

[5] *Lives*, i. 64.

[6] *Rambler* No. 208 (see above, document No. 7).

[7] Preface to the *Aeneid*, in *Critical Essays*, ed. G. Watson, 1962, ii. 252.

[8] *Works*, 1724, iii. 391.

[9] Tacitus, *Annals*, I. 69 ('what he might store away, and bring out when they had become fruitful').

required. The letter, in the *Rambler*, No. 12, from a young girl that wants a place, will illustrate this observation. . . .

Johnson is always lofty; he seems, to use Dryden's phrase, to be o'er informed with meaning,[10] and his words do not appear to himself adequate to his conception. He moves in state, and his periods are always harmonious. His Oriental Tales are in the true style of Eastern magnificence, and yet none of them are so much admired as the Visions of Mirza.[11] In matters of criticism, Johnson is never the echo of preceding writers. He thinks and decides for himself. If we except the Essays on the Pleasures of Imagination,[12] Addison cannot be called a philosophical critic. His moral Essays are beautiful; but in that province nothing can exceed the *Rambler*, though Johnson used to say, that the Essay on *The burthens of mankind* (in the *Spectator* No. 558) was the most exquisite he had ever read. Talking of himself, Johnson said, 'Topham Beauclerk has wit, and every thing comes from him with ease; but when I say a good thing, I seem to labour.'[13] When we compare him with Addison, the contrast is still stronger. Addison lends grace and ornament to truth; Johnson gives it force and energy. Addison makes virtue amiable; Johnson represents it as an awful duty. Addison insinuates himself with an air of modesty; Johnson commands like a dictator; but a dictator in his splendid robes, not labouring at the plough. Addison is the Jupiter of Virgil, with placid serenity talking to Venus:

> Vultu, quo coelum tempestatesque serenat.[14]

Johnson is JUPITER TONANS: he darts his lightning, and rolls his thunder, in the cause of virtue and piety. The language seems to fall short of his ideas; he pours along, familiarizing the terms of philosophy, with bold inversions, and sonorous periods; but we may apply to him what Pope has said of Homer: 'It is the sentiment that swells and fills out the diction, which rises with it, and forms itself about it; like glass in the furnace, which grows to a greater magnitude, as the breath within is more powerful, and the heat more intense.'[15]

It is not the design of this comparison to decide between those two eminent writers. In matters of taste every reader will chuse for himself.

---

[10] Cf. *Absalom and Achitophel*, l. 158.
[11] Cf. *Rambler* Nos. 120, 190, 204, 205; *Spectator* No. 159.
[12] *Spectator* Nos. 411–21.
[13] *Journey*, 207; see Boswell, *Life*, v. 76–7.
[14] *Aeneid*, i. 255 ('With the countenance with which he [Jupiter] calms the heaven and the storms').
[15] Preface to the *Iliad*.

Johnson is always profound, and of course gives the fatigue of thinking. Addison charms while he instructs; and writing, as he always does, a pure, an elegant, and idiomatic style, he may be pronounced the safest model for imitation.

The essays written by Johnson in the *Adventurer* may be called a continuation of the *Rambler*. The *Idler*,[16] in order to be consistent with the assumed character, is written with abated vigour, in a style of ease and unlaboured elegance. It is the *Odyssey* after the *Iliad*. Intense thinking would not become the *Idler*. The first number presents a well-drawn portrait of an Idler and from that character no deviation could be made. Accordingly, Johnson forgets his austere manner, and plays us into sense.

9. George Gleig in the *Encyclopaedia Britannica*

1797

Text from third edition, 1797, ix. 299–300n.

Gleig (1753–1840), later to be Bishop of Brechin, author of a number of important contributions to the third edition of the *Encyclopaedia*, was responsible for the sympathetic article on Johnson. It was repeated with few changes in subsequent editions until replaced in the eighth by Macaulay's in some ways inferior essay. Printed here is Gleig's lengthy footnote on the *Rambler* style. See Introduction, p. 22.

The style of the *Rambler* has been much praised and much censured, sometimes perhaps by men who paid little attention to the author's views. Its defects have been petulantly caricatured, and its merits unduly exalted. To attempt a defence of all the words in it which are derived from the Latin, would be in vain: for though many of them are elegant and expressive, others are harsh, and do not easily assimilate with the English idiom. But it would be as easy to defend the use of Johnson's words as

[16] Johnson's essays appeared in the *Adventurer* 1753–4; in the *Idler* 1758–60.

the structure of all Addison's sentences; for though many of these are exquisitely beautiful, it must be confessed that others are feeble, and offend at once the ear and the mind. An ingenious essayist says, that in the *Rambler* 'the constant recurrence of sentences in the form of what have been called triplets, is disgusting to all readers'. The recurrence is indeed very frequent; but it certainly is not constant, nor we hope always disgusting: and as what he calls the triplet is unquestionably the most energetic form of which an English sentence is susceptible, we cannot help thinking, that it *should* frequently recur in detached essays, of which the object is to inculcate moral truths. He who reads *half a volume* of the *Rambler* at a sitting, will feel his ear fatigued by the close of similar periods so frequently recurring; but he who reads only one paper in the day, will experience nothing of this weariness. For purposes merely didactic, when something is to be told that was not known before, Addison's style is certainly preferable to Johnson's, and Swift's is preferable to both: but the question is, Which of them makes the best provision against that inattention by which known truths are suffered to lie neglected? There are very few moral truths in the *Spectator* or in the *Rambler* of which the reader can be totally ignorant; but there are many which may have little influence on his conduct, because they are seldom the objects of his thought. If this be so, that style should be considered as best which most rouses the attention, and impresses deepest in the mind the sentiments of the author: and therefore, to decide between the style of Addison and that of Johnson, the reader should compare the effects of each upon his own memory and imagination, and give the preference to that which leaves the most lasting impression. But it is said that Johnson himself must have recognized the fault of perpetual triplets in his style, since they are by no means frequent in his last productions. Is this a fair state of the case? His last production was *The Lives of the British Poets*, of which a great part consists of the narration of facts; and such a narration in the style of the *Rambler* would be ridiculous. Cicero's orations are universally admired; but if Caesar's commentaries had been written in that style, who would have read them? When Johnson in his biography has any important truth to enforce, he generally employs the rounded and vigorous periods of the *Rambler*; but in the bare narration he uses a simpler style, and that as well in the life of Savage, which was written at an early period, as in the lives of those which were written latest. It is not, however, very prudent in an ordinary writer to attempt a close imitation of the style of the *Rambler*; for Johnson's vigorous periods are fitted only to the weight of Johnson's thought.

10. Mudford on the 'moral utility' of the *Rambler*

1802

Text from *Critical Enquiry*, 1802, 2–47, 51–3, 58–9, 108–9.

In his *Critical Enquiry* (see No. 2), which was chiefly devoted to
Johnson as an essayist, Mudford expresses strong reservations about
the 'moral utility' of the *Rambler*; he fully acknowledges its
'sublimities'. See Introduction, p. 23.

A free and candid enquiry into his literary character still remains in some
measure open. It still remains to consider the nature and tendency of his
writings; as ethical how far adapted to common life and domestic purposes; how far they may be considered as just; and where they exhibit
marks of prejudice and misanthropy.* It still remains undecided how far
our language is indebted to him for its present elegance, perspicuity, and
energy; or to what degree of refinement he has advanced it. These are
topics which have hitherto been neglected, or at least but faintly discussed, though of acknowledged importance. But they would require
the hand of a master; and the following observations will be confined to
a few strictures on his moral writings, with, perhaps, some occasional
remarks on the preceding hints.

Before the appearance of Johnson's *Rambler* the public was possessed
of many diurnal papers. The *Tatler*, the *Guardian*, the *Spectator*, and many
others, had embraced the arduous project of instructing their countrymen, and laboured to extirpate the vices and immorality then existing.
To this effect they thought ridicule the most powerful weapon; and
employed it sometimes with dexterity, and sometimes with propriety:
every foible was exposed, and every vice abhorred; but descending too
much to the minute fopperies of giddy fashion, and prescribing rules for

* This enquiry has been in some measure pursued by Dr. Towers, in an ingenious work
of his, entitled 'An Essay on the life, character, and writings of Dr. Samuel Johnson, 1786.'

74

the adjustment of female dress, their writings were sought after rather as a recreation from satiety and listlessness, than as a manual of truth and morality.

This great defect Johnson was aware of; ambitious of distinction, his gigantic mind was upon the wing for every avenue which might lead to it; and it was doubtless a ready suggestion, that a pure body of ethics was still wanting; and, (perhaps, conscious of his own capability) he determined to commence the difficult employment. Having read much, and possessing a retentive memory, he found his mind stored with abundance of matter; Classical allusions were ready at his command, and a peculiar felicity of combination; an accurate observer of nature, he readily bared the human breast to his inspection, and detected, with uncommon penetration, the multifarious involutions of human passion. Thus qualified for the attempt, he published his first *Rambler*, March 20, 1750.

To consider every paper individually, would be a tedious and unprofitable task. Their ultimate tendency and probable effect is the thing to be discussed, and this requires to be done with as much precision, brevity and perspicuity, as possible. How far I may attain to this, is properly the decision of my readers.

Johnson naturally possessed a misanthropic way of thinking; and this had probably been greatly confirmed by the numerous disappointments of his early life. A slave, likewise, to the most absurd prejudices, which he could never overcome, for he too much indulged them, his judgment was often perverted: and he may be suspected of sometimes, endeavouring to give dignity to trifles, of which he was conscious, and of persisting in error rather than retract what he had once advanced. His misanthropy and prejudice are eminently manifest in his *Rambler*.

The great design of this work was to instruct mankind; to teach the happiness of virtue and religion; to display the horrors of vice and impiety; to inculcate a proper subordination of the passions; and to arm the mind against the vicissitudes of life. A more noble and exalted undertaking could not employ the mind of man. But to produce the proposed effect, much was required, and much which Johnson never could attain; he taught the happiness of virtue, and displayed the miseries of vice with peculiar energy; here his whole soul was employed, and he felt the indignation he expressed; but when he would support us against the contingencies of existence, his mind becomes darkened by intervening clouds of prejudice, and his arguments degenerate into sophistical declamation. Yet, in his own words, 'to have attempted much is always laudable even when the enterprise is above the strength that undertakes it; to rest below his aim is incident to every one whose fancy is active, and whose views are comprehensive.'[1]

Life, in its very sunshine, is perhaps sufficiently beset with evil; and we need not Monitors to tell us, at every step, that destruction may be the consequence. This is perpetually awakening the mind to a bitter consciousness of its situation, and barring every access to genuine pleasure, even when pursued with the most unerring virtue. The motive is unquestionably just: a desire to guard unthinking youth from the precipices which surround them, and to impress upon their hearts the conviction, that a life of heedless security is a life of guilt and misery. But this end will rarely be attained if thus sought; a perpetual alarm of probable dangers and miscarriages soon loses its effect; human judgment is not infallible; we may expect to err more frequently than to be right, and our prophecies will often be found to be erroneous. This influences the mind, and not unfrequently engenders a sceptical habit, which directly discredits every thing, on the pretence that some are false.

A young mind rising from a perusal of the *Rambler* would conceive the most melancholy ideas of human nature and human events. Mankind would appear to him as an undistinguished mass of fraud, perfidy, and deceit; oppressing the humble, exalting the base, and levelling the virtuous; awarding its suffrages and honours to the unworthy and degenerate, and turning, with disgust, from the manly struggles of the truly wise and worthy. Life would appear to him as one incessant warfare with envy, malevolence, and falshood; as the precarious tenure of a minute, never free from open assault or secret undermining; as beset on every side with misery, with want, with disease; as a road for ever obstructed by the pitfalls of infamy and remorse, and into which every step may plunge us; he will, I say, conceive this life to be a monstrous association of all possible evils, and unattended with any alleviation but religion, and unvisited by any hope but that of futurity and a MERCIFUL CREATOR.

The utility of Dr. Johnson's *Rambler* as a moral work may be justly questioned. Every thing which tends to obstruct the activity of man, and to crush well-founded hopes on this life, severely merits reprehension. The circle of our pleasures is sufficiently contracted, and our truest happiness can be derived only from the present moment; the past and future being objects either of regret or desire. To restrict them still more is of no avail, whether the end proposed be the advancement either of religion or morality; but it may be the cause of infinite injury. The gloomy representations of life as exhibited by Johnson, have this direct and only

[1] Preface to the *Dictionary*, see document No. 18.

tendency, to repress the arm of industry, to check the vigour of enterprize, to suppress rational wishes, to fill the mind with a hateful distrust
of society, and to foster the most pernicious prejudices. They are also
capable of repressing other generous sentiments of the mind which form
the most important links of human connection. In short, the papers of
the *Rambler* which relate to life, are in his own words, fit only 'to disturb
the happiness of others, to lessen the little comforts, and shorten the short
pleasures of our condition, by painful remembrances of the past, or
melancholy prognostics of the future; their only *aim* is to crush the rising
hope, to damp the kindling transport, and alloy the golden hours of
gaiety with the hateful dross of grief and suspicion.'[2]

[Lengthy examples follow, based on *Rambler* Nos. 2, 32, 144, 190.]

It is difficult to conceive a man more oppressed with melancholy, or
more governed by prejudice than Dr. Johnson. In him there is no variation; he is for ever one and the same. All his pictures are alike, and in all
we trace the reflection of a cynic. His sensations could seldom be enviable;
he must have turned away with visible horror and disgust from all that
bore the smiles of happiness, or the gaiety of mirth. . . .

Justice now demands that I should say something of the beauties of
this work, for beauties it certainly possesses. Some of them it will be
sufficient to point out, others I shall transcribe.

A noble effusion of Johnson's mind is the seventh *Rambler*, and which,
perhaps, is not exceeded by any he afterwards wrote. It contains many
just and penetrating remarks, great sublimity of sentiment, and energy
of language, originality of speculation, and a most pious and worthy end.
Johnson will perhaps never be excelled by any writer on religion. All his
papers on that subject breathe a spirit of the most elevated piety. The
solemnity of his language, the multiplicity of his ideas, the vigour of his
intellect, and the sincerity of his heart, all conspire to give an awful
dignity to his religious writings, which can hardly fail of awakening the
most obdurate mind. I confess I never rise from a perusal of this paper
without a most thorough conviction of all that it inculcates. None who
shall read it with due attention, will I think be able to deny the efficacy of
retirement for the advancement of religion. I cannot resist the pleasure of
transcribing the following paragraphs with which it concludes.

[quotes last three paragraphs.]

The allegories of Johnson, tho' not numerous are, I think, always just;
[2] *Rambler* No. 59.

and I know not whether they may not be preferred to those of Addison for strength and invention. The principal allegories of the *Rambler* are, those of Criticism, No. 3; of Hope, No. 67; the Voyage of Life, No. 102; and that of Wit and Learning, No. 22; which last exceeds any that this language can produce. It exhibits all the powers of invention in the most charming combination; of wit replete with delicacy, and of Learning guided by judgment. The allegory is in itself so complete, that I know nothing which could be added or taken away without injury; and the language is at the same time so pure and nervous, that praise is lost in admiration and delight. This alone would have conferred the title of poet upon Johnson, had his imitations of Juvenal never been written; and I doubt whether he does not rather merit it from this and his other allegories than from all the rhymes he ever published. This, indeed, was the opinion of his friend and contemporary, Dr. Goldsmith, who observed he was more a poet in his prose than in his imitations, and his authority must be allowed to have some weight even though my own opinions should be rejected. It is not merely the cadence of the syllables, or the final jingle of the words which constitute a poet; for these are trifling and mechanical; but it is that power of invention, that strength of imagery, and that vigour and variety of combination, which confer that glorious title. No reader of Johnson can be ignorant of the eminent degree in which he possesses all these qualities, and which he adorns and illustrates with all the strength of reason, all the power of eloquence, and all the harmony of language. . . .

No. 77 of the *Rambler* presents a noble specimen of virtuous indignation against the immorality of authors. It might, indeed, be recommended to the serious perusal of some writers of the present day, who would do well to listen to its dictates.—Such, I would be understood, as that gross and libidinous creature, who styles himself Peter Pindar, that violator of all morality and religion Godwin,[3] and others needless to enumerate. Johnson never employs ridicule against any vice he would extirpate; he always chuses the more solemn and efficacious powers of reason and argument. He does not strive to laugh you out of your follies or your errors, but he demonstrates with perspicuity wherein it is wrong, and where it degrades you from your station as a rational being: and then having awakened the mind to a sense of its impropriety, he displays, with inimitable majesty and force, the consequences they lead to; and, in a moral estimation, how loudly they call for repression and extinction.

[3] John Wolcot (1738–1819), the satirist who used the pseudonym 'Peter Pindar'; and the political philosopher William Godwin (1756–1836).

This it is which gives that peculiar energy to his writings, and which renders them far more valuable than those of Addison, who, by adopting ridicule for his weapon, often amused *only*, where he intended to instruct, and his precepts were frequently forgotten amid the general hilarity, which the gaiety of his essays produced; hence, where the latter is once mentioned, the former is quoted perhaps a hundred times, on account that his writings being totally divested of that unseasonable mirth, the mind is never divided by laughter and seriousness, but the effect being uniform, they make a constant and equable impression, and rarely fade off the memory.

The native vigour of Johnson's mind is finally displayed in this essay. What he censures he censures with dignity; and never degenerates into that vulgarity of diction, which sometimes characterize the most valuable productions. He is lofty and sublime; and he appeals to the heart without exciting the passions. He disdained the meanness of controversial epithets, and always maintains an innate grandeur of thought and expression which chains the attention of the reader, and forcibly impresses conviction. . . .

Apart from a moral consideration I would recommend the three papers (86, 88, 90) on Milton, as an elegant specimen of criticism, and greatly divested of that ill nature which distinguished his subsequent remarks.[4] He has determined with great precision wherein the true harmony of the English poetry consists, and has considered the versification of Milton with great judgment. These papers are indeed a valuable accession to literary criticism.

Innumerable are the beauties of this work which might be noticed; but it would he in some measure idle; for where is the person who lays any claim to learning that has not read the *Rambler* of Johnson? The History of Anningait and Ajut is pleasing;[5] and the concluding paper is a noble specimen of literary magnanimity; in which the author disclaims all protection or favour during the progress of his work, and anticipates censure by a firm avowal, that he sought only the advancement of morality, and 'that he shall never envy the honours which wit and learning obtain in any other cause, if he can be numbered among the writers who have given ardour to virtue and confidence to truth.'[6] . . .

The *Idler* does not offer much for remark. Its general character is fidelity and ease. It contains few of those blemishes which obscure the

[4] i.e. in his *Life of Milton*.
[5] Nos. 186–7.
[6] See above, document No. 7.

79

Rambler, and is thus far more valuable; but at the same time, it contains as few of its sublimities. There are not many laborious speculations or moral enquiries, which would indeed be incompatible with the assumed character, which is admirably supported throughout the whole. The *Idler* has been styled by one of his biographers,[7] the *Odyssey* after the *Iliad*. This definition is not, perhaps, very exact; but it is expressive, and I am not inclined to detect the impropriety.

Johnson's reflections on life in this work are more natural than in his *Rambler*. He seems less inclined to querulous exaggeration, and less attached to the enlargement of mournful truths; he even tells us in one of the papers, that we shall find each day possessed of its pleasures and joys;[8] a declaration not to be found, I believe, in all the *Ramblers*. He had, perhaps, seen his folly when it was too late to retract; or it might be owing to a concurrence of slight causes not now known, but which will often operate very visibly on the intellect. Whatever the reason may have been, it is very certain, that Johnson displays in the *Idler* more candour in his delineations, and more veracity in his assertions than he commonly did; and he has certainly more impartially estimated the motives and consequences of human action, and their moral rectitude and obliquity. But this I shall no longer insist upon here. It must be sufficiently known to those who have read the *Idler*; and to those who have not, the remarks will be unnecessary.

[7] Arthur Murphy; see above, document No. 8.
[8] *Rambler* No. 80.

11. Alexander Chalmers in *British Essayists*

1802

Text from *British Essayists*, 1823 edition, xvi. pp. xl–xlviii.

Chalmers (1759–1834) was well known in the early nineteenth century for editions of prose and poetry, an abridgement of Johnson's *Dictionary*, and other miscellaneous writings. His edition of *British Essayists* in forty-five volumes in 1802 included all Johnson's essays. Printed here are extracts from the preface to the *Rambler* volumes. See Introduction, p. 22.

On the general merit of this work, it is now unnecessary to expatiate: the prejudices which were alarmed by a new style and manner have long subsided; critics and grammarians have pointed out what they thought defective, or dangerous for imitation; and although a new set of objectors have appeared since the author's death the world has not been much swayed in its opinions by that hostility which is restrained until it can be vented with impunity. The few laboured, and perhaps pedantic sentences which occur, have been selected and repeated with incessant malignity, but without the power of depreciation; and they who have thus found Johnson to be obscure and unintelligible, might with similar partiality celebrate Shakspeare only for his puns and his quibbles. Luckily, however, for the taste and improvement of the age, these objections are not very prevalent, and the general opinion, founded on actual observation, is, that although Dr. Johnson is not to be imitated with perfect success, yet the attempt to imitate him, where it has neither been servile nor artificial, has elevated the style of every species of literary composition. In every thing, we perceive more vigour, more spirit, more elegance. He not only began a revolution in our language, but lived till it was almost completed.

With respect to the plan of the *Rambler*, he may surely be said to have executed what he intended: he has successfully attempted the propagation of truth; and boldly maintained the dignity of virtue. He has accumulated in this work a treasure of moral science, which will not be soon exhausted. He has laboured to refine our language to grammatical purity, and to clear it from colloquial barbarisms, licentious idioms, and irregular combinations. Something he *certainly* has added to the elegance of its construction, and something to the harmony of its cadence.[1]

Comparisons have been formed between the *Rambler* and its predecessors, or rather between the genius of Johnson and of Addison, but have generally ended in discovering a total want of resemblance. As they were both original writers, they must be tried, if tried at all, by laws applicable to their respective attributes. But neither had a predecessor. We can find no humour like Addison's; no energy and dignity like Johnson's. They had nothing in common but moral excellence of character; they could not have exchanged styles for an hour. Yet there is one respect in which we must give Addison the preference, *more general utility*. His writings would have been understood at any period; Johnson's would have perhaps been unintelligible a century ago, and are calculated for the more improved and liberal education, now so common. In both, however, what was peculiar was natural. The earliest of Dr. Johnson's works confirm this; from the moment he could write at all, he wrote in stately periods; and his conversation, from first to last, abounded in the peculiarities of his composition. In general we may say, with Seneca, *Riget eius oratio, nihil in ea placidum, nihil lene.*[2] Addison's style was the direct reverse of this.—If the *Lives of the Poets* be thought an exception to Dr. Johnson's general habit of writing, let it be remembered that he was for the most part confined to dates and facts, to illustrations and criticisms, and quotations; but when he indulged himself in moral reflections, to which he delighted to recur, we have again the rigour and loftiness of the *Rambler*, and only miss some of what have been termed his *hard words*.

Addison principally excelled in the observation of manners, and in that exquisite ridicule he threw on the minute improprieties of life. Johnson, although by no means ignorant of life and manners, could not descend to familiarities with tuckers and commodes, with fans and hoop-petticoats. A scholar by profession, and a writer from necessity, he loved to bring forward subjects so near and dear as the disappointments of authors—the dangers and miseries of literary eminence—anxieties of literature—contrariety of criticism—miseries of patronage—value of fame—causes of the contempt of the learned—prejudices and caprices of criticism—vanity of an author's expectations—meanness of dedication—necessity of literary courage; and all those other subjects which relate to

---

1 *Rambler* No. 208 (see above, document No. 7).
2 'His style is stiff; there is nothing gentle, nothing smooth in it.'

authors and their connexion with the public. Sometimes whole papers are devoted to what may be termed the personal concerns of men of literature; and incidental reflections are everywhere interspersed for the instruction or caution of the same class.

When he treats of common life and manners, it has been observed that he gives to the lowest of his correspondents the same style and lofty periods; and it may also be noticed, that the ridicule he attempts is in some cases considerably heightened by this very want of accommodation of character. Yet it must be allowed that the levity and giddiness of coquets and fine ladies, are expressed with great difficulty in the Johnsonian language. It has been objected also that even the names of his ladies have very little of the air either of court or city, as Zosima, Properantia, &c. Every age seems to have its peculiar names of fiction. In the *Spectator's* time, the Damons and Phillises, the Amintors, Amandas, and Cleoras, &c. were the representatives of every virtue, and every folly. These were succeeded by the Philamonts, Tenderillas, Timoleons, Seomanthes, Pantheas, Adrastas, and Bellimantes; names to which Mrs. Heywood gave currency in her *Female Spectator*;[3] and from which at no great distance of time Dr. Johnson appears to have taken his Zephyrettas, Trypheruses, Nitellas, Misotheas, Vagarios, and Flirtillas.

His first attempt at characteristic familiarity occurs in No. 12, in a letter from a young girl who wants a place; and in my opinion it is the most successful: the style is seldom turgid, and it has a considerable portion of humour; a quality in which it is now acknowledged Dr. Johnson excelled, although one of his biographers seems to think he did not know it.[4] It was a considerable time before I was fully convinced that Dr. Johnson wrote this letter, so little appears of his usual manner: it attacks a species of cruelty which he could not often have witnessed; and when he came to revise the original *Ramblers*, he made fewer alterations in this than in any other: a delicacy which he always observed with regard to his correspondents. But the paper is undoubtedly his, and evinces an accurate observation of common life.

With respect to humour, the following papers may be enumerated as pregnant proofs that he possessed that quality: No. 46, on the mischiefs of rural fiction; 51, on the employments of a housewife in the country; 59, Suspirius, or the human screech-owl, from which Dr. Goldsmith took his character of Croaker; 61, a Londoner's visit to the country; 73, the lingering expectation of an heir; 82, the virtuoso's account of his

---

[3] Eliza Haywood, *The Female Spectator*, 1744–6.
[4] Arthur Murphy (document No. 8).

rarities; 101, a proper audience necessary to a wit; 113, 115, history of Hymenæus's courtship; 116, the young trader's attempt at politeness; 117, the advantages of living in a garret; 119, Tranquilla's account of her lovers; 123, the young trader turned gentleman; 138, the character of Mrs. Busy; 141, the character of Papilius; 157, the scholar's complaint of his own bashfulness; 161, the revolutions of a garret; 165, the impotence of wealth, the visit of Serotinus to the place of his nativity; 177, an account of a club of antiquaries; 192, love unsuccessful without riches; 197, 198, the history of a legacy-hunter; 200, Asper's complaint of the insolence of Prospero; and 206, the art of living at the cost of others. If these papers are not allowed to contain humour, if the characters are not drawn and the stories related with that quality which forces a smile at the expense of absurdity, and delights the imagination by the juxta-position of unexpected images and allusions, it will be difficult to say where genuine humour is to be found. If it has not the ease, and sometimes the good-nature of Addison, this is saying no more than that it is not Addison's humour: neither is it that of Swift or Arbuthnot. This does not take from its originality, nor weaken the influence it produces upon contempt, the passion to which humour more particularly addresses itself. It ought to be observed also that the greater part of the subjects enumerated above are new in the history of Essay-writing: and the few that were touched by former writers, such as the virtuoso's rarities, recommend themselves to the fancy by new combinations and sportive fictions.

But the religious and moral tendency of the *Rambler* is, after all, its principal excellence, and what entitles it to a higher praise than can be earned by the powers of wit or of criticism. On subjects connected with the true interests of man, what our author has said of Goldsmith may with much more truth be applied to himself, *Nullum quod tetigit non ornavit*.[5] If we do not discover in his essays the genius which invents, we have a wonderful display of those powers of mind which, second only to the genius of the poet, most happily illustrate, and almost instantly strike conviction. Whatever position Dr. Johnson lays down, is laid down with irresistible force; it is not new, but we wonder that we have before heard it with indifference; it is perhaps familiar, and yet we receive it with the welcome of a discovery. Whatever virtue he praises, receives dignity and strength; and whatever vice he exposes, becomes more odious and contemptible. To select examples from a work so well known would be superfluous; yet one paper, No. 148, on parental cruelty, which has not

5 Boswell, *Life*, iii. 82. ('He never touched any subject but he adorned it.')

generally been pointed out by his critics, has ever appeared to me pre-eminent in every grace of moral expostulation. Men who have not seen much of life, and who believe cautiously of human depravity, cannot think it possible that such a paper should ever be read without improvement; yet without any very extensive knowledge of what is daily passing in the world, we may be allowed to assert with the author, that there are some on whom its persuasions may be lost.

[quotes 'He that can bear' to 'the force of reason', *Rambler* No. 148.]

Instances might be multiplied in which common truths and common maxims are supported by an eloquence no-where else to be found; and in which the principles of human nature are explained with a facility and truth which could result only from what appears to have been the author's favourite study, the study of the heart. Yet this distinguishing characteristic of the *Rambler*, added to a style by no means familiar, may have rendered it a less agreeable companion to a very numerous class of readers, than other works of the kind. It is certainly not a book for the uneducated part of the world, nor for those who, whatever their education, read only for their amusement. In the comparison of books with men, it may be said that the *Rambler* is one of those which are at first repulsive, but which grow upon us on a further acquaintance. Accordingly those who have read it oftenest are most sensible of its excellence: it will not please at first sight, nor suit the gay who wish to be amused, nor the superficial who cannot command attention. It is to be studied as well as read; and the few objections that have been made to it, would have probably been retracted, if the objectors had returned frequently to the work, and examined whether the author had preferred any claims which could not fairly be granted. It cannot be too often repeated that the *Rambler* is not a work to be hastily laid aside; and that they who from the apparent difficulties of style and manner have been led to study it attentively, have been amply rewarded by the discovery of new beauties; and have been ready to confess, what it would be now extremely difficult to disprove, that literature, as well as morals, owes the greatest obligations to this writer; and that since the work became popular, every thing in literature or morals, in history or dissertation, is better conceived, and better expressed—conceived with more novelty, and expressed with greater energy.

12. William Hazlitt on the *Rambler*

1819

Text from *Lectures*, 1819, 195–201.

Before Hazlitt (1778–1830) published his *Lectures on the English Comic Writers* in 1819, virtually all critics preferred Johnson's essays to those of Addison. Hazlitt vigorously dissented from the general opinion. See Introduction, pp. 22–3.

The dramatic and conversational turn which forms the distinguishing feature and greatest charm of the *Spectator* and *Tatler*, is quite lost in the *Rambler* by Dr. Johnson. There is no reflected light thrown on human life from an assumed character, nor any direct one from a display of the author's own. The *Tatler* and *Spectator* are, as it were, made up of notes and memorandums of the events and incidents of the day, with finished studies after nature, and characters fresh from the life, which the writer moralises upon, and turns to account as they come before him: the *Rambler* is a collection of moral Essays, or scholastic theses, written on set subjects, and of which the individual characters and incidents are merely artificial illustrations, brought in to give a pretended relief to the dryness of didactic discussion. The *Rambler* is a splendid and imposing common-place-book of general topics, and rhetorical declamation on the conduct and business of human life. In this sense, there is hardly a reflection that had been suggested on such subjects which is not to be found in this celebrated work, and there is, perhaps, hardly a reflection to be found in it which had not been already suggested and developed by some other author, or in the common course of conversation. The mass of intellectual wealth here heaped together is immense, but it is rather the result of gradual accumulation, the produce of the general intellect, labouring in the mine of knowledge and reflection, than dug out of the quarry, and dragged into the light by the industry and sagacity of a single mind. I am not here saying that Dr. Johnson was a man without originality, compared with the ordinary run of men's minds, but he was not a man of original thought or genius, in the sense in which Montaigne or Lord

Bacon was. He opened no new vein of precious ore, nor did he light upon any single pebbles of uncommon size and unrivalled lustre. We seldom meet with any thing to 'give us pause'; he does not set us thinking for the first time. His reflections present themselves like reminiscences; do not disturb the ordinary march of our thoughts; arrest our attention by the stateliness of their appearance, and the costliness of their garb, but pass on and mingle with the throng of our impressions. After closing the volumes of the *Rambler*, there is nothing that we remember as a new truth gained to the mind, nothing indelibly stamped upon the memory; nor is there any passage that we wish to turn to as embodying any known principle or observation, with such force and beauty that justice can only be done to the idea in the author's own words. Such, for instance, are many of the passages to be found in Burke, which shine by their own light, belong to no class, have neither equal nor counterpart, and of which we say that no one but the author could have written them! There is neither the same boldness of design, nor mastery of execution in Johnson. In the one, the spark of genius seems to have met with its congenial matter: the shaft is sped; the forked lightning dresses up the face of nature in ghastly smiles, and the loud thunder rolls far away from the ruin that is made. Dr. Johnson's style, on the contrary, resembles rather the rumbling of mimic thunder at one of our theatres; and the light he throws upon a subject is like the dazzling effect of phosphorus, or an *ignis fatuus* of words. There is a wide difference, however, between perfect originality and perfect common-place: neither ideas nor expressions are trite or vulgar because they are not quite new. They are valuable, and ought to be repeated, if they have not become quite common; and Johnson's style both of reasoning and imagery holds the middle rank between startling novelty and vapid common-place. Johnson has as much originality of thinking as Addison; but then he wants his familiarity of illustration, knowledge of character, and delightful humour.—What most distinguishes Dr. Johnson from other writers is the pomp and uniformity of his style. All his periods are cast in the same mould, are of the same size and shape, and consequently have little fitness to the variety of things he professes to treat of. His subjects are familiar, but the author is always upon stilts. He has neither ease nor simplicity, and his efforts at playfulness, in part, remind one of the lines in Milton:—

————— The elephant
To make them sport wreath'd his proboscis lithe.[1]

[1] *Paradise Lost*, IV. 345–7 (misquoted).

His Letters from Correspondents, in particular, are more pompous and unwieldy than what he writes in his own person. This want of relaxation and variety of manner has, I think, after the first effects of novelty and surprise were over, been prejudicial to the matter. It takes from the general power, not only to please, but to instruct. The monotony of style produces an apparent monotony of ideas. What is really striking and valuable, is lost in the vain ostentation and circumlocution of the expression; for when we find the same pains and pomp of diction bestowed upon the most trifling as upon the most important parts of a sentence or discourse, we grow tired of distinguishing between pretension and reality, and are disposed to confound the tinsel and bombast of the phraseology with want of weight in the thoughts. Thus, from the imposing and oracular nature of the style, people are tempted at first to imagine that our author's speculations are all wisdom and profundity: till having found out their mistake in some instances, they suppose that there is nothing but common-place in them, concealed under verbiage and pedantry; and in both they are wrong. The fault of Dr. Johnson's style is, that it reduces all things to the same artificial and unmeaning level. It destroys all shades of difference, the association between words and things. It is a perpetual paradox and innovation. He condescends to the familiar till we are ashamed of our interest in it: he expands the little till it looks big. 'If he were to write a fable of little fishes,' as Goldsmith said of him, 'he would make them speak like great whales.'[2] We can no more distinguish the most familiar objects in his descriptions of them, than we can a well-known face under a huge painted mask. The structure of his sentences, which was his own invention, and which has been generally imitated since his time, is a species of rhyming in prose, where one clause answers to another in measure and quantity, like the tagging of syllables at the end of a verse; the close of the period follows as mechanically as the oscillation of a pendulum, the sense is balanced with the sound; each sentence, revolving round its centre of gravity, is contained with itself like a couplet, and each paragraph forms itself into a stanza. Dr. Johnson is also a complete balance-master in the topics of morality. He never encourages hope, but he counteracts it by fear; he never elicits a truth, but he suggests some objection in answer to it. He seizes and alternately quits the clue of reason, lest it should involve him in the labyrinths of endless error: he wants confidence in himself and his fellows. He dares not trust himself with the immediate impressions of things, for fear of compromising his dignity; or follow them into their consequences, for

[2] Boswell, *Life*, ii. 231.

fear of committing his prejudices. His timidity is the result, not of ignorance, but of morbid apprehension. 'He runs the great circle, and is still at home.'[3] No advance is made by his writings in any sentiment, or mode of reasoning. Out of the pale of established authority and received dogmas, all is sceptical, loose, and desultory: he seems in imagination to strengthen the dominion of prejudice, as he weakens and dissipates that of reason; and round the rock of faith and power, on the edge of which he slumbers blindfold and uneasy, the waves and billows of uncertain and dangerous opinion roar and heave for evermore. His *Rasselas* is the most melancholy and debilitating moral speculation that ever was put forth. Doubtful of the faculties of his mind, as of his organs of vision, Johnson trusted only to his feelings and his fears. He cultivated a belief in witches as an out-guard to the evidences of religion; and abused Milton, and patronised Lauder,[4] in spite of his aversion to his countrymen, as a step to secure the existing establishment in church and state. This was neither right feeling nor sound logic.

[3] Cowper, *The Task*, iv. 119.
[4] William Lauder (d. 1771), literary forger. See Boswell, *Life*, i. 228–31.

13. Johnson's *Plan of a Dictionary of the English Language*

August 1747

Johnson's aspirations as expressed in 1747 were not all to be realized in the finished *Dictionary*; but the *Plan* remains a significant critical document as his first extensive statement on lexicography. It was published in the form of a letter to Lord Chesterfield.

In the first attempt to methodise my ideas, I found a difficulty which extended itself to the whole work. It was not easy to determine by what rule of distinction the words of this dictionary were to be chosen. The chief intent of it is to preserve the purity and ascertain the meaning of our English idiom; and this seems to require nothing more than that our language be considered so far as it is our own; that the words and phrases used in the general intercourse of life, or found in the works of those whom we commonly stile polite writers, be selected, without including the terms of particular professions, since, with the arts to which they relate, they are generally derived from other nations, and are very often the same in all the languages of this part of the world. This is perhaps the exact and pure idea of a grammatical dictionary; but in lexicography, as in other arts, naked science is too delicate for the purposes of life. The value of a work must be estimated by its use: It is not enough that a dictionary delights the critic, unless at the same time it instructs the learner; as it is to little purpose, that an engine amuses the philosopher by the subtilty of its mechanism, if it requires so much knowledge in its application, as to be of no advantage to the common workman.

[discusses lexicographical problems, including spelling, pronunciation, and etymology.]

Thus, my Lord, will our language be laid down, distinct in its minutest subdivisions, and resolved into its elemental principles. And who upon this survey can forbear to wish, that these fundamental atoms of our speech might obtain the firmness and immutability of the primogenial and constituent particles of matter, that they might retain their substance while they alter their appearance, and be varied and compounded, yet not destroyed.

But this is a privilege which words are scarcely to expect; for, like their author, when they are not gaining strength, they are generally losing it. Though art may sometimes prolong their duration, it will rarely give them perpetuity, and their changes will be almost always informing us, that language is the work of man, of a being from whom permanence and stability cannot be derived.

[discusses syntax and the definition and classification of words.]

With regard to questions of purity, or propriety, I was once in doubt whether I should not attribute too much to myself in attempting to decide them, and whether my province was to extend beyond the proposition of the question, and the display of the suffrages on each side; but I have been since determined by your Lordship's opinion, to interpose my own judgment, and shall therefore endeavour to support what appears to me most consonant to grammar and reason. Ausonius thought that modesty forbad him to plead inability for a task to which Cæsar had judged him equal.

Cur me posse negem posse quod ille putat?[1]

And I may hope, my Lord, that since you, whose authority in our language is so generally acknowledged, have commissioned me to declare my own opinion, I shall be considered as exercising a kind of vicarious jurisdiction, and that the power which might have been denied to my own claim, will be readily allowed me as the delegate of your Lordship.

In citing authorities, on which the credit of every part of this work must depend, it will be proper to observe some obvious rules, such as of preferring writers of the first reputation to those of an inferior rank, of noting the quotations with accuracy, and of selecting, when it can be conveniently done, such sentences, as, besides their immediate use, may give pleasure or instruction by conveying some elegance of language, or some precept of prudence, or piety.

[1] Ausonius, *Preface to the Emperor Theodosius*, l. 12 ('Why should I say that I cannot do what he thinks I can').

It has been asked, on some occasions, who shall judge the judges? And since with regard to this design, a question may arise by what authority the authorities are selected, it is necessary to obviate it, by declaring that many of the writers whose testimonies will be alleged, were selected by Mr. Pope, of whom I may be justified in affirming, that were he still alive, solicitous as he was for the success of this work, he would not be displeased that I have undertaken it.

It will be proper that the quotations be ranged according to the ages of their authors, and it will afford an agreeable amusement, if to the words and phrases which are not of our own growth, the name of the writer who first introduced them can be affixed, and if, to words which are now antiquated, the authority be subjoined of him who last admitted them. Thus for *scathe* and *buxom*, now obsolete, Milton may be cited.

> . . . . The mountain oak
> Stands *scath'd* to heaven . . .
> . . . He with broad sails
> Winnow'd the *buxom* air. . . .[2]

By this method every word will have its history, and the reader will be informed of the gradual changes of the language, and have before his eyes the rise of some words, and the fall of others. But observations so minute and accurate are to be desired rather than expected, and if use be carefully supplied, curiosity must sometimes bear its disappointments.

This, my Lord, is my idea of an English Dictionary, a dictionary by which the pronunciation of our language may be fixed, and its attainment facilitated; by which its purity may be preserved, its use ascertained, and its duration lengthened. And though, perhaps, to correct the language of nations by books of grammar, and amend their manners by discourses of morality, may be tasks equally difficult; yet as it is unavoidable to wish, it is natural likewise to hope, that your Lordship's patronage may not be wholly lost; that it may contribute to the preservation of antient, and the improvement of modern writers; that it may promote the reformation of those translators, who for want of understanding the characteristical difference of tongues, have formed a chaotic dialect of heterogeneous phrases; and awaken to the care of purer diction, some men of genius, whose attention to argument makes them negligent of stile, or whose rapid imagination, like the Peruvian torrents, when it brings down gold, mingles it with sand.

When I survey the Plan which I have laid before you, I cannot, my

[2] *Paradise Lost*, i. 613; v. 270 (misquoted).

Lord, but confess, that I am frighted at its extent, and, like the soldiers of Cæsar, look on Britain as a new world, which it is almost madness to invade. But I hope, that though I should not complete the conquest, I shall at least discover the coast, civilize part of the inhabitants, and make it easy for some other adventurer to proceed farther, to reduce them wholly to subjection, and settle them under laws.

We are taught by the great Roman orator, that every man should propose to himself the highest degree of excellence, but that he may stop with honour at the second or third;[3] though therefore my performance should fall below the excellence of other dictionaries, I may obtain, at least, the praise of having endeavoured well, nor shall I think it any reproach to my diligence, that I have retired without a triumph from a contest with united academies and long successions of learned compilers. I cannot hope in the warmest moments, to preserve so much caution through so long a work, as not often to sink into negligence, or to obtain so much knowledge of all its parts, as not frequently to fail by ignorance. I expect that sometimes the desire of accuracy, will urge me to superfluities, and sometimes the fear of prolixity betray me to omissions; that in the extent of such variety I shall be often bewildred, and in the mazes of such intricacy, be frequently entangled; that in one part refinement will be subtilised beyond exactness, and evidence dilated in another beyond perspicuity. Yet I do not despair of approbation from those who knowing the uncertainty of conjecture, the scantiness of knowledge, the fallibility of memory, and the unsteadiness of attention, can compare the causes of error with the means of avoiding it, and the extent of art with the capacity of man; and whatever be the event of my endeavours, I shall not easily regret an attempt which has procured me the honour of appearing thus publickly,

My Lord,
Your Lordship's
Most Obedient and
Most Humble Servant,
SAM. JOHNSON

[3] Possibly paraphrased from Cicero, *Brutus*, 97.

14. Foreign notice of the *Plan*

1747

The text is a translation of the original printed by J. H. Sledd and G. J. Kolb, *Dr. Johnson's Dictionary*, Chicago, 1955, 219 n.132.

Evidence of European interest was provided by a flattering notice in the *Bibliothèque raisonnée des ouvrages des savans* (published in Amsterdam) for July–September 1747, in the section entitled 'Nouvelles Literaires, *De Londres*'.

It is not surprising that few nations have reputable dictionaries of their own language. The task is as laborious as it is unglamorous, and is appropriate for a society rather than an individual. It is to their Academy that the French are indebted for all their dictionaries. Although, till now, a similar institution may have been very desirable in this city, for some time a single individual has been working on a complete dictionary, and he has just published the *Plan* in a Letter to Lord Chesterfield. This nobleman, accustomed to promoting useful projects and knowing better than anyone else the beauties and the hazards of the English language, has encouraged the author—by the name of Johnson—to undertake his thankless task. The writer expounds in his Letter the method and the rules which he intends to follow. We cannot improve on the discrimination revealed in his survey or the nicety of the details which he offers as examples. His work convinces us that in order to be a good critic one must be a good philosopher. The history of words is inextricably bound up with the history of ideas, and common sense is no less necessary than literary knowledge to study a language in its development and its eccentricities, which often cease to appear so when the causes are unravelled. Mr. Johnson brings to his work everything necessary for success, and even those who have not made a special study of English can profitably read a Letter written with such lucidity and unusual elegance. If the dictionary is characterised by the same qualities, Englishmen will find it a book well worth waiting for.

15. Chesterfield in the *World*

1754

Text from the *World*, Nos. 100–1, 28 November and 5 December, 1754, in 1794 edition, ii. 294–305.

In November and December 1754 Lord Chesterfield contributed to the *World* (a periodical published by Dodsley) two essays 'puffing' the forthcoming *Dictionary*. Despite the postscript to the first, it is likely that Dodsley encouraged Chesterfield to write them. The publication of the essays gave the appearance of active interest on Chesterfield's part between 1747 and 1754; in fact he had shown none; hence the irritation in Johnson's famous letter (No. 17). Though the essays were anonymous their authorship was made public when they were reprinted in the *Scots Magazine*, December 1754 (the *Gentleman's Magazine* and the *London Magazine* also reprinted them in the same month). Read objectively, the first essay is courteous and polished; its final paragraphs—like much of the second essay—are affected and condescending. See Introduction, p. 4.

(a) I heard the other day with great pleasure from my worthy friend Mr. Dodsley, that Mr. Johnson's English Dictionary, with a grammar and history of our language prefixed, will be published this winter, in two large volumes in folio.

I had long lamented that we had no lawful standard of our language set up, for those to repair to, who might chuse to speak, and write it grammatically and correctly: and I have as long wished that either some one person of distinguished abilities would undertake the work singly, or that a certain number of gentlemen would form themselves, or be formed by the government, into a society for that purpose. The late ingenious Doctor Swift proposed a plan of this nature to his friend (as he thought him) the lord treasurer Oxford, but without success; precision and perspicuity not being in general the favourite objects of ministers, and perhaps still less so of that minister than any other.

Many people have imagined that so extensive a work would have been best performed by a number of persons, who should have taken their several departments, of examining, sifting, winnowing (I borrow this image from the Italian *Crusca*) purifying, and finally fixing our language, by incorporating their respective funds into one joint stock. But whether this opinion be true or false, I think the public in general, and the republic of letters in particular, greatly obliged to Mr. Johnson, for having undertaken and executed so great and desirable a work. Perfection is not to be expected from man; but if we are to judge by the various works of Mr. Johnson, already published, we have good reason to believe that he will bring this as near to perfection as any one man could do. The plan of it, which he published some years ago, seems to me to be a proof of it. Nothing can be more rationally imagined, or more accurately and elegantly expressed. I therefore recommend the previous perusal of it to all those who intend to buy the dictionary, and who, I suppose, are all those who can afford it.

The celebrated dictionaries of the Florentine and French academies owe their present size and perfection to very small beginnings. Some private gentlemen of Florence, and some at Paris, had met at each other's houses to talk over and consider their respective languages: upon which they published some short essays, which essays were the embrios of those perfect productions, that now do so much honour to the two nations. Even Spain, which seems not to be the soil where, of late at least, letters have either prospered, or been cultivated, has produced a dictionary, and a good one too, of the Spanish language, in six large volumes in folio.

I cannot help thinking it a sort of disgrace to our nation, that hitherto we have had no such standard of our language; our dictionaries at present being more properly what our neighbours the Dutch and the Germans call theirs, WORD BOOKS, than dictionaries in the superior sense of that title. All words, good and bad, are there jumbled indiscriminately together, insomuch that the injudicious reader may speak, and write as inelegantly, improperly, and vulgarly as he pleases, by and with the authority of one or other of our WORD-BOOKS.

It must be owned that our language is at present in a state of anarchy; and hitherto, perhaps, it may not have been the worse for it. During our free and open trade, many words and expressions have been imported, adopted, and naturalized from other languages, which have greatly enriched our own. Let it still preserve what real strength and beauty it may have borrowed from others, but let it not, like the Tarpeian maid, be overwhelmed and crushed by unnecessary foreign ornaments. The time for discrimination seems to be now come. Toleration, adoption and naturalization have run their lengths. Good order and authority are now necessary. But where shall we find them, and at the same time the obedience due to them? We must have recourse to the old Roman expedient in times of confusion, and chuse a dictator. Upon this principle I give my vote for Mr. Johnson to fill that great and arduous post. And I hereby declare that I make a total surrender of all my rights and privileges in the English language, as a free-born British subject, to the said Mr. Johnson, during the term of his dictatorship. Nay more; I will not only obey him, like an old Roman, as my dictator, but, like a modern Roman, I will implicitly believe in him as my pope, and hold him to be infallible while in the chair; but no longer. More than this he cannot well require; for I presume that obedience can never be expected when there is neither terror to enforce, nor interest to invite it.

I confess that I have so much honest English pride, or perhaps prejudice about me, as to think myself more considerable for whatever contributes to the honour, the advantage, or the ornament of my native country. I have therefore a sensible pleasure in reflecting upon the rapid progress which our language has lately made, and still continues to make all over Europe. It is frequently spoken, and almost universally understood, in Holland; it is kindly entertained as a relation in the most civilized parts of Germany; and it is studied as a learned language, though yet little spoke, by all those in France and Italy, who either have, or pretend to have, any learning.

The spreading the French language over most parts of Europe, to the degree of making it almost an universal one, was always reckoned among the glories of the reign of Lewis the fourteenth. But be it remembered, that the success of his arms first opened the way to it; though at the same time it must be owned, that a great number of most excellent authors who flourished in his time, added strength and velocity to its progress. Whereas our language has made its way singly by its own weight and merit, under the conduct of those leaders, Shakespear, Bacon, Milton, Locke, Newton, Swift, Pope, Addison, &c. A nobler sort of conquest, and a far more glorious triumph, since graced by none but willing captives!

These authors, though for the most part but indifferently translated into foreign languages, gave other nations a sample of the British genius. The copies, imperfect as they were, pleased, and excited a general desire of seeing the originals; and both our authors and our language soon became classical.

97

But a grammar, a dictionary, and a history of our language, through its several stages, were still wanting at home, and importunately called for from abroad. Mr. Johnson's labours will now, and, I dare say, very fully, supply that want, and greatly contribute to the farther spreading of our language in other countries. Learners were discouraged by finding no standard to resort to, and consequently thought it incapable of any. They will now be undeceived and encouraged.

There are many hints and considerations relative to our language, which I should have taken the liberty of suggesting to Mr. Johnson, had I not been convinced that they have equally occurred to him: but there is one, and a very material one it is, to which perhaps he may not have given all the necessary attention. I mean the genteeler part of our language, which owes both its rise and progress to my fair country-women, whose natural turn is more to the copiousness, than to the correction of diction. I would not advise him to be rash enough to proscribe any of those happy redundancies, and luxuriances of expression, with which they have enriched our language. They willingly inflict fetters, but very unwillingly submit to wear them. In this case his task will be so difficult, that I design, as a common friend, to propose in some future paper, the means which appear to me the most likely to reconcile matters.

P.S. I hope that none of my courteous readers will upon this occasion be so uncourteous, as to suspect me of being a hired and interested puff of this work; for I most solemnly protest, that neither Mr. Johnson, nor any person employed by him, nor any bookseller or booksellers concerned in the success of it, have ever offered me the usual compliment of a pair of gloves or a bottle of wine; nor has even Mr. Dodsley, though my publisher, and, as I am informed, deeply interested in the sale of this dictionary, so much as invited me to take a bit of mutton with him.

(b) When I intimated in my last paper some distrust of Mr. Johnson's complaisance to the fair part of his readers, it was because I had a greater opinion of his impartiality and severity as a judge, than of his gallantry as a fine gentleman. And indeed I am well aware of the difficulties he would have to encounter, if he attempted to reconcile the polite, with the grammatical part of our language. Should he, by an act of power, banish and attaint many of the favourite words and expressions with which the ladies have so profusely enriched our language, he would excite the indignation of the most formidable, because the most lovely part of his readers: his dictionary would be condemned as a system of tyranny, and he himself, like the last Tarquin, run the risque of being deposed. So popular and so powerful is the female cause! On the other hand, should he, by an act of grace, admit, legitimate, and incorporate into our language those words and expressions, which, hastily begot, owe their birth to the incontinency of female eloquence, what severe censures might he not justly apprehend from the learned part of his readers, who do not understand complaisances of that nature?

For my own part, as I am always inclined to plead the cause of my fair fellow subjects, I shall now take the liberty of laying before Mr. Johnson those arguments which upon this occasion may be urged in their favour, as introductory to the compromise which I shall humbly offer and conclude with.

Language is indisputably the more immediate province of the fair sex: there they shine, there they excel. The torrents of their eloquence, especially in the vituperative way, stun all opposition, and bear away in one promiscuous heap, nouns, pronouns, verbs, moods and tenses. If words are wanting (which indeed happens but seldom) indignation instantly makes new ones, and I have often known four or five syllables that never met one another before, hastily and fortuitously jumbled into some word of mighty import.

Nor is the tender part of our language less obliged to that soft and amiable sex: their love being at least as productive as their indignation. Should they lament in an involuntary retirement the absence of the adored object, they give new murmurs to the brook, new sounds to the echo, and new notes to the plaintive Philomela. But when this happy copiousness flows, as it often does, into gentle numbers, good Gods! how is the poetical diction enriched, and the poetical licence extended! even in common conversation, I never see a pretty mouth opening to speak, but I expect, and am seldom disappointed, some new improvement of our language. I remember many very expressive words coined in that fair mint. I assisted at the birth of that most significant word, flirtation, which dropped from the most beautiful mouth in the world, and which has since received the sanction of our most accurate laureat in one of his comedies. Some inattentive and undiscerning people have, I know, taken it to be a term synonimous with coquetry; but I lay hold of this opportunity to undeceive them, and eventually to inform Mr. Johnson, that flirtation is short of coquetry, and intimates only the first hints of approximation, which subsequent coquetry may reduce to those preliminary articles, that commonly end in a definitive treaty.

I was also a witness to the rise and progress of that most important verb, to fuzz; which if not of legitimate birth, is at least of fair extraction. As I am not sure that it has yet made its way into Mr. Johnson's literary retirement, I think myself obliged to inform him that it is at present the most useful, and the most used word in our language; since it means no less than dealing twice together with the same pack of cards, for luck's sake, at WHIST.

Not contented with enriching our language by words absolutely new, my fair country-women have gone still farther, and improved it by the application and extension of old ones to various and very different significations. They take a word and change it, like a guinea into shillings for pocket money, to be employed in the several occasional purposes of the day. For instance, the adjective VAST and its adverb VASTLY mean any thing, and are the fashionable words of the most fashionable people. A fine woman (under this head I comprehend all fine gentlemen too, not knowing in truth where to place them properly) is VASTLY obliged or VASTLY offended, VASTLY glad, or VASTLY sorry. Large objects are VASTLY great, small ones are VASTLY little; and I had lately the pleasure to hear a fine woman pronounce, by a happy metonymy, a very small gold snuff-box that was produced in company to be VASTLY pretty, because it was VASTLY little. Mr. Johnson will do well to consider seriously to what degree he will restrain the various and extensive significations of this great word.

Another very material point still remains to be considered; I mean the orthography of our language, which is at present very various and unsettled.

We have at present two very different orthographies, the PEDANTIC, and the POLITE; the one founded upon certain dry crabbed rules of etymology and grammar, the other singly upon the justness and delicacy of the ear. I am thoroughly persuaded that Mr. Johnson will endeavour to establish the former; and I perfectly agree with him, provided it can be quietly brought about. Spelling, as well as music, is better performed by book, than merely by the ear, which may be variously affected by the same sounds. I therefore most earnestly recommend to my fair country-women, and to their faithful, or faithless servants, the fine gentlemen of this realm, to surrender, as well for their own private, as for the public utility, all their natural rights and privileges of mis-spelling, which they have so long enjoyed, and so vigorously exerted. I have really known very fatal consequences attend that loose and uncertain practice of AURICULAR ORTHOGRAPHY; of which I shall produce two instances as a sufficient warning.

A very fine gentleman wrote a very harmless innocent letter to a very fine lady, giving her an account of some trifling commissions which he had executed according to her orders. This letter, though directed to the lady, was, by the mistake of a servant, delivered to, and opened by the husband; who finding all his attempts to understand it unsuccessful, took it for granted that it was a concerted cypher, under which a criminal correspondence, not much to his own honour or advantage, was secretly carried on. With the letter in his hand, and rage in his heart, he went immediately to his wife, and reproached her in the most injurious terms with her supposed infidelity. The lady, conscious of her own innocence, calmly requested to see the grounds of so unjust an accusation; and being accustomed to the AURICULAR ORTHOGRAPHY, made shift to read to her incensed husband the most inoffensive letter that ever was written. The husband was undeceived, or at least wise enough to seem so: for in such nice cases one must not peremptorily decide. However, as sudden impressions are generally pretty strong, he has been observed to be more suspicious ever since.

The other accident had much worse consequences. Matters were happily brought, between a fine gentleman and a fine lady, to the decisive period of an appointment at a third place. *The place where* is always the lover's business, *the time when* the lady's. Accordingly an impatient and rapturous letter from the lover signified to the lady the house and street *where*; to which a tender answer from the lady assented, and appointed the time *when*. But unfortunately, from the uncertainty of the lover's AURICULAR ORTHOGRAPHY, the lady mistook both house and street, was conveyed in a hackney chair to a wrong one, and in the hurry and agitation which ladies are sometimes in upon those occasions, rushed into a house where she happened to be known, and her intentions consequently discovered. In the mean time the lover passed three or four hours at the right place, in the alternate agonies of impatient and disappointed love, tender fear, and anxious jealousy.

Such examples really make one tremble; and will, I am convinced, determine my fair fellow-subjects and their adherents, to adopt, and scrupulously conform to Mr. Johnson's rules of true ORTHOGRAPHY by book. In return to this concession, I seriously advise him to publish, by way of appendix to his great work, a genteel Neological dictionary, containing those polite, though perhaps not strictly grammatical words and phrases, commonly used, and sometimes understood, by the BEAU MONDE. By such an act of toleration, who knows but he may, in time, bring them within the pale of the English language? The best Latin dictionaries have commonly a short supplemental one annexed, of the obsolete and barbarous Latin words, which pedants sometimes borrow to shew their erudition. Surely then, my country-women, the enrichers, the patronesses, and the harmonizers of our language, deserve greater indulgence. I must also hint to Mr. Johnson, that such a small supplemental dictionary will contribute infinitely to the sale of the great one; and I make no question but that under the protection of that little work, the great one will be received in the genteelest houses. We shall frequently meet with it in ladies dressing-rooms, lying upon the harpsichord, together with the knotting bag, and signor Di-Giardino's[1] incomparable concertos; and even sometimes in the powder-rooms of our young nobility, upon the same shelf with their German-flute, their powder mask, and their four-horse whip.

16. Johnson writes to Thomas Warton

1 February 1755

Life, i. 278.

Johnson informs Warton that the *Dictionary* is finished.

Dear Sir

I wrote to you some weeks ago but believe did not direct accurately, and therefore know not whether you had my letter. I would likewise write to your brother[2] but know not where to find him. I now begin to see land, after having wandered, according to Mr. Warburton's phrase, in this vast sea of words.[3] What reception I shall meet with on the shore I know not, whether the sound of bells and acclamations of the people which Ariosto talks of in his last Canto[4] or a general murmur of dislike, I

---

[1] Felice de Giardini (1716–96), brilliant Italian violinist.
[2] The critic, Joseph Warton.
[3] From the Preface to Warburton's edition of Shakespeare (1747).
[4] *Orlando Furioso*, c. 46, st. 2.

know not whether I shall find upon the coast, a Calypso that will court, or a Polypheme that will resist. But if Polypheme comes, have at his eye.

I hope however the criticks will let me be at peace for though I do not much fear their skill or strength, I am a little afraid of myself, and would not willingly feel so much ill-will in my bosom as literary quarrels are apt to excite.

17. Johnson's letter to Chesterfield

7 February 1755

Life, i. 261–3.

Johnson refused to allow Chesterfield the seeming responsibility for his growing prominence in the literary world (see No. 15). The letter is a brilliant display of controlled venom; but by implication it is also an unequivocal declaration by a professional writer of his allegiance to the reading public. Any hint of patronage was offensive to Johnson. The letter, though known at once to 'the town', was not published until Boswell issued it in pamphlet form in 1790; it sold for half a guinea.

February 7, 1755.

My Lord,

I have been lately informed, by the proprietor of the *World*, that two papers, in which my *Dictionary* is recommended to the publick, were written by your Lordship. To be so distinguished, is an honour, which, being very little accustomed to favours from the great, I know not well how to receive, or in what terms to acknowledge.

When, upon some slight encouragement, I first visited your Lordship, I was overpowered, like the rest of mankind, by the enchantment of your address; and could not forbear to wish that I might boast myself *Le vainqueur du vainqueur de la terre*;[1]—that I might obtain that regard for

[1] Boileau, *L'Art Poétique*, iii. 272.

which I saw the world contending; but I found my attendance so little encouraged, that neither pride nor modesty would suffer me to continue it. When I had once addressed your Lordship in publick, I had exhausted all the art of pleasing which a retired and uncourtly scholar can possess. I had done all that I could; and no man is well pleased to have his all neglected, be it ever so little.

Seven years, my Lord, have now past, since I waited in your outward room, or was repulsed from your door; during which time I have been pushing on my work through difficulties, of which it is useless to complain, and have brought it at last, to the verge of publication, without one act of assistance, one word of encouragement, or one smile of favour. Such treatment I did not expect, for I never had a Patron before.

The shepherd in Virgil[2] grew at last acquainted with Love, and found him a native of the rocks.

Is not a Patron, my Lord, one who looks with unconcern on a man struggling for life in the water, and, when he has reached ground, encumbers him with help? The notice which you have been pleased to take of my labours, had it been early, had been kind; but it has been delayed till I am indifferent and cannot enjoy it; till I am solitary, and cannot impart it; till I am known, and do not want it. I hope it is no cynical asperity not to confess obligations where no benefit has been received, or to be unwilling that the Publick should consider me as owing that to a Patron, which Providence has enabled me to do for myself.

Having carried on my work thus far with so little obligation to any favourer of learning, I shall not be disappointed though I should conclude it, if less be possible, with less; for I have been long wakened from that dream of hope, in which I once boasted myself with so much exaltation,

My Lord,

Your Lordship's most humble,

Most obedient servant,

Sam. Johnson.

[2] *Eclogues*, viii. 43.

18. Johnson's Preface

1755

Text from the version corrected by Johnson for the fourth edition, 1773.

Johnson explains and justifies his lexicographical procedures; gives a view of the scope of his achievement; and while asserting his claim to distinction, frankly confesses the shortcomings of his *Dictionary*. Subsequently critics often censured him for defects he had already admitted. See Introduction, p. 24.

It is the fate of those who toil at the lower employments of life, to be rather driven by the fear of evil, than attracted by the prospect of good; to be exposed to censure, without hope of praise; to be disgraced by miscarriage, or punished for neglect, where success would have been without applause, and diligence without reward.

Among these unhappy mortals is the writer of dictionaries; whom mankind have considered, not as the pupil, but the slave of science, the pionier of literature, doomed only to remove rubbish and clear obstructions from the paths through which Learning and Genius press forward to conquest and glory, without bestowing a smile on the humble drudge that facilitates their progress. Every other authour may aspire to praise; the lexicographer can only hope to escape reproach, and even this negative recompense has been yet granted to very few.

I have, notwithstanding this discouragement, attempted a dictionary of the *English* language, which, while it was employed in the cultivation of every species of literature, has itself been hitherto neglected; suffered to spread, under the direction of chance, into wild exuberance; resigned to the tyranny of time and fashion; and exposed to the corruptions of ignorance, and caprices of innovation.

When I took the first survey of my undertaking, I found our speech copious without order, and energetick without rules: wherever I turned my view, there was perplexity to be disentangled, and confusion to be regulated; choice was to be made out of boundless variety, without any established principle of selection; adulterations were to be detected, without a settled test of purity; and modes of expression to be rejected or received, without the suffrages of any writers of classical reputation or acknowledged authority.

Having therefore no assistance but from general grammar, I applied myself to the perusal of our writers; and noting whatever might be of use to ascertain or illustrate any word or phrase, accumulated in time the materials of a dictionary, which, by degrees, I reduced to method, establishing to myself, in the progress of the work, such rules as experience and analogy suggested to me; experience, which practice and observation were continually increasing; and analogy, which, though in some words obscure, was evident in others.

[discusses orthography.]

In this part of the work [orthography], where caprice has long wantoned without controul, and vanity sought praise by petty reformation, I have endeavoured to proceed with a scholar's reverence for antiquity, and a grammarian's regard to the genius of our tongue. I have attempted few alterations, and among those few, perhaps the greater part is from the modern to the ancient practice; and I hope I may be allowed to recommend to those, whose thoughts have been perhaps employed too anxiously on verbal singularities, not to disturb, upon narrow views, or for minute propriety, the orthography of their fathers. It has been asserted, that for the law to be *known*, is of more importance than to be *right*. Change, says *Hooker*, is not made without inconvenience, even from worse to better.[1] There is in constancy and stability a general and lasting advantage, which will always overbalance the slow improvements of gradual correction. Much less ought our written language to comply with the corruptions of oral utterance, or copy that which every variation of time or place makes different from itself, and imitate those changes, which will again be changed, while imitation is employed in observing them.

This recommendation of steadiness and uniformity does not proceed from an opinion, that particular combinations of letters have much influence on human happiness; or that truth may not be successfully taught by modes of spelling fanciful and erroneous: I am not yet so lost in lexicography, as to forget that *words are the daughters of earth, and that things are the sons of heaven*.[2] Language is only the instrument of science, and words are but the signs of ideas: I wish, however, that the instrument

[1] *Ecclesiastical Polity*, 1594, iv. 14.   [2] Hindu proverb.

might be less apt to decay, and that signs might be permanent, like the things which they denote.

[on his etymological procedure.]

The etymology, so far as it is yet known, was easily found in the volumes where it is particularly and professedly delivered; and, by proper attention to the rules of derivation, the orthography was soon adjusted. But to COLLECT the WORDS of our language was a task of greater difficulty: the deficiency of dictionaries was immediately apparent; and when they were exhausted, what was yet wanting must be sought by fortuitous and unguided excursions into books, and gleaned as industry should find, or chance should offer it, in the boundless chaos of a living speech. My search, however, has been either skilful or lucky; for I have much augmented the vocabulary.

[on his principles of selection in the word-list.]

Many words yet stand supported only by the name of Bailey, Ainsworth, Philips,[3] or the contracted Dict. for Dictionaries subjoined; of these I am not always certain that they are read in any book but the works of lexicographers. Of such I have omitted many, because I had never read them; and many I have inserted, because they may perhaps exist, though they have escaped my notice: they are, however, to be yet considered as resting only upon the credit of former dictionaries. Others, which I considered as useful, or know to be proper, though I could not at present support them by authorities, I have suffered to stand upon my own attestation, claiming the same privilege with my predecessors of being sometimes credited without proof.

The words, thus selected and disposed, are grammatically considered; they are referred to the different parts of speech; traced, when they are irregularly inflected, through their various terminations; and illustrated by observations, not indeed of great or striking importance, separately considered, but necessary to the elucidation of our language, and hitherto neglected or forgotten by English grammarians.

That part of my work on which I expect malignity most frequently to fasten, is the Explanation; in which I cannot hope to satisfy those, who are perhaps not inclined to be pleased, since I have not always been able to satisfy myself. To interpret a language by itself is very difficult; many

---

[3] Nathan Bailey (d. 1742), Robert Ainsworth (1660–1743) and Edward Phillips (1630–?96), lexicographers whom Johnson acknowledges as his sources. He worked from an interleaved copy of Bailey's Dictionarium Britannicum.

words cannot be explained by synonimes, because the idea signified by them has not more than one appellation; nor by paraphrase, because simple ideas cannot be described. When the nature of things is unknown, or the notion unsettled and indefinite, and various in various minds, the words by which such notions are conveyed, or such things denoted, will be ambiguous and perplexed. And such is the fate of hapless lexicography, that not only darkness, but light, impedes and distresses it; things may be not only too little, but too much known, to be happily illustrated. To explain, requires the use of terms less abstruse than that which is to be explained, and such terms cannot always be found; for as nothing can be proved but by supposing something intuitively known, and evident without proof, so nothing can be defined but by the use of words too plain to admit a definition. . . .

Some words there are which I cannot explain, because I do not understand them; these might have been omitted very often with little inconvenience, but I would not so far indulge my vanity as to decline this confession: for when *Tully* owns himself ignorant whether *lessus*, in the twelve tables, means a *funeral song*, or *mourning garment*;[4] and *Aristotle* doubts whether οὔρευς, in the *Iliad*, signifies a *mule*, or *muleteer*, I may surely, without shame, leave some obscurities to happier industry . . .

[the difficulties posed by definition.]

All the interpretations of words are not written with the same skill, or the same happiness: things equally easy in themselves, are not all equally easy to any single mind. Every writer of a long work commits errours, where there appears neither ambiguity to mislead, nor obscurity to confound him; and in a search like this, many felicities of expression will be casually overlooked, many convenient parallels will be forgotten, and many particulars will admit improvement from a mind utterly unequal to the whole performance.

But many seeming faults are to be imputed rather to the nature of the undertaking, than the negligence of the performer. Thus some explanations are unavoidably reciprocal or circular, as *hind, the female of the stag*; *stag, the male of the hind*: sometimes easier words are changed into harder, as *burial* into *sepulture* or *interment*, *drier* into *desiccative*, *dryness* into *siccity* or *aridity*, *fit* into *paroxysm*; for the easiest word, whatever it be, can never be translated into one more easy. But easiness and difficulty are merely relative, and if the present prevalence of our language should invite foreigners to this dictionary, many will be assisted by those words which

4 Cicero, *Laws*, II. xxiii, 59.

now seem only to increase or produce obscurity. For this reason I have endeavoured frequently to join a *Teutonick* and *Roman* interpretation, as to CHEER, to *gladden*, or *exhilarate*, that every learner of *English* may be assisted by his own tongue.

The solution of all difficulties, and the supply of all defects, must be sought in the examples, subjoined to the various senses of each word, and ranged according to the time of their authours.

When I first collected these authorities, I was desirous that every quotation should be useful to some other end than the illustration of a word; I therefore extracted from philosophers principles of science; from historians remarkable facts; from chymists complete processes; from divines striking exhortations; and from poets beautiful descriptions. Such is design, while it is yet at a distance from execution. When the time called upon me to range this accumulation of elegance and wisdom into an alphabetical series, I soon discovered that the bulk of my volumes would fright away the student, and was forced to depart from my scheme of including all that was pleasing or useful in *English* literature, and reduce my transcripts very often to clusters of words, in which scarcely any meaning is retained; thus to the weariness of copying, I was condemned to add the vexation of expunging. Some passages I have yet spared, which may relieve the labour of verbal searches, and intersperse with verdure and flowers the dusty desarts of barren philology.

The examples, thus mutilated, are no longer to be considered as conveying the sentiments or doctrine of their authours; the word for the sake of which they are inserted, with all its appendant clauses, has been carefully preserved; but it may sometimes happen, by hasty detruncation, that the general tendency of the sentence may be changed: the divine may desert his tenets, or the philosopher his system.

Some of the examples have been taken from writers who were never mentioned as masters of elegance or models of stile; but words must be sought where they are used; and in what pages, eminent for purity, can terms of manufacture or agriculture be found? Many quotations serve no other purpose, than that of proving the bare existence of words, and are therefore selected with less scrupulousness than those which are to teach their structures and relations.

My purpose was to admit no testimony of living authours, that I might not be misled by partiality, and that none of my cotemporaries might have reason to complain; nor have I departed from this resolution, but when some performance of uncommon excellence excited my veneration, when my memory supplied me, from late books, with an example that was wanting, or when my heart, in the tenderness of friendship, solicited admission for a favourite name.

So far have I been from any care to grace my pages with modern decorations, that I have studiously endeavoured to collect examples and authorities from the writers before the restoration, whose works I regard as *the wells of English undefiled*,[5] as the pure sources of genuine diction. Our language, for almost a century, has, by the concurrence of many causes, been gradually departing from its original *Teutonick* character, and deviating towards a *Gallick* structure and phraseology, from which it ought to be our endeavour to recal it, by making our ancient volumes the groundwork of stile, admitting among the additions of later times, only such as may supply real deficiencies, such as are readily adopted by the genius of our tongue, and incorporate easily with our native idioms.

But as every language has a time of rudeness antecedent to perfection, as well as of false refinement and declension, I have been cautious lest my zeal for antiquity might drive me into times too remote, and croud my book with words now no longer understood. I have fixed *Sidney*'s work for the boundary, beyond which I make few excursions. From the authours which rose in the time of *Elizabeth*, a speech might be formed adequate to all the purposes of use and elegance. If the language of theology were extracted from *Hooker* and the translations of the Bible; the terms of natural knowledge from *Bacon*; the phrases of policy, war, and navigation from *Raleigh*; the dialect of poetry and fiction from *Spenser* and *Sidney*; and the diction of common life from *Shakespeare*, few ideas would be lost to mankind, for want of *English* words, in which they might be expressed.

It is not sufficient that a word is found, unless it be so combined as that its meaning is apparently determined by the tract and tenour of the sentence; such passages I have therefore chosen, and when it happened that any authour gave a definition of a term, or such an explanation as is equivalent to a definition, I have placed his authority as a supplement to my own, without regard to the chronological order, that is observed.

Some words, indeed, stand unsupported by any authority, but they are commonly derivative nouns or adverbs, formed from their primitives by regular and constant analogy, or names of things seldom occurring in books, or words of which I have reason to doubt the existence.

There is more danger of censure from the multiplicity than paucity of examples; authorities will sometimes seem to have been accumulated without necessity or use, and perhaps some will be found, which might,

[5] Spenser, *Faerie Queene*, IV. ii. 32.

without loss, have been omitted. But a work of this kind is not hastily to be charged with superfluities: those quotations, which to careless or unskilful perusers appear only to repeat the same sense, will often exhibit, to a more accurate examiner, diversities of signification, or, at least, afford different shades of the same meaning: one will shew the word applied to persons, another to things; one will express an ill, another a good, and a third a neutral sense; one will prove the expression genuine from an ancient authour; another will shew it elegant from a modern: a doubtful authority is corroborated by another of more credit; an ambiguous sentence is ascertained by a passage clear and determinate; the word, how often soever repeated, appears with new associates and in different combinations, and every quotation contributes something to the stability or enlargement of the language.

When words are used equivocally, I receive them in either sense; when they are metaphorical, I adopt them in their primitive acceptation.

I have sometimes, though rarely, yielded to the temptation of exhibiting a genealogy of sentiments, by shewing how one authour copied the thoughts and diction of another: such quotations are indeed little more than repetitions, which might justly be censured, did they not gratify the mind, by affording a kind of intellectual history.

The various syntactical structures occurring in the examples have been carefully noted; the licence or negligence with which many words have been hitherto used, has made our stile capricious and indeterminate; when the different combinations of the same word are exhibited together, the preference is readily given to propriety, and I have often endeavoured to direct the choice.

Thus have I laboured by settling the orthography, displaying the analogy, regulating the structures, and ascertaining the signification of *English* words, to perform all the parts of a faithful lexicographer: but I have not always executed my own scheme, or satisfied my own expectations. The work, whatever proofs of diligence and attention it may exhibit, is yet capable of many improvements: the orthography which I recommend is still controvertible, the etymology which I adopt is uncertain, and perhaps frequently erroneous; the explanations are sometimes too much contracted, and sometimes too much diffused, the significations are distinguished rather with subtilty than skill, and the attention is harrassed with unnecessary minuteness.

The examples are too often injudiciously truncated, and perhaps sometimes, I hope very rarely, alleged in a mistaken sense; for in making this collection I trusted more to memory, than, in a state of disquiet and embarrassment, memory can contain, and purposed to supply at the review what was left incomplete in the first transcription.

Many terms appropriated to particular occupations, though necessary and significant, are undoubtedly omitted; and of the words most studiously considered and exemplified, many senses have escaped observation.

Yet these failures, however frequent, may admit extenuation and apology. To have attempted much is always laudable, even when the enterprize is above the strength that undertakes it: To rest below his own aim is incident to every one whose fancy is active, and whose views are comprehensive; nor is any man satisfied with himself because he has done much, but because he can conceive little. When first I engaged in this work, I resolved to leave neither words nor things unexamined, and pleased myself with a prospect of the hours which I should revel away in feasts of literature, with the obscure recesses of northern learning, which I should enter and ransack; the treasures with which I expected every search into those neglected mines to reward my labour, and the triumph with which I should display my acquisitions to mankind. When I had thus enquired into the original of words, I resolved to show likewise my attention to things; to pierce deep into every science, to enquire the nature of every substance of which I inserted the name, to limit every idea by a definition strictly logical, and exhibit every production of art or nature in an accurate description, that my book might be in place of all other dictionaries whether appellative or technical. But these were the dreams of a poet doomed at last to wake a lexicographer. I soon found that it is too late to look for instruments, when the work calls for execution, and that whatever abilities I had brought to my task, with those I must finally perform it. To deliberate whenever I doubted, to enquire whenever I was ignorant, would have protracted the undertaking without end, and, perhaps, without much improvement; for I did not find by my first experiments, that what I had not of my own was easily to be obtained: I saw that one enquiry only gave occasion to another, that book referred to book, that to search was not always to find, and to find was not always to be informed; and that thus to persue perfection, was, like the first inhabitants of Arcadia, to chace the sun, which, when they had reached the hill where he seemed to rest, was still beheld at the same distance from them.

I then contracted my design, determining to confide in myself, and no longer to solicit auxiliaries, which produced more incumbrance than assistance: by this I obtained at least one advantage, that I set limits to my work, which would in time be ended, though not completed.

Despondency has never so far prevailed as to depress me to negligence; some faults will at last appear to be the effects of anxious diligence and persevering activity. The nice and subtle ramifications of meaning were not easily avoided by a mind intent upon accuracy, and convinced of the necessity of disentangling combinations, and separating similitudes. Many of the distinctions which to common readers appear useless and idle, will be found real and important by men versed in the school philosophy, without which no dictionary ever shall be accurately compiled, or skilfully examined.

[Johnson reluctantly admits the inability of a lexicographer to 'fix our language' and prevent 'those alterations which time and chance' inevitably effect. He surveys the causes of change.]

If the changes that we fear be thus irresistible, what remains but to acquiesce with silence, as in the other insurmountable distresses of humanity? It remains that we retard what we cannot repel, that we palliate what we cannot cure. Life may be lengthened by care, though death cannot be ultimately defeated: tongues, like governments, have a natural tendency to degeneration; we have long preserved our constitution, let us make some struggles for our language.

In hope of giving longevity to that which its own nature forbids to be immortal, I have devoted this book, the labour of years, to the honour of my country, that we may no longer yield the palm of philology, without a contest, to the nations of the continent. The chief glory of every people arises from its authours: whether I shall add any thing by my own writings to the reputation of *English* literature, must be left to time: much of my life has been lost under the pressures of disease; much has been trifled away; and much has always been spent in provision for the day that was passing over me; but I shall not think my employment useless or ignoble, if by my assistance foreign nations, and distant ages, gain access to the propagators of knowledge, and understand the teachers of truth; if my labours afford light to the repositories of science, and add celebrity to *Bacon*, to *Hooker*, to *Milton*, and to *Boyle*.

When I am animated by this wish, I look with pleasure on my book, however defective, and deliver it to the world with the spirit of a man that has endeavoured well. That it will immediately become popular I have not promised to myself: a few wild blunders, and risible absurdities, from which no work of such multiplicity was ever free, may for a time furnish folly with laughter, and harden ignorance in contempt; but useful diligence will at last prevail, and there never can be wanting some who distinguish desert; who will consider that no dictionary of a living tongue ever can be perfect, since while it is hastening to publication, some words are budding, and some falling away; that a whole life cannot be spent upon syntax and etymology, and that even a whole life would not be sufficient; that he, whose design includes whatever language can express, must often speak of what he does not understand; that a writer will sometimes be hurried by eagerness to the end, and sometimes faint with weariness under a task, which *Scaliger* compares to the labours of the anvil and the mine;[6] that what is obvious is not always known, and what is known is not always present; that sudden fits of inadvertency will surprize vigilance, slight avocations will seduce attention, and casual eclipses of the mind will darken learning; and that the writer shall often in vain trace his memory at the moment of need, for that which yesterday he knew with intuitive readiness, and which will come uncalled into his thoughts to-morrow.

In this work, when it shall be found that much is omitted, let it not be forgotten that much likewise is performed; and though no book was ever spared out of tenderness to the authour, and the world is little solicitous to know whence proceeded the faults of that which it condemns; yet it may gratify curiosity to inform it, that the *English Dictionary* was written with little assistance of the learned, and without any patronage of the great; not in the soft obscurities of retirement, or under the shelter of academick bowers, but amidst inconveniences and distraction, in sickness and in sorrow. It may repress the triumph of malignant criticism to observe, that if our language is not here fully displayed, I have only failed in an attempt which no human powers have hitherto completed. If the lexicons of ancient tongues, now immutably fixed, and comprised in a few volumes, be yet, after the toil of successive ages, inadequate and delusive; if the aggregated knowledge, and co-operating diligence of the *Italian* academicians, did not secure them from the censure of *Beni*;[7] if the embodied criticks of *France*, when fifty years had been spent upon their work, were obliged to change its oeconomy, and give their second edition another form, I may surely be contented without the praise of perfection, which, if I could obtain, in this gloom of solitude, what would it avail me? I have protracted my work till most of those whom I wished to please have sunk into the grave, and success and miscarriage are empty sounds: I therefore dismiss it with frigid tranquillity, having little to fear or hope from censure or from praise.

6 J. J. Scaliger (1540–1609), 'In lexicorum compilatores', *Poemata Omnia*, Berlin, 1864, 38.
7 P. Beni (1552?–1625), Italian classical scholar.

19. Adam Smith, unsigned review
Edinburgh Review

May 1755, i, 61–73

The anonymous reviewer of the *Dictionary* in the *Edinburgh* was Adam Smith (1723–90), then Professor of Moral Philosophy at Glasgow (where Boswell heard him lecture in 1759). The review was reprinted in the *Scots Magazine*, November 1755; in abbreviated form, as an addendum to Adelung's essay (No. 21) in 1798; in the *European Magazine*, 1802; as well as in Smith's *Works*, 1811. See Introduction, pp. 4, 24.

The present undertaking is very extensive. A dictionary of the English language, however useful, or rather necessary, has never been hitherto attempted with the least degree of success. To explain hard words and terms of art seems to have been the chief purpose of all the former compositions which have borne the title of English dictionaries. Mr. Johnson has extended his views much farther, and has made a very full collection of all the different meanings of each English word, justified by examples from authors of good reputation. When we compare this book with other dictionaries, the merit of its author appears very extraordinary. Those which in modern languages have gained the most esteem, are that of the French academy, and that of the academy Della Crusca. Both these were composed by a numerous society of learned men, and took up a longer time in the composition, than the life of a single person could well have afforded. The dictionary of the English language is the work of a single person, and composed in a period of time very inconsiderable, when compared with the extent of the work. The collection of words appears to be very accurate, and must be allowed to be very ample. Most words, we believe, are to be found in the dictionary that ever were almost suspected to be English; but we cannot help wishing, that the author had trusted less to the judgment of those who may consult him, and had oftener passed his own censure upon those words which are not of approved use, tho' sometimes to be met with in authors of no mean name.

Where a work is admitted to be highly useful, and the execution of it intitled to praise; the adding, that it might have been more useful, can scarcely, we hope, be deemed a censure of it. The merit of Mr. Johnson's dictionary is so great, that it cannot detract from it to take notice of some defects, the supplying which, would, in our judgment, add a considerable share of merit to that which it already possesses. Those defects consist chiefly in the plan, which appears to us not to be sufficiently grammatical. The different significations of a word are indeed collected; but they are seldom digested into general classes, or ranged under the meaning which the word principally expresses. And sufficient care has not been taken to distinguish the words apparently synonomous. The only method of explaining what we intend, is by inserting an article or two from Mr. Johnson, and by opposing to them the same articles, digested in the manner which we would have wished him to have followed.

[Smith selects 'but' and 'humour' as his examples.]

These instances may serve to explain the plan of a Dictionary which suggested itself to us. It can import no reflection upon Mr. Johnsons Dictionary that the subject has been viewed in a different light by others; and it is at least a matter of curiosity to consider the different views in which it appears. Any man who was about to compose a dictionary or rather a grammar of the English language, must acknowledge himself indebted to Mr. Johnson for abridging at least one half of his labour. All those who are under any difficulty with respect to a particular word or phrase, are in the same situation. The dictionary presents them a full collection of examples; from whence indeed they are left to determine, but by which the determination is rendered easy. In this country, the usefulness of it will be soon felt, as there is no standard of correct language in conversation; if our recommendation could in any degree incite to the perusal of it, we would earnestly recommend it to all those who are desirous to improve and correct their language, frequently to consult the dictionary. Its merit must be determined by the frequent resort that is had to it. This is the most unerring test of its value; criticisms may be false, private judgments ill-founded; but if a work of this nature be much in use, it has received the sanction of the public approbation.

20. Horne Tooke's *Diversions of Purley*

1786

Text from *Diversions*, ed. R. Taylor, 1829, i. 211–12.

John Horne Tooke (1736–1812)—'one of the most systematically frantic etymologists who ever lived' (Sledd and Kolb, *Dr. Johnson's Dictionary*, 183)—had nothing favourable to say about Johnson's work. His political radicalism, support for Wilkes, and sympathy for the American colonies sharpened his antagonism to Johnson. The following extract (from the chapter on conjunctions) includes a characteristically contemptuous reference, together with a dismissive footnote (later quoted by Webster, No. 22). See Introduction, pp. 4, 24.

LEST.

Junius[1] only says 'LEST, *least*, minimus. v. *little.*' Under *Least*, he says— 'LEAST, *lest*, minimus. Contractum est ex ἐλάχιστος. v. *little,* parvus.' And under *Little*, to which he refers us, there is nothing to the purpose.

Skinner[2] says—'LEST, ab A.S. Læs, minus, q.d. *quo minus hoc fiat.*'

S. Johnson says,—'LEST, Conj. (from the Adjective *Least*) *That not.*'

This last deduction is a curious one indeed; and it would puzzle as sagacious a reasoner as S. Johnson to supply the middle steps to his conclusion from *Least* (which always however means *some*) to '*That not*' (which means *none at all*). It seems as if, when he wrote this, he had already in his mind a presentiment of some future occasion in which such reasoning would be convenient. As thus,—'The Mother Country, the seat of government, must necessarily enjoy the greatest share of dignity, power, rights, and privileges: an united or associated kingdom must

---

[1] Francis Junius (1589–1677), *Etymologicum Anglicanum*, 1743.
[2] Stephen Skinner (1623–67), *Etymologicon Linguae Anglicanae*, ed. Thomas Henshaw, 1671.

have in some degree a smaller share; and their colonies the *least* share;'—
that is, (according to S. Johnson*) *None of any kind.*

21. A German view of the *Dictionary*

1798

Text from *Three Philological Essays*, 1798, clxix–clxxxii.

A German lexicographer who pronounced with unusual authority
on the *Dictionary* was Johann Christoph Adelung (1732–1806). The
full title in English of his *Neues Grammatisch-kritischen Wörterbuch
der Englischen*, Leipzig, 1783–96, reads: 'New grammatical-critical
dictionary of the English language for Germans; principally from
the great English work of Mr. Samuel Johnson, designed according
to his fourth edition and enlarged with many entries, definitions
and examples'. Adelung's *Three Philological Essays*, translated by
A. F. M. Willich, appeared in London in 1798; the third essay is
entitled 'On the relative merits and demerits of Johnson's English
Dictionary'. It is printed here almost entire. See Introduction, pp. 5,
24–5.

The English are in possession of a very copious Dictionary of their
language, with which the late DR. SAMUEL JOHNSON has presented

---

* Johnson's merit ought not to be denied to him; but his Dictionary is the most imperfect and faulty, and the least valuable of any of his productions; and that share of merit
which it possesses, makes it by so much the more hurtful. I rejoice however, that though the
least valuable, he found it the most profitable: for I could never read his Preface without
shedding a tear. And yet it must be confessed, that his *Grammar* and *History* and Dictionary
of what *he calls* the English language, are in all respects (except the bulk of the latter) most
truly contemptible performances; and a reproach to the learning and industry of a nation,
which could receive them with the slightest approbation.

Nearly one third of this Dictionary is as much the language of the Hottentots as of the
English; and it would be no difficult matter so to translate any one of the plainest and most
popular numbers of the *Spectator* into the language of that Dictionary, that no mere Englishman, though well read in his own language, would be able to comprehend one sentence
of it.

It appears to be a work of labour, and yet is in truth one of the most idle performances
ever offered to the public: compiled by an author who possessed not one single requisite for
the undertaking, and, being a publication of a set of booksellers, owing its success to that
very circumstance which alone must make it impossible that it should deserve success.

them, and of which the fourth edition appeared (London, 1773) with some additions, in two large Folio Volumes, comprising upwards of thirty Alphabets, or 716 Sheets of letter-press*.

As the completeness of this work, together with the critical and philosophic manner, which the author follows, has been frequently the subject of great praise, not only in England, but also in other countries, by recommending it as a model of a useful Dictionary for any language; I was induced to think, that an accurate abridgment of this work might of itself suffice, to supply so important a defect in German literature. Nor indeed had I directed my views further, when I resolved upon publishing an English–German Dictionary, designed chiefly for the use of my countrymen. But upon a more minute inquiry into the merits of Johnson's work, I very soon discovered, that this performance, notwithstanding the many advantages it possesses, is replete with great imperfections. —As these imperfections are of such a nature, as to exhibit themselves more remarkably in an abridgment, translated into German, than they perhaps do appear in the original; and as the principal utility, which the Germans expect from such an undertaking, might thus have been much diminished, I was obliged to submit to a more arduous task than I was, at first, inclined to undertake.

This assertion will not be considered as unjust, when I shall point out, individually, the principal requisites to a Dictionary, and remark upon every point, how far *Johnson* has performed his duty, and wherein *I* have endeavoured to improve upon him.

1. In the number of words.
2. In the value and dignity of every word, whether it be quite obsolete or current; and in the latter case, whether it is used in the more elevated, poetical, social, or vulgar style.
3. In the grammatical nature of the word, to which I also refer the orthography, the mark of the accent, and the pronunciation.
4. In the etymology or derivation.
5. In the decomposition of the principal idea denoted by the word;— either by means of a definition, or by a synonymous *German* word;— and in the analysis of the different significations.
6. In the illustration of words by examples; and,
7. In the grammatical combination, or the use of every word, with respect to the syntax.

Conformable to this division of the subject, I shall offer some remarks upon each of these particular points.

* This computation is made from the first Edition, Lond. 1755.

I. Concerning the number and the practical use of words, I expected to find the work of Johnson in its greatest perfection. In a book, consisting of 2864 pages, large folio, and four times reprinted, I hoped to meet with the whole treasure, or at least with the most necessary and current words, of the English language. But, in this respect, my disappointment was great; and those, who have consulted Johnson's Dictionary with the same view, will agree with me, that upon this very point he displays his weakest side. We must however do him the justice to allow, that with respect to terms of science, and written language, his work is very complete; but it is defective in social language, in the language of civil life, and in the terms of arts and manufactures. His defect in the last-mentioned branches, the author himself acknowledges in the preface, and makes this strange apology for it, 'that he found it impossible to frequent the workshops of mechanics, the mines, magazines, ship-yards, &c. in order to inquire into the different terms and phrases, which are peculiar to these pursuits.' Yet this is a great desideratum to foreigners, and considerably detracts from the merit of a work of this nature; for these are the precise cases, in which they have most frequent occasion for consulting a Dictionary. To this head we may refer the names of plants, fishes, birds, and insects, frequently occurring in common life, of which a great number are wanting in the work of Johnson; though this deficiency might have been most easily supplied, as there certainly is no want of botanical books and publications on Natural History, in the English language. In order to show the extent of this deficiency, in a particular instance, I shall only remark, that in the single work containing the last voyage of Capt. Cook, in two moderate volumes, octavo, (published 1782) there occur nearly one hundred words, relating partly to navigation, partly to Natural History, that cannot be found in Johnson's or other Dictionaries.

It will be admitted, that a dictionary of a language ought to possess the greatest possible degree of completeness, particularly with respect to names and technical terms, which are more rarely employed in common language, and the meaning of which cannot be conjectured from the context. As such words frequently become an object of research, I have found myself under the disagreeable necessity of filling up these chasms as far as my time, my plan, and my source of information would admit. Thus I have increased the stock of words, occurring in Johnson's and other English Dictionaries of distinguished merit, with a great number (perhaps several thousands) of words which were wanting; especially such as concern the objects of the animal and vegetable kingdoms, of the English constitution, and of various other departments. With regard to the laws, manners, and customs of England, I have availed myself of the well known work of Entick.[1]

The proper names of countries, places, and persons, when deviating from the genuine orthography, I have likewise more correctly stated, and added such as have been omitted in Johnson's and other dictionaries.

For the improvement of terms in social language, I am much indebted to Boyer's English and French Dictionary.[2] But as I had, in this respect, placed more confidence in Johnson than I could justify after a careful examination of his work; and as, on this account, I did not bestow the portion of time requisite to a close comparison with other Dictionaries, I readily confess, that there remains much to be done yet, especially with the assistance of the latest English productions in the department of Belles Lettres. For, in latter times, the English language appears to have undergone the same changes as the French and German.

II. It is well known, that all the words of a language do not possess an equal value or degree of currency: some of them are entirely obsolete, but still occur in writings, which are studied in modern times, for instance, in the translation of the Bible, in Shakespeare, Spenser, &c.; others are peculiar to poetical language; again, others are current only in certain provinces, or in particular situations of life; and still others are vulgar, and exploded from the more dignified written style, as well as from the polite circles of conversation. It is one of Johnson's great merits, that he has carefully attended to this distinction; I have likewise marked it, in my English and German Dictionary, with equal attention; and I have pointed out the most necessary of these distinctions, by means of particular signs or characters.

III. Next to the preceding, I consider the grammatical designation of every word as the most important part of a good Dictionary; and under this head I place not only the orthography, the accentuation, and pronunciation, but also the classification of a word, to whatever class it belongs as a part of speech, and finally, its inflection; whether it be regularly or irregularly declined or conjugated. Upon this point, also, Johnson is in most instances very correct; excepting that he does not always distinguish the substantive from the adverb, and this again from the adjective; an imperfection which, with the aid of some general ideas of grammar, I have had no great difficulty to remedy.—In the spelling of words, Johnson has adopted the method prevalent among all sensible people, and consigned the orthographic disputes to those, who, from

---

[1] John Entick, *New Latin and English Dictionary*, 1771.
[2] Abel Boyer, *The Royal Dictionary*, 1699; frequently revised.

want of more important knowledge, have no other means of obtaining reputation. For my part, I saw no reason for differing from Johnson on this head.

[on accentuation in the English language.]

In the remaining part of grammatical determinations of words, I have followed Johnson as my guide, and carefully distinguished the neuter from the active form of verbs: though, in a few instances, I have been induced to differ from him, when he had mistaken the neutral use of an active verb for a neuter verb.

IV. The proximate derivation of a word is a matter of importance in all languages; for upon this circumstance depends not only the full idea or intelligibility of words, but likewise their orthography. Johnson has sensibly perceived this difficulty, and consequently has shortly pointed out the immediate derivatives, 'in cases where he was acquainted with them;' and I must add, 'that he has done it in such a manner as appeared to him the most proper.' For, upon this particular head, his Dictionary is very defective. When an English word is derived from the French or Latin, he does not easily mistake its proximate root; in words, that are obvious derivations of familiar Anglo-Saxon terms, he is equally successful. But in most other cases, he proves himself a shallow etymologist: and as his own notions of the origin of languages were not very clear, he is frequently led into great errors. Thus he considers the words, with whose origin he is unacquainted, either as *fortuitous* and *cant words*, or he derives them frequently in the absurdest manner from words nearly corresponding in sound, while he aims at explaining them in three or four different ways; for instance, 'to *chirp*,' derived from, 'to chear up, to make cheerful, &c.' yet this word obviously comes from the vernacular German, *tschirpen* or *zirpen*, 'to twitter like birds.' This may serve as a specimen of the manner, in which he searches for the source of one river in the mouth of another, which is altogether different from the former. Here I have had frequent opportunities of correcting him; particularly as SKINNER was his principal hero in etymology, and as Johnson himself was unacquainted with the German and other languages related to it. . . .

V. To ascertain the principal and peculiar signification of a word, from which the others, if there be any, must be derived, has been my next employment. This, indeed, is always the most difficult point in a Dictionary; a point, which not only presupposes correct ideas of the origin of languages, but also the most precise knowledge of every word, and of its use from the earliest periods. The whole of this knowledge must be founded upon a sufficient number of works, written by men who lived in the different ages, in which the language was spoken. But as we possess no such number of works in any language, as is sufficient to make us acquainted with all the words, that are or have been current in it; it may be easily conjectured, that the primitive signification of every word cannot be pointed out with precision. But even in cases where this is possible, it requires the most careful examination of all the ancient monuments of a language, that are still preserved, together with much sound philosophy in order to avoid falling into dreams and fancies; and deriving, in an arbitrary manner, the words from one another. In etymology, as soon as it carried him beyond the proximate derivation of a word, my predecessor has not been very successful. For, even in the latter case, he relied too much upon the authority of others; and it evidently appears from his Dictionary, that the structure of language did not induce him to philosophical inquiries. On this account, we can form no great expectations, and we must be satisfied with his classification of the different meanings of words, so as they in every instance appeared to him most proper. His want of knowledge in etymology, however, is attended with this advantage, that it has guarded him against a thousand follies, to which the pseudo-etymologists, of all languages and climates, are very liable.

[briefly censures Johnson for being unnecessarily 'liberal with a variety of significations' of words.]

It is a very common practice among the compilers of Dictionaries, to point out the signification of a word, by means of a synonymous expression used in another language. A small share of correct philological knowledge must convince every one of the impropriety and disadvantage of this practice. There are no words completely synonymous in any language; nor can any two words, from different languages, be considered as synonymous. And although in languages, that bear strong marks of affinity to one another, there should be two words of common origin, or even radically the same, such as 'ground' with the German *Grund*; 'to go,' with the German *gehen*; they still deviate in the indirect significations, or, at least, in the application to individual cases. The safest and most rational method, therefore, is to resolve every signification into other words, or to give a clear and, if possible, concise definition of it. I am sensible, that in this manner the idea of a word cannot be exhausted, nor is it possible to point out this idea with all its shades and subtle modifications. I further admit, that this developement of the idea is not in all instances practicable; since the meaning of a word, in many cases, is so obscure that it cannot be made perspicuous. Yet, at the same time, where this expedient is applicable, it affords the most certain method of exhibiting a competent notion of every word and its significations; while it serves to promote a clear and just knowledge of things in general. This, therefore, is one of the most important advantages of Johnson's *Dictionary*: for the author possessed a very happy talent of displaying the idea of a word in a concise, intelligible, and pertinent manner. In this respect, I have throughout followed him as my guide, except where I was obliged to contract the significations of words, which he had unnecessarily accumulated, and consequently to search for an appropriate and more comprehensive idea.

Johnson has not avoided the common error of lexicographers, who have either neglected to state the names of plants and animals, or have done it in a very vague and undetermined manner. He commonly dismisses the names of vegetables with the addition, '*a plant.*' Thus he forsakes the reader, where a guide is most anxiously looked for. [Adelung has corrected this defect in his German dictionary.]

VI. In order to supply the imperfect definitions of words, the signification of which cannot be fully collected from the notion contained in the definition, it is a necessary point in a Dictionary, to illustrate them by examples. From these illustrations, this additional advantage results, that the grammatical use of a word, and its combination with other parts of speech, can be rendered more conspicuous. Johnson is very liberal with his examples, and not unfrequently prodigal to excess. The greater number of them, he has extracted from poetical works, as he had employed much of his time in publishing the English poets. I have made it my study, to hold a middle course, and to select from the rich store of Johnson's examples the most concise and pertinent, especially in such cases as appeared to require an example, to show the precise meaning or the grammatical use of a word. As, however, his examples and the whole stock of his words principally relate to the language of authors or 'written language;' I have endeavoured to supply the obvious want of examples for the purposes of social life, from the above quoted English and French Dictionary, by BOYER; a work, the phrases and exemplifications of which are principally of the latter kind.

VII. Concerning the practical application of words, when in connexion with others, Johnson has bestowed great attention upon the most important cases, in which every word may occur. His accuracy in this respect has induced me to adopt his examples, without attempting to change or improve them. [concludes by discussing problems facing the compiler of an English–German dictionary.]

22. An American view of the *Dictionary*

1807

The *Letter to Dr. David Ramsay*, New Haven, 1807, by the American lexicographer, Noah Webster (1758–1843). See Introduction, pp. 4, 25.

Sir,

I received, a few days past, your favor of June 20th, in which you inform me that the 'prejudices against any American attempts to improve Dr. Johnson, are very strong in that city.' This intelligence is not wholly unexpected; for similar prejudices have been manifested in some parts of the northern states. A man who has read with slight attention the history of nations, in their advances from barbarism to civilization and science, cannot be surprised at the strength of prejudices long established, and never disturbed. Few centuries have elapsed, since many men lost their lives or their liberty, by publishing NEW TRUTHS; and not two centuries have past, since Galileo was imprisoned by an ecclesiastical court, for defending the truth of the Copernican System, condemned to do penance for three years, and his book burnt at Rome, as containing dangerous and damnable heresies. This example is cited as one of a multitude which the history of man presents to our view; and if it differs in *degree*, it accords in *principle*, with the case now before the American public.

Philology, as it respects the origin and history of words, and the principles of construction in sentences, is, at this moment, in a condition somewhat similar to that of astronomy under the system of Tycho Brahe, with the solar system revolving round this terrestrial ball. And if gentlemen, who never suspected the weakness of the principles which they have been taught in their schools, should be alarmed at the suggestion, and utter a few anathemas against the discoverers, it should be remembered that evidence will gradually undermine their prejudices, and demolish the whole system of error. Imprisonment and death are no longer the penalties inflicted on the publishers of truth; and the man who is deterred by opposition and calumny, from attacking what he knows to be fundamentally wrong, is no soldier in the field of literary combat.

I know your love of letters, and your disposition to give a patient and candid attention to discussions and details of facts which may elucidate any interesting branch of literature. I have therefore taken the liberty to address to you a few remarks and statements, intended as a brief sketch only of the errors and imperfections in Johnson's *Dictionary*, and the Lexicons of other languages, now used as classical books in our seminaries of learning. These remarks I shall transmit to you through the medium of the press.

It is well known that Johnson's *Dictionary* has been, for half a century, a standard authority in the English Language, from which all later compilers have drawn their materials. That his work is, in some respects, erroneous and defective, has long been known in Great-Britain, and Mason has lately ventured to attempt, and with some success, to supply the defects and correct the errors.[1] Two or three other compilers in England are engaged in a like undertaking; but these gentlemen seem to be deficient in the scheme of their work.

A few years ago, Mr. Horne Tooke undertook to investigate the origin of the English particles; and in his researches, discovered that Lexicographers had never become acquainted with these classes of words, and in remarking on their errors, he takes occasion to express his opinion of Johnson's *Dictionary* in the following terms.—*Diversions of Purley*, vol. I, p. 182.

[quotes 'Johnson's merit ought not . . . deserve success.'[2]]

These animadversions, which are directly opposed to popular opinion, coming from a man who had penetrated deeply into the history of our language, are calculated to excite curiosity, and deserve a careful examination.

Extravagant praise of any human production, like indiscriminate censure, is seldom well founded; and both are evidences of want of candor or want of discernment. On a careful examination of the merits of Johnson's *Dictionary*, it will unquestionably appear that the blind admiration which would impose it upon the world as a very accurate and indisputable authority, errs as much upon one extreme, as the pointed condemnation of the whole work, does upon the other. But it is the fate of man to vibrate from one extreme to another. The great intellectual powers of Dr. Johnson, displayed in many of his works, but especially

1 George Mason, *A Supplement to Dr. Johnson's Dictionary*, 1803.
2 See document No. 20.

in his *Rambler* and his *Rasselas*, have raised his reputation to high distinction, and impressed upon all his opinions a stamp of *authority*, which gives them currency among men, without an examination into their intrinsic value. The character of correctness which he merited and obtained from his ethical writings, on subjects of which all men can judge, has been very naturally transferred to his philological works, on which few men are competent to decide.—Yet nothing is more natural than that his writings on men and manners should be correct, as their correctness must depend chiefly on observation and on reading that requires little labor; while his *Dictionary*, the accuracy of which must depend on minute distinctions or laborious researches into unentertaining books, may be left extremely imperfect and full of error.

These circumstances however are seldom considered; and Johnson's writings had, in Philology, the effect which Newton's discoveries had in Mathematics, to interrupt for a time the progress of this branch of learning; for when any man has pushed his researches so far beyond his contemporaries, that all men despair of proceeding beyond him, they will naturally consider his principles and decisions as the limit of perfection on that particular subject, and repose their opinions upon his authority, without examining into their validity. 'Ubi aut præteriri aut æquari eos posse desperavimus, studium cum spe senescit.' Velleius Paterculus. lib. 1. 17.[3]

In the preface to Johnson's *Dictionary*, we have a splendid specimen of elevated composition, not indeed perfectly free from faults, but generally correct in diction as well as in principle.

In the history of the English Language, the author has proved himself very imperfectly acquainted with the subject. He commences with a most egregious error, in supposing the Saxon language to have been introduced into Britain in the fifth century, after the Romans had abandoned the island; whereas, nothing is better attested in history than that the branch of the Teutonic, which constitutes the basis of our present language, was introduced by the Belgic tribes, which occupied all the southern parts of the island at the time, and evidently long before Caesar invaded the country. Equally erroneous is his assertion that the Saxons and Welsh were nations totally distinct. The number of words of Celtic original plainly discoverable in the English language, is much greater than Johnson supposed; and the affinity of those nations is more fully manifested by numerous Celtic words found in the German, Swedish

---

[3] 'Where we have despaired of the possibility of their being surpassed or equalled, enthusiasm grows old along with hope.'

and other Teutonic dialects. But there is demonstration of that affinity in two facts, which seem to have escaped observation—first, the use of the same *relative pronoun* by the Irish and Scotch of Celtic origin, as well as by the Greeks, Romans, and every Teutonic nation—and second, by the construction of some of the cases of nouns.

This part of Johnson's work, as well as his Grammar, which is chiefly extracted from Wallis' *Grammar*,[4] if they are not 'contemptible performances', to use Tooke's language, are wretchedly imperfect. They abound with errors; but the principal fault is, that they contain very few of the material and important facts which would serve to illustrate the history of the language, and of the several nations from which it is derived. This field of inquiry has never been fully explored; it is a fruitful field, and hereafter the cultivation of it is to produce a valuable harvest of historical information.

In a brief survey of the work under consideration, a few general faults in the execution of it will be named.

1. *The insertion of a multitude of words that do not belong to the language.* These words Johnson informs us, are inserted on the authority of Bailey, Ainsworth and Phillips[5]—but they are confessedly terms which have never been used in oral or written English. *Language* consists of words uttered by the *tongue*; or written in books for the purpose of being read. Terms which are not authorised by either of these modes of communicating ideas, are no part of a language, and have no claim to a place in a dictionary.—Such are the following—*Adversable, advesperate, adjugate, agriculation, abstrude, injudicable, epicosity, crapulence, morigerous, tenebrosity, balbucinate, illachrymable,* &c. The number of this class of words is not known; but it probably rises to two thousand or more. Some of them are omitted by Sheridan, Walker, Jones, Perry, Entick, Hamilton, &c. but most of them are retained in all the English Dictionaries, and Ash has been careful to preserve them all.[6] These words seem to have been anglicized from the Latin language, and inserted by the first compilers of English Dictionaries, in their vocabularies, as candidates for employ-

[4] John Wallis, *Grammatica linguae Anglicanae*, 1653.

[5] Nathan Bailey, *Universal Etymological English Dictionary*, 1721, and *Dictionarium Britannicum*, 1730; Robert Ainsworth, Latin *Thesaurus*, 1736; Edward Phillips, *The New World of English Words*, 1658.

[6] Thomas Sheridan, *A General Dictionary of the English Language*, 1780; John Walker, *A Critical Pronouncing Dictionary*, 1791; Stephen Jones, *Sheridan Improved. A general pronouncing and explanatory dictionary*, 1796; William Perry, *Synonymous, Etymological, and Pronouncing Dictionary*, 1805; John Entick, *New Latin and English Dictionary*, 1771; Joseph Hamilton, *Johnson's Dictionary in miniature*, 1799; John Ash, *The New and Complete Dictionary*, 1775.

ment; but having never been called into service, they stand like impertinent intruders into good company; a sort of unwelcome guests, who are treated with coldness and neglect. They no more belong to the English language than the same number of Patagonian words; and the insertion and retention of them in English dictionaries is a violation of all the rules of lexicography. Had a native of the United States taken a *fiftieth* part of the same liberty, in a similar production, the admirers of Johnson, and other English writers, would have branded him with the most pointed opprobrium.

2. Another class of material errors in the great work of Dr. Johnson, proceed from an injudicious selection of authorities. Among the authors cited in support of his definitions, there are indeed the names of Tillotson, Newton, Locke, Milton, Dryden, Addison, Swift and Pope; but no small portion of words in his vocabulary, are selected from writers of the 17th century, who, though well versed in the learned languages, had neither taste nor a correct knowledge of English. Of these writers, Sir Thomas Brown seems to have been a favorite; yet the style of Sir Thomas is not English; and it is astonishing that a man attempting to give the world a standard of the English Language should have ever mentioned his name, but with a reprobation of his style and use of words. The affectation of Latinity was indeed a common vice of authors from the revival of letters to the age of Queen Ann; but Brown in attempting to write Latin-English, exceeded all his contemporaries, and actually rendered himself unintelligible. The following examples will afford a specimen of his pedantry and ill taste:

The effects of their activity are not precipitously *abrupted*, but gradually proceed to their cessations.

Authors are also suspicious, nor greedily to be swallowed, who write of secrets, to deliver antipathies, sympathies, and the occult *abstrusities* of things.

The intire or broken *compagination* of the magnetical fabric.

Some have written rhetorically and *concessively*, not controverting, but assuming the question, which, taken as granted, advantaged the illation.

Its fluctuations are but motions subservient, which winds, shelves, and every interjacency *irregulates*.

Separated by the voice of God, things in their species come out in uncommunicated varieties and *inrelative* seminalities.

See Johnson's *Dictionary*, under the words in Italics.

There are probably, thousands of similar passages in Johnson's *Dictionary*, cited as authorities for the use of words which no other English writer and no English speaker ever used; words which, as Horne Tooke says, are no more English than the language of the Hottentots. Were the only evil of introducing such authorities, to swell the size of the book with nonsense, we might consent to overlook the injury; but Johnson has suffered thousands of these terms to pass as *authorized English words*, by which means the student is apt to be misled, especially before his taste is formed by extensive reading. Indeed some writers of age and judgement are led by Johnson's authority to the use of words which are not English, and which give their style an air of pedantry and obscurity; and not unfrequently, to the use of words which do not belong to the language. Thus in a letter of ——, published not long ago, respecting Burr's conspiracy,[7] the writer spoke of matters of *dubiosity*—doubtless upon the authority of English Dictionaries, transcribed from Johnson's, who cites Sir Thomas Brown for the use of this barbarous word. So from an illegitimate word used by Thompson, *infracted*, Johnson took the liberty to form the verb *infract*, which has been frequently used for the true word *infringe*, and doubtless upon his sole authority. From a careful examination of this work, and its effect upon the language, I am inclined to believe that Johnson's authority has multiplied instead of reducing the number of corruptions in the English language. Let any man of correct taste cast his eye on such words as denominable, opiniatry, ariolation, assation, ataraxy, clancular, comminuible, conclusible, dedentition, deuteroscopy, digladiation, dignotion, cubiculary, discubitory, exolution, exenterate, incompossible, incompossibility, indigitate, &c. and let him say whether a dictionary which gives *thousands* of such terms, as *authorized English words*, is a safe standard of writing. From a general view of the work, I am confident the number of words inserted which are not authorized by any English writer, and those which are found only in a single pedantic author, like Brown, and which are really no part of the language, amount to four or five thousand; *at least a tenth part of the whole number*.

The evils resulting from this injudicious selection of words are not limited to the sphere of Johnson's work; had this been the case, the increased bulk of the book, by the insertion of useless words, would, in a degree, have been a remedy for the evils, by circumscribing its sale and use. But most of these words are transcribed into all the later compilations

---

[7] Aaron Burr (1756–1836), American political leader, was involved in a scheme to invade Mexico and set up a Mexican government independent of Spain.

—Ash, Walker, Sheridan, &c. and even the pocket Dictionaries are swelled in size by a multitude of unused and barbarous words. Nor does the evil rest here; some terms are copied into the dictionaries of foreign languages; and a German or a Spaniard who is learning English, must suppose all these terms to be really a part of our language; he will of course learn them as such, and introduce them into his discourse and writings, until corrected by a familiar acquaintance with the language now spoken. Johnson's *Dictionary* therefore furnishes no standard of correct English: but in its present form, tends very much to corrupt and pervert the language.

3. It is questionable how far vulgar and cant words are to be admitted into a Dictionary; but one thing must be acknowledged by any man who will inspect the several dictionaries in the English language, that if any portion of such words are inadmissible, Johnson has transgressed the rules of lexicography beyond any other compiler; for his work contains more of the lowest of all vulgar words, than any other now extant, Ash excepted. It may be alledged that it is the duty of a lexicographer to insert and define all words found in English books: then such words as *fishify*, *jackalent*, *parma-citty*, *jiggumbob*, *conjobble*, *foutra*, &c. are legitimate English words! Alas, had a native of the United States introduced such vulgar words and offensive ribaldry into a similar work, what columns of abuse would have issued from the Johnsonian presses, against the wretch who could thus sully his book and corrupt the language. But Shakespeare and Butler need such words in their writings!!! Yes, vulgar manners and characters must be represented by vulgar language; the writer of plays must accommodate his language to his audience; the rabble in the galleries are entitled to their share of amusement; and a part of every play must be composed of obscenity and vulgar ribaldry. In this manner, the lowest language and the coarsest manners are exhibited before a promiscuous audience, and derive some importance from the reputation of the writer and of the actors. From plays they pass into other books—yes, into standard authorities; and national language, as well as morals, are corrupted and debased by the influence of the stage!

4. It has been generally believed that a prime excellence of Johnson's *Dictionary* is, the accuracy with which the different senses of words are distinguished; and uncommon praises have been bestowed upon the author's power of discrimination. On a critical attention however to his definitions, it will appear that a *want of just discrimination* is one of the principal defects of his works; and that to this defect, we may ascribe

innumerable errors, and no small part of the superfluous bulk of the *Dictionary*. Let the reader attend to the following examples.

Larceny: Petty theft. Exemplification: 'Those laws would be very unjust, that should chastize murder and *petty larceny* with the same punishment.' *Spectator*.

This is all that Johnson has given us for definition and illustration of the word *larceny*; and every lawyer must observe that the definition is incorrect. *Larceny* comprehends every species of *theft*; not only grand and petty larceny, but burglary and robbery; tho the latter are usually arranged as separate crimes.—The author seems not to have understood the word; his definition is taken from the passage in the *Spectator*; and the word *petty*, in that passage, which should form no part of the definition, is prefixed to *larceny*. This is a very common fault with our author; not understanding the term, or *not discriminating* between the true sense of the term by itself, and its sense in *connection*, he often takes a part of the passage selected for illustration, and incorporates it into the definition. Thousands of examples of this negligence are to be found in his *Dictionary*.—See a similar error under the word *obelisk*, which, in its character as a reference, the author defines to be a 'mark of *censure* in the margin of a book'—evidently because, Grew, in the passage cited for illustration, used it in that sense. But certainly an obelisk is as often used, as a reference to things indifferent or worthy of *praise*, as to things worthy of *censure*. Let the following definitions be noted:

Industrious.
1. Diligent, laborious, assiduous, opposed to *slothful*.
'Frugal and *industrious* men are commonly friendly to the established government.' *Temple*.
2. Laborious to a particular end; opposite to *remiss*.
'He himself being excellently learned, and *industrious* to seek out the truth of all things concerning the original of his own people, hath set down the testimony of the ancients truly.' *Spenser*.

> 'Let our just censures
> Attend the true event, and put we on
> *Industrious* soldiership.' *Shakespeare*.
> 'His thoughts were low:
> To vice *industrious*; but to nobler deeds,
> Timorous and slothful.' *Milton*.

3. Designed; done for the purpose.
'The *industrious* perforation of the tendons of the second joints of fingers and toes, draw the tendons of the third joints through.' *More*.

'Observe carefully all the events which happen either by an occasional occurrence of various causes, or by the *industrious* application of knowing men.' *Watts.*

It may be questioned whether the second definition of *industrious*, above recited, is necessary, as distinct from the first. What difference is there in the sense of the *word*, whether it marks a habit of application to *one* object or to *twenty*? If any distinction should be thought necessary, it should rather be noted under the first head in the following manner:— 'Diligent, laborious, assiduous; denoting a habit of diligent application to business in general, or to a particular object.'—This however is not very material.

But in the third definition, the author has evidently mistaken the use of the term. The '*industrious* perforation of tendons,' does not signify an *industry*, designed or for a particular purpose, any more than in every other case. The word *industrious* is used to denote a perforation *made with industry*, that is, with diligence and care—the epithet being applied to the *effect* instead of the cause. So also the *industrious* application of knowing men, in the passage from Watts, means *their* application bestowed with *diligence*. The industry of men is always directed to some object, and generally to one object at a time; but this particular or general application requires no distinction of definition. Indeed, upon this system of explanation, the application of a word to any and every purpose would require a separate definition. Probably one fourth of Johnson's definitions are of this kind—serving not only to swell the size of the book, without use, but rather to embarrass and mislead the student, than to enlighten him.

[further examples of inadequate definitions follow.]

5. Equally manifest is Johnson's *want of discrimination* in defining words nearly synonymous; or rather words which bear some portion of a common signification.

'Fraud', says the author, is 'Deceit; cheat; trick; artifice; subtilty; stratagem.' But a man may use *tricks*, *artifice*, *subtilty* and *stratagems*, in a thousand ways without *fraud*; and he may be *deceived*, without being *defrauded*. Johnson has defined the word in the loose sense which *fraud* had in Latin, without discriminating between that, and the strict technical sense which is most frequent in our language.

'Impracticable,' the author defines by 'not to be performed, unfeasible, impossible;' and 'impracticableness' by 'impossibility'. *Impossible* implies an absurdity, contradiction, or utter want of power to be, or to be done, in the abstract; but *impracticable* signifies only, not to be done by human means or by the means proposed. . . .

133

But I will not multiply examples. Let me only add, that in the course of thirty years reading, I have not found a single author who appears to have been accurately acquainted with the true import and force of terms in his own language. And a multitude of errors committed by writers, evidently from their misapprehending the import of words, are cited as authorities by Johnson, instead of being noticed with censure. Indeed, thousands of instances are to be found in modern books, of a misapplication of terms, which are clearly ascribable to the negligence and mistakes of that lexicographer.

6. Another particular which is supposed to add greatly to the value of Johnson's *Dictionary*, is the illustration of the various senses of words by passages from English authors of reputation. Yet, in fact, this will be found, on careful examination, one of the most exceptionable parts of his performance: For two reasons—First, that no small part of his examples are taken from authors who did not write the language with purity—and second, that a still larger portion of them throw not the least light on his definitions.

The first objection has been considered in the previous remarks, and proved by extracts from Brown's *Vulgar Errors*—a work which manifests the most intolerable pedantry, and a total want of taste. Would the limits of this sketch permit, I would give further illustrations, by extracts from Glanvil, Digby, Ayliffe, Peacham, L'Estrange and other authors, which Johnson has cited as authorities—writers who are so far from being models of classical purity, that they have been long since condemned for their want of taste, and are now known only by name. As far as their works have any influence, it is derived from Johnson's authority, and the passages he has cited; and as far as this authority goes, it has a tendency to corrupt the style of writing. The examples I have given prove that it has had some effect; tho fortunately not very extensive. Of the old authors cited, it is however proper to notice Shakspeare, as Johnson has quoted his works more frequently than any other, and relies much on his authority. Shakespeare was a man of little learning; and altho, when he wrote the popular language of his day, his use of words was tolerably correct, yet whenever he attempted a style beyond that, he often fell into the grossest improprieties. Thus he speaks of the *insisture* of the heavens and the planets—cords too *intrinsecate*—to *patient* a person—a *pelting* river and *pelting* farm—to *sanctuarise* murder—*sightless* stains for *offensive* stains—the *sternage* of a navy—*compunctious* visitings of nature—a *combinate* husband—of *convertite*—*conspectuity* and *corresponsive*, &c. barbarisms which every correct ear instantly condemns—and for which he certainly could plead no authority, even in the pedantic age in which he lived. Some of them perhaps may be ascribed to a license of writing which he thought justifiable—but more of them, to his want of erudition. Whatever admiration the world may bestow on the *Genius* of Shakspeare his language is full of errors, and ought not to be offered as a model for imitation.

The other objection to Johnson's quotations, is, that a great part of them throw no light on his definitions; indeed a great part of English words require no illustration. Take the following examples:

Alley—a walk in a garden.

> 'And all within were walks and *alleys* wide,
> With footing worn, and leading inward far.' *Spenser.*

'Where *alleys* are close gravelled, the earth putteth forth the first year knot grass and after, spire grass.' *Bacon.*

> '. . . Yonder *alleys* green
> Our walk at noon, with branches overgrown.' *Milton.*

> 'Come to my fair love, our morning's task we lose;
> Some labor, even the easiest life would choose;
> Ours is not great, the dangling boughs to crop,
> Whose too luxuriant growth our *alleys* stop.' *Dryden.*

> 'The thriving plants, ignoble broomsticks made,
> Now sweep those *alleys* they were born to shade.' *Pope.*

Now, let me inquire, is any man, after reading all these passages, better acquainted with the meaning of *alley*? Do the passages throw the smallest light on the definition? Certainly they do not. The quotations serve no purpose but to show that Spenser, Bacon, Milton, Dryden and Pope used the word *alley* for a walk in a garden. And what then? Does any reader of English want all these authorities to show the word to be legitimate? Far from it. Nineteen twentieths of all our words are so common, that they require no proof at all of legitimacy. Yet the example here given is by no means the most exceptionable for the number of authorities cited. The author sometimes offers thirty or forty lines to illustrate words which every man, woman and child understands as well as Johnson. Thirty-five lines of exemplification under the word *froth*, for example, are just as useless in explaining the word, as would be the same number of lines from the language of the six nations.

'Finger,' says Johnson, 'is the flexible member of the hand by which men catch and hold.'—Now to prove this he cites passages from six authors.

'The *fingers* and thumb in each hand consist of fifteen bones—there being three to each finger.' *Quincy.*

'. . . . . . You seem to understand me,
By each at once her choppy *finger* laying
Upon her skinny lips.' *Shakespeare.*

'Diogenes, who is never said
For aught that ever I could read
To whine, put *fingers* in the eye and sob,
Because he had never another tub.' *Hudibras.*

'The hand is divided into four *fingers* bending forward, and one opposite to them bending backwards, and of greater strength than any of them singly, which we call the thumb, to join with them severally or united; whereby it is fitted to lay hold of objects of any size or quantity.' *Ray.*

'A hand of vast extension, and a prodigious number of *fingers* playing upon all the organ pipes of the world, and making every one sound a particular note.' *Keil.*

'Poor Peg sewed, spun, and knit for a livelihood, till her *fingers'* ends were sore.' *Arbuthnot.*

Here we arrive at the end of the author's exemplification of this sense of *finger*—and except a little anatomical knowledge from Quincy and Ray, what have we learnt from these long quotations? Why, surely nothing—except what we all knew before, that English authors have used the word *finger* just as the word is now used.

One half of the whole bulk of Johnson's *Dictionary* is composed of quotations equally useless. *One half* of all the money that has been paid for the book, and which, in fifty years, must have been a very great amount, has been taken from the purchasers for what is entirely useless. Whether this mode of constructing the work was intended for the benefit of the compiler, or whether it was a speculation of the booksellers, as Mr. Tooke has suggested, is hardly worth an inquiry—but I am confident in the assertion, that the superfluous size of the work operates as one of the grossest impositions ever practiced on the public. Ainsworth's illustrations of Latin words, which are, beyond comparison, the most judicious in plan and execution, are comprised in less than one third of the compass.

7. The last defect in Johnson's *Dictionary*, which I shall notice, is the inaccuracy of the etymologies. As this has been generally considered as the least important part of a Dictionary, the subject has been little

investigated, and is very imperfectly understood, even by men of science. —Johnson scarcely entered the threshold of the subject. He consulted chiefly Junius and Skinner;[8] the latter of whom was not possessed of learning adequate to the investigation—and Junius, like Vossius, Scaliger[9] and most other etymologists on the continent, labored to deduce all languages from the Greek. Hence these authors neglected the principal sources of information, which were to be found only in the north of Europe, and in the west of Ireland and Scotland. In another particular, they all failed of success—they never discovered some of the principal modes in which the primitive radical words were combined to form the more modern compounds. On this subject therefore almost *every thing remains to be done.*

To give very numerous examples of Johnson's errors in etymology would exceed the limits prescribed to these remarks. Two or three examples must serve as specimens of the general tenor of his work.

'School', Johnson deduces from the Latin *schola*—French école. He then gives for definitions—1st. A house of discipline and instruction. 2. a place of literary education; a university. 3. a state of instruction. 4. system of doctrine as delivered by particular teachers. 5. the age of the church and form of theology succeeding that of the fathers. Here the author first mistakes the origin of the word, and omits wholly the primary sense, and that which is still its principal sense.

School is of Teutonic origin, *scole, scolu,* denoting a multitude or great number collected. We have the original sense in a *school* of fish; which has been corrupted, by blundering writers, into *shoal* or *shole.* From this root the Romans had their *schola,* and not from the Greek *scholé, otium,* as Ainsworth supposes. Hence the first and principal sense of the word, which Johnson has overlooked, is a *number of persons collected* for the purpose of receiving instruction. The *persons* thus assembled constitute the *school.* The other senses are derivative.

Side Johnson deduces from *side,* Saxon—*sijde,* Dutch; but what the word originally expressed, he does not inform us; then beginning his definitions with 'the part of animals fortified by ribs'—he proceeds through eight senses of the word, without ever glancing at the original and most important idea which it was intended to express.

Side is from the Saxon, *sid,* broad, wide—the original idea is, that side is the *broad part* of a thing, opposed to the ends or narrow part. In the

[8] See above, p. 117n.
[9] Gerardus Vossius, *Etymologicon linguae Latinae,* 1662; Julius Caesar Scaliger, *De causis linguae Latinae,* 1540.

same manner, the Latins took their *latus*, side, from *latus*, broad. From this sense, are easily deduced all the uses of the word—tho in some instances, its uses have deviated from the primitive sense.

From not understanding the radical terms, it has happened that Johnson, like all other lexicographers, has often, not to say generally, begun his definitions at the wrong end—beginning with a remote, collateral or figurative sense, and placing the *original* meaning the very *last* in order. Ainsworth's Latin Dictionary, the best specimen of Lexicography extant, is liable to the same objection; and from the same cause, a want of etymological knowledge.

As this subject involves so large a portion of errors, that I hardly know where to begin or what to select, from the mass of mistakes and imperfections, I shall not pursue the attempt to notice Johnson's errors; but to enable the reader more easily to comprehend the uses of a correct deduction of words from their originals, and to see the miserable state of this species of learning in Europe, as well as in this country, I will present an example of real etymology; having first stated the opinion of the standard authors.

'Censeo,' says Vossius, 'cum varie sumatur, et difficile dictu sit, quae notio sit princeps, difficile est enim indicare quam originem habeat.'[10] After stating the difficulty of arriving at the primitive idea and the origin of the word, he proceeds in his usual manner, to offer the conjectures of learned men. He mentions the Hebrew, *ks*, to *count* or *number*, as one of the words from which authors have deduced it. And Parkhurst[11] actually deduces the word from this Hebrew root, inserting *n*, to make out the orthography. Vossius labors through half a column with his conjectures, and leaves the word where he found it. Ainsworth says nothing on the subject.

'*King*,' says Johnson, 'is a contraction of the Teutonic *cuning* or *cyning*, which signified *stout* or *valiant*.' *Can*, *con* and *ken* the same author refers to the Teutonic verb, *cunnan*, to know—and there he leaves us.

But all these difficulties vanish, when we recur to the primitive Celtic, in which language *kcan*, *ccan*, *chean* or *ken* signified the *head*, as it still does in the Irish and Erse. The word being gutturally pronounced, modern authors write it with a different initial consonant; but this creates no difficulty.

From this term, denoting the *head* of the human body, were formed

---

[10] 'I consider—when it is taken in various ways it is difficult to say what is the principal notion, for it is difficult to indicate what origin it has.'

[11] John Parkhurst, *Hebrew and English Lexicon*, 1762.

the Gothic *kunnan* and the Saxon *cunnan*—to know—this operation of the mind being supposed to be seated in the *head*. Hence our modern *con* and *ken*, both having primarily the same idea. Hence our modern *can* which is only a dialectical variation of con and ken, and originally signified to *know*—its modern application to express physical power, rather than intellectual, is of a recent date—and the transition is easy from *know*—to, *know to do*—and thence, to *be able to do*. . . .

These examples will show what etymology *is*, in the books now published, and what I intend it *shall be* in my proposed work. I can affirm that nearly one half of what is called etymology in Vossius, Junius, Skinner, Johnson and Ainsworth, consists of groundless conjectures, or in statements that throw not a ray of light on the subject.

The errors of Johnson's *Dictionary* have been the subject of much complaint in Great Britain. . . .

I can assure these gentlemen [Mason and Croft] and the American public that the errors in Johnson's *Dictionary* are *ten times* as numerous as they suppose; and that the confidence now reposed in its accuracy, is the *greatest injury to philology* that now exists. I can assure them further that if any man, whatever may be his abilities in other respects, should attempt to compile a new Dictionary, or amend Johnson's, without a profound knowledge of etymology, he will unquestionably do as much harm as good.

If this representation of the imperfections of Johnson's *Dictionary* is just, it may be asked, what are the excellencies in the work to which it owes its reputation? To this inquiry the answer is obvious: Dr. Johnson has given many definitions of words which his predecessors had omitted, and added illustrations which, in many instances, are very valuable. These real improvements could not fail to be duly appreciated; while the display of erudition in numerous extracts from English writers, con-curring with the reputation which the author derived from his other writings, have led the public to repose an undue confidence in his opinions.—This is probably the sense in which we are to understand Mr. H. Tooke, in the passage cited, in which he declares that the portion of merit which the *Dictionary* possesses, renders it the more dangerous. Indeed, in any branch of literature, nothing is so dangerous as the errors of a great man.

But the great advances in Philology which have been made in Europe, within the last twenty years, enable us to disabuse ourselves of these prepossessions. And I am firmly persuaded that, whatever prejudices my fellow citizens now entertain, they will be satisfied, at a period not very

139

remote, that this subject is far better understood now, than it was in the age of Dr. Johnson. . . .

[refers to the need for an American dictionary and the minimal interest shown in it by his countrymen.]

But I must put an end to these remarks, for a volume would not contain the truths that I might unfold on this subject. Let me only add, what I am prepared, by a minute examination of this subject, to affirm, that not a single page of Johnson's *Dictionary* is correct—every page requires amendments or admits of material improvement. This remark, with some abatement, is true also of the Greek and Latin Dictionaries now used in our seminaries of learning.

Our Grammars are equally defective and erroneous. Most of the principles of construction in our language are established, so as to admit of no controversy. But of the *doubtful points*, which a critical knowledge of the history of our language is required to adjust, not half of them have been correctly settled by Lowth[12] and his followers: and I have no hesitation in affirming, that the grammars now taught in our schools, *introduce more errors than they correct*. Neither Lowth nor Johnson understood the Saxon or Primitive English, without which no man can compile a real English Grammar.

The discoveries of Mr. H. Tooke, as Darwin has remarked, unfold, at a single flash, the true theory of language which had lain, for ages, buried beneath the learned lumber of the schools. That author, however, has left the investigation incomplete. I shall pursue it with zeal—and undoubtedly with success.

Accept my respects,

N. WEBSTER.

NEW HAVEN, OCT. 1807.

[12] Robert Lowth, *A Short Introduction to English Grammar*, 1762.

RASSELAS

19 April 1759

23. Owen Ruffhead, unsigned review, *Monthly Review*

May 1759, xx, 428–37

Ruffhead (1723–69) was the author of political, legal and, later, biographical works. See Introduction, pp. 25–6.

The method of conveying instruction under the mask of fiction or romance, has been justly considered as the most effectual way of rendering the grave dictates of morality agreeable to mankind in general. The diversity of characters, and variety of incidents, in a romance, keeps attention alive; and moral sentiments find access to the mind imperceptibly, when led by amusement: whereas dry, didactic precepts, delivered under a sameness of character, soon grow tiresome to the generality of readers.

But to succeed in the romantic way of writing, requires a sprightliness of imagination, with a natural ease and variety of expression, which, perhaps, oftener falls to the lot of middling writers, than to those of more exalted genius: and therefore, we observe, with less regret, of the learned writer of these volumes, that *tale-telling* evidently is not his talent. He wants that graceful ease, which is the ornament of romance; and he stalks in the solemn buskin, when he ought to tread in the light sock. His stile is so tumid and pompous, that he sometimes deals in *sesquipedalia*, such as *excogitation, exaggeratory,* &c. with other hard compounds, which it is difficult to pronounce with composed features—as *multifarious, transcendental, indiscerpible,* &c. When we meet with instances of this inflated stile, we can scarce forbear calling upon the writer, in the words of Martial—

Grande cothurnati pone Maronis opus.[1]

This swelling language may shew the writer's learning, but it is certainly no proof of his elegance. If indeed he had put it into the mouth of a pedant only, nothing could be more apt: but unhappily he has so little conception of the propriety of character, that he makes the princess speak in the same lofty strain with the philosopher; and the waiting woman harangue with as much sublimity as her royal mistress.

With regard to the matter of these little volumes, we are concerned to say, that we cannot discover much invention in the plan, or utility in the design. The topics which the writer has chosen have been so often handled, they are grown threadbare: and with all his efforts to be original, his sentiments are most of them to be found in the Persian and Turkish tales, and other books of the like sort; wherein they are delivered to better purpose, and cloathed in a more agreeable garb. Neither has the end of this work any great tendency to the good of society. It is calculated to prove that discontent prevails among men of all ranks and conditions—the knowledge of which, we may acquire without going to Ethiopia to learn it.

But the inferences which the writer draws from this general discontent are by no means just. He seems to conclude from thence, that felicity is a thing ever in prospect, but never attainable. This conclusion, instead of exciting men to laudable pursuits, which should be the aim of every moral publication, tends to discourage them from all pursuits whatever; and to confirm them in that supine indolence, which is the parent of vice and folly: and which, we dare say, it is not the worthy author's design to encourage.

It does not follow, that because there are discontented mortals in every station of life, that therefore every individual, in those several stations, is discontented. Whatever men may conclude in the gloom of a closet, yet if we look abroad, we shall find Beings who, upon the whole, afford us a moral certainty of their enjoying happiness. A *continued* or constant series of felicity is not the lot of human nature: but there are many who experience frequent returns of pleasure and content, which more than counterbalance the occasional interruptions of pain and inquietude. Such may be deemed really happy, who, in general, feel themselves so; and that there are many such, we see no reasonable cause to doubt.

We are apt to conclude too much from the restless disposition of

[1] *Epigrams*, v. 5. 8. (Presumably intended to mean as in the original: '[Do not] place [yourself beside] the mighty work of lofty Maro [Virgil]'.)

mankind, and to consider the desire which men express of changing their condition, as a constant mark of discontent and infelicity. But though this is often the case, it is not always so. On the contrary, our eagerness to shift the scene frequently makes a part of present enjoyment. The earnestness with which we pursue some probable, though distant, attainment, keeps the mind in a state of agreeable agitation, which improves its vigour. Be our condition what it will, the mind will soon grow torpid, and a *tedium* will ensue, unless we substitute some pursuit seemingly unconnected with our present state. Our fondness for change, however, does not *always* proceed from discontent merely on account of our present station, or from an expectation of greater and more permanent happiness in prospect. A wise man follows some distant pursuit, not as an *ultimate*, which is to ensure him felicity; but as a *medium* to keep the mind in action, and counterwork the inconveniences with which every state is attended. He is sensible that, when he attains his wishes, he shall still want something to diversify attention, and that further pursuits will be necessary to favour the active progress of the mind: such distant pursuits therefore, as they often engage the mind agreeably, are so far present enjoyments. But it is time to introduce our Author to the reader's acquaintance.

This little work is divided into chapters; in the first of which we are presented with a romantic, but high wrought, description of a palace, or rather prison, in a recess called the Happy Valley. In this place, provided with every thing which art and nature could supply, to render it agreeable, the Prince, who had been immured here from his infancy, grows discontented; and his discontent inclines him to meditate his escape. In this disposition of mind, he becomes intimate with Imlac, a man of learning, with a taste for poetry; and who had travelled over a great part of the globe. He entertains the Prince with the relation of his travels, and in the course of his narrative, he gives a description of the advantages enjoyed by the European nations.

'They are surely happy,' said the Prince, 'who have all these conveniences, of which I envy none so much as the facility with which separated friends interchange their thoughts.'

'The Europeans,' answered Imlac, 'are less unhappy than we, but they are not happy. Human life is every where a state, in which much is to be endured, and little to be enjoyed.'

The Prince's answer displays a simplicity of nature and goodness of heart, which is perfectly amiable and engaging.

[quotes ch. 12 'I am not yet willing' to 'rather specious than useful'.]

Here many striking and pertinent observations might have been made by Imlac, by way of reply. He might have proved the impossibility of 'filling every day with pleasure.' He might have shewn, that even wisdom and virtue, the parents of felicity, were sometimes nevertheless the sources of uneasiness and inquietude: that the perfection of our intellectual faculties, often leads to discover defects, which pain us in the observation: that the delicacy of our moral principles often subjects us to inconveniences, to which less susceptible dispositions are strangers. He might have observed to the Prince, that let his conduct in the choice of wife and friends be ever so wise, yet nevertheless his scheme of pleasure might be liable to interruption, from the loss or distress of those friends; and still much more subject to be disturbed by any disaster affecting those more intimate and dear connexions of wife and children: that these accidents, not to mention the shock of separation, might imbitter many days with sorrow. But Imlac, however, is suffered to pursue his narration without any comment on the Prince's visionary scheme of bliss.

At length the Prince, with the assistance of Imlac, makes his escape with him from the Happy Valley, together likewise with his sister, and her favourite maid. Having passed through a diversity of scenes, and observed a variety of characters, the Prince at last meets with a wise and happy man.

[quotes ch. 18 'As he was one day' to 'in every one's power'.]

Here the Writer presents us with an abstract of the Stoical tenets; which, in the event, he turns to ridicule. The Prince, who had obtained leave to visit his moral lecturer, found him one day inconsolable for the loss of an only daughter. Rasselas urged to him the precepts which he himself had so powerfully enforced. 'Has Wisdom,' said the Prince, 'no strength to arm the heart against calamity? Consider that external things are naturally variable, but truth and reason are always the same.' 'What Comfort,' said the mourner, 'can truth and reason afford me? Of what effect are they now, but to tell me that my daughter will not be restored?' Rasselas, however, was not disgusted with philosophy.

[quotes ch. 22 'He [Rasselas] went often to' to 'purify his heart'.]

The learned reader will perceive that, in this extract, the writer has availed himself of the arguments of Tully. But let us attend to the continuation of the debate.

[quotes remainder of ch. 22.]

In the character of this sage, the writer intends to expose the absurdity of the Epicurean doctrine: and it must be confessed, that he has taken an ingenious way of shewing its futility, by making the philosopher found a system of happiness upon a maxim which he is incapable of explaining intelligibly.

Rasselas was full of perplexities, and still continued doubtful concerning the way to happiness. At length, his sister and he agreed to divide between them the work of observation. The prince was to pursue his scarch in the splendour of courts, while she ranged through the scenes of humbler life.

When they met, they compared their remarks, and each found the other unsuccessful in the pursuit. Among other evils which infest private life, the princess Nekayah instances marriage.

[quotes ch. 26 'Some husbands arc imperious' to 'celibacy has no pleasures'.]

This extravagant declamation may entertain those who have read little and thought less, but to others it will probably appear trite, inconclusive, and fallacious. When the writer tells us, that 'marriage has many pains, but celibacy has no pleasures,' we must confess, that the antithesis is striking; but is the opposition just? If the author is a married man, we smile at his mistake; if he is single, and writes from his own feelings, we commiserate his condition.

After a pause in the conversation, Rasselas, whose remarks on the condition of high life are but slender and imperfect, observes, that quiet is not the daughter of grandeur.

[quotes ch. 27 'The highest stations' to 'patience must suppose pain'.]

How unnaturally is this debate supported? The prince, with all the simplicity of a credulous virgin, fondly imagines that people in humble station 'have nothing to do but to love and to be loved, to be virtuous and to be happy;' while the princess opposes his delusion with bold, manly, and masterly sentiments, enforced with all the energy of declamation. Rasselas, like an innocent and tender pupil, is documented by his philosophic sister, who shews him the folly of his visionary expectations. One would imagine that they had changed sexes: for surely that fond hope and pleasing delusion had been more natural on her side: and those deep sentiments and spirited remonstrances had been more becoming in the prince. Nekayah might have related her observations; but the reflections resulting from them should have been reserved for Rasselas.

In a short time, they renew the conversation concerning marriage.

[quotes ch. 28 'I know not, said the princess' to 'indissoluble compacts'.]

By this argument, to say nothing of the strange language in which the lady is made to express herself, marriage is not placed in a more favourable light than celibacy was just before. In short, all that we can conclude from this conversation is, that a married life is very wretched, and a single one very miserable. For our parts, we are of opinion, that each state has its advantages and its inconveniencies. But to make a just comparison between both, we must admit all collateral circumstances to be equal. Thus for instance, if we suppose two men and two women, in whom the circumstances of intellect, morals, and disposition are equal, and that one couple is married while the other remains single, certainly we should not hesitate to conclude, that the married pair have the best prospect of enjoying the most perfect felicity human nature is capable of possessing.

After further researches, the prince and princess meet with an astronomer, who imagined that for five years he had possessed the regulation of the weather, and the distribution of the seasons. This species of frenzy gives room for a very sensible chapter on the dangerous prevalence of imagination.

The astronomer, however, is cured of his frenzy by intercourse with the world; and the tale draws to a conclusion, in which, as the writer frankly acknowledges, nothing is concluded. They find that happiness is unattainable, and remain undetermined in their choice of life. As nothing is concluded, it would have been prudent in the author to have said nothing. Whoever he is, he is a man of genius and great abilities; but he has evidently misapplied his talents. We shall only add, that his title-page will impose upon many of Mr. Noble's[2] fair customers, who, while they expect to frolic along the flowery paths of romance, will find themselves hoisted on metaphysical stilts, and born aloft into the regions of syllogistical subtlety, and philosophical refinement.

[2] Francis Noble, proprietor of a well-known circulating library.

24. Unsigned notice, *Annual Register*

1759, ii, 447–9

The instruction which is found in most works of this kind, when they convey any instruction at all, is not the predominant part, but arises accidentally in the course of a story planned only to please. But in this novel the moral is the principal object, and the story is a mere vehicle to convey the instruction.

Accordingly the tale is not near so full of incidents, nor so diverting in itself, as the ingenious author, if he had not had higher views, might easily have made it; neither is the distinction of characters sufficiently attended to: but with these defects, perhaps no book ever inculcated a purer or sounder morality; no book ever made a more just estimate of human life, its pursuits, and its enjoyments. The descriptions are rich and luxuriant, and shew a poetic imagination not inferior to our best writers in verse. The style, which is peculiar and characteristical of the author, is lively, correct, and harmonious. It has however in a few places an air too exact and studied.

The ideas which travellers have given us of a mountain in which the branches of the royal family of Abissinia are confined, though it may not be very well founded in fact, affords a ground for the most striking description of a terrestial paradise, which has ever been drawn; in this the author places the hero of his tale.

[Seven paragraphs of quotation follow, including the description of the Happy Valley and the account of Rasselas's discontent.]

In consequence of these reflections [Rasselas] contrives to escape out of the valley; but if the hero of the tale was not happy in this situation, we are not to be surprised, that he did not find happiness in his excursion into the world at large.

Though the author has not put his name to the work, there is no doubt that he is the same who has before done so much for the improvement of our taste and our morals, and employed a great part of his life in an astonishing work for fixing the language of this nation; whilst this nation, which admires his works, and profits by them, has done nothing for the author.

25. William Mudford on *Rasselas*

1802

From the *Critical Enquiry into the Moral Writings of Dr. Samuel Johnson*, 80–5 (see No. 2). See Introduction, p. 26.

Rasselas has been considered as the masterpiece of Johnson, and has received very extensive and indeed merited commendation. But admiration of the man will often hurry us beyond deserved praise, and sink us in the meanness of hyperbole; and I fear this is sometimes the case with the *Prince of Abyssinia*. The language is harmonious, the arguments are acute, and the reflections are novel—but with all its splendour it exhibits a gloomy and imperfect picture. An excuse may indeed be offered for the melancholy scenes of life contained in this performance, which must be denied to the *Rambler*. Every one knows that *Rasselas* was composed to obtain money to behold an expiring parent whom Johnson tenderly loved; and it may be supposed that the gloom occasioned by such an approaching event, might in some measure tincture his writings. It is also to be remembered that he wrote it in want. These are indeed *raisons de convenance*, and might be admitted, did the *Prince of Abyssinia* stand out as an exception to his other writings: But as it is too much like all his other speculations upon life, we may justly conclude, that the same *Rasselas* would have been produced had he written it in the sunshine of plenty, and in the gaiety of happiness.

What has been said of the *Rambler* may be said of *Rasselas*. It is entitled to every praise which can be bestowed on language, on sentiment, and on argument; it is the production of a mind abundant in allusion, and capable of sublimity. It no where falls off from its dignity, but is uniformly grand even to a fault; for hence arises a want of discrimination which is remarkably obvious. The prince and princess, the waiting maid, the man of learning, and the robber, all discourse in the same exalted style, and reason with the same energy and perspicuity. Yet this is a fault which may be pardoned, in consideration of the advantages which we reap from it. . . .

The plan proposed in composing *Rasselas* was to shew the vanity of all human wishes, and how much our most ardent designs may be frustrated by the will of heaven, or by the agency of their fellow creatures. This is indeed a common subject, and I fear a useless one, at least, when treated in the manner which Johnson has done. I know no advantage which mankind can reap from being told that life is one continued scene of misery, and that no condition can afford its possessor happiness. This information, if it were true, every man must know without being told, and as it is false, every man must despise. This is the doctrine of *Rasselas*, and this is exemplified by a variety of adventures; yet I may still read and admire it as a pleasing tale, and exhibiting pleasing ideas: but it excites no tumultuous sensations, nor awakens any sympathy; hence it is soon forgotten; the reader finds in it nothing which he has been accustomed to experience or believe; nothing which bears any resemblance to the real events of life; nor any situations which he can assimilate to his mind. The disquisitions which it contains are indeed valuable, but as they are literary, they can have but few admirers.

26. Mrs Barbauld, *The British Novelists*

1810

Text from 1820 edition, xxvi. pp. i–viii.

Anna Laetitia Barbauld (1743–1825), the immensely productive miscellaneous writer and educationist, included *Rasselas* in her fifty-volume series, *The British Novelists*. Given here is her preface. See Introduction, p. 26.

Hercules, it is said, once wielded the distaff; and the Hercules of literature, Dr. Johnson, has not disdained to be the author of a novel. To say the truth, nothing which he has written has more the touch of genius than *Rasselas, Prince of Abyssinia*: nor do any of his performances bear stronger marks of his peculiar character. It is solemn, melancholy and philosophical. The frame of the story is an elegant and happy exertion of fancy. It was probably suggested to his mind from recollections of the impression made upon his fancy by a book which he translated when he first entered on his literary career, namely, *Father Lobo's Account of a Voyage to Abyssinia*.[1]

In that country, it is said, the younger branches of the royal family, instead of being sacrificed, as in some of the Eastern monarchies, to the jealousy of the reigning sovereign, are secluded from the world in a romantic and beautiful valley, where they are liberally provided with every thing that can gratify their tastes or amuse their solitude. This recess, which Dr. Johnson calls *the happy valley*, he has described with much richness of imagination. It is represented as being shut in by inaccessible mountains, and only to be entered through a cavern closed up with massy gates of iron, which were thrown open only once a year, on the annual visit of the emperor. At that time artists and teachers of every kind, capable of contributing to the amusement or solace of the princes, were admitted; but once admitted, they were immured for life with the royal captives. Every charm of nature and every decoration of art is supposed to be collected in this charming spot, and that its inhabitants had been, in general, content with the round of amusements provided for them, till at length Rasselas, a young prince of a sprightly and active genius, grows weary of an existence so monotonous, and is seized with a strong desire of seeing the world at large. In pursuance of this project, he contrives to dig a passage through the mountain, and to escape from this paradise with his favourite sister Nekayah and her attendant, and the philosopher who had assisted them in their enterprise, and who, being previously acquainted with the world, is to assist their inexperience. They are all equally disgusted with the languor of sated desires and the inactivity of unvaried quiet, and agree to range the world in order to make their *choice of life*.

The author, having thus stretched his canvass, proceeds to exhibit and to criticize the various situations and modes of human existence; public life and private; marriage and celibacy; commerce, rustic employments, religious retirement, &c., and finds that in all there is something good and something bad—that marriage has many pains, but celibacy has no pleasures; that the hermit cannot secure himself from vice, but by retiring from the exercise of virtue; that shepherds are boors, and philosophers—only men. Unable to decide amidst such various appearances of good and evil, and having seen enough of the world to be disgusted with it, they end their search by resolving to return with the first oppor-

[1] Published in 1735.

tunity in order to end their days in the happy valley; and this, to use the author's words in the title of his last chapter, is 'the conclusion, in which nothing is concluded.'

Such is the philosophic view which Dr. Johnson and many others have taken of life; and such indecision would probably be the consequence of thus narrowly sifting the advantages and disadvantages of every station in this mixt state, if done without that feeling reference to each man's particular position, and particular inclinations, which is necessary to incline the balance. If we choose to imagine an insulated being, detached from all connexions and all duties, it may be difficult for mere reason to direct his choice; but no man is so insulated: we are woven into the web of society, and to each individual it is seldom dubious what *he* shall do. Very different is the search after abstract good, and the pursuit of what a being born and nurtured amidst innumerable ties of kindred and companionship, feeling his own wants, impelled by his own passions, and influenced by his own peculiar associations, finds best for *him*. Except he is indolent or fastidious, he will seldom hesitate upon his choice of life. The same position holds good with regard to duty. We may bewilder ourselves in abstract questions of general good, or puzzle our moral sense with imaginary cases of conscience; but it is generally obvious enough to every man what duty dictates to him, in each particular case, as it comes before him.

The proper moral to be drawn from *Rasselas* is, therefore, not that goods and evils are so balanced against each other that no unmixed happiness is to be found in life,—a deduction equally trite and obvious; nor yet that a reasoning man can make no choice,—but rather that a *merely* reasoning man will be likely to make no choice,—and therefore that it becomes every man to make early that choice to which his particular position, his honest partialities, his individual propensities, his early associations impel him. Often does it happen that, while the over-refined and speculative are hesitating and doubting, the plain honest youth has secured happiness. Without this conclusion, the moral effect of the piece, loaded as it is with the miseries of life, and pointing out no path of action as more eligible than another, would resemble that of *Candide*,[2] where the party, after all their adventures, agree to plant cabbages in their own garden: but the gloomy ideas of the English philosopher are softened and guarded by sound principles of religion.

Along with Voltaire, he strongly points and perhaps exaggerates the

[2] Published in 1759, only a few weeks after *Rasselas* was written.

miseries of life; but instead of evading their force by laughing at them, or drawing from them a satire against Providence, which *Candide* may be truly said to be, our author turns the mind to the solid consolations of a future state: 'All,' says he, 'that virtue can afford is quietness of conscience, and a steady prospect of a future state: this may enable us to endure calamity with patience, but remember that patience must suppose pain.'

Such is the plan of this philosophical romance, in the progress of which the author makes many just strictures on human life, and many acute remarks on the springs of human passions; but they are the passions of the species, not of the individual. It is life, as viewed at a distance by a speculative man, in a kind of bird's-eye view; not painted with the glow and colouring of an actor in the busy scene: we are not led to say, 'This man is painted naturally,' but, 'Such is the nature of man.' The most striking of his pictures is that of the philosopher, who imagined himself to have the command of the weather, and who had fallen into that species of insanity by indulging in the luxury of solitary musing, or what is familiarly called castle-building. His state is strikingly and feelingly described, and no doubt with the peculiar interest arising from what the author had felt and feared in his own mind; for it is well known that at times he suffered under a morbid melancholy near akin to derangement, which occasionally clouded his mighty powers; and no doubt he had often indulged in these unprofitable abstractions of thought, these seducing excursions of fancy.

The following remark ought to startle those who have permitted their mind to feed itself in solitude with its own creations and wishes. 'All power of fancy over reason is a degree of insanity; but while this power is such as we can control or repress, it is not visible to others, nor considered as any depravation of the mental faculties. In time, some particular train of ideas fixes the attention, all other intellectual gratifications are rejected. By degrees the reign of fancy is confirmed; she grows first imperious, and in time despotic; then fictions begin to operate as realities, false opinions fasten upon the mind, and life passes away in dreams of rapture or of anguish.'

Rasselas is, perhaps, of all its author's works, that in which his peculiar style best harmonizes with the subject. That pompous flow of diction, that measured harmony of periods, that cadenced prose which Dr. Johnson introduced, though it would appear stiff and cumbrous in the frame of a common novel, is sanctioned by the imitation, or what our authors have agreed to call imitation, of the Eastern style, a style which has been commonly adopted in *Almoran and Hamet*,[3] *Tales of the Genii*,[4] and other works, in which the costume is taken from nations whose remoteness destroys the idea of colloquial familiarity. We silence our reason by the laws we have imposed upon our fancy, and are content that both Nekayah and her female attendant, at the sources of the Nile, or the foot of the Pyramid, should express themselves in language which would appear unnaturally inflated in the mouths of a young lady and her waiting-maid conversing together in London or in Paris. It has been remarked, however, that Nekayah, it is difficult to say why, is more philosophical than her brother.

It has been already mentioned that the frame of this piece was probably suggested by the author's having some years before translated an account of Abyssinia. It may be remarked by the way, how different an idea of the country and its inhabitants seems to have been entertained at that time, from that which is suggested by the accounts of Bruce and Lord Valentia.[5] Thomson, who probably took his ideas from the voyage-writers of the time, represents the country of 'jealous Abyssinia' as a perfect paradise, 'a world within itself; disdaining all assault;' and mentions the 'palaces, and fanes, and villas, and gardens, and cultured fields' of this innocent and amiable people with poetic rapture.[6] We must suppose that Father Lobo never had the honour of dancing with them on a gala-day.

Rasselas was published in 1759, and was then composed for the purpose of enabling the author to visit his mother in her last illness, and for defraying the expenses of her funeral. It was written with great rapidity; for the author himself has told us that it was composed in the evenings of one week, sent to the press in portions as it was written, and never reperused when finished. It was much read, and has been translated into several languages. Rich indeed must be the stores of that mind which could pour out its treasures with such rapidity, and clothe its thoughts, almost spontaneously, in language so correct and ornamented.

Perhaps the genius of Dr. Johnson has been in some measure mistaken. The ponderosity of his manner has led the world to give him more credit for science, and less for fancy, than the character of his works will justify. His remarks on life and manners are just and weighty, and show a

[3] By John Hawkesworth, 1761.

[4] Translated from the Persian of Horam, son of Asmar, by Sir C. Morell, 1764, and frequently republished.

[5] James Bruce, *Travels to Discover the Source of the Nile*, 1790; George Annesley, Earl of Mountnorris, *Voyages and Travels . . .*, 1809.

[6] James Thomson, *Summer* (1727), ll. 752, 769–73.

philosophical mind, but not an original turn of thinking. The novelty is in the style; but originality of style belongs to that dress and colouring of our thoughts in which imagination is chiefly concerned.

In fact, imagination had great influence over him. His ideas of religion were awful and grand, and he had those feelings of devotion which seldom subsist in a strong degree in a cold and phlegmatic mind; but his religion was tinctured with superstition, his philosophy was clouded with partialities and prejudices, his mind was inclined to melancholy.

In the work before us he has given testimony to his belief in apparitions, and has shown a leaning towards monastic institutions. Of his discoveries in any region of science posterity will be able to speak but little; but in his *Ramblers* he will be considered as having formed a new style, and his *Rasselas*, and *Vision of Theodore*, must give him an honourable place among those writers who deck philosophy with the ornamented diction and the flowers of fancy.

It should not be forgotten to be noticed in praise of *Rasselas*, that it is, as well as all the other works of its author, perfectly pure. In describing the happy valley, he has not, as many authors would have done, painted a luxurious bower of bliss, nor once throughout the work awakened any ideas which might be at variance with the moral truths which all his writings are meant to inculcate.

27. Johnson's *Proposals* for his edition of Shakespeare

1 June 1756

From the *Proposals for Printing, by Subscription, the Dramatick Works of William Shakespeare*, which declared Johnson's editorial intentions and promised the edition for 1757.

All the former criticks have been so much employed on the correction of the text, that they have not sufficiently attended to the elucidation of passages obscured by accident or time. The editor will endeavour to read the books which the authour read, to trace his knowledge to its source, and compare his copies with their originals. If in this part of his design he hopes to attain any degree of superiority to his predecessors, it must be considered, that he has the advantage of their labours; that part of the work being already done, more care is naturally bestowed on the other part; and that, to declare the truth, Mr. Rowe and Mr. Pope were very ignorant of the ancient English literature; Dr. Warburton was detained by more important studies; and Mr. Theobald,[1] if fame be just to his memory, considered learning only as an instrument of gain, and made no further enquiry after his authour's meaning, when once he had notes sufficient to embellish his page with the expected decorations.

With regard to obsolete or peculiar diction, the editor may perhaps claim some degree of confidence, having had more motives to consider the whole extent of our language than any other man from its first

[1] Nicholas Rowe's edition of Shakespeare, 1709; Pope's, 1725; Lewis Theobald's, 1733; William Warburton's, 1747.

formation. He hopes, that, by comparing the works of Shakespeare with those of writers who lived at the same time, immediately preceded, or immediately followed him, he shall be able to ascertain his ambiguities, disentangle his intricacies, and recover the meaning of words now lost in the darkness of antiquity.

When therefore any obscurity arises from an allusion to some other book, the passage will be quoted. When the diction is entangled, it will be cleared by a paraphrase or interpretation. When the sense is broken by the suppression of part of the sentiment in pleasantry or passion, the connection will be supplied. When any forgotten custom is hinted, care will be taken to retrieve and explain it. The meaning assigned to doubtful words will be supported by the authorities of other writers, or by parallel passages of Shakespeare himself.

The observation of faults and beauties is one of the duties of an annotator, which some of Shakespeare's editors have attempted, and some have neglected. For this part of his task, and for this only, was Mr. Pope eminently and indisputably qualified: nor has Dr. Warburton followed him with less diligence or less success. But I have never observed that mankind was much delighted or improved by their asterisks, commas, or double commas;[2] of which the only effect is, that they preclude the pleasure of judging for ourselves, teach the young and ignorant to decide without principles; defeat curiosity and discernment, by leaving them less to discover; and at last shew the opinion of the critick, without the reasons on which it was founded, and without affording any light by which it may be examined.

The editor, though he may less delight his own vanity, will probably please his reader more, by supposing him equally able with himself to judge of beauties and faults, which require no previous acquisition of remote knowledge. A description of the obvious scenes of nature, a representation of general life, a sentiment of reflection or experience, a deduction of conclusive argument, a forcible eruption of effervescent passion, are to be considered as proportionate to common apprehension, unassisted by critical officiousness; since, to conceive them, nothing more is requisite than acquaintance with the general state of the world, and those faculties which he must always bring with him who would read Shakespeare.

But when the beauty arises from some adaptation of the sentiment to customs worn out of use, to opinions not universally prevalent, or to any accidental or minute particularity, which cannot be supplied by

[2] Pope and Warburton indicated favourite passages by these means.

common understanding, or common observation, it is the duty of a commentator to lend his assistance.

The notice of beauties and faults thus limited will make no distinct part of the design, being reducible to the explanation of obscure passages.

The editor does not however intend to preclude himself from the comparison of Shakespeare's sentiments or expression with those of ancient or modern authours, or from the display of any beauty not obvious to the students of poetry; for as he hopes to leave his authour better understood, he wishes likewise to procure him more rational approbation.

The former editors have affected to slight their predecessors: but in this edition all that is valuable will be adopted from every commentator, that posterity may consider it as including all the rest, and exhibiting whatever is hitherto known of the great father of the English drama.

CONDITIONS

I. That the book shall be elegantly printed in eight volumes in octavo.
II. That the price to subscribers shall be two guineas; one to be paid at subscribing, the other on the delivery of the book in sheets.
III. That the work shall be published on or before Christmas 1757.

28. From Johnson's Preface to the first edition

1765

I can say with great sincerity of all my predecessors, what I hope will hereafter be said of me, that not one has left Shakespeare without improvement, nor is there one to whom I have not been indebted for assistance and information. Whatever I have taken from them it was my intention to refer to its original authour, and it is certain, that what I have not given to another, I believed when I wrote it to be my own. In some perhaps I have been anticipated; but if I am ever found to encroach upon the remarks of any other commentator, I am willing that the honour, be it more or less, should be transferred to the first claimant, for his right, and his alone, stands above dispute; the second can prove his pretensions only to himself, nor can himself always distinguish invention, with sufficient certainty, from recollection.

They have all been treated by me with candour, which they have not been careful of observing to one another. It is not easy to discover from what cause the acrimony of a scholiast can naturally proceed. The subjects to be discussed by him are of very small importance; they involve neither property nor liberty; nor favour the interest of sect or party. The various readings of copies, and different interpretations of a passage, seem to be questions that might exercise the wit, without engaging the passions. But, whether it be, that 'small things make mean men proud,'[1] and vanity catches small occasions; or that all contrariety of opinion, even in those that can defend it no longer, makes proud men angry; there is often found in commentaries a spontaneous strain of invective and contempt, more eager and venomous than is vented by the most furious controvertist in politicks against those whom he is hired to defame.

Perhaps the lightness of the matter may conduce to the vehemence of the agency; when the truth to be investigated is so near to inexistence, as to escape attention, its bulk is to be enlarged by rage and exclamation: That to which all would be indifferent in its original state, may attract notice when the fate of a name is appended to it. A commentator has indeed great temptations to supply by turbulence what he wants of dignity, to beat his little gold to a spacious surface, to work that to foam which no art or diligence can exalt to spirit.

The notes which I have borrowed or written are either illustrative, by which difficulties are explained; or judicial, by which faults and beauties are remarked; or emendatory, by which depravations are corrected.

The explanations transcribed from others, if I do not subjoin any other interpretation, I suppose commonly to be right, at least I intend by acquiescence to confess, that I have nothing better to propose.

After the labours of all the editors, I found many passages which appeared to me likely to obstruct the greater number of readers, and thought it my duty to facilitate their passage. It is impossible for an expositor not to write too little for some, and too much for others. He can only judge what is necessary by his own experience; and how long soever he may deliberate, will at last explain many lines which the

[1] *2 Henry VI*, IV. i. 106 ('. . . base men . . .').

learned will think impossible to be mistaken, and omit many for which the ignorant will want his help. These are censures merely relative, and must be quietly endured. I have endeavoured to be neither superfluously copious, nor scrupulously reserved, and hope that I have made my authour's meaning accessible to many who before were frighted from perusing him, and contributed something to the publick, by diffusing innocent and rational pleasure.

The compleat explanation of an authour not systematick and consequential, but desultory and vagrant, abounding in casual allusions and light hints, is not to be expected from any single scholiast. All personal reflections, when names are suppressed, must be in a few years irrecoverably obliterated; and customs, too minute to attract the notice of law, such as modes of dress, formalities of conversation, rules of visits, disposition of furniture, and practices of ceremony, which naturally find places in familiar dialogue, are so fugitive and unsubstantial, that they are not easily retained or recovered. What can be known, will be collected by chance, from the recesses of obscure and obsolete papers, perused commonly with some other view. Of this knowledge every man has some, and none has much; but when an authour has engaged the publick attention, those who can add any thing to his illustration, communicate their discoveries, and time produces what had eluded diligence.

To time I have been obliged to resign many passages, which, though I did not understand them, will perhaps hereafter be explained, having, I hope, illustrated some, which others have neglected or mistaken.

[Johnson discusses his editorial procedure.]

Perhaps I may not be more censured for doing wrong, than for doing little; for raising in the publick expectations, which at last I have not answered. The expectation of ignorance is indefinite, and that of knowledge is often tyrannical. It is hard to satisfy those who know not what to demand, or those who demand by design what they think impossible to be done. I have indeed disappointed no opinion more than my own; yet I have endeavoured to perform my task with no slight solicitude. Not a single passage in the whole work has appeared to me corrupt, which I have not attempted to restore; or obscure, which I have not endeavoured to illustrate. In many I have failed like others; and from many, after all my efforts, I have retreated, and confessed the repulse. I have not passed over, with affected superiority, what is equally difficult to the reader and to myself, but where I could not instruct him, have owned my ignorance. I might easily have accumulated a mass of seeming learning upon easy scenes; but it ought not to be imputed to negligence, that, where nothing was necessary, nothing has been done, or that, where others have said enough, I have said no more.

Notes are often necessary, but they are necessary evils. Let him, that is yet unacquainted with the powers of Shakespeare, and who desires to feel the highest pleasure that the drama can give, read every play from the first scene to the last, with utter negligence of all his commentators. When his fancy is once on the wing, let it not stoop at correction or explanation. When his attention is strongly engaged, let it disdain alike to turn aside to the name of Theobald and of Pope. Let him read on through brightness and obscurity, through integrity and corruption; let him preserve his comprehension of the dialogue and his interest in the fable. And when the pleasures of novelty have ceased, let him attempt exactness, and read the commentators.

Particular passages are cleared by notes, but the general effect of the work is weakened. The mind is refrigerated by interruption; the thoughts are diverted from the principal subject; the reader is weary, he suspects not why; and at last throws away the book, which he has too diligently studied.

Parts are not to be examined till the whole has been surveyed; there is a kind of intellectual remoteness necessary for the comprehension of any great work in its full design and its true proportions; a close approach shews the smaller niceties, but the beauty of the whole is discerned no longer.

It is not very grateful to consider how little the succession of editors has added to this authour's power of pleasing. He was read, admired, studied, and imitated, while he was yet deformed with all the improprieties which ignorance and neglect could accumulate upon him; while the reading was yet not rectified, nor his allusions understood; yet then did Dryden pronounce 'that Shakespeare was the man, who, of all modern and perhaps ancient poets, had the largest and most comprehensive soul. All the images of nature were still present to him, and he drew them not laboriously, but luckily: When he describes any thing, you more than see it, you feel it too. Those who accuse him to have wanted learning, give him the greater commendation: he was naturally learned: he needed not the spectacles of books to read nature; he looked inwards, and found her there. I cannot say he is every where alike; were he so, I should do him injury to compare with him the greatest of mankind. He is many times flat and insipid; his comick wit degenerating into clenches, his serious swelling into bombast. But he is always great, when some great occasion is presented to him: No man can say, he ever had a fit subject for his wit, and did not then raise himself as high above the rest of poets,

Quantum lenta solent inter viburna cupressi.'[2]

It is to be lamented, that such a writer should want a commentary; that his language should become obsolete, or his sentiments obscure. But it is vain to carry wishes beyond the condition of human things; that which must happen to all, has happened to Shakespeare, by accident and time; and more than has been suffered by any other writer since the use of types, has been suffered by him through his own negligence of fame, or perhaps by that superiority of mind, which despised its own performances, when it compared them with its powers, and judged those works unworthy to be preserved, which the criticks of following ages were to contend for the fame of restoring and explaining.

Among these candidates of inferiour fame, I am now to stand the judgment of the publick; and wish that I could confidently produce my commentary as equal to the encouragement which I have had the honour of receiving. Every work of this kind is by its nature deficient, and I should feel little solicitude about the sentence, were it to be pronounced only by the skilful and the learned.

[2] Dryden, *Essay of Dramatick Poesie*, ed. James T. Boulton, 1964, 87–8. The Latin line is from Virgil, *Eclogues*, I. 25 ('as cypresses usually do among the bending osiers').

29. George Colman, unsigned notice, *St. James's Chronicle*

10–15 October 1765

Text from Colman's *Prose on Several Occasions*, 1787, ii. 59f.

Colman (1732–94), the dramatist and essayist, was clearly 'one who loved mischief' (Boswell, *Life*, ii. 436); but he was also a scholar (he translated Terence and, later, Horace) and a seasoned critic. See Introduction, p. 26.

Johnson's Shakespeare! published! When?—this Morning—What, at last!—*vix tandem*, 'egad! he has observed Horace's Rule of *nonum in annum.*—*Keep the Piece nine Years*, as Pope says[1]—I know a Friend of mine that subscribed in Fifty-six— &c. &c. &c.

Such perhaps is the Language of some little Witling, who thinks his satirical Sallies extremely poignant and severe; but the Appearance of any Production of Mr Johnson cannot fail of being grateful to the literary World; and, come when they will, like an agreeable Guest, we are sure to give them a hearty Welcome, though perhaps we may have betrayed some little Impatience at their not coming sooner. Nor have the Public in general been deceived. None but Subscribers have a Right to complain; and they, I suppose, in general, meant to show their Respect for Mr Johnson, rather than to give themselves a Title of becoming clamorous Creditors.

But granting our Editor to be naturally indolent—and naturally indolent we believe him to be—we cannot help wondering at the Number, Vastness, and Excellence of his Productions. A Dictionary of our Language; a Series of admirable Essays in the *Rambler*, as well as, if we are not misinformed, several excellent ones in the *Adventurer*; an Edition of Shakespeare; besides some less considerable Works, all in the Space of no very great Number of Years! and all these the Productions of a mere Idler!—We could wish that there were a few more such indolent Men in these Kingdoms.

[1] Horace, *Ars Poetica*, l. 388; Pope, *Epistle to Dr. Arbuthnot*, l. 40.

[quotes liberally from Preface; and concludes:]

After having finished the critical Examen of his Author, Mr Johnson next proceeds to a Recapitulation of his several Editors, accompanied with Remarks on their various Merits and Demerits. Of Rowe and Pope he speaks very candidly, and justly; of Theobald, (hitherto undoubtedly the most meritorious Editor of Shakespeare) we think that he speaks too hardly; and of Hanmer, much too favourably. Of the last Right Rev. Annotator[2] on our Author he speaks respectfully, though freely; and to atone for the Liberties taken with him, Mr Johnson sacrifices to his Resentment the Authors of the *Canons of Criticism*, and *the Revisal of Shakespeare's Text*.[3] In short, Mr J. treats Dr. W. as termagant Wives do their Husbands, who will let nobody call them to Account but themselves. . . .

On the whole, this Preface, as it is an elaborate, so it is also a fine Piece of Writing. It possesses all the Virtues and Vices of the peculiar Stile of its Author. It speaks, perhaps, of Shakespeare's Beauties too sparingly, and of his Faults too hardly; but it contains, nevertheless, much Truth, good Sense, and just Criticism.

[2] William Warburton, Bishop of Gloucester.
[3] Thomas Edwards and Benjamin Heath.

30. William Kenrick, unsigned review, *Monthly Review*

October–November 1765, xxxiii, 285–301, 374–89

Both the *Critical Review* (November–December 1765) and the *Monthly Review* expressed disappointment at Johnson's overall performance. The former remarked: 'Mr. Johnson has at last brought the child to light; but alas! in the delivery it has received, so many unhappy squeezes, pinches, and wrenches, that the healthful constitution of the parent alone can prevent it from being lame and deformed for ever' (xx, 321). But this reviewer was lightweight, a literary Sparkish compared with the Dennis-like rigour of Kenrick in the *Monthly*. Boswell is rather scornful and patronizing towards him; but though Kenrick was later the libeller of Goldsmith and Garrick, it would be foolish to underestimate his critical ability. See Introduction, pp. 5, 26.

It is a circumstance very injurious to the productions even of the best writers, that the public prepossession is up in their favour before they make their appearance; especially if such prepossession hath been kept any considerable time in a state of expectation and suspense: delay being in itself a kind of disappointment, which prepares the mind for a still greater mortification, and even disposes us to conceive ourselves disappointed if we are not gratified with something superior to what we had at first a right to expect. A number of apologies are ready, and various are the pleas admitted, in justification of a precipitated performance. Errour and inadvertence are imputed, as natural effects, to haste; and even ignorance itself finds a convenient shelter under the pretence of rapidity of composition. A very different fate attends on those works, whose publication, having been long promised and frequently deferred, is supposed to be delayed only to render them by so much the more valuable when they appear, as their appearance may have been procrastinated.

Under this disadvantage lies the present edition of Shakespeare; a poet, who least requires, and most deserves, a comment, of all the writers his age produced. We cannot help thinking it, therefore, a misfortune almost as singular as his merit, that, among so many ingenious scholiasts that have employed themselves in elucidating his writings, hardly one of them hath been found in any degree worthy of him. They all seem to have mistaken the route, in which only they could do honour to themselves, or be useful to the reader. Engaged in the piddling task of adjusting quibbles, and restoring conundrums, they have neglected the illustration of characters, sentiments and situations. Instead of aspiring to trim the ruffled bays that have a little obscured his brow, they have been laboriously and servilely employed in brushing the dirt from his shoes. Instead of strewing flowers, and planting fresh laurels, on his tomb, they have been irreverently trampling down the turf, that had otherwise covered his dust with perpetual verdure. From the present Editor, it is true, we hoped better things. But what shall we say? when he himself confesses, that, as to 'the poetical beauties or defects of his author, he hath not been very diligent to observe them: having given up this part of his design to chance and caprice.' This is surely a strange concession to be made by the author of the proposals for printing this work by subscription! We were by them given to understand, that the Editor would proceed in a manner very different from his predecessors; and were encouraged to hope that Shakespeare would no longer be commented on, like a barren or obsolete writer; whose works were of no other use than to employ the sagacity of antiquarians and philologers. But perhaps our Editor found the task, of commenting on Shakespeare as a *poet*, much more difficult than he had conceived it to be. It might sound as harsh in the ear of the public, to tax a writer whom it hath so much honoured by its approbation, with want of capacity for writing such a commentary, as it doubtless would, in the ears of Dr. Johnson, to hear himself charged with want of application to it, when he acknowledges the great encouragement he has had the honour of receiving for that purpose. We should be very tender, be the occasion what it would, of laying any writer of acknowledged merit under the necessity of pleading guilty either to the charge of ignorance or indolence. But we cannot help subscribing to the opinion of a very ingenious critic, when he affirms, that 'every writer is justly chargeable with want of knowledge when he betrays it on the subject he is treating of, let him be ever so capable of treating other subjects, or however justly founded may be his reputation for learning in general.'[1] It hath been observed, in some remarks already published on this occasion, that

[1] Thomas Edwards, *Canons of Criticism*, 1748.

our Editor's notes, few and exceptionable as they are, lay claim to our admiration, if we reflect on the extreme indolence of the Writer; who is naturally an *idler*.[2] How far such a plea may be satisfactory to the purchasers of this edition, we know not; but we have too high an opinion of the Editor's character, to think he will more readily acquiesce under the imputation of ingratitude than under that of incapacity. At the same time, however, we cannot but express our apprehensions, that every judicious reader, who may accompany us through a fair and impartial review of his preface and commentary, will think, with us, that there are many evident marks of the want of ingenuity or industry in the Commentator.

We find little in the first five pages of our Editor's preface, but trite and common-place reflections, on our veneration for antiquity, and on the general talents of Shakespeare; delivered in that pompous style which is so peculiar to himself, and is so much admired by some kind of readers. In some places, however, he is less verbose; and then he is generally sensible, instructive and entertaining.

[quotes 'Shakespeare is above all writers' to 'progress of the passions'.]

After bestowing this just elogium on Shakespeare, our editor proceeds to exculpate him from the censures of Rhymer, Dennis, and Voltaire; entering particularly into a defence of the tragi-comedy, or that mixed kind of drama, which hath given such great offence to the minor critics. He states the fact, and considers it thus:

[quotes 'Shakespeare's plays are not in' to 'pleasure consists in variety'.]

We do not feel the force of this reasoning; though we think the critics have condemned this kind of drama too severely. What follows also is to us a little problematical. Dr. Johnson prefers Shakespeare's comic scenes to his tragic: in the latter, he says, 'there is always something wanting, while the former often surpasses expectation or desire. His tragedy seems to be skill, and his comedy instinct.' As this is a general assertion, unsupported by any particular examples, we cannot very easily controvert it; but we are apt to suspect it is founded in a great degree on the preference which the Editor himself may possibly be disposed to give to comedy in general. Different auditors, as he observes, have different habitudes; so that, were we to put this assertion to the proof by particular applications, we should possibly find *quot homines tot sententiæ*.[3]

[2] See document No. 29.
[3] Terence, *Phormio*, II. 2. 14 ('as many opinions as men').

After having enumerated the various excellencies of this great poet, our Editor proceeds to mention his faults; faults, says he, '*sufficient to obscure and overwhelm any other merit.*' The first defect he charges him with, is, indeed, a very capital one; from which we should be glad, and shall endeavour, to exculpate him.

[quotes 'His first defect' to 'independant on time or place'.]

'No question,' says our Editor, in another place, 'can be more innocently discussed than a dead poet's pretensions to renown.' But, tho' this be true, some tenderness surely should be felt for his probity. Shakespeare is here charged with 'sacrificing virtue to convenience,' for no other reason than that he seemed more careful to please than instruct, and to write without any moral purpose. But if it be admitted, as our Editor actually admits, that a system of social duty may be selected from his writings, and that his precepts and axioms were virtuous; we may justly ask, whether they are less so for dropping casually from him? Must a writer be charged with making a sacrifice of virtue, because he does not professedly inculcate it? Is every writer *ex professo* a parson or a moral philosopher? It is doubtless always the *moralist*'s duty, to strive at least, to make the world better; but we should think it no inconsiderable merit in a *comic-poet*, to be able to divert and amuse the world without making it worse; especially if he should occasionally drop such virtuous precepts and axioms, as would serve to form a system of social duty. We are, for these reasons, so far from thinking that the barbarity of his age cannot extenuate the fault here censured, that we think he stands in need of no other excuse than our Editor hath on another occasion made for him, viz. his ignorance of poetical composition. He did not know that the rules of criticism required the drama to have a particular moral; nor did he conceive himself bound, as a *poet*, to write like a *philosopher*. He carries his persons, therefore, indifferently through right and wrong, for the same reason as he makes them laugh and cry in the same piece; and is justifiable on the same principles; it is a strict imitation of nature; and Shakespeare is the Poet of Nature. Were our Poet now living, and possessed of Dr. Johnson's critical knowledge, we presume he would make no more nor greater sacrifices of *virtue* to *convenience* than his Editors may have done. Shakespeare, it is true, hath depicted none of

Those faultless monsters which the world ne'er saw;[4]

He did not presume to limit the designs of providence to the narrow

[4] John Sheffield, *An Essay on Poetry*, 1682, l. 195.

bounds of poetical justice; but hath displayed the sun shining, as it really does, both on the just and the unjust.

The next fault our immortal Poet is charged with, is the want of connection and consistence in his plots; from which charge, with all the aggravating circumstances enumerated by the learned Editor, we shall not undertake to defend him, any more than from the charge, of paying no regard to distinction of time or place. It is certain he makes no scruple of giving, to one age or nation, the customs, institutions, and opinions of another, not only at the expence of likelihood, but even of possibility. But surely our Editor will admit that the barbarity of his age may extenuate this fault; since, by his own confession, Shakespeare was not the only violater of chronology in his time: Sidney, his contemporary, who wanted not the advantages of learning, having, in his *Arcadia*, confounded the pastoral with the feudal times, the days of innocence, quiet and security, with those of turbulence, violence, and adventure.

Shakespeare is said to be seldom very successful in his comic scenes, when he engages his characters in raillery or repartee, or as Dr. Johnson more quaintly expresses it, 'reciprocations of smartness and contests of sarcasm.' Their jests, we are told, are commonly gross and their pleasantry licentious: nor will, it seems, the barbarity of his age excuse our Poet with regard to this defect, any more than the former. For our part, however, we think that Shakespeare is sometimes peculiarly happy in hitting off that kind of sheer wit; for which some modern writers, particularly Congreve and Farquhar, have been so generally admired. The reciprocations of smartness between Benedick and Beatrice in *Much-ado-about-Nothing*, are scarce inferior to any thing of the kind; and tho' we cannot pretend that the dialogue of his gentlemen and ladies, is so delicate and refined, as that of Cibber and some other writers, it is full as witty, and not a jot more licentious, than what we frequently find in Vanbrugh and Congreve, who had not the barbarity of the age to plead in excuse.

As to the quirks and quibbles of Shakespeare's clowns, which sometimes infect the graver parts of his writings, we cannot be of Dr. Johnson's opinion. He affirms that 'A quibble is to Shakespeare, what luminous vapours are to the traveller; he follows it at all adventures, it is sure to lead him out of his way, and sure to engulf him in the mire. It has some malignant power over his mind, and its fascinations are irresistible. Whatever be the dignity or profundity of his disquisition, whether he be enlarging knowledge or exalting affection, whether he be amusing attention with incidents, or enchaining it in suspense, let but a quibble spring up before him, and he leaves his work unfinished. A quibble is the golden apple for which he will always turn aside from his career, or stoop from his elevation. A quibble, poor and barren as it is, gave him such delight, that he was content to purchase it, by the sacrifice of reason, propriety and truth. A quibble was to him the fatal *Cleopatra* for which he lost the world, and was content to lose * it.'

Quaintly as all this is expressed, and boldly as it is asserted, we cannot be persuaded that Shakespeare's native genius was not too sublime to be so much captivated with the charms of so contemptible an object. How poorly soever it might descend to trifle with an *ignis fatuus* by owl-light, we cannot think an eagle, soaring in the direct beams of the meridian sun, could be allured, to look down with pleasure on the feeble glimmerings of a rush-light. It is not impossible, indeed, that the necessity of accommodating himself in this particular so frequently to the humour and taste of the times, had rendered a practice habitual to him, which his own better taste and judgment could not fail to condemn. We do therefore readily adopt Sir Thomas Hanmer's defence of Shakespeare, with regard to this point. It must be remembered, says that judicious Editor, that 'our poet wrote for the stage, rude and unpolished as it then was; and the vicious taste of the age must stand condemned for the poor witticisms and conceits that fell from his pen; since he hath left upon record a signal proof how much he despised them. In his play of the *Merchant of Venice*, a clown is introduced quibbling in a miserable manner; upon which one who bears the character of a man of sense makes the following reflection: *How every fool can play upon a word! I think the best grace of wit will shortly turn into silence, and discourse grow commendable in none but parrots.* He could hardly have found stronger words to express his indignation at those false pretences to wit then in vogue; and therefore tho' such trash is frequently interspersed in his writings, it would be unjust to cast it as an imputation upon his taste and judgment as a writer.'[5]

We shall leave our Readers to determine, whether what the present

* Doth not this whole paragraph serve egregiously to prove, that, altho' our Editor may not be fond of down-right punning, he takes full as much delight in starting and hunting down a poor conceit as he affirms Shakespeare did? We will venture to assert, indeed, that this is a species of quibbling, which, barren and pitiful as it is, seems to give the critic himself so much delight, that he is 'content to purchase it, by the sacrifice of reason, propriety and truth.'

[5] Preface to *Shakespeare* edn, 1743, in *Eighteenth Century Essays on Shakespeare*, ed. D. Nichol Smith, 1903, 94.

Editor hath above advanced, is sufficient to invalidate this plea; or whether they will take the Editor's word for Shakespeare, rather than Shakespeare's word for himself.

In speaking of our poet's faults in tragedy, the Editor says, 'his performance seems constantly to be worse as his labour is more. The effusions of passion which exigence forces out, are for the most part striking and energetic; but whenever he solicits his invention, or strains his faculties, the offspring of his throes is *tumour, meanness, tediousness, and obscurity*.' And again—'His declamations or set-speeches are commonly cold and weak, for his power was the power of nature; when he endeavoured, like other tragic writers, to catch opportunities of amplification, and instead of inquiring what the occasion demanded, to show how much his stores of knowledge could supply, he seldom escapes without the *pity* or *resentment* of his reader.' It is a pity our Editor does not refer us to the particular passages, that justify these general assertions. For, admitting the truth of them, yet if it be very seldom, as we will venture to say it is, that Shakespeare appears reduced to the necessity of straining his faculties; if he be hardly ever endeavouring, like other tragic poets, at amplification, or to make an impertinent display of his knowledge, what shall we say to the candour of that commentator, who lays hold of a few defects, *ubi plura nitent*,[6] on which to found a general charge against his author? Were we disposed to be as harsh and severe on the learned Annotator, as the Annotator himself hath been on his GREAT, INIMITABLE Author, we might here appeal to the public, to decide which of them most demands our *pity* or merits our *resentment*.

He goes on.——'It is incident to Shakespeare to be now and then entangled with an unwieldy sentiment, which he cannot well express, and will not reject; he struggles with it a while, and if it continues stubborn, comprises it in such words as occur, and leaves it to be disintangled and evolved by those who have more leisure to bestow upon it.'

We know not whether this *incident* might not be called with more propriety a misfortune rather than a fault, and be imputed with greater justice to the then imperfect state of our language than to Shakespeare. But be this as it may; certain it is, that if our poet be sometimes entangled with his sentiments for want of words, our Editor is not seldom entangled with his, through a multiplicity of them; or, if he may understand his own meaning, it is not always the case with his reader, who, as he says of the poet, struggles with it for a while, and if it continues stubborn,

[6] Horace, *Ars Poetica*, l. 351 ('where more things shine').

leaves it comprised in the words that invelop it, to be disintangled and evolved by those who have more leisure to bestow upon it. It is possible that, in this, he may betray the want of patience, though we cannot admit that he betrays a want of judgment; being fully of opinion with our Editor, that where the language is intricate the thought is not always subtle, nor the image always great where the line is bulky. 'The equality of words to things,' as he justly observes, 'is very often neglected, and trivial sentiments and vulgar ideas disappoint the attention, to which they are recommended by sonorous epithets and swelling figures.'

Having thus endeavoured to prove the faults of Shakespeare 'sufficient to obscure and *overwhelm any other merit*,' our Editor attempts dexterously to change sides, and to stand up in his defence, against those who have accused him, of violating those laws, which have been instituted and established by the joint authority of poets and of critics; we mean, the unities of action, place and time.

'From the censure, which this irregularity may bring upon him,' says Dr. Johnson, 'I shall with due reverence to that learning which I must oppose, adventure to try how I can defend him.'

It happens, however, very unluckily for our Editor, that, in spite of that respect which he is so notoriously ready to pay to his opponents, he shews himself to be as indifferent a pleader *for* Shakespeare as he hath proved *against* him. Nay, we entertain some suspicion that the critical Reader will, on a due consideration of what is hereafter advanced, be apt to think Dr. Johnson too little acquainted with the nature and use of the drama, to engage successfully in a dispute of so much difficulty as that which relates to the breach or observation of the dramatic unities.

To begin with the first. If we except the historical plays of Shakespeare, where these unities are never looked for; in his other works our Editor says, he has well enough preserved the *unity of action*. 'He has not indeed,' continues he, 'an intrigue regularly perplexed and regularly unravelled; he does not endeavour to hide his design only to discover it, for this is seldom the order of real events, and Shakespeare is the poet of nature: but his plan has commonly what Aristotle requires, a beginning, a middle and an end; one event is concatenated with another, and the conclusion follows by an easy consequence.' All this, however, might be said of many simple histories, that make no pretences to unity of action. Their merely having a beginning, middle, and end, is not sufficient. Aristotle's meaning is more distinctly explained by Bossu, thus: 'The causes and design of any action constitute the beginning of it: the effect of such causes, and the difficulties attending the execution of such design, are the middle of it; and the unravelling or obviating these difficulties are the end of it.'[7] It is not our business here to contend, whether Shakespeare be, or be not, defensible in this particular; it is enough for us to enquire how far our Editor hath actually defended him. Laying authorities however aside, we cannot, on the principles of commonsense, conceive, how any dramatic Writer can be justly said to have preserved the unity of action, who hath confessedly shewn no regard to those of time and place; with which we apprehend it to be very strictly connected. Certain at least it is, that, if any considerable time should elapse between, or space divide, the two parts of an action, we should be more apt to consider them as two distinct and different actions, than as united parts of one and the same action. This will be made more evident by our enquiry into the nature of these unities, and their essentiality to the drama. Before we enter on this point, however, we shall make some remarks on the supposed necessity, on which, Dr. Johnson conceives, the observation of these unities is founded. To enable the Reader fully to comprehend the subject in dispute, we shall quote the whole of what our Editor hath advanced on this curious topic; which we are the more readily led to do, on account of his own suggestion, that it is 'not dogmatically but deliberatively, written; and may recall the principles of the drama to a new examination.'

[quotes 'The necessity of observing the unities' to 'see their imitation'.]

Plausible as these arguments may at first sight appear, we will venture to say there is hardly one of them that does not seem false, or foreign to the purpose. We apprehend that the assumption, on which our Editor proceeds, is not true. The observation of these unities may be necessary without requiring the dramatic fable in its *materiality* (as this writer terms it) to be either credited or credible. It is not requisite, in order to justify the necessity of such observation, that the Spectator should *really imagine* himself one hour in Alexandria and the next at Rome; or that he should actually *believe* the transactions of months and years to pass in a few hours. The dramatic unities if necessary, are necessary to support the *apparent probability*, not the *actual credibility* of the drama. Our learned Editor may not probably distinguish the difference; but Cicero will tell him *nihil est tam* INCREDIBILE, *quod non dicendo fiat* PROBABILE:[8] and if such be the power of oratory, can we

---

[7] *Monsieur Bossu's Treatise of the Epick Poem*, trans. by 'W.J.', 2nd edn, 1719, i. 183–4.

[8] *Paradoxa Stoicorum*, praef. 1 ('There is nothing so unbelievable as not to become probable by being told').

doubt that a similar effect is produced by theatrical representation? Now, it is the senses and the passions, and not the imagination and understanding, that are in both these cases immediately affected. We do not pretend to say that the spectators are not always in their senses; or that they do not know (if the question were put to them) that the stage is only a stage, and the players only players. But we will venture to say, they are often so intent on the scene, as to be absent with regard to every thing else. A spectator, properly affected by a dramatic representation, makes no reflections about the fiction or the reality of it, so long as the action proceeds without grossly offending, or palpably imposing on the senses. It is very true that a person, going to Drury-lane to see the Tragedy of *Venice Preserved*,[9] knows, when he places himself in the pit, that he is in the theatre at London, and not in Venice. But the curtain is no sooner drawn up than he begins to be interested in the business of the scene, the orchestra vanishes, and the views of St. Mark and the Rialto dispose him (not to think how *he* came *there* but) to see and hear what is to be *done* and *said* there. When his attention is fully engaged to the fable, and his passions affected by the distress of the characters, he is still farther removed from his own character and situation; and may be conceived *quatenus* a spectator, to be rather at Venice than at London. The image of Mr. Garrick, it is true, is painted on the retina of his eye, and the voice of Mrs. Cibber mechanically affects the tympanum of his ear: but it is as true also that he sees only the transports of Jaffier and listens only to the ravings of Belvidera. And yet there is no frenzy, no calenture in the case; the man may be as much in his senses as Horace, when he supposed the same deception might happen to himself, under the like influence of theatrical magic:

> Ille per extentum funem mihi posse videtur
> Ire poeta; meum qui pectus inaniter angit,
> Irritat, mulcet, falsis terroribus implet,
> Ut magus; et modo me Thebis, modo ponit Athenis.[10]

The spectator is unquestionably deceived; but the deception goes no farther than the passions, it affects our sensibility but not our understanding: and is by no means so powerful a delusion as to affect our *belief*. There is a species of probability, which is necessary to be adhered

---

9 By Thomas Otway, 1682. David Garrick and Mrs Cibber acted together in this play, as Jaffier and Belvidera respectively.

10 *Epistles*, II. i. 210–13 ('I think that poet is able to walk a tightrope, who with airy nothings wrings my heart, inflames, soothes, fills it with vain alarms like a magician, and sets me down now at Thebes, now at Athens').

to, even to engage the attention of the senses, and affect our passions; but this regards the *representation* and not the *materiality* of the fable. The *incredulus odi*,[11] of Horace, hath been cited with too great latitude of construction. It can hardly be supposed that the poet should stigmatize himself for incredulity, merely because he could not believe that Progne was metamorphosed into a bird, or Cadmus into a serpent. Or, supposing he might, why should he use the verb *odi?* Why should he *hate* or *detest* a thing merely because he thought it incredible? It is natural indeed to hate whatever offends, or is shocking to, the senses. The truth is, these terms are directly applied to the *form,* or *representation,* and not to the materiality of the fable; as is evident on perusing the context. The whole passage runs thus;

> Aut agitur res in Scenis, aut acta refertur,
> Segnius irritant animos demissa per aurem,
> Quam quæ sunt oculis subjecta fidelibus, et quæ
> Ipse sibi tradit spectator. Non tamen intus
> Digna geri, promes in scenam: multaque tolles
> Ex oculis, quæ mox narret facundia præsens.
> Ne pueros *coram populo* Medea trucidet;
> Aut humana *palam* coquat exta nefarius Atreus;
> Aut in avem Progne vertatur, Cadmus in anguem.
> Quodcunque *ostendis* mihi *sic*, incredulus odi.[12]

We find no objection made to the credibility of these fables in themselves, (for on this the auditor may not give himself the trouble to bestow a single reflection) but to the unseemliness or improbability that must necessarily attend their representation on the stage: by which means the senses would be offended with a palpable absurdity, not the understanding be imposed on by a falsehood. For he allows that the very same things may be agreeably related which will not bear to be represented.—But to return to our Editor. That the judgment never mistook any dramatic representation we readily admit; but that our senses frequently do, is certain, from the effect it hath on our passions. Nay, Dr. Johnson himself, after all the pains he takes to prove the drama

---

[11] *Ars Poetica*, l. 188 ('I discredit and abhor').

[12] Ibid, ll. 179–88 ('Either an event is acted on the stage, or the action is narrated. Less vividly is the mind stirred by what finds entrance through the ears than by what is brought before the trusty eyes, and what the spectator can see for himself. Yet you will not bring upon the stage what should be performed behind the scenes, and you will keep much from our eyes which an actor's ready tongue will narrate anon in our presence; so that Medea is not to butcher her boys before the people, nor impious Atreus cook human flesh upon the stage, nor Procne be turned into a bird, Cadmus into a snake. Whatever you thus show me, I discredit and abhor.'

absolutely incredible, is reduced, for want of making this necessary distinction, to confess that it really *is credited*. 'It will be asked,' says he, 'how the drama moves, if it is not credited? It is credited with all the credit due to a drama.' The method he takes, to evade this evident contradiction, is, by adopting the sophistry of those philosophers, who strive to account for the emotions of pity, gratitude, generosity and all the nobler passions, from a retrospect to that of self-love. The drama is credited, says Dr. Johnson, 'whenever it moves, as a just picture of a real original; as representing to the auditor what he would himself feel, if he were to do or suffer what is there feigned to be suffered or to be done. The reflection that strikes the heart* is not, that the evils before us are real evils, but that they are evils to which we ourselves may be exposed.' Now nothing is more certain than that those spectators, who are most affected by dramatic representation are usually the least capable of making a comparison between the picture and the original. There are also few auditors that can put themselves in the place of the characters represented; and we believe still fewer who are moved because they reflect that they themselves are exposed to the evils represented on the stage. The audience are moved by mere mechanical motives; they laugh and cry from mere sympathy at what a moment's reflection would very often prevent them from laughing or crying at all. 'If there be any fallacy,' continues our Editor, 'it is not that we fancy the players, but that we fancy ourselves unhappy for a moment; but we rather lament the possibility than suppose the presence of misery, as a mother weeps over her babe, when she remembers † that death may take it from her. The delight of Tragedy proceeds from our consciousness of fiction; if we thought murders and treasons real they would please no more.' In reply to this, it may be safely affirmed, that we neither fancy the players nor ourselves unhappy: our imagination hath nothing to do with the immediate impressions whether of joy or sorrow; we are in this case merely passive, our organs are in unison with those of the players on the stage, and the convulsions of grief or laughter are purely involuntary.

* This language is not quite so correct as might be expected from a writer so capable of expressing himself philosophically. The heart is often affected without any appeal to the judgment; nor is it necessary, in order to work upon our sensibility, to address the understanding. This is more frequently and more easily done by addressing the passions immediately through the senses.

† Is this an accurate use of the verb *remember*? Can we be properly said to *remember* what is yet to come, or what may never come at all? The meaning is, that she *recollects* the precept or maxim which inculcates the probability of death's depriving her of her child: but this is imperfectly expressed. Indeed this preface is not, in general, written with that precision and accuracy of style, which distinguishes some other of this celebrated Author's writings.

As to the delight we experience from Tragedy, it no more proceeds directly from a consciousness of fiction, than the pleasure we reap from Comedy; but is the physical consequence of having the transient sense of pain or danger excited in us by sympathy, instead of actually and durably feeling it ourselves. Hence that diminution of pain, which gives rise to the pleasing sensation, to which the ingenious Author of the *Enquiry into the Origin of our Ideas of the Sublime and Beautiful*, gives the name of *delight*.[13] And hence it is that such persons, who are most affected with the distress of a Tragedy, are generally most delighted with its representation.

(discusses how actuality is related to drama, and the value of the unities.)

Dr. Johnson questions whether Shakespeare knew the unities and rejected them by design, or deviated from them by happy ignorance. It is impossible perhaps to determine this point; but we think it pretty clear, that, whether he learned the rules of the drama from the writings of the ancients or not, he was better versed in them than any of his successors that did. What should hinder Shakespeare from drinking knowledge at the fountain-head as well as the ancients? Must all knowledge be called *ignorance*, that is not obtained at second-hand, by means of books? It is proper for those, who cannot go alone, to be led by others; but Shakespeare was the fondling of Nature, and needed not the leading-strings of Aristotle. It does not follow, however, that the practice of the one, and the precepts of the other, are incompatible. It is by no means necessary that Nature's strong and vigorous offspring should be confined to that strict regularity of diet and regimen which is requisite to support the weak and puny nurslings of art. They both, however, pursue the same objects, and attain them nearly by the same means. Hence, though it should be true, that Shakespeare was

　　　　——above the critic's law,
And but from Nature's fountains scorn'd to draw,[14]

he might not deviate essentially from the general law of the Stagyrite, although he did not servilely adopt his particular rules. Indeed the point is almost universally given up with regard to the unity of *place*; the preservation of which gives rise to more improbabilities than the breach of it.—But to return to that of action. There is no doubt but

---

[13] Edmund Burke, *Philosophical Enquiry into . . . the Sublime and Beautiful*, 1757, ed. James T. Boulton, 1958, 35–7.
[14] Pope, *Essay on Criticism*, ll. 132–3.

Shakespeare hath taken many exceptionable liberties in this respect, for want of a due attention to the mechanical part of composition. And this he hath done in common with the first dramatic poets among the ancients*. Nor is he, in this particular, to be justified by any thing his Editor hath advanced: for the unity of action must not only be so far observed as to preserve the unity of character, but also so far as to preserve an apparent unity of design in the fable.

As to the unity of time, Dr. Johnson is also strangely mistaken, with regard to its essentiality in the drama. 'A play read (says he) affects the mind like a play acted. It is therefore evident that the action is not supposed to be real, and it follows, that between the acts a longer or shorter time may be allowed to pass, and that no more account of space or duration is to be taken by the auditor of a drama, than by the reader of a narrative, before whom may pass in an hour the life of a hero, or the revolutions of an empire.' Here again our Editor seems to betray a want of acquaintance with the conduct and effects of the drama.———It is very certain that a longer or shorter time may be allowed to pass between the acts, provided the union of character be preserved, and nothing intervene between the two parts of the action but the lapse of time; there is yet a wide difference between the auditor of a drama and the reader of a narrative. Few things can be represented in the same time they are related; so that it would be impossible to *represent* the whole life of an hero, or the revolutions of an empire, in the same time as the history of them might be read. It is indeed impossible for the action represented to seem to be longer than the actual time of representation; for, as we before observed, it is the senses, and not the imagination, that is immediately employed on the representation.

Dr. Johnson indeed says, that 'time is, of all modes of existence, most obsequious to the imagination; a lapse of years is as easily conceived as a passage of hours. In contemplation we easily contract the time of real actions, and therefore willingly permit it to be contracted when we only see their imitation.'

In this argument, however, as in almost all his other reasoning on the subject, the conclusion hath little to do with the premises. During the actual representation of an action, we are not *contemplating*, but *observing*; and it is impossible for us either to shorten or to prolong the time of such representation: but when it ceases, as at the end of an act, or even in shifting the scene, the attention of the senses being taken off, the imagination is at liberty to act during the interval; which, however

* See Aristotle's *Poetics*, Chap. VI.

177

short, is sufficient for the purpose. And hence we see that the frequent shifting of the scenes, though it may break in upon the restrictions of action and place, it affords an opportunity of preserving that of time, together with the first and grand rule of probability. It is pleasant enough to see how the French critics, who affect to abide by the strictest observance of the unities, perplex themselves to excuse Corneille for the multiplicity of incidents in the *Cid*; the hero of which fights two duels, marches against the enemy, returns, is brought to a solemn trial; fights again, and finds means to reconcile himself to his mistress, whose father he had slain; and all this in the space of four and twenty hours. Now, it is certain, that all these actions, if properly disposed in succession, and judiciously divided, might be so represented as never to break in upon dramatic probability.

The French, indeed, in support of the unity of place, maintain that the stage never should be empty during the act; in consequence of their observance of this rule, however, they are guilty of much greater absurdities than would arise from shifting the scene. It is mentioned, as an instance of consummate skill in Corneille, that he hath provided, in one of his plays, for keeping the stage full, while one of the characters goes to the field to fight, and returns conqueror. Now had this supposed combat passed during the interval between the acts, or even during the shifting of the scene, it had not transgressed the bounds of dramatic probability, because it then had passed during the interlude of the imagination; but the audience would not fail of perceiving the improbability of a combat's being fought while they had been listening to some twenty or thirty lines, spoken by the persons of the stage. The unity of time, is, indeed, so far essential to the drama, that the successive actions represented must be confined to the time of actual representation; although the intervals between them may be as long as the poet pleases, consistent with the preservation of the unity of character, and that of the design of the fable.

In respect to the unity of place; it appears more than probable, that the pretended necessity of it originally arose from the imperfect state of the ancient theatres, as it is plain that the French poets have absurdly involved themselves in the most ridiculous perplexities by adopting it to an unnecessary degree. There can be no doubt, however, that it is so far essential to the drama, as it is necessary to preserve the unity of action: for as the interval of time may in some cases be so great as to vary the personality, or destroy the unity of character, so the transition of place may be so great as to destroy the unity of the action. We should not be more vehement, indeed, than Dr. Johnson, in reproaching a poet who should make his first act pass in Venice, and his next in Cyprus, provided they were both so nearly related as when Shakespeare wrote his *Othello*; but we should have no great opinion of the dramatic conduct of a piece, the first scene of which should be laid in England, and the last in China· In any other respect, however, it is certain that the unity of place is unnecessary to the modern drama, as the attention of the spectator is always diverted from the action of the piece, and the imagination is at liberty during the change of the scene.—It appears, on the whole, that the unities are essential to the drama, though not in that degree as hath been asserted by the critics; so that the result of Dr. Johnson's enquiries concerning them, is as erroneous as his supposition of the necessity on which they were founded.

[quotes Johnson's remarks on Shakespeare's general characteristics, and on previous editors.]

Our Editor proceeds next to give an account of what he hath done, or attempted to do himself, and to apologize for what he hath not done, or confessedly found himself unable to do. We cannot help being somewhat apprehensive, however, that the readers of this part of Dr. Johnson's preface, will be apt to think he hath, in more places than one, betrayed a consciousness of the want of application in his pretended endeavours, as well as of the ill success attending them. There runs, indeed, through the whole of this preface, such a mixed and inconsistent vein of praise and censure respecting others; and of boasting and excuse regarding himself, that we think we discover it to be the production of a wavering pen, directed by a hand equally wearied and disgusted with a task, injudiciously undertaken, and as indolently pursued. We shall take our leave of it therefore with one more quotation, which may serve farther to confirm what is here advanced:

[quotes 'Perhaps I may not be more censured' to 'I have said no more'.]

As to the work itself; the present Editor hath prefixed the several prefaces of Pope, Theobald, Hanmer and Warburton, as also the dedication and preface of Heminge and Condell, and Shakespeare's life by Mr. Rowe. Of Mr. Pope's notes the Editor hath retained the whole; in order, as he says, that no fragment of so great a writer may be lost. With Dr. Johnson's leave, however, as Mr. Pope's attempts on Shakespeare do so little honour to his memory, a future editor who affected to revere that memory ought to have suppressed them; at least those of them which were the most exceptionable.—Of Theobald's notes, the *weak, ignorant, mean, faithless, petulant, ostentatious* Theobald, the present Editor hath generally retained those which he retained *himself* in his second edition; and these, we must acquaint our Readers, are not a few nor unimportant.—Of Sir Thomas Hanmer's notes, Dr. Johnson professes, and we find no reason to disbelieve him, that he hath inserted them all.—To Dr. Warburton he is still more obliged than to any of the preceeding commentators, at least in point of quantity.— To the author of the *Canons of Criticism* he is also equally obliged in point of quality; but we know not to what cause we must impute it, that the Editor is so extremely sparing of confessing his obligations, from this quarter.

As to the Editor's own notes, it possibly will not be expected they should be so numerous, or so important, as those he had an opportunity of borrowing from his predecessors: the Reader will meet with some of them, however, here and there interspersed among the rest, and like the rest, *bona quædam, mala, mediocra*. If the Reader should complain that these are too few and insignificant, we can only impute their paucity and want of importance to a notion entertained by the Editor (the most unfortunate sure that ever entered into the head of a commentator!) that the Reader is more, and better pleased with what he finds out himself, than with what the most sagacious scholiast can point out to him. But this plea, if admitted, would of course be urged too far, and even supersede the task of any commentator at all. Indeed Dr. Johnson seems full as little solicitous about the success of his annotations, as he could possibly be about the composing them; it is to be wished, however, for the sake of his own reputation, that he had always treated the poet with the same candour as he *professes* to have observed toward his brother commentators.

31. William Kenrick, *Review of Johnson's Shakespeare*

November 1765

Extracts from the *Review*, 1765, iv–v, x–xvi, 82–90.

The full title of this book-length attack is: *A Review of Doctor Johnson's New Edition of Shakespeare, in which the ignorance, or inattention of that editor is exposed, and the poet defended from the persecution of his commentators.* Kenrick's strictures were confined to the first three volumes of the edition; more were promised on the other five; they never appeared. See Introduction, pp. 5, 26–7.

. . . the intent and design . . . is plainly what is set forth in the title, viz. to defend the text of Shakespeare from the *persecution* of his commentators.

The Reviewer is well aware that Dr. Johnson's self-sufficiency may suggest a more sinister view. For, he doubts not, that gentleman *thinks* of himself, what he has *said* of Dr. Warburton, that he has 'a name sufficient to confer celebrity on those who can exalt themselves into antagonists;'[1] and hence he may possibly impute the present work to the motive which he insinuates to have actuated the opponents of that writer. The allusion, also, of the eagle and owl, which he quotes from *Macbeth*, may, with a very little latitude of construction, be applied as well to himself and the Reviewer, as to Dr. Warburton and his antagonist.

> An Eagle, tow'ring in his pride of place,
> Was, by a mousing owl, hawk'd at and kill'd.[2]

For tho', Dr. Johnson having neither preferment in the church, nor post in the state, the word *place* may seem to want that strict propriety the critics require; yet, if we reflect how nearly *places* and *pensions* are allied,

[1] Preface; see *Shakespeare*, 99–100.
[2] Ibid., 100.

there is not one of Shakespeare's commentators who would make any scruple of substituting one word for the other, reciprocally, and alternately, as he thought the case might require. There is no doubt also that, on this occasion, the word pension would be preferred; as a pension must be universally allowed, *cæteris paribus*, to be better than a place, to a man so fond of doing but little; as it is apprehended the reader will think is the case with Dr. Johnson. . . .

The republic of letters is a perfect democracy, where, all being equal, there is no respect of persons, but every one hath a right to speak the truth of another, to censure without fear, and to commend without favour or affection. Nor is the *literary* community of less dignity than the *political*. Popularity and influence, indeed, may be obtained, for a while, by sinister means in both; but though birth and wealth may confer eminence and power in the one, not the descent of an Alexander, nor the riches of Crœsus, confer prerogative or authority in the other.

In the primitive state of society, a superiority of intellectual abilities was the foundation of all civil pre-eminence; and hence the sceptre continued to be swayed by superior wisdom through a succession of ages. The acquisitions of science and learning were held among the ancients, in no less esteem than those of conquest, and in as much greater than the possessions of royalty, as a chaplet of laurel was preferred to a coronet of mere gems and gold. Xenophon reaped more honour from his *Cyropædia*, than from the famous retreat of the ten thousand; and Cæsar still more from his commentary, than from all the military exploits recorded in it. As to the examples of modern times; to say nothing of James and Christina, lest it be objected that one was a weak man, and the other a foolish woman, we have seen the kings of Prussia and of Poland, the Alexander and the Nestor of our age, ambitious to become authors, and be made denizons of our little state. Frederick hath been more than once heard to say, he would give his crown, and Stanislaus, if he had not lost it, would have given another, to possess the scientific fame of Leibnitz, or the literary reputation of Voltaire.

Is it, by the way, then, to be wondered at, that a private individual, like Samuel Johnson, should be even preposterously elated at finding that homage paid to him, which has been in vain solicited by sovereigns, and is refused even to the King on his throne? Graduated by universities, pensioned by his prince, and surrounded by pedagogues and poetasters, he finds a grateful odour in the incense of adulation; while admiring booksellers stand at a distance, and look up to him with awful reverence, bowing the knee to Baal, and holding in fearful remembrance the exemplary fate of Tom Osborne; presumptuous Tom Osborne! who, braving the vengeance of this paper-crowned idol, was, for his temerity, transfixed to his mother-earth by a thundering folio![3] It may be a pity to disturb Dr. Johnson from so pleasing a reverie, and to dissipate so agreeable a scene of delusion; he will exclaim doubtless, with the honest citizen of Argos.

> Pol me occidistis——
> ————— cui sic extorta voluptas,
> Et demptus per vim mentis gratissimus error.[4]

But, if the interests of our literary state require it, it cannot be doubted that the mere gratification of an individual ought to be given up for the good of the whole community.

But to proceed to the *third* and last head of our discourse: the object of which is the effects or consequences of the following Review. These, like the subject of our preface, may be divided also into three parts. In the *first* place, it is presumed the injuries done to the name of Shakespeare will be in a great measure repaired, and the lustre of his tarnished honour restored. In the *second*, it is feared Dr. Johnson will suffer not a little in his literary reputation; and in the *last*, it may be suspected, that the proprietors will be injured in the sale of the work.

In regard to the *first*; the pleasure, which it is presumed every true Englishman will feel, at the attempt to do justice to his favourite poet, will sufficiently exculpate the author, had it been necessary to practise a still greater severity in effecting it.

With respect to the *second*, it may not be improper for the writer to offer something in his justification.

[argues that critics should not hesitate to expose 'unworthy' writers 'for fear of depriving an impostor of the reputation on which he plumes himself'.]

As to the last point, viz. the interest of the proprietors; the Reviewer thinks it very problematical whether this will be affected either way. He hath indeed known books sometimes sell the better for being publicly censured: but, be this as it may, he can truly aver that he meant them no harm; for, though it is possible that one or other of them may have sometimes failed a little in that respect to the writer, which he thinks an author has a right to expect of his bookseller, and his bookseller, if he is

[3] See Boswell, *Life*, i. 154.
[4] Horace, *Epistles*, II. ii. 138–40 ('Truly you have killed me . . . for thus you have robbed me of a pleasure and forcibly taken away the dearest illusion of my heart').

wise, will be ready to pay him, yet he does not harbour so much resentment against any of them, as to wish to hurt their interest. If unluckily it should turn out, however, that the sale of Dr. Johnson's edition of Shakespeare should be hence obstructed, and that it should only *hobble*, instead of taking a *run*; the proprietors have nothing to do, but to engage the Reviewer, if they can, or some body else, to furnish them with a better edition. Nor will this be a difficult task, although it would be an arduous and noble one, to give the public such a commentary as the writings of this incomparable Bard deserve.

To detain the reader but a moment longer.—Dr. Johnson, having acted, in the outrage he hath committed on Shakespeare, just like other sinners, not only by doing those things he ought not to have done, but by leaving undone those things he ought to have done; his sins of omission are not less important, though much more numerous, than those of commission. Indeed, nothing is more usual with commentators in general, than to display their own sagacity on obvious passages, and to leave the difficult ones to be explained by the sagacity of their readers★. The Reviewer, however, cannot be supposed here to have given a compleat commentary himself; indeed he hath been able only to include in the following sheets some few remarks on the most glaring blunders and defects that occur in this new edition; of which such wonderful things were promised and expected; and to which, having seen the prophecy fulfilled, we may apply, with as much justice as ever it was applied to any thing, that well-known quotation from Horace.

> Quid dignum tanto feret hic promissor hiatu?
> Parturiunt montes: nascetur ridiculus mus![5]

[Four examples are given here to illustrate Kenrick's commentary on Johnson's alleged 'blunders and defects': the observations on Johnson's notes to *Love's Labour's Lost*, IV, iii, 25; IV, iii, 161; V, ii, 884; and *Winter's Tale*, IV, iv, 21.]

Vol. II. Page 165.

KING. So sweet a kiss the golden sun gives not
　　　To those fresh morning drops upon the rose,
　　　As thy eye-beams, when their fresh rays have smote
　　　The night of dew, that on my cheeks down flows.

★ Dr. Johnson, indeed, says, in his Preface: 'Not a single passage in the whole work has appeared to me corrupt, which I have not attempted to restore; or obscure, which I have not endeavoured to illustrate.' How he hath succeeded in these attempts, the reader is left to judge for himself on perusal of the following sheets.

---

5 Horace, *Ars Poetica*, ll. 138-9 ('What will this braggart produce in keeping with such boasts? Mountains will labour, a mouse causing laughter will be born').

On this passage Dr. Johnson hath the following note.

The night of dew, that on my cheeks down flows.] I cannot think the *night of dew* the true reading, but know not what to offer.

That is very strange! Dr. Johnson.—Why, thou must have no more invention in thee than there is in a leaden plummet: thy pegasus must be confined and hoodwinked like a horse in a mill; or surely something would have suggested itself to a writer who declares, that 'not a single passage, in this whole work, has appeared to him corrupt, which he has not attempted to restore!'*—I would be far from seeking to depreciate the success of our editor's *modest industry*: but I am afraid the purchasers of his book will be apt to think, from many such slovenly notes as this, that both his *industry* and *modesty* are pretty well matched. It is evident, from the context, that the king, being over head and ears in love, employs himself, as people usually do in that situation,

> Wasting the live-long hours away,
> In tears by night, and sighs by day.

What objection then could our editor have to substituting *nightly dew*, instead of *night of dew*. If we are not absolutely certain the poet wrote so, there is a moral presumption, a great probability, of it: but whether he did or not, the alteration is certainly an amendment, and a very harmless one. It would also have served a little to save the credit of the editor; who, whatever might be his intentions before he begun his work, sufficiently shews, by the work itself, that he regarded not what he had promised when he did it; and, by his Preface, that he knew as little what he *had done* when it was finished.

Vol. II. Page 170.

BIRON. O me, with what strict patience have I sat
   To see a king transformed to a knot!

Here, indeed! we see our editor *attempting* to restore a passage, which appears to him corrupt.—Mark the success!—

To see a king transformed to a knot!] *Knot* has no sense that can suit this place. We may read *sot*. The rhymes in this play are such as that *sat* and *sot* may be well enough admitted.

What! have you lost your *hearing* and *judgment* too, Mr. Editor, as well as your *memory* and *invention?*—Do you not know that even *sot*

* See Dr. Johnson's Preface [*Shakespeare*, 110].

185

and *sot* cannot be admitted into any verse as English rhymes; and do you think the matter mended with *sot* and *sat*?

Besides, do you see no impropriety in Biron's calling the King, to his face, a blockhead or fool, because truly he was in love; especially when he is conscious he is himself in the same situation? Add to this, that so gross an expression is totally inconsistent with the fine strain of raillery that runs through the whole of his speech. This attempt, therefore, of our editor at *restoration*, is evidently a very unlucky one, and is excusable only as the unsuccessful endeavour of *modest industry*.

But why doth Dr. Johnson conclude this passage to be corrupted? If he thinks the rhymes *sot* and *sat* admissible, surely he can have no objection to our pronouncing *sat* after the broad orthoëpy of the vulgar; in which case it would be a much less exceptionable rhyme to *knot* than what he is willing to admit.—But he says, 'knot hath no sense that can suit this place.' He might have found, however, by turning to almost any dictionary, excepting his own, that a *knot* is a small bird, well known in many parts of England, and is called *avis Canuti* by the naturalists; as it is said, because king Canutus was very fond of such birds. It is, indeed, a delicious kind of water-fowl. Now, as Biron hath said but just before, speaking of the King,

> Shot, by heav'n! proceed, sweet Cupid; thou has thumpt
> him with thy *bird-bolt* under the left pap;

I cannot, for my part, see any objection to his comparing him in this passage to a wounded *knot*. If my readers do, I have done. They will do me the justice, however, to own, that, if I am not possessed of Dr. Johnson's *ingenuity* and *modesty*, I shew at least as much *industry* in defending the text of Shakespeare, as he does in pulling it to pieces.

Vol. II. Page 222.

SONG.

When daizies pied and violets blue,
And lady-smocks all silver white;
And cuckow-buds of yellow hue,
Do paint the meadows with delight.

Dr. Warburton says, we should read *much-bedight*, which is very proper and elegant.—The present editor quotes Dr. Warburton's note; to which he adds the following short animadversion.

Much less elegant than the present reading.

Undoubtedly it is: and I have here only to ask Dr. Johnson, why he excludes the notes of Theobald, when they have been sufficiently exploded by other writers; and yet pesters his readers with those of Dr. Warburton, which stand exactly in the same predicament?

The ingenious author of the *Canons of Criticism* objected, long ago, to this proposed emendation of Dr. Warburton's; judiciously observing, that if *bedight* means *bedecked* or *adorned*, the meadows being *bedight* already, they little need painting.—But Dr. Johnson seems to be so much influenced by the *respect due to high place*, that he seems determined to avoid the name of Edwards, as much as possible, for fear of offending the bishop.

Vol. II. Page 298.

PERDITA. ————— even now I tremble
To think your father, by some accident,
Should pass this way, as you did: Oh, the fates!
How would he look, to see his work, so noble,
Vilely bound up!

Here Dr. Johnson hath found Shakespeare tripping again.—Hear what he says.

His work so noble, &c.] It is impossible for any man to rid his mind of his profession. The authorship of Shakespeare has supplied him with a metaphor, which, rather than he would lose it, he has put, with no great propriety, into the mouth of a country maid. Thinking of his own works, his mind passed naturally to the binder. I am glad he has no hint at an editor.

We have here also, another aukward attempt of our editor at wit and pleasantry. But, why wilt thou, Dr. Johnson, persist thus in playing at bob-cherry, when the prize hangeth so high above thine head, and such a weight of lead is incumbent on thy heels? I have already advised thee, in the fullness of my heart, and, as Cicero says, non otii abundantiâ, sed amoris erga te,[6] not to be so forward to display thy wit. I told thee before, and I tell thee again, thou hast it not in thee, being as unable to divert the reader with thy pleasantry, as to convince him of Shakespeare's impropriety.—Again, why, Dr. Johnson, art thou glad that Shakespeare hath no hint at an editor? Dost thou think he would have thrown out any censures that might reach *thee?*—No—that incomparable bard was, as thou sayest, the poet of nature, and drew his characters from the life: and nature had not produced in that age so arrogant, and at the same

[6] *Epistulae ad Familiares*, vii. 1 ('not that I have nothing better to do, but I have plenty of affection for you').

time so dull an animal, as the present commentator on Shakespeare. There were pedants and pedagogues, it is true, in his day; he has depicted an Holofernes and a Sir Hugh Evans. But these were slight excrescences, mushrooms, champignons, that perished as the smoke of the dunghill evaporated, which reared them. A modern editor of Shakespeare is, on the contrary, a fungus attached to an oak; a male agaric of the most astringent kind, that, while it disfigures its form, may last for ages to disgrace the parent of its being.

But, to lay aside metaphor; not Burgerdischius, Gronovius, nor any one of the whole tribe of Dutch commentators, from the first of them to the last, hath proceeded through his author with more phlegm and frigidity, than Dr. Johnson hath gone through Shakespeare*. It is hard to say, indeed, who is the dullest scholiast of the dullest writer of antiquity. But Dr. Johnson has the singular honour of being the dullest annotator on the brightest of all those who have succeeded the revival of letters.

* And here lies the difference between Dr. Warburton and Dr. Johnson, whose commentaries I place both on a footing with regard to their utility, as they are themselves pretty equal with respect to that arrogance with which they have treated the public, the living patrons of Shakespeare. In the commentary of Dr. Warburton, however, we have all the fire and spirit of a restif imagination, bridled in by as perverse an understanding: whereas, in that of Dr. Johnson, we see but too plainly the waywardness of senescence struggling with the weakness of puerility.

It may be thought strange that I should treat Dr. Johnson's pretensions to wit so contemptuously, when it is notorious that his bons-mots have been constantly repeated for these ten years past in taverns and in coffeehouses, at dinners, and over tea-tables, to the great gratification of his admirers, and the edification of their hearers. Nay, it is well known, that a certain literary projector, excited by the success of BEN *Johnson's* jests, had schemed the publication of the *Johnsoniana*, under the name of our editor, intending to insert on his title page, instead of *O rare* BEN! *O brave* SAM!—But I know not how, yet so it happened, that, upon enquiry, the projector could not muster up above a dozen *genuine* jokes worth printing. It was found that most of the wise sayings, smart repartees, pregnant puns, and cramp conundrums, imputed to him, had been forged or invented for him by his friends and acquaintance.

32. James Barclay, *Examination of Mr. Kenrick's Review*

1766

Extracts from *Examination*, 1766, iii–viii, 57.

'A young student of Oxford, of the name of Barclay, wrote an answer to Kenrick's review of Johnson's Shakespeare. Johnson was at first angry that Kenrick's attack should have the credit of an answer. But afterwards, considering the young man's good intention, he kindly noticed him, and probably would have done more, had not the young man died' (Boswell, *Life*, i. 498). Johnson's champion, aged nineteen, was an undergraduate of Balliol. See Introduction, p. 27.

Literary reputation, says a certain elegant moralist, is bestowed by the joint applauses of the generality, and destroyed by the malignity of individuals. Forbidding as this opinion may be to every eager candidate for literary fame, yet I am afraid the late attack upon Mr. Johnson's character will in some measure verify the observation.

Indeed a charge urged with such confidence, and backed with such delusive sophistry, can scarce fail of hurting him with the ignorant and unwary; with the learned and ingenious, his reputation must for ever remain unshaken.——The reader, I suppose, is ready to anticipate me in my declaration concerning the design of the following Examination. He will easily conclude, that to rescue injured merit from the hands of presuming arrogance, is the sole end of the performance before him.

Before I proceed, I must observe, that the parties attacking and attacked are equally unknown to me, and that I sat down to examine the extraordinary claims of the former, divested of any predilection for the one or prejudice against the other.

Upon the publication of Mr. Johnson's *Shakespeare*, the expectations of the generality, it must be owned, were greatly disappointed: They had been induced to expect from his avowed learning and ingenuity, a compleat commentary upon the works of their immortal bard; but through the concurring circumstances of inattention in the Editor, and sanguine expectation in the reader, the performance, I am afraid, has incurred the public censure.

This being a true state of the case, the injured party has certainly a right to complain, and an open declaration of the general sense would not have been unjust: But let me add, the manner in which it is conveyed to Mr. Johnson is UNJUST AND UNWARRANTABLE.

A deference is certainly due to established fame, and decorum to those members of the community who have been honoured with the public approbation: IT IS A DOWNRIGHT AFFRONT TO NATIONAL AP-PROBATION, TO STIGMATISE THAT MAN WITH IGNORANCE, WHO HAS BEEN SELECTED FROM THE COLLECTIVE LEARNED AS PECULIARLY DESERVING THEIR FAVOURS.

Little, I believe, did any person *wish* to see Mr. Johnson treated with irreverence, or attacked with malevolence, and still less *think* to see him represented as a self-sufficient literary impostor. Will posterity believe that an *obscure* man has dared to do this, and prefix his name to the libel? that he has dared to give the lie to the applause of domestic seminaries and foreign academies? Such an attempt, I hope, needs no comment with the friends of candour and merit. Would that Mr. Johnson were to stand or fall by their determination! But human wishes are not to transgress the bounds of moral probability; and as the prejudiced, ignorant, and unwary, arrogate the liberty of decision equally with the qualified judge, an analysis of the Reviewer's offences against criticism and decency is altogether necessary.

I suppose I need not remind the reader that W. Kenrick proposed in his advertisements, to detect the IGNORANCE AND INDOLENCE of the late Editor, intending, as it is natural to conclude, to give the reader a sample of his abusive powers. What could not the public expect from a writer, who in the most summary manner informed them of that which a common genius would at least take a volume to demonstrate, *viz.* Mr. Johnson's IGNORANCE? As much struck must they have been at his ingenuity, who could convert an advertisement into a VIRULENT LIBEL.

It was a natural question in every reader of such prefatory abuse, Who is this W. Kenrick? What works have proceeded from his pen sufficient to countenance this unaccountable charge? To these inter-rogatories, few, very few, could make a satisfactory answer, and the world was apt to conclude, THAT A MAN WHOM NO BODY KNEW, HAD ATTACKED A MAN WHOM EVERY BODY KNEW.

To obviate these mortifying questions, while the Review was in the press, the friends of Mr. Kenrick gave out that he was a *prime hand* in the *Monthly Review*, and consequently a man of profound erudition and extensive abilities: The consequence some may say does not flow from the premises; but in spite of such infidels, the argument was admitted by the many as conclusive, and W. Kenrick revered accordingly.

In the space between the advertisement and publication, the friends of Mr. Johnson suspended their judgments; and though they thought it *passing strange* that his learning and ingenuity should pass muster with Oxford, and Dublin, at home, and the academy Del Crusca abroad, and at last be insinuated as fictitious by W. Kenrick; yet reasoned they, This discovery may have been reserved for him alone, and it is unreasonable to suppose he would dogmatize in the public prints in so uncommon a manner, without great foundation for his positiveness.

At length the performance appears, with the extraneous recommendations of a fine type, white paper, and the internal advantages of petulant raillery. Instead of convincing argument, it fobs us off with unmeaning sophistry; and instead of its demonstrating the author to be a critical writer, it betrays him to be the uninteresting RETAILER of trite silly ABUSIVE ANECDOTES.

It is indeed a matter of great surprise to every liberal reader, to find such a vast profusion of LITERARY DIRT spattered over the face of the Reviewer's performance: Does Mr. Kenrick imagine a few errors of judgment can authorise the vile epithets and personal abuse with which he urges his claim? No, surely! Common decency and the general voice discountenance such proceedings.

But upon what foundation is this general charge of ignorance supported? Upon the result of a mature examination of Mr. Johnson's *collective works?* By no means; for in them the critic and the scholar every where plead in his favour, and, if I may use such an argument *coram Aristarcho nostro*,[1] the christian and moralist.

Mr. Kenrick, it seems, was sensible of the impropriety of such an important charge proceeding from one with whom the public has not had any acquaintance in the literary walk: To obviate this, he kindly informs us, the world is obliged to him for the EPISTLES TO LORENZO, which no body reads; and a translation of the infidel Rousseau's *Emilius*, which no body ought to read.[2]

Any man, unhackney'd in the ways of writers, would be led to

---

[1] 'Before our Aristarchus' (the famous Alexandrian critic).
[2] *Epistles to Lorenzo*, published 1756; the Rousseau translation in 1762.

imagine, from the general good reception with which they are received, that scurrility and paradox are necessary ingredients in every composition, as most likely to introduce the Author to publick notice. To lead the reader through the inextricable mazes of a paradox, till you bring him to an unexpected meaning, like a Chinese Hah! hah! is now become fashionable. To be esteemed ingenious, we must lay down a proposition, the palpable absurdity of which stares every body in the face, and then, —do what? Assault common sense (that obstinate enemy of such heterodox opinions,) with a storm of logic and a peal of syllogisms. But where is your application, sneers Mr. Kenrick?—My application? Why, you have given into this fashion with a witness; and that your pamphlet might go down the glibber, made it one continued PARA-DOXICAL LIBEL. After all, perhaps, some excuse may be urged in extenuation of 'the heresies of paradox.' They contribute to set off the writer's ingenuity in the eye of the reader, but even this can by no means be predicated of scurrility, for IT IS A RECEIVED AXIOMATICAL TRUTH, THAT DULNESS AND ABUSE SELDOM MAKE THEIR APPEARANCE BUT IN THE ABSENCE OF REASON AND ARGU-MENTATION. Such is the frailty of human nature, that when *we are hard put to it* for fair disputation, we cannot for the life of us keep clear from the stink-pots of Billingsgate; imitating in this respect, the ignorant and unequal boxer, who, when he cannot cope with his adversary by mere honest bruising, flies for assistance to dirt and other offensive weapons.

Many are the conjectures of the public concerning the reasons for such ungentleman-like treatment used by the Reviewer towards Dr. Warburton and Mr. Johnson. He himself declares in his preface, he has never been disobliged by either of these gentlemen. Shall I hazard a conjecture, gentle reader, and endeavour to account for such behaviour? Here it is.

Mr. Johnson, it is well known, joins to the COMPLEAT SCHOLAR, yes, the compleat scholar, Mr. Kenrick, the BELIEVING CHRISTIAN. It is well known by those who are acquainted with the creed of the Reviewer, that to the RAILING author he joins the UNBELIEVING CAVILLER*. Here then the difficulty vanishes. The Reviewer thinks it

* This supposition is not founded upon hearsay, but a perusal of Mr. Kenrick's various performances. His *Epistles to Lorenzo* proceed upon deistical principles, and those of the blackest, most detestable nature,—UNIVERSAL SCEPTICISM; for if I mistake not, he proposes raising an altar to The unknown God—A kindred mode of thinking led him to the translation of Rousseau's *Emilius*, a book pregnant with the most blasphemous notions. And in the *Review* before me, he makes such a jest of the language of inspiration, as to apply it to a ludicrous occasion! Judge, then, reader, if the charge above is ill founded.

strange, any man *above* the degree of a natural, should be found on the side of CHRISTIANITY; and as it is not likely Mr. Johnson should, on the instance of Mr. Kenrick, or Lorenzo's friend, subscribe to the infidel's articles of faith, he wants to reduce him to the degree of a natural: This we know is not very uncommon with *gentlemen of Mr. Kenrick's kidney*, as may be proved from the treatment the bishop of Gloucester, and his dead friend Pope, received from the hands of the abusive, the infidel Bolingbroke.[3]

The Reviewer's first attack being levelled against the two greatest supporters our religion can boast, may we not reasonably expect in a short time, a farther attempt upon other CHURCH CHAMPIONS, until at length he prove, THAT AS ALL CHRISTIANS ARE FOOLS, SO, NONE BUT A FOOL WOULD BE A CHRISTIAN?

[Barclay provides a page-by-page commentary on Kenrick's *Review*. His retort to Kenrick's remarks on Johnson's note on *Love's Labour's Lost*, IV, iii, 161 (No. 31) will serve as an example.]

Mr. Johnson owns himself at a loss for the meaning of *Knot*; and his opponent, through his sleep, tells him, 'The Poet meant a *bird* called a *Knot*, alias *Avis Canuti*.' Mr. Kenrick! awake, Mr. Kenrick. Rub your eyes and look about you. You should never sit down to criticise when you are sleepy, man; you see, what comes of it—Incoherent raving—When you are broad awake, I shall ask you, Why of all the species of birds must a *water-fowl*, and of these the *Knot*, be picked out for the King to be changed into? Indeed, Sir, you must shake off this drowsiness: I have perceived it to be creeping upon you this long time, but here we catch you *napping* indeed! Downright sleepy talk; I wish it may not grow into a lethargy before you doze through the eight volumes of Mr. Johnson's *Shakespeare*. But now you are pretty well awake, let me ask you, how you came to dream of the *Knot*? Belike you sat down to write with a belly full of them: I cannot account any other way for such an expected meaning for the word—Let us however endeavour to come at the real signification, fresh and fasting.

[3] In Bolingbroke's *Familiar Letter to the most Impudent Man Living*, 1749.

33. Voltaire, 'Art Dramatique', in *Questions sur l'Encyclopédie*

1770

Translated from *Oeuvres*, Paris, 1878, xvii. 397.

Voltaire is classed with Dennis and Rymer in Johnson's Preface; their objections to Shakespeare's portrayal of Romans and kings are dismissed: 'These are the petty cavils of petty minds.' Boswell remarks: 'Voltaire, in revenge, made an attack on Johnson ... I pressed him to answer. He said, he perhaps might; but he never did' (*Life*, i. 498–9).

I cast my eyes over an edition of Shakespeare produced by Mr. Samuel Johnson. I found that he describes as 'petty minds' those foreigners who are astonished to find in plays by the great Shakespeare that 'a Roman senator should play the buffoon and a king should appear drunk on the stage'.[1] Far be it from me to suspect that Mr. Johnson is given to clumsy jokes or is over-addicted to wine; but I find it rather extraordinary that he should include buffoonery and drunkenness among the beauties of the tragic theatre; the reason he gives for doing so is not less remarkable. 'The poet', he says, 'overlooks the casual distinction of condition and country, as a painter who, satisfied with having painted the figure, neglects the drapery.' The comparison would have been more accurate if he had been speaking of a painter who introduced ridiculous clowns into a noble subject, or portrayed Alexander the Great mounted on an ass at the battle of Arbela and the wife of Darius drinking with the rabble in a common tavern.

[1] *Shakespeare*, 65–6.

34. Schlegel, *Lectures on Dramatic Art and Literature*

1808

Translated by John Black (Bohn edition, 1846), 360–1, 365.

The German translator of Shakespeare and Romantic critic, August Wilhelm von Schlegel (1767–1845), proposed in his lectures to rescue Shakespeare from what he regarded as the misguided criticism of English, mainly eighteenth-century, writers. Johnson was numbered amongst them. See Introduction, pp. 8, 27.

The English critics are unanimous in their praise of the truth and uniform consistency of [Shakespeare's] characters, of his heart-rending pathos, and his comic wit. Moreover, they extol the beauty and sublimity of his separate descriptions, images, and expressions. This last is the most superficial and cheap mode of criticising works of art. Johnson compares him who should endeavour to recommend this poet by passages unconnectedly torn from his works, to the pedant in Hierocles, who exhibited a brick as a sample of his house.[1] And yet how little, and how very unsatisfactorily does he himself speak of the pieces considered as a whole! Let any man, for instance, bring together the short characters which he gives at the close of each play, and see if the aggregate will amount to that sum of admiration which he himself, at his outset, has stated as the correct standard for the appreciation of the poet. It was, generally speaking, the prevailing tendency of the time which preceded our own (and which has shown itself particularly in physical science,) to consider everything having life as a mere accumulation of dead parts, to separate what exists only in connexion and cannot otherwise be conceived, instead of penetrating to the central point and viewing all the parts as so many irradiations from it. Hence nothing is so rare as a critic who can elevate himself to the comprehensive contemplation of a

---

[1] *Hieroclis Commentarius in Aurea Carmina*, ed. P. Needham, 1709, 462. Cf. Johnson, *Shakespeare*, 62.

work of art. Shakespeare's compositions, from the very depth of purpose displayed in them, have been especially liable to the misfortune of being misunderstood. Besides, this prosaic species of criticism requires always that the poetic form should be applied to the details of execution; but when the plan of the piece is concerned, it never looks for more than the logical connexion of causes and effects, or some partial and trite moral by way of application; and all that cannot be reconciled therewith is declared superfluous, or even a pernicious appendage. . . . In this they altogether mistake the rights of poetry and the nature of the romantic drama, which, for the very reason that it is and ought to be picturesque, requires richer accompaniments and contrasts for its main groups. In all Art and Poetry, but more especially in the romantic, the Fancy lays claims to be considered as an independent mental power governed according to its own laws. . . .

Johnson has objected to Shakespeare that his pathos is not always natural and free from affectation.[2] There are, it is true, passages, though comparatively speaking very few, where his poetry exceeds the bounds of actual dialogue, where a too soaring imagination, a too luxuriant wit, rendered a complete dramatic forgetfulness of himself impossible. With this exception, the censure originated in a fanciless way of thinking, to which everything appears unnatural that does not consort with its own tame insipidity. Hence an idea has been formed of simple and natural pathos, which consists in exclamations destitute of imagery and nowise elevated above everyday life. But energetical passions electrify all the mental powers, and will consequently, in highly-favoured natures, give utterance to themselves in ingenious and figurative expressions. It has often been remarked that indignation makes a man witty; and as despair occasionally breaks out into laughter, it may sometimes also give vent to itself in antithetical comparisons.

[2] *Shakespeare,* 74.

35. Coleridge on Johnson's *Shakespeare*

1811–16

The first two extracts are taken from Coleridge's 'Lectures on Shakespeare and Milton', (Nos. 6 and 12), delivered November 1811–January 1812 (*Coleridge's Essays and Lectures on Shakespeare . . .*, 1907, 413–4, 477–8); the third comes from a letter to Daniel Stuart, 13 May 1816 (*Letters from the Lake Poets to Daniel Stuart*, 1889, 262–3).

I have been induced to offer these remarks, in order to obviate an objection made against Shakespeare on the ground of the multitude of his conceits.[1] I do not pretend to justify every conceit. . . . The notion against which I declare war is, that when ever a conceit is met with it is unnatural. People who entertain this opinion forget, that had they lived in the age of Shakespeare, they would have deemed them natural. Dryden in his translation of Juvenal has used the words 'Look round the world,'[2] which are a literal version of the original; but Dr. Johnson has swelled and expanded this expression into the following couplet:—

> Let observation, with extensive view,
> Survey mankind from China to Peru;
> > *Vanity of Human Wishes.*

mere bombast and tautology; as much as to say, 'Let observation with extensive observation observe mankind extensively.'[3]

Had Dr. Johnson lived in the time of Shakespeare, or even of Dryden, he would never have been guilty of such an outrage upon common sense and common language; and if people would, in idea, throw themselves back a couple of centuries, they would find that conceits, and even puns, were very allowable, because very natural. Puns often arise out of a mingled sense of injury, and contempt of the person in-

---

[1] Cf. Johnson, *Shakespeare*, 74.

[2] *Tenth Satire of Juvenal*, l. 1 ('Look round the Habitable World').

[3] Coleridge apparently relished this jibe; he repeated it on at least four other occasions. See *Shakespearean Criticism*, ii. 170; *Letters*, iv. 1031; *Miscellaneous Criticism*, ed. T. M. Raysor, 1936, 225–6, 439.

flicting it, and, as it seems to me, it is a natural way of expressing that mixed feeling. I could point out puns in Shakespeare, where they appear almost as if the first openings of the mouth of nature—where nothing else could so properly be said.

Another objection has been taken by Dr. Johnson, and Shakespeare has been taxed very severely. I refer to the scene where Hamlet enters and finds his uncle praying, and refuses to take his life, excepting when he is in the height of his iniquity. To assail him at such a moment of confession and repentance, Hamlet declares,

> Why, this is hire and salary, not revenge.
> *Act III, Scene 3.*

He therefore forbears, and postpones his uncle's death, until he can catch him in some act

> That has no relish of salvation in't.

This conduct, and this sentiment, Dr. Johnson has pronounced to be so atrocious and horrible, as to be unfit to be put into the mouth of a human being.[4] The fact, however, is that Dr. Johnson did not understand the character of Hamlet, and censured accordingly: the determination to allow the guilty King to escape at such a moment is only part of the indecision and irresoluteness of the hero.

It is among the feebleness of our nature, that we are often to a certain degree acted on by stories gravely asserted, of which we yet do most religiously disbelieve every syllable. Nay, which perhaps, we happen to know to be false. The truth is, that images and thoughts possess a power in and of themselves, independent of that act of the judgement or understanding by which we affirm or deny the existence of a reality correspondent to them. Such is the ordinary state of the mind in dreams. . . . Add to this a voluntary lending of the Will to this suspension of one of its own operations (i.e. that of comparison and consequent decision concerning the reality of any sensuous Impression) and you have the true theory of stage illusion—equally distant from the absurd notion of the French critics, who ground their principles on the principle of an absolute *de*lusion, and of Dr. Johnson who would persuade us that our judgements are as broad awake during the most masterly representation of the deepest scenes of *Othello*, as a philosopher would be during the exhibition of a magic lanthorn with Punch and

4 *Shakespeare*, 990.

Joan, and Pull Devil Pull Baker, &c on its painted Slides. Now as extremes always meet, this dogma of our dogmatic critic and soporific Irenist would lead by inevitable consequence to that very doctrine of the unities maintained by the French Belle Lettrists, which it was the object of his strangely overrated contradictory and most illogical Preface to Shakespear, to overthrow.

36. Hazlitt, *Characters of Shakespear's Plays*

1817

Extracts from the Preface to *Characters of Shakespear's Plays*, 1817, xv–xxiii. See Introduction, pp. 8, 27.

[quotes from Schlegel's *Lectures*, 'by far the best account of the plays of Shakespear that has hitherto appeared.']

We have the rather availed ourselves of this testimony of a foreign critic in behalf of Shakespear, because our own countryman, Dr. Johnson, has not been so favourable to him. It may be said of Shakespear, that 'those who are not for him are against him': for indifference is here the height of injustice. We may sometimes, in order 'to do a great right, do a little wrong.'[1] An overstrained enthusiasm is more pardonable with respect to Shakespear than the want of it; for our admiration cannot easily surpass his genius. We have a high respect for Dr. Johnson's character and understanding, mixed with something like personal attachment: but he was neither a poet nor a judge of poetry. He might in one sense be a judge of poetry as it falls within the limits and rules of prose, but not as it is poetry. Least of all was he qualified to be a judge of Shakespear, who 'alone is high fantastical.'[2] Let those who have a prejudice against Johnson read Boswell's *Life* of him: as those whom he has prejudiced against Shakespear should read his *Irene*. We do not say that a man to be a critic must necessarily be a poet: but to be a good critic, he ought

[1] *Merchant of Venice*, IV. i. 216.
[2] *Twelfth Night*, I. i. 15.

not to be a bad poet. Such poetry as a man deliberately writes, such, and such only will he like. Dr. Johnson's Preface to his edition of Shakespear looks like a laborious attempt to bury the characteristic merits of his author under a load of cumbrous phraseology, and to weigh his excellences and defects in equal scales, stuffed full of 'swelling figures and sonorous epithets.'[3] Nor could it well be otherwise; Dr. Johnson's general powers of reasoning overlaid his critical susceptibility. All his ideas were cast in a given mould, in a set form: they were made out by rule and system, by climax, inference, and antithesis:—Shakespear's were the reverse. Johnson's understanding dealt only in round numbers: the fractions were lost upon him. He reduced everything to the common standard of conventional propriety; and the most exquisite refinement or sublimity produced an effect on his mind, only as they could be translated into the language of measured prose. To him an excess of beauty was a fault; for it appeared to him like an excrescence; and his imagination was dazzled by the blaze of light. His writings neither shone with the beams of native genius, nor reflected them. The shifting shapes of fancy, the rainbow hues of things, made no impression on him: he seized only on the permanent and tangible. He had no idea of natural objects but 'such as he could measure with a two-foot rule, or tell upon ten fingers':[4] he judged of human nature in the same way, by mood and figure: he saw only the definite, the positive, and the practical, the average forms of things, not their striking differences—their classes, not their degrees. He was a man of strong common sense and practical wisdom, rather than of genius or feeling. He retained the regular, habitual impressions of actual objects, but he could not follow the rapid flights of fancy, or the strong movements of passion. That is, he was to the poet what the painter of still life is to the painter of history. Common sense sympathises with the impressions of things on ordinary minds in ordinary circumstances: genius catches the glancing combinations presented to the eye of fancy, under the influence of passion. It is the province of the didactic reasoner to take cognizance of those results of human nature which are constantly repeated and always the same, which follow one another in regular succession, which are acted upon by large classes of men, and embodied in received customs, laws, language, and institutions; and it was in arranging, comparing, and arguing on these kind of general results, that Johnson's excellence lay. But he could not quit his hold of the common-place and mechanical, and apply the general rule

[3] *Shakespeare*, 74.
[4] Burke, *Second Letter on a Regicide Peace*, 1796, para. 7.

to the particular exception, or shew how the nature of man was modified by the workings of passion, or the infinite fluctuations of thought and accident. Hence he could judge neither of the heights nor depths of poetry. Nor is this all; for being conscious of great powers in himself, and those powers of an adverse tendency to those of his author, he would be for setting up a foreign jurisdiction over poetry, and making criticism a kind of Procrustes' bed of genius, where he might cut down imagination to matter-of-fact, regulate the passions according to reason, and translate the whole into logical diagrams and rhetorical declamation. Thus he says of Shakespear's characters, in contradiction to what Pope had observed, and to what every one else feels, that each character is a species, instead of being an individual. He in fact found the general species or *didactic* form in Shakespear's characters, which was all he sought or cared for; he did not find the individual traits, or the *dramatic* distinctions which Shakespear has engrafted on this general nature, because he felt no interest in them. Shakespear's bold and happy flights of imagination were equally thrown away upon our author. He was not only without any particular fineness of organic sensibility, alive to all the 'mighty world of ear and eye,'[5] which is necessary to the painter or musician, but without that intenseness of passion, which, seeking to exaggerate whatever excites the feelings of pleasure or power in the mind, and moulding the impressions of natural objects according to the impulses of imagination, produces a genius and a taste for poetry. According to Dr. Johnson, a mountain is sublime, or a rose is beautiful; for that their name and definition imply. But he would no more be able to give the description of Dover cliff in *Lear*, or the description of flowers in *The Winter's Tale*, than to describe the objects of a sixth sense; nor do we think he would have any very profound feeling of the beauty of the passages here referred to. A stately common-place, such as Congreve's description of a ruin in the *Mourning Bride*, would have answered Johnson's purpose just as well, or better than the first; and an indiscriminate profusion of scents and hues would have interfered less with the ordinary routine of his imagination than Perdita's lines, which seem enamoured of their own sweetness—

——Daffodils
That come before the swallow dares, and take
The winds of March with beauty; violets dim,
But sweeter than the lids of Juno's eyes,
Or Cytherea's breath.—[6]

---

[5] Wordsworth, *Tintern Abbey*, ll. 105–6.　　　[6] *Winter's Tale*, IV. iv. 118–22.

No one who does not feel the passion which these objects inspire can go along with the imagination which seeks to express that passion and the uneasy sense of delight accompanying it by something still more beautiful, and no one can feel this passionate love of nature without quick natural sensibility. To a mere literal and formal apprehension, the inimitably characteristic epithet, 'violets *dim*,' must seem to imply a defect, rather than a beauty; and to any one, not feeling the full force of that epithet, which suggests an image like 'the sleepy eye of love,'[7] the allusion to 'the lids of Juno's eyes' must appear extravagant and un-meaning. Shakespear's fancy lent words and images to the most refined sensibility to nature, struggling for expression: his descriptions are identical with the things themselves, seen through the fine medium of passion: strip them of that connection, and try them by ordinary conceptions and ordinary rules, and they are as grotesque and barbarous as you please!—By thus lowering Shakespear's genius to the standard of common-place invention, it was easy to show that his faults were as great as his beauties; for the excellence, which consists merely in a conformity to rules, is counterbalanced by the technical violation of them. Another circumstance which led to Dr. Johnson's indiscriminate praise or censure of Shakespear, is the very structure of his style. Johnson wrote a kind of rhyming prose, in which he was as much compelled to finish the different clauses of his sentences, and to balance one period against another, as the writer of heroic verse is to keep to lines of ten syllables with similar terminations. He no sooner acknowledges the merits of his author in one line than the periodical revolution of his style carries the weight of his opinion completely over to the side of objection, thus keeping up a perpetual alternation of perfections and absurdities. We do not otherwise know how to account for such assertions as the following:—

In his tragic scenes, there is always something wanting, but his comedy often surpasses expectation or desire. His comedy pleases by the thoughts and the language, and his tragedy, for the greater part, by incident and action. His tragedy seems to be skill, his comedy to be instinct.[8]

Yet after saying that 'his tragedy was skill,' he affirms in the next page,

His declamations or set speeches are commonly cold and weak, *for his power was the power of nature*: when he endeavoured, like other tragic writers, to catch opportunities of amplification, and instead of inquiring what the occasion

---

[7] Cf. Pope, *First Epistle of the Second Book of Horace*, l. 150.
[8] *Shakespeare*, 69.

demanded, to shew how much his stores of knowledge could supply, he seldom escapes without the pity or resentment of his reader.

Poor Shakespear! Between the charges here brought against him, of want of nature in the first instance, and of want of skill in the second, he could hardly escape being condemned. And again,

But the admirers of this great poet have most reason to complain when he approaches nearest to his highest excellence, and seems fully resolved to sink them in dejection, or mollify them with tender emotions by the fall of greatness, the danger of innocence, or the crosses of love. What he does best, he soon ceases to do. He no sooner begins to move than he counteracts himself; and terror and pity, as they are rising in the mind, are checked and blasted by sudden frigidity.[9]

In all this, our critic seems more bent on maintaining the equilibrium of his style than the consistency or truth of his opinions.—If Dr. Johnson's opinion was right, the following observations on Shakespear's Plays must be greatly exaggerated, if not ridiculous. If he was wrong, what has been said may perhaps account for his being so, without detracting from his ability and judgment in other things.

[9] Ibid., 74.

POLITICAL PAMPHLETS

1770–5

---

37. Unsigned review of *The False Alarm*, *Critical Review*

January 1770, xxix, 54–7

The False Alarm, Johnson's first political pamphlet, endeavoured to vindicate the Commons' action in declaring Colonel Luttrell the member for Middlesex, despite the overwhelming electoral victory of John Wilkes in May 1769.

This writer marches against the Goliah of sedition, clad in the simple, but impenetrable, armour of truth and philosophy. He fortifies himself with few or no precedents from the journals, nor does he rear the ponderous spear of law, but the weapons he employs are keen and irresistible.

After an introduction upon the advancement of civil wisdom for quieting the minds of men, and the difficulty which it encounters in its progress; he considers the ferment that now rages in this nation as propagated from papers, petitions, and pamphlets. 'It may,' says he, 'not be improper to lay before the public the reflections of a man who cannot favour the opposition, for he thinks it wicked; and cannot fear it, for he thinks it weak.'

The case of Mr. Wilkes naturally takes the lead in this argumentation. As to the person of Mr. Wilkes, 'lampoon itself,' says he, 'would disdain to speak ill of him, of whom no man speaks well. It is sufficient that he is expelled the house of commons, and confined in gaol as being legally convicted of sedition and impiety.'

Notwithstanding the high opinion we have of this author, we cannot help thinking that he resembles the man in the play, who laughs with the tear in his eye. His even proclaiming the opposition to be weak, may be justly considered as an implied declaration that it is strong; and we are sorry to see so able a champion encounter so feeble an adversary. As to the character of Mr. Wilkes, we may affirm, that what is here said of him does no service to the cause in which this author has engaged.

After some arch ridicule thrown out against imaginary grievances of the Middlesex electors, he observes that that county, distinguished from the city, has no claim to particular consideration; and he thinks that the confinement of Mr. Wilkes cannot at all meliorate his morals, nor is it a sufficient reason why he should come out of gaol a legislator. He next examines some of the most specious arguments for his eligibility into parliament, notwithstanding his expulsion. He observes that where there is a possibility of offence, there should be a possibility of punishment; and that 'a member of the house of commons cannot be cited for his conduct in parliament before any other court; and therefore, if the house cannot punish him, he may attack with impunity the rights of the people, and the title of the king.'—Our author's reasoning upon this head, and upon the powers of the house of commons is shrewd and sensible. As in some cases the members of parliament are above the controul of the courts of law, civil order undoubtedly requires that they should be under the jurisdiction of their respective houses, that they may not abuse such an exemption. He then states the case of Mr. Wilkes, his expulsion, his incapacitation, his re-election, and the admission of Mr. Luttrell upon a minority of votes; and according to him 'the question must be, whether a smaller number of legal votes, shall not prevail against a greater number of votes not legal. It must be considered, that those votes only are legal which are legally given; and that those only are legally given, which are given for a legal candidate.'

This we think is a full and a fair state of the case. Our author then examines 'whether a man expelled, can be so disqualified by a vote of the house, as that he shall be no longer eligible by lawful electors.' To prove the affirmative of this proposition he appeals to the unwritten law of social nature, and to the great and pregnant principle of political necessity. 'If,' says he, 'the commons have only the power of dismissing for a few days the man whom his constituents can immediately send back, if they can expel but cannot exclude, they have nothing more than nominal authority, to which perhaps obedience never may be paid.'

This writer quotes Mr. Selden[1] as an advocate for the power of perpetual disability being lodged in the commons. As he does not quote

[1] John Selden (1584–1654), eminent constitutional lawyer.

the particular passage of Selden where this doctrine is found, we must suppose that he alludes to the words of the speech of that great man against Sir Edward Sawyer. If that is the passage in question, though we allow it is very pregnant, we cannot think it amounts to the power of a perpetual disability, for all that Selden says is 'to maintain the privileges of our house, we can fine as well as the lords. And as they disable lords from sitting there, so we can disable any member of our own house from sitting here.' After all, it is very possible that this writer might have had some other passage of Selden in his view, which has not come to our knowledge.

After some farther reasoning on the same subject, which we think conclusive to prove that expulsion infers exclusion, he shews the absurdity of supposing that expulsion is only a dismission of the representative to his constituents, who may, if they think proper, re-elect and return him to the same parliament. 'This,' says our author, (in a stile which may be thought a little lexiphantic,) 'is plausible but not cogent. It is a scheme of representation, which would make a specious appearance in a political romance, but cannot be brought into practice among us, who see every day the towering head of speculation bow down unwillingly to grovelling experience.' He then shews, that 'expulsion without exclusion might very often be desirable; some, for instance, buy the favour of others which perhaps they may gratify by the act which provoked the expulsion. In short, was that the case, none would dread expulsion but those who bought their elections, and who would be obliged to buy them again at a higher price.' He proceeds to expose the futility of all arguments drawn from an act of the 4th and 5th of queen Anne, and which means no more than a permission for the electors to re-chuse those members whose seats may be vacated by their accepting a place of profit. He examines with great accuracy several other arguments that have been alleged against the power of exclusion upon expulsion; and, we think, undeniably proves that they all operate directly against the re-admission of Mr. Wilkes into this parliament. He then examines the groundless alarms that have been circulated among the people on this occasion. 'Outcries,' says he, 'uttered by malignity, and ecchoed by folly; general accusations of indeterminate wickedness, and obscure hints of impossible designs, dispersed among those that do not know their meaning, by those that know them to be false, have disposed part of the nation, though but a small part, to pester the court with ridiculous petitions.'

We next meet with a very entertaining account of the progress of a petition, and the means of obtaining names to it; and our author seems to think that that great engine of sedition has recoiled upon its authors. 'They thought,' says he, 'that the terms they sent were terms of weight, which would have amazed all and stumbled many; but the consternation is now over, and their foes stand upright, as before.'

We shall here take our leave of this writer, who finishes his publication by recapitulating the insults and indignities that have been offered to the person of his majesty; and we heartily wish that he may prophesy truly as to the inefficacy and end of all our public commotions.

38. Unsigned review of *The False Alarm*, *Monthly Review*

January 1770, xlii, 62–6

Among other able writers who have appeared in aid of the opposition, or the defence of the administration, amidst the out-cry of *grievances* and *apprehensions* on the one side, and of *faction* and *sedition* on the other,—a genius of the highest eminence in the science of MORALS, and in POLITE LITERATURE, after some years of silence and solitude, hath at length broke from his retirement, *rambled* into the field of POLITICS, and gratefully drawn his pen in the support of that government by which he is himself so generously supported.

The performance is intended to shew that the late alarms which have been given to the people are false, and their fears groundless. It consists of argument, declamation, and ridicule. We shall present to our Readers a specimen of what he has offered to the consideration of the public, under each of these heads.

DECLAMATION

[quotes first five paragraphs.]

We shall make no other observation on the foregoing passage, than—that it is extremely characteristic of the writer.

ARGUMENT

In discussing the question 'whether a member expelled, can be so disqualified by a vote of the house, as that he shall be no longer eligible by lawful electors?' he has the following argument against those who maintain 'that expulsion is only a dismission of the representative to his constituents, with such a testimony against him as his sentence may comprise.'

[quotes 'and that if his constituents, notwithstanding' to 'buy them again at a higher price', *Works*, 1792, viii. 77–8.]

This *back stroke*, by which many of our author's friends in that House whose wisdom and rectitude he is now so zealously vindicating, are, perhaps, *harder hit* than he was aware of, seems not much unlike the action represented in the noted picture of the country-parson and his wife, riding double:—while the good man is lifting his staff on high, to smite his sluggish beast, he unwittingly breaks the head of the poor woman who sits behind him.

RIDICULE

The following account of the progress of a *petition* has *humour*, at least, if not the most scrupulous *verity*.

[quotes 'An ejected placeman' to 'tax upon his windows', *Works*, viii. 87–90.]

After all, however, that ingenuity itself may find to urge in behalf of the measures of administration, and the power, wisdom, and justice of parliaments, ought not some regard to be had to the plain common-sense of the people, who, as an acute writer observes*, '*feel* that the right of election, that great foundation and best security of all their other rights, has been violently taken away from them, by the *sole* authority of *those*, who were chosen for their defence.'

* 'Essay on the Middlesex Election.'

39. Percival Stockdale, *The Remonstrance*

1770

Extract from pp. 15–19.

Stockdale (1736–1811) was for a time editor of the *Critical Review* and of the *Universal Magazine*, and later biographer of Waller (see *Lives*, i. 267 n. 4) and Thomson.

[Britons are urged to abandon belief in the 'Pretended patriotism' of men like Wilkes and William Beckford, and to rely on trustworthy guides like Johnson.]

> And you, great JOHNSON, to your latest breath,
> Shall find your ruling object strong in death;
> Such in those moments as in all the past,
> 'Receive thy votary, Heaven,' shall be your last.
> Thou nobly singular, immortal man!
> Whom nought could e'er divert from virtue's plan!
> The cruel straits, with genius oft at strife,
> Which make a feeling nature sick of life;
> A mortal stab to fine existence give,
> And kill the man who should for ever live;
> Thy steddy purpose never could controul,
> Nor check one vigorous effort of thy soul.
> Thy glorious purpose didst thou still sustain,
> And fortune frowned, and envy snarled in vain.
> Can the dim taper supersede the day?
> Can buzzing myriads hide the solar ray?
> Ah! no: these objects hardly meet the sight;
> As VENUS dwindles on returning light.
>
> Never wilt thou retain the hoarded store,
> In virtue affluent, but in metal poor;
> Thou feelest, oft, the sympathy of grief,

And oft thy hand extends the kind relief:
The tears of orphans melt thee as they roll;
The widow's misery shakes the sage's soul.

Thy honest censure, and thy honest praise,
Perhaps ill suit our false, and polished days;
Timid politeness says thou art severe;
But simple virtue loves the tongue sincere.
Say, to a blockhead, is it love, or spite,
To mortify him ne'er again to write;
To rescue from his own aerial views,
A solitary man without a muse?

Great is thy prose; great thy poetic strain;
Yet to dull coxcombs are they great in vain.
When weak opponents would thy strength defeat,
Thy words, like babbling parrots, they repeat;
But mixed with theirs, the vigour all is fled,
The letter living, but the spirit dead:
Their want of powers these insects will not see;
Bombast in them, is the sublime in thee.
Say, should a swain a royal mandate bear?
Say, should a dwarf the warriour's plumage wear?
Poorly a GARRICK, HOLLAND strove to show,[1]
In frantic terror, or in plaintive woe.

At length thy Sovereign gave his bounteous aid
To worth sequestered in the private shade.
Pensions, thus fixed, an equal honour bring
To the deserving subject, and the King:
Yet at thy pension rave the callous tribe,
Who bluster only to obtain a bribe.
Must pensions always honesty discard?
Should merit never meet it's just reward?
'Pensioner JOHNSON,' bawls the venal knave:
But has thy conduct marked thee for a slave?
Find in the man some more material flaw;
Nor public guilt from public honour draw.

[1] Charles Holland (1733–69), a pupil of Garrick, was widely condemned for servile imitations of his master. Cf. Churchill, *The Rosciad*, 1761, ll. 323–36.

The throb of virtue is to them unknown;
And hence they form thy image from their own.
Keen in their breasts the lust of gold they feel;
For gold they would destroy the public weal;
Shake o'er the land oppression's iron rod,
Betray their father, and blaspheme their GOD.

Go on, heroic man! thy setting sun
Will sink, majestic, as thy race begun;
A favourite, thou, of Heaven, and of the Nine;
Through BRITAIN's latest ages born to shine:
Heedless of censure, when for justice warm,
And from thy conscience flowed the *False Alarm*.

40. John Wilkes, *A Letter to Samuel Johnson LL.D.*

1770

Extracts from pp. 5–8, 32–8, 50–4.

In *The False Alarm* Wilkes is described as a 'retailer of sedition and obscenity'; Johnson adds for good measure that 'lampoon itself would disdain to speak ill of him, of whom no man speaks well.' Experienced in abuse, Wilkes here replies anonymously to Johnson's. See Introduction, pp. 6, 28.

Sir,
Without hesitation or apology, I address myself to Y O U, as the undoubted author of the ministerial rhapsody that has been so industriously circulated under the title of *The False Alarm*. You have ambitiously declared yourself the spitter forth of that effusion of servility and bombast. You *could not* have been concealed.—Whilst the tenets it spreads abroad might

have directed us to you, as to a probable source, the strain in which they are delivered marks you decisively.

But allow me, Sir, to ask you, for what class of reader your reasonings are intended? or, for whose benefit you have *stalked* forth from your Vocabulary, an Orator of Polysyllables?

Your great friends could not, surely, exact this service from you, for their own sakes. Men who resolve without waiting for conviction, will persist without wishing for a defence. And for the rest of us, *the rabble of England, who might all sink into non-existence without any sensible effect on the state;*[1] WE, doubtless, are either unworthy of your high instruction, or, at least, (permit us to say) not capable of profiting by it.

Believe me, Sir, *the intellectual sight* of ordinary freeholders is liable to be *offusqued* by a *superfluous glare* of erudition. The dimension of OUR understanding is not of the proper magnitude to admit of *sesquipedalian documents*. OUR undisciplined taste is apt to be nauseated by the *reduplicated evomition* of unknown idioms. If you would adapt yourself to OUR faculties, you must sink into language of a lower stature than *hendecasyllables*. WE are not skilled to estimate the *weight of terms*,[2] by their *literal* contents.

I am ready, however, to acknowledge that your book may be well enough calculated for the region, where (as I understand) it has been most greedily devoured. A certain protuberancy of diction may be very edifying to the maids of honour; and the inflation of your periods cannot fail to find a passage into that quarter where the ERSE is said to have been *the reigning dialect*.[3]

It shall be my humble, but laborious province, to endeavour to reduce your lofty speculations to the level of vulgar apprehension; not so much with a view to unwind a thread of refined sophistry, of which indeed you have observed a commendable frugality; still less to investigate candid argument, of which it is not easy to discover a trace; but to develope what little meaning you may have wished to impart, by dissipating the *cloud of words* in which it is at present involved, and by exhibiting it in the form in which it must destroy itself, the language of common sense.

[scornfully rejects arguments which justify his being disqualified as a parliamentary candidate.]

But what are we to think of your total defection *from yourself*? of such

---

[1] *False Alarm*, in *Works*, viii. 84.

[2] Ibid., viii. 92.

[3] An allusion to the Scot, Lord Bute, who was Prime Minister when Johnson's pension was granted; he was a favourite target for radical abuse.

a shameful revolt from principles long and strenuously, and even honourably maintained? Your friends *may pity*; the public abominates.

Your original sentiments concerning placemen and pensioners[4] are as notorious to the world as your inveteracy against *the Scotch*. You have at length, it seems, discovered *worth* and *dignity* in the former; and are so perfectly reconciled to the latter, as to have deviated (in despite of nature) into an *attempt at humour* in their defence, holding out to public ridicule the unwieldy exhibition of the gambols of a colossus!—But the merits of Lord Bute are superabundant; and, let me add, his discernment is not of the meanest; by a well-placed *pension of three hundred pounds a year* he has expiated his own sins and those of his country.

Yet, surely, if it be upon such terms that you are become a PENSIONER, it were far better to return back to that poor but honest state, when you and the miserable *Savage**, on default of the pittance that should have secured your quarters at the club, were contented—*in the open air*—to growl at the *moon*, and Whigs, and Walpole, and the house of Brunswick.[5]

But, if the wages of prostitution, once tasted, are too delicious to be relinquished, you must, at least, be sensible, that they are not to be enjoyed but by the loss of all respect and consideration with the public. A reflection, one would think, that might have secured you from the indiscretion of attempting to impose unwelcome falshoods on the ignorant or superficial, by the mere weight of your authority. The gross and virulent insults you have affectedly thrown out against Mr. WILKES, (who is confessedly the favourite of the public, whose private friendships are extensive and sincere; yet of whom you chuse to assert, that he is spoken well of by no man[6]) are not more scandalous than they are injudicious.

The greater part of the world do not appear to acquiesce in the criminality of the charges that have been alleged against that gentleman; *although* he has been singled out for the RE-PUBLICATION† of a paper that had been re-published before in almost all the journals in the kingdom, and *although* his servant was bribed to rob him of a poem[7] which he

* The unfortunate Mr. Richard Savage.
† It is remarkable, that the *original* ground of Mr. Wilkes's expulsion (as set forth in the votes) was his being the *author* of Number 45, of the *North Briton*; an allegation that never was revoked. And yet he has at no time been even accused, judicially, of the fact.

---

[4] In his *Dictionary* Johnson had defined 'pensioner' as 'a dependant', 'a slave of state hired by a stipend to obey his master'.
[5] Cf. Boswell, *Life*, i. 164.   [6] *False Alarm*, in *Works*, viii. 67.
[7] *Essay on Woman*, 1762. For printing the *Essay* and reprinting the *North Briton* No. 45, Wilkes was banished in 1764.

had scrupulously shut up from the general eye. The poem, indeed, by the common accounts of it, is not much more defensible than the shocking vices of your employers: but the disgust naturally excited in liberal minds by indecency, is, in this instance, lost in the abhorrence of the means by which evidence was obtained against its PUBLISHER.*

But it is not enough to load Mr. Wilkes with crimes. You charge the Freeholders of the first county in England with re-electing him upon the recommendation of those crimes. I must ask you plainly, Sir, is it your intention, in this passage, *to lend a lie the confidence of truth?*[8] or do you seriously believe, that even the most insignificant borough that your masters command, would adopt the interest of any person whatsoever, merely on the merit of sedition and obscenity?—I give you the alternative of being infamous or contemptible.

The freeholders of Middlesex (men of plain sense, and of an honesty that has stood unshaken against all the assaults of corruption, and all the intimidations of power) did not select Mr. WILKES for their representative, in so distinguished a manner, in reward of the crimes imputed to him—an insinuation that must rouze the indignation of every man of honour in the kingdom—but in acknowledgment of substantial benefits obtained by that gentleman to the constitution of this country; in detestation of the unjust, illegal, oppressive, and ungentlemanly means put in practice to convict him; and in order to mark to the present age and to latest posterity, that the man who encounters the attacks of despotism with fortitude and perseverance, shall never want the avowed protection, and generous support of the great body of the people of England.

But, at every step, you advance in brutal insolence. These noble spirits might, in your judgment it seems, 'all sink into non-existence, without any other effect, than that there would be room made for a NEW RABBLE,'[9] who, by parity of absurdity, might perish in their turn, with as little detriment to the state.

We are not at a loss to discover, to what quarter you are indebted for a mode of thinking and of speaking that has never before been endured in any country pretending to freedom.

[Wilkes continues his vilification of Johnson as a government hack.]

---

* In the next edition of your *Dictionary*, you will hardly fail to insert the following new acceptation of a verb. 'To PUBLISH (from the Latin *publicare*) to suppress; to keep private; to *lock up* in a scrutore.'—You know whither to go for your *authority*.

---

8 *False Alarm*, in *Works*, viii. 78; *London*, l. 56.
9 Ibid., viii. 84.

Your book supplies all the materials of an answer to itself. In one place, you suppose expulsions to be very rare: in another your argument turns upon the idea of their frequency.[10]

You tell us, at setting out, that the House cannot subsist without the power of incapacitation: In another passage, you are at much pains to prove that this power is *ineffectual* to any essential purposes of the constitution, which can only be secured by the permanency of a statute.[11]

It is your established principle, that the House have an absolute, uncontrolable power of *expelling any one of their members:* yet, when it suits your occasions, you maintain expressly *'that there cannot exist,* with respect to the same subject, *at the same time, an absolute power to chuse, and an absolute power to reject.'*[12] This indeed, is to do business effectually: it is to *interdict* every candidate, and make the vote of every elector *useless* and *dead.*

In the midst of these contradictions, there is one point in which you are consistent. You discover in every line a rooted attachment to *'the unhappy family'* whom *'the gloomy, sullen William'* drove out:—and, in the blindness of your zeal, or in the candor of Jacobitism, when you even mean to pay a compliment to the best of princes,[13] you are betrayed into the detestable and traiterous insinuation, that he is the only king since the Revolution, whose character, or whose measures, have borne any resemblance to those of the abdicated line.

You expressly accuse the party whose cause I am maintaining, 'of having endeavoured to alienate the affections of the people from *the only* king, who, *for almost a century,* has much appeared to desire, or much endeavoured to deserve them.'[14]

It is impossible to misunderstand you. A *complete* century would have left us amidst the infamies of the Second *Charles*; but you are habituated to the name of *James,* and are determined to bring us down to the æra of your abomination, the glorious Revolution.—Yet, surely, the *good Anne* might have been excepted, for the merit of the pious purposes of her last four years.—But I repress myself.—It is but too notorious, that you are not the only person who has been suffered to approach St. James's, with all the principles and prejudices of St. *Germains.*[15] What better, then, was to be expected, than unheard-of exertions of unconstitutional powers, on

[10] Ibid., viii. 87, 78.
[11] Ibid., viii. 81.
[12] Ibid., viii. 68–9, 81.
[13] George III.
[14] *Works,* viii. 93.
[15] The court of the deposed James II.

215

the part of administration: and the prostitution of some HIRELING PEN, in the cause of passive obedience and non-resistance, but thinly veiled in their new-fangled disguise of A GREAT AND PREGNANT PRINCIPLE OF POLITICAL NECESSITY?[16]

I am, &c. &c.

THE AUTHOR.

41. Joseph Towers, *A Letter to Dr. Samuel Johnson*

1775

Extracts from pp. 1–17, 43–8.

This (anonymous) pamphlet was the most distinguished contribution to the controversy provoked by Johnson's political writings; it seemed to 'impress him much' (Boswell, *Life*, ii. 316). The author, Dr Joseph Towers (1737–99), was a well-known dissenting minister and political controversialist. See Introduction, pp. 6, 10, 28.

Sir,

When a man, who has rendered himself eminent by his productions in morals, and in polite literature, engages in political contentions, and in those which are apprehended to be of great national importance, it may reasonably be expected of such a writer, that he should distinguish himself not by party violence and rancour, but by moderation and by wisdom: and that at least he should not wholly lose sight of that liberality of sentiment, which should characterize the scholar; nor of that decency and politeness, which should adorn the gentleman. But unhappily your political productions have been chiefly remarkable for bitterness of invective, unjust and uncandid representations, the most bigotted

[16] *Works*, viii. 74.

prejudices against them whom you oppose, and the highest strains of contemptuous insolence. You have written in a manner which must degrade you in the judgment of the impartial public, in a manner utterly unworthy of a great, or liberal, or philosophic mind, and for which even your being a royal pensioner cannot apologize.

When I first heard that a pension had been conferred upon you by those in power, I hoped that it might have been given as the reward of merit. I knew that your literary labours, your elaborate *Dictionary*, and other works, in which you had displayed great force of genius, extensive knowledge, and uncommon powers of language, had given you a just claim to public support and encouragement. I thought it not impossible, that those by whom your pension was procured, might have been satisfied with rewarding your ingenuity, without imposing any services on you unworthy of your character. But the use that has been since made of you, renders it sufficiently apparent, that a pension was conferred on you with other views. It now seems probable, that your known Jacobitical principles, which, however strange it may be thought, appear now to be in high estimation at court, were among your chief recommendations; and that it was these, added to the hope of employing you in the service of your new masters, which really occasioned your being placed in the list of royal pensioners.

It has been said, that few men are capable of bearing prosperity well; and if receiving a pension may be considered as a species of prosperity, it appears sufficiently evident, that this has not had a favourable effect either upon your head, or upon your heart. Not one truly valuable piece has issued from your pen, since you received the royal bounty. From that time, your native pride and arrogance appear to have been augmented; and your latter pieces are far from breathing that virtuous spirit, by which your former writings were generally distinguished. Instead of employing your talents in the service of the republic of letters, and in benefitting mankind, you are now dwindled into the rancorous writer of a party; and produce only such performances as the *False Alarm*, the *Thoughts on the transactions respecting Falkland's Islands*, and the *Patriot*.

During the last reign, you were generally considered as one of the most bigotted Jacobites in the kingdom. It is commonly said, that you scarcely ever spoke of the family on the throne with any degree of temper or decency; and you not unfrequently exhibited in your writings your aversion to the government. It was then a subject of your most pathetic complaints, that England was *oppressed with excise*, that it was a *cheated* and a *groaning nation*, and a *beggar'd land*. We were then cursed with a *pensioned band*, and with *hireling senators*; and it was a *thoughtless age lull'd to* SERVITUDE.[1]

You then wished for those happy days of old, when justice was uprightly and impartially administered. You sighed for the age of Alfred, because, as you inform us,

> Fair Justice then, without constraint ador'd,
> Held high the steady scale, but deep'd the sword;
> No spies were paid, no SPECIAL JURIES known,
> Blest Age! but ah! how diff'rent from our own![2]

But whatever evils the nation suffered from an iniquitous government in the last reign, they are, it seems, happily removed in the present; so that you can now discover nothing to complain of, but the turbulence and wickedness of the popular party.

As this country was so much oppressed, and laboured under such a variety of evils, in the reign of George the Second, it may amuse a speculative man to enquire, by what means so happy a revolution in public affairs has been effectuated in the Reign of George the Third. Are our taxes lessened? No. Is the nation freed from *excise*? No. Are the rights of the subject more religiously preserved? No. Is Justice more impartially administered in our courts of law? No. Are *special juries* less frequent? No. Has the commerce of the nation been encreased, and its interests better attended to? No. Are our Parliaments more incorrupt, and less under the influence of the court? No. What is it then that has so wonderfully changed the face of public affairs, as entirely to reconcile the author of the RAMBLER to the government? The whole may be answered in one short sentence. The grievances of the kingdom are removed; the nation is no more in a groaning or a sinking state; for DR. SAMUEL JOHNSON HAS A PENSION. It follows, as a necessary consequence, that wisdom presides over our councils, that all complaints against the administration must be unjust and unreasonable, and that we have the happiness to possess 'a government approaching nearer to perfection, than any that experience has known, or history related!'[3]

You have observed, (*False Alarm*, p. 28 [*Works*, viii. 80]) that 'the acceptance of a *place* contaminates no character;' and you have probably the same ideas of the acceptance of a pension. But surely the characters of those men are contaminated, who are induced by a place, to sacrifice the rights of their country; or by a pension to write in defence of

---

[1] *London*, ll. 29, 91, 65, 200–1, 213, 60.   [2] Ibid., ll. 250–3.

[3] *False Alarm*, in Johnson's *Works*, 1792, viii. 90.

measures that are oppressive and iniquitous. As to your engaging in vindication of an arbitrary administration, some allowance ought, perhaps, to be made, for that attachment to despotic principles which you early imbibed, and by which you have so often distinguished yourself. That bigotry which could lead you to celebrate in the highest strains of panegyric, that most eminent high-church saint, archbishop LAUD, and that zeal in favour of tyranny which could induce you to deplore the death of the Earl of STRAFFORD,[4] may perhaps be pleaded in extenuation of your conduct. And as you appear to have been always disposed to justify the tyranny of the Stuarts, you were already half prepared to defend despotic proceedings under a prince of another family. Though your Jacobite prejudices gave you a predilection in favour of the Stuarts, yet it might somewhat reconcile you to the government of the House of Hanover, if you had reason to believe that principles were now adopted at court, similar to those of that family, whose attempts to enslave the nation had been the cause of their expulsion from the throne. But whatever allowances may be made to you on this account, you are still extremely censurable for those notorious fallacies and misrepresentations, and that gross scurrility, with which your late political productions so much abound.

As a specimen of the moderation and civility with which you have expressed yourself concerning the party whom you oppose, I shall collect a few of the rhetorical flowers, and polite phrases, which are scattered throughout your political pieces in such bountiful profusion. Of JUNIUS you say, that *he burst into notice with a blaze of impudence*; and of Mr. WILKES that he was *a varlet driven out of the House with public infamy*. The popular party are stiled by you *a despicable faction, bellowers of sedition, ruffians who would gain power by mischief and confusion*, and *those who having fixed their hopes on public calamities, sit like vultures waiting for a day of carnage*. You also say, 'Of this faction what evil may not be credited? They have hitherto shewn *no virtue*, and very little wit, beyond that mischievous cunning, for which it is held by Hale that *children may be hanged*.'—You have also discovered, that they are more wicked than the Devil.—'As they have not the wit of Satan, they have not his virtue.' —'Their hope is malevolence, and their good is evil.' And you likewise complain of *the howl of Plebeian patriotism*, and *the howling violence of patriotic rage*.[5]

---

[4] *Vanity of Human Wishes*, ll. 131, 168.

[5] *Thoughts on the Transactions respecting Falkland's Islands*, in *Works*, viii. 120–39; *False Alarm*, in *Works*, viii. 80.

Is this the language of a man whose understanding has been refined by literature? Is this the language of a scholar, a gentleman, or a philosopher? In the heat of a political controversy, such scurrillity might not have been wondered at in low and vulgar minds; but surely something better might have been justly expected from a teacher of morals, and a professed improver of our language. Nor do the terms in which you have expressed yourself of them whom you oppose, convey a very favourable idea of your heart. The utmost stretch of candour cannot lead any man to suppose, that you believe one half of the evil that you have said of the popular party. You must be the most prejudiced man in the kingdom if you do: and if you do not, have you any right to be considered as a man of principle, or probity?

Such is your rancour against all who have engaged in any opposition to the court, that you cannot express yourself with decency even of the Earl of CHATHAM. The eloquence of that illustrious nobleman, who is unquestionably one of the greatest ornaments of his age and country, is described by you under the contemptuous appellation of *feudal gabble*, and you observe that it will be happy for him, 'if the nation shall at last dismiss him to nameless obscurity.'[6] But however highly you may estimate your own talents, be assured, that you will be extremely fortunate in this respect, if your fame should be as lasting as that of the Earl of CHATHAM, whose name will be mentioned with distinguished honour in the annals of this country, so long as any records of it shall be preserved.

The people are frequently honoured by you with the polite appellation of *the rabble*; and the citizens of London, and the freeholders of Middlesex, are also spoken of by you with similar contempt. They have been both active in the opposition to the court, and must therefore experience the effects of your loyal indignation. The inhabitants of London, have, indeed, long been under obligations to you, for the genteel terms in which you have spoken of their city. It was thus described by you many years since:

> LONDON, *the needy villain's general home,*
> *The common sewer of Paris and of Rome.*[7]

The freeholders of Middlesex have also the honour to be thus distinguished by you: 'Mr. Wilkes, and the freeholders of Middlesex, might all sink into non-existence, without any other effect, than that

---

[6] *Thoughts on the Transactions respecting Falkland's Islands*, in *Works*, viii. 118.
[7] *London*, ll. 93–4.

there would be room made for a *new rabble*, and a new retailer of sedition and obscenity.'[8] It is needless to make any remarks on this passage. It is equally characterized by politeness and humanity.

In your last political publication, *the Patriot*, speaking of the opponents of government, you say, 'The greater, far the greater number of those who rave, and rail, and enquire, and accuse, neither suspect, nor fear, nor care for the public; but hope to force their way to riches by virulence and invective, and are vehement and clamorous, only that they may be sooner hired to be silent.'[9] That this assertion is notoriously untrue, must be evident to every man who will consider it. A great majority of those who are dissatisfied with the measures of government, and who testify their discontent, cannot possibly have any hope of acquiring riches by their opposition, or cherish any hope of being bribed to silence. But you have, with an equal disregard to truth, also passed a similar unjust and undistinguishing censure of the popular party, in the *False Alarm*. You there commend the King for having neglected or *forgotten* the many petitions sent to him from different parts of the kingdom; because you say, 'he might easily know, that what was presented as the sense of the people, was the sense only of the *profligate* and *dissolute*.'[10] That this is a gross falshood must be evident to every candid person in the kingdom, of whatever party. Among those who approved of the petitions to the throne, and who joined in their complaints of those grievances of which the petitions contained an enumeration, were many of the worthiest persons in this country; and not a few who were distinguished both by abilities and learning, as well as by integrity. Surely then neither party violence, nor the influence of a pension, can be pleaded even by your friends as a justification of what you have written. Nor can you possibly vindicate yourself, unless you think it right to support the cause of your patrons, not only by a total disregard of candour, but by the most gross deviations from truth and justice.

You observe in *the Patriot*, p. 1. that 'at the end of every seven years comes the *Saturnalian season*, when the people of Great Britain may *please themselves* with the choice of their representatives. This happy day has now arrived, somewhat sooner than it could be claimed.' Your comparison here of the period of election with a Roman festival, wherein the *slaves* were put on a level with their *masters*, appears to convey in it a compliment to your countrymen not of the most delicate

[8] *False Alarm*, in *Works*, viii. 84.
[9] *Patriot*, in *Works*, viii. 144.
[10] *False Alarm*, in *Works*, viii. 92.

kind. And as to your remark, that *this happy day has arrived somewhat sooner than it could be claimed*, for which you seem to suppose that the people are under some obligation to administration, it is, I believe, far from being generally apprehended, that the unexpected dissolution of the parliament arose from any desire to gratify, or to serve the people. And if it was done with the views that are supposed, little gratitude can be due from them on that account.

In the course of those observations wherein you profess to point out the marks which distinguish true patriots from those who falsely assume that character, you say, 'Some claim a place in the list of Patriots by an acrimonious and unremitting opposition to the court. This mark is by no means infallible. Patriotism is not necessarily included in rebellion.'[11] Was it your design here to insinuate, that *opposition to the court* and *rebellion* are synonimous terms? Something like this appears to have been intended. That opposition to administration merely for the sake of opposition, or when engaged in from private views, is not Patriotism, may readily be granted. But if the prevailing measures of government are unjust, pernicious, and despotic, the purest public virtue would dictate an opposition to such an administration: and it is natural and reasonable for the people to consider those as their friends, who distinguish themselves by their opposition to measures of this kind. With whatever caution the people may elect their representatives, they are often liable to be deceived. But they always act rightly in electing such men for members of the House of Commons, whom they believe to be friends of freedom, and disposed to join in a vigorous opposition to all schemes for aggrandizing the power of the crown, or depriving the people of their rights.

You say, *Patriot*, p. 4 [*Works*, viii. 143], that 'a man may hate his king, yet not love his country.' I shall not dispute this assertion, because I consider yourself as an evidence of its truth. In the last reign, no man suspected you of any affection for the King: and yet there were reasons to believe that you had not much more for your country. When the rest of the nation were rejoicing at the advantage which they had gained over their enemies by the conquest of Louisbourgh, you seemed to view it with disgust; and therefore wrote an Essay in the *Idler*, calculated to depreciate the merit of the English in that capture, and to lessen the general joy on the occasion, under the pretence of shewing the partiality of national historians. You remark in that essay, that 'there is no crime more infamous than the violation of truth.'[12] It would have been much

---

[11] *Patriot*, in *Works*, viii. 143.   [12] *Idler* No. 20.

for your reputation as a moral man, if you had attended more to this consideration in your late political productions.

[There follow over 20 pages of analysis and rebuttal of Johnson's political principles and judgments on a wide range of topics including the Quebec Act, the late proceedings respecting the Americans, and the conduct of the previous Parliament. Towers concludes:]

It is somewhat curious to observe, how much your Jacobitism is apt to break forth, notwithstanding your present zeal in support of the government of a Prince of the House of Hanover. All your newly acquired loyalty to George III cannot make you forget your much-favoured House of Stuart, nor wholly remove your attachment to it. It was too deeply rooted, and become too natural to you, to be totally eradicated:

Naturam expelles furca, tamen usque recurret.[13]

In the *False Alarm*, p. 51 [*Works*, viii. 94], you say, that 'the struggle in the reign of Anne was to exclude or restore an *exiled King*.' This exiled King was the Pretender. And notwithstanding the many resplendent virtues which you have discovered in his present majesty, you are far from paying any compliments to his predecessors since the expulsion of the House of Stuart. For you inform us, that the prince from whom you received your pension, and in whose reign of consequence your loyalty commenced, is 'the only king, who, for *almost a century*, has appeared to desire, or much endeavoured to deserve, the affections of the people.'[14] The caution, and attention to chronology, with which you express yourself here, is truly admirable; you compliment his present majesty, but take care to exclude from your list of those Kings, who deserved the affections of the people, William III, George I, and George II. At the same time, leaving room for your readers to draw all honourable conclusions in favour of their predecessors, the Stuarts; whom you have entirely excepted from your censure; and, indeed, it ought to be remembered, that if, peradventure, they had a few faults, they were amply atoned for by that divine and hereditary right, which resided in their sacred persons!

You observe of Falkland's Island, *Patriot*, p. 20 [*Works*, viii. 150], 'that it is a bleak and barren spot in the Magellanic ocean, of which no use could be made, unless it were a place of exile for the hypocrites of

[13] Horace, *Epistles*, I. x. 24 ('You may drive out Nature with a pitchfork, yet she will always hurry back').
[14] *False Alarm*, in *Works*, viii. 93.

Patriotism.' But, perhaps, a better use might be made of it. It would at least be well adapted for the reception of men, who, though born under a free constitution of government, have no sense of its value, or concern for its preservation; who are ready to prostitute their talents in the service of every minister who will employ them; or who have so much attachment to despotic principles, as to be for ever incapable of becoming real friends to that public liberty, by which this country has been so long, and so honourably distinguished. Men of slavish principles must ever be unworthy members of a free state. And as to yourself, however unwilling you may now be, when you can bask in beams of royal favour, to remove to a spot like this, there was a time when you seemed to languish for such a retreat: when you pathetically exclaimed,

> Has Heav'n reserv'd, in pity to the poor,
> No pathless waste, or undiscover'd shore?
> No secret island in the boundless main?
> No peaceful desart, yet UNCLAIM'D BY SPAIN?
> Quick let us rise, the happy seats explore,
> And bear OPPRESSION'S INSOLENCE no more.[15]

It is a misfortune which has attended your political writings, that they have degraded your own character, without rendering much service to those by whom you were employed. I believe no writer of your abilities ever engaged in politics, whose productions were of so little effect, and so unprofitable to his patrons. And you may in many respects be considered as a memorable instance of human weakness. For though you have given evidences of great force of genius, you have at the same time discovered such little prejudices, and such bigotted attachments, as would have disgraced a common understanding.

You will probably, with that haughtiness which is natural to you, but which even your best friends must acknowledge to be a considerable flaw in your character, affect to disregard whatever can be offered against your conduct, or your writings. But should you ever again really be influenced by those principles of virtue, which you have so forcibly inculcated on others, you will regret that your time has been misemployed in the vindication of measures, which should have excited the indignation of every honest man. I would, however, wish you to remember, should you again address the public under the character of a political writer, that luxuriance of imagination, or energy of language, will ill compensate for the want of candour, of justice, and of truth.

---

[15] London, ll. 170–5.

And I shall only add, that should I hereafter be disposed to read, as I heretofore have done, the most excellent of all your performances, THE RAMBLER, the pleasure which I have been accustomed to find in it will be much diminished by the reflexion, that the writer of so moral, so elegant, and so valuable a work, was capable of prostituting his talents in such productions, as the *False Alarm*, the *Thoughts on the Transactions respecting Falkland's Islands*, and the *Patriot*.

I am Sir,

Your very humble Servant.

42. *Tyranny Unmasked*

1775

Extracts from pp. 2–11, 79–90.

This anonymous pamphlet is representative of the response provoked by Johnson's final excursion into political writing, *Taxation no Tyranny* (March 1775). See Introduction, p. 28.

In deference to truth and fact, it must be observed, that reason and argument have for some time plainly decided the matter in favour of American exemption. Without doors, the much boasted supremacy of Parliament, to tax an unrepresented and unrepresentable part of British subjects, hath hardly a single mouth left to echo it. Within the two great national assemblies, *the question* now decides, for government, those measures, which government no longer strives to discuss. It may still go on to adopt such as may promise success to it in its present struggle with America; but the generality are nevertheless unanimous, that America cannot constitutionally be taxed here.

In this state of the matter, when all men had hitherto weighed it by law and constitution, as applied to the specific circumstances of the American Colonies, and when thus *put in the balance* it began to shew itself *wanting* on the side of government; steps forth a most redoubted ministerial champion, who tells us that *Taxation is no Tyranny*: thus shaking off at once all the shackles of local circumstances, specific rights, and constitutional liberties; cutting asunder the several knots, which all former combatants, finding themselves bound by them, had patiently tried to untie; and, with his own right arm, laying the Americans on their backs, stunned, silenced, crippled, defeated, at the mercy of government.

Nothing indeed can be more decisive than the principle, which this advocate has chosen to convey the sense of his performance. It scorns exactness, as it scorns all fear. It scorns limitations, it scorns circumstances; rejecting all mesne views, it darts to an universal conclusion at once: *Taxation is no Tyranny*. We must consider this as an universal proposition. At least, it must be meant as a catch-word, to lay hold of those, who cannot reason; or to make those who can, and who think America injured, distrust for a moment, at least, their reasonings. And truly, if men can be brought to swallow this proposition, it will prove an effectual *quietus* to silence the Americans, and to allay all the present ferments, excited by American taxation, in the British Empire. But, was ever a more daring proposition offered to mankind? one more insulting to common understanding? 'Tis too absurd to deserve a confutation. To attempt to give it one by ever so little reasoning, would be an abuse and waste of sense. But to Englishmen the assertion is attended with double shame and effrontery: though it is entirely of a piece with what tyrants, and the tools of tyrants, even in this nation, have ever wished to establish; and therefore, though not new to Englishmen, yet the more unpardonable by them, who have ever shewn their indignation against it, and risen in fury to crush it. Methinks, therefore, the Author might have chosen a more cautious and decent sentiment for the index to his pamphlet; one more near to truth, one less irritating to Englishmen. But these are times, perhaps, for ministerial advocates to try, what Tory-doctrines may be disseminated.

The pamphlet before us evidently fathers itself upon one of such principles. And here, before I proceed further in this thought, I cannot help remarking, that it is exceedingly odd to find, so early as in the third generation from the time that we put an absolute exclusion, as we thought, upon Toryism from the government of these realms, Toryism now again making its way upon us in open publications, countenanced even by an administration. This is indeed exceedingly grievous to all honest men; because, if government approves it, it teaches others the worst lesson against itself; as it insinuates, by a most odious implication, an injury done to those, who lost the crown of England for their Tory principles.

If it should be found further, that the writer of the pamphlet above-mentioned is so much distinguished by the immediate notice of government as to be *pensioned*; the remark I have just made will require other and stronger terms to be given to it, before it will adequately express my feelings. Fame strongly confirms this circumstance; and fixes that production on an eminent lexicographer, who has, on former occasions, drawn his pen to gloss over the bad measures of this very administration, and to save them, when gasping for life. If we may judge indeed from the internal marks of style and diction, I know not any writer to whom we should be more apt to ascribe so *operose a deduction*,[1] than to that same person, whose very *operose* pen hath consummated more works of *operosity*, than that perhaps of any man existing; and now (if this fame be true) is more *operose* than ever, having the defence of a minister added to its other *operosities*—the vindication of dark and difficult Machiavelian politics supcradded to, perhaps superseding, the plain and pleasurable pursuit of science and the muses. Yet, notwithstanding these appearances, I can hardly concur in fixing this production on that gentleman: Because, on one hand, though he is pensioned, I have no doubt he would never convict himself out of his own mouth, nor invite the obloquy of the world, by becoming so very a pensioner, or (in his own words) so very *a slave of state*, as to be *hired by* his *stipend to obey his master* in all things: And yet, having once passed that definition, he must (if this production be his) inevitably have damned his own definition, or have damned himself for a slave. On another hand, when I consider with what singular virulence that gentleman has, all his life-long, written of the *Revolution* and the *House of Hanover*; I can as little believe that he would undertake the vindication of a minister in these days, as that a minister should employ him—reversing what rulers have ever shewn (I will not be so harsh as to say here to *traitors*, but) to *deserters*, and the *half-converted* of every kind, by *loving* and *trusting* the *deserter*, however they might *love* the *desertion*.

What effect that pamphlet hath had upon the public, I know not. But if it hath operated upon others, as it hath done upon myself, it must have rivetted all who have read it in an unalterable conviction, that America is unjustly dealt with. I understand however, that a great man in office hath thought proper to become the herald of its merits.[2] He said there was

---

[1] *Taxation no Tyranny*, in *Works*, viii. 156.

[2] Perhaps the Prime Minister, Lord North, who, as Chancellor of Oxford University, on 23 March 1775 proposed the award to Johnson of the degree of Doctor in Civil Law.

an abundance of wit in it. Whether there be this or not, every one will judge for himself. But if there be no *argument*, or only little of it, I cannot see what all its *wit* can be worth. In my judgment, *wit* has no sort of business in the present question, nor can be employed in it, without bespeaking those who employ it to be, even in their own consciousness, on the worst side. I grant however, on recollection, that people may be *outwitted* of their *property*: and when that property cannot otherwise be fairly obtained, I know of no other mean but *wit*, by which it can be come at. I am one of the first to believe, that if the property of the Americans is wrested from them by British Taxation, it must be by *outwitting* them. In this view, therefore, I wonder not at all that the *wit* of that pamphlet should be so well spoken of. For if *that* be the ministerial battery against the property of the Americans, perhaps he that proclaimed the *wit*, and he that wrote it, may be equally dexterous in playing it off.

Whatever figure this gentleman may make in *wit*, he makes, I will venture to say, a very poor one in *argument*. If he be that Colossus of knowledge above hinted at, never could he have let himself down lower. Not even, when he attempted to palliate the wretched timidity, which sacrificed to our enemies the Falkland Islands and the honour of this nation together, was he more unfortunate, than when he vindicates the present blustering despotic measures against our fellow-subjects in America. But, in candor, I cannot lay the blame on the writer, but on his cause. *There is no making bricks without straw. Ex nihilo nihil fit.*[3] Not all the wit, nor all the industry of man, not all the learning of *Johnson*, can strike abundance out of that which is barren, reason out of that which is absurd, nor make palpable wrong appear to be right. Accordingly, the writer of that pamphlet, whoever he is, hath left the ministerial cause very lamely defended. Whoever looks for argument from him, must be disappointed: Whoever is convinced by him, must be previously determined to be so convinced. No subject can be more loosely treated. There is an evident shyness in him at coming to the point. If ever he does so, he seems impatient in his situation, and eager to quit it. He dwells chiefly on the outlines of his subject, where his observations are seldom pertinent, oftner bold than exact. He seems to promise himself more from plausibility than truth; and to make invective, of which he is ever exceedingly profuse, supply the place of argument. Thus, notwithstanding the high-sounding title he has given to his book, we find it not in any degree proved: After all the expectations we were bid to form from that, and

[3] 'Nothing comes to exist out of nothing', a recurrent idea in Lucretius, *De Rerum Naturâ.*

the name given to the writer, what has he told us? but that *the mountain labour'd, and brought forth a mouse.*[4]

[follows the course of Johnson's argument and, 'having . . . rendered the fabric of [his] *vision a baseless one*', draws to his conclusion.]

He comes next to the cardinal hinge on which the whole question turns;—turns by the moderation and affectionate dispositions of the Americans, who are unwilling to push the rights of their chartered constitution to that utmost line which would encircle them as distinct states, and therefore say, that, as dependant on the parliament of England, they cannot be taxed in England, because *taxation and representation are inseparable.* I must observe, that having smothered this swelling argument within him, through so many labouring pages, he apparently expires with uttering it, as if it exhausted his whole vital breath. He is able just to follow the first utterance of it with a page and an half; and then, after panting a little with the *old member*, he collects his breath again for about two pages more upon it, and DIES. For as to what follows, in long quotations from the continental congress, occasional sarcasms, and the beautiful analogy from *Truro*,[5] I am convinced every body will think, what he himself knows, that they were only intended to bring his pamphlet to bear Eighteen Pence.

But it were fit he should give us a reason why he treats this, which is the very marrow of the question, so briefly and so lightly. We have it. It *carries sound without meaning*. It is a pity these sort of writers cannot agree with one another. For Mr. *Hume* says, in his *History of England*, that it is the point *of which the English were ever*, WITH REASON, *particularly jealous*.[6]

As *a sound without meaning* our author accordingly treats it. Every reader of him must have observed, that it is not his meaning to come into close quarters. It is his continual effort to subtilize, when he ought to reason; and to convert into air, what is founded on rocks. The reader will recollect, that when he was obliged to notice that principle, which gives the very foundation to *representation*, viz. 'the natural right of the people to have a *consent* in their own laws;' he tried to make us believe it was a *sound without meaning*.[7] He is at the same game again here. Representation, when brought to fact, he tells us, vanishes in delusion. It is a thing, *whose*

[4] Horace, *Ars Poetica*, l. 139. Cf. *The Art of Poetry by Boileau, Made English* by Dryden, l. 701.
[5] *Works*, viii. 194–7.
[6] Hume and Smollett, *History of England*, 1762, 1846 edn, 502, 517, 538 *et al.*
[7] *Works*, viii. 173.

whole effects, expected or desired, we feel, but cannot discern. It is, in short, (to wrap up his idea in the justest image) a sort of guardian-angel hovering over this isle, whose benign influence we actually participate, but without knowing where or when it rests itself: and as it thus hovers over us, it may as easily take America in the sweep of its flight, as confine itself within the air encircled by the British Channel. This is *representation.*—As our author plainly chuses to keep off the ground, so I do not chuse to fight the air; and therefore I shall leave him to the honour and happiness of his own vision. . . .

Thus I have taken notice of all that appears in our author's pamphlet worthy either of my animadversion, or of taking up the reader's time. He is welcome to all that follows in the remaining pages. I must say, a stronger proof cannot be given, that administration finds itself run to earth, upon the merits of the great question now depending between itself and America, than in the publication of that pamphlet. It had been better, *that it had never been born.*[8] The world might then have given them credit for many weighty arguments in their own breasts. But now they have exposed *the nakedness of their land.*[9] Like honest men, they have published their case; but, like unfortunate men, they have lost the verdict. There is but one method left for consistency: Having appealed to the public, they should abide by the public voice, and resign at least the measures, which neither art nor eloquence can defend.

A *Colossus* in argument is like a lighted beacon in the country; it draws all men forth from their retirements. Such a one is in some sort a general challenger. And when a *Goliath* contemptuously throws down his glove to the whole forces of human kind, no wonder if a stripling *David* should go forth to meet him. He may count it honour, even to be defeated.

[8] Cf. Matthew 26: 24.
[9] Cf. Genesis 42:9.

43. Robert Fergusson, '*To Dr.* Samuel Johnson: *Food for a new Edition of his* Dictionary'

21 October 1773

Text from the *Weekly Magazine*, Edinburgh.

Published before the completion of Johnson's Scottish tour, this poem was one of the earliest public reactions to the notorious English visitor. Fergusson's reference to Wilkes and Churchill, together with his sustained parody of Johnson's allegedly pedantic style in the manner of Campbell's *Lexiphanes* (No. 62), associate him with three of Johnson's leading antagonists of the 1760s. See Introduction, pp. 6–7, 29.

> *Let* Wilkes *and* Churchill *rage no more,*
> *Tho' scarce provision, learning's good:*
> *What can these hungry's next implore?*
> *Even* Samuel Johnson *loves our food.*
>
> RODONDO

GREAT PEDAGOGUE, whose literanian lore,
With SYLLABLE and SYLLABLE conjoin'd,
To transmutate and varyfy, has learn'd
The whole revolving scientific names
That in the alphabetic columns lie,
Far from the knowledge of mortalic shapes,

As we, who never can peroculate
The miracles by thee miraculiz'd,
The Muse silential long, with mouth apert
Would give vibration to stagnatic tongue,
And loud encomiate thy puissant name,
Eulogiated from the green decline
Of Thames's banks to Scoticanian shores,
Where *Loch-lomondian* liquids undulize.

To meminate thy name in after times,
The mighty Mayor in each regalian town
Shall consignate thy work to parchment fair
In roll burgharian, and their tables all
Shall fumigate with fumigation strong:
SCOTLAND, from perpendicularian hills,
Shall emigrate her fair MUTTONIAN store,
Which late had there in pedestration walk'd,
And o'er her airy heights perambuliz'd.

Oh, blackest execrations on thy head,
EDINA shameless! tho' he came within
The bounds of your NOTATION; tho' you knew
His HONORIFIC name, you noted not,
But basely suffer'd him to chariotize
Far from your tow'rs, with smoke that nubilate,
Nor drank one amicitial swelling cup
To welcome him convivial. BAILIES all,
With rage inflated, Catenations* tear,
Nor ever after be you vinculiz'd,
Since you that sociability denied
To him whose potent Lexiphanian stile
Words can PROLONGATE, and inswell his page
With what in others to a line's confin'd.

Welcome, thou verbal potentate and prince!
To hills and vallies, where emerging oats
From earth assurge our pauperty to bay,
And bless thy name, thy dictionarian skill,
Which there definitive will still remain,
And oft be speculiz'd by taper blue,
While youth STUDENTIOUS turn thy folio page.

Have you as yet, in per'patetic mood,

* Catenations, *vide* chains. JOHNSON.

Regarded with the texture of the eye
The CAVE CAVERNICK, where fraternal bard,
CHURCHILL, depicted pauperated swains
With thraldom and bleak want, reducted sore,[1]
Where Nature, coloriz'd, so coarsely fades,
And puts her russet par'phenalia on?
Have you as yet the way explorified,
To let lignarian chalice, swell'd with oats,
Thy orofice approach? Have you as yet,
With skin fresh rubified by scarlet spheres,
Applied BRIMSTONIC UNCTION to your hide,
To terrify the SALAMANDRIAN fire
That from involuntary digits asks
The strong allaceration?—Or can you swill
The USQUEBALIAN flames of *whisky* blue
In fermentation strong? Have you apply'd
The kelt aerian to your Anglian thighs,
And with renunciation assigniz'd
Your breeches in LONDONA to be worn?
Can you, in frigor of Highlandian sky,
On heathy summits take nocturnal rest?
It cannot be—You may as well desire
An alderman leave *plumb-puddenian* store,
And scratch the tegument from pottage-dish,
As bid thy countrymen, and thee conjoin'd,
Forsake stomachic joys. Then hie you home,
And be a malcontent, that naked hinds,
On lentiles fed, can make your kingdom quake,
And tremulate Old England libertiz'd.

[1] Cf. Charles Churchill, *The Prophecy of Famine, A Scots Pastoral,* 1763, ll. 311–34.

44. Ralph Griffiths, unsigned review, *Monthly Review*

January–February 1775, lii, 57–65, 158–62

Griffiths (1720–1803) was the founder of the *Monthly Review* in 1749.

Scotland seems to be daily so much increasing in consideration with her sister-kingdom, that tours to the Highlands, and voyages to the isles, will possibly become the fashionable *routes* of our virtuosi, and those who travel for mere amusement. Mr. Pennant has led the way,[1] Dr. Johnson has followed; and with such precursors, and the sanction of such examples, what man of spirit and curiosity will forbear to explore these remote parts of our island, with her territorial appendages,—of which, indeed, and of the public advantages which *might* be derived from them, we have hitherto been shamefully ignorant.

Dr. Johnson's book may be regarded as a valuable supplement to Mr. Pennant's two accounts of his northern expeditions,—the more *properly* supplemental, as it is a very different performance, on the same subject; both Writers concurring in the general representation, where the track in which they proceed, and the subjects they view, happen to be the same (which is not very frequently the case) and disagreeing in no circumstance of importance.

Mr. Pennant travels, chiefly, in the character of the naturalist and antiquary; Dr. Johnson in that of the moralist and observer of men and manners. The former describes whatever is remarkable in the face of the country—the extraordinary productions of Nature—the ruins, the relics, and the monuments of past times; the latter gives us his observations on the common appearances and productions of the soil and climate, with the customs and characteristics of the inhabitants, just as particulars and circumstances chanced to present themselves to his notice. The ingenious Cambrian delights in painting sublime scenes, and

---

[1] Thomas Pennant, naturalist, antiquarian and traveller; published his *Tour in Scotland*, 1771, and *A Tour in Scotland and Voyage to the Hebrides*, 1774–6.

pleasing pictures; while the learned English Rambler seems rather to confine his views to the naked truth,—to moralize on the occurrences of his journey, and to illustrate the characters and situation of the people whom he visited, by the sagacity of remark, and the profundity of reflection.

None of those who have the pleasure of a personal acquaintance with Dr. Johnson, will suppose that he set out with many prejudices in *favour* of that country. With what opinion of it he returned, will be seen from the extracts we shall give from his observations.

[by summary and quotation traces the route of Johnson's journey.]

'ALL travel,' says our reflecting and philosophizing Rambler, 'has its advantages. If the passenger visits better countries, he may learn to improve his own, and if fortune carries him to worse, he may learn to enjoy it.' One of these advantages may, indeed, be most comfortably drawn from this survey of a cluster of islands, of which it is confessed, 'that they have not many allurements, but to the mere lover of *naked nature.*' For, 'the inhabitants are thin, provisions are scarce, and desolation and penury give little pleasure.'

As the enjoyment of this satisfaction may, however, (to the *national* English Reader) be mingled with some degree of malignant exultation, we do not, at present, feel so much desire to gratify him, as to pass on, directly, to matters of higher curiosity.—Besides, with regard to those circumstances of description, which chiefly serve but to mark the natural disparity between the southern and northern parts of our island, enough of them are to be found in the former part of this article.

The public attention hath been much excited by the altercations to which this work hath given birth, concerning the *Earse* language, and our Author's opinion as to the originality and authenticity of *Ossian's* Poems, as published by the ingenious Mr. Macpherson. We shall therefore preextract what the learned traveller has inserted, on that subject, in the work before us.

[quotes fourteen paragraphs of Johnson's views on Erse and Ossian.]

Such is the opinion, and such are the reasonings of our learned Author, in relation to the *northern Homer* and his supposed writings. To these arguments, nothing hath been opposed, by the champions for Ossian, but railing and ridicule, in the news-papers; together with an Advertisement from Mr. Becket, the Bookseller, declaring that the original was publickly exposed, during several months, at his shop, for the examination of the curious. But still it does not appear in what language that same *original* was written; and our honest publisher hath, since, modestly declined his part in the controversy: it is even said that, in private, among his friends, he makes no scruple of acknowledging that he is no better acquainted with the *Earse*, than Dr. Johnson himself.

The appearance of an *inclination* in our Author to believe in the *second sight*, (the notion of which hath so long, and so seriously obtained in the Highlands and the Isles) hath given rise to some pleasantry at the Doctor's expence. He does not, however, profess his entire faith in this species of prophecy. He declares that, on a strict inquiry into the subject, he never could 'advance his curiosity to conviction.' But he acknowledges that he 'came away at last, only willing to believe.'—This will, no doubt, extort a smile even from the gravest of our Readers; but all who have perused the Doctor's book must allow that he seems to have made the most, and the best, that could be made, of so very singular an investigation: and that he hath thrown out some observations on the subject, which only a man of genius could have offered. And the most infidel reader must subscribe to the justice of the Doctor's remark, that he, and his companion, would have had but 'little claim to the praise of curiosity if they had not endeavoured, with particular attention, to examine the question of the *second sight*.' He adds, 'Of an opinion received for centuries by a whole nation, and supposed to be confirmed through its whole descent, by a series of successive facts, it is desirable that the truth should be established, or the fallacy detected.'

The Doctor's remark, and intention, are equally entitled to our approbation; but the misfortune is, that, still, with regard to this question, there is no *truth established*, nor *fallacy detected*.

We must now, for the present, take leave of this very able and entertaining writer; but not without expressing our thanks for the pleasure we have received in the perusal of his animated and instructive narration.

As to any little defects that may possibly be espied in this work, by the minute critic, we have not, at this time, either leisure or inclination to engage in the search of them.—Indeed, the modesty, and dignity of simplicity, with which this philosophic traveller concludes his volume, are sufficient to turn the edge of all true and liberal criticism.

[quotes the final paragraph of the *Journey*.]

45. Anonymous, *Remarks on a Voyage to the Hebrides, in a letter to Samuel Johnson LL.D.*

1775

Extracts from pp. 1–6, 34–6. See Introduction, p. 29.

SIR,

It cannot be denied, that he who publishes his speculations to the world, submits them to the animadversion of every reader; the following observations therefore on your *Tour to the Hebrides*, need little apology; that work containing remarks sufficient to move passions less *irritable* than those which commonly warm a Scotchman's breast; and the world will not be surprized to find, that he who is said to 'prefer his country to truth,'[1] should prefer it also to prejudice, and to you.

I shall not endeavour to reduce to method what I have to say upon this occasion, but my remarks shall follow each other as nearly as possible, in the order of those observations which occasion them; and if, in imitation of so great a model, I should now and then quit the common path, 'to view a solitary shrub, or a barren rock,' I hope for excuse.

A man is not likely to be a very unprejudiced traveller through a country which he has held for forty years in contempt: *ocular* demonstration may convince him that his opinions were erroneous, but *no* demonstration will oblige him to retract: he whose errors have acquired a kind of classic authority, will not easily confess one of so long a standing, though founded on misapprehension or mistake; and much less will he be inclined to retract an error which arose from the malice of his heart.

The contemptible ideas you have long entertained of Scotland and its inhabitants, have been too carefully propagated, not to be universally known; and those who read your *Journey*, if they cannot applaud your candour, must at least praise your consistency, for you have been very careful not to contradict yourself. Your prejudice, like a plant, has gathered strength with age—the shrub which you nursed so many years in the hothouse of confidential conversation, is now become a full-grown tree, and planted in the open air.

[1] Cf. Boswell, *Life*, ii. 311.

I, Sir, who am almost as superstitious as yourself, could not help regarding your description of *Inch Keith*, the first object of your attention, as ominous of what was to follow. 'Inch Keith is nothing more than a rock, covered with a thin layer of earth, not wholly bare of grass, and very fertile of thistles.'[2] It immediately struck me, that your book would be something like this rock, 'a barren work, covered with a thin layer of merit; not only void of truth, but very fertile of prejudice:'—how far it may agree with this description, those only who have seen what you have seen, can judge.

Immortal Buchanan![3] If yet thy sacred spirit has any influence on the scenes of thy earthly existence, let a blasting fog consume the present productions of that holy place, where thou wert wont to exalt thy Creator! And yet this, so much complained of, vegetable congregation, may as much display the glory of God, and be as acceptable in His sight, as those who, though endowed with reason, 'draw near him only with their lips, whilst their hearts are far from Him.'[4] Let not him complain that an episcopalian chapel is turned into a green-house, who would not hesitate to convert a presbyterian kirk into a privy.

What can be said for the alienated college? do you think there are not professors sufficient for the students? if there be, surely they will not be less assiduous because they are better paid; the Scotch clergy do not become negligent of their duty in proportion as their income is augmented.

He who is determined to say whatever he can in prejudice of an object, will not only be apt to say untruths, but even improbabilities. When you said that 'a tree might be a show in Scotland,'[5] you certainly overshot your mark; such an assertion will never be believed, no, not though Dr. Johnson had sworn it. I will not say it is improbable you saw no trees, for much of the eastern coast of England, as well as of Scotland, is more naked of wood than the inland country; and the greater part of the road between Edinburgh and Inverness (at least the road which you travelled) is often upon the sands, and always near the sea. And yet I think you must have passed the Bridge of Don with your eyes shut. Middleton of Seaton took, perhaps, no notice of you; and you in return, disdained to take notice of his beautiful seat, whose surrounding woods adjoin to that bridge.

You saw few trees in that part of Scotland through which you passed,

[2] *Journey*, 4.
[3] George Buchanan (1506–82), poet and scholar, was Principal of St. Leonard's College, St. Andrews, 1566–70.
[4] Isaiah 29: 13.
[5] *Journey*, 9.

and you modestly insinuate, there are none in Scotland; a Scotchman who had traversed the north-west side of London, might affirm by the same rule, that there is not a corn field in England. Scotland, however, has its extensive and well-grown woods, as well as England; and you might have reclined, in every county, under the oak or the pine of an hundred years old.

It must not be denied, that the north of Scotland is universally destitute of hedges; for which I can recollect only one good reason. Hedges and trees are in general a mark of distinction peculiar to Gentlemen's seats: a farmer no sooner attempts to inclose his fields with a hedge, or ornament them with a row of trees, than he becomes the object of the Laird's jealousy or avarice; — he is supposed to be rich, his rent is raised, and he is compelled to the alternative of starving on his farm, or quitting it. To this may be added, that a farmer in Scotland is not allowed to lop even the wood which he has planted: the loppings, without which no farmer's houses are built, must be purchased of the Laird at his own price.

[there follow nearly thirty pages of censorious comment on a wide variety of Johnson's remarks. Concludes:]

I conclude with a parody on your own words,—'To propagate error, by refusing evidence, is a degree of insolence with which the world was not *till now* acquainted; but stubborn audacity, is the last refuge of detection.'[6]

These are far from being all the observations which a more attentive perusal of your book might have given birth to; but these will perhaps be sufficient to convince the unprejudiced, that veracity and candour are not always to be expected from grey hairs. Should they prompt some abler pen to vindicate a country and a people, which you have taken so much pains to asperse, they will not have been written in vain.

Of all the various readers into whose hands your book may fall, it is almost impossible to say to whom it can prove useful, unless it be to him who would perfect himself in the illiberal art of insinuation, or to him who loves to accumulate subjects for national abuse. To the former it will be a complete manual; and there is hardly a misfortune, a folly, or a vice, that it will not enable the latter to ascribe to *poor Scotland*, on the indubitable authority of Dr. Johnson. Let him, then, who may in future have occasion to prove that a Scotchman is poor, dirty, lazy, foolish, ignorant, proud, an eater of kail, a liar, a brogue-maker, or a thief; and that Scot-

6 Cf. *Journey*, 107.

land is a barren wilderness; let him apply to your book, for there he will find ample authority.

'You had long desired,' you say, 'to visit Scotland;'[7] the desire was invidious, for it was to discover the nakedness of a sister. The flame of national rancour and reproach has been for several years but too well fed—you too have added your faggot, and well deserved the thanks of your friends; but whether you have merited those of the Scotchman who procured you the means of subsistence,[8] or of the Monarch by whose bounty you are fed, is a question which your own conscience must determine.

46. James McIntyre, 'On Samuel Johnson, who wrote against Scotland'

1775

Translated from the text of the MacLagan Manuscript printed in the *Transactions of the Gaelic Society of Inverness*, xxii (1898), 177–8.

Four Gaelic songs are extant which vigorously trounce 'the London savant' for the 'insult, contempt and defamation' which he allegedly lavished on his Scottish hosts. Three appeared in Gillie's *Collection of Ancient and Modern Gaelic Poems and Songs*, Perth, 1786; the fourth is given below.

Indeed I do not believe that the monster's ancestral root Is of the Clan MacIan [Johnson]: Rather he was begotten to his mother By a stranger with the nature of Venus.

A boor without manners full of spite; a slave who is disrespectful to himself. The best meat when it spoils Will double its smell of corruption.

You are a slimy, yellow-bellied frog, You are a toad crawling along

7 Ibid., 3.
8 Bute (see above, p. 212n.).

the ditches, You are a lizard of the waste, Crawling and creeping like a reptile.

You are a filthy caterpillar of the fields; You are an ugly, soft, sluggish snail; You are a tick [such as] it is not easy to draw from What you grip in your claws.

You are the weedings of the garden, You are the straw and the chaff of the winnowing, When productive seed is sown; You are a dun-coloured heap of tobacco.

You are the malingerer from battle, You are the kite of the birds. You are now the secret jest of the bards. Among fish you are the cub of the dogfish.

Or that sullen beast the devil fish; You are the brat in the midst of filth, The badger with its nose in his buttocks three quarters of a year, A sheep-tick that is called the leech.

Foul is the wealth that you share, And if it were not that I do not like the name of satirist, I myself would earnestly desire to abuse you.

47. Donald McNicol, *Remarks on Dr. Samuel Johnson's Journey to the Hebrides*

1779

Extracts from pp. 1–15, 242–3, 364–71.

Boswell refers to this work as 'a scurrilous volume, larger than Johnson's own, filled with malignant abuse, under a name, real or fictitious, of some low man in an obscure corner of Scotland' (*Life*, ii. 308). The *Remarks* is certainly malevolent; it is lengthy (371 pages); but the author could not be dismissed as 'some low man'. McNicol (1736–1802) was a learned minister (of Lismore in Argyll), an antiquary, and a Celtic poet in his own right. His book was republished together with Johnson's *Journey* in one volume, at Glasgow, 1817. (James 'Ossian' Macpherson may have collaborated with McNicol on the original publication.) See Introduction, pp. 7, 29.

Travelling through the different kingdoms of Europe has greatly prevailed, of late years, among men of curiosity and taste. Some are led abroad by the mere love of novelty; others have a more solid purpose in view, a desire of acquiring an extensive knowledge of mankind. As the observations of the former are generally of a cursory nature, and seldom extend beyond the circle of their private acquaintance, it is from the latter only that we can expect a more public and particular information relative to foreign parts. Some ingenious and valuable productions of this kind have lately made their appearance; and when a man communicates, with candour and fidelity, what he has seen in other countries, he cannot render a more agreeable or useful service to his own.

By such faithful portraits of men and manners, we are presented with a view of the world around us, as it really is. Our Author, like a trusty guide, conducts us through the scenes he describes, and makes us acquainted with the inhabitants; and thus we reap all the pleasures and advantages of travel, without the inconveniencies attending it. There is no country so contemptible as not to furnish some things that may please, nor is any arrived to that degree of perfection as to afford no matter of dislike. When, therefore, no false colouring is used, to diminish what is commendable, or magnify defects, we often find reason to give up much of our supposed superiority over other nations. Hence our candour increases with our knowledge of mankind, and we get rid of the folly of prejudice and self-conceit; which is equally ridiculous in a people as individuals, and equally an obstacle to improvement.

It were to be wished that the Treatise, which is the subject of the following sheets, had been formed on such a plan as has been now mentioned, as it would be a much more agreeable task to commend than censure it. But it will appear, from the sequel, how far its author has acquitted himself with that candour which could inform the curious, or undeceive the prejudiced.

When it was known, about two years ago, that Dr. Samuel Johnson, a man of some reputation for letters, had undertaken a tour through Scotland, it was naturally enough expected, that one of his contemplative turn would, some time or other, give a public account of his journey. His early prejudices against the country were sufficiently known; but every one expected a fair, if not a flattering, representation, from the narrative of grey hairs. But there was another circumstance which promised a collateral security for the Doctor's fair dealing. Mr. Pennant,[1] and other gentlemen of abilities and integrity, had made the same tour before him, and, like men of liberal sentiments, spoke respectfully of the Scotch nation. It was thought, therefore, that this, if nothing else, would prove a check on his prepossessions, and make him extremely cautious, were it only for his own sake, how he contradicted such respectable authorities.

Neither of these considerations, however, had any weight. The Doctor hated Scotland; that was the *master-passion*, and it scorned all restraints. He seems to have set out with a design to give a distorted representation of every thing he saw on the north side of the Tweed; and it is but doing him justice to acknowledge, that he has not failed in the execution.

But consistency has not always been attended to in the course of his narration. He differs no more from other travellers, than he often does from himself, denying at one time what he has asserted at another, as prejudice, or a more generous passion, happened, by turns, to prevail;

---

[1] See above, p. 234n.

which, to say no worse, is but an aukward situation for a man who makes any pretensions to be believed.

At the same time I am not so partial to my country, as to say that Dr. Johnson is always in the wrong when he finds fault. On the contrary, I am ready to allow him, as, I believe, will every Scotchman, that the road through the mountains, from Fort Augustus to Glenelg, is not quite so smooth as that between London and Bath; and that he could not find, in the huts or cottages at *Anoch* and *Glensheals*, the same luxuries and accommodations as in the inns on an English post-road. In these, and such like remarks, the Doctor's veracity must certainly remain unimpeached. But the bare merit of telling truth will not always atone for a want of candour in the intention. In the more remote and unfrequented parts of a country, little refinement is to be expected; it is, therefore, no less frivolous to examine them with too critical an eye, than disingenuous to exhibit them as specimens of the rest. This, however, has been too much the practice with Dr. Johnson, in his account of Scotland; every trifling defect is eagerly brought forward, while the more perfect parts of the piece are as carefully kept out of view. If other travellers were to proceed on the same plan, what nation in Europe but might be made to appear ridiculous?

The objects of any moment, which have been chiefly distinguished by that *odium* which Dr. Johnson bears to every thing that is Scotch, seem to be—the Poems of Ossian,—the whole Gallic language,—our seminaries of learning,—the Reformation,—and the veracity of all Scotch, and particularly Highland narration. The utter extinction of the two former seems to have been the principal motive of his journey to the North. To pave the way for this favourite purpose, and being aware that the influence of tradition, to which all ages and nations have ever paid some regard in matters of remote antiquity, must be removed, he resolves *point blank* to deny the validity of all Scotch, and particularly Highland narration. . . .

From the first appearance of Ossian's Poems in public,[2] we may date the origin of Dr. Johnson's intended tour to Scotland; whatever he may pretend to tell us, in the beginning of his narration. There are many circumstances to justify this opinion; among which a material one is, that a gentleman of undoubted honour and veracity, who happened to be at London soon after that period, informed me upon his return to the country, that Caledonia might, some day, look for an unfriendly visit

[2] *Fragments of Ancient Poetry collected in the Highlands of Scotland*, 1760, was James Macpherson's first publication of 'Ossian'.

from the Doctor. So little able was he, it seems, to conceal his ill-humour on that occasion, that it became the subject of common discourse; and the event has fully verified what was predicted as the consequence.

In the year 1773 he accomplished his purpose; and sometime in the year following he published an account of his journey, which plainly shews the spirit with which it was undertaken. All men have their prejudices more or less, nor are the best always without them; but so sturdy an instance as this is hardly to be met with. It is without example, in any attempt of the like kind that has gone before it; and it is to be hoped, for the sake of truth and the credit of human nature, it will furnish none to such as may come after.

[McNicol claims that he is 'perfectly free from narrowness of national prejudice'.]

My first intention was to write what I had to say on this subject in the form of an Essay. Upon farther consideration, however, the method I have now adopted appeared the most eligible; as, by citing the Doctor's own words, the Public will be the better enabled to judge what justice is done to his meaning. This plan, on account of the frequent interruptions, may not, perhaps, render the performance so entertaining to some readers; but it gives an opportunity for a more close investigation, and to such as are not possessed of the Doctor's book, it will, in a great measure, supply its place.

That the reader may not be disappointed, I must tell him before-hand, that he is not to expect, in the following sheets, what Dr. Johnson calls 'ornamental splendors.' Impartiality of observation shall be more attended to than elegance of diction; and if I appear sometimes severe, the Doctor shall have no reason to say I am unjust. He is to be tried all along by his own evidence; and, therefore, he cannot complain, if, 'out of his own mouth, he is condemned.'

Dr. Johnson informs us, that he set out from Edinburgh, upon his intended peregrination, the 18th of August 1773. This must undoubtedly appear an uncommon season of the year for an old frail inhabitant of London to undertake a journey to the Hebrides, if he proposed the tour should prove agreeable to himself, or amusing to the Public. Most other travellers make choice of the summer months, when the countries through which they pass are seen to most advantage; and as the Doctor acknowledges he had been hitherto but little out of the metropolis, one should think he would have wished to have made the most of his journey. But it was not beauties the Doctor went to find out in Scotland, but defects; and for the northern situation of the Hebrides, the advanced time of the year suited his purpose best.

He passes over the city of *Edinburgh* almost without notice; though surely its magnificent castle, its palace, and many stately buildings, both public and private, were not unworthy of a slight touch, at least, from the Doctor's pencil. Little, therefore, is to be expected from a man who would turn his back on the capital with a supercilious silence. But, indeed, he is commonly very sparing of his remarks where there is any thing that merits attention; though we find he has always enough to say where none but himself could find matter of observation.

[follows Johnson's account step by step. Only the remarks on his attitude to Gaelic and Ossian are given.]

There has been occasion to observe, oftener than once, that it was the great object of the Doctor's *Journey*, to find out some pretence or other for denying the authenticity of the ancient compositions in the *Gaelic* language; and now that design begins to unfold itself beyond a possibility of doubt. To effect his purpose, he takes a short but very ingenious method. He finds it only necessary to say, that no Bards have existed for some centuries; that, as nothing was then written in the *Gaelic* language, their works must have perished with themselves; and consequently, that every thing now attributed to them, by their modern countrymen, must be false and spurious.[3]

As the Doctor gives no authority for the facts, from which he draws this inference, he might as well have remained at home, as he says upon another occasion, and have fancied to himself all that he pretends to have heard on this subject. His bare word, without leaving *Fleet-street*, would have been just as good as his bare word after returning from the *Hebrides*. A *Journey*, however, was undertaken; though there is every reason to believe, that it was not so much with a view to obtain information, as to give a degree of sanction to what he had before resolved to assert. . . .

The Doctor concludes his observations on the Poems of *Ossian*, by passing two very severe reflections; the one of a personal, the other of a national kind. As what he says is pretty remarkable, I shall give it in his own words.

'I have yet,' says he, 'supposed no imposture but in the publisher;' and, a little after, he adds, 'The Scots have something to plead for their easy reception of an improbable fiction: they are seduced by their

[3] *Journey*, 104–8.

fondness for their supposed ancestors. A Scotchman must be a very sturdy moralist, who does not love *Scotland* better than truth; he will always love it better than inquiry; and, if falsehood flatters his vanity, will not be very diligent to detect it.'[4]

As an imposture is the last thing of which a gentleman can be supposed guilty, it is the last thing with which he ought to be charged. To bring forward such an accusation, therefore, without proof to establish it, is a *ruffian* mode of impeachment, which seems to have been reserved for Dr. *Johnson,* There is nothing in his *Journey to the Hebrides* to support so gross a calumny, unless we admit his own *bare* assertions for arguments; and the publisher, if by the publisher he means Mr. *Macpherson,*[5] is certainly as incapable of an imposture, as the Doctor is of candour or good manners.

The indelicacy of such language is obvious. A gentleman would not have expressed himself in that manner, for his own sake; a man of prudence would not have done it, for fear of giving just offence to Mr. Macpherson. But the Doctor seems to have been careless about the reputation of the first of those characters; and the malignity of his disposition seems to have made him overlook the foresight generally annexed to the second. Though he was bold in his assertions, however, I do not find he has been equally courageous in their defence. His mere allegation on a subject which he could not possibly understand, was unworthy of the notice of the gentleman accused; but the language, in which he expressed his doubts, deserved chastisement. To prevent this, he had age and infirmities to plead; but not content with that security, which, I dare venture to say, was sufficient, he declared, when questioned, that he would call the laws of his country to his aid. Men, who make a breach upon the laws of good manners, have but a scurvy claim to the protection of any other laws.

Nor will our traveller come better off with the public, in his more general assault. No man, whose opinion is worth the regarding, will give credit to so indiscriminate a calumny: the Doctor, therefore, has exhibited this specimen of his rancour to no other purpose, than either to gratify the prejudiced, or to impose upon the weak and credulous. If any thing can be inferred from what he says, it is only this, that he himself is not so 'very sturdy a moralist' as to love *truth* so much as he hates *Scotland.*

Soon after this, he tells us, that he left *Sky* to visit some other islands.

[4] Ibid., 108.
[5] James Macpherson (1736–96), alleged translator of the Ossianic poems.

But as his observations, through that part of his *Journey*, present nothing new, I shall not follow him in his progress; and the reader, I believe, as well as myself, will have no objection to be relieved, from his long attendance on so uncouth a companion. We shall leave him, therefore, to rail, in the old way, at the poverty, ignorance, and barbarity of the inhabitants; while, with a peculiar consistency, he acknowledges plenty, intelligence, and politeness, every where. Neither shall we disturb his meditations among the ruins of *Iona*; but permit him to tread that *once* hallowed spot with reverential awe, and demonstrate the *true* spirit of his faith, by mourning over the 'dilapidated monuments of ancient sanctity.'[6]

When he tells us, page 376 [146], that men bred in the universities of *Scotland* obtain only a mediocrity of knowledge between learning and ignorance, he contradicts his own attestations to the contrary in a thousand different places. I formerly compared this passage with his *elogiums* on the Highland clergy; I must now contrast it with what he mentions in two or three pages after. 'We now,' says he, 'returned to *Edinburgh*, where I passed some days with men of learning, whose names want no advancement from my commemoration.'[7] It was somewhat careless in the Doctor, to say no worse, to hold so very different a language in page 379, while the censure passed on our universities, but so little before, must be recent in the reader's memory. But a regard to the *trifling* forms of consistency seems never to have been an object of his attention.

It happens luckily, however, that the reputation of the *Scots* for learning rests upon a better foundation than the opinion of Dr. *Johnson*. The testimony of the world is in their favour; and, against that, *his* praise or censure can have but little weight. The three learned professions bear witness to their knowledge and talents. In physic they stand un-rivalled; and in the pulpit and at the bar they have no superiors.

But, besides professional merit, the Scots have long occupied every other department of literature; and they have distinguished themselves in each. The province of history is, in a manner, yielded up to them; they have added largely to the various stores of philosophy and the mathe-matics; and, in criticism and the *belles lettres*, they have discovered abili-ties, and acquired applause. Though they seldom descend to the *ludicrous*, yet they have not wanted writers, who have made some figure in that walk. If the Doctor doubts the fact, I shall refer him, for information, to the author of *Lexiphanes*.[8]

[6] *Journey*, 131.   [7] Ibid., 147.   [8] Archibald Campbell (see document No. 62).

I shall now take a final leave of Dr. *Johnson*. That he set out with an intention to traduce the *Scots* nation, is evident; and the account he gives of his Journey shews, with what a stubborn malignity he persevered in that purpose. Every line is marked with prejudice; and every sentence teems with the most illiberal invectives. If he has met with some correction, in the course of this examination, it is no more than he ought to have expected; unless he feels in his own mind, what his pride perhaps will not allow him to acknowledge, that misrepresentation and abuse merit no passion superior to contempt.

48. Edward Dilly to James Boswell

26 September 1777

Life, iii. 110–11.

The letter from Dilly (1732–79), one of the most reputable London booksellers, describes the genesis of the *Lives of the English Poets*. See Introduction, p. 13.

Dear Sir,

You will find by this letter, that I am still in the same calm retreat, from the noise and bustle of London, as when I wrote to you last. I am happy to find you had such an agreeable meeting with your old friend Dr. Johnson; I have no doubt your stock is much increased by the interview; few men, nay I may say, scarcely any man, has got that fund of knowledge and entertainment as Dr. Johnson in conversation. When he opens freely, every one is attentive to what he says, and cannot fail of improvement as well as pleasure.

The edition of the Poets, now printing, will do honour to the English press; and a concise account of the life of each authour, by Dr. Johnson, will be a very valuable addition, and stamp the reputation of this edition superiour to any thing that is gone before. The first cause that gave rise to this undertaking, I believe, was owing to the little trifling edition of the Poets, printing by the Martins, at Edinburgh, and to be sold by Bell, in London. Upon examining the volumes which were printed, the type was found so extremely small, that many persons could not read them; not only this inconvenience attended it, but the inaccuracy of the press was very conspicuous. These reasons, as well as the idea of an invasion of what we call our Literary Property,[1] induced the London Booksellers to

[1] 'It has always been understood by *the trade*, that he, who buys the copy-right of a book from the authour, obtains a perpetual property' (Boswell, *Life*, i. 438).

print an elegant and accurate edition of all the English Poets of reputation, from Chaucer to the present time.

Accordingly a select number of the most respectable booksellers met on the occasion; and, on consulting together, agreed, that all the proprietors of copy-right in the various Poets should be summoned together; and when their opinions were given, to proceed immediately on the business. Accordingly a meeting was held, consisting of about forty of the most respectable booksellers of London, when it was agreed that an elegant and uniform edition of *The English Poets* should be immediately printed, with a concise account of the life of each authour, by Dr. Samuel Johnson; and that three persons should be deputed to wait upon Dr. Johnson, to solicit him to undertake the Lives, *viz.* T. Davies, Strahan, and Cadell. The Doctor very politely undertook it, and seemed exceedingly pleased with the proposal. As to the terms, it was left entirely to the Doctor to name his own: he mentioned two hundred guineas[2]: it was immediately agreed to; and a farther compliment, I believe, will be made him. A committee was likewise appointed to engage the best engravers, *viz.* Bartolozzi, Sherwin, Hall, &c. Likewise another committee for giving directions about the paper, printing, &c. so that the whole will be conducted with spirit, and in the best manner, with respect to authourship, editorship, engravings, &c. &c. My brother will give you a list of the Poets we mean to give, many of which are within the time of the Act of Queen Anne, which Martin and Bell cannot give, as they have no property in them; the proprietors are almost all the booksellers in London, of consequence. I am, dear Sir,

Ever your's,

EDWARD DILLY.

[2] 'Johnson's moderation in demanding so small a sum is extraordinary. Had he asked one thousand, or even fifteen hundred guineas, the booksellers, who knew the value of his name, would doubtless readily have given it. They have probably got five thousand guineas by this work in the course of twenty-five years.' Note by Edmond Malone, 4th edn of Boswell's *Life*, 1804.

49. Advertisement to the *Lives*

15 March 1779

Text from the last edition (1783) in Johnson's lifetime. The final
paragraph was not included in the first edition. See Introduction,
p. 13.

The Booksellers having determined to publish a Body of English Poetry,
I was persuaded to promise them a Preface to the Works of each Author;
an undertaking, as it was then presented to my mind, not very extensive
or difficult.

My purpose was only to have allotted to every Poet an Advertisement,
like those which we find in the French Miscellanies, containing a few
dates and a general character; but I have been led beyond my intention,
I hope, by the honest desire of giving useful pleasure.

In this minute kind of History, the succession of facts is not easily
discovered, and I am not without suspicion that some of Dryden's works
are placed in wrong years. I have followed Langbaine,[1] as the best
authority for his plays; and if I shall hereafter obtain a more correct
chronology will publish it, but I do not yet know that my account is
erroneous.

Dryden's *Remarks on Rymer* have been somewhere printed before.
The former edition I have not seen. This was transcribed for the press
from his own manuscript.

As this undertaking was occasional and unforeseen, I must be supposed to have engaged in it with less provision of materials than might
have been accumulated by longer premeditation. Of the later writers at
least I might, by attention and enquiry, have gleaned many particulars,
which would have diversified and enlivened my Biography. These
omissions, which it is now useless to lament, have been often supplied by
the kindness of Mr. Steevens and other friends; and great assistance has
been given me by Mr. Spence's *Collections*,[2] of which I consider the
communication as a favour worthy of public acknowledgement.

---

[1] Gerard Langbaine (1656–92), *Account of the English Dramatick Poets*, 1691.

[2] Joseph Spence (1699–1768). His *Anecdotes, observations and characters of Mr. Pope and
other eminent persons of his time* was first published in 1820 (ed. S. W. Singer). (Cf. Boswell,
Life, iv. 63.)

50. Edmund Cartwright, unsigned review, *Monthly Review*

July–September 1779, lxi, 1–10, 81–92, 186–91;
August–December 1781, lxv, 100–12, 353–62, 408–11;
February 1782, lxvi, 113–27

The ten volumes of Johnson's *Prefaces, Biographical and Critical to
the Works of the English Poets*—soon to be known as the *Lives of
the English Poets*—appeared in 1779 (four volumes) and 1781 (six).
The Revd Edmund Cartwright (1743–1823) became the rector
of a Leicestershire parish in 1779 but is best known for his invention
of the power-loom. He was a close friend of George Crabbe (see
the *Life of Crabbe by his son*, 1947 edition, 117). See Introduction,
pp. 7, 29.

The long-expected beautiful edition of the English poets has at length
made its appearance. Promises that are delayed too frequently, end in
disappointment; but to this remark the present publication is an
exception. We must ingenuously confess, that, from the first of its being
advertised, we considered Dr. Johnson's *name* merely as a lure which the
proprietors of the work had obtained, to draw in the unwary purchaser;
taking it for granted that he would have just allotted, as he owns he
originally intended, to every poet, an advertisement, like those which
are found in the French miscellanies, containing a few dates, and a general
character; an undertaking, as he observes, not very tedious or difficult;
and, we may add, an undertaking also that would have conferred not
much reputation upon the Writer, nor have communicated much
information to his readers. Happily for both, *the honest desire of giving
useful pleasure*, to borrow his own expression, has led him beyond his
first intention. This honest desire is very amply gratified. In the walk of
biography and criticism, Dr. Johnson has long been without a rival. It
is barely justice to acknowledge that he still maintains his superiority.
The present work is no way inferior to the best of his very celebrated
productions of the same class.

Of the four volumes of his Prefaces already published (more lives being promised), the first is allotted to Cowley and Waller, the second to Milton and Butler, the third is appropriated entirely to Dryden, and the fourth is divided between poets of inferior name, Denham, Sprat, Roscommon, Rochester, Yalden, Otway, Duke, Dorset, Halifax, Stepney, Walsh, Garth, King, J. Philips, Smith, Pomfret, and Hughes.

In the narrative of Cowley's life there is little, except the manner in which it is told, that is new; but this deficiency, which was not in the Biographer's power to remedy, is fully compensated for in the review of his writings, which abounds in original criticism. Cowley's poetical character is introduced with an account of a race of writers who appeared about the beginning of the seventeenth century, whom Dr. Johnson terms the *Metaphysical Poets*.

[quotes paras. 51–63, 'The metaphysical poets' to 'Milton disdained it'.]

He then proceeds to illustrate his remarks by examples, in the selection of which he is singularly happy. Of these examples the limits of the present Article will not admit of more than the following from Dr. Donne. It is a most curious specimen of *metaphysical gallantry*:

> As the sweet sweat of roses in a still,
> As that which from chaf'd musk-cat's pores doth trill,
> As the almighty balm of th' early East,
> Such are the sweet drops of my mistress' breast.
> And on her neck her skin such lustre sets,
> They seem no sweat drops, but pearl coronets:
> Rank sweaty froth thy mistress' brow defiles.

'In all these examples it is apparent,' as the Critic judiciously remarks, 'that whatever is improper or vicious, is produced by a voluntary deviation from nature in pursuit of something new and strange; and that the writers fail to give delight, by their desire of exciting admiration.'

'To chuse the best, among many good, is one of the most hazardous attempts of criticism.' Dr. Johnson ventures, however, to recommend Cowley's first piece, which he tells us ought to be inscribed *To my Muse*, for the want of which the second couplet is without reference. The Ode to Wit, he pronounces to be almost without a rival; and in the verses upon Crashaw, which apparently, says he, excel all that have gone before them, there are beauties which common authors may justly think not only above their attainment, but above their ambition. It were to be wished that a poet, of whom Cowley could speak in such terms of admiration as are to be met with in the verses alluded to, had been admitted into the present collection, or at least that some specimens of his works had been preserved in it.

In speaking of the Pindarique Ode of the last century, Dr. Sprat, the former biographer of Cowley, tells us, that the *irregularity of numbers is the very thing* which makes *that kind of poesy fit for all manner of subjects*. But, continues his present historian, he should have remembered that what is fit for every thing can fit nothing well.

[quotes paras. 141–3, 'The great pleasure of verse' to 'supply its place'.]

While he was upon this subject, we could have wished to have had Dr. Johnson's sentiments on the present pedantic affectation of dividing the English Ode into Strophè, Antistrophè, and Epode. Had the same reasons for such division subsisted now, as prevailed in the times of Pindar, our ode-writers would certainly have had some excuse for adopting it. We may be told, indeed, that this practice has the sanction of the *highest poetical authority*, we mean that of the late Mr. Gray; but in answer to this we may observe, that as no authority can sanctify absurdity, neither should it prevail with us to adopt what both common sense and reason are compelled to disapprove.

The neglect and obscurity of Cowley's principal poem the *Davideis*, is accounted for both from the choice of his subject, and from the performance of the work.

[quotes paras. 147 8, 'Sacred History' to 'they were made'.]

It is not to be supposed that in a poem labouring with these disadvantages, his critic will find much to admire. His character of the *Davideis* is contained in few words: 'In the perusal of the *Davideis*, as of all Cowley's works, we find wit and learning unprofitably squandered. Attention has no relief; the affections are never moved; we are sometimes surprised, but never delighted, and find much to admire, but little to approve. Still however it is the work of Cowley, of a mind capacious by nature, and replenished by study.'

It is something singular that neither Dr. Johnson nor a former Editor of the *select* works of this writer take any notice of the following beautiful ode which David is supposed to sing under the windows of Michal's chamber, when he first declares his passion to her:

[quotes 'Awake, awake, my lyre'.]

The elegance and harmony of this little piece ought, before this, to have intitled it to selection. Indeed there are an hundred and thirty lines immediately preceding it, in which the characters of the two sisters, Merab and Michal, are drawn with great happiness, that merit notice, if it were for nothing but this, that they are totally free from every characteristic fault with which this Writer is charged. But this is not all their merit; they abound with beauties *which common writers may justly think not only above their attainment, but above their ambition.*

The character of Cowley, in which we perceive no marks of partiality, is thus concluded:

[quotes final paragraph.]

The preface to the works of Waller comes next in succession. The moral and political character of this applauded writer are developed with great skill and acuteness. Ever attentive to the more important interests of mankind, and sensible that biography ought to be a lesson of virtue, Dr. Johnson never omits to intersperse, amongst the different parts of his narration, either maxims of prudence or reflexions on the conduct of human life; something that may either direct the judgment or meliorate the heart. In the lives of Waller and his cotemporary poets he has proceeded farther; he has made them the vehicles of his political orthodoxy. As we profess the principles of universal toleration, we shall leave his political opinions to themselves. Were we, indeed, disposed to controvert them, it might be considered as an unnecessary trouble. There will never want combatants to attack a man of Dr. Johnson's reputation, when the attack is to be made on a vulnerable part.

As the limits of our Review will not permit us to accompany our Biographer through the whole extent of his criticism on this Writer, we shall confine ourselves chiefly to that part of it which is allotted to his sacred poems, which do not please, we are told, like some of his other works.

[quotes paras. 134–41, 'It has been the frequent' to 'the sidereal hemisphere'.]

It is thus that he very properly accounts for the failure of Waller in his sacred poems, and not their being written, as his former Editor supposes, after his genius had passed the zenith.

'That natural jealousy which makes every man unwilling to allow much excellence in another, always produces a disposition to believe that the mind grows old with the body; and that he, whom we are now forced to confess superior, is hastening daily to a level with ourselves.

By delighting to think this of the living, we learn to think it of the dead; and Fenton,[1] with all his kindness for Waller, has the luck to mark the exact time when his genius passed the zenith, which he places at his fifty-fifth year. This is to allot the mind but a small portion. Intellectual decay is doubtless not uncommon; but it seems not to be universal. Newton was in his eighty-fifth year improving his Chronology, a few days before his death; and Waller appears not, in my opinion, to have lost at eighty-two any part of his poetical powers.'

Some writers carry this fanciful idea of Fenton's still farther, asserting that, though judgment may retain its vigour to a more distant period, imagination gradually decays at thirty-six. Were arguments wanting to confute such groundless assertions, we need only adduce the instance of the learned and ingenious Critic whose observations are now before us. He, certainly, has passed the zenith allotted to imagination, and probably the farther term which Fenton assigns to the genius of Waller, and yet his writings betray no abatement of intellectual abilities: his imagination still retains the full vigour of youth.—But enough of this trifling; let us return to Waller.

[quotes para. 150, 'The general character' to 'his imitators', and 153, 'But of the praise' to 'excelled it'.]

MILTON.

The active part which Milton took in the public transactions of the times he lived in, will ever subject him to the misrepresentations of partiality or prejudice. In the biographical part of the preface before us, we have observed some passages not totally free from the influence of one of these principles.

In the openings of the narrative, after mentioning some other particulars of his family, we are told that 'his father had two sons, John the poet, and Christopher, who studied the law, and adhered, as the law taught him, to the King's party. After the accession of King James, he was knighted, and made a judge; but, his constitution being too weak for business, he retired before any disreputable compliances became necessary.' Fenton says, 'by too easy a compliance with the doctrines of the court, both religious and civil, he attained to the dignity of being made a judge of the Common Pleas, of which he died divested not long after the Revolution.' As he is said to have adhered *to what the law taught him*, we will hope, though there doth not seem much reason to believe,

---

1 Elijah Fenton (1683–1730) published *Works of Waller*, 1729; he was also the editor and biographer of Milton.

that he retired before any disreputable compliances became necessary. Yet, when the disposition of the times is considered, it is far from probable that he should have been advanced from the obscurity of chamber practice, which he followed, to sit as a judge in the court of Common Pleas, unless his readiness of compliance had been previously known. But, perhaps, as he adhered, as the law taught him, to King Charles's party, the biographer thought him entitled to some little indulgence.

[comments on Milton at Cambridge.]

When the biographer comes to that part of Milton's life when he returned from abroad, he tells us, that 'hearing of the differences between the King and parliament, he thought it proper to hasten home, rather than pass his life in foreign amusements while his countrymen were contending for their rights. At his return he hired a lodging at the house of one Russel a taylor, in St. Bride's Church-yard, and undertook the education of John and Edward Philips, his sister's sons. Finding his rooms too little, he took a house and garden in Aldersgate-street. Here he received more boys to be boarded and instructed.' He then breaks off his narrative to exclaim, 'Let not our veneration for Milton forbid us to look with some degree of merriment on great promises and small performance, on the man who hastens home, because his countrymen are contending for their liberty, and, when he reaches the scene of action, vapours away his patriotism in a private boarding-school.'

What the Doctor finds to excite merriment we own ourselves ignorant of. Whatever might be Milton's patriotism, it was necessary he should live. To do this with competence and convenience, he undertook the education of youth. The necessity of this is acknowledged. 'His allowance was not ample, and he supplied its deficiencies by an honest and useful employment.' That he promised more than other men in the like situations may be doubted; that he performed less is what no man can have the hardiness to affirm. He had not been above a year in England before he signalized himself, and assisted the cause which he espoused, by his treatise of *Reformation*, in two books. This work was soon followed by another, and that, in the year following, by a third. With what propriety, therefore, are we to look with merriment at *his vapouring away his patriotism in a private boarding-school?* In what follows we fully agree with our Author:

[quotes paras. 36–7, 'This is the period' to 'absurd misapprehension'.]

Notwithstanding we give full credit to the justness of these remarks, we cannot think it impossible but Milton might make many improvements upon the modes of education which at that time might prevail; he certainly was capable of striking out new roads to learning that might possibly be shorter and easier than those that were usually travelled. For, though it be true 'that the speed of the best horseman must be limited by the power of his horse,' yet, were Dr. Johnson to ride a fox-chace, he would find that his speed would depend not only upon the power of his horse, but also upon the choice of his ground.

[quotes paras. 38–41, 'The purpose of Milton' to 'and avoids evil'.]

That those authors are to be read at schools which supply most axioms of prudence, most principles of moral truth, and most materials of conversation, is too evident to be denied: that these purposes are best served by poets, orators, and historians, such as are commonly read at schools, may be doubted. It may be doubted also how far the present question can be any way influenced by the example of Socrates. His methods of instruction seem to differ as much from the modes of education which Dr. Johnson means to defend, as it is possible for Milton's to do. We should apprehend the innovators who are here opposed, never intended to 'turn off attention from life to nature:' they seem to have been actuated by the more rational idea of uniting the study of nature with the knowledge of life. Does not our Author, with respect to Milton, in some degree acknowledge as much? 'One part of his method,' says he, 'deserves general imitation. He was careful to instruct his scholars in religion. Every Sunday was spent upon theology.'

'Of institutions we may judge by their effects. From this wonder-working academy, I do not know that there ever proceeded any man very eminent for knowledge: its only genuine product, I believe, is a small History of Poetry, written in Latin by his nephew, of which perhaps none of my readers has ever heard.'

When it is considered how small must have been the number of Milton's scholars, it is matter of wonder rather than of reproach, that even one should ever rise to literary distinction. Were the history of all the schools through the kingdom to be enquired into, we should not find above one scholar in five hundred that ever attains to a like degree of eminence.

Milton, as may naturally be supposed, was an advocate for the liberty of the press. He published a book on that subject, intituled, *Areopagitica, a speech of Mr. John Milton for the liberty of unlicensed printing.*

[quotes para. 58, 'The danger of such unbounded liberty' to 'hang a thief'.]

To those who wish not to favour the designs of arbitrary power, no such problem [of danger from unrestrained printing] is to be found in the whole science of government. The arguments by which it is attempted to make this grand question problematical might be allowed to have some weight, provided they were altogether true. That every dreamer of innovations propagates his projects is acknowledged; is it therefore true that there is no settlement? That every murmurer at government diffuses his discontent is acknowledged likewise; but have we, therefore, no peace? That every sceptic in theology teaches his follies is not to be denied; yet Dr. Johnson will surely not be so hardy as to affirm that we have no religion. In those countries where the press is restrained have they more religion? Or, indeed, have they so much? So far from suspecting that religion is injured by the liberty which every one enjoys of diffusing his own opinions, we are rather disposed to believe she is benefited by it. Were doubt and objection never to be started, it is probable that truth would be but seldom inquired into: were not error to be confuted, truth could never be established: were the attack of the sceptic and infidel to be suspended, the champions of religion would forget the use of their weapons; the centinel would sometimes sleep upon guard. It is by a scrutiny into the principles of religion that the duties of religious obligation are more forcibly impressed upon the mind; and were it not for the sceptic in theology, such a scrutiny would be but rarely thought of or attended to. The illustration of his argument is by no means analogous: an author's motives for publication may be many and laudable; a thief can enter your house from no motive but to steal: if an author offend against the laws of society, he may be detected and punished; or if he escape, his bondsmen, as we may call them, the printer and publisher, are responsible for his crime. A thief may break into your house, and it is true that you may hang him, provided *he be caught*. But what security is there that he *will* be caught, or if not, who is there to make compensation for the injury he may have done you? All this is to be supposed before the analogy between the thief and the author can hold good. Were it, indeed, to be the case, there would be as little to apprehend from the one as the other. If the moment we were robbed the thief were certain to be detected and hanged, a bolt to our doors would be an unnecessary precaution.

Milton's character is drawn in no amiable colours. According to Dr. Johnson, he labours under a suspicion of such atrocious villany as ought not, but upon the strongest grounds, to be admitted of any man.

[quotes paras. 64–5, 'While he contented himself' to 'wanted to accuse'.]

That the regicides were not the forgers of the prayer in question,[2] if we may judge from such evidence as appears, is more likely than that they were. That the use of it by adaptation was innocent, nobody will deny. To charge the author of *Icon Basilike* with the use of this prayer as with a heavy crime, was illiberal and indecent. But what circumstance in the life of Milton can warrant the suspicion that he either inserted it himself, or was privy to the insertion of it by others? Whatever might be his political errors, his moral character has been ever unimpeached; his regard for truth seems to have been inviolable; his religion appears to be free from every taint of hypocrisy; 'he lived in a confirmed belief of the immediate and occasional agency of Providence;' how can we imagine then that he had *so little fear in him of the true all-seeing Deity*, as to be the perpetrator of such deliberate iniquity? But setting every argument that may be drawn from these considerations aside, there was a meanness in it too despicable for the pride of Milton ever to have submitted to.

The most culpable part of Milton's conduct seems to be his adulation of Cromwell. . . .

Though it be not improbable that Milton's republicanism might be, in some degree, founded 'in petulance, impatient of controul, and pride disdainful of superiority,' yet he surely was able to give some better reason for adopting republican principles than that *a popular government was the most frugal; for the trappings of a monarchy would set up an ordinary commonwealth*. Though it be shallow policy, as Dr. Johnson observes, 'to suppose money the chief good, and though the support and expense of a Court be, for the most part, only a particular kind of traffic, by which money is circulated, without any *national impoverishment*,' yet it is equally true that the extravagance of a Court, by taking from *the many* to lavish on *the few*, may be guilty of great *national injury*.

Through the whole of his narrative Dr. Johnson seems to have no great partiality for Milton as a man: as a poet, however, he is willing to allow him every merit he is entitled to. In the examination of his poetical works he begins with his juvenile productions. The first that offer themselves to him are his Latin pieces. 'These,' says he, 'are lusciously elegant; but the delight which they afford is rather by the exquisite imitation of the ancient writers, by the purity of the diction, and the

[2] A prayer from Sidney's *Arcadia* which was inserted into *Eikon Basilike*, a book of meditations supposed to be those used by Charles I.

harmony of the numbers, than by any power of invention, or vigour of sentiment.' This character, we apprehend, will generally suit our modern Latin poetry; but we may particularly except that noble ode of Mr. Gray's, written at the Grande Chartreuse, and some few others; there are not many of the *poemata Anglorum* that contain 'much power of invention or vigour of sentiment.'

[quotes paras. 177–9, 'The English poems' to 'dandling the kid'.]

On *Lycidas* his censures are severe, and well enforced: he is of opinion no man could have fancied that he read *Lycidas* with pleasure, had he not known its author. *L'Allegro* and *Il Penseroso* are of different estimation. These he acknowledges to be two noble efforts of the imagination. But the greatest of his juvenile performances is the Mask of *Comus*; 'in which,' says the Critic, 'may very plainly be discovered the dawn or twilight of *Paradise Lost*. Milton appears to have formed very early that system of diction, and mode of verse, which his maturer judgment approved, and from which he never endeavoured nor desired to deviate.

Nor does *Comus* afford only a specimen of his language; it exhibits likewise his power of description, and his vigour of sentiment, employed in the praise and defence of virtue. A work more truly poetical is rarely found; allusions, images, and descriptive epithets, embellish almost every period with lavish decoration. As a series of lines, therefore, it may be considered as worthy of all the admiration with which the votaries have received it. As a drama it is deficient.' This deficiency is unfolded in a masterly manner.

The Sonnets come next to be considered. These were written in different parts of Milton's life, upon different occasions. 'They deserve not,' we are told, 'any particular criticism; for of the best it can only be said, that they are not bad; and perhaps only the eighth and the twenty-first are truly entitled to this slender commendation. The fabric of a sonnet, however adapted to the Italian language, has never succeeded in ours, which, having greater variety of termination, requires the rhymes to be often changed.'

Of the inconveniency of *the fabric of a sonnet* many of our writers seem to have been aware, having deviated, and, as we think, judiciously, from the strict Italian model, by giving to their rhymes a greater liberty of change. But even of the legitimate sonnet we are not without many beautiful examples: no one will doubt this assertion who has read Mr. Warton's.

We are far from thinking the sonnet, especially when emancipated from the unnecessary restraint under which it has hitherto laboured, to be ill adapted to the English language. By uniting the elegance and dignity of the ode with the simplicity and conciseness of the ancient epigram, it seems to be a species of composition well suited to convey effusions of tenderness and affection; such incidental effusions, we mean, as flow not from a confluence of various ideas, but such rather as proceed from a single sentiment.

The *Paradise Lost* comes next to be examined: 'A Poem, which, considered with respect to design, may claim the first place, and with respect to performance, the second among the productions of the human mind.' Dr. Johnson's criticism on this immortal work extends through fifty pages. To give any adequate idea of it would much exceed our present limits. We cannot, however, resist the temptation of presenting our Readers with one extract from it:

[quotes paras. 229–33, 'The thoughts which are' to 'its fertility'.]

The above extract is given, not as having peculiar excellence, but merely as, from its detached nature, it best admitted of selection.

Of this truly excellent analysis and criticism, it is scarcely hyperbolical to affirm that it is executed with all the skill and penetration of Aristotle, and animated and embellished with all the fire of Longinus. It is every way worthy of its subject: the *Paradise Lost* is a poem which the mind of Milton only could have produced; the criticism before us is such as, perhaps, the pen of Johnson only could have written.

[several *Lives* are speedily passed over, mainly by means of quotation.]

In characterising the poetry of Matthew Prior, Dr. Johnson, in more instances than one, deviates from the general opinion of its excellence. Many circumstances, indeed, concurred to elevate Prior's poetical character higher than its intrinsic merit alone would possibly have raised it. The single circumstance of his exaltation (which was always considered, as in fact it was, the consequence of literary attainments), by speedy gradations from the station of a tavern-boy to the rank of an ambassador, would naturally impress the world with an idea of very uncommon superiority. Prior's works are considered as composing Tales, Love-verses, Occasional Poems, *Alma*, and *Solomon*. 'His Tales are written with great familiarity and great spriteliness: the language is easy, but seldom gross, and the numbers are smooth, without the appearance of care.' But it is a doubt with Dr. Johnson, whether he be the original author of any tale which he has given us.

On his Love-verses the critic is particularly severe; and, if one or two pieces be excepted, justly so. And even in those, it is wit and gallantry, rather than passion, that entitles them to notice. A man, like Prior, connecting himself with drabs of the lowest species, must be incapable of feeling either the warmth of a true passion, or the refinements of an elegant one.

[quotes paras. 56–7, 'In his Amorous Effusions' to 'disappointment to himself'.]

That Dr. Johnson's objections to the scope and tendency of the last mentioned poem are just, no one will, we presume, be hardy enough to dispute; but it is at the same time much to be doubted whether many will agree with him in thinking it a dull and tedious dialogue. Were the question to be asked, which of Prior's poems has been most generally read? we are of opinion, it would be determined in favour of *Henry and Emma*. What every one reads can hardly be thought tedious and dull.

[quotes thirty-six paras. from the *Life of Pope*, with virtually no comment.]

The eighth volume of this amusing work contains the Lives of Swift, Gay, Broome, Pitt, Parnel, A. Philips, and Watts. As it furnishes little that is new, we shall pass on to the subsequent volume, which opens with that well-known specimen of elegant Biography, the life of Savage.

The only variation from the former copies of this work that we have noted, is in the following passage. 'In the publication of this performance (the Tragedy of *Sir Thomas Overbury*) he was more successful, for the rays of genius that glimmered in it, that glimmered through all the mists which poverty *and Cibber* had spread over it, procured him the notice and esteem of many persons,' &c. To foist in a stigma upon a man so many years after he has lain peaceably in his grave, has the appearance of something singularly disingenuous and unmanly. Indeed, whenever Dr. Johnson has occasion to speak of Cibber, it is with an acrimony that, in any other man, we should suspect must have proceeded from personal resentment. Cibber's dulness has been so long the butt of ridicule with every pretender to wit, that we are surprised any writer, who affects originality of sentiment, should condescend to divert himself and his readers with so stale a topic. There is no pleasure, as Dr. Johnson elsewhere observes, in chacing a school-boy to his common-places.[3]

In characterizing Thomson's merit as a poet, his Biographer nearly

[3] *Lives*, iii. 436.

coincides with the general opinion. As a man, however, the representation of his character is not so favourable. In the early part of life, while friendless and indigent, he is represented as soliciting kindness by servile adulation; and when afterwards he had the means of gratification, it is insinuated, that he was grossly sensual. What authorities there are for the former part of this character appear not: the latter, in opposition to the suffrages of the most respectable of his cotemporaries, rests solely on the testimony of the unprincipled and profligate Savage.

We are told that 'Thomson, in his travels on the continent, found or fancied so many evils arising from the tyranny of other governments, that he resolved to write a very long poem, in five parts, upon Liberty.' In this passage the Biographer seems to have brought himself into a dilemma: either there are no evils arising from the tyranny of arbitrary governments; or Thomson was a man of no observation. To which will Dr. Johnson subscribe?

[on the source of biographical information about Hammond.]

Dr. Johnson appears not to have recollected that Hammond's Elegies, the two last excepted, are taken almost literally from Tibullus. Considered merely in the light of translations they have a merit that translations rarely possess. Were it not for the Roman imagery, that is sometimes injudiciously retained, no one, unacquainted with the originals, would suspect that Hammond wrote not from his immediate feelings. To say that 'it would be hard to find in all his productions three stanzas that deserve to be remembered,' is certainly the height of prejudice. The Doctor forgets, that although at his time of life the subject of a love elegy may be totally uninteresting, it is not the case with every one, and we doubt not that at a certain period there are those who read them with greater avidity than even LONDON, or the VANITY OF HUMAN WISHES.

Dr. Johnson is at a loss to tell why Hammond, or other writers, have thought the quatrain of ten syllables elegiac. The character of elegy, he adds, is gentleness and tenuity. So long as some of the most violent and impetuous of the passions are the subjects of elegy, so long will this be an imperfect and mistaken definition.

The next life that offers itself is that of Collins: a writer whose imperfections and peculiarities are lost in the blaze of genius. But hear what Dr. Johnson says—'His diction was often harsh, unskilfully laboured, and injudiciously selected. He affected the obsolete when it was not worthy of revival; and he puts his words out of the common order, seeming to think, with some later candidates for fame, that not to write prose is certainly to write poetry. His lines commonly are of slow motion, clogged and impeded with clusters of consonants. As men are often esteemed who cannot be loved, so the poetry of Collins may sometimes extort praise when it gives little pleasure.'

[generous quotation from the *Life of Young*.]

The next in succession is Dyer; the slender particulars of whose life being already known, it were needless to repeat them.

In the year 1757 he published *The Fleece*, his greatest poetical work; 'of which,' says Dr. Johnson, 'I will not suppress a ludicrous story. Dodsley the bookseller was one day mentioning it to a critical visiter, with more expectation of success than the other could easily admit. In the conversation the author's age was asked; and being represented as advanced in life, *He will*, said the critic, *be buried in woollen.*'

With most profound submission to the recorder of this ludicrous story, as it is here called, the critical visiter's remark is, surely, as lame an attempt at wit as ever disgraced the vilest pages of the vilest jest book.

Of *Grongar Hill*, Dyer's earliest production, we are told, that when it is once read, it will be read again; of the *Ruins of Rome*, that the title raises greater expectation than the performance gratifies. And of *The Fleece*, which never became popular, that it is now universally neglected, and that little can be said likely to recal it to attention.

[quotes last two paragraphs on Dyer.]

We fear it is more owing to a decline of poetical taste than to any defects that are here pointed out, that Dyer's *Fleece* has been so undeservedly neglected. Indeed, if the time would permit, it would be no difficult undertaking to prove, that the greatest part of the objections that Dr. Johnson has raised against this excellent poem might with equal justice be brought against the *Georgics* of Virgil, a performance which, nevertheless, will be admired as long as poetry is understood.

[quotes from *Lives* of Mallet, Shenstone, Akenside, Lyttleton, and West; then finally turns to Johnson's remarks on Gray, and quotes paras. 32–49 on *The Progress of Poesy* and *The Bard*: 'My process has now' to 'ill directed'.]

Dr. Johnson sets out with telling his Readers, that *he is one of those that are willing to be pleased*, and that, consequently, he would be glad to find the meaning of the first stanza of the *Progress of Poetry*. It seems rather, that he is less desirous of finding the meaning of it himself, than of preventing others from finding it. Nothing can be more obvious and intelligible, we had almost said trite, than the allegory with which the *Progress of Poetry* commences. It is true, there is an inaccuracy in suffering the concealed idea to break through the figurative expression, as it does in the seventh line:

> Now the rich stream *of music* winds along.

Of this, little as it can add to the embarrassment of the scene, the Critic has, however, spared no pains to avail himself.

The objection to the second stanza (part of which, indeed, is borrowed from Pindar) will lose much of its force if we advert only to the almost inseparable connection between the poetry of the ancients and their mythology: we shall then perceive, that the influence of the poetical art upon the inhabitants of Greece may not be improperly described by classical imagery.

What is said of the second ternary of stanzas will be found, we are of opinion, a continued tissue of misrepresentation. 'The first,' says he, 'endeavours to tell something, and would have told it, *had it not been crossed by Hyperion.*' The liberality and candour of this criticism will best appear, by confronting it with the beautiful passage against which it is levelled:

> Man's feeble race what ills await,
> Labour, and penury, the racks of pain,
> Disease, and Sorrow's weeping train,
> And death, sad refuge from the storms of fate!
> The fond complaint, my song, disprove,
> And justify the laws of Jove.
> Say, has he giv'n in vain the heav'nly Muse?
> Night, and all her sickly dews,
> Her spectres wan, and birds of boding cry,
> He gives to range the dreary sky:
> Till down the eastern cliffs afar
> Hyperion's march they spy, and glitt'ring shafts of war.

Gray is next represented as telling his readers that the caverns of the North and the plains of Chili are the residence of *Glory and generous Shame.* Whoever will look into the stanza from whence this information is collected, will find that he says no such thing. All that he tells his readers (divesting it of its poetical language) is, that there have been poets even among the natives of Greenland and Chili; and that in those breasts, that are susceptible of the impressions of poetry, there is the residence of Glory,

And generous shame,
Th' unconquerable Mind, and Freedom's holy flame—

An assertion not only poetical, but, if taken with that degree of latitude with which a general assertion ought to be, philosophically true.

It was sufficient to assert, that *The Bard* is but a copy from the Prophecy of Nereus (an assertion, however, which every one will not, probably, agree to), without degrading it by a charge of a still meaner plagiarism: it certainly required singular ingenuity to find out, that the abrupt manner in which it opens was suggested by the ballad of Johnny Armstrong! The weaving of the winding-sheet may be given up: Gray was no Spitalfields poet.

That 'his odes are marked by glittering accumulations of ungraceful ornaments, that strike rather than please; and that his images are magnified by affection,' will, at least, be thought severe: but it is, surely, more than severe to say, that 'he has a strutting kind of dignity, and that he is tall by walking on tip-toe.'

It is not to be wondered at, if, to the professed admirers of Mr. Gray, the manner in which he has been treated by Dr. Johnson should appear not only hostile, but malignant: and if they once entertain an opinion that there is malignity in his censure, they will suspect, it is to be feared, that there is treachery in his praise; the passage, upon which he has bestowed his warmest commendations, being, perhaps, the most exceptionable that the severity of criticism could have selected. It is that in which he accounts for Milton's blindness:

Nor second he, that rode sublime
Upon the seraph wings of extasy,
The secrets of th' abyss to spy,
He passed the flaming bounds of place and time:
The living throne, the sapphire-blaze,
Where angels tremble while they gaze,
He saw; but blasted with excess of light,
Clos'd his eyes in endless night.

It is not to be denied that the images he employs are splendidly magnificent: but that the exertions of intellectual vision should extinguish the poet's corporeal eyes, is a forced and unnatural idea. It is one of those false and hyperbolical thoughts, which, though they may possibly be admired in the poetry of Spain, the chaste simplicity of classical composition ought not to admit of. But even supposing the possibility of the fact, the consequence is inadequate to its cause; so that, whichever way the sentiment be examined, it comes under the class of the false sublime: for if just, it is an anticlimax; if not, it is bombast. And yet it is this sentiment which Dr. Johnson has particularly marked as 'poetically true and happily imagined.'

But, peace to the manes of the Poet!

The eagle tow'ring in his pride of place[4]

is still an eagle, notwithstanding a defective feather in his wing.

After the minute and particular attention that has been bestowed upon these volumes as they came before us in succession, to enter into a general discussion of them collectively would be superfluous. It may not, however, be unnecessary to observe, notwithstanding they contain a fund of profound and original criticism, which, perhaps, no other pen but the Doctor's could have supplied, that some caution is, nevertheless, required to peruse them with advantage. Instances too frequently occur, in which the Critic's judgment seems altogether under the dominion of predilection or prejudice. To think for himself in critical, as in all other, matters, is a privilege to which every one is undoubtedly intitled: this privilege of critical independence, an affectation of singularity, or some other principle, not immediately visible, is for ever betraying him into a dogmatical spirit of contradiction to received opinions. Of this there need no farther proofs than his almost uniform attempt to depreciate the writers of blank verse, and his rough treatment of Gray. He observes of Shenstone, that he set little value upon those parts of knowledge which he had not cultivated himself; his own taste of poetry seems in some degree regulated by a similar standard: method, ratiocination, and argument, especially if the vehicle be rhyme, oftentimes obtaining his regard and commendation, while the bold and enthusiastic, though perhaps irregular, flights of imagination, are past by with perverse and obstinate indifference. It is not, then, to be wondered at, that the panegyrist of Blackmore should withhold from Collins and Gray what he has bestowed upon Savage and Yalden. Through the whole of his performance the desire of praise, excepting in the case of some very favourite author, is almost always overpowered by his disposition to censure; and while beauties are passed over 'with the neutrality of a stranger and the coldness of a critic,' the slightest blemish is examined with microscopical sagacity. The truth of this observation is particularly obvious when he descends to his cotemporaries; for whom, indeed, he appears to have little more brotherly kindness than they might have expected

4 Cf. *Macbeth*, II. iv. 12.

at Constantinople. And so visibly does the fastidiousness of his criticism increase, as his work approaches to a conclusion, that his Readers will scarcely forbear exclaiming, with honest Candide, What a wonderful genius is this Pococurante! Nothing can please him![5]

51. Unsigned review, *Critical Review*

May–June 1779, xlvii, 354–62, 450–3; August 1781, lii, 81–92

The reviewer's general opening remarks are given, together with his response to the *Life of Gray* for comparison with No. 50.

As the general character of every polished nation depends in a great measure on its poetical productions, too much care cannot be taken, in works of this nature, to impress on foreigners a proper idea of their merit. This task was perhaps never so well executed as in the performance before us. Our poetical militia, cloathed in the new uniform which the editors have here bestowed upon them, make a most respectable figure, both with regard to numbers and appearance. The text is, in general, correct, the paper not too white or glossy, but neat and clean, and the type sharp and elegant; though for eyes turned of fifty it may be thought rather too small. We could have wished, for the sake of uniformity, that the *Lives of the Poets*, instead of making a number of distinct volumes, had been prefixed to the works of the several authors, and in the same type. But to this we suppose the booksellers had some weighty and substantial objections, which will appear in due time. In the mean while, we must be content with what Dr. Johnson has found leisure to give his poets; some few a long life, some a short one, and some none at all. What we already have is however worthy of the writer; and, like the rest of his works, both amusing and instructive.

Biography, so far at least as it is concerned about little men, is not very entertaining, except when it has the additional grace of novelty to recommend it. The life of a poet is seldom read twice; and when the few

5 *Candide*, chapter 25.

interesting circumstances, or diverting anecdotes that can be picked up concerning him, are once known, curiosity is satisfied: to run over the same ground, therefore, when there could be little hopes of starting fresh game, to be obliged to tell the same tale which had been often repeated, was a task that could not promise to the undertaker much pleasure, or flatter him with the hopes of much additional fame by the execution of it: it was a labour which few men would have had courage and patience enough to engage in; and in which we at the same time firmly believe no man but Dr. Johnson would have performed so well. He has proved, indeed, that a man of genius, penetration, and sagacity, can always, even from old and worn-out materials, strike out something new and entertaining.

The *Lives of the Poets*, as far as they go (and we hope soon to have more of them) are well written, and as the painters say, in his best manner. This writer has, we know, been censured for a pompous phraseology: with what degree of justice we leave our readers to determine. Certain it is, that very little of this kind appears in the work before us; and for that little we are made ample amends by a variety of judicious reflections on men and manners, sensible and lively observations, together with many excellent criticisms on the most striking passages, equally just and impartial.

The writers of poetical lives seem in general to imagine themselves bound in honour to deal in nothing but panegyrics, and it is looked upon as a kind of petty treason in the biographer to see any fault in the hero of his history. This however is by no means the case with Dr. Johnson; if he has erred, it is rather perhaps on the other side, as his remarks on some of our best poets, particularly Milton and Waller, whose political opinions by no means coincided with his own, may be thought rather too severe. . . .

Dr. Johnson then enters into a minute examination of the several stanzas of *The Bard*, and concludes his criticism on the Odes by observing that they 'Are marked by glittering accumulations of ungraceful ornaments . . . His art and his struggle are too visible, and there is too little appearance of ease or nature.'[1]

Whether the whole of this free censure is strictly just and well founded, we will not pretend to determine. Certain it is, however, at least in our opinion, that no man ever acquired a high reputation at so easy a rate, or received such *great wages* for so *little work*, as Mr. Gray.—On his *Elegy in a Country Church-Yard*, we agree with Dr. Johnson, that too much praise cannot well be lavished; at the same time we think with him, that Gray's

[1] *Lives*, iii. 440.

Odes, as well as his other little performances, have been much over-rated. The reputation of a poet in this country is, indeed, a matter very fluctuating and uncertain. Whilst he lives, and perhaps many years afterwards, a proper and unbiassed judgment of his real merit is seldom found. It is a long time before whim and caprice, prejudice and partiality subside; and the true character is not often ascertained, till that of the man is entirely forgotten. Gray has been placed by his sanguine admirers by the side of Dryden and Pope. Dr. Johnson seems to have levelled him with the minor bards of a much inferior rank: half a century hence he may, perhaps, be fixed in his right and proper station,

> Behind the foremost, and before the last.

In the mean time, as the twig inclined too much one way, we are obliged to Dr. Johnson for bending strongly towards the other, which may make it strait at last.

52. William Cowper's opinions of the *Lives*

1779–91

Text from *Letters*, ed. J. G. Frazer, 1912, i. 38–40, 170–4, 283–4; ii. 280.

Cowper (1731–1800) records the immediate response of a sensitive poet whose roots were in the Augustan period but whose sensibility was Romantic. His Whig sympathies, his passion for Milton (whose poems he proposed to edit and whose Italian and Latin poems he translated), and his Evangelical religion made it peculiarly difficult for Cowper to be an enthusiast for Johnson. See Introduction, pp. 20, 30.

---

31 October 1779, to the Revd William Unwin:
I have been well entertained with Johnson's biography, for which I thank you: with one exception, and that a swingeing one, I think he has acquitted himself with his usual good sense and sufficiency. His treatment of Milton is unmerciful to the last degree. A pensioner is not likely to spare a republican; and the Doctor, in order, I suppose, to convince his royal patron of the sincerity of his monarchial principles, has belaboured that great poet's character with the most industrious cruelty. As a man, he has hardly left him the shadow of one good quality. Churlishness in his private life, and a rancorous hatred of everything royal in his public, are the two colours with which he has smeared all the canvass. If he had any virtues, they are not to be found in the Doctor's picture of him; and it is well for Milton, that some sourness in his temper is the only vice with which his memory has been charged; it is evident enough that if his biographer could have discovered more, he would not have spared him. As a poet, he has treated him with severity enough, and has plucked one or two of the most beautiful feathers out of his Muse's wing, and trampled them under his great foot. He has passed sentence of condemnation upon *Lycidas*, and has taken occasion, from that charming poem, to expose to ridicule, (what is indeed ridiculous enough,) the childish prattlement of pastoral compositions, as if *Lycidas* was the prototype and pattern of them all. The liveliness of the description, the sweetness of the numbers, the

273

classical spirit of antiquity that prevails in it, go for nothing. I am convinced by the way, that he has no ear for poetical numbers, or that it was stopped by prejudice against the harmony of Milton's. Was there ever any thing so delightful as the music of the *Paradise Lost*? It is like that of a fine organ; has the fullest and the deepest tones of majesty, with all the softness and elegance of the Dorian flute. Variety without end and never equalled, unless perhaps by Virgil. Yet the Doctor has little or nothing to say upon this copious theme, but talks something about the unfitness of the English language for blank verse, and how apt it is, in the mouth of some readers, to degenerate into declamation. Oh! I could thresh his old jacket, till I made his pension jingle in his pocket.

I could talk a good while longer, but I have no room; our love attends you.—Yours affectionately,

W. C.

5 January 1782, to Unwin:
But what shall we say of his old fusty-rusty remarks upon *Henry and Emma*?[1] I agree with him, that morally considered both the knight and his lady are bad characters, and that each exhibits an example which ought not to be followed. The man dissembles in a way that would have justified the woman had she renounced him; and the woman resolves to follow him at the expense of delicacy, propriety, and even modesty itself. But when the critic calls it a dull dialogue, who but a critic will believe him? There are few readers of poetry of either sex, in this country, who cannot remember how that enchanting piece has bewitched them, who do not know, that instead of finding it tedious, they have been so delighted with the romantic turn of it, as to have overlooked all its defects and to have given it a consecrated place in their memories, without ever feeling it a burthen. I wonder almost, that, as the Bacchanals served Orpheus, the boys and girls do not tear this husky, dry commentator limb from limb, in resentment of such an injury done to their darling poet. I admire Johnson as a man of great erudition and sense; but when he sets himself up for a judge of writers upon the subject of love, a passion which I suppose he never felt in his life, he might as well think himself qualified to pronounce upon a treatise on horsemanship, or the art of fortification.

17 January 1782, to Unwin:
I am glad we agree in our opinion of King Critic, and the writers on whom he has bestowed his animadversions. It is a matter of indifference

[1] In *Life of Prior*, *Lives*, ii. 202–3.

to me whether I think with the world at large or not, but I wish my friends to be of my mind. The same work will wear a different appearance in the eyes of the same man according to the different views with which he reads it; if merely for his amusement, his candour being in less danger of a twist from interest or prejudice, he is pleased with what is really pleasing, and is not over curious to discover a blemish, because the exercise of a minute exactness is not consistent with his purpose. But if he once becomes a critic by trade, the case is altered. He must then at any rate establish, if he can, an opinion in every mind, of his uncommon discernment, and his exquisite taste. This great end he can never accomplish by thinking in the track that has been beaten under the hoof of public judgement. He must endeavour to convince the world, that their favourite authors have more faults than they are aware of, and such as they have never suspected. Having marked out a writer universally esteemed, whom he finds it for that very reason convenient to depreciate and traduce, he will overlook some of his beauties, he will faintly praise others, and in such a manner as to make thousands, more modest, though quite as judicious as himself, question whether they are beauties at all. Can there be a stronger illustration of all that I have said, than the severity of Johnson's remarks upon Prior, I might have said the injustice? His reputation as an author who, with much labour indeed, but with admirable success, has embellished all his poems with the most charming ease, stood unshaken till Johnson thrust his head against it. And how does he attack him in this his principal fort? I cannot recollect his very words, but I am much mistaken indeed if my memory fails me with respect to the purport of them. 'His words,' he says, 'appear to be forced into their proper places; there indeed we find them, but find likewise that their arrangement has been the effect of constraint, and that without violence they would certainly have stood in a different order.'[2] By your leave, most learned Doctor, this is the most disingenuous remark I ever met with, and would have come with a better grace from Curl or Dennis.[3] Every man conversant with verse-writing knows, and knows by painful experience, that the familiar style is of all styles the most difficult to succeed in. To make verse speak the language of prose, without being prosaic,—to marshal the words of it in such an order as they might naturally take in falling from the lips of an extempory speaker, yet without meanness, harmoniously, elegantly, and without seeming to

---

[2] *Lives*, ii. 209.
[3] Edmund Curll (1675–1747), the rascally bookseller; John Dennis (1657–1734), the irascible critic.

displace a syllable for the sake of the rhyme, is one of the most arduous tasks a poet can undertake. He that could accomplish this task was Prior; many have imitated his excellence in this particular, but the best copies have fallen far short of the original. And now to tell us, after we and our fathers have admired him for it so long, that he is an easy writer indeed, but that his ease has an air of stiffness in it, in short, that his ease is not ease, but only something like it, what is it but a self-contradiction, an observation that grants what it is just going to deny, and denies what it has just granted, in the same sentence, and in the same breath? But I have filled the greatest part of my sheet with a very uninteresting subject. I will only say, that as a nation we are not much indebted, in point of poetical credit, to this too sagacious and unmerciful judge; and that for myself in particular, I have reason to rejoice that he entered upon and exhausted the labours of his office before my poor volume could possibly become an object of them.

21 March 1784, to Unwin:
Last night I made an end of reading Johnson's *Prefaces*; but the number of poets whom he has vouchsafed to chronicle being fifty-six [52], there must be many with whose history I am not yet acquainted. These, or some of these, if it suits you to give them a part of your chaise, when you come, will be heartily welcome. I am very much the biographer's humble admirer. His uncommon share of good sense, and his forcible expression, secure to him that tribute from all his readers. He has a penetrating insight into character, and a happy talent of correcting the popular opinion, upon all occasions where it is erroneous; and this he does with the boldness of a man who will think for himself, but, at the same time, with a justness of sentiment that convinces us he does not differ from others through affectation, but because he has a sounder judgement. This remark, however, has his narrative for its object, rather than his critical performance. In the latter, I do not think him always just, when he departs from the general opinion. He finds no beauties in Milton's *Lycidas*. He pours contempt upon Prior, to such a degree, that were he really as undeserving of notice as he represents him, he ought no longer to be numbered among the poets. These, indeed, are the two capital instances in which he has offended me. There are others less important, which I have not room to enumerate, and in which I am less confident that he is wrong. What suggested to him the thought that the *Alma* was written in imitation of *Hudibras*,[4] I cannot conceive.

[4] *Lives*, ii. 205.

18 March 1791, to the Revd Walter Bagot:

I did not call in question Johnson's true spirit of poetry, because he was not qualified to relish blank verse (though, to tell you the truth, I think that but an ugly symptom); but if I did not express it I meant however to infer it from the perverse judgment that he has formed of our poets in general; depreciating some of the best, and making honourable mention of others, in my opinion not undeservedly neglected. I will lay you sixpence that, had he lived in the days of Milton, and by any accident had met with his *Paradise Lost*, he would neither have directed the attention of others to it, nor have much admired it himself. Good sense, in short, and strength of intellect, seem to me, rather than a fine taste, to have been his distinguished characteristics. But should you still think otherwise, you have my free permission; for so long as you have yourself a taste for the beauties of Cowper, I care not a fig whether Johnson had a taste or not.

53. Francis Blackburne, *Remarks on Johnson's Life of Milton*

1780

Extracts from pp. 21–6, 85–9, 98–101, 122–8.

The *Remarks* was published anonymously by the Revd Francis Blackburne (1705–87), rector of Richmond and prebendary of York. It was reprinted from his *Memoirs* (1780) of the republican Thomas Hollis; this fact clarifies Blackburne's purpose. For him Milton was a distinguished 'patron of public liberty' whereas Johnson was a friend of 'despotism'. See Introduction, p. 30.

Milton only, for the present, is our client, and only Milton the prose-writer, who, in that character, must ever be an eye-sore to men of Dr. Johnson's principles; principles that are at enmity with every patron of public liberty, and every pleader for the legal rights of Englishmen, which, in their origin, are neither more nor less than the natural rights of all mankind.

Milton, in contending for these against the tyrant of the day and his abettors, was serious, energetic, and irrefragable. He bore down all the silly sophisms in favour of despotic power like a torrent, and left his adversaries nothing to reply, but the rhetoric of Billingsgate, from which Lauder,[1] in the end of his pamphlet, intituled, *King Charles I. vindicated, &c.* has collected a nosegay of the choicest flowers; and pity it was, that he was too early to add his friend Johnson's character of Milton the prose-writer to the savoury bouquet.

When the Doctor found, on some late occasions, that his crude abuse and malicious criticisms would not bring down Milton to the degree of contempt with the public which he had assigned him in the scale of prose-writers; he fell upon an expedient which has sometimes succeeded in particular exigencies. In one word, he determined to write his Life.

[1] William Lauder (d. 1771), literary forger. (See Boswell, *Life*, i. 228–9.) His pamphlet appeared in 1754.

There are no men so excellent who have not some personal or casual defect in their bodily frame, some aukward peculiarity in their manners or conversation, some scandalous calumny tacked to their private history, or some of those natural failings which distinguish human from angelic beings.

On the other hand, few men are so totally abandoned and depraved as to have no remnants of grace and goodness, no intervals of sobriety, no touches of regret for departed innocence, no sense of those generous passions which animate the wise and good to praise-worthy actions, or no natural or acquired abilities to abate the resentment of the reputable public, and to atone, in some degree, for their immoralities.

A man of genius, who has words and will to depress or raise such characters respectively, will consider little in his operations upon them, but the motives and occasions which call for his present interference; and the world who know the artificer will make it no wonder that the encomiast and apologist of the profligate Richard Savage should employ his pen to satyrize and calumniate the virtuous John Milton.

[quotes opening paragraph of *Life of Milton*.]

The uniformity of editions is commonly the bookseller's care, and the necessity of such uniformity generally arises from the taste of the public; of which, among the number of names exhibited in the title-pages of these volumes, there must be many competent judges. It would be a pity however that a conformity to this taste should engage Dr. Johnson in writing this *Life*, to go beyond what would *more properly* have contented himself; the least intimation from the Biographer of the *impropriety* of a *new narrative* would, we are persuaded, have made the undertakers of the edition contented with the Doctor's plan.

He might not indeed have found the means to introduce certain particulars, which embellish his *new narrative*, into his notes on Mr. Fenton's abridgement,[2] in which there is a vein of candor that does the writer more honour than the ingenuity of his performance; not to mention the different judgment, from that of Dr. Johnson, formed by Mr. Fenton, on some of Milton's poetical pieces.

We therefore believe this *new narrative* was calculated rather for Dr. Johnson's private *contentment* than the necessities of the edition. . . .

It is hardly necessary to apprize a reader of Milton's prose-works that his ideas of *usurpation* and *public liberty* were very different from those of Dr. Johnson. In the Doctor's system of government public liberty is the

[2] See above, p. 257n.

free grace of an *hereditary* monarch, and limited in kind and degree, by his gracious will and pleasure; and consequently to controul his arbitrary acts by the interposition of good and wholesome laws is a *manifest usurpation* upon his prerogative. Milton allotted to the people a considerable and important share in political government, founded upon original stipulations for the rights and privileges of free subjects, and called the monarch who should infringe or encroach upon these, however qualified by lineal succession, a tyrant and an usurper, and freely consigned him to the vengeance of an injured people. Upon Johnson's plan, there can be no such thing as public liberty. Upon Milton's, where the laws are duly executed, and the people protected in the peaceable and legal enjoyment of their lives, properties, and municipal rights and privileges, there can be no such thing as *usurpation*, in whose hands soever the executive power should be lodged. From this doctrine Milton never swerved; and in that noble apostrophe to Cromwell, in his Second Defense of the people of England, he spares not to remind him, what a wretch and a villain he would be, should he invade those liberties which his valour and magnanimity had restored. If, after this, Milton's employers deviated from *his* idea of their duty, be it remembered, that he was neither in their secrets, nor an instrument in their arbitrary acts or encroachments on the legal rights of the subject; many (perhaps the most) of which were to be justified by the necessity of the times, and the malignant attempts of those who laboured to restore that wicked race of despotic rulers, the individuals of which had uniformly professed an utter enmity to the claims of a free people, and had acted accordingly, in perfect conformity to Dr. Johnson's political creed. On another hand, be it observed, that in those State-letters, latinized by Milton, which remain, and in those particularly written in the name of the Protector Oliver, the strictest attention is paid to the dignity and importance of the British nation, to the protection of trade, and the Protestant religion, by spirited expostulations with foreign powers on any infraction of former treaties, in a style of steady determination, of which there have been few examples in subsequent times. A certain sign in what esteem the British government was held at that period by all the other powers of Europe. And as this was the only province in which Milton acted under that government which Dr. Johnson calls an usurpation, let his services be compared with those performed by Dr. Johnson for his present patrons; and let the constitutional subject of the British empire judge which of them better deserves the appellation of a traitor to public liberty, or have more righteously earned the *honey* of a pension. . . .

It is remarkable, that, in depreciating such of Milton's writings as thwart Dr. Johnson's political notions, the censure is always accompanied with some evil imputation upon the writer's head or his heart. He observes of his serious tracts in general, that *Hell grows darker at his frown*; borrowing, to make his abuse more tasty, an expression from Milton himself.[3] In his treatises *of civil power in ecclesiastical cases*, and *of the means of removing hirelings out of the church*, 'He gratified his malevolence to the clergy.' In writing his pamphlet called, *A ready and easy way to establish a free commonwealth*, 'He was *fantastical* enough to think, that the nation, agitated as it was, might be settled by it;' and his notes upon a sermon of Dr. Griffiths, 'were foolish, and the effect of *kicking* when he could not *strike*.'[4]

If controversial fame were thus to be purchased, Dr. Johnson might be esteemed the first of writers in that province, for no man ever expressed his abuse in a more inimitable style of abuse. And though he may sometimes create suspicions that he has either never read, or does not understand the writings he so peremptorily censures; yet the vehicle is pleasing, and the reputation he has gained by his labours of more general utility precludes all examination, and he expects his scandalous chronicle should be licensed and received upon his own bare word.

'For Milton to complain of evil tongues,' says the Doctor, 'required impudence at least equal to his other powers; Milton, whose warmest advocates must allow, that he never spared any asperity of reproach, or brutality of insolence.'[5]

Milton wrote in a public contest for public liberty: and he generally in that contest was upon the *defensive*. The asperity of his reproaches seldom exceeded the asperity of the wickedness upon which those reproaches were bestowed.

Brutality is a word of an ill sound, and required some instances to justify the imputation of it. When these are given, we will readily join issue in the trial, whether Milton or his adversaries were the more brutal or more insolent. They who would reduce mankind to a *brutal* slavery, under the despotism of a lawless tyrant, forfeit all claim to the rationality of human beings; and no tongue can be called *evil* for giving them their proper appellation. . . .

In conclusion, the good Doctor turns evesdropper; and, to warn the public against the principles of the miscreant Milton, condescends to

[3] *Lives*, i. 104. The Miltonic allusion is to *Paradise Lost*, II. 719.
[4] *Lives*, i. 125–6.
[5] Ibid., i. 140.

inform us of what passed in the domestic privacies of his family. 'Milton's character, in his domestic relations, was severe and arbitrary.' How does he know this? 'His family consisted of women,' he tells you, 'and there appears, in his books, something like a Turkish contempt of females, as subordinate and inferior beings.' A most heinous offence! enough to muster the whole multitude of English Amazons against him. But the question is not concerning what is in his books, but what passed in his kitchen and parlour. We want instances; and here they are: 'That his own daughters might not break the ranks, he suffered them to be depressed by a mean and penurious education.'[6]

The impudence of Belial would be abashed at so gross a misrepresentation. Milton's daughters grew impatient of reading what they did not understand; this impatience 'broke out more and more into expressions of uneasiness.' What had they now to expect from their Turkish father? what! but stripes and imprisonment in a dark chamber, and a daily pittance of bread and water. No such matter. They were relieved from their task, and 'sent out to learn some curious and ingenious sorts of manufacture that were proper for women to learn, particularly imbroideries in gold and silver.'[7] And how far this branch of education was from being either mean or penurious in those days, the remains of these curious and ingenious works, performed by accomplished females of the highest and noblest extraction, testify to this very day.

To account for this tyranny of Milton over his females, the Doctor says, 'He thought woman made only for obedience, and man only for rebellion.'[8]

In the first member of this quaint antithesis the Doctor perhaps did not guess far amiss at Milton's *thought*. He seems to have been of St. Paul's opinion, that 'women were made for obedience.'[9] But Paul and Milton had different ideas of rebellion from those of Dr. Johnson. That Prynne, Burton, and Bastwick,[10] were *rebels* in Dr. Johnson's scale, no one can doubt. And yet they had certainly an equal right to insist upon the privileges of Englishmen against Dr. Laud[11] and his assessors, as Paul had to plead those of a Roman citizen against the chief captain Lysias; and

[6] Ibid., i. 157.

[7] Edward Phillips, *Life of Milton*, in Milton's *Letters of State*, 1694, xliii.

[8] *Lives*, i. 157.

[9] 1 Corinthians 14: 34.

[10] William Prynne (1600–69), Henry Burton (1578–1648), John Bastwick (1593–1654); all anti-episcopal writers.

[11] William Laud (1573–1645), Archbishop of Canterbury under Charles I; executed 'for endeavouring to subvert the laws and to overthrow the Protestant religion'.

even to require that the said Archbishop should repair to the several prisons of these sufferers to ask their pardon, and to conduct them in person and with honour out of their confinement; as was done in the case of Paul and Silas, by the magistrates of Philippi; who (however the Biographer may stomach the idea of such a humiliation of this magnanimous prelate) seem to have understood the honour due to the laws of their country, and the rights of free citizens, something better than either Abp. Laud or Dr. Johnson.

But after all, would Dr. Johnson lead us to the converse of the sentiment he ascribes to Milton, as a tenet of his own orthodoxy? What his family-connexions with females may be we profess not to know; but we cannot believe that he is so far in love with petticoat-government, as to subscribe to the proposition, that 'men are made only for obedience, and women only for rebellion.'

But here we take our leave of his *new narrative*; leaving his strictures on Milton's poetry to the examination of critics by profession; all of whom, we are persuaded, will not approve them merely because they came from Dr. Johnson. They will observe that they are tainted throughout with the effects of an inveterate hatred to Milton's politics, with which, as the Biographer of a Poet the author of *Paradise Lost*, the Critic had very little to do.

54. Horace Walpole on the *Life of Pope*

14 April 1781

Text from *Correspondence of Walpole and William Mason*, 1851, i. 171–2.

Boswell remarked with notable understatement that Horace Walpole (1717–97) 'never was one of the true admirers of Johnson' (*Life*, iv. 314). Walpole's barbed comments on Johnson are numerous; one must suffice: 'Johnson was an odious and mean character . . . with all the pedantry he had all the gigantic littleness of a country schoolmaster' (*Memoirs of the Reign of George III*, 1845, iv. 297). William Mason, to whom he wrote the letter below, himself regarded Johnson as 'a bear upon stilts' (Boswell, *Life*, ii. 347 n.3).

Sir Joshua Reynolds has lent me Dr. Johnson's Life of Pope, which Sir Joshua holds to be a *chef-d'oeuvre*. It is a most trumpery performance and stuffed with all his crabbed phrases and vulgarisms, and much trash as anecdotes; you shall judge yourself:—he says, that all he can discover of Pope's correspondent Mr. Cromwell[1] is that he used to hunt in a tie-wig. The *Elegy on the Unfortunate Lady* he says, *signifies the amorous fury of a raving girl*; and yet he admires the subject of *Eloïsa's Epistle to Abelard*. The machinery in *The Rape of the Lock* he calls *combinations of skilful genius with happy casuality*, in English I guess a *lucky thought*; publishing proposals is turned into emitting them.[2] But the 66th page is still more curious, it contains a philosophic solution of Pope's not transcribing the whole *Iliad* as soon as he thought he should, and it concludes with this piece of bombast nonsense, *he that runs against time has an antagonist not subject to casualties.* Pope's house here he calls *the house to which his residence afterwards procured so much celebration*, and that *his vanity produced a grotto where necessity enforced a passage*; and that, *of his intellectual character, the constituent and fundamental principle was good sense, a prompt and intuitive perception of*

1 Henry Cromwell (*c.* 1658–1728), critic and poet. 2 *Lives*, iii. 101, 105, 104, 112.

consonance and propriety.[3] Was poor good sense ever so unmercifully over-laid by a babbling old woman! How was it possible to marshal words so ridiculously? He seems to have read the ancients with no view but of pilfering polysyllables, utterly insensible to the graces of their simplicity, and these are called standards of biography! I forgot he calls Lord Hervey's challenging Pulteney, *summoning him to a duel*.[4] Hurlothrumbo talked plain English in comparison of this wight on stilts,[5] but I doubt I have wearied you,—send me something to put my mouth in taste again.

55. William Fitzthomas, *Cursory Examination of Dr. Johnson's Strictures on the Lyric Performances of Gray*

1781

One of several writers who took strong exception to Johnson's unsympathetic treatment of Gray was the Revd William Windsor Fitzthomas; he published his pamphlet anonymously. Anna Seward, a fervent admirer of Gray, complimented Fitzthomas on his vindication of the poet: 'You have stretched the giant at your feet' (*Letters*, 1811, ii. 147). The compliment was partisan. See Introduction, pp. 7, 30.

The polite and literary world has, of late, been laid under fresh obliga-tions to Dr. Johnson, for his excellent biographical and critical prefaces to the works of the most eminent English poets. These prefaces, as it is well known, are written with the Doctor's usual precision, vigour, and clearness of style; his usual methodical arrangement, and discriminative judgment; and, for the most part, with his usual candour and critical

---

[3] Ibid., iii. 117, 134, 135, 216.
[4] Ibid., iii. 178.
[5] *Hurlothrumbo*, 1729, a popular burlesque written by Samuel Johnson (1691–1773), the Manchester dancing-master.

justice. On the perusal, however, of his remarks on the writings of Gray, I was instantly struck by his unfair, and unusual mode of criticism, as well as by his total deviation from the common track of popular opinion. His strictures on Gray, seem to be influenced by, I know not what, prejudice; and he takes up Gray's lyricks, apparently, with a fixed resolution to condemn them.

It was not, altogether, the ambition of erecting a temporary shed, under the shadow of so noble a structure as that of Dr. Johnson's literary reputation, which induced me to offer to the public the following hasty remarks. A certain love of truth and of justice, even in the meerest trifles, so natural to the human mind; together with a hope of in some measure vindicating, the poetical reputation of the late excellent Mr. Gray, from the too severe, and hyper critical censures of our modern Aristarchus, has made me a candidate for the *immortality of a week*; and excited a desire of adding somewhat to the heap of pamphlets, with which literature is already so much oppressed.

I shall begin with the Doctor's remarks on the two *Sister Odes*;[1] upon which, perhaps on account of their enjoying a peculiar portion of the public approbation, he seems, in a peculiar manner, to exercise his critical and dictatorial severity.

Of the first stanza of the ode on the progress of poetry, he observes, that, 'Gray seems in his rapture to confound the images of *spreading sound* and *running water*.' To prevent a frequent and troublesome application to the poet, I choose to lay the whole passage before the reader. The ode opens thus:

> Awake, Æolian Lyre, awake,
> And give to rapture all thy trembling strings.
> From Helicon's harmonious springs
> A thousand rills their mazy progress take:
> The laughing flowers, that round them blow,
> Drink life and fragrance as they flow.
> Now the rich stream of music winds along,
> Deep, majestic, smooth and strong,
> Through verdant vales, and Ceres' golden reign:
> Now rowling down the steep amain,
> Headlong, impetuous, see it pour:
> The rocks, and nodding groves, rebellow to the roar.

In his notes on this stanza, Gray professes that his intention is to imitate the usual model of all lyric performances, the odes of Pindar. Now it is

[1] *Lives*, iii. 436–8.

one of Pindar's well-known and characteristic peculiarities, to incorporate for the most part his similes, with his subject. Gray therefore as an imitator, unites the image of poetry, (which as it was of old ever accompanied and regulated by the lyre, he calls music,) to that of the simile, a majestic stream of flowing water. He then, in order to shew the power of poetry in enobling and adorning every subject, metaphorically describes it as taking its course like a gently-flowing and majestic river, through *verdant vales and Ceres' golden reign*, enriching the adjacent country with *life and fragrance*: and lastly to characterise the vehement and passionate kind of poetry, as *rowling down the steep amain*, and causing the *rocky banks* and *pendent groves* to *rebellow to its roar*.

'But,' objects the Doctor, 'where does *music*, however *smooth and strong*, after having visited the *verdant vales*, *rowl down the steep amain*, so as that *rocks and nodding groves rebellow to the roar?*'

I have before observed, that this is evidently said of music and poetry in their primitive conjunction: but let us, for the present, suppose it to be spoken of music alone.—Can the Doctor, though avowedly insensible of the effects of music, be likewise so ignorant of the art, as not to know that there is admissible in it as great a variety of style, as in either of its sister arts? Are not both ancient and modern musicians allowed the power of, in some degree, exciting, as well as soothing, the passions of the more susceptible part of mankind? Is there not a rapid and impetuous style of music, as well as a grave and equable one? By what image can this impetuous style of music be, with greater metaphorical propriety, illustrated, than by the foregoing one! How can the effects of poetry be more happily typified, than by those of its sister art, music*!

The Doctor then dismisses this stanza, by observing, that, 'if this be said of *music*, it is nonsense; if it be said of *water*, it is nothing to the purpose'; and thus leaves us suspended between the horns of an apparent dilemma.

But to forbid its being said of music in its separate state, is, in a manner, to interdict the use of all figurative decoration. It is to deny an artist the assistance of the necessary implements of his trade. We must all be well aware that this passage, literally understood, is stark nonsense when applied to either of the arts.—But it is, most evidently, a simile interwoven with the subject, and by the poet designed to characterise the more vehement and empassioned kind of poetry, in its original union

---

* The analogical resemblance between these two noble arts, is indeed so perfect, that music may, with some propriety, be said to furnish a system of colours, for the ornament of the chiaro-oscuro of poetical sentiment.

with music; and, to a mind not previously and designedly rendered insensible to its beauty, cannot fail of conveying an image, perfectly clear and distinct; and ideas, in the highest degree vivid and sublime.

We find the whole of the second stanza of this ode, included in one general censure: 'It is unworthy', says the critic, 'of further notice. Criticism disdains to chace a school-boy to his common places'. He pays not the least attention to the effect of the transition and contrast, both with respect to the versification, and the subject. He gives us not the least encouragement to approve of those beautiful lines, with which the second stanza commences:

> Oh! sovereign of the willing soul,
> Parent of sweet and solemn breathing airs,
> Enchanting shell! the Sullen cares,
> And frantic passions hear thy soft controul.

The remaining part of this stanza is a very close imitation*, (not to say translation) of part of the first Pythian ode of Pindar; and, consequently, retains a leaven of that mythological fiction, in which all the ancient poets so greatly delighted.—The Doctor's observations concerning the interweaving the old mythology into modern performances, are undoubtedly just and rational. There is indeed something so puerile, frigid, and uninteresting in the greater part of the mythological fictions, as inevitably to repel the attention of every reader, not wholly devoted to the antique. But there is no general rule without its exceptions: the fiction before us is so pleasing to the imagination, and the lines it is contained in, so poetical and animated, that very few classical readers would, I think, wish this stanza cancelled.

On the third stanza, the Doctor's strictures are chiefly verbal: and few, I believe, will choose to contradict Dr. Johnson's verbal criticism. He does not, however, dismiss this stanza, without remarking its pleasing effect on the ear.

I now accompany the critic to the first, of the second ternary of stanzas; which, as we are informed, 'endeavours to tell something, and would have told it, had it not been crossed by Hyperion'.—It is indeed crossed by Hyperion: but in like manner is the *Essay on Criticism*, crossed by the *Alpine traveller*; the *Campaign*, by the *destroying Angel*;[2] and many

---

* The passage imitated by Gray, begins at the latter part of line 11, of Pindar's first Pythian, and ends with the beginning of line 21.

---

[2] Pope's *Essay on Criticism*, 1711, ll. 225–32; Addison's *Campaign*, 1704, in *Works*, ed. G. W. Greene, 1891, i. 187–8. (See *Lives*, ii. 130–1.)

other excellent poems, by many other excellent illustrative similes. Gray, to use the Doctor's expression, here 'endeavours to tell', (and to the greater part of his readers will, I believe, appear actually to enumerate) the various, and unavoidable evils, the black train of misfortunes incident to human life: and, from their existence, endeavours likewise to prove the great utility of poetry, by its well-known power, in some measure to divert or alleviate them. Which position, (still uniting the subject and simile) he illustrates by the similitude of the *solar light*, driving away the ill-omened birds of darkness, and dispersing the gloom and terrors of the night.—But this union of the subject and simile seems, unaccountably enough, for ever to lie in the Doctor's way; and to prove an eternal *stumbling block* to his critical sagacity. If he does not approve of this union, why does he not tell us so?—But, if we may be allowed to judge from appearances, the Doctor either does not, or *will not*, observe this intentional union.

The remark on the non-dependence of the conclusion on the premises of the following stanza, is acute and judicious.

Stanza the third 'sounds big', as we are informed, 'with *Delphi*, and *Egean*, and *Illissus*, and *Meander*, and *hallowed fountain*, and *solemn sound*'. —If to *talk big* be a liberty that may be granted to the *Muses* at all, it may be allowed, I think, as an exclusive privilege, to the *lyric Muse*. Dignified sound, is such a requisite auxiliary to her usual elevation of sentiment, as to be, in a manner, inseparable from her, without degrading her to a level with the rest of the choral band. It cannot, however, be denied by Gray's greatest admirers, but that he is too fond of superfluous splendour; of accumulating and crouding his images; and of overloading his lines with unnecessary, though not unmeaning epithets. On the Doctor's observation* on the position in the latter part of this stanza, I must beg leave a little to dilate.

Gray's position is, briefly, this: After descanting on the natural connection between poetry, liberty, and all the nobler virtues, and its abhorrence of, and desertion from all those countries in which *tyrant power* and *coward vice* prevail, he exemplifies by a cursory view of the present state of those countries in which poetry once particularly flourished, and by its emigration from Greece to Italy, and from Italy to England, as each became unworthy of its independent dignity and

---

* His observation is this: Gray's 'position is at last false: in the time of Dante and Petrarch, from whom he derives our first school of poetry, Italy was over-run by *tyrant power* and *coward vice*; nor was our state much better when we first borrowed the Italian arts'.

immaculate purity.—The thought is ingenious, and the attempt laudable; and must give the highest pleasure to every true lover of the fine arts: and if it be difficult to support this position by historical fact, it is, in my opinion, no less difficult by the same method to overthrow it.

It is certain that poetry is a shrub which has sometimes taken root, and put forth its fairest blossoms in a barren and, apparently, ungrateful soil. Poetical genius seems, on a retrospect, to have started up casually, as it were in the course of nature, without much dependence on the moral or political state of the countries to which it owed its origin. There have, no doubt, been times in which poetical merit has been particularly encouraged; and poetry, of course, more cultivated by ambitious pretenders. There have, we know, been times in which it has even been admitted to a share in the legislature: but in general it may be said of genius, that as no encouragement whatever can originally produce it, so no discouragement or difficulties can extinguish its noble ardour, when produced.

In England, it is particularly hard to point out the golden age of poetry: its greatest poetical luminaries have, for the most part, appeared singly; they have not often shone in constellations of uniformly diffused lustre. But it will somewhat tend to the support of Gray's hypothesis, if we remark, that the more noble and original works, those which bid the fairest for immortal praise, were mostly produced in ages conspicuous for the exertion of the nobler virtues; and in countries distinguished by an unremitting ardour for liberty and independence.

The Doctor's remarks on the first of the third ternary of stanzas are eminently judicious, and unexceptionably just.

It is observable of the next stanza, that our great critic has singled out for commendation almost the only thing that former critics have chosen to reprobate. This thing is the poetical account of Milton's blindness. Whether it be commended justly, or not, it is certain a reader of very moderate abilities and poetical experience may decide.—With regard to the car of Dryden, I can by no means agree with the Doctor, that it will suit every rider. Gray, as he tells us in his notes, means here to characterise the *sounding energy* and *stately march* of Dryden's versification: and he has done it very happily and discriminatively in the following lines:

> Behold where Dryden's less presumptuous car,
> Wide o'er the fields of glory, bear
> Two coursers of ethereal race,
> With necks in thunder clothed, and long-resounding pace.

Can these lines, with equal propriety, be applied to Waller, Prior, Addison, or even Pope himself? Surely not!

We are now arrived at the concluding stanza, of which the Doctor, apparently, unwilling to praise where he cannot blame, says nothing at all. Few readers, however, of any poetical discernment or feelings, will, I think, acquiesce in this neglect. Few, but those of the dullest heads and coldest hearts, can, I am persuaded, read this part of the ode, without feeling in a peculiar manner, the effect of the transition, the beauty of the imagery, and the glowing warmth of the diction.—The circumstance of Dryden's having written but one ode of the sublime and truly lyric kind, and suddenly withdrawing his masterly hand from those chords he knew so well to strike, is here exquisitely expressed by the image of a musician, unexpectedly pausing in the midst of his strain:

> Hark, his hands the lyre explore!
> Bright-eyed Fancy hovering o'er
> Scatters from her pictured urn
> Thoughts that breathe and words that burn.
> But ah! 'tis heard no more –

The remainder of the stanza must necessarily appear feeble after animation like this!

I cannot help remarking here, that the Doctor's critical process with Gray, differs, considerably, from that which he makes use of towards every other writer. He is with Gray more verbal, logical, and minute, where these critical niceties ought, in reason, least of all to be practised. He is less observant of the versification and imagery; and for the most part declines giving us either a general, or comparative character of the pieces under inspection.

[examines Johnson's comments on *The Bard*.]

I am now arrived at the end of my collateral remarks: and hope I have, to the reader's satisfaction, shown the visible injustice of some of the great critic's remarks, and the no less visible futility of others. The Doctor dismisses these odes with a general observation, which would, I think, be rendered more just, and characteristic of the poet's merit, were it invertedly parodied in the following manner:

These odes are distinguished by splendid accumulations of the most graceful ornaments; they strike no less than please: the images are amplified by an imagination eminently poetical; the language is, for the most part, void of harshness. The mind of the writer seems to glow with that enthusiasm, which ever will be deemed by frigid critics unnatural, in proportion as it is unusual, or unknown to them. He has a kind of native dignity, and is tall without *walking in stilts*. His art and his struggle are but little visible, disguised under the becoming veil of ease and nature.

I cannot take leave of the reader without subjoining an observation, which, no doubt, has occurred to many.

After all these remarks, these severe strictures, I much suspect, that the Doctor offers us but an *artificial copy* of his sentiments, with regard to this truly elegant and original writer. Is it reasonable to imagine, considering the well-known taste and discernment of Dr. Johnson, that he should *really* be so callous to that beautiful simplicity which runs through many of Gray's productions? Or, considering his just, and truly discriminated decisions on the merits of every other writer, that he should really be so insensible to the inexpressible dignity and animation which reign in these particular odes?—It seems most probable, therefore, that the Doctor, looking upon the great, and almost unexampled reputation of this writer as somewhat superior to his real merit, might think that he was doing the public a piece of service, by 'bending the twig the contrary way'; and, by confining Gray's fame within its proper bounds, render it more solid and durable.—If this were his design, it must be, I think, the general opinion, that he has greatly over-acted his part in the critical drama.

56. Unsigned review, *Annual Register*

1782, xxv, 203–8

Text from second edition, 1791, 203–4.

This review of the second group of *Lives* provides a representative journalistic stock-taking of the undertaking as a whole.

Though the merits of this learned performance have been long since the subject of discussion, and its reputation be established on the most universal applause, yet the uniformity of our plan, and the respect due to a name so justly celebrated, require that we should connect with our former remarks some observations on the last six volumes of this valuable work.

Perhaps no age or country has ever produced a species of criticism more perfect in its kind, or better calculated for general instruction, than the publication before us: for whether we consider it in a literary, philosophical, or a moral view, we are at a loss whether to admire most the author's variety and copiousness of learning, the soundness of his judgement, or the purity and excellence of his character as a man.

It is surely of importance to the rising generation to be supplied in the most elegant walk of literature with a guide, who points out what is beautiful in writing as well as in action, who uniformly blends instruction with amusement, who informs the understanding, and rectifies the judgement, while he mends the heart.

But notwithstanding the general popularity of this performance, and an uncommon degree of decision in its favour, it was not to be expected that a work of this nature, indeed that any work, should pass totally without exception, or without censure. In some instances it has divided the opinions of the learned, in a few it has provoked the severity of criticism; with what propriety the public have judged from the pamphlets that have appeared, particularly in defence of Gray. That the doctor was not over zealous to allow him the degree of praise that the public voice had pretty universally assigned him, is, we think, sufficiently apparent. Partiality to his beautiful elegy, had perhaps allotted him a rank above his general merits: that justice was the object of the biographer, we cannot doubt; but in combating opinions we suppose to be erroneous, we are extremely subject to fall ourselves into the opposite extreme, and to this we are inclined to attribute whatever deviations from the general accuracy of the author may be met with in the course of this work. In this opinion we are confirmed by instances on the other side, where the doctor seems to give hyperbolical praise to names, which had perhaps been suffered to lie under too much neglect and oblivion. Whether the origin of something like an attachment to a particular set of notions, or a set of men, may be explained upon this principle, we leave our readers to determine. That our learned author's judgement has been warped on some subjects, where party has an influence, is the opinion of probably the greater number of his admirers; and if it be true, it is a decisive argument to show the prevalence of prejudice, and that the strongest understanding is not always proof against its inroads.

[the remainder of the review consists chiefly of quotation.]

57. Robert Potter, *Inquiry into some passages in Dr. Johnson's Lives of the Poets*

1783

Extracts from pp. 1–7, 14–16, 36–8.

The Revd Robert Potter (1721–1804) was a country clergyman, schoolmaster, and translator of Aeschylus; he acknowledged Johnson's literary distinction but regretted his insensitivity to writers such as Gray, Collins, and Shenstone. See Introduction, pp. 19, 30.

Just Criticism, directed by superior learning and judgement, and tempered with candor, must at all times have an happy influence on the public taste, and of course be favourable to the interests and credit of literature. . . . Every age is not so happy as to produce an Addison; yet the present age owes much to the vigorous and manly understanding of Dr. Johnson: this truly respectable writer was early and deservedly distinguished by his great abilities, and the public has so long been habituated to receive and submit to his decisions, that they are now by many considered as infallible. Some years ago he wrote the life of Savage, a man neither amiable nor virtuous, but of a singular character formed from singular circumstances of distress, which never happened before, probably will never happen again in the life of any other man: undeserved distress has a claim to pity; and pity has always in it some mixture of love, which wishes to palliate the failings of the unfortunate sufferer; Dr. Johnson has the feelings of humanity warm at his honest heart; he has therefore with a free and spirited indignation stigmatized the unnatural mother, and to her unrelenting cruelty ultimately refers the faults of the unhappy son, faults which truth would not allow him to suppress, nor his virtue incline him to defend. In his account of Savage as a Poet, he places his genius in the fairest light, and makes just apologies for his inaccuracies. This little tract was written with an animated glow of sentiment, a vigorous and clear expression, and a pleasing candor sometimes perhaps stretched a little beyond the line of judgement: it pleased; it must always please: no wonder then that the public expressed no small degree of satisfaction, when it was known that this celebrated author was engaged in writing the Lives of the most eminent English Poets, with critical observations on their works; much was expected from his knowledge and judgement; but high raised expectations are frequently disappointed: in these volumes, amidst the many just observations, the solid sense, and deep penetration which even his enemies must admire, his warmest friends find some passages which they must wish unwritten or obliterated.

It is not my intention to follow the Biographer through all the lives he has written; but, after a few cursory remarks, these pages will be confined to his observations on Lyric Poetry, particularly on the Odes of Mr. Gray. As I shall have frequent occasions to dissent from the Critic's judgement, I shall give my reasons freely and firmly, but with great respect to his understanding and virtues.

'With the political tenets of the writer, I have nothing to do; my business is with his criticism:'[1] yet it were to be wished that the spirit of party had not been so warmly diffused through this work; it is often disagreeable, but in the *Life of Milton* it is disgusting: not that I am inclined to defend the religious or political principles of our great poet; I know too well the intolerant spirit of that liberty, which worked its odious purposes through injustice, oppression, and cruelty: but it is of little consequence to the present and future ages whether the author of *Paradise Lost* was Papist or Presbyterian, Royalist or Republican; it is the Poet that claims our attention: if however in the life of Milton it were necessary to take notice of the part he bore in those disastrous times, it might have been more eligible to have imitated the moderation of J. Philips, who, though he wrote more than seventy years nearer those times, when the facts were yet fresh on mens memories, checked his expression of the abhorrence of them, through respect to his master, with this beautiful apostrophe,

> And had that other Bard,
> Oh, had but he, that first ennobled song
> With holy raptures, like his Abdiel been,
> 'Mongst many faithless, strictly faithful found;
> Unpity'd he should not have wail'd his orbs,
> That roll'd in vain to find the piercing ray,

---

[1] Cf. 'With the philosophical or religious tenets of the author I have nothing to do; my business is with his poetry' (*Life of Akenside*), *Lives*, iii. 417.

And found no dawn, by dim suffusion veil'd!
But he—However, let the Muse abstain,
Nor blast his fame, from whom she learn'd to sing
In much inferior strains.—[2]

We are also sorry to see the masculine spirit of Dr. Johnson descending to what he perhaps in another might call 'anile garrulity.' In reading the life of any eminent person we wish to be informed of the qualities which gave him the superiority over other men: when we are poorly put off with paltry circumstances, which are common to him with common men, we receive neither instruction nor pleasure. We know that the greatest men are subject to the infirmities of human nature equally with the meanest; why then are these infirmities recorded? Can it be of any importance to us to be told how many pair of stockings the author of the *Essay on Man* wore?[3] Achilles and Thersites eat, and drank, and slept; in these things the Hero was not distinguished from the Buffoon: are we made the wiser or the better by being informed that the Translator of Homer stewed his Lampreys in a silver saucepan?[4] Who does not blush when he finds recorded that idle story of a nameless critic, who said of the author of *The Fleece, He will be buried in woolen*?[5] Is this held up for wit? Is it intended as a sarcasm on Dyer? Is it not an insult to the understanding of the reader? Let me stop a moment to speak of this writer. 'Dyer is not a poet of bulk or dignity sufficient to require an elaborate criticism.'[6] Does Dr. Johnson estimate poetical merit, as Rubens did feminine beauty, *by the stone?* Well then might he recommend Blackmore to us. If *The Fleece* be now universally neglected, let me join my testimony to that of Akinside, that such neglect is a reproach to the reigning taste; the poem is truly classical: to say that 'Dyer's mind was not unpoetical,'[7] is parsimonious praise; he had a benevolent heart, a vigorous imagination, and a chastised judgement; his style is compact and nervous; his numbers have harmony, spirit, and force.

On they move
Indissolubly firm; nor obvious hill,
Nor streit'ning vale, nor wood, nor stream divides
Their perfect ranks.—[8]

The present passion for anecdotes may make these levities pardonable: but when the narrative goes further, and reflects upon the social and moral character of a worthy person, it must be taken up in an

---

[2] John Philips, *Cyder*, 1708, i. 767–76.   [3] *Lives*, iii. 197.   [4] Ibid., iii. 200.
[5] Ibid., iii. 345.   [6] Ibid., iii. 345.   [7] Ibid., iii. 346.   [8] *Paradise Lost*, VI. 68–71.

higher tone. We are carefully informed of the avidity of Addison, of the eagerness with which he laid hold on his proportion of the profits arising from the papers of the *Spectator*, of his unmerciful exaction of an hundred pounds lent by him to Steele.[9] If this be true, it only shows that Addison had not 'exalted his moral to divine:' but the intervention of more than sixty years has not yet obliterated the remembrance of his gentle manners and benevolent disposition: that Steele was not an œconomist is well known; but what authority Dr. Johnson has for saying that Addison reclaimed his loan by an execution, we are not told: I am told by the best authority that it is an absolute falsehood. This vindication is due to the memory of a man, who was universally respected whilst he lived, and 'of whose virtue it is a sufficient testimony, that the resentment of party has transmitted no charge of any crime;' 'who taught, with great justness of argument and dignity of language, the most important duties, and sublime truths;' 'who employed wit on the side of virtue and religion, purified intellectual pleasure, separated mirth from indecency,' enlightened and refined the age in which he lived, 'and excited such an emulation of intellectual elegance, that, from his time to our own, life has been gradually exalted, and conversation purified and enlarged.'[10]

This purity, this enlargement leads us to resent the cruel manner in which Dr. Johnson speaks of the Lady, who is the subject of Hammond's Elegies[11]: an old Goth would not have been guilty of such an indelicacy: but whatever character her lover, or his Biographer, may have bequeathed her, those, who were so happy as to be acquainted with her, speak of her as a very excellent and amiable woman. This offence against truth and good manners is the more inexcusable, as Dr. Johnson had opportunities enough of informing himself of the Lady's real character. With regard to Hammond, whether Mr. Shiels[12] was misled by false accounts I cannot determine; but that this Poet was not the Son of Anthony Hammond, who was allied to Sir Robert Walpole by marrying his Sister, I can assure the public upon the authority of that respectable family.[13] His Elegies certainly have faults, which the Critic is eagle-eyed to discover; but they have beauties, against which he shuts his eyes; a younger man might perhaps say with Spenser,

[9] *Lives*, ii. 81, 106.

[10] Ibid., ii. 118, 96, 126, 146.

[11] Ibid., ii. 314.

[12] Robert Shiels (d. 1753) whose memoir of Hammond Johnson used; he was one of Johnson's amanuenses for the *Dictionary*.

[13] See *Lives*, ii. 313 n.l.

Such one's ill judge of love, that cannot love,
Ne in their frozen hearts feel kindly flame.
For-thy they ought not thing unknown reprove,
Ne natural affection faultless blame.[14]

'Why Hammond, *or other writers,* have thought the quatrain of ten syllables elegiac, it is difficult to tell.' Perhaps the difficulty is not great; the next sentence may serve to explain it; 'the character of the Elegy is gentleness and tenuity;' no other measure in the English language glides with such easy sweetness, and in such a gentle strain of melody. 'But this Stanza has been pronounced by Dryden, whose knowledge of English metre was not inconsiderable, to be the most magnificent of all the measures which our language affords.'[15] The critic himself accounts for this opinion of Dryden, 'Davenant was perhaps *at this time* his favourite author, though *Gondibert* never appears to have been popular; and from Davenant he learned to please his ear with the stanza of four lines alternately rhymed.'[16] The elegant Aikins, in their dissertation on *Gondibert*,[17] have adverted to its measure with propriety and fine taste. But it is not for nothing that this opinion of Dryden is held out to us: Mr. Gray's Elegy is written in this metre; it had been too desperate to have hazarded an open attack on that poem; the Critic therefore shelters himself behind the authority of Dryden, and seems to direct his censure against Hammond, whilst the shaft is aimed at Gray.

[introduces the subject of the ode and thus turns to Johnson's criticism of Gray's poetry. This topic occupies the second half of the book.]

Sublimity is the essential and characteristic perfection of the Ode; where this can be attained by 'the placid beauties of methodical deduction', that artful course is pursued; but it is more often seized by a rapid and impetuous transition; yet this is always under the controul of some nice connexion, is never vague and wanton, never loses sight of its important object. The Ode is daring, but not licentious; though it is great, it disclaims 'the proud irregularity of greatness'.

Collins was the first of our poets that reached its excellence: his mind was impressed with a tender melancholy, but without any mixture of that sullen gloom which deadens its powers; it led him to the softest sympathy, that most refined feeling of the human heart; his faculties

[14] *Faerie Queene*, IV. i. 2.
[15] *Lives*, ii. 316.
[16] Ibid., i. 425.
[17] J. and A. L. Aikin, *Miscellaneous Pieces in Prose*, 1773, 138–89.

were vigorous, and his genius truly sublime; his style is close and strong, and his numbers in general harmonious. He was well acquainted with Æschylus and Euripides, and drew deep from their fountains: his thoughts had a romantic cast, and his imagination a certain wild grandeur, which sometimes perhaps approaches to the borders of extravagance; but this led him to descriptions and allegories wonderfully poetical; such for instance is the Antistrophe in his *Ode to Liberty*, and the first part of his *Ode to Fear*; Æschylus himself has not a bolder conception, and the grandeur of thought is as greatly expressed. Dr. Johnson speaks of this sublime Poet with a tenderness which reflects honour on himself; he allows him sometimes to have sublimity and splendor, but in the coldness of criticism expresses some disapprobation of his allegorical imagery, and is unjust to his harmony.

The want of a good taste in a professed Critic is a mental blindness which totally incapacitates him for the discharge of the high office he has assumed; but the want of good manners is an offence against those laws of decorum which, by guarding the charities of society, render our intercourse with each other agreeable: yet there is in some persons a blunt and surly humour, which prides itself in despising these laws of civility; and often with an awkward affectation of pleasantry they play their rude gambols to make mirth, and

> Wallowing unwieldy, enormous in their gait,
> Tempest the ocean.[18]

To whatever liberal motive this conduct may possibly be imputed, we are told by an excellent writer that 'there is a certain expression of style and behaviour which verges towards barbarism; and that it is a degree of barbarism to ascribe nobleness of mind to arrogance of phrase or insolence of manners.' If there is a writer who, more than others, has a claim to be exempted from this pelting petulance, Mr. Gray has that claim: his own polished manners restrained him from ever giving offence to any good man, his warm and chearful benevolence endeared him to all his friends; though he lived long in a college, he lived not *sullenly* there, but in a liberal intercourse with the wisest and most virtuous men of his time; he was perhaps the most learned man of the age, but his mind never contracted the rust of pedantry; he had too good an understanding to neglect that urbanity which renders society pleasing; his conversation was instructing, elegant, and agreeable; superior knowledge, an exquisite taste in the fine arts, and above all purity of

18 Milton, *Paradise Lost*, VII. 411–12.

morals and an unaffected reverence for religion made this excellent person an ornament to society and an honour to human nature.

[records his own response to Gray's odes in opposition to Johnson's.]

I cannot quit this subject without taking a review of the Ode. The Bard, as Dr. Beattie, who caught the enthusiasm of the Poet, finely observes, 'just escaped from the Massacre of his brethren, under the complicated agitations of grief, revenge, and despair, and surrounded with the scenery of rocks, mountains, and torrents, stupendous by nature, and now rendered hideous by desolation, imprecates perdition upon the bloody Edward.'[19] The effect of this imprecation on the tyrant and his warrior chiefs is greatly represented by images of varied terror; the king's crested pride was dismayed;

> Stout Glo'ster stood aghast in speechless trance:
> To arms! cried Mortimer, and couch'd his quiv'ring lance.

The description of the Bard adds to the great ideas of Raphael and Milton a wild dignity of sorrow which strikes us with awe. His lamentations over his slaughtered brethren call for revenge in strains of dreadful harmony. Amidst these woe-wild notes he sees their spirits sitting on a distant cliff, and weaving the ample winding-sheet of Edward's race; on this, 'seized with prophetic enthusiasm, he foretells in the most alarming strains, and typifies by the most dreadful images, the disasters that were to overtake his family and descendents.'[20] And now, 'The work is done.' The airy images melt away in a track of light that fires the western skies. Yet other visions, visions of glory, now burst upon his sight; he beholds in a prophetic extasy a succession of genuine kings, of the line of Tudor, regain their sovereignty; the deep sorrows of his lyre are now changed to measures of transport and rapture; he hails the Bards of future times, whose voices reach his ear, and with strains of defiance and triumph, seeing his death inevitable, (like the poor mariner that leaps from his burning ship into the sea) to preserve himself from the outrages of his enemies he plunges from the mountain's height into the roaring tide below.

The wild and romantic scenery, the strength of conception, the boldness of the figures, the terrible sublimity, the solemn spirit of prophecy, and the animated glow of visions of glory render this 'the finest Ode in the world.' The language of Gray is always pure, peculiarly

[19] James Beattie, *Essays . . . on Poetry and Music*, Dublin, 1778, ii. 255.
[20] Ibid., ii. 255.

compact and nervous, ever appropriated to his subject; when that is gay and smiling, his diction is elegant and glittering; in the sober reflections of saintly melancholy it is grave and solemn; and it rises with an elevated dignity along with the boldest flights of his sublime imagination; and his numbers, regulated by a fine taste and a nice ear, have through all their various modulations a rich and copious harmony. Gray inherited the ample pinion of the Theban Eagle, and sails with supreme dominion through the azure deep of air; but he never sinks to that humiliating lowness to which not want of genius, but the poverty of his subject often depresses the Theban's fluttering pennons: he therefore has a claim to the highest rank in the realms of Lyric Poety. This testimony to his merit would from any lover of literature have been an act of justice; but from the translator of Æschylus,[21] who owes so much to him, it is a debt of Gratitude.

What could induce Dr. Johnson, who as a good man might be expected to favour goodness, as a scholar to be candid to a man of learning, to attack this excellent person and poet with such outrage and indecency, we can only conjecture from this observation, 'there must be a certain sympathy between the book and the reader to create a good liking.' Now it is certain that the Critic has nothing of this sympathy, no portion nor sense of that vivida vis animi,[22] that etherial flame which animates the poet; he is therefore as little qualified to judge of these works of imagination, as the shivering inhabitant of the caverns of the North to form an idea of the glowing sun that flames over the plains of Chili.

Dr. Johnson knows well that 'all Truth is valuable, and that satyrical criticism may be considered as useful, when it rectifies error and improves judgement; he that refines the publick taste is a publick benefactor.'[23] Under this idea he will value the truth of these observations; and upon a more careful review of this Ode of Gray he will perhaps discover that it has some little use, that it promotes one truth; 'it makes kings fear to be tyrants, tyrants to manifest their tyrannical humours.'[24] Few indeed are the pages any where to be found from which some useful instruction may not be derived by those who are disposed to receive it; even these may be a lesson to literary tyrants to bear their faculties meekly, to favour the Progress of Poetry, and to spare the Bard.

[21] Potter's own translation was published in 1777.
[22] Lucretius, De Rerum Naturâ, i. 72 ('lively energy of mind').
[23] Lives, iii. 242.
[24] Sidney, An Apology for Poetry, in Prose Works, ed. A. Feuillerat, 1963, iii. 23.

58. Sir John Hawkins, *Life of Samuel Johnson LL.D.*

1787

The first edition of Hawkins's *Life* was published in March 1787; the second, with many additions and corrections, appeared three months later. Extract from second edition, 534–8.

Hawkins is not without his merits as a biographer but, for the most part, his critical comments on Johnson's writings are perfunctory. Below are his remarks on the *Lives of the English Poets*, which he considered the most celebrated of the works by the man he describes elsewhere as 'the greatest proficient in vernacular erudition, and one of the ablest critics of his time' (p. 441). See Introduction, p. 33.

The book came abroad in the year 1778, in ten small volumes, and no work of Johnson has been more celebrated. It has been said to contain the soundest principles of criticism, and the most judicious examen of the effusions of poetic genius, that any country, not excepting France, has to shew; and so much of this is true, that, in our perusal of it, we find our curiosity, as to facts and circumstances, absorbed in the contemplation of those penetrating reflections and nice discriminations, which are far the greater part of it.

It is, nevertheless, to be questioned, whether Johnson possessed all the qualities of a critic, one of which seems to be a truly poetic faculty. This may seem a strange doubt, of one who has transfused the spirit of one of Mr. Pope's finest poems into one written by himself in a dead language,[1] and, in two instances, nearly equalled the greatest of the Roman satyrists. By the poetic faculty, I mean that power which is the result of a mind stored with beautiful images, and which exerts itself in creation and description: of this Johnson was totally devoid. His organs, imperfect as they were, could convey to his imagination but little of that intelligence

[1] Johnson translated Pope's 'Messiah' into Latin. See *Poems*, 29–36.

which forms the poetic character, and produces that enthusiasm which distinguishes it. If we try his ability by Shakespeare's famous description;

> The poet's eye, in a fine frenzy rolling,
> Doth glance from Heaven to earth, from earth to Heaven;
> And, as imagination bodies forth
> The forms of things unknown, the poet's pen
> Turns them to shapes, and gives to airy nothing
> A local habitation, and a name:[2]

he will appear deficient. We know that he wanted this power; that he had no eye that could be said to roll or glance, and, therefore, that all his conceptions of the grandeur and magnificence of external objects, or beautiful scenes, and extensive prospects, were derived from the reports of others, and consequently were but the feeble impressions of their archetypes; so that it may be questioned whether, either waking or sleeping,

> Such sights as youthful poets dream,[3]

were ever presented to his view.

This defect in his imaginative faculty, may well account for the frigid commendation which Johnson bestows on Thomson, and other of the descriptive poets, on many fine passages in Dryden, and on the *Henry and Emma* of Prior. Moral sentiments, and versification, seem chiefly to have engaged his attention, and on these his criticisms are accurate, but severe, and not always impartial. His avowed fondness for rhyme is one of the blemishes in his judgment: he entertained it in opposition to Milton, and cherished it through the whole of his life; and it led him into many errors. Dryden had his doubts about the preference of rhyme to blank verse; and I have heard Johnson accuse him for want of principle in this respect and of veering about in his opinion on the subject. No such imputation could fasten on himself.

That Johnson had no sense of the harmony of musical sounds, himself would frequently confess, but this defect left him not without the power of deriving pleasure from metrical harmony, from that commixture of long and short quantities, which the laws of prosody have reduced to rule, and from whence arises a delight in those whose ear is unaffected by consonance. The strokes on the pulsatile instruments, the drum for instance, though they produce monotonous sounds, have, if made by

---

[2] *Midsummer Night's Dream*, v. i. 12-17.
[3] *L'Allegro*, l. 129.

rule, mathematical ratios of duple and triple, with numberless fractions, and admit of an infinite variety of combinations, which give pleasure to the auditory faculty; but of this Johnson seems also to have been insensible. That his own numbers are so harmonious as, in general, we find them, must have been the effect of his sedulous attention to the writings of Dryden and Pope, and the discovery of some secret in their versification, of which he was able to avail himself.

If Johnson be to be numbered among those poets in whom the powers of understanding, more than those of the imagination, are seen to exist, we have a reason for that coldness and insensibility which he so often discovers in the course of this work; and, when we recollect that he professed himself to be a fastidious critic, we are not to wonder, that he is sometimes backward in bestowing applause on passages that seem to merit it. In short, he was a scrupulous estimator of beauties and blemishes, and possessed a spirit of criticism, which, by long exercise, may be said to have become mechanical. So nicely has he balanced the one against the other, that, in some instances, he has made neither scale preponderate, and, in others, by considering the failings of his authors as positive demerit, he has left some celebrated names in a state of reputation below mediocrity. A spirit like this, had before actuated him in his preface to Shakespeare, in which, by a kind of arithmetical process, subtracting from his excellencies his failings, he has endeavoured to sink him in the opinion of his numerous admirers, and to persuade us, against reason and our own feelings, that the former are annihilated by the latter.

His censures of the writings of lord Lyttelton, and of Gray, gave great offence to the friends of each: the first cost him the friendship of a lady, whose remarks on the genius of Shakespeare have raised her to a degree of eminence among the female writers of this time;[4] and the supposed injury done by him to the memory of Gray, is resented by the whole university of Cambridge. The character of Swift he has stigmatized with the brand of pride and selfishness, so deeply impressed, that the marks thereof seem indelible. In the praises of his wit, he does him no more than justice; of his moral qualities, he has made the most; and of his learning, of which Swift possessed but a very small portion, he has said nothing. Few can be offended at Johnson's account of this man, whose arrogance and malevolence were a reproach to human nature; and in whose voluminous writings little is to be found, that can conduce to the improvement or benefit of mankind, or, indeed, that it beseemed a clergyman to publish.

4 Mrs Elizabeth Montagu, (see p. 408 n. 45).

In his own judgment of the lives of the poets, Johnson gave the preference to that of Cowley, as containing a nicer investigation and discrimination of the characteristics of wit, than is elsewhere to be found. Others have assigned to Dryden's life the pre-eminence. Upon the whole, it is a finely written, and an entertaining book, and is likely to be coeval with the memory of the best of the writers whom it celebrates.

59. Robert Potter, *The Art of Criticism as exemplified in Dr. Johnson's Lives of the Most Eminent English Poets*

1789

Extracts from pp. 109, 172–5, 189–94.

This work was an expanded version of Potter's 'Remarks' which appeared in the *Gentleman's Magazine*, October 1781 – March 1782 (li, 463–7, 506–10, 561–4; lii, 24–6, 116–18). It is more fragmented and censorious than No. 57. The section on Shenstone is included to illustrate a kind of rapturous delight that was quite alien to Johnson's critical temper. See Introduction, pp. 30, 32.

LANSDOWNE,[1]

It may be perceived from our author's mean opinion of him, was a lover as well as lord: as to his poetry, I have a better opinion of it than our author, whose mind was, in some respects, as narrow as a crane's neck.

AS TO SHENSTONE,

Johnson's and his mind were so diametrically opposite, that they were like the elephant and rhinoceros; and in the story of the wooden book,[2]

[1] George Granville. See *Lives*, ii. 286–96.
[2] *Lives*, iii. 348.

Johnson chose rather to burlesque learning than to omit so idle a jest: nevertheless, of the two, it must be admitted, that Shenstone was at least as far removed from being a piece of timber as himself, who a little resembled King Log. For as to the stanzas of Shenstone, 'to which' (says Johnson) 'if any mind denies its sympathy, it has no acquaintance with love or nature;'[3]—the reader should be informed, that it is said that he had no perception of their beauty till it was pointed out to him; but whether the sketches exhibited by him for laying out pleasure-grounds were his, I know not. Shenstone brings to mind Tickell's lines addressed to Addison:

> Ne'er was to the bow'rs of bliss convey'd
> A purer spirit, or more welcome shade.—[4]

which however were, I suppose, too mythological for our author. Be that as it might, the concluding criticism is really cruel: but it is beyond the power of Johnson's libel on this tender poet, Hammond, Gray, &c., of his ironical commendation of Addison, as himself has given out, or of any pedagogue's contempt, to destroy their reputation; although he introduces Gray with his knotted club to knock down the gentle Shenstone, to be himself knocked down at last by our blind Polypheme in the wantonness of his might. He makes Lyttleton too give him a stroke,[5] in the spirit of him who furnished the monkies with clubs to belabour one another for his diversion.

The Doctor, as always, sickens at the idea of any thing rural. Were it not vain to argue against a person who possessed but three out of the five senses, being destitute of that of taste and sight, one might have asked him who wrote London, whether great cities do not afford something sickening, distressing, or horrible, at every step by day or by night. Too true it is, that the savageness of mankind renders rural, as well as other scenes, often sickening and odious; but the scenes of pastoral may be supposed to be laid in Arcadia, or rather indeed in fancied Arcadia. But if we will not in this admit fiction allowed to every kind of poetry, but insist on truth, ancient, or perhaps some modern, realities may afford some satisfaction. It may not be impossible, that as the belief of the true God has always been preserved in some corner of the world, so the genuine simplicity of nature may have been quite extinct. But otherwise, the pastoral poet may revert to the state of man before the

---

[3] Ibid., iii. 356.
[4] Thomas Tickell, 'To the Earl of Warwick, on the Death of Mr Addison', 1721, ll. 45–6.
[5] Lives, iii. 351, 354.

fall. At all times grazing flocks are certainly a pleasing sight: though, in modern times, those who deem themselves of the better sort, annex, like the lowest of mankind whom they nevertheless despise, no idea of entertainment to the prospect of them, but sordidness: they, I will not say, like our biographer, have not the least relish of nature as it is solely God's. If according to a remark of Pope's, in his essay on pastoral, only the pleasing objects of rural life should be presented to view,[6] that of a shepherd in Britain at this day has agreeable circumstances. Let one figure to himself a fine spring morning; the sun rising over a distant hill, bespangling the wide surrounding lawn with pearl, the harmless smiling flocks cropping it, and the lark singing over his head, whilst perhaps the thought of his fair one attunes his own voice to the carrol and the song. If moreover he has a genius for verse, or music to entertain his long leisure, the comparison with sequestered scenes of Arcadia will not seem preposterous. But withal, the reader of pastoral, as of romance, may please himself with the natural congenial idea of a future immortal state, realizing, and more than realizing, the sweet tranquil descriptions of Arcadian and Elysian vales, or of golden castles and ivory gates turning to angelic harmony, such as it never entered the imagination of poet to conceive. Regarding the pastoral of romance, as better than past, as prophetic of what is to come; of, for ought we know, Paradise Regained, when the thoughts of the butcher shall not mingle with the sights of the flocks and herds. . . .

CONCLUSION.

These *Lives*, which furnish the literary of a century, and contain many good morsels of criticism, &c. may be named with Plutarch's, on account of the veins of pleasantry interspersed; but if we compare the numerous apothegms recorded by Plutarch, with the few recited by Johnson, we shall find our author's greatly superior, and be apt to conclude that both Plutarch's heroes and himself entertained but an indifferent notion of repartee. These two great biographers also resemble each other in possessing a considerable spice of the old woman.

The characteristics of Dr. Johnson were general and extensive classical erudition, strong sense, and accurate observation; which seasoned with dry humour and sly detraction, rather than Dryden's free, and Pope's pungent wit, have rendered his classical erudition equally immortal. Strange, and a pity it was, that with his great qualities, he, or rather his posthumous editors, should make the world the confessor of his weak-

---

[6] In *Poems of Alexander Pope*, ed. John Butt, 1963, 120.

nesses, and of his methodism, commixed as they were with literary butchery and savageness. Indeed his character consisted of contradictions. Though his piety was great, and he feared not man, but God, nor any dangers of death, yet he trembled at the thoughts of it. His piety was of the kind, that, haughty and arrogant as it was, would have held the world in the fetters of slavery and priestcraft, whilst the precepts inculcated in these *lives* run counter both to divinity and christian morality. He thought that every one but himself should submit to the great, whilst he despised all men but Popes and Kings, and his father among the rest. As his own character was inconsistent, so his countrymen, nine in ten of whom despised his principles, and nine in ten of the remainder his uncouth manner approaching to savageness, though he was enamoured of a smooth luxurious age, adored him. So devoted was he to the ways of the world, that in this latter work, he, as Bacon says of Machiavel,[7] taught rather what men do, than what they ought to do, as Bacon himself taught by example.

Of his works; though they have little of originality, and his style has a certain atrabiliousness, and his tissue of paragraphs an unpleasing quaintness, it must be confessed that his *Dictionary*, *Rambler*, and the two imitative translations of Juvenal, &c. are very excellent; and that these *Lives of the English Poets* contain a fund of very valuable general criticism, and that his remarks on Pope's Epitaphs are singularly acute,[8] and, for the most part, just. But the coarseness of his constitution, his vigorous mind being perhaps vitiated or degraded by the grossness of his body, vibrated not to the delicate touches of a Shenstone and a Hammond, nor even to the stronger hand of a Gray, but gravitated by the weight of that in which it was inclosed to earth. Johnson's feelings were more ordinary than fine, which indeed accounts for his popularity; more nervous than elevated; and I take Hawkesworth to have been at least his equal in sublimity, and that the author of the *Adventurer*[9] deserves one history of his life.

Johnson was in literature what the first Pitt was in politics, both being alike rough and overbearing. And it would, methinks, be no disagreeable speculation for a moment, how such violent spirits would have assorted on the national theatre? But, as according to Johnson, Garrick was mute in a court of law,[10] and the Lord Chief Justice would probably make

[7] Bacon, *Advancement of Learning*, II. xxi. 9.
[8] *Lives*, iii. 254–72.
[9] John Hawkesworth (1715?–73).
[10] *Journey*, 322–3; see Boswell, *Life*, v. 243.

but an indifferent figure on the stage, so it is probable that he, whose knowledge much exceeded Pitt's, would have borne the bell in conversation, as he easily did in the company of Chesterfield, but would not have been a match for either in Parliament; though it is not likely that he would have brooked total silence, as did, according to report, the whole House of Commons, at one period of Chatham's greatness. How was it at the club, of which Charles Fox and Burke were members? When the Doctor ridiculed Lord Mansfield for being the pack-horse of the law,[11] he might have remembered that himself had been a lexicographical pioneer.

Johnson seldom writes to the fancy; nor visibly ironically so as to discover such a purpose to the reader; but in a continual jog-trot of didactic, allowing no holiday. He constantly addresses himself to the understanding; makes no excursions into the regions of spirits, beyond 'this visible diurnal sphere,' nor essays knowledge denied to 'ears of flesh and blood;' nor even wishes to stray beyond the walks of mere modern life, back to the regions of Gothic fancy. His timid, impalpable, dreary religion permitted him not to expatiate in the field of hypothesis and conjecture; reveries, vain, perhaps, yet amusing; the food of the soul, and a refuge from the miseries and calamities of life. Terribly afraid of free-thinking, though not hostile to free-eating, he immersed in dogma and superstition, fearing to make use of reason as a mediator between extremes. He had the anxiety and yearning of the psalmist without the joy and exultation: such as repel from a pleasant contemplation of the Deity, and instead of imparting delight, make men shrink back from eternity, and exhibit the idea of death terrible; such as pluck away the rose buds of ideal hope from the hour of the separation of soul and body, and point it only with thorns. But these maladies, and his other defects and faults, candour will partially set down to his frame of body, ill adapted to a perfect mind, and acknowledge him, with whose anecdotes the press teemed, to have been no inconsiderable person, but a great author, notwithstanding his *Dictionary* is imperfect, his *Rambler* pompous, his *Idler* inane, his *Lives* unjust, his poetry inconsiderable, his learning common, his ideas vulgar, his *Irene* a child of mediocrity, his genius and wit moderate, his precepts worldly, his politics narrow, and his religion bigoted.

[11] *Journey*, 427; see Boswell, *Life*, v. 395.

60. Anna Seward's opinions of the *Lives*

1789-97

Text from *Letters*, ed. A. Constable, 1811, ii. 307-8; v. 31-2.

Anna Seward (1747 1809), the ample 'Swan of Lichfield', was capable of a sympathetic response to Johnson (see Introduction, pp. 21, 22, 31); she was also capable of malevolence. There appears to be calculated malice in the two letters printed here. Her correspondents were the Revd Thomas Whalley, prebendary of Wells and minor poet, and Thomas Park the antiquary.

7 April 1789, to Whalley:
I do not think it fair to appeal to Johnson's critical tribunal for arbitration on any poetic subject, except indeed his dictionary, which, for verbal authority, may generally be relied upon. In his critical dissertations, the *Lives of the Poets*, he is too perpetually stimulated by rival-hating envy, to perplex and mislead concerning the true merits of the art, and the respective claims of the artists, to have his decisions referred to in disputes of this nature. You observe 'that, having never written sonnets, he could have no bias upon his judgment from jealousy.' Now Johnson has not attempted Pindaric odes any more than sonnets; it may, therefore, with equal force, be alleged, that, no clashing interest existing, we may rely upon his judgment, as inevitably impartial, when he decides upon their claims. Yet how unjust, how despicable is his wretched contempt of Gray's noble odes! Remember, also, his contempt for the sweet, the matchless *Lycidas* of our immortal Bard; and, I am sure, you will confess that, either a wretched depravity of taste, or a lying spirit of criticism, incapacitates his dogmas for becoming umpires between literary friends, when they differ about any thing Milton has written. He decide, indeed! who asserts in his life of that poet, that nobody closes the leaves of the *Paradise Lost* with any wish of ever opening them again!!![1] Surely it is strange that you should say of *him*, who could *so* say, that 'Milton has, on

[1] *Lives*, i. 183.

311

the whole, had due honour from Johnson.' To me it appears, that whatever praise he gives Milton, was for the purpose of giving an air of impartiality to his injustice, and keener edge to his sarcasms. But that his malice to Milton is so glaring, he might have a better right than yourself to dislike the sonnets of that poet, since his hatred to blank verse was allowed, and since they partake so much of its nature. That my opinions do not blindly follow the whistling of a great name, my confession that I cannot read a canto of Spenser without weariness may evince.

21 December 1797, to Park:

After Johnson rose himself into fame, it is well known that he read no other man's writings, living or dead, with that attention without which public criticism can have no honour, or, indeed, common honesty. If genius flashed upon his maturer eyes, they ached at its splendour, and he cast the book indignantly from him. All his familiarity with poetic compositions, was the result of juvenile avidity of perusal; and their various beauties were stampt upon his mind, by a miraculous strength and retention of memory. The wealth of poetic quotation in his admirable *Dictionary*, was supplied from the hoards of his early years. They were very little augmented afterwards.

In subsequent periods, he read verse, not to appreciate, but to depreciate its excellence. His first ambition, early in life, was poetic fame; his first avowed publication was in verse. Disappointed in that darling wish, indignant of less than first-rate eminence, he hated the authors, preceding or contemporary, whose fame, as poets, eclipsed his own.[2] In writing their lives, he gratified that dark passion, even to luxury. The illiberal propensity of mankind in general, to be gratified by the degradation of eminent talents, favoured his purpose. Wit and eloquence gilded injustice, and it was eagerly swallowed*.

* Miss Seward's strictures, in this and some of the preceding letters, on Dr Johnson's character as a critic, may, to many readers, appear perhaps to be carried too far: yet they have lately received a sanction from a writer of the highest authority, whose candour is no less conspicuous than his penetration or his eloquence, and whose situation precludes him from all suspicion of being here influenced by local prejudices. It is in the following fine strain of moral indignation that Mr Stewart expresses himself upon this subject.

'Among our English poets, who is more vigorous, correct, and polished than Dr Johnson, in the few poetical compositions which he has left? Whatever may be thought of his claims to originality of genius, no person who reads his verses can deny that he possessed a sound taste in this species of composition; and yet how wayward and perverse, in many instances, are his decisions, when he sits in judgment on a political adversary, or when he

---

[2] Gillray attributed a similar motive to Johnson, in a cartoon of 1783. See M. D. George, *Hogarth to Cruikshank*, 1967, Plate 121.

61. Thomas De Quincey, 'Postscript respecting Johnson's Life of Milton'

1859

Text from *Collected Writings*, ed. D. Masson, 1890, iv. 114–7.

The date of composition of this piece is not known; it was first published (under the title of a 'Prefatory Memorandum') in the collected edition of De Quincey's writings in 1859. It is perhaps the most hostile response to one of the *Lives*. De Quincey regards Johnson as 'the worst enemy that Milton and his great cause have ever been called upon to confront; the worst as regards undying malice!' (p. 105).

[De Quincey claims that Johnson was determined to put a mine under 'the most consecrated of Milton's creations', *Paradise Lost*.]

Into this great *chef-d'oeuvre* of Milton it was no doubt Johnson's secret determination to send a telling shot at parting. He would lodge a little *gage d'amitié*, a farewell pledge of hatred, a trifling token (trifling, but such things are not estimated in money) of his eternal malice. Milton's admirers might divide it among themselves; and, if it should happen to fester and rankle in their hearts, so much the better; they were heartily welcome to the poison: not a jot would he deduct for himself if a thousand times greater. O Sam! kill us not with munificence. But now, as I must close within a minute or so, what *is* that pretty souvenir of gracious detestation with which our friend took his leave? The *Paradise Lost*, said he, in effect, is a wonderful work; wonderful; grand beyond

treads on the ashes of a departed rival! To myself (much as I admire his great and various merits, both as a critic and as a writer), human nature never appears in a more humiliating form, than when I read his *Lives of the Poets*; a performance which exhibits a more faithful, expressive, and curious picture of the author, than all the portraits attempted by his biographers; and which, in this point of view, compensates fully, by the *moral* lessons it may suggest, for the *critical* errors which it sanctions. The errors, alas! are not such as any one who has perused his imitations of Juvenal can place to the account of a bad taste; but such as had their root in weaknesses, which a noble mind would be still more unwilling to acknowledge.'—*Philosophical Essays*, by Dugald Stewart, [1810] 491.

all estimate; sublime to a fault. But—well, go on, we are all listening. But—I grieve to say it, wearisome. It creates a world of admiration (*one* world, take notice); but—oh, that I, senior offshoot from the house of Malagrowthers,[1] should live to say it!—ten worlds of ennui; one world of astonishment; ten worlds of *taedium vitae.* Half and half might be tolerated—it is often tolerated by the bibulous and others; but one against ten? No, no!

This, then, was the farewell blessing which Dr. Johnson bestowed upon *Paradise Lost*! What is my reply? The poem, it seems, is wearisome; Edmund Waller called it *dull*. A man, it is alleged by Dr. Johnson, opens the volume; reads a page or two with feelings allied to awe; next he finds himself rather jaded; then sleepy; naturally shuts up the book; and forgets ever to take it down again.[2] Now, when any work of human art is impeached as wearisome, the first reply is wearisome to *whom*? For it so happens that nothing exists, absolutely nothing, which is not at some time, and to some person, wearisome or potentially disgusting. There is no exception for the works of God. 'Man delights not me, nor woman either,'[3] is the sigh which breathes from the morbid misanthropy of the gloomy but philosophic Hamlet. Weariness, moreover, and even sleepiness, is the natural reaction of awe or of feelings too highly strung; and this reaction in some degree proves the sincerity of the previous awe. In cases of that class, where the impressions of sympathetic veneration have been really unaffected, but carried too far, the mistake is—to have read too much at a time. But these are exceptional cases: to the great majority of readers the poem is wearisome through mere vulgarity and helpless imbecility of mind; not from overstrained excitement, but from pure defect in the *capacity* for excitement. And a moment's reflection at this point lays bare to us the malignity of Dr. Johnson. The logic of that malignity is simply this: that he applies to Milton, as if separately and specially true of *him*, a rule abstracted from human experience spread over the total field of civilisation. All nations are here on a level. Not a hundredth part of their populations is capable of any unaffected sympathy with what is truly great in sculpture, in painting, in music, and by a transcendent necessity in the supreme of Fine Arts—Poetry. To be popular in any but a meagre comparative sense as an artist of whatsoever class is to be *confessedly* a condescender to human infirmities. And, as to the test which Dr. Johnson, by implication, proposes as trying the merits of Milton in his greatest work, viz. the degree in which it was read, the

---

[1] Malachi Malagrowther, a pseudonym used (in 1826) by Sir Walter Scott.
[2] *Lives*, i. 183.   [3] *Hamlet*, II. ii. 312.

Doctor knew pretty well,—and when by accident he did *not* was inexcusable for neglecting to inquire,—that by the same test all the great
classical works of past ages, Pagan or Christian, might be branded with
the mark of suspicion as works that had failed of their paramount purpose, viz. a deep control over the modes of thinking and feeling in each
successive generation. Were it not for the continued succession of
academic students having a contingent *mercenary* interest in many of the
great authors surviving from the wrecks of time, scarcely one edition of
fresh copies would be called for in each period of fifty years. And, as to
the arts of sculpture and painting, were the great monuments in the
former art, those, I mean, inherited from Greece, such as the groups, &c.,
scattered through Italian mansions, the Venus, the Apollo, the Hercules,
the Faun, the Gladiator, and the marbles in the British Museum, purchased by the Government from the late Lord Elgin,[4]—stripped of their
metropolitan advantages, and left to their own unaided attraction in
some provincial town, they would not avail to keep the requisite officers
of any establishment for housing them in salt and tobacco. We may
judge of this by the records left behind by Benjamin Haydon[5] of the
difficulty which *he* found in simply upholding their value as wrecks of
the Phidian era. The same law asserts itself everywhere. What is *ideally*
grand lies beyond the region of ordinary* human sympathies; which
must, by a mere instinct of good sense, seek out objects more congenial
and upon their own level. One answer to Johnson's killing shot, as he
kindly meant it, is that our brother is not dead but sleeping.[6] Regularly
as the coming generations unfold their vast processions, regularly as
these processions move forward upon the impulse and summons of a
nobler music, regularly as the dormant powers and sensibilities of the
intellect in the working man are more and more developed, the *Paradise
Lost* will be called for more and more: less and less continually will there
be any reason to complain that the immortal book, being once restored
to its place, is left to slumber for a generation. So far as regards the Time
which is coming; but Dr. Johnson's insulting farewell was an arrow

* In candour I must add—*if uncultured*. This will suggest a great addition to the one in
a hundred whom I have supposed capable of sympathy with the higher class of models.
For the majority of men have had no advantages, no training, no discipline. [De Quincey]

---

[4] The Elgin Marbles—the work of Pheidias (*c.* 440 B.C.)—from the Parthenon at Athens,
were collected by the Earl of Elgin (1766–1841) and sold to the British Government. They
were placed in the British Museum in 1816.

[5] Historical painter (1786–1846), one of the few who recognised the distinguished
quality of the Marbles.

[6] Matthew 9: 24.

feathered to meet the Past and Present. We may be glad at any rate that the supposed neglect is not a wrong which Milton does, but which Milton suffers. Yet that Dr. Johnson should have pretended to think the case in any special way affecting the reputation or latent powers of Milton,—Dr. Johnson, that knew the fates of Books, and had seen by moonlight, in the Bodleian, the ghostly array of innumerable books long since departed as regards all human interest or knowledge—a review like that in Beranger's[7] Dream of the First Napoleon at St. Helena, reviewing the buried forms from Austerlitz or Borodino, horses and men, trumpets and eagles, all phantom delusions, vanishing as the eternal dawn returned,—might have seemed incredible except to one who knew the immortality of malice,—that for a moment Dr. Johnson supposed himself seated on the tribunal in the character of judge, and that Milton was in fancy placed before him at the bar,

Quem si non aliqua nocuisset, mortuus esset.[8]

[7] Jean Pierre de Béranger (1780–1857), French poet.
[8] Adapted from Virgil, *Eclogues*, III. 15 (intended to mean: 'whom, if he had not harmed in some way, he would have died').

62. Archibald Campbell, *Lexiphanes, a Dialogue, Imitated from Lucian*

1767

Text from pp. 1–10, 70–2.

According to Boswell, Campbell (1726?–80) was 'a Scotch purser in the navy' (*Life*, ii. 44). His purpose was—in words from *Hudibras* on his title-page—to ridicule the 'Babylonish Dialect Which learned Pedants much affect'; his method (in Boswell's words) was to apply 'Johnson's "words of large meaning" to insignificant matters', a standard satirical technique of the century. Though Boswell thought *Lexiphanes* could not harm Johnson, it gained considerable notoriety; a second edition was published in 1767, a third in 1783. See Introduction, p. 5.

ARGUMENT.

Mr. J——n or the English Lexiphanes and the Critick meet. After some compliments past between them, Lexiphanes rehearses his Rhapsody. It contains a rant about Hilarity and a Garret; Oroonoko's[1] adventure with a Soldier; his own journey to Highgate, and adventures there and on the road; his return to London, and lawsuit about his horse; his walk to Chelsea, where he plays at skittles; his being frightened by a calf on his return, which he mistakes for the Cock-lane Ghost;[2] his amours and disappointments at a Bagnio. He is now interrupted by the Critick, who takes him to task for his hard words and affected style, and thinking him mad, applies to a Physician passing by, who proves to be the British Lucretius. He repeats a great many verses, and the Critick gets

[1] *Oroonoko* (*c.* 1678), a novel by Aphra Behn.
[2] The supposed ghost at 33 Cock Lane, Smithfield. Many people believed or alleged that Johnson was deceived by the imposture; but see Boswell, *Life*, i. 406–8.

rid of him with some difficulty. Another Doctor comes up, who is the Critick's friend. They talk together upon Lexiphanes's cafe, and other matters concerning taste and writing. They force him to swallow a potion which makes him throw up many of his hard words. The Doctor goes to a consultation, and the Critick instructs Lexiphanes how to avoid his former faults, and write better for the future.

LEXIPHANES.

A

DIALOGUE.

CRITICK. J——N. FIRST PHYSICIAN.
SECOND PHYSICIAN.

CRITICK.

See J——N yonder, our English Lexiphanes, marching along with a huge folio under his arm. Some new piece I'll warrant, in the stile of his *Ramblers*. I shall be well entertained, if he is in a reading humour; a thing he is often fonder of than many of his hearers.

J——N.

Most happily occurred, my very benevolent convivial associate. Behold. A novel exhibition which is purely virginal, and which has never been critically * surveyed by any annual or diurnal retailer of literature, in this so signal † a metropolis.

CRITICK

What! a new romance, or a second *Rasselas of Abyssinia?*

J——N.

Without dubiety you misapprehend this dazzling scintillation of conceit in totality‡, and had you had that constant recurrence to my oraculous dictionary, which was incumbent upon you from the§

---

* Rambler No. 10, *critically condemned.*

† I beg leave to observe here once for all, that I do not intend to confine myself to a close imitation of Lexiphanes's manner of writing only, but propose to shew by example the absurdity of hard words, and affectation in general. For instance, the words *novel* and *signal* are not much used by Lexiphanes, that I remember, but Gordon, in his Tacitus, is mighty fond of them.[3] They are here affected, as they generally are in Gordon, yet have been used by some of our best writers, though very sparingly. But bad authors have the same influence on words, that the dregs of the people have upon dress.

‡ *Rambler*, No. 141.

§ *Rasselas, vehement injunctions of haste. Rambler*, No. 26, *monitory letters.*

---

[3] Thomas Gordon (d. 1750) published his translation of Tacitus in 1728.

vehemence of my monitory injunctions, it could not have escaped you that the word novel exhibits to all men dignified by literary honours and scientifical accomplishments, two discrepant significations. The one imports that which you have affixed to it, a romance or fiction, such as the tale of Ajut and Anningait, or the Prince of Abyssinia *; but that in which I have at present used it, signifies new, recent, hodiernal. And indeed the eye of critical discernment will perceive, that there is a most exquisite elegancy in conferring that appellation upon a recent and hodiernal production. But I am afraid that I shall ransack vacuity, and strike out in vain flashes of instruction from the fortuitous collision of happy incidents,† for your intellects are exhausted,‡ or distorted,§ their fortresses are betray'd to rebels, and their children excited to sedition, ‖ and you are now labouring under an intellectual famine, and want the banquet of the lady Pekuah's conversation¶.

CRITICK.

Excuse, dear sir, the dullness of my apprehension. But pray what is the subject of this new piece?

J———N.

It is a rhapsody or a characteristical essay, an assemblage calculated to enhance and diversify convivial festivity. But you must understand, that I totally anti-rhapsodize Ashley.

CRITICK.

What then! you don't retail your characters in small quantities, as Ashley his punch, *pro bono publico?* We have them wholesale. But there are many of that name, and I should rather imagine, as 'tis a rhapsody, you mean my Lord Shaftsbury.[4]

J———N.

You arread me aright. And, indeed, this** luxuriant efflorescence of my wit would have been utterly inexplicable to any but one of your sagacity of conjecture, acuteness of comprehension, and facility of

---

* Tales and romances of our author well known [*Rambler* Nos. 186–7, and *Rasselas*].
† *Ram.* No. 154. ‡ *Rass.* [chapter 3]. § *Ram.* No. 95.
‖ *Rass.* [chapter 18]. ¶ *Rass.* [chapter 39]. ** *Ram.* No. 141.

---

4 Anthony Ashley Cooper, 3rd Earl of Shaftesbury (1671–1713), author of *Characteristicks*, 1711.

penetration*. You are one of those gigantick and stupenduous intelligences who grasp a system by intuition†.

CRITICK.

Well, then give us a sample of your work, that I may not be altogether deprived of so great a feast, for I promise myself it will be as good as a cup of Nectar‡.

J——N.

Deject then§ exaggeratory obloquy below the horizon of your prospects,‖ without the servility of adulation afford openness of ears, sedulity of thought, and stability of attention¶. But above all ** expulse hereditary aggregates and agglomerated asperities which may obumbrate your intellectual luminaries with the clouds of obscurity, or obthurate the porches of your intelligence with the adscititious excrement of critical malevolence.

CRITICK.

Begin boldly, my good friend, there are neither agglomerated asperities nor hereditary aggregates about me††.

* This is quite in Lexiphanes's style. He is mighty fond of ending a sentence with three phrases of this sort, for the most part equally superfluous and insignificant. When he hath done this, no doubt he thinks he hath rounded off the period well, and hath added something to the harmony of its cadence. *Ram.* No. 208. Innumerable examples of this kind are to be met with in his writings. One I found in the very paragraph whence I took the last quotation *Colloquial barbarisms, licentious idioms, and irregular combinations. Ram.* 208. Another I met with, as I just now cast my eye on the first number of his third volume. *The prejudice of faction, the stratagem of intrigue, and the servility of adulation. Ram.* No. 106. These may very properly be called *Triads.* But sometimes, and when he is disposed to be more eloquent than common, he mounts it up to a *Quaternion,* of which there are likewise many examples in his *Ramblers.*

† *Ram.* No. 108. If one could suspect such an original genius as Lexiphanes of being a plagiary, he hath borrowed *grasp a system by intuition,* from king Phys, in *the Rehearsal,* who *grasps a storm with the eye of reason.*[5] Akenside, our poetical, or rather blank-verse Lexiphanes, has an expression of much the same nature,

> When despair shall grasp
> His agonizing bosom.
>> *Pleas. of Imag.* b. ii. v. 491.

‡ Almost literal from Lucian.
§ *Rasselas.*
‖ *Ram.* No. 2.
¶ Here's another Triad *more Lexiphanico.*
** Gordon's Tacitus.
†† In the place answering this, in the original, Lucian tells Lexiphanes, that he has no vermin about him, neither lice nor fleas; a play upon words which it was impossible to preserve in the copy.

---

[5] Buckingham, *The Rehearsal,* 1671, II. i.

J———N.

Consider well how I have conglomerated this atchievement of erudition, the insinuation of its exordial sentences*, the selection of its diction, and resplendency of its sentiment.

CRITICK.

It must be all that, if yours. But I pray you begin†.

J———N.

I shall inchoate with one of it's most delicious morsels of eloquence, and shall at the same time be curt‡. Perpend§, and receive my sayings with a stedfast ear‖. But I obsecrate that in the interim you would, by a proper secession, facilitate my enjoyment of the light, whilst I, by the fortuitous liquefaction of spectacular lenses, and their concordant adaptation to my poral regions, meliorate and prolong its fruition¶.

After our post-meridional refection, rejoined Hypertatus, we will

---

* *Exordial verses. Ram. No.* 158.

† What goes before is a pretty close copy of Lucian, the same conceits and playing upon words as near as the different turn of the two languages would allow. For instance, Lexiphanes tells Lucian, that he antisymposiazes Aristo, which was Plato's original name, but by which he was little known. In the same manner J———n tells the Critick, who, in this dialogue, acts the part of Lucian, that he anti-rhapsodizes Ashley, a name, at least, never used when one speaks of my Lord Shaftsbury. Lucian's Lexiphanes is a pert conceited fop, whereas mine, like his living original, is a grave solemn affected pedant and coxcomb. Lucian's *Symposium*, as far as we can now know of the matter, is an original. But my Rhapsody is mostly taken from the *Ramblers* with some few quotations and parodies from the *Elements of Criticism*, *Night-Thoughts*, *Pleasures of Imagination*, *Centaur not Fabulous*, and Warton's *Essay on Pope*.⁶ Lucian has jumbled together a parcel of the strangest incoherent stuff and nonsense that can well be imagined. I hope I have equall'd him in this point, however short I may have fallen in other articles.

‡ *Elements of Criticism.*   § Pistol in Shakespear [*Henry V*, IV. iv. 8].

‖ *Pleas. of Imag.* B. 2. l. 306.

¶ 'Tis supposed that in this sentence Lexiphanes means no more than that the critic should step aside while he puts on his spectacles. For some of the hard words, and quaint phrases, consult *Rambler*, No. 9.

And now Lexiphanes begins to read his Rhapsody, conceived in the following words: *After our postmeridional refection, rejoined Hypertatus, &c.* and continues reading till interrupted by the critic. The fragment here given, without either beginning or ending, is supposed to be only a small part of a larger work; for Mr. J———n tells us, he *inchoates with one of its most delicious morsels of eloquence*. Lucian begins and ends his *Symposium* in the same abrupt manner, and though it be in itself a matter of perfect indifference, I thought it better to follow the example of so great an original.

---

⁶ Lord Kames, *Elements of Criticism*, 1762; Edward Young, *Night Thoughts*, 1742–5, and *Centaur not Fabulous*, 1754; Mark Akenside, *Pleasures of Imagination*, 1744; Joseph Warton, *Essay on . . . Pope*, i., 1756.

regale with a supernumerary compotation of convivial ale, so adapted to exhilarate the young, and animate the torpor of hoary wisdom with sallies of wit, bursts of merriment, and an unintermitted stream of jocularity. From this assemblage of festivity we will unanimously extrude those screech-owls whose only care is to crush the rising hope, to damp the kindling transport, and allay the golden hours of gaiety with the hateful dross of grief and suspicion. Such is Suspirius, whom I have now known fifty-eight years and four months, who has intercepted the connubial conjunction of two hundred and twenty six reciprocal hymeneal solicitors by prognostications of infelicity, and has never yet passed an hour with me in which he has not made some attack upon my tranquillity, by representing to me, that the imbecillities of age, and infirmities of decrepitude are coming fast upon me. Indeed to those whose timidity of temper subjects them to extemporaneous impressions, who suffer by fascination, and catch the contagion of misery, it is extreme infelicity to live within the compass of a screech-owl's voice. Therefore let us avoid Suspirius with a studied sedulity, and should we fortuitously meet him in the multifarious confluxes of men, let us repress the solicitude of his advances with a frigid graciousness*. . . .

CRITICK.

Have done, Mr J———n, for God's sake have done. We have had enough of ascending and reciting. Besides, I guess what follows is neither fit for you to read nor me to hear. This, however, is not all I find fault with. Where the D——l! have you collected all this trash of hard words? from what magazine or repository have you raked together these perverse terms and absurd phrases, wherewith you have be-spattered me, who never did you any wrong, at so unmerciful a rate? Some, I see, are of your own invention; for others you must have ransacked the old musty volumes of former times, justly disregarded when first written, and now deservedly forgotten. The rest I perceive you have gleaned up, with infinite pains, from Greek and Latin, from scholastick writers, and books on the abstruse sciences. And you think you have done a mighty pretty feat, that you have performed an eminent service to learning, when you have wriggled in, over head and shoulders, a new-fashioned long-tailed word, what in your own phrase I would call a *vermicular* word, or a dark term of art, without considering whether it be proper to the subject, suited to the capacity of your readers, or

---

* For most of the hard words, quaintnesses, and absurdities of style in this paragraph, consult the character of Suspirius the screech-owl, in the *Rambler* No. 59.

indeed whether it be an English word or not. You are the unfittest person of any I know for what you have undertaken, to compile a dictionary. Though 'tis indeed no wonder you should be employed by booksellers in such a work.

63. Johnson defends his style

1777

Life, iii. 173-4.

In Baretti's Review, which he published in Italy, under the title of *Frusta Letteraria*,[1] it is observed, that Dr. Robertson the historian had formed his style upon that of '*Il celebre Samuele Johnson*.' My friend himself was of that opinion: for he once said to me, in a pleasant humour, 'Sir, if Robertson's style be faulty, he owes it to me; that is, having too many words, and those too big ones.'

I read to him a letter which Lord Monboddo[2] had written to me, containing some critical remarks upon the style of his *Journey to the Western Islands of Scotland*. His Lordship praised the very fine passage upon landing at Icolmkill;[3] but his own style being exceedingly dry and hard, he disapproved of the richness of Johnson's language, and of his frequent use of metaphorical expressions. JOHNSON. 'Why, Sir, this criticism would be just, if in my style, superfluous words, or words too big for the thoughts, could be pointed out; but this I do not believe can be done. For instance; in the passage which Lord Monboddo admires, "We were now treading that illustrious region," the word *illustrious*, contributes nothing to the mere narration; for the fact might be told without it: but it is not, therefore, superfluous; for it wakes the mind to peculiar attention, where something of more than usual importance is to

[1] Giuseppe Marc Antonio Baretti (1719-89), critic and miscellaneous writer, edited his review October 1763 - January 1765. (See Boswell, *Life*, iii. 503.)
[2] James Burnett, Lord Monboddo (1714-99), Scottish judge.
[3] *Journey*, 134-5. (See Boswell, *Life*, v. 334.)

be presented. "Illustrious!"—for what? and then the sentence proceeds to expand the circumstances connected with Iona. And, Sir, as to metaphorical expression, that is a great excellence in style, when it is used with propriety, for it gives you two ideas for one;—conveys the meaning more luminously, and generally with a perception of delight.'

64. Horace Walpole, 'General Criticism of Dr. Johnson's Writings'

c. 1779

Text from British Museum Add. MS 37728, f. 34–5v.

First published (though differing at many points from the manuscript version given here) in Walpole's *Works*, 1798, iv. 361–2. Most of it was written before 1779 (see *Walpole's Correspondence*, ed. W. S. Lewis, Yale, 1965, xxxiii. 89 n.25).

Dr Johnstone's Works have obtained so much reputation, & the Execution of them, from partiality to his abilities, has been rated so far above his merit, that without detracting from his capacity or his Learning, it may be usefull to caution young Authors against partiality to his Style & manner, both of which are uncommonly vicious & unworthy of Imitation by any Man who aims at excellence in writing his own Language.

A marked manner, when It runs thro all the compositions of any Master, is a defect in itself, & indicates a deviation from Nature. The Writer betrays his having been struck by some predominant Tint, & his Ignorance of Nature's Variety. Yet it is true that the greatest Masters of composition are so far imperfect, that they always leave some marks by which We may discover their hand. He approaches the nearest to universality, whose Works do not put it in the power of our Quickness or depth of Sagacity to observe certain characteristic touches that ascertain the specific Author.

Johnston's Works are all as easily distinguished as if he were an affected Writer; for exuberance is a fault as well as Quaintness. There is Sense in almost every thing Johnstone says; he is often profound, and a just reasoner—I mean, when Prejudice, bigotry, and arrogance do not cloud or debase his Logic. He is benevolent in the application of his morality; dogmatically uncharitable in the dispensation of his Censures; and equally so, when he differs with his Antagonist on general Truths or partial doctrines.

The first Criterion that stamps J's works for his, is the loaded Style.—I will not call it Verbose, tho strictly proper, because Verbosity generally implies unmeaning Verbiage—a censure he does not deserve. I have allowed & do allow that most of his words have an adequate, & frequently an illustrating purport—the true use of epithets—but then his words are indiscriminately select, & too forcefull for ordinary occasions. They form a hardness of diction, & a muscular toughness that destroy all ease & simplicity. Every Sentence is as high coloured as any. No paragraph improves; the position is as robust as the demonstration; & the weakest part of the paragraph, I mean, in the effect, not in the Solution, is generally the Conclusion. He illustrates till he fatigues. This fault is so usual with him, he is so apt to explain the same thought by three different set of phrases heaped on each other, that if I did not condemn his laboured coinage of words, I would call his threefold inundation of parallel expressions Triptology.

He prefers learned Words to the simple & common—& on every occasion. He is never simple, elegant, or light. He destroys more Enemies with the Weight of his Shield than with his spear, & had rather make 3 mortal wounds in the same part than one. This Monotony, the grievous effect of Pedantry & Self-conceit, prevents him from ever being eloquent. He excites no passion but indignation; his Writings send the Reader away more satiated than pleased. If he attempts humour, he makes yr reason smile, without making you gay; because the Study that his learned mirth demands, annihilates chearfullness. It is the clumsy gambol of a lettered Elephant. We wonder that so grave an Animal should have strayed into the province of the Ape, yet admire that practice should have given the bulky Quadruped so much agility.

Upon the whole, Johnston's Style appears to me so encumbered, so void of ear & harmony, & consequently so harsh & unpliable that I know no modern Writer whose works coud be read aloud with so little satisfaction. I question whether one should not read a page of equal length in any modern Author in a minute's time less than one of Johnstons, all proper pauses & accents duly attended to in Both.

His works are the Antipodes of Taste, & he a Schoolmaster of truth, but never its parent; for his doctrines have no novelty, and are never inculcated with indulgence either to the froward child, or to the Dull one. He has set nothing in a new light, yet is as diffuse as if we had every thing to learn. Modern Writers have improved on the Ancients only by conciseness: Dr. Johnstone, like the Chymists of Laputa, endeavours to carry back what has been digested to its pristine & crude principles. He is a Standing proof that the Muses leave works unfinished, if they are not embellished by the graces.

65. Robert Burrowes, 'Essay on the Stile of Doctor Samuel Johnson', Nos. I and II

1786

Text from the *Transactions of the Royal Irish Academy*, Dublin, 1787, i. 27–56.

The Revd Robert Burrowes read his two papers on Johnson's style to the Academy on 13 March and 13 November 1786; Boswell rightly thought that in them Burrowes had 'analysed the composition of Johnson and pointed out its peculiarities with much acuteness' (*Life*, iv. 386). See Introduction, p. 31.

As the primary and immediate desire of every reader must necessarily be to understand the meaning of his author, of all the faults of stile obscurity must be the most obvious and offensive. . . .

That Johnson's stile is obscure, the testimony of all unlearned readers abundantly confirms; and from the same authority the cause may be stated to be his perpetual affectation of expressing his thoughts by the use of polysyllables of Latin derivation: a fault, which confines to men of erudition the most animating enforcements to virtue and the most salutary rules of conduct, by disqualifying all who have not been made acquainted by a liberal education with the Latin appellations for things, or those, from whose memories the common use of the English names has in course of time effaced them. And let it not be said that such a class is beneath the attention of an author, when it is considered that almost the whole female world, from the circumstances of their education are necessarily included in it. They learn the words of their language from conversation or familiar books; but with whom are they to converse, or what volumes of musty pedantry are they to ransack, to be enabled to peruse the writings of Johnson without frequent recourse to his dictionary? Nor has this wilful exclusion of the unlearned readers served as a means of conciliating the favour of the learned, who, though they understand Latin, in an English work expect to find English; and whatever may be the peculiarities of their own stile, are forward enough to discover and reprobate those of others.

Thus Dr. Johnson observes, that Milton formed his stile on a perverse and pedantic principle: he was desirous 'to use English words with a foreign idiom.'[1] But Milton's poetry, if indeed a defence be necessary, is sufficiently defended by established poetic license: and for his prose, let it be observed, that his subjects were learned, and I may say technical, and his readers of such description as left it matter of indifference whether they should be addressed in English or in Latin: that he was engaged in repeated controversies with foreigners, and his works designed to persecute the fortunes of the exiled monarch over the continent, and written, in some sort officially, by the Latin secretary to Cromwell. But surely that principle, which has led Johnson to seek for remote words, though with the English idiom, is no less pedantic than Milton's, and much more injurious by its obscurity. The reader who knows the single words may perhaps be able to overcome the difficulties of the arrangement, but for ignorance of the single words no remedy can with efficacy be applied. Johnson has besides no peculiarity of situation to plead in excuse, but has on the contrary adopted his pedantic principle against the dissuasive influence of circumstances. From the writer of an English dictionary, there might reasonably be expected a nice selection of words, purely and radically English, or at least the use of such only as had been indisputably admitted into the language: and the complexion of his readers, as well as the popular subjects he treated of, were such as might be thought to

[1] *Lives*, i. 190.

furnish little temptation to learned and antiquated phraseology. Indeed, if rules for periodical essays are to be drawn from the practice of their great English original, Mr. Addison, as the rules of epic poetry from Homer's, nothing can be more opposite to their true character; for as their professed intent is the improvement of general manners, their stile, as well as their subjects, should be levelled to understandings of every description.

It may be said, however, in favour of Johnson, that the great lawgivers of criticism have indulged writers of eminence in a license for calling in the aid of foreign words. But this indulgence, which of right belongs only to poetry, and the more dignified kinds of prose, is even granted to them with but a sparing hand, 'dabitur licentia sumpta pudenter.'[2] Our Author, who in his poems has made but little use of this privilege, has in his prose, extended a limited sufferance to the most unqualified permission and encouragement: he has preferred, on all occasions where a choice was to be made, the remote word of Latin derivation to the received English one, and has brought in the whole vocabulary of natural philosophy, to perplex and encumber familiar English writing. I do not speak of a few words scattered rarely through his works, but of the general character of his stile appearing in every page; not of single acts, but of confirmed and prevailing habits, of new-raised colonies, disdaining an association with the natives, and threatening the final destruction of our language. The reader, at his first perusal of the Rambler, finds himself bewildered in a labyrinth of long and learned words, distracted with foreign sounds, and exiled from his native speech, in perpetual want of an interpreter: disgusted at the intrusion of so many phrases to which he has been hitherto a stranger, he labours out a passage through the palpable obscure, and, when he has at last gained the golden prize, laments that so much time should have been wasted, in overcoming the unnecessary obstacles to its approach.

[numerous examples follow.]

There are however two occasions on which this fault appears yet more extravagant and ridiculous. The first of these is, where personages of different descriptions are introduced as writing in their own characters; for what can be more absurd than to suppose a similarity of stile, and particularly where that stile is so far from a simple one, in the writings of persons supposed to be of different ages, tempers, sexes and occupations. Yet all the correspondents of the Rambler seem infected with the same

[2] Horace, Ars Poetica, l. 51 ('the liberty will be granted if taken with moderation').

literary contagion, and the Johnsonian distemper to have been equally communicated to all. Thus Papilius talks of 'garrulity, erratic industry, and heterogenous notions dazzling the attention with sudden scintillations of conceit.' Victoria 'passes through the cosmetic discipline, covered with emollients, and punished with artificial excoriations.' Misocapelus tells of his 'officinal state, adhesions of trade, and ambulatory projects;' and Hypertatus describes the 'flaccid sides of a foot-ball swelling out into stiffness and extension,' and talks of 'concentration of understanding, barometrical pneumatology,' and 'tenuity of a defecated air.'[3] In such writings the hand of the master must be immediately perceived; the existence of the imaginary correspondents cannot even for a moment be believed, and the Rambler stands convicted of an ineffectual and unnecessary attempt to raise his own consequence by forging letters to himself.

The second occasion on which this fault is equally glaring, is where ordinary or perhaps mean subjects become necessary to be treated of; and a few instances from our author may well warrant my asserting that on such occasions, as he himself says less deservedly of Dr. Young,— 'burlesque cannot go beyond him.'[4] Thus a calamity which will not admit being complained of, is in Johnson's language, such as 'will not justify the acerbity of exclamation, or support the solemnity of vocal grief:' to deny and to profess, are to 'pronounce the monosyllables of coldness and the sonorous periods of respectful profession:' when the skillet is watched on the fire, we see it 'simmer with the due degree of heat, and snatch it off at the moment of projection:' for sun-set, we read 'the gentle coruscations of declining day;' and for washing the face with exactness, we have, 'washing with oriental scrupulosity.'[5] Mean and vulgar expressions cannot have a more powerful recommendation than that one of the ablest writers in the English language could only thus avoid them.

Johnson was a writer of too attentive and critical observation to be ignorant of this remarkable peculiarity of his own stile. In the last paper of his *Rambler*, where he treats of his work as a classical English composition, he takes notice of, and by a defence, which if admitted would justify and recommend it, shews himself not a little prejudiced in its favour. After declaring, with some ostentation, that 'he has laboured to refine our language to grammatical purity, and to clear it from colloquial

---

[3] See *Rambler* Nos. 141, 130, 133, 123, 117.
[4] *Lives*, iii. 398.
[5] *Rambler* Nos. 200, 194, 51, 135; *Lives*, iii. 55.

barbarisms, licentious idioms, and irregular combinations;' that 'something perhaps he has added to the elegance of its construction, and something to the harmony of its cadence;' he proceeds to subjoin the following passage: 'When common words were less pleasing to the ear, or less distinct in their signification, I have familiarized the terms of philosophy by applying them to known objects and popular ideas; but have rarely admitted any word not authorized by former writers: for I believe that whoever knows the English tongue in its present extent, will be able to express his thoughts, without farther help from other nations.'[6] The first of these reasons for substituting, in place of a received familiar English word, a remote philosophical one, such as are most of Johnson's Latin abstract substantives, is its being more pleasing to the ear. But this can only be deemed sufficient by those who would submit sense to sound, and for the sake of being admired by some, would be content not to be understood by others. And though, in some instances, for the sake of tempering the constitutional roughness of the English language, this might be admitted, yet it never can be contended for in such latitude, as would justify the practice of our author. This he well knew, and accordingly defending hard words in an essay in his *Idler*, he insists largely on the second plea, the greater distinctness of signification. 'Difference of thoughts,' he says, 'will produce difference of language: he that thinks with more extent than another, will want words of larger meaning; he that thinks with more subtilty, will seek for terms of more nice discrimination.'[7] In this argument there is certainly some degree of weight, and the exact appropriation and perspicuity of Johnson's words in some measure confirms it. But that language, which he does not admit to have sunk beneath Milton, would surely have been sufficient to have supported him; and, as he himself observes, 'though an art cannot be taught without its proper terms, yet it is not always necessary to teach the art: in morality it is one thing to discuss the niceties of the casuist, and another to direct the practice of common life.' Let the nature of periodical publications determine, which should be more properly the object of the author. But he is not reduced to the alternative: if the testimony of many English authors of eminence, confirmed experimentally by their own practice, is to be relied on, exactness of thought is not necessarily at variance with familiar expression: and if this union was not impossible, would not some endeavour to effect it have deserved the attention of Johnson? Of Johnson who, while his dictionary proves such accurate and copious

[6] See document No. 7.
[7] *Idler* No. 70.

knowledge of the powers of our received words, as could not have failed of accomplishing the patriotic task, however arduous, gives in his other works the stronger reason to lament, that his prejudices in favour of a vicious and affected stile should have prevented his undertaking it.

But this fault is surely committed without excuse, in every case where the language furnishes a received word adequate to the distinct communication of the idea: and that many such have innocently incurred Doctor Johnson's displeasure must be abundantly evident to every reader. A page of his writings, compared with one of any of our eminent English authors on the same subject, will furnish many instances, which cannot be accounted for by attention to harmony of sound, or distinctness of signification: instances, to be ascribed merely to that wantonness of habit which after quoting Congreve's declaration, that 'he wrote the *Old Batchelor* to amuse himself in his recovery from a fit of sickness,' thinks proper, a few lines after, to explain it in Johnson's words, by saying, 'the *Old Batchelor* was written in the languor of convalescence.'[8] It would seem that the aunt of Bellaria,[9] who gives the writings of the Rambler to her niece for her perusal, and promises to tell her the meaning of any word she should not understand, has undertaken a task, which the author himself suspects to be not unnecessary, and the reader has reason to apprehend she will scarcely be able to accomplish.

Johnson says indeed, he has rarely admitted any word, not authorized by former writers: but where are we to seek authorities for 'resuscitation, orbity, volant, fatuity, divaricate, asinine, narcotic, vulnerary, empireumatic, papilionaceous,' and innumerable others of the same stamp, which abound in and disgrace his pages? For 'obtund, disruption, sensory or panoply,' all occurring in the short compass of a single essay in the *Rambler*?[10] Or for 'cremation, horticulture, germination and decussation,' within a few pages in his *Life of Browne*?[11] They may be found, perhaps, in the works of former writers, but they make no part of the English language. They are the illegitimate offspring of learning by vanity; adopted indeed, but not naturalized, and though used, yet not authorized: For if use can sufficiently authorize, there is no description of improper words, which can be condemned. Technical words may be defended from Dryden and Milton, obsolete from Shakespeare, vulgar from Swift and Butler. Johnson's fault lies in this, that he has made such frequent use of remote and abstruse words of Latin original, that his meaning often becomes unintelligible to readers not possessed of a

---

[8] *Lives*, ii. 214.   [9] *Rambler* No. 191.   [10] Ibid. No. 78.
[11] See *Works*, 1792, xii. 283–6.

considerable degree of learning; and whether these words were now first made by him, or having been made by others, had been hitherto denied admittance into the current language, is a matter of perfect indifference.

It must be allowed that these terms are restrained by our author to such precision, that they cannot often resign their places to others more familiar, without some injury to the sense. But such is the copiousness of our language, that there are few ideas on ordinary subjects, which an attentive examination will find incommunicable in its ordinary words. Though we may not have a term to denote the existence of a quality in the abstract, we may perhaps find one to denote it in the concrete; and even though there may be none to express any mode of its existence, there may readily occur one to express its direct negation. It is the business of the writer who wishes to be understood, to try all possible variations of the grammatical structure of his sentence, to see if there be not some which may possibly make known his thought in familiar words. But that this was not the practice of Johnson, his compositions and his celebrated fluency afford the strongest evidence. He seems to have followed the first impulse of his mind in the structure of his sentence, and when he found in his progress no English word at hand to occupy the predetermined place, it was easy to supply the deficiency by calling in a Latin one.

Of this overbearing prejudice, which thus subdued a strongly rational understanding, and misled a judgment eminently critical, it may not be useless to enquire the reasons. To the first and principal of these, no man can be a stranger who has so read the works of Johnson as to have formed a just notion of the peculiar genius of the author. Possessed of the most penetrating acuteness and resolute precision of thought, he delights to employ himself in discriminating what common inaccuracy had confounded, and of separating what the grossness of vulgar conception had united. A judgment, thus employed (as he would perhaps himself describe it) in subtilizing distinctions, and dissociating concrete qualities to the state of individual existence, naturally called for language the most determinate, for words of the most abstract significations. Of these common speech could furnish him with but a scanty supply. Familiar words are usually either the names of things actually subsisting, or of qualities denoted adjectively, by reference to those substantives to which they belong: besides, common use gives to familiar words such a latitude of meaning, that there are few which it does not admit in a variety of acceptations. Johnson, unwilling to submit to this inconvenience, which, in every country, to avoid a multiplicity of terms, had been acquiesced in, sought out those remote and abstruse Latin derivatives, which as they had for the most part hitherto been used but once, were as yet appropriated to one signification exclusively. What the natural bent of his genius thus gave birth to, his successive employments strengthened to maturity.

[illustrates Johnson's knowledge of Latin and determination to display it.]

Yet let me not conclude this part of my subject with too unfavourable an impression of our author. As I have stated fully the faults of his words, it is but candid to declare their merits. They are formed according to the exact analogy of the English language; they are forcible and harmonious; but, above all, they are determinate. Discriminated from each other, and appropriated each to one idea, they convey, to such as understand the author's language, his genuine sense, without superfluity and without mutilation. The distinctions of words esteemed synonimous, might from his writings be accurately collected. For thoughts the most definite, he has language the most precise; and though his meaning may sometimes be obscure, it can never be misunderstood. . . .

As there are no modern writings higher in public estimation than Doctor Johnson's, and as there are none which abound more in appropriate marks of stile, there are none which can with more advantage be made the subject of critical enquiry. On their obvious and distinguishing characteristic, the too frequent use of Latin derivatives, I have already discoursed at large. I shall in this essay consider such other peculiarities of Johnson's stile as, though less apt to be taken notice of, will it is presumed when noticed be readily recognized.

And of all these the merit or demerit must rest with full force on Johnson: for, however the stile of his compositions may correspond with his stile of conversation, and however extraordinary and perhaps authentic the stories his biographers tell of his fluency may be, yet nothing in his works can fairly be ascribed to carelessness. His stile in writing, which he had formed early, became familiar by abundant practice, and in the course of a long continued life of dissertation became also his stile of speaking. His authoritative decisions on the merit of all our English authors demand, and his constant employment in critical disquisition should have enabled him to grant it without injury to his literary character, that his own stile should be fairly subjected to animadversion: nor should negligence, which will never be insisted on in diminution of his merit, be admitted as a sufficient plea in extenuating his faults.

As his peculiarities cannot be ascribed to carelessness, so neither are they the effect of necessity. Few of them would have appeared, had Johnson, intent only on communicating his ideas, despised all aids of embellishment. But that this did not suit his ideas of literary perfection, we are sufficiently informed in his remarks on the stile of Swift; an author who has at least this merit, that he has escaped all those faults which the critic has fallen into. The easy and safe conveyance of meaning Johnson there declares to be 'not the highest praise: against that inattention with which known truths are received, it makes,' he says, 'no provision; it instructs, but it does not persuade.'[12] Our author seems therefore to have thought it necessary, in conformity with his own principle, to introduce into his stile certain ornaments, which, in his opinion, would prove the effectual means of captivating attention; and these ornaments, too laboriously sought for, and used without sufficient variety, have become the peculiarities of his stile. I shall comprize the principal of them under two heads, as arising either from his endeavours after splendor and magnificence, or from his endeavours after harmony; for to these two heads they may almost all be referred.

Not that it is denied, that magnificence and harmony are objects worthy an author's regard; but the means made use of to attain these, if not skilfully selected, may fail of their intended effect; may substitute measurement for harmony, and make that only pompous which was designed to be magnificent. On dignified subjects they are no doubt to be attended to, for the stile should always be proportioned to the subject; but on familiar and meaner topics they should, by a parity of reasoning, be avoided: and however well adapted to excite attention, it may be remarked, that in general they rather fix it on the expression, than on the sentiment, and too often cloy that appetite they were intended but to stimulate.

Johnson's study of splendor and magnificence, by inducing him as much as possible to reject the weaker words of language, and to display only the important, has filled his pages with many peculiarities. His sentences, deprived of those feeble ties which restrained them to individual cases and circumstances, seem so many detached aphorisms, applicable to many other particulars, and certainly more dignified as more universal. But though he may have employed this art with some advantage, it is yet hardly to be recommended. Johnson's thoughts were so precise, and his expressions so minutely discriminated, that he was able to keep the leading circumstances of the particular case distinctly in view, and in the form of an universal sentence implicitly to insinuate them to the reader: an injudicious imitator, by generalizing his expres-

[12] *Lives*, iii. 52.

sions, might in some instances make that false which under restrictions might have been true; and in almost all, make that obscure which otherwise would have been perspicuous.

As every substantive presents a determinate image to the mind, and is of course a word of importance, Johnson takes care to crowd his sentences with substantives, and to give them on all occasions the most distinguished place. The instrument, the motive, or the quality therefore, which ordinary writers would have in the oblique case, usually takes the lead in Johnson's sentences; while the person, which in connected writing is often expressed by some weak pronoun, is either intirely omitted, or thrown into a less conspicuous part. Thus, 'fruition left them nothing to ask, and innocence left them nothing to fear,'—'trifles written by idleness and published by vanity,'—'wealth may, by hiring flattery or laying diligence asleep, confirm error and harden stupidity.'[13] This practice doubtless gives activity and importance, but caution must be used to prevent its exceeding the bounds of moderation. When the person is to be dethroned from its natural pre-eminence, it is not every quality which has sufficient dignity to assume its place: besides, in narration, or continued writing of any sort, the too frequent change of leading objects in sentences contributes to dissipate the attention, and withdraw it from the great and primary one: and even in Johnson's hands this ornament has become too luxuriant, when affections, instead of being personified, are absolutely humanized, and we are teized with the repeated mention of 'ear of greatness,'—'the bosom of suspicion,'—and 'the eye of wealth, of hope, and of beauty.'[14]

This attachment to substantives has led him, wherever it was possible by a change of construction, to substitute them in place of the other parts of speech; instead therefore of the usual construction, where the adjective agrees with the substantive, he forms a new substantive from the adjective, which governs the other in the possessive case. Thus, instead of 'with as easy an approach,' he always writes, 'with the same facility of approach:' instead of 'with such lively turns, such elegant irony, and such severe sarcasms,'—he says, 'with such vivacity of turn, such elegance of irony, and such asperity of sarcasm.'[15] When the effect produced no otherwise arises from the substantive, than as possessed of the quality which the adjective denotes, this change of construction is an happy one: it expresses that which is necessary in the thought, by a necessary member

[13] Lives, i. 174; ii. 295; Rambler No. 58.
[14] Rambler Nos. 153, 54.
[15] Journey, 4; Rambler No. 26.

of the sentence; whereas the usual form lays the whole stress of the idea on a word, which, without the smallest injury to the construction, may be safely removed. An instance however may shew, that Johnson sometimes uses it where the same reasoning would shew it to be absolutely improper. 'Steele's imprudence of generosity, or vanity of profusion,' he says, 'kept him always incurably necessitous.'[16]—Here, since Steele's generosity could not have kept him necessitous if it had not been excessive or imprudent, 'imprudence of generosity' is proper: but as his being vain of profusion, if he had not actually been profuse, never could have produced this effect; since his vanity is but the very remote cause of that which his profusion would have effected, whether he had been vain of it or not, 'vanity of profusion' is an improper expression.

This ambition of denoting every thing by substantives has done considerable violence to Johnson's constructions:—'places of little frequentation,'—'circumstances of no elegant recital,'—'with emulation of price,'—'the library which is of late erection,'—'too much temerity of conclusion,'—'Phillips's addiction to tobacco,' are expressions of affected and ungraceful harshness.[17] This, however, is not the worst fault such constructions may have, for they often become unnecessarily obscure: as 'he will continue the road by annual elongation;' that is, by compleating some additional part of it each year:—'Swift now lost distinction;'[18] that is, he could not now distinguish his acquaintances. Many of the substantives too which are thus introduced, are words absolutely foreign to the language: as 'ebriety of amusement,'—'perpetual perflation,'—'to obtain an obstruction of the profits, though not an inhibition of the performance,'—'Community of possession must always include spontaneity of production.'[19] One of our most usual forms of substantives, the participle of the verb used substantively, to give room for such introduced words he has on all occasions studiously avoided: Yet Dr. Louth would scarcely have given the rule for a construction repugnant to the genius of our language;[20] and some arguments will be necessary to prove that the words, 'renewing, vanishing, shadowing and recalling,' should give place to 'renovation, evanescence, adumbration and revocation,' when it is considered, that all who understand English know the meaning of the former, while the latter are intelligible to such only of them as understand Latin; but of this I have elsewhere treated fully.

[16] *Lives*, ii. 81.
[17] *Journey*, 118, 43, 4, 7; *Rambler* No. 63; *Lives*, i. 316.
[18] *Journey*, 118; *Lives*, iii. 48.
[19] *Rambler* No. 167; *Journey*, 72; *Rambler* No. 131.
[20] Robert Lowth (1710–87) published his *Introduction to English Grammar* in 1762.

Johnson's licentious constructions however are not to be conceived as flowing entirely from his passion for substantives. His endeavours to attain magnificence, by removing his stile from the vulgarity, removed it also from the simplicity of common diction, and taught him the abundant use of inversions and licentious constructions of every sort. Almost all his sentences begin with an oblique case, and words used in uncommon significations, with Latin and Greek idioms, are strewed too plentifully in his pages. Of this sort are the following: 'I was only not a boy'—'Part they did'—'Shakespeare approximates the remote'—'Cowley was ejected from Cambridge'—'Brogues are a kind of artless shoes'—'Milk liberal of curd.'[21] Such expressions it is unnecessary to mark with censure; they bear in themselves an harshness so repulsive, that easy writing must be held in more than ordinary contempt, when they are considered as patterns worthy of imitation.

Metaphorical expression is one of those arts of splendor which Johnson has most frequently employed; and while he has availed himself of all its advantages, he has escaped most of its concomitant faults. Here is no muse, which in one line is a horse and in the next a boat;[22] nor is there any pains requisite to keep the horse and boat from singing. Johnson presents to your view no chaos of discordant elements, no feeble interlining of the literal with the figurative. In his metaphors and similes the picture is always compleat in itself, and some particulars of exact resemblance are distinctly impressed upon the reader. What image can be more beautiful than that which represents the beginnings of madness as 'the variable weather of the mind, the flying vapours which from time to time cloud reason without eclipsing it?' Or what more apposite than that which calls Congreve's personages 'a sort of intellectual gladiators?'[23]

Sometimes, indeed, it must be acknowledged, his metaphors succeed each other in too quick succession, and are followed up too elaborately: but to commit this fault he was solicited by temptations scarcely to be resisted. Much of his life had been consumed in enquiring into the various acceptations of each word, all of which except the primary one are so many metaphorical uses of it; so that every word suggested many metaphors to his mind, presenting also from his quotations a variety of other terms of the same class, with which it would wish to be associated. Thus *ardour*, which in his preface to his *Dictionary*, he observes, is never used to denote material heat, yet to an etymologist would naturally suggest it;

[21] *Lives*, ii. 20; iii. 422; *Shakespeare*, 65; *Lives*, i. 5; *Journey*, 44, 74.
[22] *Lives*, ii. 128.
[23] Ibid., ii. 97, 228.

and Johnson accordingly, speaking of the '*ardour* of posthumous fame,' says that 'some have considered it as little better than *splendid* madness; as a *flame kindled* by pride and *fanned* by folly.'[24] Thinking of a deep stratagem, he is naturally led from the depth to the surface, and declares 'that Addison knew the heart of man from the *depths* of stratagem to the *surface* of affectation.'[25] His subjects too were such as scarcely could be treated of without figurative diction: the powers of the understanding require the aid of illustration to become intelligible to common readers. But to enquire how our author illustrates them, is to detect the greatest and almost the only fault in his metaphors. 'The mind stagnates without external ventilation'—'An intellectual digestion, which concocted the pulp of learning, but refused the husks'—'An accumulation of knowledge impregnated his mind, fermented by study, and sublimed by imagination.'[26] From such illustrations common readers will, it is feared, receive but little assistance. The sources from which his allusions are borrowed are so abstruse and scientific, and his expressions so studiously technical, that even those who most commend his similes as apposite, cannot pretend that many of them are explanatory.

Of the peculiarities of Johnson's stile, which I proposed to treat of under my second head, as arising from his study of harmony, the principal I may call the parallelism of his sentences; which admits no clause, without one or two concomitants, exactly similar in order and construction. There is scarcely a page of the *Rambler* which does not produce abundant instances of this peculiarity: and what is the ornament, which, if introduced so often, can be always introduced happily? Or what is the ornament, however happily introduced, which will not disgust by such frequent repetitions? Johnson's mind was so comprehensive, that no circumstance occurred to him unaccompanied by many others similar; no effect, without many others depending on the same or similar causes. So close an alliance in the thought naturally demanded a corresponding similitude in the expression: yet surely all similar circumstances, all the effects of each cause, are not equally necessary to be communicated; and as it is acknowledged that even a continued poem of pure iambics would disgust, variety must appear an indispensably necessary ingredient to harmony. Were we even to admit then, that in any particular triod the construction of one of its clauses could not be altered without injuring the harmony of the sentence, yet a regard to the harmony of the whole treatise will occasionally make such an alteration necessary.

[24] *Rambler* No. 49.   [25] *Lives*, ii. 121.
[26] *Rambler* No. 101; *Lives*, i. 3, 183.

But these parallel sentences are not always faultless in themselves. Sometimes, though indeed rarely, a word is used without a definitive appropriation to that to which it is annexed; as in this instance, 'Omnipotence cannot be exalted, infinity cannot be amplified, perfection cannot be improved:'[27] where the exact relation between amplitude and infinity, and between improvement and perfection, is not at all kept up by exaltation being applied to Omnipotence. Sometimes two words are introduced, which answer hardly any other purpose than to make the parallelism more conspicuous, by adding a new member to each clause. Thus, in the following passage, 'grows too slothful for the labour of contest, too tender for the asperity of contradiction, and too delicate for the coarseness of truth;'[28] where labour, asperity and coarseness are sufficiently implied in slothful, tender and delicate. Sometimes too the parallelism itself is unnecessarily obtruded on the reader, as 'quickness of apprehension and celerity of reply,' where 'celerity' having precisely the same meaning as 'quickness,' could only have been introduced to make up the parallelism: 'Nothing is far-sought or hard-laboured' where the first adverb is essential to the sense, and the last only to the sound.[29] 'When two Englishmen meet, their first talk is of the weather, they are in haste to tell each other what each must already know, that it is hot or cold, bright or cloudy, windy or calm.'[30] Such uninteresting enumerations, since they contribute nothing to the meaning, we can only suppose introduced, as our author observes of some of Milton's Italian names, to answer the purposes of harmony.

It were unjust however not to declare, that many of his parallelisms are altogether happy. For antithesis indeed he was most eminently qualified; none has exceeded him in nicety of discernment, and no author's vocabulary has ever equalled his in a copious assortment of forcible and definite expressions. Thus, in his comparison of Blackmore's attack on the dramatic writers with Collier's, 'Blackmore's censure,' he says, 'was cold and general, Collier's was personal and ardent: Blackmore taught his readers to dislike, what Collier incited them to abhor.'[31] But it is useless to multiply instances of that which all must have perceived, since all his contrasts and comparisons possess the same high degree of accuracy and perfection. From the same cause may be inferred the excellence of his parallel sentences, where praise-worthy qualities are separated from their concomitant faults, or kindred effects are disunited: as where he calls Goldsmith 'a man who had the art of being minute without

[27] *Lives*, i. 292.   [28] *Rambler* No. 74.   [29] Ibid. No. 177; *Lives*, i. 64.
[30] *Idler* No. 11.   [31] *Lives*, ii. 241.

tediousness, and general without confusion; whose language was copious without exuberance, exact without constraint, and easy without weakness.'[32] But Johnson's triods occur so frequently, that I find myself always led aside to wonder, that all the effects from the same cause should be so often discovered reducible to the mystical number three: I torment myself to find a reason for that particular order in which the effects are recited, and I am involuntarily delayed to consider, whether some are not omitted which have a right to be inserted, or some enumerated which due discretion would have suppressed. Surely I must be singular in my turn of thought, or this art of attention, which thus leads away from the main subject, cannot be an happy one.

His desire of harmony has led him to seek even for the minute ornament of alliteration. Thus, he says, 'they toil without prospect of praise, and pillage without hope of profit.'—'Shakespeare opens a mine, which contains gold and diamonds in inexhaustible plenty, though clouded by incrustations, debased by impurities, and mingled with a mass of meaner minerals.'[33] Alliteration indeed is so often casual, and so often necessary, that it is difficult to charge it on an author's intentions. But Johnson employs it so frequently, and continues it through so many words, as in the instances given above, that when we consider too how nearly allied it is as an ornament to parallelism, we have I think sufficient grounds to determine it not involuntary.

Under this head I shall beg leave to mention one peculiarity of Johnson's stile, which though it may not have arisen, at least not entirely, from his endeavours after harmony, yet discovers itself obviously to the reader by its effects upon the ear; I mean the studied recurrence of the same words in the latter part of the sentence, which had appeared in the former; the favourite ornament of his *Idler*, as parallelisms are of the *Rambler*, and used not unfrequently in the *Lives of the Poets*. As the use of it is attended with many advantages and many disadvantages, the author who would adopt it should watch it with a suspicious eye. If restrained within the bounds of moderation, it is on many occasions the most lively, concise, perspicuous and forcible mode of expressing the thought. Since the words too at their return naturally recall to the mind the antecedent members of the sentence, it may be considered as a valuable assistant in imprinting the thought upon the memory. It has also this additional advantage, that as unfairness in reasoning often arises from change of terms, so where the terms are not changed, we are apt to presume the

32 Ibid., ii. 49.
33 *Rambler* No. 144; *Shakespeare*, 84.

reasoning to be fair. Thus, where we read in the *Life of Savage* the following sentence, 'As he always spoke with respect of his master, it is probable the mean rank in which he then appeared did not hinder his genius from being distinguished or his industry from being rewarded; and if in so low a state he obtained distinctions and rewards, it is not likely they were gained but by genius and industry.'[34] In this instance the perspicuity of the reasoning seems to have been preserved through such a chain of propositions, merely by the artifice of returning the same words a second time to the reader's observation. But the unrestrained use of this art is perhaps one of the greatest faults an author can adopt. A fault, which burlesques grave subjects by communicating impressions of levity, and on occasions less serious, instead of being sprightly degenerates into quaintness: which for disquisition and reasoning gives us nothing but point and epigram; by a constrained conciseness often betrays to obscurity, and where most successful, leads but to trite retorts and verbal oppositions, which the reader has already anticipated, and perhaps already rejected.

Were Johnson however to be charged with negligence, it might be most fairly on the subject of harmony. There are many passages in his works where sounds almost similar are suffered to approach too near each other; and though some of these are too palpable to be passed over unnoticed by the author, yet I can never think any ear so incorrect as to adopt sameness and monotony for harmony. Either way however Johnson is culpable, and his alternative is either a faulty principle, or a negligence in his practice.

Yet his pages abound with memorials of close attention to harmony; unfortunately with memorials equally deserving of censure; with heroic lines and lyric fragments. Thus, he says, 'Pope foresaw the future efflorescence of imagery just budding in his mind, and resolved to spare no art or industry of cultivation; the soft luxuriance of his fancy was already shooting, and all the gay varieties of diction were ready at his hand to colour and embellish it.' 'I will chase the deer, I will subdue the whale, resistless as the frost of darkness, and unwearied as the summer sun.'[35] Surely this is to revive the Pindaric licentiousness, to confound the distinction between prose and poetry, to introduce numbers by study while negligence admits rhymes, and to annihilate the harmony of prose, by giving the reader an obvious opportunity to compare it with the harmony of versification.

Indeed all the peculiarities of Johnson's stile, pursued to their excess,

[34] *Lives*, ii. 325.   [35] Ibid., iii. 103–4; *Rambler* No. 187.

tend to raise prosaic composition above itself: they give the admirers of Gray a fit occasion of retorting 'the glittering accumulation of ungraceful ornaments, the double double toil and trouble, the strutting dignity which is tall by walking on tip-toe,'[36] which have so harshly been objected to their favourite. Simplicity is too often given up for splendor, and the reader's mind is dazzled instead of being enlightened.

I shall now conclude this enquiry into the peculiarities of Johnson's stile with remarking, that if I have treated more of blemishes than beauties, I have done it, not so much to pass censure on Johnson, as to give warning to his imitators. I have indeed selected my instances from his writings: but in writings so numerous, who is there that would not sometimes have indulged his peculiarities in licentiousness? I have singled him out from the whole body of English writers, because his universally acknowledged beauties would be most apt to induce imitation; and I have treated rather on his faults than his perfections, because an essay might comprize all the observations I could make upon his faults, while volumes would not be sufficient for a treatise on his perfections.

[36] *Lives*, iii. 440.

66. Anna Seward on Johnson's prose style

1795

Extract from *Letters*, 1811, iv. 54–6.

Seward's correspondent was Johnson's friend William Seward (1747–99). She gives a specific example of Johnson's ability vividly to excite his reader's imagination. The contrast to be made is with Macaulay's allegation about his habit of 'padding out a sentence with useless epithets' (see No. 80).

17 May 1795, to Seward:

Dr Johnson, whose sophistry in criticism has been fatal to the general poetic taste of this period, elevated the style of prose composition much above the water-gruel mark. His splendid example demonstrates, that efflorescence and strength of language united, are necessary to form the perfection of writing in prose as well as in verse; and the brilliant diction of Gibbon and Berrington,[1] equally proves the dull mistake of supposing a plain unornamented style necessary, even to history itself.

Johnson's *Tour to the Hebrides* shows us the possibility of giving, by the graces of language, an exquisite charm to many observations and descriptions, which, without those verbal graces, would disgust by their want of essential importance. If he had plainly told us, that the channels of the rivers and of the brooks in the Highlands were much wider than the streams that occupied them at the season he travelled through those tracks;— that such disproportionate breadth of channel was occasioned by the frequent and sudden floods;—and that such depth and rapidity after rain, combined with their general shallowness to prevent their containing fish: we should certainly have thought the information dully unimportant, and have probably exclaimed—'Pshaw! who knows not that the generally shallow streams of mountainous countries, often deep by flood, must, in dry seasons, have larger beds than they fill, and cannot possibly sustain fish?' But who, that is not insensible to the magic of fine style, can read the information without delight, as he thus imparts it?

[1] Edward Gibbon (1737–94); Joseph Berington (1746–1827).

We passed many rivers and rivulets which commonly ran, with a clear shallow stream, over an hard pebbly bottom. These channels, which seem so much wider than the water they convey would naturally require, are formed by the violence of wintry floods, produced by the accumulation of innumerable streams that fall from the hills, and bursting away, with resistless impetuosity, make themselves a passage proportioned to their mass.

Such capricious and temporary waters cannot be expected to produce fish. The rapidity of the wintry deluge sweeps them away, and the scantiness of the summer stream would hardly sustain them above the ground. This is the reason why, in fording the northern rivers, no fishes are seen, as in England, wandering in the water.[2]

By the picturesque power of the numerous epithets, in the first sentence, we are placed on the brink of those currents, while they are hurrying through their broad and stony channel, and we seem to stand amidst the wild scenes through which they flow. In the second, the image of the more vital English rivers and brooks is brought distinctly to the eye, by that fine poetic expression, 'wandering in the water.'

67. Nathan Drake on the influence of Johnson's style

1809

Extract from *Essays . . . illustrative of the Rambler, Adventurer, and Idler*, 1809, i. 198–201, 280–6.

By profession a physician, Drake (1766–1836) was well known as an essayist and miscellaneous writer. See Introduction, pp. 31–2.

The public had been accustomed, in the pages of the *Spectator*, to great variety of style, to a fascinating gaiety of manner, and to a perpetual interchange of topic, and it was not therefore hastily taught to relish the solemn and majestic tone of the preceptive *Rambler*. It gradually gained ground, however, with the learned, the wise, and the good; and

[2] *Journey*, 34.

though not more than five hundred of each paper were taken off during its publication in numbers, as soon as it was collected into volumes, its circle of attraction began rapidly to enlarge. Yet that it acquired enthusiastic admirers, if not numerous yet select, even from its earliest appearance, may be drawn from contemporary publications; from the newspapers of the day, from the *Gentleman's Magazine*, and from *The Student*, a miscellany of which, in the second essay of this volume, we have exhibited a passage of high praise in favour of the *Rambler*.[1] Fresh proofs, however, of an early and zealous support of this paper, have very lately appeared in the *Correspondence* of Richardson, edited by Mrs. Barbauld, and which, as singularly striking and curious, cannot fail of being acceptable to my readers. In a letter to Mr. Cave, dated August 9th, 1750, the author of *Clarissa* thus forcibly expresses his opinion:

Though I have constantly been a purchaser of the *Ramblers* from the first five that you was so kind as to present me with, yet I have not had time to read any further than those first five, till within these two or three days past. But I can go no further than the thirteenth, now before me, till I have acquainted you that I am inexpressibly pleased with them. I remember not any thing in the *Spectators* that I read, for I never found time—(alas! my life has been a trifling busy one) to read them all, that half so much struck me; and yet I think of them highly.

I hope the world tastes them; for its own sake, I hope the world tastes them; the author I can only guess at. There is but one man, I think, that could write them; I desire not to know his name; but I should rejoice to hear that they succeed; for I would not, for any consideration, that they should be laid down through discouragement.

I have, from the first five, spoke of them with honour. I have the vanity to think that I have procured them admirers; that is to say, *readers*. And I am vexed that I have not taken larger draughts of them before, that my zeal for their merit might have been as glowing as now I find it.

Excuse the overflowing of a heart highly delighted with the subject; and believe me to be an equal friend to Mr. Cave and the Rambler, as well as

Their most humble servant,

S. RICHARDSON.

To this, Mr. Cave in a letter written August the 13th, 1750, replies,

that Mr. Johnson is the *Great Rambler*; being, as you observe, the only man who can furnish two such papers in a week, besides his other great business, and has not been assisted with above three.

I may discover to you that the world is not so kind to itself as you wish it. The

---

[1] See above, document No. 6.

encouragement, as to sale, is not in proportion to the high character given to the work by the judicious, not to say the raptures expressed by the few that do read it; but its being thus relished in numbers, gives hope that the sets must go off; as it is a fine paper, and, considering the late hour of having the copy, tolerably printed.

When the author was to be kept private, (which was the first scheme,) two gentlemen, belonging to the prince's court, came to me to enquire his name, in order to do him service; and also brought a list of seven gentlemen to be served with the *Rambler*. As I was not at liberty, an inference was drawn, that I was desirous to keep to myself so excellent a writer. Soon after, Mr. Doddington sent a letter directed *to the Rambler*, inviting him to his house, when he should be disposed to enlarge his acquaintance. In a subsequent number a kind of excuse was made, with a hint that a good writer might not appear to advantage in conversation.

I have had letters of approbation from Dr. Young, Dr. Hartley, Dr. Sharpe, Miss C——, &c. &c. most of them, like you, setting them in a rank equal, and some superior, to the *Spectators*, (of which I have not read many for the reasons which you assign;) but, notwithstanding such recommendation, whether the price of *two-pence*, or the unfavourable season of their first publication, hinders the demand, no boast can be made of it.

These letters clearly evince that the uncommon merit of the *Rambler* was very soon appreciated by men of taste and genius. . . .

The publication of the *Rambler* produced a very rapid revolution in the tone of English composition; an elevation and dignity, an harmony and energy, a precision and force of style, previously unknown in the history of our literature, speedily became objects of daily emulation; and the school of Johnson increased with such celerity, that it soon embraced the greater part of the rising literary characters of the day, and was consequently founded on such a basis as will not easily be shaken by succeeding modes. Of his immediate contemporaries, who strove to wield the weapons of Achilles, Mr. Courtenay, in his 'Poetical Review of the moral and literary Character of Dr. Johnson,'[2] has given us, in very elegant verse, the following discriminative catalogue:

[see below, pp. 369–70.]

To the celebrated scholars which Mr. Courtenay has thus commemorated for their casual imitation of the style of Johnson, may be *now* added many more writers of acknowledged genius, and whose works are calculated to impart a very increased value to the language in which they are composed. The resemblance has with many of them

[2] Published 1786.

been unintentional, and is consequently a strong proof of the wide influence which the diction of Johnson had already acquired over the literature of his country. When such writers as Dr. Robertson, Dr. Blair, Mr. Gibbon, Mr. Burke, Dr. Leland, Madame D'Arblay, Dr. Ferguson, Dr. Knox, Dr. Stuart, Dr. Parr, Dr. Gillies, Archdeacon Nares, Mr. Mackenzie, Mr. Chalmers, Mr. Roscoe, and Dr. Anderson, can be brought forward as having, in a greater or less degree, founded their style on that of the author of the *Rambler*, it may be presumed that the merits of the model which they had chosen, or unconsciously imitated, must have been great. In fact, the adoption of the style of Johnson by the Critic, the Orator, and the Historian, has been frequently attended with the best effects; as the weight, the splendor, and dignity of the subjects have often been such as would most happily harmonize with the strong and nervous periods of their prototype. On topics of a more familiar kind, however; on topics which detail the history of minute manners, where humour, irony, and delicate satire are demanded; it surely would be no mark of judgment to employ the elaborate and sonorous phraseology so uniformly characteristic of the lucubrations of the *Rambler*. The Novel and the familiar periodical Essay seldom require the grand and stately march of the Johnsonian period; Goldsmith, Mackenzie, and Madam D'Arblay have occasionally adopted, it is true, the splendour and force of Johnson with great felicity; but the general cast of their diction is widely different; on the contrary, the Essays of Dr. Knox,[3] though truly valuable for their moral and literary wealth, are, in point of composition, too studiously and exclusively copies from this great master. It has been too generally forgotten, indeed, that, bold, impressive, and magnificent as is the language of Johnson when occupied on themes of great importance, it has frequently been his misfortune to lavish it upon subjects too delicate to support its weight; on subjects where ease and plainness only were required, where sonorous words served only to excite burlesque, and elaborate periods only to encumber.

To him, however, who possesses a correct taste and a strong discriminate judgment, the study of the style of Johnson must be attended with the best results; he will have before him specimens of the noblest and the richest diction of which our literature can boast; a diction, indeed, from its nature considerably limited in its due application; but when employed on subjects of true dignity and serious moment, to record the labours of the hero or the legislator, or to clothe with fresh

[3] Vicesimus Knox (1752–1821); his *Winter Evenings; or, Lucubrations on Life and Letters,* published 1788.

energy the maxims of virtue and of piety, perhaps unparalleled in the powers of impression.

If we turn from the style of the *Ramblers*, to the consideration of their merit in the delineation of character and the exhibition of humour, we shall find abundant reason to conclude that Johnson was a most accurate and discriminating observer of human life in all its various shades and modifications. Though destined, during the most vigorous portion of his existence, to obtain a precarious, and very often a most scanty support, by the daily labours of his pen, he was yet enabled, in consequence of his powers, and rapidity of execution, to pass much of his time in the bosom of society. Excelling in conversation, expert in appreciating and drawing forth the talents of his companions, and often anxious, from morbid sensation, to escape from himself, he delighted not only in the frequent association of his intimate friends, but in that variety and information which are to be derived from mingling with every class of mankind. As he affirmed of himself, he had been 'running about the world more than almost any body;'[4] and the result of this habit was, in a mind uncommonly retentive and acute, a most exuberant fund of character and anecdote.

To stores thus ample and rich was added a strong but peculiar vein of humour; widely different, indeed, from the delicate and indirect satire of Addison, but nearly as powerful, and much more highly coloured. Had the language of Johnson been more plastic and accommodating, this talent would have appeared still more prominent; for, owing to the unvarying swell of his diction, which almost necessarily induces a tone of mind inimical to ridicule, his object has sometimes escaped the penetration of his readers; though it must be noticed, that occasionally the humour has been unintentionally heightened by the singular contrast of style and subject.

4 Boswell, *Life*, i. 215.

68. Sir James Mackintosh, private journal

December 1811

Journal entry from R. J. Mackintosh, *Memoirs of Sir James Mackintosh*, 1835, ii. 166–71.

In the course of a general estimate of Johnson, Mackintosh (1765–1832)—politician, lawyer, and historian—assesses his contribution to the development of English prose style. See Introduction, pp. 20, 31.

Dr. Johnson had a great influence on the taste and opinions of his age, not only by the popularity of his writings, but by that colloquial dictatorship which he exercised for thirty years in the literary circles of the capital. He was distinguished by vigorous understanding and inflexible integrity. His imagination was not more lively than was necessary to illustrate his maxims; his attainments in science were inconsiderable, and in learning, far from the first class; they chiefly consisted in that sort of knowledge which a powerful mind collects from miscellaneous reading and various intercourse with mankind. From the refinements of abstruse speculation he was withheld, partly perhaps by that repugnance to such subtleties which much experience often inspires, and partly also by a secret dread that they might disturb those prejudices in which his mind had found repose from the agitations of doubt. He was a most sagacious and severely pure judge of the actions and motives of men, and he was tempted by frequent detection of imposture to indulge somewhat of that contemptuous scepticism respecting the sincerity of delicate and refined sentiments, which affected his whole character as a man and a writer.

In early youth he had resisted the most severe tests of probity. Neither the extreme poverty nor the uncertain income to which the virtue of so many men of letters has yielded, even in the slightest degree weakened his integrity, or lowered the dignity of his independence. His moral principles (if the language may be allowed) partook of the vigour of his understanding. He was conscientious, sincere, determined; and his pride was no more than a steady consciousness of superiority in the most valuable qualities of human nature; his friendships were not only firm, but generous, and tender beneath a rugged exterior; he wounded none of those feelings which the habits of his life enabled him to estimate; but he had become too hardened by serious distress not to contract some disregard for those minor delicacies, which become so keenly susceptible in a calm and prosperous fortune. He was a Tory, not without some propensities towards Jacobitism, and a high Churchman, with more attachment to ecclesiastical authority and a splendid worship than is quite consistent with the spirit of Protestantism. On these subjects he neither permitted himself to doubt nor tolerated difference of opinion in others. The vigour of his understanding is no more to be estimated by his opinions on subjects where it was bound by his prejudices, than the strength of a man's body by the efforts of a limb in fetters. His conversation, which was one of the most powerful instruments of his extensive influence, was artificial, dogmatical, sententious, and poignant, adapted, with the most admirable versatility, to every subject as it arose, and distinguished by an almost unparalleled power of serious repartee. He seems to have considered himself as a sort of colloquial magistrate, who inflicted severe punishment from just policy. His course of life led him to treat those sensibilities, which such severity wounds, as fantastic and effeminate, and he entered society too late to acquire those habits of politeness which are a substitute for natural delicacy.

As a man, then, Johnson had a masculine understanding, clouded on important subjects by prejudice, a conscience pure beyond the ordinary measure of human virtue, a heart full of rugged benevolence, and a disregard only for those feelings in controversy or in conversation, of which he had not learnt the force, or which he thought himself obliged to wound. As a writer, he is memorable as one of those who effect a change in the general style of a nation, and have vigour enough to leave the stamp of their own peculiarities upon their language.

In the progress of English style, three periods may be easily distinguished. The first period extended from Sir Thomas More to Lord Clarendon. During great part of this period, the style partook of the rudeness and fluctuation of an unformed language, in which use had not yet determined the words that were to be English. Writers had not yet discovered the combination of words which best suits the original structure and immutable constitution of our language: where the terms were English, the arrangement was Latin—the exclusive language of learning, and that in which every truth in science, and every model of elegance, was contemplated by youth. For a century and a half, ineffectual attempts were made to bend our vulgar tongue to the genius of the language supposed to be superior; and the whole of this period, though not without a capricious mixture of coarse idiom, may be called the Latin, or pedantic age, of our style.

In the second period, which extended from the Restoration to the middle of the eighteenth century, a series of writers appeared, of less genius indeed than their predecessors, but more successful in their experiments to discover the mode of writing most adapted to the genius of the language. About the same period that a similar change was effected in France by Pascal, they began to banish from style learned as well as vulgar phraseology, and to confine themselves to the part of the language naturally used in general conversation by well-educated men. That middle region, which lies between vulgarity and pedantry, remains commonly unchanged, while both extremes are equally condemned to perpetual revolution. Those who select words from that permanent part of a language, and who arrange them according to its natural order, have discovered the true secret of rendering their writings permanent, and of preserving that rank among the classical writers of their country, which men of greater intellectual power have failed to attain. Of these writers, whose language has not yet been slightly superannuated, Cowley was probably the earliest, as Dryden and Addison were assuredly the greatest.

The third period may be called the Rhetorical, and is distinguished by the prevalence of a school of writers, of which Johnson was the founder. The fundamental character of the Rhetorical style is, that it employs undisguised art, where classical writers appear only to obey the impulse of a cultivated and adorned nature. As declamation is the fire of eloquence without its substance, so rhetoric consists in the forms of eloquence without its spirit. In the schools of the rhetorician, every ornament of composition is made by a rule; where ornaments are natural, the feeling from which they spring, if it be tempered, performs the office of taste, by regulating their number, and adapting them to the occasion; but those who fabricate them by rule, without this natural regulator, have no security against unseasonable and undistinguishing profusion. These writers have not the variety of nature, but the uniformity of a Dutch garden.

As the English classical writers had been led by the nature of their subjects as well as the bent of their genius, to cultivate a temperate elegance, rather than to emulate the energy and grandeur of their less polished predecessors, so Johnson and his followers, in their attempt (which was partly successful) to impart more vigour and dignity to the general style, receded so far from vulgarity as to lose all ease and variety, and so exclusively preferred terms of Latin origin, as to sacrifice all that part of the English language on which its peculiar character depends. With Latin words they attempted also the renewal of those inversions and involutions which the syntax of that language allows, but which, after a vain effort of a century, had been banished from ours. All their words were thrown into one mould, and their periods came up in the same shape. As the mind of Johnson was robust, but neither nimble nor graceful, so his style, though sometimes significant, nervous, and even majestic, was void of all grace and ease, and being the most unlike of all styles to the natural effusion of a cultivated mind, had the least pretensions to the praise of eloquence. During the period, now near a close, in which he was a favourite model, a stiff symmetry and tedious monotony succeeded to that various music with which the taste of Addison diversified his periods, and to that natural imagery which the latter's beautiful genius seemed with graceful negligence to scatter over his composition. They who had not fancy enough to be ornamental, sought to distinguish themselves by being artificial; and, though there were some illustrious exceptions, the general style had all those marks of corrupt taste which Johnson himself had so well satirised in his commendation of the prose of Dryden, and of which he has admirably represented the opposite in his excellent criticism on Addison. His earlier writings abound most with examples of these faults of style. Many of his Latin words in an English shape no imitator has ventured to adopt; others have already dropped from the language, and will soon be known only in Dictionaries. Some heaviness and weariness must be felt by most readers at the perusal of essays on life and manners, written like the *Rambler*; but it ought never to be forgotten that the two most popular writers of the eighteenth century, Addison and Johnson, were such efficacious teachers of virtue, that their writings may be numbered among the causes which in an important degree have contributed to preserve and to improve the morality of the British nation.

His *Dictionary*, though distinguished neither by the philosophy nor by the erudition which illustrate the origin and history of words, is a noble monument of his powers and his literary knowledge, and even of his industry, though it betrays frequent symptoms of that constitutional indolence which must have so often overpowered him in so immense a labour.

Towards the end of his life, when intercourse with the world had considerably softened his style, he published his *Lives of the English Poets*, a work of which the subject ensures popularity, and on which his fame probably now depends. He seems to have poured into it the miscellaneous information which he had collected, and the literary opinions which he had formed, during his long reign over the literature of London. The critical part has produced the warmest agitations of literary faction. The time may perhaps now be arrived for an impartial estimate of its merits. Whenever understanding alone is sufficient for poetical criticism, the decisions of Johnson are generally right. But the beauties of poetry must be felt before their causes are investigated. There is a poetical sensibility which in the progress of the mind becomes as distinct a power as a musical ear or a picturesque eye. Without a considerable degree of this sensibility it is as vain for a man of the greatest understanding to speak of the higher beauties of poetry, as it is for a blind man to speak of colours. To adopt the warmest sentiments of poetry, to realise its boldest imagery, to yield to every impulse of enthusiasm, to submit to the illusions of fancy, to retire with the poet into his ideal worlds, were dispositions wholly foreign from the worldly sagacity and stern shrewdness of Johnson. As in his judgment of life and character, so in his criticism on poetry, he was a sort of Freethinker. He suspected the refined of affectation, he rejected the enthusiastic as absurd, and he took it for granted that the mysterious was unintelligible. He came into the world when the school of Dryden and Pope gave the law to English poetry. In that school he had himself learned to be a lofty and vigorous declaimer in harmonious verse; beyond that school his unforced admiration perhaps scarcely soared; and his highest effort of criticism was accordingly the noble panegyric on Dryden. His criticism owed its popularity as much to its defects as to its excellencies. It was on a level with the majority of readers—persons of good sense and information, but of no exquisite sensibility, and to their minds it derived a false appearance of solidity from that very narrowness which excluded those grander efforts of imagination to which Aristotle and Bacon confined the name of poetry. If this unpoetical character be considered, if the force of prejudice be estimated, if we bear in mind that in this work of his old age we must expect to find him enamoured of every observation which he had thrown into a striking form, and of every paradox which he had supported with brilliant success, and that an old man seldom warmly

353

admires those works which have appeared since his sensibility has become sluggish and his literary system formed, we shall be able to account for most of the unjust judgments of Johnson, without recourse to any suppositions inconsistent with honesty and magnanimity. Among the victories gained by Milton, one of the most signal is that which he obtained over all the prejudices of Johnson, who was compelled to make a most vigorous, though evidently reluctant, effort to do justice to the fame and genius of the greatest of English poets. The alacrity with which he seeks every occasion to escape from this painful duty in observation upon Milton's Life and Minor Poems sufficiently attest the irresistible power of *Paradise Lost*. As he had no feeling of the lively and graceful, we must not wonder at his injustice to Prior. Some accidental impression, concurring with a long habit of indulging and venting every singularity, seems necessary to account for his having forgotten that Swift was a wit. As the *Seasons* appeared during the susceptible part of Johnson's life, his admiration of Thomson prevailed over the ludicrous prejudice which he professed against Scotland, perhaps because it was a Presbyterian country. His insensibility to the higher poetry, his dislike of a Whig university, and his scorn of a fantastic character, combined to produce that monstrous example of critical injustice which he entitles the *Life of Gray*.

Such is the character which may be bestowed on Johnson by those who feel a profound reverence for his virtues, and a respect approaching to admiration for his intellectual powers, without adopting his prejudices, or being insensible to his defects.

69. Coleridge's opinions on Johnson's style

1818–33

Extracts from his lecture on style, 1818 (*Coleridge's Essays and Lectures* . . ., 1907, 324–5) and table-talk (edn. 1835, ii, 216–18, 274–5).

After the Revolution, the spirit of the nation became much more commercial, than it had been before; a learned body, or clerisy, as such, gradually disappeared, and literature in general began to be addressed to the common miscellaneous public. That public had become accustomed to, and required, a strong stimulus; and to meet the requisitions of the public taste, a style was produced which by combining triteness of thought with singularity and excess of manner of expression, was calculated at once to soothe ignorance and to flatter vanity. The thought was carefully kept down to the immediate apprehension of the commonest understanding, and the dress was as anxiously arranged for the purpose of making the thought appear something very profound. The essence of this style consisted in a mock antithesis, that is, an opposition of mere sounds, in a rage for personification, the abstract made animate, far-fetched metaphors, strange phrases, metrical scraps, in every thing, in short, but genuine prose. Style is, of course, nothing else but the art of conveying the meaning appropriately and with perspicuity, whatever that meaning may be, and one criterion of style is that it shall not be translateable without injury to the meaning. Johnson's style has pleased many from the very fault of being perpetually translateable; he creates an impression of cleverness by never saying any thing in a common way. The best specimen of this manner is in Junius,[1] because his antithesis is less merely verbal than Johnson's. Gibbon's manner is the worst of all; he has every fault of which this peculiar style is capable.

4 July 1833

Dr. Johnson's fame now rests principally upon Boswell. It is impossible

[1] The pseudonym adopted by the unknown writer who contributed a series of virulent letters to the *Public Advertiser*, 1769–72.

not to be amused with such a book. But his *bow-wow* manner must have had a good deal to do with the effect produced;—for no one, I suppose, will set Johnson before Burke,—and Burke was a great and universal talker;—yet now we hear nothing of this except by some chance remarks in Boswell. The fact is, Burke, like all men of genius who love to talk at all, was very discursive and continuous; hence he is not reported; he seldom said the sharp short things that Johnson almost always did, which produce a more decided effect at the moment, and which are so much more easy to carry off. Besides, as to Burke's testimony to Johnson's powers, you must remember that Burke was a great courtier; and after all, Burke said and wrote more than once that he thought Johnson greater in talking than in writing, and greater in Boswell than in real life.

1 November 1833

Dr. Johnson seems to have been really more powerful in discoursing *viva voce* in conversation than with his pen in hand. It seems as if the excitement of company called something like reality and consecutiveness into his reasonings, which in his writings I cannot see. His antitheses are almost always verbal only; and sentence after sentence in the *Rambler* may be pointed out to which you cannot attach any definite meaning whatever. In his political pamphlets there is more truth of expression than in his other works, for the same reason that his conversation is better than his writings in general.

70. Charles Churchill, 'Pomposo' in *The Ghost*

1762

Text from third edition of Book II, second edition of Book III;
see *Poetical Works*, ed. D. Grant, 1956, 97–8, 126–7.

Book II containing the first portrait of Johnson as 'Pomposo'
appeared in March 1762. Before Book III, containing the second,
was published in October 1762, Churchill had struck up his friendship with John Wilkes and Johnson had accepted a royal pension.
See Introduction, pp. 5, 19.

> POMPOSO (insolent and loud,
> Vain idol of a *scribbling* crowd,
> Whose very name inspires an awe,
> Whose ev'ry word is Sense and Law,
> For what his Greatness hath decreed,
> Like Laws of PERSIA and of MEDE,
> Sacred thro' all the realm of *Wit*,
> Must never of Repeal admit;
> Who, cursing flatt'ry, is the tool
> Of ev'ry fawning flatt'ring fool;
> Who Wit with jealous eye surveys,
> And sickens at another's praise;
> Who, proudly seiz'd of *Learning*'s throne,
> Now damns all Learning but his own;
> Who scorns those common wares to trade in,
> *Reas'ning, Convincing,* and *Persuading,*
> But makes each Sentence current pass
> With *Puppy, Coxcomb, Scoundrel, Ass*;
> For 'tis with *him* a certain rule,
> The Folly's prov'd, when he calls Fool;

Who, to increase his native strength,
Draws words, six syllables in length,
With which, assisted with a frown
By way of Club, he knocks us down;
Who 'bove the Vulgar dares to rise,
And sense of *Decency* defies,
For this same *Decency* is made
Only for Bunglers in the trade;
And, like the *Cobweb Laws*, is still
Broke thro' by *Great ones* when they will)—
POMPOSO, with *strong sense* supplied,
Supported, and confirm'd by *Pride*,
His Comrades' terrors to beguile,
Grinn'd horribly a ghastly smile:[1]
Features so horrid, were it light,
Would put the Devil himself to flight. . . .

Horrid, *unwieldy, without Form,*
Savage, as OCEAN in a Storm,
Of size prodigious, in the rear,
That Post of Honour, should appear
POMPOSO; *Fame* around should tell
How he a slave to int'rest fell,
How, for *Integrity* renown'd,
Which Booksellers have often found,
He for *Subscribers* baits his hook,
And takes their cash—but where's the Book?[2]
No matter where—*Wise* Fear, we know,
Forbids the robbing of a Foe,
But what, to serve our private ends,
Forbids the cheating of our Friends?
No Man alive, who would not swear
All's *safe,* and therefore *honest* there.
For spite of all the learned say,
If we to Truth attention pay,
The word *Dishonesty* is meant
For nothing else but *Punishment.*

[1] Cf. Milton, *Paradise Lost,* II. 846.
[2] Proposals were issued and subscribers sought for Johnson's edition of Shakespeare in 1756; the edition did not appear until 1765.

Fame too should tell, nor heed the threat
Of Rogues, who Brother Rogues abet,
Nor tremble at the terrors hung
Aloft, *to make her hold her tongue,*
How to all Principles untrue,
Nor fix'd to *old* Friends, nor to *New*,
He damns the *Pension* which he takes,
And loves the STUART he forsakes.[3]
NATURE (who justly regular
Is very seldom known to err,
But now and then in *sportive mood*,
As some *rude* wits have understood,
Or *through much work requir'd in haste*,
Is with a random stroke disgrac'd)
POMPOSO form'd on *doubtful* plan,
Not quite a *Beast*, nor quite a *Man*,
Like—*God knows what*—for never yet
Could the most subtle human Wit,
Find out a Monster, which might be
The Shadow of a *Simile*.

[3] Johnson was nominated for his pension by John Stuart, Earl of Bute.

71. John Wilkes, *North Briton*
Nos. XI and XII

5–12 August 1762

Text from *North Briton*, second edition, 1771, 34–5.

Wilkes (1727–97), then M.P. for Aylesbury, and Churchill produced the first issue of the *North Briton* on 5 June 1762 to attack the new ministry of George III's favourite, the Earl of Bute. Wilkes was responsible for Nos. xi and xii. See Introduction, p. 5.

I have only *two* words to settle with the BRITON[1] this week. They are *glorification* and *vouchsafement*. He says that *I have twice twitted him in the teeth* (a most elegant phrase) *with the word* GLORIFICATION *printed in Italics.* He *affirms that* it is an *English* word, to be found in all the common dictionaries, and *to be* met *with more than once in Scripture.* I never denied that it was an *English* word, but I ridiculed it as a *cant* word of the illiberal and illiterate *Scottish Presbyterians*; and it found favour among their long-winded divines, only because it was so long, and mouthed so well. I will say, however, that I have not met with it in Scripture, and I am satisfied that he cannot name one text where it is to be found.

Now for *vouchsafement*. He says, *I could wish he would settle the authenticity of the word* VOUCHSAFEMENTS, *used as a substantive, a word which I do not remember to have seen in any dictionary or writer of reputation.* What so ignorant a fellow *has* seen, I do not know; but I know he *may* see the word *vouchsafement*, as a substantive too, in *Johnson's English Dictionary*, and the great *Boyle* quoted as the authority for it. I hope *Johnson* is *a writer of reputation*, because as a writer he has just got a pension of 300*l. per ann.* I hope too that he is become a friend to this constitution and the family on the throne, now he is thus nobly provided for: but I know he has much to *unwrite*, more to *unsay*, before he will be forgiven by the true friends of the present illustrious family, for what he has been *writing* and *saying* for many years. As to the *Briton*, he

[1] A weekly periodical inaugurated on 29 May 1762 by Smollett in Lord Bute's interest.

is so ignorant and foolish, I shall for the future *vouchsafe* him a very small share of my attention; for as every body has left off *reading*, it is high time that I should leave off *answering him.*

Numb. XII. Saturday, August 12, 1762.

Pensions, which reason to the worthy gave,
Add fresh dishonour to the fool and knave.

ANON.

TO THE NORTH BRITON.

SIR,

I do not know in any controversy so sure a method of coming at truth, which is always the pretence, though so seldom the real object of modern enquiries, as a just and strict definition of all the words and phrases of any importance, which are afterwards to be in use. This practice is universal, excepting only in *theological* and *political* controversy. If I take up a book of mathematics, the writer defines in the very first page, what a *triangle,* a *circle,* or a *trapezium* is; and then argues closely from the precise and accurate ideas of each, which the author and reader have previously settled. A book of fortification as regularly sets out with explaining to me what a *bastion,* a *demi-lune,* or a *hornwork* is. I have read much religious controversy; for, unhappily, there is as little agreement between the ministers of the gospel, as between the ministers of state. I do not, however, remember to have found in any of our divines a satisfactory definition of *faith, free-will, or predestination.* We are not yet arrived at the same accuracy, with respect to the meaning of these words, as of a *circle* or a *square.* The same remark will hold true in *political* controversy. Who has with any precision defined the words *faction* or *patriot?* The word *favourite* alone we have of late pretty fully understood the force of, both from the definitions of the MONITOR[2] and of the NORTH BRITON: yet give me leave to say, Sir, that neither of you have reached the force and closeness of expression in the great lexicographer, Mr. JOHNSON, who defines a *favourite* to be *a mean wretch, whose whole business is by any means to please.* But whether the word has been well defined or not, in former periods of the English history, the effect of it has been very fully felt, and even at this hour it is never uttered without the most unjust passion and ill-founded resent-

[2] A weekly paper in the Whig interest, founded in 1755 by Richard Beckford and edited by John Entick.

ment, as if the nation was now smarting from the sad consequences of its reality, and exertion in pride and insolence.

The word *pension* likewise has of late much puzzled our politicians. I do not recollect that any one of them has ventured at a definition of it. Mr. *Johnson*, as he is now a *pensioner*, one should naturally have recourse to, for the truest literary information on this subject. His definition then of a *pension* is, *an allowance made to any one without an equivalent. In England it is generally understood to mean pay given to a state hireling for treason to his country*. And under the word *pensioner* we read, 1. *One who is supported by an allowance paid at the will of another: a dependant*. 2. *A slave of state, hired by a stipend to obey his master*. But with submission to this great prodigy of learning, I should think both definitions very erroneous. Is the said Mr. *Johnson a dependant?* Or is he *a slave of state hired by a stipend to obey his master?* There is according to him, no alternative. Is his *pension, understood to be pay given him as state hireling for treason to his country?* Whoever gave it him, must then have read *London*, a Poem, &c. &c. and must have mistaken all his *distant hints* and *dark allusions*. As Mr. *Johnson* therefore has, I think, failed in this account, may I, after so great an authority, venture at a short definition of so intricate a word? A *pension* then I would call *a gratuity during the pleasure of the Prince for services performed, or expected to be performed, to himself or to the state*. Let us consider the celebrated Mr. *Johnson* and a few other late pensioners, in this light.

Mr. *Johnson's* many writings in the cause of liberty, his steady attachment to the present Royal Family, his gentleman-like compliments to his Majesty's grandfather, and his decent treatment of the parliament, intitle him to a share of the royal bounty. It is a matter of astonishment that *no notice* has till now been taken of him by government for some of the most *extraordinary* productions, which appeared with the name of *Samuel Johnson*; a name sacred to *George and Liberty*. No man, who has read only one poem of his, *London*, but must congratulate the good sense and discerning spirit of the minister, who bestows such a part of the public treasure on this distinguished friend of the public, of his master's family, and of the constitution of this country. The rewards are *now* most judiciously given to those who have supported, not to those who have all their lives written with bitterness, and harangued with virulence, against the government. With all due deference to the first minister's discernment, I rather think that Mr. *Johnson* (as merit *of this kind* must now be rewarded) might have been better provided for in another way: I mean at the board of *Excise*. I am desirous of seeing him one of the *commissioners*, if not at the head of that board, that the gentlemen there may cease to be *wretches hired by those to whom excise is paid.* His definition of *excise* is, that it *is a hateful tax levied upon commodities, and adjudged not by the common judges of property, but wretches hired by those to whom excise is paid.* Is the *excise* still on the same footing? I wish to know who *hires* these *wretches*, the *commissioners of excise.* Mr. *Johnson* says, *those to whom excise is paid!* If that is indeed the case, I am not at a loss to find out *to whom excise is paid*, nor who of consequence, in Mr. Johnson's idea, *hires these wretches.*

72. William Blake, 'An Island in the Moon'

c. 1784

Text from *Complete Writings*, ed. Geoffrey Keynes, 1966, 54.

The speakers in this brief extract from Blake's rombustious satire are 'Suction the Epicurean' (probably representing his favourite brother Robert) and 'Quid the Cynic' (the poet himself). See Introduction, p. 32.

'I say, this evening we'll all get drunk—I say—dash! —an Anthem, an Anthem!' said Suction.
  'Lo the Bat with Leathern wing [1]
  Winking & blinking,
  Winking & blinking,
  Winking & blinking,
  Like Doctor Johnson.'
Quid. 'Oho', said Dr. Johnson
   To Scipio Africanus,
   'If you don't own me a Philosopher,
   I'll kick your Roman Anus.'

[1] Cf. Collins, 'Ode to Evening', ll. 9–10.

Suction. 'Aha', To Dr. Johnson
Said Scipio Africanus,
'Lift up my Roman Petticoat
And kiss my Roman Anus.'

73. John Courtenay, *A Poetical Review of the Literary and Moral Character of the late Samuel Johnson LL.D.*

1786

Extracts from pp. 10–27.

Courtenay (1741–1816), M.P. for Tamworth and well known in the Commons for his ironic wit, was a member of the 'Literary Club' and one to whom Boswell turned for advice about his *Life of Johnson* (see *Life*, iv. 542, 557). Boswell quotes from the *Poetical Review* (see No. 75). Courtenay's poem is liberally provided with notes. See Introduction, pp. 18, 31.

[illustrates the strange paradoxes in Johnson's character.]

But who to blaze his frailties feels delight,
When the great Author rises to our sight?
When the pure tenour of his life we view,
Himself the bright exemplar that he drew?
Whose works console the good, instruct the wise,
And teach the soul to claim her kindred skies.
By grateful bards his name be ever sung,
Whose sterling touch has fix'd the English tongue!
Fortune's dire weight, the patron's cold disdain,
'Shook off, like dew-drops from the lion's mane;'*

* 'The incumbrances of fortune were shaken from his mind, like dew-drops from the lion's mane.' Johnson's *Preface to his edition of Shakspeare.*

Unknown, unaided, in a friendless state,
Without one smile of favour from the great;
The bulky tome his curious care refines,
Till the great work in full perfection shines:
His wide research and patient skill displays
What scarce was sketch'd in ANNA's golden days;
What only learning's aggregated toil
Slowly accomplish'd in each foreign soil
Yet to the mine though the rich coin he trace,
No current marks his early essays grace;
For in each page we find a massy store
Of English bullion mix'd with Latian ore:
In solemn pomp, with pedantry combin'd,
He vents the morbid sadness of his mind;
In scientifick phrase affects to smile,
Form'd on Brown's turgid Latin-English style;*
Where oft the abstract in stiff state presides,
And measur'd numbers, measur'd periods guides:
But all propriety his *Ramblers* mock,
When Betty prates from Newton and from Locke;
When no diversity we trace between
The lofty moralist and gay fifteen.†—
Yet genius still breaks through the encumbering phrase;
His taste we censure, but the work we praise:
There learning beams with fancy's brilliant dyes,
Vivid as lights that gild the northern skies;
Man's complex heart he bares to open day,
Clear as the prism unfolds the blended ray:
The picture from his mind assumes its hue,
The shade's too dark, but the design still true.
   Though Johnson's merits thus I freely scan,
And paint the foibles of this wond'rous man;
Yet can I coolly read, and not admire,

---

* The style of the *Ramblers* seems to have been formed on that of Sir Thomas Brown's *Vulgar Errors* and *Christian Morals*.

† See Victoria's Letter, *Rambler*, No. 130.—'I was never permitted to sleep till I had passed through the cosmetick discipline, part of which was a regular lustration performed with bean-flower water and may-dews; my hair was perfumed with a variety of unguents, by some of which it was to be thickened, and by others to be curled. The softness of my hands was secured by medicated gloves, and my bosom rubbed with a pomade prepared by my mother, of virtue to discuss dimples, and clear discolorations.'

When Learning, Wit and Poetry conspire
To shed a radiance o'er his moral page,
And spread truth's sacred light to many an age:
For all his works with innate lustre shine,
Strength all his own, and energy divine:
While through life's maze he darts his piercing view,
His mind expansive to the object grew.

   In judgment keen he acts the critick's part,
By reason proves the feelings of the heart;
In thought profound, in nature's study wise,
Shews from what source our fine sensations rise;
With truth, precision, fancy's claims defines,
And throws new splendour o'er the poet's lines.*

   When specious sophists with presumption scan
The source of evil, hidden still from man;†
Revive Arabian tales,‡ and vainly hope
To rival St. John, and his scholar, Pope;§
Though metaphysicks spread the gloom of night,
By reason's star he guides our aching sight;
The bounds of knowledge marks; and points the way
To pathless wastes, where wilder'd sages stray;
Where, like a farthing linkboy, J[enyn]s stands,
And the dim torch drops from his feeble hands.

   Impressive truth, in splendid fiction drest,||
Checks the vain wish, and calms the troubled breast;
O'er the dark mind a light celestial throws,
And sooths the angry passions to repose:
As oil effus'd illumes and smooths the deep,
When round the bark the swelling surges sweep.—
With various stores of erudition fraught,
The lively image, the deep-searching thought,
Slept in repose;—but when the moment press'd,

   * See his admirable *Lives of the Poets*, and particularly his Disquisition on metaphysical and religious poetry.
   † See his Review of Soame Jennings's *Essay on the Origin of Evil*; a masterpiece of composition, both for vigour of style and precision of ideas.
   ‡ Pope's or rather Bolingbroke's system was borrowed from the Arabian metaphysicians.
   § The scheme of the *Essay on Man* was given by Lord Bolingbroke to Pope.
   || See that sublime and beautiful Tale, *The Prince of Abyssinia*; and *The Rambler*, No. 65, 204, &c. &c.

The bright ideas stood at once confess'd;
Instant his genius sped its vigorous rays,
And o'er the letter'd world diffus'd a blaze:
As womb'd with fire the cloud electrick flies,
And calmly o'er the horizon seems to rise;
Touch'd by the pointed steel, the lightning flows,
And all the expanse with rich effulgence glows.
   Soft-ey'd compassion with a look benign,
His fervent vows he offer'd at thy shrine;
To guilt, to woe, the sacred debt was paid,
And helpless females bless'd his pious aid;
Snatch'd from disease, and want's abandon'd crew,
Despair and anguish from their victims flew:
Hope's soothing balm into their bosoms stole,
And tears of penitence restor'd the soul.
   But hark, he sings! the strain ev'n Pope admires;
Indignant Virtue her own bard inspires;
Sublime as Juvenal, he pours his lays,
And with the Roman shares congenial praise:—
In glowing numbers now he fires the age,
And Shakspeare's sun relumes the clouded stage.*
   So full his mind with images was fraught,
The rapid strains scarce claim'd a second thought;
And with like ease his vivid lines assume
The garb and dignity of ancient Rome.—
Let college *versemen* flat conceits express,
Trick'd out in splendid shreds of Virgil's dress;
From playful Ovid cull the tinsel phrase,
And vapid notions hitch in pilfer'd lays;
Then with mosaick art the piece combine,
And boast the glitter of each dulcet line:
Johnson adventur'd boldly to transfuse
His vigorous sense into the Latian muse;
Aspir'd to shine by unreflected light,
And with a Roman's ardour *think* and write.
He felt the tuneful Nine his breast inspire,
And, like a master, wak'd the soothing lyre:
Horatian strains a grateful heart proclaim,

* See [Johnson's] Prologue spoken by Mr. Garrick in 1747, on the opening of Drury-Lane theatre.

While Sky's wild rocks resound his Thralia's name.[1]—
Hesperia's plant, in some less skillful hands,
To bloom a while, factitious heat demands;
Though glowing Maro a faint warmth supplies,
The sickly blossom in the hot-house dies:
By Johnson's genial culture, art, and toil,
Its root strikes deep, and owns the fost'ring soil;
Imbibes our sun through all its swelling veins,
And grows a native of Britannia's plains.
    How few distinguish'd of the studious train
At the gay board their empire can maintain!
In their own books intomb'd their wisdom lies;
Too dull for talk, their slow conceptions rise:
Yet the mute author, of his writings proud,
For wit unshewn claims homage from the crowd;
As thread-bare misers, by mean avarice school'd,
Expect obeisance from their hidden gold.—
In converse quick, impetuous Johnson press'd
His weighty logick, or sarcastick jest:
Strong in the chace, and nimble in the turns,
For victory still his fervid spirit burns;
Subtle when wrong, invincible when right,
Arm'd at all points, and glorying in his might,
Gladiator-like, he traverses the field,
And strength and skill compel the foe to yield.—
Yet have I seen him, with a milder air,
Encircled by the witty and the fair,
Ev'n in old age with placid mien rejoice
At beauty's smile, and beauty's flattering voice.—
With Reynolds' pencil, vivid, bold, and true,
So fervent Boswell gives him to our view.
In every trait we see his mind expand;
The master rises by the pupil's hand;
We love the writer, praise his happy vein,
Grac'd with the naiveté of the sage Montaigne.
Hence not alone are brighter parts display'd,
But ev'n the specks of character portray'd:
We *see* the Rambler with fastidious smile

---

[1] Johnson wrote a Latin ode to Mrs Thrale in Skye on 6 September 1773. See *Poems*,
280–1.

Mark the lone tree, and note the heath-clad isle;
But when the heroick tale of Flora charms,*
Deck'd in a kilt, he wields a chieftain's arms:
The tuneful piper sounds a martial strain,
And Samuel sings, 'The King shall have his ain':
Two Georges in his loyal zeal are slur'd,
A gracious pension only saves the third!—
  By Nature's gifts ordain'd mankind to rule,
He, like a Titian, form'd his brilliant school;
And taught congenial spirits to excel,
While from his lips impressive wisdom fell.
Our boasted GOLDSMITH felt the sovereign sway;
To him we owe his sweet yet nervous lay.
To Fame's proud cliff he bade our Raphael rise;
Hence REYNOLDS' pen with REYNOLDS' pencil vyes.
With Johnson's flame melodious BURNEY glows,[2]
While the grand strain in smoother cadence flows.
And thou, MALONE,[3] to critick learning dear,
Correct and elegant, refin'd, though clear,
By studying him, first form'd that classick taste,
Which high in Shakspeare's fane thy statue plac'd.
Near Johnson STEEVENS[4] stands, on scenick ground,
Acute, laborious, fertile, and profound.
Ingenious HAWKESWORTH[5] to this school we owe,
And scarce the pupil from the tutor know.
Here early parts accomplish'd JONES[6] sublimes,
And science blends with Asia's lofty rhimes:
Harmonious JONES! who in his splendid strains
Sings Camdeo's sports, on Agra's flowery plains;
In Hindu fictions while we fondly trace
Love and the Muses, deck'd with Attick grace.
Amid these names can BOSWELL be forgot,

* The celebrated Flora Macdonald. See Boswell's *Tour*.

---

[2] Dr Charles Burney (1726–1814), musician and author.
[3] Edmond Malone (1741–1812), described by Boswell as 'one of the best criticks of our age' (*Life*, v. 78 n. 5).
[4] George Steevens (1736–1800), Shakespearean editor.
[5] John Hawkesworth (1715?–73), edited the *Adventurer*.
[6] Sir William Jones (1746–94), the distinguished orientalist, produced his *Poesos Asiaticae Commentariorum Libri Sex*, 1774, at an early age.

Scarce by North Britons now esteem'd a Scot?
Who to the sage devoted from his youth,
Imbib'd from him the sacred love of truth;
The keen research, the exercise of mind,
And that best art, the art to know mankind.—
Nor was his energy confin'd alone
To friends around his philosophick throne;
Its influence wide improv'd our letter'd isle,
And lucid vigour mark'd the general style:
As Nile's proud waves, swol'n from their oozy bed,
First o'er the neighbouring meads majestick spread;
Till gathering force, they more and more expand,
And with new virtue fertilise the land.
  Thus sings the Muse, to Johnson's memory just,
And scatters praise and censure o'er his dust;
For through each checker'd scene a contrast ran,
Too sad a proof, how great, how weak is man!
Though o'er his passions conscience held the rein,
He shook at dismal phantoms of the brain:
A boundless faith that noble mind debas'd,
By piercing wit, energick reason grac'd:
A generous Briton, yet he seem'd to hope
For James's grandson, and for James's Pope:
Though proudly splenetick, yet idly vain,
Accepted flattery, and dealt disdain.—
E'en shades like these, to brilliancy ally'd,
May comfort fools, and curb the Sage's pride.
  Yet Learning's sons, who o'er his foibles mourn,
To latest time shall fondly view his urn;
And wond'ring praise, to human frailties blind,
Talents and virtues of the brightest kind;
Revere the man, with various knowledge stor'd,
Who science, arts, and life's whole scheme explor'd;
Who firmly scorn'd, when in a lowly state,
To flatter vice, or court the vain and great;*
Whose heart still felt a sympathetick glow,
Prompt to relieve man's variegated woe;
Who even shar'd his talents with his friends;

* It is observable that Dr. Johnson did not prefix a dedication to any one of his various works.

By noble means who aim'd at noble ends;*
Whose ardent hope, intensely fixed on high,
Saw future bliss with intellectual eye.
Still in his breast Religion held her sway,
Disclosing visions of celestial day;
And gave his soul, amidst this world of strife,
The blest reversion of eternal life:
By this dispell'd, each doubt and horrour flies,
And calm at length in holy peace he dies.
 The sculptur'd trophy, and imperial bust,
That proudly rise around his hallow'd dust,
Shall mould'ring fall, by Time's slow hand decay'd,
But the bright meed of virtue ne'er shall fade.
Exulting Genius stamps his sacred name,
Enroll'd for ever in the dome of Fame.

74. Joseph Towers, *An Essay on the Life, Character, and Writings of Dr. Samuel Johnson*

1786

Extracts from the *Essay*, 6–8, 40–59, 101–2, 114–24.

See headnote to No. 41; see Introduction, pp. 32–3.

It was very pardonable in Mr. Tyers,[1] and the other zealous friends of Dr. Johnson, to speak somewhat too highly of his character. The warmth of attachment to the memory of a deceased friend, was a sufficient apology for their conduct. But positions must not too hastily be admitted, which are not supported by fact, and which are not consistent with a just regard

---

* 'Who noble ends by noble means obtains.' Pope. [*Essay on Man*, IV. 233.]

---

[1] Thomas Tyers, *A Biographical Sketch of Dr. Johnson*, 1785 (in *Johnsonian Miscellanies*, ii).

to the honour of human nature. It seems also injurious to the interests of religion and virtue, to represent Dr. Johnson as a pattern of human excellence. Better models might undoubtedly be pointed out. He had great virtues, but he had also too many striking and apparent faults, to be considered as a proper object of indiscriminate imitation. Highly as he thought of himself, his attachment to the interests of virtue was too sincere to have suffered him to countenance such an opinion. When, in his last illness, he said to his surrounding friends, 'Don't live such a life as I have done,'[2] he had no idea of being considered as a man of exemplary piety and virtue. There have been many men, who were more uniformly pious, and more uniformly benevolent, than Dr. Johnson, and who had neither his arrogance, nor his bigotry; and such men, in a moral and religious view, were superior characters. There were such men before the death of this celebrated writer, and there can be no reasonable doubt but that such men are yet remaining.

Having made these remarks, I think it here proper to observe, that I am totally devoid of the least inclination to degrade injuriously the character of Dr. Johnson; and that I only wish to see it equitably and accurately ascertained, in such a manner as shall do justice to his real excellencies, without injury to the interests either of virtue or of truth.

[comments follow on all Johnson's major writings; it is possible only to give a selection.]

His *History of Rasselas, Prince of Abissinia*, which was published in 1758, is elegantly written, and contains striking remarks upon the vanity of human pursuits, and the unsatisfactory nature of human enjoyments; together with a variety of acute observations on men and manners. But the representations given in it of human life are extremely gloomy, and more gloomy than are warranted by truth or reason. The character of Imlac is well sustained, and his enumeration of the qualifications of a poet is highly eloquent; but in some of the conversations between Rasselas and Nekayah, the princess is made too profound a philosopher. The character of the Arabian chief, by whom Pekuah was captured, is well delineated; and the disquisition concerning marriage is amusing and instructive. It is observable, that in this work the reality of apparitions is strongly maintained; and the remarks which it contains on disorders of the intellect, and the dangerous prevalence of imagination, seem to have taken their rise from those fears of some derangement of understanding,

---

[2] Tyers, in *Johnsonian Miscellanies*, ii. 336.

and that morbid melancholy, with which Johnson was not unfrequently afflicted.

The *Idler*, which was finished in the year 1760, has, perhaps, hardly yet obtained the reputation which it deserves. It is not equal to the *Rambler*; but it is, upon the whole, a very pleasing collection of essays, and there are some papers in it of great excellence. Among the best papers in the *Idler* are those on the robbery of time, on the retirement of Drugget, on the imprisonment of debtors, on the uncertainty of friendship, admonitions on the flight of time, the journey of Will Marvel, on the necessity of self-denial, on the vanity of riches, on the decline of reputation, on the progress of arts and language, on the fate of posthumous works, the history of translations, on the sufficiency of the English language, and on the obstructions of learning.* Some of the characters in other papers are also well drawn; and it is a circumstance rather curious, that the character of SOBER, in the 31st number, should have been intended by Johnson, as Mrs. Piozzi informs us it was,[3] as a satirical description of himself.

His edition of SHAKESPEARE was published in the year 1765; it had been long delayed; and, perhaps, at last, did not fully answer the expectations of the public; but many of his notes are valuable, and the short strictures at the end of the several plays are written with his usual vigour. His preface is also a composition of great merit; though there are parts of it which have somewhat of affectation, and somewhat of inconsistency; but it contains many fine passages; and some of his remarks respecting the unities of time and place are original, acute, and rational. In characterizing the preceding commentators of our great dramatic poet, he has treated Theobald with too much severity, and appears not to have done him justice as an editor of Shakespeare; but he is partial to Warburton, and speaks of the opponents of that prelate with a degree of contempt which they certainly did not deserve. Since the publication of Dr. Johnson's edition of Shakespeare, our great dramatic poet has been farther elucidated, and his plays enriched with many valuable notes, by the successive labours of Mr. Steevens, Mr. Malone, Mr. Reed, and other gentlemen.

Of the POLITICAL WRITINGS of Dr. Johnson, it would be injurious to the interests of truth, and to the common rights of human nature, to speak in terms of much commendation, in any other view except as to their style. His *False Alarm* was published in 1770, and chiefly relates

---

* Numbers 14, 16, 22, 23, 43, 49, 52, 59, 62, 63, 64, 65, 68, 69, 91, 94.

3 See *Johnsonian Miscellanies*, i. 178.

to the proceedings respecting Mr. Wilkes in the case of the Middlesex election, and to the petitions and public meetings which were occasioned by that transaction. His *Falkland's Islands* appeared the following year, and his *Patriot* in 1774. In the latter he ridiculed the pretensions to patriotism of the leaders of the popular party, opposed the claims of the colonies to be exempted from taxation by the British parliament, and defended the Quebec act.

In these political productions many positions are laid down, in admirable language, and in highly polished periods, which are inconsistent with the principles of the English constitution, and repugnant to the common rights of mankind. As a political writer, he makes much more use of his rhetoric than of his logic, and often gives his readers high sounding declamation instead of fair argument. And, indeed, in characterizing those who differ from him in sentiment, he seems sometimes to pay so little attention to truth, equity, or candour, that, in perusing his pieces, we are inclined readily to assent to a proposition of his own, that 'there is no credit due to a rhetorician's account either of good or evil.'[4] However we may respect the memory of Johnson, and however unwilling we may be to speak of him with harshness, those who impartially peruse his political publications will be obliged to confess, that few party pamphlets have appeared in this country, which contain greater malignity of misrepresentation. Even Swift, who carried the rancour of party to a great height, hardly equalled the malignity of Johnson's representations of those who differed from himself on political subjects. It seems difficult to suppose, that he could seriously believe many things that he has advanced, concerning those whose political sentiments were different from his own; and, if he did not, it is still more difficult to vindicate his conduct.

The petitions presented to the King about the year 1769, and in which many of the best and worthiest men in the kingdom undoubtedly concurred, are represented by Dr. Johnson as containing 'the sense only of the profligate and dissolute.'[5] And he was such an enemy to public assemblies of the people, and so little inquired whether what he advanced was truth in matters of this kind, that he maintained, that 'meetings held for directing representatives are seldom attended but by the idle and the dissolute.'[6] No man who had ever attended many meetings of that kind could be of this opinion; and next to a man's advancing things which he knows to be false, is his asserting things which he cannot know to be true.

[4] Life of Roger Ascham, in *Works*, 1792, xii. 321.
[5] *Works*, viii. 92.   [6] *The Patriot*, in *Works*, viii. 149.

In 1775, he published his *Taxation no Tyranny*; *an answer to the resolutions and address of the American congress*. The style of this pamphlet must
appear extraordinary to those who are acquainted with the termination
of the great contest, which then subsisted between Great-Britain and the
American colonies. The terms which he employs in speaking of the
congress, of the people of America, and of their cause, are grossly indecent, and unworthy of a man of letters, a Christian or a philosopher.
They reflect dishonour only on himself, and we are grieved that such
sentiments should be couched in such language, and should proceed from
such a man.

Dr. Johnson contended, that the parliament of Great-Britain had 'a
legal and constitutional power of laying upon the Americans any tax or
impost, whether external or internal, upon the product of land, or the
manufactures of industry, in the exigencies of war, or in the time of
profound peace, for the defence of America, for the purpose of raising
a revenue, or for any other end beneficial to the empire;' and that they
had 'a right to bind them by statutes, and to bind them in all cases whatsoever.'[7] Every impartial man is now convinced of the injustice and
ridiculousness of these claims; and there are few who do not lament that
any attempts were ever made to enforce them.

It must always be regretted, that a man of Johnson's intellectual powers
should have had so strong a propensity to defend arbitrary principles
of government. But on this subject, the strength of his language was not
more manifest than the weakness of his arguments. In apology for him,
it may be admitted, that he was a Tory from principle, and that much of
what he wrote was conformable to his real sentiments. But to defend all
that was written by him, his warmest friends will find impossible. In all
his political writings, the passages which are, perhaps, the most worthy
of regard, and the best supported by principles of reason, are those in
which he has introduced such arguments, as should prevent nations from
being too ready to engage in war. The inhabitants of this country have
always had too great a propensity of this kind; and it is on this subject
only that I would recommend to them some attention to Dr. Johnson as
a politician.

It was in the autumn of the year 1773, that he undertook his journey
to the Hebrides, or Western islands of Scotland; of which he published
an account in the year 1775. This is a very masterly performance; for,
besides a very pleasing account of his journey, it also contains a variety
of acute observations on human life, and many curious incidental remarks

[7] *Works,* viii. 171–2.

relative to the history of literature, with which Dr. Johnson was very intimately conversant. In this journey he was accompanied by Mr. Boswell; and the habitual good humour of this gentleman, his vivacity, his love of literature, and his personal attachment to Johnson, together with his natural influence in Scotland, must have rendered him a very agreeable companion to him, during the course of his tour to the Hebrides. Of this journey Mr. Boswell has himself since published an account, which is highly entertaining, and which appears to contain a very natural, exact, and faithful representation, not only of the incidents which occurred during the tour, but also of the very singular manners of his learned and celebrated friend.

In 1779, when he was seventy years of age, he published his *Lives of the Poets*, which seem to have been the most popular of all his productions. These, considered as compositions, and as abounding with strong and acute remarks, and with many very fine, and some even sublime passages, have unquestionably great merit; but if they be regarded merely as containing narrations of the lives, delineations of the characters, and strictures on the works of the authors concerning whom he wrote, they are far from being always to be depended on; the characters are sometimes partial, and there is sometimes too much malignity of misrepresentation; to which, perhaps, may be added, no inconsiderable portion of erroneous criticism.

The first life which occurs in this collection is that of COWLEY, which is very favourably written, and contains an elaborate criticism on his works. The false taste, which so frequently appears in the productions of that poet, is treated by his biographer with sufficient indulgence; and we are apt to be somewhat surprized, that so fastidious a critic, as Johnson sometimes was, should descant so copiously on such petty conceits, as Cowley frequently exhibits. He is unjustly partial to Cowley in the preference which he gives to his Latin poetry over that of Milton; but his observations on the writings of the metaphysical poets are novel and ingenious.

The second life in this collection is that of WALLER, of whom Dr. Johnson says, that, in 1640, he 'produced one of those noisy speeches which disaffection and discontent regularly dictate; a speech filled with hyperbolical complaints of imaginary grievances.'[8] This *noisy speech*, as our author terms it, was dictated by good sense and real patriotism. The complaints in it were not hyperbolical, and the grievances that Waller enumerated were real, and not imaginary. The grievances of which he

[8] *Lives*, i. 255.

complained were the encroachments of prerogative on the rights of the people, the imprisoning their persons without law, and the power assumed by the king of taxing his subjects, and seizing their property, without the authority of parliament; and the language of the complaints made by him on this subject was not too strong for the occasion. He afterwards made a speech in favour of episcopacy: but with this his biographer was better pleased, and speaks in terms of high commendation. The character of Waller by Clarendon is given by Johnson at full length: upon which it may not be improper to observe, that the noble historian's account is in several particulars manifestly erroneous; and as it is said that Waller had some animosity against Clarendon, it seems equally apparent, that the latter wrote the character of the poet under the influence of sentiments of personal dislike.

In his life of MILTON, he has spoken in the highest terms of the abilities of that great poet, and has bestowed on his principal poetical compositions the most honourable encomiums: but he has very injuriously misrepresented his character and conduct as a man. He could not endure those high sentiments of liberty, which Milton was so ardently desirous to propagate. He viewed with aversion the man, who had dared publickly to defend the execution of King Charles the First. There is something curious, in tracing the conduct of Johnson with respect to Milton, and in observing the struggle which there was in his mind concerning him, resulting from his reverence for him as a poet, and his rooted dislike against him as a political writer. It can hardly be doubted, but that his aversion to Milton's politics, was the cause of that alacrity, with which he joined with Lauder, in his infamous attack on our great epic poet, and which induced him to assist him in that transaction. But Johnson was unacquainted with the imposture; and, when it was discovered, urged Lauder to an open recantation. It is well known, that the forgeries of Lauder were completely detected by Dr. Douglas, and that by that ingenious and able writer Milton was sufficiently vindicated from the charge of plagiarism. But it is, perhaps, not generally known, that Lauder died, some years since, in very indigent circumstances, at Barbadoes.

It seems to have been by way of making some compensation to the memory of Milton, for the share he had in the attack of Lauder, that Johnson wrote the prologue that was spoken by Garrick, at Drury-lane theatre, in 1750, on the performance of the mask of *Comus*, for the benefit of Milton's grand-daughter; and in which the following lines appear to refer to the detection of Lauder:

At length our mighty Bard's victorious lays,
Fill the loud voice of universal praise,
And baffled spite, with hopeless anguish dumb,
Yields to renown the centuries to come.[9]

But many years after, when his *Lives of the Poets* appeared, his old dislike to Milton's politics was again manifested; and we see strikingly exhibited, in his account of him, his reverence for his talents, and his aversion for his principles. . . .

The principal fault of Johnson, as a biographical writer, seems to have been, too great a propensity to introduce injurious reflections against men of respectable character, and to state facts unfavourable to their memory, on slight and insufficient grounds. Biographical writers in general are charged with the contrary fault, too great a partiality in favour of the persons whose lives they undertake to relate. Impartiality should certainly be aimed at; and the truth should be given, when it can be obtained. But truth, at least the whole truth, is often not attainable; and, in doubtful cases, candour and equity seem to dictate, that it is best to err on the favourable side. No benefit can be derived to the interests either of virtue, or of learning, by injurious representations of men eminent for genius and literature.

Notwithstanding the errors, and instances of partiality and misrepresentation, which occasionally occur in the *Lives of the Poets*, they contain so many accurate and just observations on human nature, such original and curious remarks on various literary subjects, and abound with so many beauties of style, that they cannot be perused by any reader of taste without a great degree of pleasure. Besides their general merit as compositions, they also contain many particular passages of distinguished excellence. The character of Gilbert Walmsley, in the life of Edmund Smith, is finely drawn; the account, in the life of Addison, of the rise and progress of the *Tatler*, *Spectator*, and *Guardian*, and of the effects produced by those admirable essays on the manners of the nation, is just and curious; and there are many excellent observations on the modes of study, and on literary composition.

The style of Johnson appeared suited to his peculiar character, and mode of thinking. It seems too learned for common readers; and, on the first publication of his *Ramblers*, many complaints were made of the frequent recurrence of hard words in those essays. It was with a view to this accusation against him, that he wrote that essay in the *Idler* [No. 70], which contains a defence of the use of hard words, and in which he

[9] See *Poems*, 240–1.

remarks, that 'every author does not write for every reader.' He was not ambitious of illiterate readers, and was willing to resign them to those writers whose productions were better adapted to their capacities. 'Difference of thoughts,' says he, 'will produce difference of language. He that thinks with more extent than another will want words of larger meaning. He that thinks with more subtilty will seek for terms of more nice discrimination.' It is certain, that passages sometimes occur in his writings, which are not very intelligible to ordinary readers. Thus, in the preface to his *Dictionary*, he puts the following question: 'When the radical idea branches out into parallel ramifications, how can a consecutive series be formed of senses in their nature collateral?'

He was occasionally fond of antithesis and of alliteration; and his periods are sometimes too artificial, and his phrases too remote from the ordinary idiom of our language. But notwithstanding the peculiarity of his style, he has seldom made use of words not to be found in preceding writers. 'When common words,' says he, 'were less pleasing to the ear, or less distinct in their signification, I have familiarized the terms of philosophy by applying them to known objects and popular ideas; but have rarely admitted any word not authorized by former writers.'[10] He considered himself as having contributed to the improvement of the English language. He says in his last *Rambler*, 'I have laboured to refine our language to grammatical purity, and to clear it from colloquial barbarisms, licentious idioms, and irregular combinations. Something, perhaps, I have added to the elegance of its construction, and something to the harmony of its cadence.' Whatever may be the faults of his style, it has certainly great strength and great dignity, and his periods are often highly polished; and, perhaps, it would be difficult to point out any of his contemporaries, by whom the English language was written with equal energy.

When the great intellectual powers that Dr. Johnson possessed are considered, and the rapidity with which he finished his compositions, when he could prevail on himself to sit down to write, little doubt can be entertained, but that he might have produced much more than he did: and it was probably this consciousness that occasioned his frequent self-reproaches. The works, however, that he did produce, were very considerable, and such as will undoubtedly secure to him a great and lasting reputation.

With a slight sketch of some of the principal features of his character, I shall conclude this Essay.

[10] *Rambler* No. 208; see above, document No. 7.

He possessed extraordinary powers of understanding, which were much cultivated by study, and still more by meditation and reflection. His memory was remarkably retentive, his imagination uncommonly vigorous, and his judgment keen and penetrating. He had a strong sense of the importance of religion; his piety was sincere, and sometimes ardent; and his zeal for the interests of virtue was often manifested in his conversation and in his writings. The same energy, which was displayed in his literary productions, was exhibited also in his conversation, which was various, striking, and instructive; and, perhaps, no man ever equalled him for nervous and pointed repartees.

The great originality which sometimes appeared in his conceptions, and the perspicuity and force with which he delivered them, greatly enhanced the value of his conversation; and the remarks that he delivered received additional weight from the strength of his voice, and the solemnity of his manner. He was conscious of his own superiority; and when in company with literary men, or with those with whom there was any possibility of rivalship or competition, this consciousness was too apparent. With inferiors, and those who readily admitted all his claims, he was often mild and gentle: but to others, such was often the arrogance of his manners, that the endurance of it required no ordinary degree of patience. He was very dextrous at argumentation; and, when his reasonings were not solid, they were at least artful and plausible. His retorts were so powerful, that his friends and acquaintance were generally cautious of entering the lists against him; and the ready acquiescence, of those with whom he associated, in his opinions and assertions, probably rendered him more dogmatic than he might otherwise have been. With those, however, whom he loved, and with whom he was familiar, he was sometimes chearful and sprightly, and sometimes indulged himself in sallies of wit and pleasantry. He spent much of his time, especially in his latter years, in conversation; and seems to have had such an aversion to being left without company, as was somewhat extraordinary in a man possessed of such intellectual powers, and whose understanding had been so highly cultivated.

He sometimes discovered much impetuosity and irritability of temper, and was too ready to take offence at others; but when concessions were made, he was easily appeased. For those from whom he had received kindness in the earlier part of his life, he seemed ever to retain a particular regard, and manifested much gratitude towards those by whom he had at any time been benefited. He was soon offended with pertness, or ignorance: but he sometimes seemed to be conscious of having answered the questions of others with too much roughness; and was then desirous to discover more gentleness of temper, and to communicate information with more suavity of manners. When not under the influence of personal pique, of pride, or of religious or political prejudices, he seems to have had great ardour of benevolence; and, on some occasions, he gave very signal proofs of generosity and humanity.

He was naturally melancholy, and his views of human life appear to have been habitually gloomy. This appears in his *Rasselas*, and in many passages of his writings. It was also a striking part of the character of Dr. Johnson, that with powers of mind that did honour to human nature, he had weaknesses and prejudices that seemed suited only to the lowest of the species. His piety was strongly tinctured with superstition; and we are astonished to find the author of the *Rambler* expressing serious concern, because he had put milk into his tea on a Good Friday.[11] His custom of praying for the dead, though unsupported by reason or by scripture, was a less irrational superstition. Indeed, one of the great features of Johnson's character, was a degree of bigotry, both in politics and in religion, which is now seldom to be met with in persons of a cultivated understanding. Few other men could have been found, in the present age, whose political bigotry would have led them to style the celebrated JOHN HAMPDEN 'the zealot of rebellion;'[12] and the religious bigotry of the man, who, when at Edinburgh, would not go to hear Dr. Robertson preach, because he would not be present at a Presbyterian assembly, is not easily to be paralleled in this age, and in this country. His habitual incredulity with respect to facts, of which there was no reasonable ground for doubt, as stated by Mrs. Piozzi,[13] and which was remarked by Hogarth,[14] was also a singular trait in his character; and especially when contrasted with his superstitious credulity on other occasions. To the close of life, he was not only occupied in forming schemes of religious reformation, but even to a very late period of it, he seems to have been solicitous to apply himself to study with renewed diligence and vigour. It is remarkable, that, in his sixty-fourth year, he attempted to learn the Low Dutch language;[15] and, in his sixty-seventh year, he made a resolution to apply himself 'vigorously to study, particularly of the Greek and Italian tongues.'[16]

[11] Boswell, *Life*, iv. 203.
[12] *Lives*, i. 249.
[13] *Anecdotes*, in *Johnsonian Miscellanies*, i. 243.
[14] Ibid., i. 241.
[15] Boswell, *Life*, ii. 263.
[16] Ibid., iii. 90.

The faults and foibles of JOHNSON, whatever they were, are now descended with him to the grave; but his virtues should be the object of our imitation. His works, with all their defects, are a most valuable and important accession to the literature of England. His political writings will probably be little read, on any other account than for the dignity and energy of his style; but his *Dictionary*, his moral essays, and his productions in polite literature, will convey useful instruction, and elegant entertainment, as long as the language in which they are written shall be understood; and give him a just claim to a distinguished rank among the best and ablest writers that England has produced.

75. James Boswell, *The Life of Samuel Johnson LL.D.*

16 May 1791

Extracts from the *Life*, third edition, 1799 (see edition by G. Birkbeck Hill and L. F. Powell, 1934, i. 25–6, 192–204, 208–9, 213–24, 255, 291–6, 340–2, 496–8; ii. 111–3, 300–8, 311–7; iv. 34–9, 63–5, 424–30).

Boswell undoubtedly exercised the major formative influence on Johnson's posthumous reputation. 1,200 copies of the *Life* were sold in three months; a second edition was published in 1793; others followed in 1799, 1804, 1807 and 1811. Many were alarmed and shocked by the avid desire shown by Boswell and scores of others to record the minutiae of Johnson's career. Burke's remark vividly registers their view: 'How many maggots have crawled out of that great body' (W. Roberts, *Memoirs of Hannah More*, 1834, ii. 101). But Burke also expressed what was to become the dominant nineteenth-century attitude: that Boswell's *Life* 'was a greater monument to Johnson's fame, than all his writings put together' (*Life*, i. 10 n.1).

The extracts direct attention almost exclusively to Boswell's comments on Johnson's writings; they thus provide only a partial view of the influence he exerted on Johnson's reputation. It was his presentation of the *man* 'equalled by few in any age' which mainly caught the interest of later generations. See Introduction, pp. 8, 32–5.

To write the Life of him who excelled all mankind in writing the lives of others, and who, whether we consider his extraordinary endowments, or his various works, has been equalled by few in any age, is an arduous, and may be reckoned in me a presumptuous task.

Had Dr. Johnson written his own life, in conformity with the opinion which he has given, that every man's life may be best written by himself;[1] had he employed in the preservation of his own history, that clearness of narration and elegance of language in which he has embalmed so many eminent persons, the world would probably have had the most perfect example of biography that was ever exhibited. But although he at different times, in a desultory manner, committed to writing many particulars of the progress of his mind and fortunes, he never had persevering diligence enough to form them into a regular composition. Of these memorials a few have been preserved; but the greater part was consigned by him to the flames, a few days before his death.

As I had the honour and happiness of enjoying his friendship for upwards of twenty years; as I had the scheme of writing his life constantly in view; as he was well apprised of this circumstance, and from time to time obligingly satisfied my inquiries, by communicating to me the incidents of his early years; as I acquired a facility in recollecting, and was very assiduous in recording, his conversation, of which the extraordinary vigour and vivacity constituted one of the first features of his character; and as I have spared no pains in obtaining materials concerning him, from every quarter where I could discover that they were to be found, and have been favoured with the most liberal communications by his friends; I flatter myself that few biographers have entered upon such a work as this, with more advantages; independent of literary abilities, in which I am not vain enough to compare myself with some great names who have gone before me in this kind of writing. . . .

1749: ÆTAT. 40.]—In January, 1749, he published *The Vanity of Human Wishes, being the Tenth Satire of Juvenal imitated*. He, I believe, composed it the preceding year. Mrs. Johnson, for the sake of country air, had lodgings at Hampstead, to which he resorted occasionally, and there the greatest part, if not the whole, of this Imitation was written. The fervid rapidity with which it was produced, is scarcely credible. I have heard him say, that he composed seventy lines of it in one day, without putting one of them upon paper till they were finished. I remember when I once regretted to him that he had not given us more of Juvenal's Satires, he said he probably should give more, for he had them all in his head; by which I understood, that he had the originals and correspondent allusions floating in his mind, which he could, when he pleased, embody and render permanent without much labour. Some of them, however, he observed were too gross for imitation.

The profits of a single poem, however excellent, appear to have been

1 *Idler* No. 84.

very small in the last reign, compared with what a publication of the same size has since been known to yield. I have mentioned, upon Johnson's own authority, that for his *London* he had only ten guineas; and now, after his fame was established, he got for his *Vanity of Human Wishes* but five guineas more, as is proved by an authentick document in my possession.

It will be observed, that he reserves to himself the right of printing one edition of this satire, which was his practice upon occasion of the sale of all his writings; it being his fixed intention to publish at some period, for his own profit, a complete collection of his works.[2]

His *Vanity of Human Wishes* has less of common life, but more of a philosophick dignity than his *London*. More readers, therefore, will be delighted with the pointed spirit of *London*, than with the profound reflection of *The Vanity of Human Wishes*. Garrick, for instance, observed in his sprightly manner, with more vivacity than regard to just discrimination, as is usual with wits, 'When Johnson lived much with the Herveys, and saw a good deal of what was passing in life, he wrote his *London*, which is lively and easy. When he became more retired, he gave us his *Vanity of Human Wishes*, which is as hard as Greek. Had he gone on to imitate another satire, it would have been as hard as Hebrew.'

But *The Vanity of Human Wishes* is, in the opinion of the best judges, as high an effort of ethick poetry as any language can shew. The instances of variety of disappointment are chosen so judiciously, and painted so strongly, that, the moment they are read, they bring conviction to every thinking mind. That of the scholar must have depressed the too sanguine expectations of many an ambitious student. That of the warrior, Charles of Sweden is, I think, as highly finished a picture as can possibly be conceived.

Were all the other excellencies of this poem annihilated, it must ever have our grateful reverence from its noble conclusion; in which we are consoled with the assurance that happiness may be attained, if we 'apply our hearts'[3] to piety:

[quotes ll. 343–68.]

Garrick being now vested with theatrical power by being manager of Drury-lane theatre, he kindly and generously made use of it to bring out Johnson's tragedy, which had been long kept back for want of encouragement. But in this benevolent purpose he met with no small difficulty from the temper of Johnson, which could not brook that a drama which

[2] It was never published.   [3] Psalm 90: 12.

he had formed with much study, and had been obliged to keep more than the nine years of Horace,[4] should be revised and altered at the pleasure of an actor. Yet Garrick knew well, that without some alterations it would not be fit for the stage. A violent dispute having ensued between them, Garrick applied to the Reverend Dr. Taylor to interpose. Johnson was at first very obstinate. 'Sir, (said he) the fellow wants me to make Mahomet run mad, that he may have an opportunity of tossing his hands and kicking his heels.' He was, however, at last, with difficulty, prevailed on to comply with Garrick's wishes, so as to allow of some changes; but still there were not enough.

Dr. Adams was present the first night of the representation of *Irene*, and gave me the following account: 'Before the curtain drew up, there were catcalls whistling, which alarmed Johnson's friends. The Prologue, which was written by himself in a manly strain, soothed the audience, and the play went off tolerably, till it came to the conclusion, when Mrs. Pritchard, the heroine of the piece, was to be strangled upon the stage, and was to speak two lines with the bow-string round her neck. The audience cried out "*Murder! Murder!*" She several times attempted to speak; but in vain. At last she was obliged to go off the stage alive.' This passage was afterwards struck out, and she was carried off to be put to death behind the scenes, as the play now has it. The Epilogue, as Johnson informed me, was written by Sir William Yonge. I know not how his play came to be thus graced by the pen of a person then so eminent in the political world.[5]

Notwithstanding all the support of such performers as Garrick, Barry, Mrs. Cibber, Mrs. Pritchard, and every advantage of dress and decoration, the tragedy of *Irene* did not please the publick. Mr. Garrick's zeal carried it through for nine nights, so that the author had his three nights' profits; and from a receipt signed by him, now in the hands of Mr. James Dodsley, it appears that his friend Mr. Robert Dodsley gave him one hundred pounds for the copy, with his usual reservation of the right of one edition.

Irene, considered as a poem, is intitled to the praise of superiour excellence. Analysed into parts, it will furnish a rich store of noble sentiments, fine imagery, and beautiful language; but it is deficient in pathos, in that delicate power of touching the human feelings, which is the principal end of the drama. Indeed Garrick has complained to me, that Johnson not only had not the faculty of producing the impressions

---

[4] *Ars Poetica*, l. 388.
[5] Yonge (d. 1755) was Secretary at War in Walpole's government.

of tragedy, but that he had not the sensibility to perceive them. His great friend Mr. Walmsley's prediction, that he would 'turn out a fine tragedy-writer,'[6] was, therefore, ill-founded. Johnson was wise enough to be convinced that he had not the talents necessary to write successfully for the stage, and never made another attempt in that species of composition.

When asked how he felt upon the ill success of his tragedy, he replied, 'Like the Monument;' meaning that he continued firm and unmoved as that column. And let it be remembered, as an admonition to the *genus irritabile*[7] of dramatick writers, that this great man, instead of peevishly complaining of the bad taste of the town, submitted to its decision without a murmur. He had, indeed, upon all occasions, a great deference for the general opinion: 'A man (said he) who writes a book, thinks himself wiser or wittier than the rest of mankind; he supposes that he can instruct or amuse them, and the publick to whom he appeals, must, after all, be the judges of his pretensions.' . . .

1750: ÆTAT. 41.]—In 1750 he came forth in the character for which he was eminently qualified, a majestick teacher of moral and religious wisdom. The vehicle which he chose was that of a periodical paper, which he knew had been, upon former occasions, employed with great success. The *Tatler*, *Spectator*, and *Guardian*, were the last of the kind published in England, which had stood the test of a long trial; and such an interval had now elapsed since their publication, as made him justly think that, to many of his readers, this form of instruction would, in some degree, have the advantage of novelty. A few days before the first of his Essays came out, there started another competitor for fame in the same form, under the title of *The Tatler Revived*, which I believe was 'born but to die'.[8] Johnson was, I think, not very happy in the choice of his title, *The Rambler*, which certainly is not suited to a series of grave and moral discourses; which the Italians have literally, but ludicrously, translated by *Il Vagabondo*; and which has been lately assumed as the denomination of a vehicle of licentious tales, *The Rambler's Magazine*. He gave Sir Joshua Reynolds the following account of its getting this name: 'What *must* be done, Sir, *will* be done. When I was to begin publishing that paper, I was at a loss how to name it. I sat down at night upon my bedside, and resolved that I would not go to sleep till I had fixed its title. *The Rambler* seemed the best that occurred, and I took it.'

With what devout and conscientious sentiments this paper was undertaken, is evidenced by the following prayer, which he composed and

---

6 Boswell, *Life*, i. 102.   7 Horace, *Epistles*, II. ii. 102 ('fretful tribe').
8 Pope, *Essay on Man*, II. 10.

offered up on the occasion: 'Almighty GOD, the giver of all good things, without whose help all labour is ineffectual, and without whose grace all wisdom is folly; grant, I beseech Thee, that in this undertaking thy Holy Spirit may not be with-held from me, but that I may promote thy glory, and the salvation of myself and others: grant this, O LORD, for the sake of thy son JESUS CHRIST. Amen.'

The first paper of the *Rambler* was published on Tuesday the 20th of March, 1750; and its authour was enabled to continue it, without interruption, every Tuesday and Friday, till Saturday the [14]th of March, 1752, on which day it closed. This is a strong confirmation of the truth of a remark of his, which I have had occasion to quote elsewhere,[9] that 'a man may write at any time, if he will set himself doggedly to it;' for, notwithstanding his constitutional indolence, his depression of spirits, and his labour in carrying on his *Dictionary*, he answered the stated calls of the press twice a week from the stores of his mind, during all that time; having received no assistance, except four billets in No. 10, by Miss Mulso, now Mrs. Chapone; No. 30, by Mrs. Catharine Talbot; No. 97, by Mr. Samuel Richardson, whom he describes in an introductory note as 'An author who has enlarged the knowledge of human nature, and taught the passions to move at the command of virtue;' and Numbers 44 and 100, by Mrs. Elizabeth Carter.

Posterity will be astonished when they are told, upon the authority of Johnson himself, that many of these discourses, which we should suppose had been laboured with all the slow attention of literary leisure, were written in haste as the moment pressed, without even being read over by him before they were printed. It can be accounted for only in this way; that by reading and meditation, and a very close inspection of life, he had accumulated a great fund of miscellaneous knowledge, which, by a peculiar promptitude of mind, was ever ready at his call, and which he had constantly accustomed himself to clothe in the most apt and energetick expression. Sir Joshua Reynolds once asked him by what means he had attained his extraordinary accuracy and flow of language. He told him, that he had early laid it down as a fixed rule to do his best on every occasion, and in every company; to impart whatever he knew in the most forcible language he could put it in; and that by constant practice, and never suffering any careless expressions to escape him, or attempting to deliver his thoughts without arranging them in the clearest manner, it became habitual to him. . . .

As the *Rambler* was entirely the work of one man, there was, of course,

[9] *Journey*, 184; see *Life*, v. 40.

such a uniformity in its texture, as very much to exclude the charm of variety; and the grave and often solemn cast of thinking, which distinguished it from other periodical papers, made it, for some time, not generally liked. So slowly did this excellent work, of which twelve editions have now issued from the press, gain upon the world at large, that even in the closing number the authour says, 'I have never been much a favourite of the publick.'

Yet, very soon after its commencement, there were who felt and acknowledged its uncommon excellence. Verses in its praise appeared in the newspapers; and the editor of the *Gentleman's Magazine* mentions, in October, his having received several letters to the same purpose from the learned.[10] *The Student, or Oxford and Cambridge Miscellany*, in which Mr. Bonnell Thornton and Mr. Colman were the principal writers, describes it as 'a work that exceeds any thing of the kind ever published in this kingdom, some of the *Spectators* excepted,—if indeed they may be excepted.' And afterwards, 'May the publick favours crown his merits, and may not the English, under the auspicious reign of GEORGE the Second, neglect a man, who, had he lived in the first century, would have been one of the greatest favourites of AUGUSTUS.'[11] This flattery of the monarch had no effect. It is too well known, that the second George never was an Augustus to learning or genius. . . .

I profess myself to have ever entertained a profound veneration for the astonishing force and vivacity of mind, which the *Rambler* exhibits. That Johnson had penetration enough to see, and seeing would not disguise the general misery of man in this state of being, may have given rise to the superficial notion of his being too stern a philosopher. But men of reflection will be sensible that he has given a true representation of human existence, and that he has, at the same time, with a generous benevolence displayed every consolation which our state affords us; not only those arising from the hopes of futurity, but such as may be attained in the immediate progress through life. He has not depressed the soul to despondency and indifference. He has every where inculcated study, labour, and exertion. Nay, he has shewn, in a very odious light, a man whose practice is to go about darkening the views of others, by perpetual complaints of evil, and awakening those considerations of danger and distress, which are, for the most part, lulled into a quiet oblivion. This he has done very strongly in his character of Suspirius,[12] from which Goldsmith took that of Croaker, in his comedy of *The Good-natured*

10 See document No. 67.   11 See document No. 6.
12 *Rambler* No. 59.

Man, as Johnson told me he acknowledged to him, and which is, indeed, very obvious.

To point out the numerous subjects which the *Rambler* treats, with a dignity and perspicuity, which are there united in a manner which we shall in vain look for anywhere else, would take up too large a portion of my book, and would, I trust, be superfluous, considering how universally those volumes are now disseminated. Even the most condensed and brilliant sentences which they contain, and which have very properly been selected under the name of *Beauties*,[13] are of considerable bulk. But I may shortly observe, that the *Rambler* furnishes such an assemblage of discourses on practical religion and moral duty, of critical investigations, and allegorical and oriental tales, that no mind can be thought very deficient that has, by constant study and meditation, assimilated to itself all that may be found there. No. 7, written in Passion-week on abstraction and self-examination, and No. 110, on penitence and the placability of the Divine Nature, cannot be too often read. No. 54, on the effect which the death of a friend should have upon us, though rather too dispiriting, may be occasionally very medicinal to the mind. Every one must suppose the writer to have been deeply impressed by a real scene; but he told me that was not the case; which shews how well his fancy could conduct him to the 'house of mourning.'[14] Some of these more solemn papers, I doubt not, particularly attracted the notice of Dr. Young, the authour of *The Night Thoughts*, of whom my estimation is such, as to reckon his applause an honour even to Johnson. I have seen some volumes of Dr. Young's copy of the *Rambler*, in which he has marked the passages which he thought particularly excellent, by folding down a corner of the page; and such as he rated in a super-eminent degree, are marked by double folds. I am sorry that some of the volumes are lost. Johnson was pleased when told of the minute attention with which Young had signified his approbation of his Essays.

I will venture to say, that in no writings whatever can be found *more bark and steel for the mind*, if I may use the expression; more that can brace and invigorate every manly and noble sentiment. No. 32 on patience, even under extreme misery, is wonderfully lofty, and as much above the rant of stoicism, as the Sun of Revelation is brighter than the twilight of Pagan philosophy. I never read the following sentence without feeling my frame thrill: 'I think there is some reason for questioning whether the body and mind are not so proportioned, that the one can bear all

[13] *The Beauties of Johnson*, 1781. See Introduction, p. 14.
[14] Ecclesiastes 7: 4.

which can be inflicted on the other; whether virtue cannot stand its ground as long as life, and whether a soul well principled will not be sooner separated than subdued.'

Though instruction be the predominant purpose of the *Rambler*, yet it is enlivened with a considerable portion of amusement. Nothing can be more erroneous than the notion which some persons have entertained, that Johnson was then a retired author, ignorant of the world; and, of consequence, that he wrote only from his imagination when he described characters and manners. He said to me, that before he wrote that work, he had been 'running about the world,' as he expressed it, more than almost any body; and I have heard him relate, with much satisfaction, that several of the characters in the *Rambler* were drawn so naturally, that when it first circulated in numbers, a club in one of the towns in Essex imagined themselves to be severally exhibited in it, and were much incensed against a person who, they suspected, had thus made them objects of publick notice; nor were they quieted till authentick assurance was given them, that the *Rambler* was written by a person who had never heard of any one of them. Some of the characters are believed to have been actually drawn from the life, particularly that of Prospero[15] from Garrick, who never entirely forgave its pointed satire. For instances of fertility of fancy, and accurate description of real life, I appeal to No. 19, a man who wanders from one profession to another, with most plausible reasons for every change. No. 34, female fastidiousness and timorous refinement. No. 82, a Virtuoso who has collected curiosities. No. [98], petty modes of entertaining a company, and conciliating kindness. No. 182, fortune-hunting. No. 194–195, a tutor's account of the follies of his pupil. No. 197–198, legacy-hunting. He has given a specimen of his nice observation of the mere external appearances of life, in the following passage in No. 179, against affectation, that frequent and most disgusting quality:

[quotes 'He that stands' to 'evidences of importance'.]

Every page of the *Rambler* shews a mind teeming with classical allusion and poetical imagery: illustrations from other writers are, upon all occasions, so ready, and mingle so easily in his periods, that the whole appears of one uniform vivid texture.

The style of this work has been censured by some shallow criticks as involved and turgid, and abounding with antiquated and hard words.

15 In No. 200.

So ill-founded is the first part of this objection, that I will challenge all who may honour this book with a perusal, to point out any English writer whose language conveys his meaning with equal force and perspicuity. It must, indeed, be allowed, that the structure of his sentences is expanded, and often has somewhat of the inversion of Latin; and that he delighted to express familiar thoughts in philosophical language; being in this the reverse of Socrates, who, it was said, reduced philosophy to the simplicity of common life. But let us attend to what he himself says in his concluding paper: 'When common words were less pleasing to the ear, or less distinct in their signification, I have familiarised the terms of philosophy, by applying them to popular ideas.' And, as to the second part of this objection, upon a late careful revision of the work, I can with confidence say, that it is amazing how few of those words, for which it has been unjustly characterised, are actually to be found in it; I am sure, not the proportion of one to each paper. This idle charge has been echoed from one babbler to another, who have confounded Johnson's Essays with Johnson's *Dictionary*; and because he thought it right in a Lexicon of our language to collect many words which had fallen into disuse, but were supported by great authorities, it has been imagined that all of these have been interwoven into his own compositions. That some of them have been adopted by him unnecessarily, may, perhaps, be allowed; but, in general they are evidently an advantage, for without them his stately ideas would be confined and cramped. 'He that thinks with more extent than another, will want words of larger meaning.'[16] He once told me, that he had formed his style upon that of Sir William Temple,[17] and upon Chambers's Proposal for his *Dictionary*.[18] He certainly was mistaken; or if he imagined at first that he was imitating Temple, he was very unsuccessful; for nothing can be more unlike than the simplicity of Temple, and the richness of Johnson. Their styles differ as plain cloth and brocade. Temple, indeed, seems equally erroneous in supposing that he himself had formed his style upon Sandys's *View of the State of Religion in the Western parts of the World*.

The style of Johnson was, undoubtedly, much formed upon that of the great writers in the last century, Hooker, Bacon, Sanderson, Hakewell,[19] and others; those 'GIANTS,' as they were well characterised by

16 *Idler* No. 70.

17 Temple (1628–99) was patron to Swift who published his *Letters*, 1700, and *Memoirs*, 1709.

18 Ephraim Chambers (d. 1740); published his *Cyclopaedia* in 1728.

19 Richard Hooker (1554?–1600); Francis Bacon (1561–1626); Robert Sanderson (1587–1663), Bishop of Lincoln; George Hakewill (1578–1649), Oxford divine.

A GREAT PERSONAGE,[20] whose authority, were I to name him, would stamp a reverence on the opinion. . . .

Yet Johnson assured me, that he had not taken upon him to add more than four or five words to the English language, of his own formation; and he was very much offended at the general licence, by no means 'modestly taken' in his time, not only to coin new words, but to use many words in senses quite different from their established meaning, and those frequently very fantastical.

Sir Thomas Brown, whose life Johnson wrote, was remarkably fond of Anglo-Latian diction; and to his example we are to ascribe Johnson's sometimes indulging himself in this kind of phraseology. Johnson's comprehension of mind was the mould for his language. Had his conceptions been narrower, his expression would have been easier. His sentences have a dignified march; and, it is certain, that his example has given a general elevation to the language of his country, for many of our best writers have approached very near to him; and, from the influence which he has had upon our composition, scarcely any thing is written now that is not better expressed than was usual before he appeared to lead the national taste.

This circumstance, the truth of which must strike every critical reader, has been so happily enforced by Mr. Courtenay, in his *Moral and Literary Character of Dr. Johnson*, that I cannot prevail on myself to withhold it, notwithstanding his, perhaps, too great partiality for one of his friends:

[quotes 'By nature's gifts' to 'fertilise the land'; see above, pp. 369–70.]

Johnson's language, however, must be allowed to be too masculine for the delicate gentleness of female writing. His ladies, therefore, seem strangely formal, even to ridicule; and are well denominated by the names which he has given them, as Misella, Zozima, Properantia, Rhodoclia.[21]

It has of late been the fashion to compare the style of Addison and Johnson, and to depreciate, I think very unjustly, the style of Addison as nerveless and feeble, because it has not the strength and energy of that of Johnson. Their prose may be balanced like the poetry of Dryden and Pope. Both are excellent, though in different ways. Addison writes with the ease of a gentleman. His readers fancy that a wise and accomplished companion is talking to them; so that he insinuates his sentiments and taste into their minds by an imperceptible influence. Johnson writes like a teacher. He dictates to his readers as if from an academical chair. They

---

[20] George III.   [21] See *Rambler* Nos. 170–1, 12, 107, 62.

attend with awe and admiration; and his precepts are impressed upon them by his commanding eloquence. Addison's style, like a light wine, pleases every body from the first. Johnson's, like a liquor of more body, seems too strong at first, but, by degrees, is highly relished; and such is the melody of his periods, so much do they captivate the ear, and seize upon the attention, that there is scarcely any writer, however inconsiderable, who does not aim, in some degree, at the same species of excellence. But let us not ungratefully undervalue that beautiful style, which has pleasingly conveyed to us much instruction and entertainment. Though comparatively weak, opposed to Johnson's Herculean vigour, let us not call it positively feeble. Let us remember the character of his style, as given by Johnson himself:

[quotes last three sentences from Johnson's *Life of Addison*.]

Johnson's papers in the *Adventurer* are very similar to those of the *Rambler*; but being rather more varied in their subjects, and being mixed with essays by other writers, upon topicks more generally attractive than even the most elegant ethical discourses, the sale of the work, at first, was more extensive. Without meaning, however, to depreciate the *Adventurer*, I must observe that as the value of the *Rambler* came, in the progress of time, to be better known, it grew upon the publick estimation, and that its sale has far exceeded that of any other periodical papers since the reign of Queen Anne. . . .

The *Dictionary, with a Grammar and History of the English Language,* being now at length published, in two volumes folio, the world contemplated with wonder so stupendous a work atchieved by one man, while other countries had thought such undertakings fit only for whole academies. Vast as his powers were, I cannot but think that his imagination deceived him, when he supposed that by constant application he might have performed the task in three years. Let the Preface be attentively perused, in which is given, in a clear, strong, and glowing style, a comprehensive, yet particular view of what he had done; and it will be evident, that the time he employed upon it was comparatively short. I am unwilling to swell my book with long quotations from what is in every body's hands; and I believe there are few prose compositions in the English language that are read with more delight, or are more impressed upon the memory, than that preliminary discourse. One of its excellencies has always struck me with peculiar admiration; I mean the perspicuity with which he has expressed abstract scientifick notions. As an instance of this, I shall quote the following sentence: 'When the radical idea branches out into parallel ramifications, how can a consecutive series be formed of senses in their own nature collateral?' We have here an example of what has been often said, and I believe with justice, that there is for every thought a certain nice adaptation of words which none other could equal, and which, when a man has been so fortunate as to hit, he has attained, in that particular case, the perfection of language.

The extensive reading which was absolutely necessary for the accumulation of authorities, and which alone may account for Johnson's retentive mind being enriched with a very large and various store of knowledge and imagery, must have occupied several years. The Preface furnishes an eminent instance of a double talent, of which Johnson was fully conscious. Sir Joshua Reynolds heard him say, 'There are two things which I am confident I can do very well: one is an introduction to any literary work, stating what it is to contain, and how it should be executed in the most perfect manner; the other is a conclusion, shewing from various causes why the execution has not been equal to what the authour promised to himself and to the publick.'

How should puny scribblers be abashed and disappointed, when they find him displaying a perfect theory of lexicographical excellence, yet at the same time candidly and modestly allowing that he 'had not satisfied his own expectations.' Here was a fair occasion for the exercise of Johnson's modesty, when he was called upon to compare his own arduous performance, not with those of other individuals, (in which case his inflexible regard to truth would have been violated, had he affected diffidence,) but with speculative perfection; as he, who can outstrip all his competitors in the race, may yet be sensible of his deficiency when he runs against time. Well might he say, that 'the *English Dictionary* was written with little assistance of the learned;'[22] for he told me, that the only aid which he received was a paper containing twenty etymologies, sent to him by a person then unknown, who he was afterwards informed was Dr. Pearce, Bishop of Rochester. The etymologies, though they exhibit learning and judgement, are not, I think, entitled to the first praise amongst the various parts of this immense work. The definitions have always appeared to me such astonishing proofs of acuteness of intellect and precision of language, as indicate a genius of the highest rank. This it is which marks the superiour excellence of Johnson's *Dictionary* over others equally or even more voluminous, and must have made it a work of much greater mental labour than mere Lexicons, or *Word-Books*, as the Dutch call them. They, who will make the experiment of trying how

[22] See document No. 18.

they can define a few words of whatever nature, will soon be satisfied of the unquestionable justice of this observation, which I can assure my readers is founded upon much study, and upon communication with more minds than my own.

A few of his definitions must be admitted to be erroneous. Thus, *Windward* and *Leeward*, though directly of opposite meaning, are defined identically the same way;[23] as to which inconsiderable specks it is enough to observe, that his Preface announces that he was aware there might be many such in so immense a work; nor was he at all disconcerted when an instance was pointed out to him. A lady once asked him how he came to define *Pastern* the *knee* of a horse: instead of making an elaborate defence, as she expected, he at once answered, 'Ignorance, Madam, pure ignorance.' His definition of *Network* has been often quoted with sportive malignity, as obscuring a thing in itself very plain. But to these frivolous censures no other answer is necessary than that with which we are furnished by his own Preface.

[quotes 'To explain requires the use' to 'admit or definition', and 'sometimes easier words' to 'one more easy'. See above, No. 18.]

His introducing his own opinions, and even prejudices, under general definitions of words, while at the same time the original meaning of the words is not explained, as his *Tory, Whig, Pension, Oats, Excise,* and a few more, cannot be fully defended, and must be placed to the account of capricious and humourous indulgence. Talking to me upon this subject when we were at Ashbourne in 1777, he mentioned a still stronger instance of the predominance of his private feelings in the composition of this work, than any now to be found in it. 'You know, Sir, Lord Gower forsook the old Jacobite interest. When I came to the word *Renegado*, after telling that it meant "one who deserts to the enemy, a revolter," I added, *Sometimes we say a* GOWER. Thus it went to the press; but the printer had more wit than I, and struck it out.'

Let it, however, be remembered, that this indulgence does not display itself only in sarcasm towards others, but sometimes in playful allusion to the notions commonly entertained of his own laborious task. Thus: '*Grub-street*, the name of a street in London, much inhabited by writers of small histories, *dictionaries*, and temporary poems; whence any mean production is called *Grub-street*.'—'*Lexicographer*, a writer of dictionaries, a *harmless drudge*.' . . .

I have been told that he regretted much his not having gone to visit his

23 Both are defined 'towards the wind'.

mother for several years, previous to her death. But he was constantly engaged in literary labours which confined him to London; and though he had not the comfort of seeing his aged parent, he contributed liberally to her support.

Soon after this event, he wrote his *Rasselas, Prince of Abyssinia*; concerning the publication of which Sir John Hawkins guesses vaguely and idly, instead of having taken the trouble to inform himself with authentick precision. Not to trouble my readers with a repetition of the Knight's reveries, I have to mention, that the late Mr. Strahan the printer told me, that Johnson wrote it, that with the profits he might defray the expence of his mother's funeral, and pay some little debts which she had left. He told Sir Joshua Reynolds that he composed it in the evenings of one week, sent it to the press in portions as it was written, and had never since read it over. Mr. Strahan, Mr. Johnston, and Mr. Dodsley purchased it for a hundred pounds, but afterwards paid him twenty-five pounds more, when it came to a second edition.

Considering the large sums which have been received for compilations, and works requiring not much more genius than compilations, we cannot but wonder at the very low price which he was content to receive for this admirable performance; which, though he had written nothing else, would have rendered his name immortal in the world of literature. None of his writings has been so extensively diffused over Europe; for it has been translated into most, if not all, of the modern languages. This Tale, with all the charms of oriental imagery, and all the force and beauty of which the English language is capable, leads us through the most important scenes of human life, and shews us that this stage of our being is full of 'vanity and vexation of spirit.'[24] To those who look no further than the present life, or who maintain that human nature has not fallen from the state in which it was created, the instruction of this sublime story will be of no avail. But they who think justly, and feel with strong sensibility, will listen with eagerness and admiration to its truth and wisdom. Voltaire's *Candide*, written to refute the system of Optimism, which it has accomplished with brilliant success, is wonderfully similar in its plan and conduct to Johnson's *Rasselas*; insomuch, that I have heard Johnson say, that if they had not been published so closely one after the other that there was not time for imitation, it would have been in vain to deny that the scheme of that which came latest was taken from the other.[25] Though the proposition illustrated by both these works was the

[24] Ecclesiastes 1 : 14.
[25] *Candide* was published in late February 1759, *Rasselas* on 19 April.

same, namely, that in our present state there is more evil than good, the intention of the writers was very different. Voltaire, I am afraid, meant only by wanton profaneness to obtain a sportive victory over religion, and to discredit the belief of a superintending Providence: Johnson meant, by shewing the unsatisfactory nature of things temporal, to direct the hopes of man to things eternal. *Rasselas*, as was observed to me by a very accomplished lady, may be considered as a more enlarged and more deeply philosophical discourse in prose, upon the interesting truth, which in his *Vanity of Human Wishes* he had so successfully enforced in verse.

The fund of thinking which this work contains is such, that almost every sentence of it may furnish a subject of long meditation. I am not satisfied if a year passes without my having read it through; and at every perusal, my admiration of the mind which produced it is so highly raised, that I can scarcely believe that I had the honour of enjoying the intimacy of such a man. . . .

In the October of this year [1765] he at length gave to the world his edition of Shakspeare, which, if it had no other merit but that of producing his Preface, in which the excellencies and defects of that immortal bard are displayed with a masterly hand, the nation would have had no reason to complain. A blind indiscriminate admiration of Shakspeare had exposed the British nation to the ridicule of foreigners. Johnson, by candidly admitting the faults of his poet, had the more credit in bestowing on him deserved and indisputable praise; and doubtless none of all his panegyrists have done him half so much honour. Their praise was, like that of a counsel, upon his own side of the cause: Johnson's was like the grave, well considered, and impartial opinion of the judge, which falls from his lips with weight, and is received with reverence. What he did as a commentator has no small share of merit, though his researches were not so ample, and his investigations so acute as they might have been, which we now certainly know from the labours of other able and ingenious criticks who have followed him. He has enriched his edition with a concise account of each play, and of its characteristick excellence. Many of his notes have illustrated obscurities in the text, and placed passages eminent for beauty in a more conspicuous light; and he has in general, exhibited such a mode of annotation, as may be beneficial to all subsequent editors.

His Shakspeare was virulently attacked by Mr. William Kenrick,[26] who obtained the degree of LL.D. from a Scotch University, and wrote for the booksellers in a great variety of branches. Though he certainly

[26] See documents Nos. 30, 31.

was not without considerable merit, he wrote with so little regard to decency and principles, and decorum, and in so hasty a manner, that his reputation was neither extensive nor lasting. I remember one evening, when some of his works were mentioned, Dr. Goldsmith said, he had never heard of them; upon which Dr. Johnson observed, 'Sir, he is one of the many who have made themselves *publick*, without making themselves *known*.'

A young student of Oxford, of the name of Barclay, wrote an answer to Kenrick's review of Johnson's Shakspeare.[27] Johnson was at first angry that Kenrick's attack should have the credit of an answer. But afterwards, considering the young man's good intention, he kindly noticed him, and probably would have done more, had not the young man died. . . .

1770: ÆTAT. 61.]— In 1770 he published a political pamphlet, entitled *The False Alarm*, intended to justify the conduct of ministry and their majority in the House of Commons, for having virtually assumed it as an axiom, that the expulsion of a Member of Parliament was equivalent to exclusion, and thus having declared Colonel Lutterel to be duly elected for the county of Middlesex, notwithstanding Mr. Wilkes had a great majority of votes.[28] This being justly considered as a gross violation of the right of election, an alarm for the constitution extended itself all over the kingdom. To prove this alarm to be false, was the purpose of Johnson's pamphlet; but even his vast powers were inadequate to cope with constitutional truth and reason, and his argument failed of effect; and the House of Commons have since expunged the offensive resolution from their Journals.[29] That the House of Commons might have expelled Mr. Wilkes repeatedly, and as often as he should be re-chosen, was not denied; but incapacitation cannot be but by an act of the whole legislature. It was wonderful to see how a prejudice in favour of government in general, and an aversion to popular clamour, could blind and contract such an understanding as Johnson's, in this particular case; yet the wit, the sarcasm, the eloquent vivacity which this pamphlet displayed, made it be read with great avidity at the time, and it will ever be read with pleasure, for the sake of its composition. That it endeavoured to infuse a a narcotick indifference, as to publick concerns, into the minds of the people, and that it broke out sometimes into an extreme coarseness of contemptuous abuse, is but too evident.

It must not, however, be omitted, that when the storm of his violence

[27] See document No. 32.
[28] On 13 April 1768 Wilkes received 1143 votes, Luttrell 296.
[29] On 3 May 1782.

subsides, he takes a fair opportunity to pay a grateful compliment to the King, who had rewarded his merit: 'These low-born railers have endeavoured, surely without effect, to alienate the affections of the people from the only King who for almost a century has much appeared to desire, or much endeavoured to deserve them.' And, 'Every honest man must lament, that the faction has been regarded with frigid neutrality by the Tories, who being long accustomed to signalise their principles by opposition to the Court, do not yet consider, that they have at last a King who knows not the name of party, and who wishes to be the common father of all his people.'

To this pamphlet, which was at once discovered to be Johnson's, several answers came out, in which, care was taken to remind the publick of his former attacks upon government, and of his now being a pensioner, without allowing for the honourable terms upon which Johnson's pension was granted and accepted, or the change of system which the British court had undergone upon the accession of his present Majesty. He was, however, soothed in the highest strain of panegyrick, in a poem called *The Remonstrance*, by the Rev. Mr. Stockdale, to whom he was, upon many occasions, a kind protector. . . .[30]

His *Journey to the Western Islands of Scotland* is a most valuable performance. It abounds in extensive philosophical views of society, and in ingenious sentiments and lively description. A considerable part of it, indeed, consists of speculations, which many years before he saw the wild regions which we visited together, probably had employed his attention, though the actual sight of those scenes undoubtedly quickened and augmented them. Mr. Orme, the very able historian,[31] agreed with me in this opinion, which he thus strongly expressed:—'There are in that book thoughts, which, by long revolution in the great mind of Johnson, have been formed and polished like pebbles rolled in the ocean!'

That he was to some degree of excess a *true-born Englishman*,[32] so as to have entertained an undue prejudice against both the country and the people of Scotland, must be allowed. But it was a prejudice of the head, and not of the heart. He had no ill will to the Scotch; for, if he had been conscious of that, he would never have thrown himself into the bosom of their country, and trusted to the protection of its remote inhabitants with a fearless confidence. His remark upon the nakedness of the country, from its being denuded of trees, was made after having travelled two

[30] See document No. 39.
[31] Robert Orme (1728–1801).
[32] *Richard II*, I. iii. 309.

hundred miles along the eastern coast, where certainly trees are not to be found near the road; and he said it was 'a map of the road' which he gave. His disbelief of the authenticity of the poems ascribed to Ossian, a Highland bard, was confirmed in the course of his journey, by a very strict examination of the evidence offered for it; and although their authenticity was made too much a national point by the Scotch, there were many respectable persons in that country, who did not concur in this; so that his judgement upon the question ought not to be decried, even by those who differ from him. As to myself, I can only say, upon a subject now become very uninteresting, that when the fragments of Highland poetry first came out, I was much pleased with their wild peculiarity, and was one of those who subscribed to enable their editor, Mr. Macpherson, then a young man, to make a search in the Highlands and Hebrides for a long poem in the Erse language, which was reported to be preserved somewhere in those regions. But when there came forth an Epick Poem in six books, with all the common circumstances of former compositions of that nature; and when, upon an attentive examination of it, there was found a perpetual recurrence of the same images which appear in the fragments; and when no ancient manuscript, to authenticate the work, was deposited in any publick library, though that was insisted on as a reasonable proof, *who* could forbear to doubt?

Johnson's grateful acknowledgements of kindnesses received in the course of this tour, completely refute the brutal reflections which have been thrown out against him, as if he had made an ungrateful return; and his delicacy in sparing in his book those who we find from his letters to Mrs. Thrale, were just objects of censure, is much to be admired. His candour and amiable disposition is conspicuous from his conduct, when informed by Mr. Macleod, of Rasay, that he had committed a mistake, which gave that gentleman some uneasiness. He wrote him a courteous and kind letter, and inserted in the news-papers an advertisement, correcting the mistake.

The observations of my friend Mr. Dempster[33] in a letter written to me, soon after he had read Dr. Johnson's book, are so just and liberal, that they cannot be too often repeated:

There is nothing in the book, from beginning to end, that a Scotchman need to take amiss. What he says of the country is true; and his observations on the people are what must naturally occur to a sensible, observing, and reflecting inhabitant of a convenient metropolis, where a man on thirty pounds a year may be better accommodated with all the little wants of life, than Col or Sir Allan.

[33] George Dempster (1732–1818), Scottish M.P. and agriculturalist.

I am charmed with his researches concerning the Erse language, and the antiquity of their manuscripts. I am quite convinced; and I shall rank Ossian, and his Fingals and Oscars, amongst the nursery tales, not the true history of our country, in all time to come.

Upon the whole, the book cannot displease, for it has no pretensions. The author neither says he is a geographer, nor an antiquarian, nor very learned in the history of Scotland, nor a naturalist, nor a fossilist. The manners of the people, and the face of the country, are all he attempts to describe, or seems to have thought of. Much were it to be wished, that they who have travelled into more remote, and of course more curious regions, had all possessed his good sense. Of the state of learning, his observations on Glasgow University show he has formed a very sound judgement. He understands our climate too: and he has accurately observed the changes, however slow and imperceptible to us, which Scotland has undergone, in consequence of the blessings of liberty and internal peace.

Mr. Knox, another native of Scotland, who has since made the same tour, and published an account of it, is equally liberal.

I have read (says he,) his book again and again, travelled with him from Berwick to Glenelg, through countries with which I am well acquainted; sailed with him from Glenelg to Rasay, Sky, Rum, Col, Mull, and Icolmkill, but have not been able to correct him in any matter of consequence. I have often admired the accuracy, the precision, and the justness of what he advances, respecting both the country and the people.

The Doctor has every where delivered his sentiments with freedom, and in many instances with a seeming regard for the benefit of the inhabitants, and the ornament of the country. His remarks on the want of trees and hedges for shade, as well as for shelter to the cattle, are well founded, and merit the thanks, not the illiberal censure of the natives. He also felt for the distresses of the Highlanders, and explodes with great propriety the bad management of the grounds, and the neglect of timber in the Hebrides.

Having quoted Johnson's just compliments on the Rasay family, he says,

On the other hand, I found this family equally lavish in their encomiums upon the Doctor's conversation, and his subsequent civilities to a young gentleman of that country, who, upon waiting upon him at London, was well received, and experienced all the attention and regard that a warm friend could bestow. Mr. Macleod having also been in London, waited upon the Doctor, who provided a magnificent and expensive entertainment in honour of his old Hebridean acquaintance.

And talking of the military road by Fort Augustus, he says,

By this road, though one of the most rugged in Great Britain, the celebrated Dr. Johnson passed from Inverness to the Hebride Isles. His observations on the country and people are extremely correct, judicious, and instructive.[34]

Mr. Tytler,[35] the acute and able vindicator of Mary Queen of Scots, in one of his letters to Mr. James Elphinstone, published in that gentleman's *Forty Years' Correspondence*, says,

I read Dr. Johnson's *Tour* with very great pleasure. Some few errours he has fallen into, but of no great importance, and those are lost in the numberless beauties of his work.

If I had leisure, I could perhaps point out the most exceptionable places; but at present I am in the country, and have not his book at hand. It is plain he meant to speak well of Scotland; and he has in my apprehension done us great honour in the most capital article, the character of the inhabitants.

His private letters to Mrs. Thrale, written during the course of his journey, which therefore may be supposed to convey his genuine feelings at the time, abound in such benignant sentiments towards the people who showed him civilities, that no man whose temper is not very harsh and sour, can retain a doubt of the goodness of his heart.

It is painful to recollect with what rancour he was assailed by numbers of shallow irritable North Britons, on account of his supposed injurious treatment of their country and countrymen, in his *Journey*. Had there been any just ground for such a charge, would the virtuous and candid Dempster have given his opinion of the book, in the terms which I have quoted? Would the patriotick Knox have spoken of it as he has done? Would Mr. Tytler, surely

— a *Scot*, if ever *Scot* there were,

have expressed himself thus? And let me add that, citizen of the world as I hold myself to be, I have that degree of predilection for my *natale solum*, nay, I have that just sense of the merit of an ancient nation, which has been ever renowned for its valour, which in former times maintained its independence against a powerful neighbour, and in modern times has been equally distinguished for its ingenuity and industry in civilized life, that I should have felt a generous indignation at any injustice done to it. Johnson treated Scotland no worse than he did even his best friends, whose characters he used to give as they appeared to him, both in light and shade. Some people, who had not exercised their minds sufficiently,

[34] John Knox, *Tour through the Highlands of Scotland*, 1787, lxviii-ix. 103.
[35] William Tytler (1711-92).

condemned him for censuring his friends. But Sir Joshua Reynolds, whose philosophical penetration and justness of thinking were not less known to those who lived with him, than his genius in his art is admired by the world, explained his conduct thus: 'He was fond of discrimination, which he could not show without pointing out the bad as well as the good in every character; and as his friends were those whose characters he knew best, they afforded him the best opportunity for showing the acuteness of his judgement.'

He expressed to his friend Mr. Windham of Norfolk,[36] his wonder at the extreme jealousy of the Scotch, and their resentment at having their country described by him as it really was; when, to say that it was a country as good as England, would have been a gross falsehood. 'None of us, (said he,) would be offended if a foreigner who has travelled here should say, that vines and olives don't grow in England.' And as to his prejudice against the Scotch, which I always ascribed to that nationality which he observed in *them*, he said to the same gentleman, 'When I find a Scotchman, to whom an Englishman is as a Scotchman, that Scotchman shall be as an Englishman to me.' His intimacy with many gentlemen of Scotland, and his employing so many natives of that country as his amanuenses,[37] prove that his prejudice was not virulent; and I have deposited in the British Museum, amongst other pieces of his writing, the following note in answer to one from me, asking if he would meet me at dinner at the Mitre, though a friend of mine, a Scotchman, was to be there:—

Mr. Johnson does not see why Mr. Boswell should suppose a Scotchman less acceptable than any other man. He will be at the Mitre.

My much-valued friend Dr. Barnard, now Bishop of Killaloe, having once expressed to him an apprehension, that if he should visit Ireland he might treat the people of that country more unfavourably than he had done the Scotch, he answered, with strong pointed double-edged wit, 'Sir, you have no reason to be afraid of me. The Irish are not in a conspiracy to cheat the world by false representations of the merits of their countrymen. No, Sir; the Irish are a FAIR PEOPLE;—they never speak well of one another.'

Johnson told me an instance of Scottish nationality, which made a very unfavourable impression upon his mind. A Scotchman, of some consideration in London, solicited him to recommend, by the weight of

[36] The politician, William Windham (1750–1810).
[37] Five of the six amanuenses employed on the *Dictionary* were Scotsmen.

his learned authority, to be master of an English school, a person of whom he who recommended him confessed he knew no more but that he was his countryman. Johnson was shocked at this unconscientious conduct.

All the miserable cavillings against his *Journey*, in newspapers, magazines, and other fugitive publications, I can speak from certain knowledge, only furnished him with sport. At last there came out a scurrilous volume,[38] larger than Johnson's own, filled with malignant abuse, under a name, real or fictitious, of some low man in an obscure corner of Scotland, though supposed to be the work of another Scotchman,[39] who has found means to make himself well known both in Scotland and England. The effect which it had upon Johnson was, to produce this pleasant observation to Mr. Seward, to whom he lent the book: 'This fellow must be a blockhead. They don't know how to go about their abuse. Who will read a five shilling book against me? No, Sir, if they had wit, they should have kept pelting me with pamphlets.' . . .

The doubts which, in my correspondence with him, I had ventured to state as to the justice and wisdom of the conduct of Great-Britain towards the American colonies, while I at the same time requested that he would enable me to inform myself upon that momentous subject, he had altogether disregarded; and had recently published a pamphlet, entitled, *Taxation no Tyranny; an Answer to the Resolutions and Address of the American Congress* [1775].

He had long before indulged most unfavourable sentiments of our fellow-subjects in America. For, as early as 1769, I was told by Dr. John Campbell, that he had said of them, 'Sir, they are a race of convicts, and ought to be thankful for any thing we allow them short of hanging.'

Of this performance I avoided to talk with him; for I had now formed a clear and settled opinion, that the people of America were well warranted to resist a claim that their fellow-subjects in the mother-country should have the entire command of their fortunes, by taxing them without their own consent; and the extreme violence which it breathed, appeared to me so unsuitable to the mildness of a Christian philosopher, and so directly opposite to the principles of peace which he had so beautifully recommended in his pamphlet respecting Falkland's Islands, that I was sorry to see him appear in so unfavourable a light. Besides, I could not perceive in it that ability of argument, or that felicity of expression, for which he was, upon other occasions, so eminent. Positive

[38] McNicol's *Remarks*, 1779. See document No. 47.
[39] Iames ('Ossian') Macpherson. (He may indeed have contributed to McNicol's book.)

assertion, sarcastical severity, and extravagant ridicule, which he himself reprobated as a test of truth, were united in this rhapsody. . . .

His pamphlets in support of the measures of administration were published on his own account, and he afterwards collected them into a volume, with the title of *Political Tracts, by the Authour of the Rambler* [1776], with this motto:

> *Fallitur egregio quisquis sub Principe credit*
> *Servitium; nunquam libertas gratior extat*
> *Quam sub Rege pio.*   CLAUDIANUS.[40]

These pamphlets drew upon him numerous attacks. Against the common weapons of literary warfare he was hardened; but there were two instances of animadversion which I communicated to him, and from what I could judge, both from his silence and his looks, appeared to me to impress him much.

One was, *A Letter to Dr. Samuel Johnson, occasioned by his late political Publications*. It appeared previous to his *Taxation no Tyranny*, and was written by Dr. Joseph Towers.[41] In that performance, Dr. Johnson was treated with the respect due to so eminent a man, while his conduct as a political writer was boldly and pointedly arraigned, as inconsistent with the character of one, who, if he did employ his pen upon politicks,

It might reasonably be expected should distinguish himself, not by party violence and rancour, but by moderation and by wisdom.

It concluded thus:

[quotes 'I would, however, wish' to 'the *Patriot*'. See above, pp. 224–5.]

I am willing to do justice to the merit of Dr. Towers, of whom I will say, that although I abhor his Whiggish democratical notions and propensities, (for I will not call them principles,) I esteem him as an ingenious, knowing, and very convivial man.

The other instance was a paragraph of a letter to me, from my old and most intimate friend, the Reverend Mr. Temple,[42] who wrote the character of Gray, which has had the honour to be adopted both by Mr. Mason and Dr. Johnson in their accounts of that poet. The words were,

How can your great, I will not say your *pious*, but your *moral* friend, support the barbarous measures of administration, which they have not the face to ask even their infidel pensioner Hume to defend.

[40] *Stilichonis*, III. 113 ('He errs who deems obedience to a prince slavery; a happier freedom never reigns than with a pious monarch').
[41] See document No. 41.
[42] The Revd William J. Temple (1739–96).

However confident of the rectitude of his own mind, Johnson may have felt sincere uneasiness that his conduct should be erroneously imputed to unworthy motives, by good men; and that the influence of his valuable writings should on that account be in any degree obstructed or lessened. . . .

1781: ÆTAT. 72.]—In 1781 Johnson at last completed his *Lives of the Poets*, of which he gives this account: 'Some time in March I finished the *Lives of the Poets*, which I wrote in my usual way, dilatorily and hastily, unwilling to work, and working with vigour and haste.' In a memorandum previous to this, he says of them: 'Written, I hope, in such a manner as may tend to the promotion of piety.'

This is the work which of all Dr. Johnson's writings will perhaps be read most generally, and with most pleasure. Philology and biography were his favourite pursuits, and those who lived most in intimacy with him, heard him upon all occasions, when there was a proper opportunity, take delight in expatiating upon the various merits of the English Poets: upon the niceties of their characters, and the events of their progress through the world which they contributed to illuminate. His mind was so full of that kind of information, and it was so well arranged in his memory, that in performing what he had undertaken in this way, he had little more to do than to put his thoughts upon paper, exhibiting first each Poet's life, and then subjoining a critical examination of his genius and works. But when he began to write, the subject swelled in such a manner, that instead of prefaces to each poet, of no more than a few pages, as he had originally intended, he produced an ample, rich, and most entertaining view of them in every respect. In this he resembled Quintilian, who tells us, that in the composition of his *Institutions of Oratory*, '*Latiùs se tamen aperiente materiâ, plus quàm imponebatur oneris sponte suscepi.*'[40] The booksellers, justly sensible of the great additional value of the copy-right, presented him with another hundred pounds, over and above two hundred, for which his agreement was to furnish such prefaces as he thought fit.

This was, however, but a small recompence for such a collection of biography, and such principles and illustrations of criticism, as, if digested and arranged in one system, by some modern Aristotle or Longinus, might form a code upon that subject, such as no other nation can shew. As he was so good as to make me a present of the greatest part of the original, and indeed only manuscript of this admirable work, I have an

[43] *Institutio Oratoria*, liber I, Prooemium 3 ('But as my matter grew under my hand, I voluntarily undertook a bigger task than had been laid upon me').

opportunity of observing with wonder the correctness with which he rapidly struck off such glowing composition. . . .

The *Life of Cowley* he himself considered as the best of the whole, on account of the dissertation which it contains on the *Metaphysical Poets*. Dryden, whose critical abilities were equal to his poetical, had mentioned them in his excellent Dedication of his Juvenal, but had barely mentioned them. Johnson has exhibited them at large, with such happy illustration from their writings, and in so luminous a manner, that indeed he may be allowed the full merit of novelty, and to have discovered to us, as it were, a new planet in the poetical hemisphere. . . .

So easy is his style in these *Lives*, that I do not recollect more than three uncommon or learned words;[44] one, when giving an account of the approach of Waller's mortal disease, he says, 'he found his legs grow *tumid;*' by using the expression his legs *swelled,* he would have avoided this; and there would have been no impropriety in its being followed by the interesting question to his physician, 'What that *swelling* meant?' Another, when he mentions that Pope had *emitted* proposals; when *published* or *issued* would have been more readily understood; and a third, when he calls Orrery and Dr. Delany, writers both undoubtedly *veracious*; when *true, honest,* or *faithful,* might have been used. Yet, it must be owned, that none of these are *hard* or *too big* words; that custom would make them seem as easy as any others; and that a language is richer and capable of more beauty of expression, by having a greater variety of synonimes. . . .

While the world in general was filled with admiration of Johnson's *Lives of the Poets,* there were narrow circles in which prejudice and resentment were fostered, and from which attacks of different sorts issued against him. By some violent Whigs he was arraigned of injustice to Milton; by some Cambridge men of depreciating Gray; and his expressing with a dignified freedom what he really thought of George, Lord Lyttelton, gave offence to some of the friends of that nobleman, and particularly produced a declaration of war against him from Mrs. Montagu, the ingenious Essayist on Shakspeare,[45] between whom and his Lordship a commerce of reciprocal compliments had long been carried on. In this war the smaller powers in alliance with him were of course led to engage, at least on the defensive, and thus I for one was excluded from the enjoyment of 'A Feast of Reason,' such as Mr.

[44] See *Lives,* i. 276; iii. 112, 26.
[45] Elizabeth Montagu (1720–1800) published her *Essay on the Writings and Genius of Shakespeare* in 1769.

Cumberland[46] has described, with a keen, yet just and delicate pen, in his *Observer*. These minute inconveniences gave not the least disturbance to Johnson. He nobly said, when I talked to him of the feeble, though shrill outcry which had been raised, 'Sir, I considered myself as entrusted with a certain portion of truth. I have given my opinion sincerely; let them shew where they think me wrong.' . . .

The character of S A M U E L J O H N S O N has, I trust, been so developed in the course of this work, that they who have honoured it with a perusal, may be considered as well acquainted with him. As, however, it may be expected that I should collect into one view the capital and distinguishing features of this extraordinary man, I shall endeavour to acquit myself of that part of my biographical undertaking, however difficult it may be to do that which many of my readers will do better for themselves.

His figure was large and well formed, and his countenance of the cast of an ancient statue; yet his appearance was rendered strange and somewhat uncouth, by convulsive cramps, by the scars of that distemper which it was once imagined the royal touch could cure, and by a slovenly mode of dress. He had the use only of one eye; yet so much does mind govern and even supply the deficiency of organs, that his visual perceptions, as far as they extended, were uncommonly quick and accurate. So morbid was his temperament, that he never knew the natural joy of a free and vigorous use of his limbs: when he walked, it was like the struggling gait of one in fetters; when he rode, he had no command or direction of his horse, but was carried as if in a balloon. That with his constitution and habits of life he should have lived seventy-five years, is a proof that an inherent *vivida vis*[47] is a powerful preservative of the human frame.

Man is, in general, made up of contradictory qualities; and these will ever shew themselves in strange succession, where a consistency in appearance at least, if not in reality, has not been attained by long habits of philosophical discipline. In proportion to the native vigour of the mind, the contradictory qualities will be the more prominent, and more difficult to be adjusted; and, therefore, we are not to wonder, that Johnson exhibited an eminent example of this remark which I have made upon human nature. At different times, he seemed a different man, in some respects; not, however, in any great or essential article, upon which he had fully employed his mind, and settled certain principles of duty,

[46] Richard Cumberland (1732–1811), author of sentimental comedies and editor of the periodical, *The Observer*.
[47] Lucretius, *De Rerum Naturâ*, i. 72 ('lively energy').

but only in his manners, and in the display of argument and fancy in his talk. He was prone to superstition, but not to credulity. Though his imagination might incline him to a belief of the marvellous and the mysterious, his vigorous reason examined the evidence with jealousy. He was a sincere and zealous Christian, of high Church-of-England and monarchial principles, which he would not tamely suffer to be questioned; and had, perhaps, at an early period, narrowed his mind somewhat too much, both as to religion and politicks. His being impressed with the danger of extreme latitude in either, though he was of a very independent spirit, occasioned his appearing somewhat unfavourable to the prevalence of that noble freedom of sentiment which is the best possession of man. Nor can it be denied, that he had many prejudices; which, however, frequently suggested many of his pointed sayings, that rather shew a playfulness of fancy than any settled malignity. He was steady and inflexible in maintaining the obligations of religion and morality; both from a regard for the order of society, and from a veneration for the GREAT SOURCE of all order; correct, nay stern in his taste; hard to please, and easily offended; impetuous and irritable in his temper, but of a most humane and benevolent heart, which shewed itself not only in a most liberal charity, as far as his circumstances would allow, but in a thousand instances of active benevolence. He was afflicted with a bodily disease, which made him often restless and fretful; and with a constitutional melancholy, the clouds of which darkened the brightness of his fancy, and gave a gloomy cast to his whole course of thinking: we, therefore, ought not to wonder at his sallies of impatience and passion at any time; especially when provoked by obtrusive ignorance, or presuming petulance; and allowance must be made for his uttering hasty and satirical sallies even against his best friends. And, surely, when it is considered, that, 'amidst sickness and sorrow,'[48] he exerted his faculties in so many works for the benefit of mankind, and particularly that he atchieved the great and admirable *Dictionary* of our language, we must be astonished at his resolution. The solemn text, 'of him to whom so much is given, much will be required,'[49] seems to have been ever present to his mind, in a rigorous sense, and to have made him dissatisfied with his labours and acts of goodness, however comparatively great; so that the unavoidable consciousness of his superiority was, in that respect, a cause of disquiet. He suffered so much from this, and from the gloom which perpetually haunted him, and made solitude frightful, that it may be said of him, 'If in

[48] See above, p. 114.
[49] Luke 12: 48.

this life only he had hope, he was of all men most miserable.'[50] He loved praise, when it was brought to him; but was too proud to seek for it. He was somewhat susceptible of flattery. As he was general and unconfined in his studies, he cannot be considered as master of any one particular science; but he had accumulated a vast and various collection of learning and knowledge, which was so arranged in his mind, as to be ever in readiness to be brought forth. But his superiority over other learned men consisted chiefly in what may be called the art of thinking, the art of using his mind; a certain continual power of seizing the useful substance of all that he knew, and exhibiting it in a clear and forcible manner; so that knowledge, which we often see to be no better than lumber in men of dull understanding, was, in him, true, evident, and actual wisdom. His moral precepts are practical; for they are drawn from an intimate acquaintance with human nature. His maxims carry convictions; for they are founded on the basis of common sense, and a very attentive and minute survey of real life. His mind was so full of imagery, that he might have been perpetually a poet; yet it is remarkable, that, however rich his prose is in this respect, his poetical pieces, in general, have not much of that splendour, but are rather distinguished by strong sentiment, and acute observation, conveyed in harmonious and energetick verse, particularly in heroick couplets. Though usually grave, and even aweful, in his deportment, he possessed uncommon and peculiar powers of wit and humour; he frequently indulged himself in colloquial pleasantry; and the heartiest merriment was often enjoyed in his company; with this great advantage, that as it was entirely free from any poisonous tincture of vice or impiety, it was salutary to those who shared in it. He had accustomed himself to such accuracy in his common conversation, that he at all times expressed his thoughts with great force, and an elegant choice of language, the effect of which was aided by his having a loud voice, and a slow deliberate utterance. In him were united a most logical head with a most fertile imagination, which gave him an extraordinary advantage in arguing: for he could reason close or wide, as he saw best for the moment. Exulting in his intellectual strength and dexterity, he could, when he pleased, be the greatest sophist that ever contended in the lists of declamation; and, from a spirit of contradiction, and a delight in shewing his powers, he would often maintain the wrong side with equal warmth and ingenuity; so that, when there was an audience, his real opinions could seldom be gathered from his talk; though when he was in company with a single friend, he would discuss a subject with genuine

[50] I Corinthians 15: 19.

fairness: but he was too conscientious to make errour permanent and pernicious, by deliberately writing it; and, in all his numerous works, he earnestly inculcated what appeared to him to be the truth; his piety being constant, and the ruling principle of all his conduct.

Such was SAMUEL JOHNSON, a man whose talents, acquirements, and virtues, were so extraordinary, that the more his character is considered, the more he will be regarded by the present age, and by posterity, with admiration and reverence.

76. Anna Seward's general estimate of Johnson

14 February 1796

Text from *Letters*, 1811, iv. 155–60.

14 February 1796, to 'Mr. Laugh of the Dewar Club':*
Sir,

THE majority are certainly right in this dispute about the meaning of the epitaph on Johnson. Dazzled by the splendour of his talents, admiration of a stupendous but imperfect Being has misled you;—has warped the judgment of a man of genius to put a forced construction upon a very obvious sense. If it was possible to construe, 'he knew envy,' as importing

---

* A literary society, often frequented by Dr Johnson, in which a dispute had arisen concerning the meaning of the epitaph on him, which appeared in the beginning of this month, in several of the newspapers, with A. Seward's signature, most unwarrantably given, and which obliged her publicly to disavow the composition. This was the epitaph:

> The groans of Learning tell that Johnson dies.
> Adieu, rough critic, of Colossal size!
> Grateful, ye virtues, round his grave attend,
> And boldly guard your energetic friend!
> Ye vices keep aloof—a foe to you!
> Yet one, the subtlest of your tribe, he knew;
> In silence, Envy, to his fame be just,
> And, tho' you stain'd his spirit, spare his dust.

his experience of it in others, yet how could the envy of others stain his spirit? If it had been written, 'and though you vex'd his spirit, spare his dust,' the meaning might have been equivocal; but with the word *stained*, dubious meaning cannot exist.

I have had frequent opportunities of conversing with that wonderful man. Seldom did I listen to him without admiring the great powers of his mind, and feeling concern and pain at the malignance of his disposition. He would sometimes be just to the virtues and literary fame of others, if they had not been praised in the conversation before his opinion was asked:—If they had been previously praised, never. His truth, so needlessly precise in common-life trifles, always yielded to the darkest jealousy I ever knew to exist in the bosom of genius. Johnson's *Lives of the Poets*, and all the records of his own life and conversation, prove that envy did deeply stain his spirit.

Frank in avowing my sentiments, it has been my fate equally to contend with the prejudiced for and against Dr Johnson; with those who attest their faith in the moral and religious perfection of that sublime teacher of perfect morality, I allege proofs from my own experience, and the anecdotes of him which are before the world, that he had overbearing haughtiness of temper, uncharitable prejudices, and envy, which betrayed him into injustice concerning the lettered fame of the celebrated, and the virtues of those who differed from him in politics and religion; all which are incompatible with a uniformly good and noble mind.

With those who deem his writings turgid, elaborate, stiff, and pedantic;—who, as a serious essayist, exalt above him the comparatively feeble Addison;—who deny all degree of excellence to his poetry, and pronounce his taste for the art grovelling and undiscerning;—in short, who deny him every thing intellectually but memory and learning:—against these, I have always maintained, that his powers, and style, in moral declamation, are far superior to Addison's, and indeed to that of every other essayist;—that his compositions are luminous, impressive, and harmonious;—that to them may be fairly imputed the immense improvement in English prose-writing within the last half-century;—that, by Latinizing our language, he has expanded its powers, and harmonized its sound. I have, indeed, granted that his style has no versatility;—that when he attempts to write in the character of *others*, he always fails;—that in the Lady Pekuah of *Rasselas*, and the Flavia and Flirtilla of the *Rambler*,[1] we always, as Mr Burke has observed, see the

[1] Nos. 84, 10.

413

enormous Johnson in petticoats;—yet have I asserted, that the dignity and grace with which he declaims, when writing on abstract themes, and in his own character—the happiness with which he unites efflorescence and strength in his diction, give him an high place on the list of genius;—that his poetry, if not quite first-rate, is very beautiful;— particularly, that the *Vanity of Human Wishes*, in which he is only indebted to Juvenal for the general idea, is an exquisite ethic poem, for I can hardly term it a satire, so gracefully does it seem to commiserate the presumptuous desires and rash pursuits of mankind.

To your question, Whom could Johnson envy? I answer, all his superiors in genius, all his equals; in short, at times, every celebrated author, living or dead.

You seem to think he has no superiors.—Great as I deem him, I cannot help feeling that he has superiors, and that in a very large degree, though they will not be found amongst our essayists, where I acknowledge his pre-eminence. Johnson was a very bright star; yet, to Shakespeare and Milton, he was but as a star to the sun.

Reflect, Sir, coolly, what are the constituent powers of superlative genius, and you will better appreciate its claims, than to assert that Johnson had no superiors. You will confess those powers to be creative fancy,—intuitive discernment into the subtlest recesses of the human heart;—exhaustless variety of style;—the Proteus ability of speaking the sentiments and language of every character, whether belonging to real or to imaginary existence; and that so naturally, as to make the reader feel that so must have spoken every man or woman, angel or fiend, fairy or monster, whose shape is assumed.

If these are the constituent powers of superlative genius, how fades the dazzling lustre of Johnson's talents before that of Shakespeare's and Milton's!

Gray was indolent, and wrote but little;—yet that little proves him the first Genius of the period in which he lived. I have been assured that he had more learning than Johnson, and he certainly was a very superior poet. Johnson felt the superiority, and for that he hated him. It was that consciousness, I verily believe, which impelled him to speak with such audacious contempt of the first lyric compositions the world has seen, of loftier subjects than Pindar's. Grander in point of imagery and language no odes can be than the odes of Gray.

Johnson's first ambition was to be distinguished as a poet, and as a poet he was first celebrated. His fine satire, *London*, had considerable reputation; yet it neither eclipsed, nor had power to eclipse, the satires

of Pope. As a dramatic poet he failed—the cold *Irene*, all whose personages speak the same spiritless, unnatural, though polished language, met
almost total neglect. Hence originated his spleen to poets; that disappointment laid the train to his indignancy against those, who, in his
primeval pursuit, had higher celebrity.

77. George Mason, Epitaph on Johnson

1796

Text from the *Gentleman's Magazine*, lxvi (1796), 758–9.

The *Gentleman's Magazine*—which, only two years before,
published Thomas Tyers's laudatory *Biographical Sketch*—
reprinted this abusive epitaph from Mason's edition of *Poems of
Thomas Hoccleve*, 1796.

> Here, peaceable at last
> are deposited the remains
> of Dr. Samuel Johnson,
> the Poet
> the Critic
> the Periodical Essayist
> the Novellist
> the Politico-polemic,
> the Lexicographer,
> Topographer,
> Biographer.
> The Public taste
> Patron of every novelty,
> Cherished his writings for a while,
> as most extraordinary specimens
> of pedantic verbosity;
> even the matchless insipidity of *Rasselas*
> was tolerated.

His political and poetical talents
differed widely from each other.
A bigoted education
had taught him to maintain
long-exploded absurdities
in maxims of government.
His own failures in poetry
made him a perfect leveler
throughout the region of the Muses.
Incompetent critic from hebetude,
Credulous retailer of calumnies;
illiberal in his censures;
Cynical in his expressions;
he acquired the literary title of
Snarler General.
To the manes of poets
whom Johnson slandered in their graves,
be this an expiatory offering.

78. Richard Cumberland, *Memoirs*

1807

Extracts from *Memoirs*, 1807, i. 353–6, 360–4.

Cumberland (1732–1811) was dramatist, novelist, and translator
of Aristophanes.

Who will say that Johnson himself would have been such a champion
in literature, such a front-rank soldier in the fields of fame, if he had not
been pressed into the service, and driven on to glory with the bayonet
of sharp necessity pointed at his back? If fortune had turned him into
a field of clover, he would have laid down and rolled in it. The mere

manual labour of writing would not have allowed his lassitude and love
of ease to have taken the pen out of the inkhorn, unless the cravings of
hunger had reminded him that he must fill the sheet before he saw the
table cloth. He might indeed have knocked down Osbourne for a
blockhead, but he would not have knocked him down with a folio of
his own writing.[1] He would perhaps have been the dictator of a club,
and wherever he sate down to conversation, there must have been that
splash of strong bold thought about him, that we might still have had
a collectanea after his death; but of prose I guess not much, of works of
labour none, of fancy perhaps something more, especially of poetry,
which under favour I conceive was not his tower of strength. I think we
should have had his *Rasselas* at all events, for he was likely enough to
have written at Voltaire, and brought the question to the test, if infidelity
is any aid to wit. An orator he must have been; not improbably a
parliamentarian, and, if such, certainly an oppositionist, for he preferred
to talk against the tide. He would indubitably have been no member of
the Whig Club, no partisan of Wilkes, no friend of Hume, no believer
in Macpherson; he would have put up prayers for early rising, and laid
in bed all day, and with the most active resolutions possible been the
most indolent mortal living. He was a good man by nature, a great man
by genius, we are now to enquire what he was by compulsion.

Johnson's first style was naturally energetic, his middle style was
turgid to a fault, his latter style was softened down and harmonized into
periods, more tuneful and more intelligible. His execution was rapid,
yet his mind was not easily provoked into exertion; the variety we find
in his writings was not the variety of choice arising from the impulse of
his proper genius, but tasks imposed upon him by the dealers in ink, and
contracts on his part submitted to in satisfaction of the pressing calls of
hungry want; for, painful as it is to relate, I have heard that illustrious
scholar assert (and he never varied from the truth of fact) that he subsisted
himself for a considerable space of time upon the scanty pittance of four-
pence halfpenny per day. How melancholy to reflect that his vast trunk
and stimulating appetite were to be supported by what will barely feed
the weaned infant! Less, much less, than Master Betty[2] has earned in one
night, would have cheered the mighty mind, and maintained the athletic
body of Samuel Johnson in comfort and abundance for a twelvemonth.
Alas! I am not fit to paint his character; nor is there need of it; *Etiam*

[1] See Boswell, *Life*, i. 154.
[2] The 'Young Roscius', William H. Betty (1791–1874); in 1803–5 he appeared extensively in Shakespearean adult roles in London, Ireland and Scotland.

mortuus loquitur:[3] every man, who can buy a book, has bought a *Boswell*; Johnson is known to all the reading world. . . .

The expanse of matter, which Johnson had found room for in his intellectual storehouse, the correctness with which he had assorted it, and the readiness with which he could turn to any article that he wanted to make present use of, were the properties in him, which I contemplated with the most admiration. Some have called him a savage; they were only so far right in the resemblance, as that, like the savage, he never came into suspicious company without his spear in his hand and his bow and quiver at his back. In quickness of intellect few ever equalled him, in profundity of erudition many have surpassed him. I do not think he had a pure and classical taste, nor was apt to be best pleased with the best authors, but as a general scholar he ranks very high. When I would have consulted him upon certain points of literature, whilst I was making my collections from the Greek dramatists for my essays in *The Observer*, he candidly acknowledged that his studies had not lain amongst them, and certain it is there is very little shew of literature in his *Ramblers*, and in the passage, where he quotes Aristotle,[4] he has not correctly given the meaning of the original. But this was merely the result of haste and inattention, neither is he so to be measured, for he had so many parts and properties of scholarship about him, that you can only fairly review him as a man of general knowledge. As a poet his translations of Juvenal gave him a name in the world, and gained him the applause of Pope. He was a writer of tragedy, but his *Irene* gives him no conspicuous rank in that department. As an essayist he merits more consideration; his *Ramblers* are in every body's hands; about them opinions vary, and I rather believe the style of these essays is not now considered as a good model; this he corrected in his more advanced age, as may be seen in his *Lives of the Poets*, where his diction, though occasionally elaborate and highly metaphorical, is not nearly so inflated and ponderous, as in the *Ramblers*. He was an acute and able critic; the enthusiastic admirers of Milton and the friends of Gray will have something to complain of, but criticism is a task, which no man executes to all men's satisfaction. His selection of a certain passage in the *Mourning Bride* of Congreve, which he extols so rapturously,[5] is certainly a most unfortunate sample; but unless the oversights of a critic are less pardonable than those of other men, we may pass this over in a work of merit, which abounds in

[3] 'Even the dead speaks' (cf. Hebrews 11 : 4).
[4] *Rambler* No. 139.
[5] *Lives*, ii. 230.

beauties far more prominent than its defects, and much more pleasing to contemplate. In works professedly of fancy he is not very copious; yet in his *Rasselas* we have much to admire, and enough to make us wish for more. It is the work of an illuminated mind, and offers many wise and deep reflections, cloathed in beautiful and harmonious diction. We are not indeed familiar with such personages as Johnson has imagined for the characters of his fable, but if we are not exceedingly interested in their story, we are infinitely gratified with their conversation and remarks. In conclusion, Johnson's æra was not wanting in men to be distinguished for their talents, yet if one was to be selected out as the first great literary character of the time, I believe all voices would concur in naming him. Let me here insert the following lines, descriptive of his character, though not long since written by me and to be found in a public print——

On Samuel Johnson.

Herculean strength and a Stentorian voice,
Of wit a fund, of words a countless choice:
In learning rather various than profound,
In truth intrepid, in religion sound:
A trembling form and a distorted sight,
But firm in judgement and in genius bright;
In controversy seldom known to spare,
But humble as the Publican in prayer;
To more, than merited his kindness, kind,
And, though in manners, harsh, of friendly mind;
Deep ting'd with melancholy's blackest shade,
And, though prepar'd to die, of death afraid—
Such Johnson was; of him with justice vain,
When will this nation see his like again?

79. Sir Walter Scott, *Lives of the Novelists*

1821–4

Extracts from *Lives of the Novelists*, Paris, 1825, ii. 79–80, 86–90.

In the tradition of Johnson's *Lives of the English Poets*, Scott wrote a series of biographical and critical prefaces for Ballantyne's 'Novelists Library'. Johnson was included as the author of *Rasselas*. Scott's opening paragraphs make it particularly clear that Boswell had provided spectacles through which succeeding generations viewed Johnson. See Introduction, p. 34.

Of all the men distinguished in this or any other age, Dr. Johnson has left upon posterity the strongest and most vivid impression, so far as person, manners, disposition, and conversation are concerned. We do but name him, or open a book which he has written, and the sound and action recall to the imagination at once his form, his merits, his peculiarities, nay, the very uncouthness of his gestures, and the deep impressive tone of his voice. We learn not only what he said, but how he said it; and have at the same time a shrewd guess of the secret motive why he did so, and whether he spoke in sport or in anger, in the desire of conviction, or for the love of debate. It was said of a noted wag that his *bons-mots* did not give full satisfaction when published because he could not print his face. But with respect to Dr. Johnson this has been in some degree accomplished; and although the greater part of the present generation never saw him, yet he is, in our mind's eye, a personification as lively as that of Siddons in *Lady Macbeth* or Kemble in *Cardinal Wolsey*.

All this, as the world well knows, arises from Johnson having found in James Boswell such a biographer as no man but himself ever had or ever deserved to have. The performance which chiefly resembles it in structure is the life of the philosopher Demonax, in Lucian; but that slight sketch is far inferior in detail and in vivacity to Boswell's *Life of Johnson*, which, considering the eminent persons to whom it relates, the quantity of miscellaneous information and entertaining gossip which it brings together, may be termed, without exception, the best parlour window book that ever was written. . . .

When we consider the rank which Dr. Johnson held, not only in literature, but in society, we cannot help figuring him to ourselves as the benevolent giant of some fairy tale, whose kindnesses and courtesies are still mingled with a part of the rugged ferocity imputed to the fabulous sons of Anak, or rather, perhaps, like a Roman dictator, fetched from his farm, whose wisdom and heroism still relished of his rustic occupation. And there were times when, with all his wisdom, and all his wit, this rudeness of disposition, and the sacrifices and submissions which he unsparingly exacted, were so great that even Mrs. Thrale seems at length to have thought that the honour of being Johnson's hostess was almost counter balanced by the tax which he exacted on her time and patience.

The cause of those deficiencies in temper and manners was no ignorance of what was fit to be done in society, or how far each individual ought to suppress his own wishes in favour of those with whom he associates; for, theoretically, no man understood the rules of good breeding better than Dr. Johnson, or could act more exactly in conformity with them, when the high rank of those with whom he was in company for the time required that he should do so. But during the greater part of his life he had been in a great measure a stranger to the higher society in which such restraint became necessary; and it may be fairly presumed that the indulgence of a variety of little selfish peculiarities, which it is the object of good breeding to suppress, became thus familiar to him. The consciousness of his own mental superiority in most companies which he frequented, contributed to his dogmatism; and when he had attained his eminence as a dictator in literature, like other potentates, he was not averse to a display of his authority: resembling, in this particular, Swift, and one or two other men of genius, who have had the bad taste to imagine that their talents elevated them above observance of the common rules of society. It must be also remarked that in Johnson's time the literary society of London was much more confined than at present, and that he sat the Jupiter of a little circle, prompt, on the slightest contradiction, to launch the thunders of rebuke and sarcasm. He was, in a word, despotic, and despotism will occasionally lead the best dispositions into unbecoming abuse of power. It is not likely that any one will again enjoy, or have an opportunity of abusing, the singular degree of submission which was rendered to Johnson by all around him.

The unreserved communications of friends, rather than the spleen of enemies, have occasioned his character being exposed in all its shadows, as well as its lights. But those, when summed and counted, amount only to a few narrow-minded prejudices concerning country and party, from which few ardent tempers remain entirely free, and some violences and solecisms in manners, which left his talents, morals, and benevolence, alike unimpeachable.

Of *Rasselas*, translated into so many languages, and so widely circulated through the literary world, the merits have been long justly appreciated. It was composed in solitude and sorrow; and the melancholy cast of feeling which it exhibits sufficiently evinces the temper of the author's mind. The resemblance, in some respects, betwixt the tenor of the moral and that of *Candide*, is so striking, that Johnson himself admitted that if the authors could possibly have seen each other's manuscript, they could not have escaped the charge of plagiarism. But they resemble each other like a wholesome and a poisonous fruit. The object of the witty Frenchman is to lead to a distrust of the wisdom of the Great Governor of the Universe, by presuming to arraign him of incapacity before the creatures of his will. Johnson uses arguments drawn from the same premises, with the benevolent view of encouraging men to look to another and a better world for the satisfaction of wishes which, in this, seem only to be awakened in order to be disappointed. The one is a fiend—a merry devil, we grant—who scoffs at and derides human miseries; the other, a friendly though grave philosopher, who shows us the nothingness of earthly hopes, to teach us that our affections ought to be placed elsewhere.

The work can scarce be termed a narrative, being in a great measure void of incident; it is rather a set of moral dialogues on the various vicissitudes of human life, its follies, its fears, its hopes, and its wishes, and the disappointment in which all terminate. The style is in Johnson's best manner; enriched and rendered sonorous by the triads and quaternions which he so much loved, and balanced with an art which perhaps he derived from the learned Sir Thomas Browne. The reader may sometimes complain, with Boswell, that the unalleviated picture of human helplessness and misery leaves sadness upon the mind after perusal. But the moral is to be found in the conclusion of the *Vanity of Human Wishes*, a poem which treats of the same melancholy subject, and closes with this sublime strain of morality:—

[quotes final ten lines of the poem.]

80. Macaulay, review of Croker's edition of Boswell's *Life of Johnson*, *Edinburgh Review*

September 1831, liv, 1–38

Extracts from *Critical and Historical Essays* (second edition, 1843), i. 391–2, 396–407.

See Introduction, pp. 8, 34.

The characteristic peculiarity of [Johnson's] intellect was the union of great powers with low prejudices. If we judged of him by the best parts of his mind, we should place him almost as high as he was placed by the idolatry of Boswell; if by the worst parts of his mind, we should place him even below Boswell himself. Where he was not under the influence of some strange scruple, or some domineering passion, which prevented him from boldly and fairly investigating a subject, he was a wary and acute reasoner, a little too much inclined to scepticism, and a little too fond of paradox. No man was less likely to be imposed upon by fallacies in argument or by exaggerated statements of fact. But if, while he was beating down sophisms and exposing false testimony, some childish prejudices, such as would excite laughter in a well managed nursery, came across him, he was smitten as if by enchantment. His mind dwindled away under the spell from gigantic elevation to dwarfish littleness. Those who had lately been admiring its amplitude and its force were now as much astonished at its strange narrowness and feebleness as the fisherman in the Arabian tale, when he saw the Genie, whose stature had overshadowed the whole sea-coast, and whose might seemed equal to a contest with armies, contract himself to the dimensions of his small prison, and lie there the helpless slave of the charm of Solomon.

[some contradictions among Johnson's attitudes.]

The judgments which Johnson passed on books were, in his own time, regarded with superstitious veneration, and, in our time, are generally treated with indiscriminate contempt. They are the judgments of a strong but enslaved understanding. The mind of the critic was hedged round by an uninterrupted fence of prejudices and superstitions. Within his narrow limits, he displayed a vigour and an activity which ought to have enabled him to clear the barrier that confined him.

How it chanced that a man who reasoned on his premises so ably should assume his premises so foolishly, is one of the great mysteries of human nature. The same inconsistency may be observed in the schoolmen of the middle ages. Those writers show so much acuteness and force of mind in arguing on their wretched data, that a modern reader is perpetually at a loss to comprehend how such minds came by such data. Not a flaw in the superstructure of the theory which they are rearing escapes their vigilance. Yet they are blind to the obvious unsoundness of the foundation. It is the same with some eminent lawyers. Their legal arguments are intellectual prodigies, abounding with the happiest analogies and the most refined distinctions. The principles of their arbitrary science being once admitted, the statute-book and the reports being once assumed as the foundations of reasoning, these men must be allowed to be perfect masters of logic. But if a question arises as to the postulates on which their whole system rests, if they are called upon to vindicate the fundamental maxims of that system which they have passed their lives in studying, these very men often talk the language of savages or of children. Those who have listened to a man of this class in his own court, and who have witnessed the skill with which he analyses and digests a vast mass of evidence, or reconciles a crowd of precedents which at first sight seem contradictory, scarcely know him again when, a few hours later, they hear him speaking on the other side of Westminster Hall in his capacity of legislator. They can scarcely believe that the paltry quirks which are faintly heard through a storm of coughing, and which do not impose on the plainest country gentleman, can proceed from the same sharp and vigorous intellect which had excited their admiration under the same roof, and on the same day.

Johnson decided literary questions like a lawyer, not like a legislator. He never examined foundations where a point was already ruled. His whole code of criticism rested on pure assumption, for which he sometimes quoted a precedent or an authority, but rarely troubled himself to give a reason drawn from the nature of things. He took it for granted that the kind of poetry which flourished in his own time, which he had been accustomed to hear praised from his childhood, and which he had himself written with success, was the best kind of poetry. In his biographical work he has repeatedly laid it down as an undeniable proposition that during the latter part of the seventeenth century, and the earlier part of the eighteenth, English poetry had been in a constant progress of improvement. Waller, Denham, Dryden, and Pope, had been, according to him, the great reformers. He judged of all works of the imagination by the standard established among his own contemporaries. Though he allowed Homer to have been a greater man than Virgil, he seems to have thought the *Æneid* a greater poem than the *Iliad*. Indeed he well might have thought so; for he preferred Pope's *Iliad* to Homer's. He pronounced that, after Hoole's translation of Tasso, Fairfax's would hardly be reprinted. He could see no merit in our fine old English ballads, and always spoke with the most provoking contempt of Percy's fondness for them. Of the great original works of imagination which appeared during his time, Richardson's novels alone excited his admiration. He could see little or no merit in *Tom Jones*, in *Gulliver's Travels*, or in *Tristram Shandy*. To Thomson's *Castle of Indolence*, he vouchsafed only a line of cold commendation, of commendation much colder than what he has bestowed on the *Creation* of that portentous bore, Sir Richard Blackmore. Gray was, in his dialect, a barren rascal. Churchill was a blockhead. The contempt which he felt for the trash of Macpherson was indeed just; but it was, we suspect, just by chance. He despised the *Fingal* for the very reason which led many men of genius to admire it. He despised it, not because it was essentially common-place, but because it had a superficial air of originality.

He was undoubtedly an excellent judge of compositions fashioned on his own principles. But when a deeper philosophy was required, when he undertook to pronounce judgment on the works of those great minds which 'yield homage only to eternal laws,' his failure was ignominious. He criticized Pope's *Epitaphs* excellently. But his observations on Shakspeare's plays and Milton's poems seem to us for the most part as wretched as if they had been written by Rymer himself, whom we take to have been the worst critic that ever lived.

Some of Johnson's whims on literary subjects can be compared only to that strange nervous feeling which made him uneasy if he had not touched every post between the Mitre tavern and his own lodgings. His preference of Latin epitaphs to English epitaphs is an instance. An English epitaph, he said, would disgrace Smollett. He declared that he would not pollute the walls of Westminster Abbey with an English epitaph on Goldsmith.[1] What reason there can be for celebrating a British writer in Latin, which there was not for covering the Roman

[1] Boswell, *Life*, iii. 85.

arches of triumph with Greek inscriptions, or for commemorating the deeds of the heroes of Thermopylæ in Egyptian hieroglyphics, we are utterly unable to imagine.

On men and manners, at least on the men and manners of a particular place and a particular age, Johnson had certainly looked with a most observant and discriminating eye. His remarks on the education of children, on marriage, on the economy of families, on the rules of society, are always striking, and generally sound. In his writings, indeed, the knowledge of life which he possessed in an eminent degree is very imperfectly exhibited. Like those unfortunate chiefs of the middle ages who were suffocated by their own chain-mail and cloth of gold, his maxims perish under that load of words which was designed for their defence and their ornament. But it is clear from the remains of his conversation, that he had more of that homely wisdom which nothing but experience and observation can give than any writer since the time of Swift. If he had been content to write as he talked, he might have left books on the practical art of living superior to the *Directions to Servants*.

Yet even his remarks on society, like his remarks on literature, indicate a mind at least as remarkable for narrowness as for strength. He was no master of the great science of human nature. He had studied, not the genus man, but the species Londoner. Nobody was ever so thoroughly conversant with all the forms of life and all the shades of moral and intellectual character which were to be seen from Islington to the Thames, and from Hyde-Park corner to Mile-end green. But his philosophy stopped at the first turnpike-gate. Of the rural life of England he knew nothing; and he took it for granted that everybody who lived in the country was either stupid or miserable. 'Country gentlemen,' said he, 'must be unhappy; for they have not enough to keep their lives in motion;'[2] as if all those peculiar habits and associations which made Fleet Street and Charing Cross the finest views in the world to himself had been essential parts of human nature. Of remote countries and past times he talked with wild and ignorant presumption. 'The Athenians of the age of Demosthenes,' he said to Mrs. Thrale, 'were a people of brutes, a barbarous people.' In conversation with Sir Adam Ferguson he used similar language. 'The boasted Athenians,' he said, 'were barbarians. The mass of every people must be barbarous where there is no printing.'[3] The fact was this: he saw that a Londoner who could not read was a very stupid and brutal fellow: he saw that great refinement of taste and

[2] Ibid., v. 108.
[3] Ibid., ii. 170-1, 211.

activity of intellect were rarely found in a Londoner who had not read much; and, because it was by means of books that people acquired almost all their knowledge in the society with which he was acquainted, he concluded, in defiance of the strongest and clearest evidence, that the human mind can be cultivated by means of books alone. An Athenian citizen might possess very few volumes; and the largest library to which he had access might be much less valuable than Johnson's bookcase in Bolt Court. But the Athenian might pass every morning in conversation with Socrates, and might hear Pericles speak four or five times every month. He saw the plays of Sophocles and Aristophanes: he walked amidst the friezes of Phidias and the paintings of Zeuxis: he knew by heart the choruses of Æschylus: he heard the rhapsodist at the corner of the street reciting the shield of Achilles, or the Death of Argus: he was a legislator, conversant with high questions of alliance, revenue, and war: he was a soldier, trained under a liberal and generous discipline: he was a judge, compelled every day to weigh the effect of opposite arguments. These things were in themselves an education, an education eminently fitted, not, indeed, to form exact or profound thinkers, but to give quickness to the perceptions, delicacy to the taste, fluency to the expression, and politeness to the manners. All this was overlooked. An Athenian who did not improve his mind by reading was, in Johnson's opinion, much such a person as a Cockney who made his mark, much such a person as black Frank before he went to school, and far inferior to a parish clerk or a printer's devil.

Johnson's friends have allowed that he carried to a ridiculous extreme his unjust contempt for foreigners. He pronounced the French to be a very silly people, much behind us, stupid, ignorant creatures. And this judgment he formed after having been at Paris about a month, during which he would not talk French, for fear of giving the natives an advantage over him in conversation. He pronounced them, also, to be an indelicate people, because a French footman touched the sugar with his fingers. That ingenious and amusing traveller, M. Simond, has defended his countrymen very successfully against Johnson's accusation, and has pointed out some English practices which, to an impartial spectator, would seem at least as inconsistent with physical cleanliness and social decorum as those which Johnson so bitterly reprehended. To the sage, as Boswell loves to call him, it never occurred to doubt that there must be something eternally and immutably good in the usages to which he had been accustomed. In fact, Johnson's remarks on society beyond the bills of mortality, are generally of much the same kind with those of honest Tom Dawson, the English footman in Dr. Moore's *Zeluco*. 'Suppose the king of France has no sons, but only a daughter, then, when the king dies, this here daughter, according to that there law, cannot be made queen, but the next near relative, provided he is a man, is made king, and not the last king's daughter, which, to be sure, is very unjust. The French footguards are dressed in blue, and all the marching regiments in white, which has a very foolish appearance for soldiers; and as for blue regimentals, it is only fit for the blue horse or the artillery.'[4]

Johnson's visit to the Hebrides introduced him to a state of society completely new to him; and a salutary suspicion of his own deficiencies seems on that occasion to have crossed his mind for the first time. He confessed, in the last paragraph of his *Journey*, that his thoughts on national manners were the thoughts of one who had seen but little, of one who had passed his time almost wholly in cities. This feeling, however, soon passed away. It is remarkable that to the last he entertained a fixed contempt for all those modes of life and those studies which tend to emancipate the mind from the prejudices of a particular age or a particular nation. Of foreign travel and of history he spoke with the fierce and boisterous contempt of ignorance. 'What does a man learn by travelling? Is Beauclerk the better for travelling? What did Lord Charlemont learn in his travels, except that there was a snake in one of the pyramids of Egypt?'[5] History was, in his opinion, to use the fine expression of Lord Plunkett, an old almanack: historians could, as he conceived, claim no higher dignity than that of almanack-makers; and his favourite historians were those who, like Lord Hailes, aspired to no higher dignity. He always spoke with contempt of Robertson. Hume he would not even read. He affronted one of his friends for talking to him about Catiline's conspiracy, and declared that he never desired to hear of the Punic war again as long as he lived.[6]

Assuredly one fact which does not directly affect our own interests, considered in itself, is no better worth knowing than another fact. The fact that there is a snake in a pyramid, or the fact that Hannibal crossed the Alps, are in themselves as unprofitable to us as the fact that there is a green blind in a particular house in Threadneedle Street, or the fact that a Mr. Smith comes into the city every morning on the top of one of the Blackwall stages. But it is certain that those who will not crack the shell of history will never get at the kernel. Johnson, with hasty

[4] John Moore, *Zeluco*, 1786, chapter 73.   [5] Boswell, *Life*, iii. 352.
[6] Ibid., ii. 366, 236–7; iii. 206n. 1.

arrogance, pronounced the kernel worthless, because he saw no value in the shell. The real use of travelling to distant countries and of studying the annals of past times is to preserve men from the contraction of mind which those can hardly escape whose whole communion is with one generation and one neighbourhood, who arrive at conclusions by means of an induction not sufficiently copious, and who therefore constantly confound exceptions with rules, and accidents with essential properties. In short, the real use of travelling and of studying history is to keep men from being what Tom Dawson was in fiction, and Samuel Johnson in reality.

Johnson, as Mr. Burke most justly observed, appears far greater in Boswell's books than in his own.[7] His conversation appears to have been quite equal to his writings in matter, and far superior to them in manner. When he talked, he clothed his wit and his sense in forcible and natural expressions. As soon as he took his pen in his hand to write for the public, his style became systematically vicious. All his books are written in a learned language, in a language which nobody hears from his mother or his nurse, in a language in which nobody ever quarrels, or drives bargains, or makes love, in a language in which nobody ever thinks. It is clear that Johnson himself did not think in the dialect in which he wrote. The expressions which came first to his tongue were simple, energetic, and picturesque. When he wrote for publication, he did his sentences out of English into Johnsonese. His letters from the Hebrides to Mrs. Thrale are the original of that work of which the *Journey to the Hebrides* is the translation; and it is amusing to compare the two versions. 'When we were taken up stairs,' says he in one of his letters, 'a dirty fellow bounced out of the bed on which one of us was to lie.' This incident is recorded in the *Journey* as follows: 'Out of one of the beds on which we were to repose started up, at our entrance, a man black as a Cyclops from the forge.'[8] Sometimes Johnson translated aloud. '*The Rehearsal*,' he said, very unjustly, 'has not wit enough to keep it sweet;' then, after a pause, 'it has not vitality enough to preserve it from putrefaction.'[9]

Mannerism is pardonable, and is sometimes even agreeable, when the manner, though vicious, is natural. Few readers, for example, would be willing to part with the mannerism of Milton or of Burke. But a mannerism which does not sit easy on the mannerist, which has been adopted on principle, and which can be sustained only by constant effort, is always offensive. And such is the mannerism of Johnson.

[7] See document No. 75, headnote.   [8] *Journey*, 43.   [9] Boswell, *Life*, iv. 320.

The characteristic faults of his style are so familiar to all our readers, and have been so often burlesqued, that it is almost superfluous to point them out. It is well known that he made less use than any other eminent writer of those strong plain words, Anglo-Saxon or Norman-French, of which the roots lie in the inmost depths of our language; and that he felt a vicious partiality for terms which, long after our own speech had been fixed, were borrowed from the Greek and Latin, and which, therefore, even when lawfully naturalised, must be considered as born aliens, not entitled to rank with the king's English. His constant practice of padding out a sentence with useless epithets, till it became as stiff as the bust of an exquisite,[10] his antithetical forms of expression, constantly employed even where there is no opposition in the ideas expressed, his big words wasted on little things, his harsh inversions, so widely different from those graceful and easy inversions which give variety, spirit, and sweetness to the expression of our great old writers, all these peculiarities have been imitated by his admirers and parodied by his assailants, till the public has become sick of the subject.

Goldsmith said to him, very wittily and very justly, 'If you were to write a fable about little fishes, doctor, you would make the little fishes talk like whales.'[11] No man surely ever had so little talent for personation as Johnson. Whether he wrote in the character of a disappointed legacy-hunter or an empty town fop, of a crazy virtuoso or a flippant coquette, he wrote in the same pompous and unbending style. His speech, like Sir Piercy Shafton's Euphuistic eloquence, bewrayed him under every disguise.[12] Euphelia and Rhodoclea talk as finely as Imlac the poet or Seged, Emperor of Ethiopia. The gay Cornelia describes her reception at the country-house of her relations, in such terms as these: 'I was surprised, after the civilities of my first reception, to find, instead of the leisure and tranquillity which a rural life always promises, and, if well conducted, might always afford, a confused wildness of care, and a tumultuous hurry of diligence, by which every face was clouded, and every motion agitated.' The gentle Tranquilla informs us, that she 'had not passed the earlier part of life without the flattery of courtship, and the joys of triumph; but had danced the round of gaiety amidst the murmurs of envy and the gratulations of applause, had been attended from pleasure to pleasure by the great, the sprightly, and the vain, and had seen her regard solicited by the obsequiousness of gallantry, the gaiety of

[10] i.e. a dandy or fop.
[11] Boswell, *Life*, ii. 231.
[12] In Walter Scott's *Monastery*, 1820.

wit, and the timidity of love.'[13] Surely Sir John Falstaff himself did not wear his petticoats with a worse grace. The reader may well cry out, with honest Sir Hugh Evans, 'I like not when a 'oman has a great peard: I spy a great peard under her muffler.'*

We had something more to say. But our article is already too long; and we must close it. We would fain part in good humour from the hero, from the biographer, and even from the editor who, ill as he has performed his task, has at least this claim to our gratitude, that he has induced us to read Boswell's book again. As we close it, the club-room is before us, and the table on which stands the omelet for Nugent, and the lemons for Johnson. There are assembled those heads which live for ever on the canvass of Reynolds. There are the spectacles of Burke and the tall thin form of Langton, the courtly sneer of Beauclerk and the beaming smile of Garrick, Gibbon tapping his snuff-box and Sir Joshua with his trumpet in his ear. In the foreground is that strange figure which is as familiar to us as the figures of those among whom we have been brought up, the gigantic body, the huge massy face, seamed with the scars of disease, the brown coat, the black worsted stockings, the grey wig with the scorched foretop, the dirty hands, the nails bitten and pared to the quick. We see the eyes and mouth moving with convulsive twitches; we see the heavy form rolling; we hear it puffing; and then comes the 'Why, sir!' and the 'What then, sir?' and the 'No, sir!' and the 'You don't see your way through the question, sir!'

What a singular destiny has been that of this remarkable man! To be regarded in his own age as a classic, and in ours as a companion! To receive from his contemporaries that full homage which men of genius have in general received only from posterity! To be more intimately known to posterity than other men are known to their contemporaries! That kind of fame which is commonly the most transient is, in his case, the most durable. The reputation of those writings, which he probably expected to be immortal, is every day fading; while those peculiarities of manner and that careless table-talk the memory of which, he probably thought, would die with him, are likely to be remembered as long as the English language is spoken in any quarter of the globe.

* It is proper to observe that this passage [*Merry Wives of Windsor*, IV. ii. 205] bears a very close resemblance to a passage in the *Rambler* (No. 20). The resemblance may possibly be the effect of unconscious plagiarism.

---

[13] See *Rambler* Nos. 42, 46, for Euphelia; No. 62 for Rhodoclia; Nos. 204–5 for Seged; No. 51 for Cornelia; No. 119 for Tranquilla.

81. Thomas Carlyle, review of Croker's edition of Boswell's *Life of Johnson, Fraser's Magazine*

May 1832, v, 379–413

Extracts from *Collected Works*, 1869, iv. 42, 55–8, 77–81, 89–106.

Though he reinforced the myopic view of Johnson found in Macaulay's review-essay, Carlyle (1795–1881) was more sensitive to the tragic depths in the English 'Ulysses'. His was a highly subjective view; Johnson had been transformed into a Carlylean hero, as his appearance in *Heroes and Hero-Worship* (1841) later confirmed. Yet, despite the mannered style, there is a compelling force in the expression of Carlyle's insights. See Introduction, pp. 8, 34

As for [Boswell's *Life*] itself, questionless the universal favour entertained for it is well merited. In worth as a Book we have rated it beyond any other product of the eighteenth century: all Johnson's own Writings, laborious and in their kind genuine above most, stand on a quite inferior level to it; already, indeed, they are becoming obsolete for this generation; and for some future generation may be valuable chiefly as Prolegomena and expository Scholia to this *Johnsoniad* of Boswell. Which of us but remembers, as one of the sunny spots in his existence, the day when he opened these airy volumes, fascinating him by a true natural magic! It was as if the curtains of the Past were drawn aside, and we looked mysteriously into a kindred country, where dwelt our Fathers; inexpressibly dear to us, but which had seemed forever hidden from our eyes. For the dead Night had engulfed it; all was gone, vanished as if it had not been. Nevertheless, wondrously given back to us, there once more it lay; all bright, lucid, blooming; a little island of Creation amid the circumambient Void. There it still lies; like a thing stationary, imperishable, over which changeful Time were now accumulating itself in vain, and could not, any longer, harm it, or hide it. . . .

Amid those dull millions, who, as a dull flock, roll hither and thither, whithersoever they are led; and seem all sightless and slavish, accomplishing, attempting little save what the animal instinct in its somewhat higher kind might teach, To keep themselves and their young ones alive, —are scattered here and there superior natures, whose eye is not destitute of free vision, nor their heart of free volition. These latter, therefore, examine and determine, not what others do, but what it is right to do; towards which, and which only, will they, with such force as is given them, resolutely endeavour: for if the Machine, living or inanimate, is merely *fed*, or desires to be fed, and so *works*; the Person can *will*, and so *do*. These are properly our Men, our Great Men; the guides of the dull host,—which follows them as by an irrevocable decree. They are the chosen of the world: they had this rare faculty not only of 'supposing' and 'inclining to think,' but of *knowing* and *believing;* the nature of their being was, that they lived not by Hearsay, but by clear Vision; while others hovered and swam along, in the grand Vanity-fair of the World, blinded by the mere Shows of things, these saw into the Things themselves, and could walk as men having an eternal loadstar, and with their feet on sure paths. Thus was there a *Reality* in their existence; something of a perennial character; in virtue of which indeed it is that the memory of them is perennial. Whoso belongs only to his own age, and reverences only *its* gilt Popinjays or soot-smeared Mumbojumbos, must needs die with it: though he have been crowned seven times in the Capitol, or seventy-and-seven times, and Rumour have blown his praises to all the four winds, deafening every ear therewith,—it avails not; there was nothing universal, nothing eternal in him; he must fade away, even as the Popinjay-gildings and Scarecrow-apparel, which he could not see through. The great man does, in good truth, belong to his own age; nay more so than any other man; being properly the synopsis and epitome of such age with its interests and influences: but belongs likewise to all ages, otherwise he is not great. What was transitory in him passes away; and an immortal part remains, the significance of which is in strict speech inexhaustible,—as that of every *real* object is. Aloft, conspicuous, on his enduring basis, he stands there, serene, unaltering; silently addresses to every new generation a new lesson and monition. Well is his Life worth writing, worth interpreting; and ever, in the new dialect of new times, of re-writing and re-interpreting.

Of such chosen men was Samuel Johnson: not ranking among the highest, or even the high, yet distinctly admitted into that sacred band; whose existence was no idle Dream, but a Reality which he transacted *awake;* nowise a Clothes-horse and Patent Digester, but a genuine Man. By nature he was gifted for the noblest of earthly tasks, that of Priesthood, and Guidance of mankind; by destiny, moreover, he was appointed to this task, and did actually, according to strength, fulfil the same: so that always the question, *How; in what spirit; under what shape?* remains for us to be asked and answered concerning him. For as the highest Gospel was a Biography, so is the Life of every good man still an indubitable Gospel, and preaches to the eye and heart and whole man, so that Devils even must believe and tremble, these gladdest tidings: 'Man is heaven-born; not the thrall of Circumstances, of Necessity, but the victorious subduer thereof: behold how he can become the "Announcer of himself and of his Freedom;" and is ever what the Thinker has named him, "the Messias of Nature".'—Yes, Reader, all this that thou hast so often heard about 'force of circumstances,' 'the creature of the time,' 'balancing of motives,' and who knows what melancholy stuff to the like purport, wherein thou, as in a nightmare Dream, sittest paralysed, and hast no force left,—was in very truth, if Johnson and waking men are to be credited, little other than a hag-ridden vision of death-sleep; some *half*-fact, more fatal at times than a whole falsehood. Shake it off; awake; up and be doing, even as it is given thee!

The Contradiction which yawns wide enough in every Life, which it is the meaning and task of Life to reconcile, was in Johnson's wider than in most. Seldom, for any man, has the contrast between the ethereal heavenward side of things, and the dark sordid earthward, been more glaring: whether we look at Nature's work with him or Fortune's, from first to last, heterogeneity, as of sunbeams and miry clay, is on all hands manifest. Whereby indeed, only this was declared, That *much Life* had been given him; many things to triumph over, a great work to *do*. Happily also he did it; better than the most.

Nature had given him a high, keen-visioned, almost poetic soul; yet withal imprisoned it in an inert, unsightly body: he that could never rest had not limbs that would move with him, but only roll and waddle: the inward eye, all-penetrating, all-embracing, must look through bodily windows that were dim, half-blinded; he so loved men, and 'never once *saw* the human face divine'![1] Not less did he prize the love of men; he was eminently social; the approbation of his fellows was dear to him, 'valuable,' as he owned, 'if from the meanest of human beings:' yet the first impression he produced on every man was to be one of aversion, almost of disgust. By Nature it was farther ordered that

[1] Milton, *Paradise Lost*, III. 44.

the imperious Johnson should be born poor: the ruler-soul, strong in its native royalty, generous, uncontrollable, like the lion of the woods, was to be housed, then, in such a dwelling-place: of Disfigurement, Disease, and lastly of a Poverty which itself made him the servant of servants. Thus was the born king likewise a born slave: the divine spirit of Music must awake imprisoned amid dull-croaking universal Discords; the Ariel finds himself encased in the coarse hulls of a Caliban. So is it more or less, we know (and thou, O Reader, knowest and feelest even now), with all men: yet with the fewest men in any such degree as with Johnson.

[It was Johnson's misfortune to encounter two major problems. First, with the decay of private patronage he had to become a professional writer and depend on public support. Second, his age was beset by 'Hypocrisy and Atheism', and traditional values both political and religious no longer commanded general acceptance.]

Such was that same 'twofold Problem' set before Samuel Johnson. Consider all these moral difficulties; and add to them the fearful aggravation, which lay in that other circumstance, that he needed a continual appeal to the Public, must continually produce a certain impression and conviction on the Public; that if he did not, he ceased to have 'provision for the day that was passing over him,' he could not any longer live! How a vulgar character, once launched into this wild element; driven onwards by Fear and Famine; without other aim than to clutch what Provender (of Enjoyment in any kind) he could get, always if possible keeping *quite* clear of the Gallows and Pillory, that is to say, minding heedfully both 'person' and 'character,'—would have floated hither and thither in it; and contrived to eat some three repasts daily, and wear some three suits yearly, and then to depart and disappear, having consumed his last ration: all this might be worth knowing, but were in itself a trivial knowledge. How a noble man, resolute for the Truth, to whom Shams and Lies were once for all an abomination, was to act in it: *here* lay the mystery. By what methods, by what gifts of eye and hand, does a heroic Samuel Johnson, now when cast forth into that waste Chaos of Authorship, maddest of things, a mingled Phlegethon and Fleet-ditch, with its floating lumber, and sea-krakens, and mud-spectres, —shape himself a voyage; of the *transient* drift-wood, and the *enduring* iron, build him a sea-worthy Life-boat, and sail therein, undrowned, unpolluted, through the roaring 'mother of dead dogs,' onwards to an eternal Landmark, and City that hath foundations? This high question is even the one answered in Boswell's Book; which Book we therefore, not so falsely, have named a *Heroic Poem;* for in it there lies the whole argument of such. Glory to our brave Samuel! He accomplished this wonderful Problem; and now through long generations we point to him, and say: Here also was a Man; let the world once more have assurance of a Man!

Had there been in Johnson, now when afloat on that confusion worse confounded of grandeur and squalor, no light but an earthly outward one, he too must have made shipwreck. With his diseased body, and vehement voracious heart, how easy for him to become a *carpe-diem*[2] Philosopher, like the rest, and live and die as miserably as any Boyce[3] of that Brotherhood! But happily there was a higher light for him; shining as a lamp to his path; which, in all paths, would teach him to act and walk not as a fool, but as wise, and in those evil days too 'redeeming the time.'[4] Under dimmer or clearer manifestations, a Truth had been revealed to him: I also am a Man; even in this unutterable element of Authorship, I may live as beseems a Man! That Wrong is not only different from Right, but that it is in strict scientific terms *infinitely* different; even as the gaining of the whole world set against the losing of one's own soul, or (as Johnson had it) a Heaven set against a Hell; that in all situations out of the Pit of Tophet, wherein a living Man has stood or can stand, there is actually a Prize of quite *infinite* value placed within his reach, namely a *Duty* for him to do: this highest Gospel, which forms the basis and worth of all other Gospels whatsoever, had been revealed to Samuel Johnson; and the man had believed it, and laid it faithfully to heart. Such knowledge of the *transcendental,* immeasurable character of Duty we call the basis of all Gospels, the essence of all Religion: he who with his whole soul knows not this, as yet knows nothing, as yet *is* properly nothing.

This, happily for him, Johnson was one of those that knew: under a certain authentic Symbol it stood forever present to his eyes: a Symbol, indeed, waxing old as doth a garment; yet which had guided forward, as their Banner and celestial Pillar of Fire, innumerable saints and witnesses, the fathers of our modern world; and for him also had still a sacred significance. It does not appear that at any time Johnson was what we call irreligious: but in his sorrows and isolation, when hope died away, and only a long vista of suffering and toil lay before him to the

2 Horace, *Odes,* I. xi. 8 ('make the most of today').
3 Samuel Boyse (1708–49), a destitute minor poet.
4 Ephesians 5: 16.

end, then first did Religion shine forth in its meek, everlasting clearness; even as the stars do in black night, which in the daytime and dusk were hidden by inferior lights. How a true man, in the midst of errors and uncertainties, shall work out for himself a sure Life-truth; and adjusting the transient to the eternal, amid the fragments of ruined Temples build up, with toil and pain, a little Altar for himself, and worship there; how Samuel Johnson, in the era of Voltaire, can purify and fortify his soul, and hold real communion with the Highest, 'in the Church of St. Clement Danes:'[5] this too stands all unfolded in his Biography, and is among the most touching and memorable things there; a thing to be looked at with pity, admiration, awe. Johnson's Religion was as the light of life to him; without it his heart was all sick, dark and had no guidance left.

He is now enlisted, or impressed, into that unspeakable shoeblack-seraph Army of Authors; but can feel hereby that he fights under a celestial flag, and will quit him like a man. The first grand requisite, an assured heart, he therefore has: what his outward equipments and accoutrements are, is the next question; an important, though inferior one. His intellectual stock, intrinsically viewed, is perhaps inconsiderable: the furnishings of an English School and English University; good knowledge of the Latin tongue, a more uncertain one of Greek: this is a rather slender stock of Education wherewith to front the world. But then it is to be remembered that his world was England; that such was the culture England commonly supplied and expected. Besides, Johnson has been a voracious reader, though a desultory one, and oftenest in strange scholastic, too obsolete Libraries; he has also rubbed shoulders with the press of Actual Life for some thirty years now: views or hallucinations of innumerable things are weltering to and fro in him. Above all, be his weapons what they may, he has an arm that can wield them. Nature has given him her choicest gift,—an open eye and heart. He will look on the world, wheresoever he can catch a glimpse of it, with eager curiosity: to the last, we find this a striking characteristic of him; for all human interests he has a sense; the meanest handicraftsman could interest him, even in extreme age, by speaking of his craft: the ways of men are all interesting to him; any human thing, that he did not know, he wished to know. Reflection, moreover, Meditation, was what he practised incessantly, with or without his will: for the mind of the man was earnest, deep as well as humane. Thus would the world, such fragments of it as he could survey, form itself, or continually tend

<hr>

[5] Boswell, *Life*, ii. 214 *et al.*

to form itself, into a coherent Whole; on any and on all phases of which, his vote and voice must be well worth listening to. As a Speaker of the Word, he will speak real words; no idle jargon or hollow triviality will issue from him. His aim too is clear, attainable; that of *working for his wages:* let him *do* this honestly, and all else will follow of its own accord.

With such omens, into such a warfare, did Johnson go forth. A rugged hungry Kerne or Gallowglass, as we called him: yet indomitable; in whom lay the true spirit of a Soldier.

[Further reflections on Johnson's life as 'a victorious Battle of a free, true Man'.]

To estimate the quantity of Work that Johnson performed, how much poorer the World were had it wanted him, can, as in all such cases, never be accurately done; cannot, till after some longer space, be approximately done. All work is as seed sown; it grows and spreads, and sows itself anew, and so, in endless palingenesia, lives and works. To Johnson's Writings, good and solid, and still profitable as they are, we have already rated his Life and Conversation as superior. By the one and by the other, who shall compute what effects have been produced, and are still, and into deep Time, producing?

So much, however, we can already see: It is now some three quarters of a century that Johnson has been the Prophet of the English; the man by whose light the English people, in public and in private, more than by any other man's, have guided their existence. Higher light than that immediately *practical* one; higher virtue than an honest PRUDENCE, he could not then communicate; nor perhaps could they have received: such light, such virtue, however, he did communicate. How to thread this labyrinthic Time, the fallen and falling Ruin of Times; to silence vain Scruples, hold firm to the last the fragments of old Belief, and with earnest eye still discern some glimpses of a true path, and go forward thereon, 'in a world where there is much to be done, and little to be known:'[6] this is what Samuel Johnson, by act and word, taught his Nation; what his Nation received and learned of him, more than of any other. We can view him as the preserver and transmitter of whatsoever was genuine in the spirit of Toryism; which genuine spirit, it is now becoming manifest, must again embody itself in all new forms of Society, be what they may, that are to exist, and have continuance— elsewhere than on Paper. The *last* in many things, Johnson was the last

[6] From Johnson's prayer 'Against inquisitive and perplexing thoughts', quoted in Boswell, *Life*, iv. 370 n. 3.

genuine Tory; the last of Englishmen who, with strong voice and wholly-believing heart, preached the Doctrine of Standing-still; who, without selfishness or slavishness, reverenced the existing Powers, and could assert the privileges of rank, though himself poor, neglected and plebeian; who had heart-devoutness with heart-hatred of cant, was orthodox-religious with his eyes open; and in all things and everywhere spoke out in plain English, from a soul wherein jesuitism could find no harbour, and with the front and tone not of a diplomatist but of a man.

This last of the Tories was Johnson: not Burke, as is often said; Burke was essentially a Whig, and only, on reaching the verge of the chasm towards which Whiggism from the first was inevitably leading, recoiled; and, like a man vehement rather than earnest, a resplendent far-sighted Rhetorician rather than a deep sure Thinker, recoiled with no measure, convulsively, and damaging what he drove back with him.

In a world which exists by the balance of Antagonisms, the respective merit of the Conservator and the Innovator must ever remain debatable. Great, in the mean while, and undoubted for both sides, is the merit of him who, in a day of Change, walks wisely, honestly. Johnson's aim was in itself an impossible one: this of stemming the eternal Flood of Time; of clutching all things, and anchoring them down, and saying, Move not!—how could it, or should it, ever have success? The strongest man can but retard the current partially and for a short hour. Yet even in such shortest retardation may not an inestimable value lie? If England has escaped the blood-bath of a French Revolution; and may yet, in virtue of this delay and of the experience it has given, work out her deliverance calmly into a new Era, let Samuel Johnson, beyond all contemporary or succeeding men, have the praise for it. We said above that he was appointed to be Ruler of the British Nation for a season: whoso will look beyond the surface, into the heart of the world's movements, may find that all Pitt Administrations, and Continental Subsidies, and Waterloo victories, rested on the possibility of making England, yet a little while, *Toryish*, Loyal to the Old; and this again on the anterior reality, that the Wise had found such Loyalty still practicable, and recommendable. England had its Hume, as France had its Voltaires and Diderots; but the Johnson was peculiar to us.

If we ask now, by what endowment it mainly was that Johnson realised such a Life for himself and others; what quality of character the main phenomena of his Life may be most naturally deduced from, and his other qualities most naturally subordinated to, in our conception of him, perhaps the answer were: The quality of Courage, of Valour; that Johnson was a Brave Man. . . .

The Courage we desire and prize is not the Courage to die decently, but to live manfully. This, when by God's grace it has been given, lies deep in the soul; like genial heat, fosters all other virtues and gifts; without it they could not live. In spite of our innumerable Waterloos and Peterloos, and such campaigning as there has been, this Courage we allude to, and call the only true one, is perhaps rarer in these last ages than it has been in any other since the Saxon Invasion under Hengist. Altogether extinct it can never be among men; otherwise the species Man were no longer for this world: here and there, in all times, under various guises, men are sent hither not only to demonstrate but exhibit it, and testify, as from heart to heart, that it is still possible, still practicable.

Johnson, in the eighteenth century, and as Man of Letters, was one of such; and, in good truth, 'the bravest of the brave.' What mortal could have more to war with? Yet, as we saw, he yielded not, faltered not; he fought, and even, such was his blessedness, prevailed. Whoso will understand what it is to have a man's heart may find that, since the time of John Milton, no braver heart had beat in any English bosom than Samuel Johnson now bore. Observe too that he never called himself brave, never felt himself to be so; the more completely *was* so. No Giant Despair, no Golgotha Death-dance or Sorcerer's-Sabbath of 'Literary Life in London,' appals this pilgrim; he works resolutely for deliverance; in still defiance steps stoutly along. The thing that is given him to do, he can make himself do; what is to be endured, he can endure in silence.

[Johnson's capacity for endurance.]

Closely connected with this quality of Valour, partly as springing from it, partly as protected by it, are the more recognisable qualities of Truthfulness in word and thought, and Honesty in action. There is a reciprocity of influence here: for as the realising of Truthfulness and Honesty is the life-light and great aim of Valour, so without Valour they cannot, in anywise, be realised. Now, in spite of all practical short-comings, no one that sees into the significance of Johnson will say that his prime object was not Truth. In conversation, doubtless, you may observe him, on occasion, fighting as if for victory;—and must pardon these ebulliences of a careless hour, which were not without temptation and provocation. Remark likewise two things: that such prize-arguings were ever on merely superficial debatable questions; and then that they were argued generally by the fair laws of battle and logic-fence, by one cunning in that same. If their purpose was excusable, their effect was harmless, perhaps beneficial: that of taming noisy mediocrity, and showing it another side of a debatable matter; to see *both* sides of which was, for the first time, to see the Truth of it. In his Writings themselves are errors enough, crabbed prepossessions enough; yet these also of a quite extraneous and accidental nature, nowhere a wilful shutting of the eyes to the Truth. Nay, is there not everywhere a heartfelt discernment, singular, almost admirable, if we consider through what confused conflicting lights and hallucinations it had to be attained, of the highest everlasting Truth, and beginning of all Truths: this namely, that man is ever, and even in the age of Wilkes and Whitefield, a Revelation of God to man; and lives, moves and has his being in Truth only; is either true, or, in strict speech, *is* not at all?

Quite spotless, on the other hand, is Johnson's love of Truth, if we look at it as expressed in Practice, as what we have named Honesty of action. 'Clear your mind of Cant;'[7] *clear* it, throw Cant utterly away: such was his emphatic, repeated precept; and did not he himself faithfully conform to it? The Life of this man has been, as it were, turned inside out, and examined with microscopes by friend and foe; yet was there no Lie found in him. His Doings and Writings are not *shows* but *performances*: you may weigh them in the balance, and they will stand weight. Not a line, not a sentence is dishonestly done, is other than it pretends to be. Alas! and he wrote not out of inward inspiration, but to earn his wages: and with that grand perennial tide of 'popular delusion' flowing by; in whose waters he nevertheless refused to fish, to whose rich oyster-beds the dive was too muddy for him. Observe, again, with what innate hatred of Cant, he takes for himself, and offers to others, the lowest possible view of his business, which he followed with such nobleness. Motive for writing he had none, as he often said, but money; and yet he wrote *so*. Into the region of Poetic Art he indeed never rose; there was no *ideal* without him avowing itself in his work: the nobler was that unavowed *ideal* which lay within him, and commanded saying, Work out thy Artisanship in the spirit of an Artist! They who talk loudest about the dignity of Art, and fancy that they too are Artistic guild-brethren, and of the Celestials,—let them consider well what manner of man this was, who felt himself to be only a hired day-labourer. A labourer that was worthy of his hire; that has laboured not as an eye-servant but as one found faithful! Neither was Johnson in those days perhaps wholly a unique. Time was when, for money, you might have

[7] Boswell, *Life*, iv. 221.

ware: and needed not, in all departments, in that of the Epic Poem, in that of the Blacking-bottle, to rest content with the mere *persuasion* that you had ware. It was a happier time. But as yet the seventh Apocalyptic Bladder (of PUFFERY) had not been rent open,—to whirl and grind, as in a West-Indian Tornado, all earthly trades and things into wreck, and dust, and consummation,—and regeneration. Be it quickly, since it must be!—

That Mercy can dwell only with Valour, is an old sentiment or proposition; which in Johnson again receives confirmation. Few men on record have had a more merciful, tenderly affectionate nature than old Samuel. He was called the Bear;[8] and did indeed too often look, and roar, like one; being forced to it in his own defence: yet within that shaggy exterior of his there beat a heart warm as a mother's, soft as a little child's. Nay generally, his very roaring was but the anger of affection: the rage of a Bear, if you will; but of a Bear bereaved of her whelps. Touch his Religion, glance at the Church of England, or the Divine Right; and he was upon you! These things were his Symbols of all that was good and precious for men; his very Ark of the Covenant: whoso laid hand on them tore asunder his heart of hearts. Not out of hatred to the opponent, but of love to the thing opposed, did Johnson grow cruel, fiercely contradictory: this is an important distinction; never to be forgotten in our censure of his conversational outrages. But observe also with what humanity, what openness of love, he can attach himself to all things: to a blind old woman, to a Doctor Levett, to a cat 'Hodge.' 'His thoughts in the latter part of his life were frequently employed on his deceased friends; he often muttered these or suchlike sentences: "Poor man! and then he died." ' How he patiently converts his poor home into a Lazaretto; endures, for long years, the contradiction of the miserable and unreasonable; with him unconnected, save that they had no other to yield them refuge! Generous old man! Worldly possession he has little; yet of this he gives freely; from his own hard-earned shilling, the half-pence for the poor, that 'waited his coming out,' are not withheld: the poor 'waited the coming out' of one not quite so poor! A Sterne can write sentimentalities on Dead Asses: Johnson has a rough voice; but he finds the wretched Daughter of Vice fallen down in the streets; carries her home on his own shoulders, and like a good Samaritan gives help to the help-needing, worthy or unworthy.[9] Ought not Charity, even in that sense, to cover a multitude of sins? No Penny-a-

[8] Boswell, *Life*, ii. 66.
[9] Ibid., ii. 119; iv. 321–2.

week Committee-Lady, no manager of Soup-Kitchens, dancer at Charity-Balls, was this rugged, stern-visaged man: but where, in all England, could there have been found another soul so full of Pity, a hand so heavenlike bounteous as his? The widow's mite, we know, was greater than all the other gifts.

Perhaps it is this divine feeling of Affection, throughout manifested, that principally attracts us towards Johnson. A true brother of men is he; and filial lover of the Earth; who, with little bright spots of Attachment, 'where lives and works some loved one,' has beautified 'this rough solitary Earth into a peopled garden.' Lichfield, with its mostly dull and limited inhabitants, is to the last one of the sunny islets for him: *Salve magna parens*![10] Or read those Letters on his Mother's death: what a genuine solemn grief and pity lies recorded there; a looking back into the Past, unspeakably mournful, unspeakably tender. And yet calm, sublime; for he must now act, not look; his venerated Mother has been taken from him; but he must now write a *Rasselas* to defray her funeral! Again in this little incident, recorded in his Book of Devotion, are not the tones of sacred Sorrow and Greatness deeper than in many a blank-verse Tragedy; —as, indeed, 'the fifth act of a Tragedy,' though unrhymed, does 'lie in every death-bed, were it a peasant's, and of straw':

Sunday, October 18, 1767. Yesterday, at about ten in the morning, I took my leave forever of my dear old friend, Catherine Chambers, who came to live with my mother about 1724, and has been but little parted from us since. She buried my father, my brother and my mother. She is now fifty-eight years old.

I desired all to withdraw; then told her that we were to part forever; that as Christians, we should part with prayer; and that I would, if she was willing, say a short prayer beside her. She expressed great desire to hear me; and held up her poor hands as she lay in bed with great fervour, while I prayed kneeling by her.

I then kissed her. She told me that to part was the greatest pain she had ever felt, and that she hoped we should meet again in a better place. I expressed, with swelled eyes and great emotion of tenderness, the same hopes. We kissed and parted; I humbly hope, to meet again, and to part no more.[11]

Tears trickling down the granite rock: a soft well of Pity springs within!—Still more tragical is this other scene: 'Johnson mentioned that he could not in general accuse himself of having been an undutiful son. "Once, indeed," said he, "I was disobedient: I refused to attend my father to Uttoxeter market. Pride was the source of that refusal, and the remembrance of it was painful. A few years ago I desired to atone for

10 Virgil, *Georgics*, II. 173 ('Hail noble parent').
11 Boswell, *Life*, ii. 43–4.

this fault." '12—But by what method?—What method was now possible? Hear it; the words are again given as his own, though here evidently by a less capable reporter:

Madam, I beg your pardon for the abruptness of my departure in the morning, but I was compelled to it by conscience. Fifty years ago, Madam, on this day, I committed a breach of filial piety. My father had been in the habit of attending Uttoxeter market, and opening a stall there for the sale of his Books. Confined by indisposition, he desired me, that day, to go and attend the stall in his place. My pride prevented me; I gave my father a refusal.—And now today I have been at Uttoxeter; I went into the market at the time of business, uncovered my head, and stood with it bare, for an hour, on the spot where my father's stall used to stand. In contrition I stood, and I hope the penance was expiatory.[13]

Who does not figure to himself this spectacle, amid the 'rainy weather, and the sneers,' or wonder, 'of the bystanders'? The memory of old Michael Johnson, rising from the far distance; sad-beckoning in the 'moonlight of memory:' how he had toiled faithfully hither and thither; patiently among the lowest of the low; been buffeted and beaten down, yet ever risen again, ever tried it anew—And oh, when the wearied old man, as Bookseller, or Hawker, or Tinker, or whatsoever it was that Fate had reduced him to, begged help of *thee* for one day,—how savage, diabolic, was that mean Vanity, which answered, No! He sleeps now; after life's fitful fever, he sleeps well:[14] but thou, O Merciless, how now wilt thou still the sting of that remembrance?—The picture of Samuel Johnson standing bareheaded in the market there, is one of the grandest and saddest we can paint. Repentance! Repentance! he proclaims, as with passionate sobs: but only to the ear of Heaven, if Heaven will give him audience: the earthly ear and heart, that should have heard it, are now closed, unresponsive forever.

That this so keen-loving, soft-trembling Affectionateness, the inmost essence of his being, must have looked forth, in one form or another, through Johnson's whole character, practical and intellectual, modifying both, is not to be doubted. Yet through what singular distortions and superstitions, moping melancholies, blind habits, whims about 'entering with the right foot,' and 'touching every post as he walked along;'[15] and all the other mad chaotic lumber of a brain that, with sun-clear intellect, hovered forever on the verge of insanity,—must that same inmost essence have looked forth; unrecognisable to all but the most observant! Accordingly it was not recognised; Johnson passed not for a fine nature,

[12] Ibid., iv. 373. [13] *Johnsonian Miscellanies*, ii. 426–7.
[14] *Macbeth*, III. ii. 23. [15] Boswell, *Life*, i. 484, 485 n. l.

but for a dull, almost brutal one. Might not, for example, the first-fruit of such a Lovingness, coupled with his quick Insight, have been expected to be a peculiarly courteous demeanour as man among men? In Johnson's 'Politeness,' which he often, to the wonder of some, asserted to be great,[16] there was indeed somewhat that needed explanation. Nevertheless, if he insisted always on handing lady-visitors to their carriage; though with the certainty of collecting a mob of gazers in Fleet Street,— as might well be, the beau having on, by way of court-dress, 'his rusty brown morning suit, a pair of old shoes for slippers, a little shrivelled wig sticking on the top of his head, and the sleeves of his shirt and the knees of his breeches hanging loose:'[17]—in all this we can see the spirit of true Politeness, only shining through a strange medium. Thus again, in his apartments, at one time, there were unfortunately no chairs. 'A gentleman who frequently visited him whilst writing his *Idlers*, constantly found him at his desk, sitting on one with three legs; and on rising from it, he remarked that Johnson never forgot its defect; but would either hold it in his hand, or place it with great composure against some support; taking no notice of its imperfection to his visitor,'—who meanwhile, we suppose, sat upon folios, or in the sartorial fashion. 'It was remarkable in Johnson,' continues Miss Reynolds (*Renny dear*), 'that no external circumstances ever prompted him to make any apology, or to seem even sensible of their existence. Whether this was the effect of philosophic pride, or of some partial notion of his respecting high-breeding, is doubtful.'[18] That it *was*, for one thing, the effect of genuine Politeness, is nowise doubtful. Not of the Pharisaical Brummellean Politeness, which would suffer crucifixion rather than ask twice for soup: but the noble universal Politeness of a man that knows the dignity of men, and feels his own; such as may be seen in the patriarchal bearing of an Indian Sachem; such as Johnson himself exhibited, when a sudden chance brought him into dialogue with his King.[19] To us, with our view of the man, it nowise appears 'strange' that he should have boasted himself cunning in the laws of Politeness; nor 'stranger still,' habitually attentive to practise them.

More legibly is this influence of the Loving heart to be traced in his intellectual character. What, indeed, is the beginning of intellect, the first inducement to the exercise thereof, but attraction towards somewhat, *affection* for it? Thus too, who ever saw, or will see, any true talent, not to speak of genius, the foundation of which is not goodness, love? From Johnson's strength of Affection, we deduce many of his intellectual

[16] Ibid., iii. 54 and n. 1.   [17] Ibid., ii. 406.
[18] *Johnsonian Miscellanies*, ii. 259–60.   [19] Boswell, *Life*, ii. 34–42.

peculiarities; especially that threatening array of perversions, known under the name of 'Johnson's Prejudices.' Looking well into the root from which these sprang, we have long ceased to view them with hostility, can pardon and reverently pity them. Consider with what force early-imbibed opinions must have clung to a soul of this Affection. Those evil-famed Prejudices of his, that Jacobitism, Church-of-Englandism, hatred of the Scotch, belief in Witches, and suchlike, what were they but the ordinary beliefs of well-doing, well-meaning provincial Englishmen in that day? First gathered by his Father's hearth; round the kind 'country fires' of native Staffordshire; they grew with his growth and strengthened with his strength: they were hallowed by fondest sacred recollections; to part with them was parting with his heart's blood. If the man who has no strength of Affection, strength of Belief, have no strength of Prejudice, let him thank Heaven for it, but to himself take small thanks.

Melancholy it was, indeed, that the noble Johnson could not work himself loose from these adhesions; that he could only purify them, and wear them with some nobleness. Yet let us understand how they grew out from the very centre of his being: nay moreover, how they came to cohere in him with what formed the business and worth of his Life, the sum of his whole Spiritual Endeavour. For it is on the same ground that he became throughout an Edifier and Repairer, not, as the others of his make were, a Puller-down; that in an age of universal Scepticism, England was still to produce its Believer. Mark too his candour even here; while a Dr. Adams, with placid surprise, asks, 'Have we not evidence enough of the soul's immortality?' Johnson answers, 'I wish for more.'[20]

But the truth is, in Prejudice, as in all things, Johnson was the product of England; one of those *good* yeomen whose limbs were made in England: alas, the last of *such* Invincibles, their day being now done! His culture is wholly English; that not of a Thinker but of a 'Scholar:' his interests are wholly English; he sees and knows nothing but England; he is the John Bull of Spiritual Europe: let him live, love him, as he was and could not but be! Pitiable it is, no doubt, that a Samuel Johnson must confute Hume's irreligious Philosophy by some 'story from a Clergyman of the Bishoprick of Durham;' should see nothing in the great Frederick but 'Voltaire's lackey;' in Voltaire himself but a man *acerrimi ingenii, paucarum literarum*; in Rousseau but one worthy to be hanged; and in the universal, long-prepared, inevitable Tendency of European Thought but a green-sick milkmaid's crotchet of, for variety's sake, 'milking the

[20] Boswell, *Life*, iv. 299.

446

Bull.'[21] Our good, dear John! Observe too what it is that he sees in the city of Paris: no feeblest glimpse of those D'Alemberts and Diderots, or of the strange questionable work they did; solely some Benedictine Priests, to talk kitchen-latin with them about *Editiones Principes.*[22] '*Monsheer Nongtongpaw!*'—Our dear, foolish John: yet is there a lion's heart within him!—Pitiable all these things were, we say; yet nowise inexcusable; nay, as basis or as foil to much else that was in Johnson, almost venerable. Ought we not, indeed, to honour England, and English Institutions and Way of Life, that they could still equip such a man; could furnish him in heart and head to be a Samuel Johnson, and yet to love them, and unyieldingly fight for them? What truth and living vigour must such Institutions once have had, when, in the middle of the Eighteenth Century, there was still enough left in them for this!

It is worthy of note that, in our little British Isle, the two grand Antagonisms of Europe should have stood embodied, under their very highest concentration, in two men produced simultaneously among ourselves. Samuel Johnson and David Hume, as was observed, were children nearly of the same year: through life they were spectators of the same Life-movement; often inhabitants of the same city. Greater contrast, in all things, between two great men, could not be. Hume, well-born, competently provided for, whole in body and mind, of his own determination forces a way into Literature: Johnson, poor, moonstruck, diseased, forlorn, is forced into it 'with the bayonet of necessity at his back.' And what a part did they severally play there! As Johnson became the father of all succeeding Tories; so was Hume the father of all succeeding Whigs, for his own Jacobitism was but an accident, as worthy to be named Prejudice as any of Johnson's. Again, if Johnson's culture was exclusively English; Hume's, in Scotland, became European;—for which reason too we find his influence spread deeply over all quarters of Europe, traceable deeply in all speculation, French, German, as well as domestic; while Johnson's name, out of England, is hardly anywhere to be met with. In spiritual stature they are almost equal; both great, among the greatest: yet how unlike in likeness! Hume has the widest, methodising, comprehensive eye; Johnson the keenest for perspicacity and minute detail: so had, perhaps chiefly, their education ordered it. Neither of the two rose into Poetry; yet both to some approximation thereof; Hume to something of an Epic clearness and method, as in his delineation of the

21 Ibid., i. 434; ii. 406 ('of the most acute intellect, but little scholarship'); ii. 11–12; i. 444.
22 Ibid., ii. 397, 399, 404.

Commonwealth Wars; Johnson to many a deep Lyric tone of plaintiveness and impetuous graceful power, scattered over his fugitive compositions. Both, rather to the general surprise, had a certain rugged Humour shining through their earnestness: the indication, indeed, that they *were* earnest men, and had *subdued* their wild world into a kind of temporary home and safe dwelling. Both were, by principle and habit, Stoics: yet Johnson with the greater merit, for he alone had very much to triumph over; farther, he alone ennobled his Stoicism into Devotion. To Johnson Life was as a Prison, to be endured with heroic faith: to Hume it was little more than a foolish Bartholomew-Fair Show-booth, with the foolish crowdings and elbowings of which it was not worth while to quarrel; the whole would break up, and be at liberty, so *soon*. Both realised the highest task of Manhood, that of living like men; each died not unfitly, in his way: Hume as one, with factitious, half-false gaiety, taking leave of what was itself wholly but a Lie: Johnson as one, with awe-struck, yet resolute and piously expectant heart, taking leave of a Reality, to enter a Reality still higher. Johnson had the harder problem of it, from first to last: whether, with some hesitation, we can admit that he was intrinsically the better-gifted, may remain undecided.

These two men now rest; the one in Westminster Abbey here; the other in the Calton-Hill Churchyard of Edinburgh. Through Life they did not meet: as contrasts, 'like in unlike,' love each other; so might they two have loved, and communed kindly,—had not the terrestrial dross and darkness that was in them withstood! One day, their spirits, what Truth was in each, will be found working, living in harmony and free union, even here below. They were the two half-men of their time: whoso should combine the intrepid Candour and decisive scientific Clearness of Hume, with the Reverence, the Love and devout Humility of Johnson, were the whole man of a new time. Till such whole man arrive for us, and the distracted time admit of such, might the Heavens but bless poor England with half-men worthy to tie the shoe-latchets of these, resembling these even from afar! Be both attentively regarded, let the true Effort of both prosper;—and for the present, both take our affectionate farewell!

Bibliography

BRONSON, BERNARD H., 'The Double Tradition of Dr. Johnson', *Journal of English Literary History*, xviii (June 1951), 90–106. Reprinted in *Eighteenth-Century Literature: Modern Essays in Criticism*, ed. James L. Clifford, New York, 1959, 285–99. An important discussion of the 'popular' and 'learned' traditions in the response to Johnson after the publication of Boswell's *Life*.

CLIFFORD, JAMES L., *Johnsonian Studies, 1887–1950: A Survey and Bibliography*, Minneapolis, 1951. A model bibliographical guide; the excellent 'Survey' is reprinted and extended to 1965 in *Samuel Johnson: A Collection of Critical Essays*, ed. Donald J. Greene, Englewood Cliffs, New Jersey, 1965, 46–62.

CLIFFORD, JAMES L., and GREENE, DONALD J., 'A Bibliography of Johnsonian Studies, 1950–1960', *Johnsonian Studies*, ed. Magdi Wahba, Cairo, 1962, 263–350. An excellent extension of the preceding item, with another valuable 'survey'.

CLIFFORD, JAMES L., and GREENE, DONALD J., *Samuel Johnson: A Survey and Bibliography of Critical Studies*, London, 1971. Combines the two preceding items, while extending their chronological scope back to Johnson's own lifetime and forward to 1968.

COURTNEY, W. P., with SMITH, D. NICHOL, *Bibliography of Johnson*, Clarendon Press, Oxford, 1915; reissued 1925. Though now out of date, contains much important material relevant to the contemporary response to Johnson. (In process of being revised; one 'Supplement to Courtney' was produced by R. W. Chapman and Allen T. Hazen in 1939, in *Oxford Bibliographical Society Proceedings*, v.)

KENNEY, WILLIAM, 'The Modern Reputation of Samuel Johnson', unpublished dissertation, Boston University, 1956.

MCGUFFIE, HELEN L., 'Samuel Johnson and the Hostile Press', unpublished dissertation, Columbia University, 1961.

MORGAN, IRA L., 'Contemporary Criticism of the Works of Johnson', unpublished dissertation, University of Florida, 1954.

NOYES, GERTRUDE, 'The Critical Reception of Johnson's *Dictionary* in the latter eighteenth century', *Modern Philology*, lii (February 1955), 175–91. Sound and authoritative.

ROWLAND, JOHN C., 'The Reputation of Dr. Samuel Johnson in England, 1779–1835', unpublished dissertation, Western Reserve University, 1962.

SLEDD, JAMES H., and KOLB, GWIN J., *Dr. Johnson's Dictionary: Essays in the Biography of a Book*, Chicago, 1955. Very thorough and judicious.

SPITTAL, JOHN K., *Contemporary Criticisms of Dr. Samuel Johnson*, John Murray, London, 1923. Unedited collection of criticism from the *Monthly Review*.

WILES, ROY M., 'The Contemporary Distribution of Johnson's *Rambler*', *Eighteenth-Century Studies*, ii (December 1968), 155–71. Illuminating analysis of the reprinting of *Rambler* essays in English provincial newspapers.

Select Index

References are grouped as follows:

I Names

II Authors of comments (brief or extensive) on Johnson, quoted in the Introduction and Text; where a writer's identity is unknown or uncertain, the title or source of his entry is given.

III References to Johnson's writings.

IV Some major aspects of discussion in the criticism of Johnson.

I

Addison, Joseph, 23, 31, 70, 97, 129, 288, 295, 307, 328, 351, 352; *Life* of, 298 (*see also* IV, Comparison with Addison)
Ainsworth, Robert, 107, 128, 137, 138
Akenside, Mark, 50, 320–1
Alves, Robert, 1
Anderson, Robert, 14
Aristotle, 7, 57, 58–9, 108, 176, 177, 263, 407; Bossu on, 171–2
Arnold, Matthew, 34, 35
Ash, John, 128, 131

Bailey, Nathan, 12, 107, 128
Bate, W. Jackson, 37
Beattie, James, 301
Blackmore, Sir Richard, *Life* of, 2, 269, 425
Blair, Hugh, 13, 347
Boileau (Despréaux), Nicolas, 61, 103
Bolingbroke, Henry St John, Viscount, 60, 193
Boyer, Abel, 121, 124
Bronson, Bernard H., 35, 449
Brooke, Henry, 59

Brown, Peter, 27
Browne, Sir Thomas, 70, 129, 130, 134, 365, 393, 422
Burke, Edmund, 10, 16, 87, 176, 200, 347, 356, 383, 413–14, 429, 438
Burney, Fanny, 31, 347
Bute, John Stuart, Earl of, 19, 29, 212, 213, 240, 359, 360
Bute, Lady Mary, 3

Cadell, Thomas, 13, 251
Chapin, Chester, 36
Chapman, R.W., 36
Cibber, Colley, 55, 168, 264
Clarendon, Edward Hyde, Earl of, 31, 350
Clifford, James, 36, 37, 449
Collins, William, 30, 299–300; *Life* of, 265–6, 269
Cooke, William, 14
Courtney, W. P., 36, 449
Cowley, Abraham, 32, 50, 70, 351; *Life* of, 254–6, 376, 408
Cowper, William, 20, 30, 89; quoted on *Lives*, 273–7
Crabbe, George, 8, 253
Curll, Edmund, 275

Daily Advertiser, 3, 63
Davie, Donald, 36
Davis, Bertram, H., 33
Dennis, John, 275
Dodsley, Robert, 4, 10, 11, 12, 43, 95, 98, 386
Dryden, John, 18, 31, 47, 70, 71, 129, 160–1, 197, 252, 272, 291, 299, 304, 351, 408; *Life* of, 306, 353
Dyer, John, *Life* of, 266, 297

Edwards, Thomas, 163, 165, 180, 187
Entick, John, 121, 128, 361
European Magazine, 115; quoted, 21

Fenton, Elijah, 257, 279
Fleischauer, Warren, 37

Gibbon, Edward, 31, 343, 347, 355
Godwin, William, 78
Graves, Richard, 30
Greene, Donald J., 36, 37, 449

Hagstrum, Jean H., 37
Hamilton, Joseph, 128
Hammond, James, *Life* of, 265, 298–9
Hanmer, Sir Thomas, 163, 169, 180
Hanway, Jonas, 9
Hawkesworth, John, 153, 309, 369
Haywood, Eliza, 83
Heath, Benjamin, 163
Hill, G. Birkbeck, 35–6
Hooker, Richard, 106, 110, 113, 392
Hume, David, 229, 447–8

Jack, Ian, 36
Jones, Stephen, 128
Junius, Francis, 117, 137, 139
Juvenal, 20, 43, 49, 78, 367, 414

Kames, Henry Home, Lord, 321
Kearsley, Thomas, 14
Kolb, Gwin J., 37, 117, 449
Krutch, Joseph W., 36

Lansdowne, George Granville, Lord, 306
Lauder, William, 89, 278, 377
Leavis, Frank R., 36
Leman, Sir Tanfield, 4
Locke, John, 70, 97, 129
London Magazine, 4, 5, 95
Longinus, 7, 263, 407
Lowth, Robert, 140, 336
Lyttleton, George, Baron *Life* of, 307, 408

McAdam, E. L., 36
Macpherson, James, 7, 235, 242, 244, 246–7, 401, 425
Maxwell, John, 4
Middlesex Journal, 6
Milton, John, 7, 30, 79, 87, 89, 92, 97, 113, 129, 414, 429, 440; on *Life* of, 257–63, 273–4, 277, 278–83, 296, 311–12, 313–16, 327, 354, 377–8, 408, 418, 425
Montagu, Elizabeth, 305, 408
More, Sir Thomas, 31, 350

Noble, Francis, 146
Nollekens, Joseph, 11

Otway, Thomas, 173

Parkhurst, John, 138
Pennant, Thomas, 234, 243
Perry, William, 128
'Peter Pindar', *see* Wolcot
Philips, Ambrose, 45
Philips, John, 296–7
Phillips, Edward, 107, 128
Pitt, William, Earl of Chatham, 309–10
Political Register, 6
Pope, Alexander, 2–3, 10, 16, 23, 26, 30, 70, 92, 97, 129, 193, 272, 288, 309, 353; as editor of *Shakespeare*, 155, 156, 160, 163, 179–80, 201; compared as poet with Johnson, 21,

44, 46, 47, 50, 414–15; *Dunciad* quoted, 18; on *Life* of, 284–5, 309, 425; on pastoral verse, 308
Powell, L. F., 36
Prior, Matthew, 30; on *Life* of, 263–4, 274–6, 304, 354
Public Advertiser, 4, 6

Raleigh, Sir Walter, 36
Robertson, William, 12, 31, 323, 347
Rousseau, Jean-Jacques, 191, 192
Rowe, Nicholas, 27, 155, 163

St. James's Chronicle, 6, 162–3
Savage, Richard, *Life* of, 10, 33, 68, 73, 264, 269, 295–6, 341
Scots Magazine, 95, 115
Scott, Joseph N., 11
Shaftesbury, Anthony Ashley Cooper, Earl of, 319, 321
Shakespeare, William, 97, 110, 121, 131, 134–5 (*see also* III, *Shakespeare*)
Sheffield, John, 167
Shenstone, William, 30; on *Life* of, 306–8
Sherbo, Arthur, 37
Sheridan, Thomas, 128, 131
Sidney, Sir Philip, 168, 261, 302
Skinner, Stephen, 117, 122, 137, 139
Sledd, James H., 37, 117, 449
Smith, D. Nichol, 36, 449
Spenser, Edmund, 110, 121, 298–9
Steele, Sir Richard, 69, 336
Stephen, Leslie, 35
Strahan, William, 13, 251
Student, 3, 345, 389; quoted, 63–4
Swift, Jonathan, 17, 70, 73, 84, 95, 97, 129, 305, 373, 421, 425

Tate, Allen, 37
Tate, Nahum, 45
Temple, Sir William, 392
Theobald, Lewis, 155, 160, 163, 180, 373

Thomson, James, 153, 425; on *Life* of, 264–5, 354

Voitle, Robert, 37
Vossius, Gerardus, 137, 138, 139
Vulliamy, C. E., 35

Walker, John, 128, 131
Waller, Edmund, on *Life* of, 256–7, 376–7
Wallis, John, 128
Warburton, William, 102, 155, 156, 163, 180, 181, 186–7, 188, 192–3, 373
Warton, Joseph, 3, 21, 321
Warton, Thomas, 102
Weekly Magazine, 6, 7, 231
Westminster Magazine, 7
Whitehall, 6
Wiles, Roy M., 11, 449
Willick, A. F. M., 5, 118
Wimsatt, W. K., 36
Wolcot, John ('Peter Pindar'), 78

Yonge, Sir William, 57, 386
Young, Arthur, 7
Young, Edward, 321, 390

II

Adelung, Johann Christoph, 5, 24–5, 115; on *Dictionary*, 118–24
Aikin, John, 21; on poems, 49–51
Annual Register, 5, 26; quoted, 147, 273–4
Austen, Jane, 8

Bancroft, Edward, 27–8
Barbauld, Anna L., 26, 49; on *Rasselas*, 149–54
Barclay, James, 27, 399; on Kenrick's *Review*, 189–93
Bentham, Jeremy, 8

Blackburne, Francis, 30; on *Life of Milton*, 278–83

Blake, William, 32; on Johnson, 363–4

Boswell, James: *Life of Johnson* quoted, 383–412 *passim*; character of *Life*, 33–4, 368–70; Carlyle on *Life*, 432, 435–6, influence of *Life*, 8, 32, 34–5, 355–6, 417–18, 420–1; Macaulay on *Life*, 423–31 *passim*; on Johnson's conversation, 384, 411–12; on his character, 409–12; on *Dictionary*, 394–6; on *Irene*, 386–7; on *Journey*, 400–5; on *Lives of Poets*, 407–8; on poems, 384–5; on political writings, 399–400, 405–7; on *Rambler*, 23, 387–91; on *Rasselas*, 5, 397–8; on *Shakespeare*, 398–9; on style, 391–4, 408; Towers on Boswell, 376

Brydges, Sir Samuel Egerton, 17

Burney, Charles, 14–15, 369

Burrowes, Robert, 8, 31; on Johnson's style, 326–42

Byron, George, Lord, 34

Callender, James, 1; on Johnson, 16, 19, 23–4

Campbell, Archibald, 1, 5, 16–17, 22, 25, 31, 33, 231, 248; on Johnson's style, 317–23

Carlyle, Thomas, 8, 32; on Johnson, 432–48

Cartwright, Edmund, on *Lives*, 7, 29, 253–70

Cave, Edward, 42–3, 69; on *Rambler*, 345–6

Chalmers, Alexander, 22, 32, 347; on *Rambler*, 81–5

Chesterfield, Philip Dormer Stanhope, fourth Earl of, 4, 9, 16, 90, 103–4; on *Dictionary*, 95–102

Churchill, Charles, 1, 5, 19, 26, 231, 233, 425; on Johnson, 357–9

Cobbett, William, on *Journey*, 1–2

Coleridge, Samuel Taylor, 8, 27, 32; on Johnson's style, 355–6; on *Shakespeare*, 197–9

Colman, George, 23–4, 26; on *Dictionary*, 162–3; on *Irene*, 22

Connoisseur, 3, 22

Courtenay, John, 18, 31, 346, 393; on Johnson, 364–71

Critical Review, 5, 6, 7, 11, 15–16, 26, 27, 28, 29, 164, 209; quoted, 204–7, 270–2

Criticism on Mahomet and Irene, A (anon.), 21–2; quoted, 52–7

Croft, Herbert, 4, 24, 139

Cumberland, Richard, 8, 408; quoted, 416–19

De Quincey, Thomas, 8; on *Life of Milton*, 313–16

Dilly, Edward, on *Lives*, 250–1

Drake, Nathan, 31–2; on Johnson's style, 344–8

Eliot, T. S., 31, 36

Essay on Tragedy, An (Hippisley?), 3, 21–2; quoted, 57–62

Fergusson, Robert, 6, 29; quoted, 321–3

Fitzthomas, William, 7, 30; on *Life of Gray*, 285–92

Garrick, David, 16, 22, 24, 50, 52, 56, 164, 173, 210, 385–6; on Johnson's *Dictionary*, 4

Gillray, James, 7, 312

Gleig, George, 22; on *Rambler*, 72–3

Goldsmith, Oliver, 15, 22, 84, 164, 347, 369, 399; on Johnson, 3, 20, 78, 88, 430

Gray, Thomas, 7, 30, 255, 262, 414; on Johnson, 20; on *Life* of, 266–9, 271–2, 285–92, 293–4, 296–302, 311, 342, 354, 408, 418

Gray's-Inn Journal, 3, 22

Griffiths, Ralph, 28; on *Journey*, 234–6

Hawkins, Sir John, 15, 33; on *Lives*, 303–6

Hazlitt, William, 8, 22, 27; on *Rambler*, 86–9; on *Shakespeare*, 199–203

Hippisley, John (?), 3; on *Irene*, 57–62

Hurd, Richard, 19–20, 32

Jones, Sir William, 369; quoted, 30

Keats, John, 21; on *Lives*, 30–1

Kenrick, William, 5, 26–7, 398–9; on *Shakespeare*, 164–88; Barclay on, 189–93

Knox, Vicesimus, 32, 347; quoted, 1

Lennox, Charlotte, on *Rambler*, 3

London, Packet, 7, 28

Lynd, Robert, 35

Macaulay, Thomas Babington, 8, 15, 34, 72, 343, 432; quoted, 422–31

McIntyre, James, on *Journey*, 240–1

Mackintosh, Sir James, 20, 30, 31; on Johnson's style, 349–54

McNicol, Donald, 7, 10, 29, 405; on *Journey*, 242–9

Malone, Edmond, 12, 13, 369; quoted 27, 251

Mason, George, 4, 32, 126, 139; epitaph on Johnson, 415–16

Montagu, Lady Mary Wortley, on *Rambler*, 3

Monthly Review, The, 1, 4, 5, 7, 15–16, 25, 26, 27–8, 29, 32, 141–6, 191; quoted 164–80, 207–8, 234–6, 253–70

Mudford, William, 8, 21, 23, 26; on poems, 44–8; on *Rambler*, 74–80; on *Rasselas*, 148–9

Murphy, Arthur, 15, 22, 32, 80, 83; on *Rambler*, 68–72

Newcastle General Magazine, 12; on *Rambler*, 11

Piozzi, Hester Lynch (Thrale), 2, 373, 381, 401, 403, 421; quoted on Johnson, 17

Potter, Robert, 19, 30, 32; on *Lives*, 295–302, 306–10

Remarks on a Voyage to the Hebrides (anon.), 29; on *Journey*, 237–40

Remembrancer, 3; on *Rambler*, 63

Review of *The False Alarm* (*Critical Review*), 204–7

Review of *The False Alarm* (*Monthly Review*), 207–8

Review of *Lives of the Poets* (*Annual Register*), 293–4

Review of *Lives of the Poets* (*Critical Review*), 270–72

Review of *Rasselas* (*Annual Register*), 147

Richardson, Samuel, 388, 425; on *Rambler*, 345

Ritson, Joseph, on *Shakespeare*, 27

Ruffhead, Owen, 5, 25–6; on *Rasselas*, 141–6

Schlegel, August Wilhelm von, 8, 27, 199; on *Shakespeare*, 195–6

Scott, Sir Walter, 17, 34; on Johnson, 420–2

Seward, Anne, 17, 30, 285; general estimate of Johnson, 412–15; his style, 22–3, 31, 343–4; on *Lives*, 311–12; on his poetry, 21

Shaw, William, 45; quoted, 9, 20–1, 44

Smart, Christopher, 23; on *Rambler*, 22, 63–4

Smith, Adam, 4, 24, 27; on *Dictionary*, 115–16

Stewart, Dugald, on *Lives*, 312–13

Stockdale, Percival, 400; on *The False Alarm*, 209–11

Strachey, G. Lytton, on *Lives*, 35

Temple, William J., 10, 32, 406–7; quoted, 17

Temple Bar, 35

Tooke, John Horne, 4, 24, 126, 130, 136, 139, 140; on *Dictionary*, 117–18

Towers, Joseph, 6, 10, 30, 34, 74, 406–7; on Johnson's character and writings, 24, 32–3, 371–82; on Johnson's political writings, 28, 216–25

Tyers, Thomas, 371–2, 415; quoted, 8, 17, 32

Tyranny Unmasked, (anon.) 28, 29; on *Taxation no Tyranny*, 225–30

Voltaire, 60, 166, 417, 437; *Candide*, 151–2, 270, 397–8, 422; on *Shakespeare*, 194

Walpole, Horace, 20, 31; on Johnson's style, 324–6; on *Life of Pope*, 284–5

Webster, Noah, 31, 117; on *Dictionary*, 4–5, 25, 125–40

Wilkes, John, 1, 5, 6, 26, 117, 204–6, 209, 231, 357, 399; on Johnson's political writing and values, 28, 211–16, 360–3

III

Adventurer, 72, 394

Advertisement to *Lives of the English Poets*, 13, 252

Dictionary of the English Language, A, 4–5, 10, 11–12, 23–5, 29, 35, 70, 81, 90–140, 162, 214, 352–3, 360–2, 382, 392, 394–6

False Alarm, The, 6, 13, 204–8, 211–16, 217–25, 373, 399–400

Idler, 12, 72, 79–80, 310, 330, 340, 373

Irene, 3, 11, 21–2, 52–62, 199, 310, 386–7, 415, 418

Journey to the Western Islands of Scotland, A, 6, 13, 28–9, 33, 36, 231–49, 323–4, 343–4, 375–6, 400–5, 428

Lives of the English Poets, 7, 13, 29–31, 33, 35, 73, 82, 250–316, 340, 353–4, 376–8, 407–8, 413, 418 (*see also* I and II *under* Cowley, Gray, Milton etc.)

Letter to Chesterfield, 16, 103–4

Patriot, The, 6, 13, 217–25, 373

Plan of a Dictionary, 4, 90–4, 96

Poems, 2, 3, 10, 20–1, 36, 42–51, 78, 197, 218, 220, 224, 303, 309, 312, 362, 384–5, 414–15, 418

Preface to a Dictionary, 24, 105–14, 127, 394

Preface to Shakespeare, 27, 157–61, 163, 166–79, 194, 195–9, 200–3

Rambler, 2, 3, 4, 9, 11, 12, 22–3, 24, 33, 47, 63–89, 127, 148, 154, 162, 225, 310, 318–23, 329–31, 335, 338, 340, 345–8, 352, 365, 378–9, 387–91, 418

Rasselas, 5, 12, 25–6, 89, 127, 141–54, 318–20, 372–3, 381, 397–8, 415, 417, 419, 422

Review of Jonas Hanway, *Essay on Tea*, 9

Shakespeare, 5, 10, 12, 26–7, 30, 155–203, 358, 373, 398–9

Taxation no Tyranny, 6, 9, 13, 27, 33, 225–30, 374, 405–7

Thoughts on Falkland's Islands, 6, 13, 27, 217–25, 373

IV

Biographer and critic, 29–31, 35, 36, 67, 69, 79, 163, 195–203, 253–316, 353–4, 376–8, 383–4, 407–9, 418–19, 423–5